The American School
1642–1993

The American School

1642–1993

THIRD EDITION

Joel Spring
State University of New York
College at New Paltz

McGraw-Hill, Inc.

New York   St. Louis   San Francisco   Auckland   Bogotá   Caracas
Lisbon   London   Madrid   Mexico City   Milan   Montreal   New Delhi
San Juan   Singapore   Sydney   Tokyo   Toronto

This book was developed by Lane Akers, Inc.

This book was set in Palatino by Better Graphics, Inc.
The editors were Lane Akers and Caroline Izzo;
the production supervisor was Kathryn Porzio.
The cover was designed by Karen K. Quigley.
Arcata Graphics/Martinsburg was printer and binder.

Cover Photo Credits
Clockwise from top right: The Bettmann Archive; Reuters/Bettmann;
UPI/Bettmann; The Bettmann Archive; Culver Pictures, Inc.;
Culver Pictures, Inc.

THE AMERICAN SCHOOL
1642–1993

4 5 6 7 8 9 0   AGM   AGM   9 0 9 8 7 6 5 4

ISBN 0-07-060539-4

Library of Congress Cataloging-in-Publication Data

Spring, Joel H.
    The American school, 1642–1993 / Joel Spring.—3rd ed.
        p.   cm.
    Rev. ed. of: The American School, 1642–1990. c1990.
    Includes index.
    ISBN 0-07-060539-4
    1. Education—United States—History.   2. Education—Social
aspects—United States—History.   I. Spring, Joel H.   American
school, 1642—1990.   II. Title.
LA205.S64   1994
370′.973—dc20   93-1645

About the Author

JOEL SPRING, professor of education at the State University of New York–
College at New Paltz, received his Ph.D. in educational policy studies from
the University of Wisconsin. His father was born a citizen of the Choctaw
Nation in Indian Territory prior to the abolishment of the Choctaw govern-
ment and the creation of Oklahoma. Professor Spring's current interest in
Native American culture and history is a reflection of his Indian background.

Professor Spring is the author of many books including *Images of American
Life: A History of Ideological Management in Schools, Movies, Radio, and Television;
American Education* (now in its sixth edition); *Wheels in the Head: Educational
Philosophies of Authority, Freedom, and Culture from Socrates to Paulo Freire;* and
*Deculturalization and the Struggle for Equality: A Brief History of the Education of
Dominated Cultures in the United States.*

Contents in Brief

PREFACE   xiii

Chapter 1   Introduction to the Third Edition: Instructional
Methodology and Historical Interpretations   1

Chapter 2   Religion and Authority in Colonial Education   4

Chapter 3   Nationalism, Moral Reform, and Charity
in the New Republic   32

Chapter 4   The Ideology and Politics of the Common School   62

Chapter 5   Organizing the American School: The
Nineteenth-Century Schoolmarm   97

Chapter 6   Education as Deculturalization: Native Americans
and Puerto Ricans   130

Chapter 7   Education and Segregation: Asians, African
Americans, and Mexican Americans   162

Chapter 8   Schooling and the New Corporate Order   188

vii

Chapter 9   Education and Human Capital   212

Chapter 10   Meritocracy: The Experts Take Charge   248

Chapter 11   The Politics of Education   280

Chapter 12   Big Bird: Movies, Radio, and Television Join
Schools as Public Educators   302

Chapter 13   The Great Civil Rights Movement   346

Chapter 14   Education and National Policy   370

Chapter 15   The Conservative Reaction and the Politics
of Education   392

INDEX   425

Contents

PREFACE   xiii

Chapter 1   Introduction to the Third Edition: Instructional
             Methodology and Historical Interpretations   1

   Ideological Management, Deculturalization, and Mass Media   3

Chapter 2   Religion and Authority in Colonial Education   4

   Authority and Social Status in Colonial New England   5
   Colonialism and Educational Policy   12
   Freedom of Thought and the Establishment of Academies   16
   Education as Social Mobility   21
   The Family and the Child   24
      Conclusion   28
      Notes   29

Chapter 3   Nationalism, Moral Reform, and Charity
             in the New Republic   32

      Noah Webster: *Nationalism and Education*   34
      Thomas Jefferson: *A Natural Aristocracy*   37

   Moral Reform and Faculty Psychology   40
   Charity Schools, the Lancasterian System, and Prisons   42
   Institutional Change and the American College   49
   Public versus Private Schools   54
      Conclusion: Continuing Issues in American Education   56
      Notes   58

Chapter 4   The Ideology and Politics of the Common School   62

    The Ideology of the Common School Movement   64
    Workingmen and the Struggle for a Republican Education   73
    The Whigs and the Democrats   77
    The Catholic Issue   81
    The Continuing Debate about the Common School Ideal   86
        Conclusion   92
        Notes   94

Chapter 5   Organizing the American School: The
              Nineteenth-Century Schoolmarm   97

    The American Teacher   98
    The Maternal Model of Instruction   109
    The Evolution of the Bureaucratic Model   114
    McGuffey's Readers and the Spirit of Capitalism   121
        Conclusion   126
        Notes   127

Chapter 6   Education as Deculturalization: Native Americans
              and Puerto Ricans   130

    Native Americans   131
    The American Board and the Civilization Fund   133
    Reservations and Boarding Schools   142
    The "Meriam Report"   147
    Puerto Ricans   148
    The Americanization of Puerto Rico   150
        Conclusion: Methods of Deculturalization and Americanization   156
        Notes   158

Chapter 7   Education and Segregation: Asians, African
              Americans, and Mexican Americans   162

    Asians   163
    African Americans   164
    Segregated Schools in the South   168
    Resisting Segregation   173
    The Second Crusade   174
    Mexican Americans   176
        Notes   185

Chapter 8   Schooling and the New Corporate Order   188

    Extending the Social Role of the School   189

The Changing Classroom—Herbart, Dewey, and Thorndike   198
  Conclusion   209
  Notes   209

Chapter 9   Education and Human Capital   212

The High School   213
*Vocational Education, Vocational Guidance, and
    the Junior High School*   226
Public Benefit or Corporate Greed?   235
The Meaning of Equality of Opportunity   242
  Notes   243

Chapter 10   Meritocracy: The Experts Take Charge   248

Meritocracy and Efficient Management   250
Measurement and Democracy   260
Special Classrooms and Bureaucratic Order   266
The University and Meritocracy   267
  Conclusion   275
  Notes   276

Chapter 11   The Politics of Education   280

The Politics of Professionalism: Teachers versus Administrators   282
The Rise of the National Education Association   289
The Political Changes of the Depression Years   292
  Conclusion   300
  Notes   300

Chapter 12   Big Bird: Movies, Radio, and Television Join
                      Schools as Public Educators   302

The Censorship Debate   303
Educators and the Movies   306
The Production Code: Creating a Political and Moral Conscience   313
Should Commercial Radio or Educators Determine National Culture?   319
Crime and Gore on Children's Radio   325
Children's Television Workshop and Sesame Street   331
  Conclusion   339
  Notes   340

Chapter 13   The Great Civil Rights Movement   346

School Desegregation   347

Busing   353
Magnet Schools   354
Native Americans   357
Indian Education: A National Tragedy   358
Mexican Americans   360
Bilingual Education: Puerto Ricans and Mexican Americans   362
The Great Civil Rights Movement Expands Its Reach   366
   Notes   367

Chapter 14   Education and National Policy   370

The Cold War and National Educational Policy   372
The War on Poverty   383
   Conclusion   389
   Notes   389

**Chapter 15   The Conservative Reaction and the Politics
                of Education**   392

The Nixon Administration and the Conservative Reaction   394
Accountability and the Increasing Power of the Standardized Test   398
The Political Nature of Classroom Instruction   400
The Politics of Education   404
School Prayer   406
Children with Special Needs   407
The Reagan Agenda   408
The Bush Years: National Standards, Choice, and Savage Inequalities   412
Choice   414
Savage Inequalities   414
Human Capital Triumphs   415
   Conclusion: Ideological Management and the History of Education   416
   Notes   420

INDEX   425

Preface

To help the reader understand the role of education in relationship to dominated cultures in the United States, I have added three new chapters to the third edition. Chapter 6, "Education and Deculturalization: Native Americans and Puerto Ricans" documents how the educational policies of the U.S. government attempted to destroy the languages and cultures of these conquered peoples. Chapter 7, "Education and Segregation: Asians, African Americans, and Mexican Americans," demonstrates how educational segregation is part of a pattern of economic exploitation. Chapter 13, "The Great Civil Rights Movement," traces the struggles of dominated cultures in the twentieth century to gain equal educational opportunity.

To emphasize the importance of mass media as a public educator in the twentieth century, I have added a section on "The Children's Television Workshop and Sesame Street" to Chapter 12 ("Big Bird: Movies, Radio, and Television Join Schools as Public Educators"). To the last chapter of the book, Chapter 15, I have added sections on "The Bush Years: National Standards, Choice, and Savage Inequalities," "Choice," and "Human Capital Triumphs."

Throughout the volume, I have rearranged and rewritten sections on historical interpretations to make them more accessible to the reader. In addition, I have updated all chapters.

I would like to thank Caroline Izzo of McGraw-Hill for her careful and thoughtful role in supervising the editing and production of this book and my editor, Lane Akers, for encouraging the addition of chapters on dominated cultures. Also, I would like to thank my wife, Naomi Silverman, for her editorial expertise and criticism, and my daughter, Dawn Toglia, for doing the arduous task of indexing.

Joel Spring

Introduction to the Third Edition: Instructional Methodology and Historical Interpretations

I wrote this book with the intention of combining a particular approach to teaching history with a broader perspective on the interpretation of the history of education. First, as I will explain in more detail below, my pedagogical method is based on the idea that the reader should be presented with a variety of historical interpretations and historical issues. The presentation of material in this fashion, I believe, allows the reader to think about history as opposed to being a passive recipient of facts.

Second, I am concerned about the broader meaning of the history of education. The history of education is one aspect of the study of the dissemination of knowledge. In modern times, educational institutions are one of the major distributors of knowledge to society, but they are not the only distributors of ideas. Recent historical interpretations, as I discuss in this book, stress the importance of the influence of differing political and economic groups on the content of knowledge that is distributed by schools. In the same fashion, political and economic pressures influence the knowledge distributed by sources other than educational institutions. I use the term *ideological management* to describe how these political and economic forces shape the dissemination of ideas in modern society.

In the conclusion to this book, I discuss the importance of ideological management in a world in which the control of ideas is considered a source of power. What people know, what they believe in, and how they interpret the world have an important effect on their choices and, consequently, their actions. In countries under centralized control, a central bureau might control the ideas distributed to the public by the public schools and the media. In

1

China this central bureau is known as the Ministry of Truth, while in Ethiopia it is known as the Ministry or Department of Ideological Management. In countries such as the United States, ideological management is a product of struggle between differing political and economic groups ranging from students and bureaucrats to business interests and social advocacy groups. This is why most recent historical writings present the public school as a contested arena. Recognizing that knowledge is power, different groups struggle for influence and control over the public schools.

To achieve the instructional goals of this book, I discuss various interpretations of historical events. My purpose is to help the reader understand that historical texts are created by historians who are concerned about particular problems and who are influenced by their own histories. I use the discussions of historical interpretations as a means of raising issues about each historical period.

For instance, the history of education in the nineteenth century could be written in a manner that does not question the social value of public schools. This type of history might result in an uncritical acceptance of public schooling. But, on the other hand, when one begins to examine the differing historical interpretations as to why public schools developed in the nineteenth century, a host of questions is raised regarding the necessity and goals of government-supported public schooling. Issues raised in this manner often force readers to think through assumptions they might hold about institutions, ideas, and the organization of society. In this manner, the reader of history becomes engaged in a dialogue with the text.

Out of this dialogue, the reader will begin to formulate his or her own interpretations about the past and present. In part, this process will involve a reshaping of images and feelings about the past. Many people do not remember the details of history, but they do develop images and emotions about past events. Therefore, thinking about history involves both an intellectual consideration of conflicting interpretations and issues and reflection about emotions and images. For example, at an early age a person might be taught a history that is designed to build an emotional attachment, in the form of patriotism, to the political and economic organization of the United States. Later in life this person's emotional feelings about the United States might be challenged if the person reads a critical history of the American past.

In addition, I believe that one's knowledge, images, and emotions regarding the past have an impact on future actions. Individuals often make decisions based on what they believe to be the historical purposes and goals of an institution. The varieties of interpretations presented in this book provide the reader with an opportunity to judge past events and think about future actions. Like historians who weave together the drama of the past, consumers of history have their own political and social opinions. By engaging in an intellectual dialogue with the historical text, readers should be able to clarify their opinions about educational institutions and about the relationship of education to other institutions and to social events.

IDEOLOGICAL MANAGEMENT, DECULTURALIZATION, AND MASS MEDIA

In this third edition, I have added chapters on "Education as Deculturalization: Native Americans and Puerto Ricans" (Chapter 6) and "Education and Segregation: Asians, African Americans, and Mexican Americans" (Chapter 7) to provide an understanding of how the management of ideas can be used for the purpose of exploitation. In the case of Native Americans and Puerto Ricans (Chapter 6), the U.S. government, after conquering Native American tribes and Puerto Rico, attempted to gain the allegiance of these groups by instituting educational policies designed to strip them of their cultures and languages. The segregation in schools of Asians, African Americans, and Mexican Americans (Chapter 7) in the late nineteenth and early twentieth centuries highlights how the management of ideas can be linked to economic exploitation.

In addition, I have added a section on "Children's Television Workshop and Sesame Street" to Chapter 12 ("Big Bird: Movies, Radio, and Television Join Schools as Public Educators"). The new section focuses on the increasing role of media as the third educator along with schools and the family. In general, the chapter is designed to provide an understanding of ideological management in the twentieth century. It deals with the link between educators and the development of radio and movies during the first half of the twentieth century. The chapter demonstrates how the interaction of political and economic forces similar to those affecting schools also influenced the ideas and values distributed by the movie and broadcasting industries. In addition, I discuss the concern of educators about the competition between public schools and these media for influence over children's minds and national culture. As a result of this concern, educators have also influenced the content of ideas distributed by movies and radio.

These additions to the book strengthen its pedagogical and interpretative purposes. Readers will find a richer set of interpretations of educational history and a broader consideration of the meaning of education in the framework of how societies disseminate ideas. I believe that the study of history is essential to understanding our society. A comprehension of history is also essential to making critical decisions about the future. To be a critical thinker about American schools requires being a critical thinker about the history of education.

CHAPTER 2

Religion and Authority in Colonial Education

Colonial education illustrates important roles that education can play in a society. In the seventeenth and eighteenth centuries, education in colonial New England was used to maintain the authority of the government and religion. People were taught to read and write so that they could obey the laws of God and the state. In addition, education in Puritan New England, with its emphasis on individual conduct, bore the seeds for the nineteenth- and twentieth-century view of education as a panacea for society. This view can be traced to the Protestant Reformation, one result of which was an emphasis on individual instruction for the development of piety with the goal of creating "the good society." Whether or not education can create the good society continues to be an important question.

In addition, education in the colonies helped to maintain social distinctions. For many, the learning of Latin and Greek in grammar schools or with tutors and attendance at a college were a means of maintaining or gaining elite status. For others, attendance at an academy was the key to social mobility. From the seventeenth century to present times, there has been a continuous debate on the role of the school in creating social classes and providing for social mobility.

Also, education was increasingly considered a means of improving the material prosperity of society. In the seventeenth and eighteenth centuries, some colonialists and Europeans believed that scientific research would improve the quality of life for all people. They believed that the key to scientific research was freedom of thought and the freedom to pursue any form of inquiry. In England, the quest for intellectual freedom resulted in the establishment of academies which, eventually, were transplanted to the American colonies.

The concern about the advancement of science and intellectual freedom raised issues regarding the control of education. As I will discuss in this chapter, some people argued that intellectual freedom could be achieved only by separating schools from religious organizations that were supported by governments. It was argued that government-supported church schools pri-

4

marily taught obedience to God and the state and, consequently, limited freedom of thought. Others argued that any control by government over education would result in despotism over the mind and a limitation of free inquiry because government officials would always use education to support their own power. The concern about freedom of thought sparked debates about whether or not education should be secular and controlled by government. Similar debates about the role of education in providing material benefits to society and the control of schools continue to present times.

Colonial education also illustrates the relationship between education and concepts of the child and family. Throughout the history of education, concepts of childhood and youth have played important roles in determining methods of instruction. A child who is thought of as being born good is treated quite differently than one who is considered to be born evil. The authoritarian quality of colonial education reflects an authoritarian family structure and a belief that the inherent evil of childhood needed to be controlled.

In summary, these themes in colonial education continue to the present. Education is still considered a means of preparing children to obey the authority of the government. People still think that education can function as a social panacea by eliminating crime, immorality, and poverty. Education is also still considered a means of maintaining social class differences, though many people still believe in the power of schools to provide social mobility. Debates continue about the potential of government-operated schools to inhibit intellectual freedom. And, increasingly through the twentieth century, public schools have adapted to the changing needs of the family.

My discussion of these themes in colonial education will begin with the role of authority and maintenance of social differences by schools in colonial New England. The next section of the chapter, "Colonialism and Educational Policy," will examine educational developments throughout the colonies. The following two sections will deal with the development of academies in England and the colonies. Important themes in these sections are intellectual freedom and social mobility. And the last section of the chapter will explore concepts of childhood and the family.

Throughout this chapter, I will be relating these themes to different historical interpretations of the colonial period. As I discussed in Chapter 1, one goal of this book is to help readers understand the importance of a historian's interpretation of our images of the past. Different historians have emphasized different themes in interpreting the development of colonial education.

AUTHORITY AND SOCIAL STATUS IN COLONIAL NEW ENGLAND

When the Puritans settled in the Massachusetts Bay Colony in the 1630s, they considered themselves to be creating a model religious commonwealth in the wilderness. Early Puritan leader John Winthrop told his fellow colonists in

1630, "We must consider that we shall be as a city upon a hill, the eyes of all people are upon us."[1] Their goal was to create the good society, which meant a well-ordered religious society that would win God's approval and be used as a model by the rest of the world.

The importance of religion in New England colonies has led some historians to emphasize the Protestant nature of colonial education and the effect of that legacy on the development of public schools in the nineteenth century. Most historians who offer this interpretation of education in seventeenth-century New England emphasize the colonists' growing faith in education as a panacea for social problems.[2] Other historians have stressed the authoritarian nature of colonial education as an example of schooling being used to maintain the power of established leadership.[3]

Ellwood Cubberley, who has portrayed the rise of the public school as a struggle between the forces of good and evil, argued that since their origins in colonial times, schools in America have gradually been transformed from instruments of religion into instruments of the state.[4] "The first schools in America were clearly the fruits of the Protestant Revolts in Europe." And of all the Protestant groups that settled in colonial America, according to Cubberley, "the Puritans who settled New England contributed most that was valuable for our future educational development."[5]

The view that the roots of American public schools lie primarily in the Protestant church and in New England has had a profound impact on the history of education. Historian Carl Kaestle has recently argued that the public school movement in the nineteenth century was essentially a result of a desire to protect a Protestant orthodoxy.[6] Catholic groups in the nineteenth century rebelled against the Protestant quality of public schools and established their own school system, and in the nineteenth and twentieth centuries Catholics referred to public schools as Protestant schools. Even in this century, after Bible reading and school prayer were banned by the U.S. Supreme Court, many religious groups protested the loss of what they believed to be the traditional Christian morality of the public schools. From the viewpoint of a historian like Cubberley, the secularization of public schooling did represent a break with tradition.

Not all historians agree with the idea of a continuity of development in schools from colonial times to the emergence of public schools in the nineteenth century. Rush Welter argued that the public school movement of the nineteenth century resulted from a consensus about the need for educated citizens in a democratic society. Welter found little in colonial education that contributed to a democratic theory of education, and he viewed colonial education as a "false start from which it was necessary to turn away before education could become a key principle of democratic faith."[7] According to Welter, colonial education was oriented toward teaching respect for authority and maintaining the existing social and religious order. This orientation was contrary, in his opinion, to the later educational emphasis on preparing citizens for independent democratic behavior.

While differences in historical interpretations of colonial education exist, no one denies the important role of religion. Within the context of the

Massachusetts Bay Colony's attempt to create a model religious common-wealth, education was considered essential to maintaining religious piety and social stability. The purpose of teaching reading and writing was to ensure not only that individuals read the Bible and religious tracts but also that they became good workers and obeyed the laws of the community. These educational goals were explicitly given in the earliest colonial law regarding education, the Massachusetts Law of 1642. This law opens with a general complaint about the neglect of parents and masters in the training of children in learning and labor and calls for the appointment of individuals to investigate the ability of children "to read and understand the principles of religion and the capital laws of this country."[8]

The religious theme received even greater emphasis five years later in the famous "Old Deluder Satan Law," enacted in 1647 in Massachusetts. This law has become famous because it required communities to establish and support schools. Specifically, the law required any community having at least fifty households to appoint a teacher to provide instruction in reading and writing and any community of one hundred or more households to establish a grammar school. The law opens with the famous words "It being the chief project of old deluder, Satan, to keep men from the knowledge of the Scriptures. . . . It is therefore ordered . . ."[9]

Several important points about these two laws should be noted. The first is the reference to masters and parents. In both the colonies and England, some children were apprenticed to a master for seven years. During the apprenticeship, the master had the responsibility for ensuring that the apprentice learned to read and write. The shortage of labor in the colonies often led to a shortening of the apprenticeship period and to the neglect by masters and parents of their obligation to provide instruction. Both these laws were intended to correct this neglect. Second, both laws made a distinction between instruction in reading-and-writing schools and in grammar schools. Unlike reading-and-writing schools, grammar schools primarily provided instruction that prepared their students for college and for leadership positions.

When historians argue that colonial schools perpetuated the existing social order, what they have in mind are the implications of the distinctions among apprenticeship, reading-and-writing schools, and grammar schools. This argument is made most forcefully by Merle Curti in *The Social Ideas of American Educators*. Curti views the history of education as primarily a conflict between people who wanted to use education to maintain their power and those who wanted education to be a means of improving conditions for all people. Curti argues that the colonial use of education as an instrument for preserving existing economic and social arrangements was rooted in European traditions. In England, for instance, the sons of the nobility were educated in the great endowed public schools, while the well-to-do middle class studied at the local grammar schools. The vast number of children of the poor were apprenticed, and the minimal instruction they received in reading and writing was for the purpose of maintaining religious conformity and the power of existing authority.

In New England as well as in the other colonies, Curti argues, the identity of interests between the dominant religious group and the ruling authorities was even closer than in Europe, which resulted in education serving to protect the existing authority structure. Curti identifies two distinct schemes of education in the colonies. One served the elite, which included merchants, planters, clergy, and lawyers. The other scheme served the rest of the population. In the southern colonies, he argues, the class system was most in evidence; there the children of the rich were educated by private tutors or attended private schools while other children received only a minimal education. In New England the class distinctions began in the reading-and-writing schools, with the children of the elite attending private dame schools and the children of the poor attending the town schools. The sharpest distinction was between children in apprenticeship and those attending grammar schools and colleges. The majority of boys were placed into apprenticeship, but the sons of the elite were sent to grammar schools and on to college. As was stated earlier, the minimal instruction in reading and writing given apprentices was solely for the purpose of teaching religious conformity and conveying an understanding of the laws of the colony. In Curti's words, "Apprentices were taught to respect their superiors and the sons of their superiors who were conning Latin Verbs and acquiring the other requisites of the culture and polish that characterized the class to which they belonged."[10]

To understand Curti's argument, the history of reading and writing instruction and the development of grammar schools must be examined. The primary content in colonial reading and writing instruction was religious and moral, whereas the grammar school emphasized the teaching of Latin and Greek as part of a Renaissance conception of the educated person.

Both reading-and-writing schools and grammar schools were products of an educational revolution that had swept England in the sixteenth century. This revolution embodied the emphasis of the Protestant Reformation on the individual's responsibility to know the word of God and learn proper religious behavior. Reading-and-writing schools, often called *petty schools*, concentrated on the teaching of reading, with some teaching of writing and ciphering. This instruction took place in a variety of places, including households, churches, and schools. Instruction was conducted using a hornbook— a piece of wood with a thin layer of horn on top bearing the letters of the alphabet and a brief prayer. A majority of these schools were conducted by a single master or mistress.

A popular form of the petty school in the colonies was the *dame school* for neighborhood children. The dame school was often conducted in the kitchen or living room of the teacher's home. These schools primarily gave instruction in reading and writing, whereas writing schools provided a more advanced level of instruction in writing and also instruction in arithmetic and the simple elements of merchants' accounts. Instruction in these schools became a prerequisite for admission to grammar school.

The content of instruction in the petty schools was primarily religious and authoritarian. The best example of this was *The New England Primer*, which became the most popular text for primary instruction.[11] The content of *The New England Primer* reflects the strong religious and authoritarian nature of colonial education. It opens with the alphabet and a guide to spelling. This section is followed by the short statement "Now the child being entered in his letters and spelling, let him learn; these and such like sentences by heart, whereby he will be both instructed in his duty and encouraged in his learning." The authoritarian context of the child's duty is presented in the first lines of the following verse, which the student was required to memorize:

> I will fear God, and honour the KING.
> I will honour my Father & Mother.
> I will obey my Superiors.
> I will Submit to my Elders.

After this verse comes "An Alphabet of Lessons for Youth"—an alphabetic listing of statements containing religious and moral maxims that the student was required to memorize:

> **A** wise son makes a glad Father, but a foolish son is the heaviness of his Mother.
> **B** etter is little with the fear of the Lord, than great treasure and trouble therewith.
> **C** ome unto CHRIST all ye that labour and are heavy laden, and He will give you rest.

This list is followed by the Lord's Prayer, the Creed, the Ten Commandments, a section called "Duty of Children towards Their Parents," a list of the books of the Old and New Testaments, and a list of numbers. Numbers are introduced with the statement "The numeral letters and figures, which serve for the ready finding of any Chapter, Psalm and Verse in the Bible." After the section on numbers comes a long exhortation given by John Rogers to his nine children in 1554 at the time the entire family was burned at the stake. The *Primer* ends with the Shorter Catechism.

A catechism is a series of questions with a set of correct answers. The child was required to memorize both the questions and the answers. The catechism in *The New England Primer* provided lessons in the basic tenets of Protestant faith. It opens with the question "What is the chief end of Man?" This question was to be answered "Man's chief end is to glorify God, and to enjoy him forever." The next question is:

> Q. What rule hath God given to direct us how we may glorify and enjoy him?
> A. The Word of God which is contained in the Scriptures of the Old and New Testament, is the only Rule to direct us how we may glorify and enjoy him.

The catechism then proceeds to take the student through a series of religious lessons to a final question on the meaning of the conclusion of the Lord's Prayer.[12]

After reading *The New England Primer*, it is not difficult to understand why a historian like Rush Welter would consider colonial education a false start on the road to a democratic education. The content of colonial education emphasized not only submission to authority but also a particular method of instruction. Students were required to memorize the entire text. The method used to teach reading and writing was not one that taught individuals to give direction to their own lives but one by which individuals would learn to submit to the laws of religion and the government. Students were not asked to analyze and give their opinions about religious texts but were taught to accept official interpretations as correct.

Chapter 9 in this book includes a discussion of the reaction in the nineteenth century to both the content and the method of this type of instruction. It is important to understand that at this point in the history of education this method of instruction and content were part of a worldview whose adherents believed the good society could be achieved only through obedience to the word of God. In other words, educational practices were consistent with the philosophy and organization of society at that time. It is also important to understand the continuity in history. For example, in the nineteenth century the most important schoolbook was Noah Webster's spelling book, which has many of the characteristics of *The New England Primer*.

The grammar school provided a strikingly different type of education than the reading-and-writing schools did. The purpose of the grammar school, in contrast to that of the petty school, was to educate the leaders of society. For instance, the typical goal of the grammar school was stated by the Hopkins Grammar School at New Haven in 1684 as "[the education] of hopeful youth in the Latin tongue, and other learned languages so far as to prepare such youths for the college and public service of the country in church and commonwealth."[13]

Historian Lawrence Cremin, in his monumental study *American Education: The Colonial Experience 1607–1783*, links the development of grammar schools to the Renaissance ideal of the educated public leader. During the Renaissance in the sixteenth century, intellectual leaders began to argue for the proper education of future leaders as the means of producing the just society. Foremost among these thinkers was Desiderius Erasmus, who in the early sixteenth century wrote a treatise titled *The Education of the Christian Prince*. This work calls for the education of a just and wise prince through the study of the Scriptures and the selected works of Plutarch, Seneca, Aristotle, Cicero, and Plato. Of great importance to the development of grammar schools is the emphasis on the study of classical Greek and Roman writers, which would, it was believed, lead to the development of civic character and be a preparation for leadership.

Cremin argues that it was a logical step for the middle class in England to see the type of education proposed by Renaissance writers such as Erasmus as a method of enhancing the social status of the middle class. This argument highlights an important distinction between education as a means of *conferring* status and education as a means of *confirming* status. In the education of a prince, the status of the prince is to be confirmed by the type of education he receives. If the middle class receives the same type of education, it enhances its social position and confers an improved status.[14]

Therefore, the grammar school became an important institution in England and the colonies for the improvement of middle-class status. This represented a great shift in the role of education, one that would have lasting results. First, by conferring status, education assumed the role of providing a degree of upward mobility. By the nineteenth century, increasing numbers of individuals began turning to education as a means of enhancing their social status. In modern times, this role for education was born with the grammar school. Second, grammar schools represented a direct threat to aristocratic control because their existence suggested that individuals could be educated to rule. An issue of concern to aristocratic leaders is the source of a society's leadership. The suggestion that an educated leadership might be superior to an inherited leadership opened the door to the consideration of republican forms of government. The argument that a systematic study of Greek and Latin authors would produce superior leaders in government and church contributed to the rapid expansion of grammar schools in England in the sixteenth century. By the time of the settlement of North America, grammar schools had become an established part of the educational landscape in England. In the colonies, as was previously mentioned, the Massachusetts Law of 1647 required the establishment of a grammar school in every town with one hundred or more households. By 1700, thirty-nine grammar schools had been founded in New England.

The typical grammar school provided a seven-year education with major emphasis on the study of Latin and minor emphasis on Greek and Hebrew. The schools were divided into eight forms and concentrated on the study of Latin grammar, Latin conversation and composition, and Latin readings. In addition, students studied Greek and Hebrew grammar and Greek literature. Cremin writes, "As a rule, mornings were devoted to grammar, afternoons to literature, Fridays to review and the testing of memorization, Saturdays to themes and Sundays to catechizing and other religious exercises."[15]

It is important to remember that the purpose of the classical education in the grammar school was to provide instruction in the wisdom of the Greeks and Romans as preparation for civic and religious responsibilities and leadership. Another step in this preparation was to receive a college education. It is significant to note that after the American Revolution, many leaders, including Thomas Jefferson, began to view American colleges as the source of republican leadership; this idea had its roots in sixteenth- and seventeenth-century educational arguments.

A first act by colonists in the Massachusetts Bay Colony was to establish Harvard College in 1636. Its founding is described in a pamphlet, *New England's First Fruits*, published in London in 1642: "After God had carried us safe to New England, and we had built our houses, provided necessaries for our liveli-hood, rear'd convenient places for God's worship, and settled the Civil Government: One of the next things we longed for, and looked after was to advance Learning, and perpetuate it to Posterity."[16] To advance learning, the colonists accepted money and books from John Harvard for the founding of Harvard College.

New England's First Fruits states clearly that the purpose of Harvard College was to ensure an educated ministry for the colony. It was feared that no replacements would be forthcoming for the religious leaders who had led the colonists from England. In the words of *New England's First Fruits,* there was a "dreading to leave an illiterate Ministry to the Churches, when our present Ministers shall lie in the Dust."[17] Thus the goal of Harvard College was to guarantee continuity in the social organization and leadership of the colony.

Studies of the occupations of Harvard graduates in the seventeenth century confirm the role of the college in educating religious and civic leaders. Roughly half, or 180, of the 368 Harvard alumni completing their studies between 1642 and 1689 became clergymen. The next largest group of alumni, 42, became public servants—governors, councillors, judges, and permanent government officials. Twenty-seven of the alumni became physicians and 13 became schoolmasters and college tutors. Occupations for 68 of the alumni could not be determined and 27 died at a young age. The remaining alumni were classified as merchants, planters, gentlemen, soldiers, mariners, and miscellaneous.[18]

After reviewing the purposes and history of reading and writing schools and of grammar schools and the establishment of Harvard College, one can understand historian Merle Curti's argument that the educational system in New England was designed to protect existing authority by providing a class system of education. Reading-and-writing schools, which the majority of the school-going population attended, provided an authoritarian education and taught only the skills necessary to read and understand religious and civil decrees. On the other hand, grammar schools and Harvard College trained society's future leadership by providing an education in the classics. It is important to understand that the latter type of education provided knowledge that was ornamental but not necessarily useful. In other words, education in the classics became a means of conferring and identifying social status.

Education in colonial New England must be understood in the context of a group of people struggling for survival in an unknown wilderness. The colonists faced many problems and experienced labor shortages that blurred social-class lines. The different forms of schooling were not a closed system in which all individuals below a certain level of social status were excluded from attendance at a grammar school. Nor was education the chief and only means of improving one's position in society. In fact, when dealing with education from the perspective of the twentieth century, one always faces the problem of attributing too much importance to its past social role. What is described here is only the early beginnings of a system that rapidly increased in importance and size during the nineteenth century.

COLONIALISM AND EDUCATIONAL POLICY

In the seventeenth century, marked differences existed among the colonial policies of the various nations with colonies in North and South America. In fact, national policies differed during the various periods of colonization. The differences in colonial policies were reflected in the educational practices of the various North American colonies. The result was sharp variations in educational practices among the different regions of North America in the seventeenth and eighteenth centuries and, in the nineteenth century, differences among the states.

Historian Lawrence Cremin's *American Education* provides an insight into the effects of colonial policies. Cremin believes that educational history has been too narrowly defined as the history of schooling. He has written educational history as the history of all institutions that have shaped American thought and character, including families, churches, libraries, museums, publishers, newspapers, and benevolent societies. As part of this general approach, Cremin emphasizes the importance of colonial policy in the transmission of culture to the New World.

The differences in English colonial policy in different regions can be understood by comparing Virginia with New England. The Virginia companies chartered in 1606 were concerned primarily with the establishment of plantations that would yield a profit. During the early years of the Virginia settlement, education was in the hands of ministers for the purposes of maintaining discipline and order and controlling the Native Americans. During these early years Virginia was above all viewed as a trading post in the wilderness. In 1609 this colonial policy changed when families were transported from England to settle on small plots of land. The colony was governed like a military outpost as opposed to an agricultural community. Education consisted of little more than colonists going to church twice daily. By the 1620s more settlers were brought to Virginia and an ordered community was established. Several unsuccessful attempts to establish schools occurred between 1618 and 1622.

The regional differences in early colonial policies created different educational traditions in Virginia and New England. As discussed earlier, the Massachusetts Bay Colony was established with a particular religious purpose and as a colony of self-sustaining families. Unlike the colony of Virginia, its major goal was not to provide a profit for English-based companies. Consequently, schooling became important as a means of sustaining a well-ordered religious commonwealth. In Virginia, on the other hand, less attention was paid to the education of the average colonist. Reading-and-writing schools were established in Virginia in the seventeenth century, but their numbers were small compared with those in New England. By 1689 Virginia had six reading-and-writing schools while Massachusetts had twenty-three.[19]

Most historians of colonial education have depicted early education in Virginia and the rest of the South as being aristocratic. Only a few pauper schools and apprenticeship training were available for the poor, but for the elite there were private pay schools and opportunities for education in the mother country. It can be argued that, within the context of colonial policy, Virginia best represented the educational policies of England in contrast to the colonies in New England. This was a result of more direct control from the mother country and the emphasis on colonization for profit.

Colonial policy in New Netherland represents a different and more complex situation. By the time of the English conquest of New Netherland in
1664, it had a population of over five thousand living in a dozen Dutch
villages and a few Puritan, Swedish, and Finnish settlements. The Dutch
villages had less self-government than the New England towns and less of a
sense of educational mission.

Before the English conquest of New Netherland, the Dutch West Indies
Company had founded schools in eleven of the twelve Dutch communities.
A struggle within the Dutch West Indies Company over schools in New
Amsterdam resulted in the company paying the cost of the schoolmaster, the
city paying for the schoolhouse and teacher's dwelling, and control administered by the local government. The English continued the practice of letting
local officials and the courts hire, remove, and supervise teachers in local schools.

A major result of the more diverse population that settled in New York
was the emergence of a variety of educational institutions. New York City
(New Amsterdam) developed a system of private schools that dominated the
educational scene until the early nineteenth century. These private schools
offered a broad range of subjects, including instruction in the practical arts.
They also served the particular needs of several religious interests and therefore avoided any major clash among the different religious factions over the
content of schooling. This would become a major issue in New York in the
nineteenth century, when public support for education was expanded. Therefore, in New York, English colonial policy involved a certain degree of respect
for religious and ethnic differences. This allowed for the development of more
diversity in educational institutions.

A similar development occurred in the settlement of Pennsylvania, but
with a major clash between German and English settlers over language usage.
In many respects, the problems encountered in Pennsylvania foreshadowed
conflicts in the nineteenth and twentieth centuries over which language
should be used in the schools. Pennsylvania is also a good example of how
colonial policy viewed education as a means of establishing the superiority of
one ethnic group over another. Here the language used in the schools was
thought to be the means by which one ethnic group could gain cultural
ascendancy over another.

William Penn, the Quaker founder of Pennsylvania, actively recruited the
oppressed from England and the Continent to settle in the New World. The
original settlement of English Quakers and Anglicans was followed by a large
German settlement of religious minorities, including Mennonites, Dunkers,
and Amish. Both the Amish and Mennonites would be in conflict with civil
authorities over the issue of schooling through the twentieth century. Groups
of other religious minorities from Scotland, Ireland, England, and Germany
also settled throughout Penn's colony. By 1766 Benjamin Franklin estimated
that the colonial population of 160,000 consisted of one-third Quakers, one-
third Germans, and one-third religious minorities from a variety of places in
Europe.[20]

Major differences existed between English control in New York and in Pennsylvania. In New York, the English attempted to Anglicize the administration of the colony while allowing diversity in cultural and social institutions. In Pennsylvania, the English embarked on a policy of "cultural Anglicization."[21] This policy was directed in particular at the Germans, who caused the greatest fears among the English settlers. A letter to John Penn in 1727 warned him about German immigration: "At this rate you will soon have a German colony here, and perhaps such a one as Britain once received from Saxony in the fifth century."[22] Concern was so great that the Pennsylvania Assembly passed a law in 1727 requiring all male German immigrants to swear an oath of allegiance to the British Crown.

The great fear was that the culture and language of the settlers would become German. As a result, proposals began to appear that would prohibit German printing houses, the publication of German government documents, and the importing of German books. Of great importance were the recommendations for the establishment of English-language schools. These were viewed as a means of countering and suppressing the expansion of German culture.

Benjamin Franklin was a major proponent of English-language schools and opponent of the expansion of German culture. He played a significant role in the establishment of charity schools, which were to be used for Anglicization. The schools originated as religious institutions for educating the poor German children of the province. Appeals for funds for the schools spread to London, where in 1753 an enthusiastic supporter of the endeavor, William Smith, proclaimed: "By a common education of English and German youth at the same schools, acquaintances and connections will be formed, and deeply impressed upon them in their cheerful and open moments. The English language and a conformity of manners will be acquired."[23]

In early 1755 the first schools were organized and a press was purchased from Franklin. Immediately the German community attacked the schools for giving a false picture of German culture. This attack caused the failure of the schools. At their peak in 1759 the schools served only 600 to 750 children, of whom two-thirds were German. By 1764 the effort was considered a failure.[24]

This brief history of the attempt to Anglicize the Germans in Pennsylvania illustrates a continuing theme in American educational history: the use of the school as a means of spreading a particular culture has resulted in tensions between organized school systems on one side, and immigrant groups, Native Americans, Mexican Americans, Puerto Ricans, and African Americans on the other. In the nineteenth century many of the religious tensions caused by Catholics' perception of the public school system as Protestant could also be considered a result of cultural differences.

Although the Germans in Pennsylvania eventually did become Anglicized, they retained their own separate German schools and churches throughout the colonial period. The result was an educational system in the colony that relied on a combination of apprenticeship, private schools, and schools operated by the different religious denominations. The attempt to

Anglicize the German population through charity schools was one of the first attempts in America to use education as a means of cultural imperialism.

The educational goals of many of the religious schools in Pennsylvania and New York were similar to those of the schools in New England. Memorization, submission, and authority were all emphasized in the instruction and the curriculum, and *The New England Primer* was used throughout these colonies. However, the pattern of development of the educational system in Pennsylvania and New York was distinctively different from that in New England and the southern colonies. New England placed an emphasis on the establishment of town schools to assure the perpetuation of religious values and obedience to the government. The southern colonies displayed little interest in the development of educational institutions except for private schools and tutors for the planter class.

These regional differences were a function of England's colonial policies. The most lasting of these differences was between the North and the South. Throughout the nineteenth century the South lagged behind the North in the development of government-operated systems of education, and in the late nineteenth and twentieth centuries the regions continued to be divided on the issue of segregated education. It was not until the 1950s and 1960s that the major differences between the educational systems of the North and the South began to fade.

FREEDOM OF THOUGHT AND THE ESTABLISHMENT OF ACADEMIES

An intellectual revolution occurred in the seventeenth and eighteenth centuries that changed the purposes of education and made possible a secular school system. This revolution encompassed two major developments. The first was the emergence of the argument that freedom of ideas is essential to the development of society. The second was a growing awareness that education and learning can be instrumental and useful in improving the conditions of society.

These developments reflected changes in political thinking that were integral in shaping the American Revolution. The belief that the maintenance of a republican society requires freedom of thought and beliefs became embodied in American political life in the words of the First Amendment to the Constitution, which prohibits Congress from making any laws that would abridge freedom of speech and the press. Both of these intellectually revolutionary concepts were also related to new developments in science and technology that promised to enhance the quality of human existence.

In England, the struggle for intellectual freedom found its outlet in the establishment of dissenting academies. The idea of the academy was brought to the colonies, where it underwent changes to meet the practical needs of the New World. An important aspect of the academy movement was that it provided a clear alternative to the classical education of the grammar schools and colleges of the seventeenth and eighteenth centuries. The academies also provided an early model for the development of the high school.

The curriculum of the academy, with its dissenting tradition and its emphasis on practical skills, made the school something more than an institution for cultivating religious and civic obedience or shaping future leaders. The academy taught ideas and skills directly related to the practical side of life and provided intellectual tools for the development of new knowledge about the material world.

The changes in thinking about schooling and freedom of ideas were part of the ideological justification of the American Revolution that appeared in pamphlets and newspapers distributed in England and the colonies during the seventeenth and eighteenth centuries. Historian Bernard Bailyn describes his study of these pamphlets and newspapers:

> It confirmed my belief that intellectual developments in the decade before Independence led to a radical idealization of the previous century and a half of American experience, and that it was this intimate relationship between Revolutionary thought and the circumstances of life in eighteenth-century America that endowed the Revolution with its peculiar force and made it so profoundly a transforming event.[25]

An early work in this revolutionary tradition, and the one most directly related to schools, was Robert Molesworth's *Account of Denmark as It Was in the Year 1692.* Molesworth's book is one of the first criticisms of the use of schooling to create obedient and submissive citizens. The purpose of his study was to find the elements that had been most important in transforming Denmark into a system of hereditary absolutism. A key to explaining this transformation was the gaining of absolute obedience of the people to the state.

Molesworth believed that obedience had been gained by linking religion to the state and making education a function of religion. He argued that religious orders preached and taught a doctrine of submission and obedience to both heavenly and earthly rulers. When religion linked arms with government, religious doctrines were used to justify tyranny, and when education was a function of a state-established religion, religious doctrines were used to justify the power of the state and to mold future citizens into a condition of obedience.

In his study of tyranny in Denmark, Molesworth writes, "Enslaving the Spirits of the People, as preparative to that of their Bodies; . . . those Foreign Princes think it their Interest that Subjects should obey without reserve, and all Priests, who depend upon the Prince, are for their own sakes obliged to promote what he esteems his Interest." After establishing the interrelationships of interests, he goes on to lament, "'Tis plain, the Education of Youth, on which is laid the very Foundation Stones of the Public Liberty, has been of late years committed to the sole management of such as make it their business to undermine it."[26]

According to Molesworth, a major service that religion performed for the state through education of youth was "to recommend frequently to them what they call the Queen of all virtues, Viz. Submission to Superiors, and an entire blind Obedience to Authority." Of even greater importance, this educational system caused the people to forget that government was a product of human actions—not divine intervention. By making government appear divine in origin, religiously controlled education could teach obedience to government as if it were obedience to divine authority. Such education taught "that the People ought to pay an Absolute Obedience to a limited Government; fall down and worship the Work of their own Hands, as if it dropt from Heaven."[27]

A major conclusion of Molesworth's study is that education, in order to contribute to liberty and freedom, must be secular and separated from religion. He called for the professor to replace the priest and for students to learn the content of their classical studies rather than just the grammar. He believed that education must be both free of religious dogma in service to the state and free to lead the learner down the path of reason.

Molesworth's criticisms of education could easily have been applied to the type of education provided in *The New England Primer* and to the reading and writing schools of the seventeenth and eighteenth centuries. His study became part of a general discussion with his two friends John Trenchard and Thomas Gordon, who provided the broadest defense of freedom of ideas and learning that had so far been offered. Their essays were distributed between 1720 and 1723 as *Cato's Letters* and were reprinted many times during the subsequent twenty-five years. These essays, which are considered a primary source for the justification of the American Revolution, provided topics for endless political discussions in public houses on both sides of the Atlantic Ocean.[28]

The essays defend freedom of thought and speech as essential to the economics and social development of a nation. In making the link between social progress and freedom, the *Letters* offer their defense in concrete terms, not merely as an appeal to abstract justice: A country needs freedom because without freedom there can be no growth in human wisdom and invention and, consequently, no progress in economic development. The authors of *Cato's Letters* believed that tyranny and slavery stop social development and improvement in human well-being, whereas freedom and liberty lead people down the road to progress and happiness.[29]

Cato's Letters define freedom of thought and speech as a right that can be abridged only to protect the freedom of others: "Without Freedom, there can be no such Thing as Wisdom; and no such Thing as public liberty, without Freedom of Speech: Which is the Right of every Man, as far as by it he does not hurt and control the Right of another." This one limitation on freedom, they declared, "is the only Check which it ought to suffer, the only Bounds which it ought to know."[30]

In linking freedom of thought to human progress, the authors of *Cato's Letters* argue that humans in their original state of nature contented themselves with "the Spontaneous Productions of Nature," but these "spontaneous" supplies proved insufficient to support increasing numbers of humans. The next step was "to open the bosom of the Earth, and, by proper Application and Culture, to extort her hidden stores." The differing degrees of prosperity that existed among nations are considered largely a product of different levels of advancement in the state of learning, which allowed the more advanced nations to enjoy greater productivity. Wisdom and art, the authors argue, promote prosperity, which in turn provides full employment, economic well-being, and a general elevation of the spirit and culture of a people. If the advancement of wisdom and learning fails to occur, unemployment will come and result in human misery. In describing the conditions that produce human misery, they write, "People, in most countries, are forced, for want of other Employment, to cut the Throats of one another, or of their neighbors; and to ramble after their Princes in all their mad conquests . . . and all to get, with great Labour, Hazard, and often with great Hunger and slaughter, a poor precarious, and momentary subsistence."[31]

The equation made in *Cato's Letters* between freedom of ideas and the good life is this: Freedom of thought and speech promotes wisdom, which in turn provides the basis for prosperity and the elimination of the crime that grows from hunger and poverty. Within the framework of this argument, tyranny must be avoided because it hinders the growth of wisdom, prosperity, and social happiness. "Ignorance of Arts and Sciences, and of everything that is good, together with Poverty, misery, and desolation, are found for the most part all together, and are all certainly produced by Tyranny."[32]

The arguments in *Cato's Letters* and in Molesworth's writings give an entirely different perspective on the nature of schooling and the role of schooling in society. In the context of their arguments, if education took place in an environment free of ideological restraints, particularly those of religion, it would be the source of material benefits for society. These arguments reflect the scientific revolution that emerged in the seventeenth century as the result of work by individuals such as Francis Bacon.

Bacon was one of the first people to see in science hope for the progress of humanity. During his life as a barrister, essayist, and scientist, he envisioned a utopia made possible by the use of the scientific method. In his book *Novum Organum* (1620), he argued that scientific experimentation would unlock the secrets of nature and usher in a golden era. His utopian novel *New Atlantis* describes a society in which the central institution is a College of Six Days Work's, devoted to the scientific study of nature.[33]

Bacon's early arguments were accepted by intellectuals such as Molesworth and the authors of *Cato's Letters*. In the eighteenth century this group of English political thinkers, scientists, inventors, and early industrialists was known as *commonwealthmen*. The scientists and inventors in the group included Matthew Boulton, James Watt, Erasmus Darwin, Samuel Galton, and Joseph Priestly.[34] All of these persons had contact with other intellectuals in Glasgow and Edinburgh and interacted freely with members of the leading philosophical societies in England.

This group of intellectuals took the argument for freedom of ideas one step further than would their counterparts in North America. They objected to government-provided systems of education as a threat to intellectual freedom. English historian Brian Simon has written about Joseph Priestly and this group of intellectuals: "In common with . . . all other dissenters, Priestly was adamantly opposed to education becoming a function of the state. Should it do so, it would not achieve the object he desired, on the contrary, it would be used to promote uniformity of thought and belief."[35] Joseph Priestly used specific examples to show the negative results of government-controlled education. For instance, he often referred to the attempt at Oxford University to discourage the reading of John Locke's *Essay on Human Understanding*. Priestly believed that any group that gained control of the educational system could greatly increase its power over the rest of society. He argued that education should encourage free inquiry and inspire the love of truth and that state-endowed education would be more committed to instilling a particular set of religious, moral, or political principles than to training the mind for the free use of reason.

Historian Caroline Robbins summarizes Priestly's ideas about state-provided education as follows: "The chief glory of human nature, the operation of reason in a variety of ways and with diversified results, would be lost. Every man should educate his children in his own manner to preserve the balance which existed among the several religious and political parties in Great Britain."[36]

In England, the institution through which the advocates of intellectual freedom expressed their beliefs became the dissenting academies established in the latter half of the seventeenth century. These academies served as refuges for Nonconformist ministers and others dissenting against the major religious and educational institutions in England. Their growth was a direct result of the closing in 1662 of Oxford and Cambridge to non-Anglicans. The dissenting academies became centers of intellectual and educational innovation as they promoted science and rejected a strictly classical curriculum. In fact, the academies introduced English as the language of instruction.

Although various types of academies served numerous purposes, many of the academies accepted the idea that science and politics were suitable subjects for the curriculum and that freedom of inquiry should be encouraged. Some academies were run by individuals; others were operated by religious denominations. The variety of schools and the commitment of most of them to intellectual freedom made the academies an important source of educational innovation in the eighteenth century. In England they were considered an alternative to older forms of higher education. When the academy idea was introduced into the colonies, it served as a model both for newly established colleges and, in the nineteenth century, for the development of the high school.

In conclusion, the intellectual revolution that fostered the importance of freedom of ideas had two significant consequences for schooling: First, it led to a different concept of the purposes of education and institutional organization. Within this framework, education was viewed as providing the intellectual tools, scientific knowledge, and inventions required to create a better society. Second, this intellectual revolution attacked the notion that the primary purpose of education was to bring people into obedience to a church or government.

EDUCATION AS SOCIAL MOBILITY

The academy movement in North America was primarily a result of the desire to provide a more utilitarian education than that provided in classical grammar schools. The North American academies were modeled after the English dissenting academies, but unlike those in England, they were not a response to exclusion from other educational institutions, nor did they place as much emphasis on intellectual freedom. In North America these institutions served two needs: They provided a useful education, and at the same time they transmitted the culture required for entrance into the middle class. In other words, they were institutions that could provide social mobility for the average citizen. They were often called *people's colleges.*

The academy movement spread rapidly in the eighteenth and nineteenth centuries. In 1855 Henry Barnard reported the existence of 6,185 academies in the United States, with a total enrollment of 263,096. As in England, the academies in North America were varied in curriculum and organization. In general, a mixture of public and private control and financing was used. Often, small towns would provide financial support to local academies under the control of a private board of trustees. The curricula of the academies tended to be flexible and adaptable to the needs of the student, although, of course, this varied from institution to institution.[37]

One of the earliest and most famous plans for an academy was Benjamin Franklin's *Proposals Relating to the Education of Youth in Pennsylvania* (1749). Ironically, the institution established to carry out his plans, which eventually became the University of Pennsylvania, failed to teach his curriculum, but nonetheless it became a widely discussed model for other academies. In many ways, Franklin's model academy embodied the elements of the life experiences that had gone into his own education. A famous phrase from his proposal states, "it would be well if [students] could be taught every Thing that is useful, and every Thing that is ornamental: But Art is long, and their Time is short. It is therefore propos'd that they learn those Things that are likely to be most useful and most ornamental."[38]

Franklin's life was a model for getting ahead in the New World. He was exposed early in life to the major types of educational institutions that existed in the colonies. Benjamin Franklin was born in Boston in 1706 and at the age of eight was sent by his father to grammar school to prepare to be a minister. His father, who became financially unable to carry through with this plan, later withdrew Franklin from the grammar school. He was sent to a school for writing and arithmetic and was made an apprentice to his brother in the

newspaper trade. Eventually he rebelled and left Boston, going to Philadelphia in 1723 to pursue his trade of printer.

Although his life in Philadelphia demonstrated the opportunities available in the New World for upward mobility, Franklin's ability eventually to
become an internationally recognized scientist and statesman was dependent
on his self-education.

The "useful" elements in Franklin's education were the skills learned in
his apprenticeship and through his reading. The "ornamental" elements, on
the other hand, were the knowledge and social skills learned through reading, writing, and debating, which provided him with the culture needed to
advance in the world. A main source of his ornamental education was a club
he organized in Philadelphia called the Junto. The Junto met every Friday
evening, and its members were required to prepare questions dealing with
morals, philosophy, and politics. Every three months they had to write an
essay and defend it to the other members. As Franklin wrote in his *Autobiography*, the purpose of the club was "mutual improvement."[39] Mutual improvement and self-education were also Franklin's reasons for founding the first
subscription library in America. He recommended to the members of the
Junto that they place all their individually owned books into a common library
for the benefit of all members. Out of this grew the idea of a subscription
library, to which library members would pay a fee for expenses and the
purchase of new books. Franklin believed that these libraries improved the
general culture of the average citizen:

> These libraries have improved the general conversation of the Americans,
> made the common tradesmen and farmers as intelligent as most gentlemen
> from other countries, and perhaps have contributed in some degree to the
> stand so generally made throughout the Colonies in defense of their privi-
> leges.[40]

The academy Franklin proposed was an institutionalized version of both
his formal schooling and his self-education. The academy proposal can also
be viewed as a model of an educational system that would confirm one's
status in the middle class or prepare one for entrance into the middle class in
eighteenth-century North America. Certainly, Franklin's *Autobiography* can be
considered a guide to social mobility in the world as he knew it.

The educational content that Franklin proposed reflects the influence of
the radical English writers who did so much to spark the American Revolution. His plan includes the study of English through reading *Cato's Letters* and
the writings of the English radical Algernon Sidney. It should be noted that
Cato's Letters had been published only a few decades before the publication of
Franklin's proposal, but in his proposal Franklin refers to them as classics.

Franklin placed a great deal of emphasis on the teaching of style in both
writing and speaking. Proper style, for Franklin, included writing clearly and
concisely and "pronouncing properly, distinctly, emphatically, not with an
even Tone, which under-does, nor a theatrical, which over-does Nature."[41] It
was style in writing and speaking that would allow an individual to move
through the social world with grace.

According to Franklin, the substance behind the style would emerge from the study of history, which in its broadest sense would be the vehicle for learning the "most useful" knowledge. In Franklin's words, "But if History be made a constant Part of their Reading . . . may not almost all Kinds of useful Knowledge be that Way introduc'd to Advantage, and with Pleasure to the Student?"[42] For Franklin, history was a vehicle for teaching morality, oratory, geography, politics, philosophy, human affairs, agriculture, technology, science, and invention. The teaching of history, combined with the teaching of style in writing and speech, would provide the "most useful and most ornamental" in learning.

Franklin's proposal heralded the beginning of the academy movement in North America. Although academies came in many forms and were governed by a variety of public and religious groups, they were all considered to be distinct from the classical grammar school. Unlike the grammar schools, the academies were conceived as institutions to provide a practical education. This is best exemplified in the wording of the constitution of the Phillips Academy, founded in 1778. It states that the founding of the academy was "for the purpose of instructing Youth, not only in English and Latin Grammar, Writing, Arithmetic, and those Sciences, wherein they are taught; but more especially to learn them the GREAT END AND REAL BUSINESS OF LIVING."[43]

Over the years the identify of the academies fluctuated: They were sometimes considered to be small colleges and at other times high schools. By the latter part of the nineteenth century, however, academies had established a primary identity as institutions providing a secondary education. Also by the end of the nineteenth century, they had become identified as institutions for educating the elite. This view of the academy had not yet emerged in the eighteenth and early nineteenth centuries.

A direct contribution by the academy movement to the development of high schools in the United States was made in 1821, when the English Classical School was founded in Boston. At that time, most academies were country boarding schools. A group of parents in Boston complained about having to send their children either outside the city to attend an academy or—the only alternative—to the Boston Latin School, where a traditional grammar school curriculum was taught. The city responded to the complaints by founding the English Classical School, which offered a curriculum typical of academies of the time, including English, geography, arithmetic, algebra, geometry, trigonometry, history, navigation, and surveying. Within a few years, the school was renamed English High School and became the first high school in the United States.

The history of dissenting academies in England and academies in North America demonstrates the interrelationship among politics, the organization of society, and education. The dissenting academies, born in the midst of revolutionary talk that quickly spread to the North American continent, were institutions reflecting the new spirit of science and industrial development. Transplanted to the New World, they became institutions for teaching what was considered useful knowledge and for providing social mobility. A real irony of history is that by the late nineteenth century the academies in the

United States served primarily to confirm the social status of elite members of society.

THE FAMILY AND THE CHILD

A popular interpretation of historical change in the United States is to view it as a process of institutional expansion and contraction. In this framework, the institution of the family is portrayed as contracting while other institutions assume roles once performed by it. In terms of the history of education, this means the school has assumed tasks previously performed by the family as educational responsibilities have shifted from the parents to the school-teacher. In addition, changes in commonly held concepts of children and of women have had a fundamental effect on the organization of education. Changes in the concept of childhood provided a basis for the belief that the proper education of children could create the ideal political and social world.

In *American Education*, Cremin interprets educational history mainly as a shifting set of institutional arrangements wherein the family had the basic responsibility for education. Cremin writes, "The household remained the single most fundamental unity of social organization in the eighteenth-century colonies and, for the vast majority of Americans, the decisive agency of deliberate cultural transmission."[44] In frontier areas, he argues, the family often assumed the functions of both church and school, whereas in more settled areas it shared these responsibilities with other institutions.

The importance of the socializing role of the family in colonial life is highlighted in John Demos's study *A Little Commonwealth: Family Life in Plymouth Colony*. Demos ascribes a variety of functions to the colonial family. First, it was a business; work was a natural part of family life, and most households were self-sufficient. Second, it was a school; parents and masters were required by law to attend to the education of their children. Third, it was a vocational institution; it transmitted skills for earning a living. Fourth, it was a church; family worship supplemented the work of formal religious institutions. Fifth, the family was a house of correction in which idle and even criminal persons were sentenced to live as servants. And last, the family was a welfare institution that functioned at various times as a hospital, orphanage, old people's home, and home for the poor."[45]

Within this broad-ranging institution was a strict hierarchy, with the father at the top and the children at the bottom. The colonial family operated on a simple premise: "He for God only, she for God in him." This meant that women were to bow to the God in men, and men were to assume the spiritual care of women. In legal matters, the married woman was at the mercy of her husband—she was without rights to own property, make contracts, or sue for damages.

Although women were dependent on men, they still had to assume responsibility for their own individual salvation, and in order to do so they had to learn how to read. This created an ambivalent situation regarding the education of women. The education of women was undertaken purely for purposes of religious control, but, ironically, even though women were considered the weaker sex with regard to intellectual capacities, they not only assumed responsibility for teaching reading within the household but also functioned as neighborhood teachers in the dame schools and, during the summer, the district schools of New England.

In general, the education of women was limited to basic reading, writing, and arithmetic, but their role as teachers in the family and in dame schools foreshadowed their dominant role as teachers in public schools in the late nineteenth and twentieth centuries. This role of teacher opened the door to further education for women and provided a career for them that became an important stepping-stone on the road to greater equality and rights.

Children in the colonial family were in a position of complete subordination to their parents. The requirement to honor one's parents extended even into adulthood. This is best exemplified by a statue of the Plymouth Colony that stated, "If any Childe or Children above sixteen years old, and of competent Understanding, shall curse or Smite their Natural Father or Mother; he or they shall be put to Death, unless it can be sufficiently testified that the Parents have been very Unchristianly negligent in the Education of such Children."[46]

Of major importance to the family was the economic function of the child. In a world where most families were financially self-sufficient, each new pair of helping hands was welcomed. After infancy, the colonial child usually helped with agricultural chores during the summer and attended school in the winter. Between the age of seven and puberty, children were fully integrated into the work force. Many times, the family would apprentice out to another family boys over the age of seven. The economic value of the child to the family was clearly demonstrated by the requirement that if the boy left home to work he was expected to pay for a substitute for his labor. Often families considered the child's value during the winter to be no more than the cost of providing board, but during the summer months the child's labor was considered essential. It is not surprising that families would resist child labor laws in the nineteenth and twentieth centuries, given the deep roots of this traditional view of the economic worth of the child to the family unit."[47]

The primary responsibility of colonial parents to their children was to raise them to live according to God's commandments. This meant caring for their physical and spiritual needs. Parental strictness was required because of a belief that all children at birth shared in the common sins of humanity. This belief is best exemplified by the alphabet in *The New England Primer* that begins,

> *A* in Adam's Fall We Sinned All
> *B* Thy Life to Mend This Book Attend.[48]

The "Book" referred to is the Bible, which was presented as the source of correction of the Original Sin in which all children were believed to have been born.

The emphasis in child rearing was to prevent children from leading a life of sin. In other words, parents had an obligation to make sure their children were good. What this meant is expressed in the following verse from *The New England Primer:*

Good Children Must

Fear God all Day	Love Christ Always,
Parents Obey,	In Secret Pray,
No False thing Say,	Mind Little Play,
By no Sin Stray,	Make no delay,

In doing Good.[49]

This attitude toward children can be understood more clearly by contrasting it with other concepts of childhood that began to be popularized in the eighteenth century. For instance, the French philosopher Jean-Jacques Rousseau believed that the child is born good and that the greatest danger in childhood is corruption by the outside world. He popularized this concept of childhood in his book *Emile* (1762). *Emile* is Rousseau's plan for the ideal education of a child. To provide Emile, the protagonist, with the best education, Rousseau isolates him from society until the onset of adolescence and places him in a country home under the supervision of a tutor who allows Emile to discover what is necessary and useful for living. The concept of education that permits the child to learn through experience and discovery was a major departure from schooling that emphasized memorization and subordination to authority.[50]

A major contrast exists between colonial ideas about child rearing and Rousseau's theory that moral education should not take place until the child has reached the age of social reasoning—adolescence. Rousseau calls this *negative education,* by which he means that learning is to be a product of experience, not moral and verbal instruction. According to Rousseau, during the early period of their development, human beings are incapable of reasoning about morality and social relations. Thus it is important to avoid placing a child in situations requiring moral choices before she or he is old enough to handle them with her or his own powers of social reasoning. Rousseau felt that books are a great plague in childhood. He did not mean by this that children should not be taught how to read, but that learning to read should be attached to experience and necessity. For example, Emile receives invitations to dinners and parties but cannot find anyone to read them to him. These experiences lead Emile to learn how to read out of self-interest and necessity. Rousseau's method of teaching reading avoids moral instruction; it is not based on a sense of duty or on a belief in an abstract good. For Rousseau, learning and knowledge are tools to be used by the individual—not tools enabling society to use the individual.

Emile demonstrates how a theory of childhood can influence actual child rearing and instruction. The colonial concept that the child is born in a state of sin required restraining children from doing evil and subjecting them to authoritarian instruction to assure a godly life. According to Rousseau, however, children are born in a state of goodness and need to be protected from the sins of the world and allowed freely to develop their basic good nature. Rousseau's concept of childhood means more freedom for the child and a more permissive form of instruction.

Emile heralded the beginning of a romantic concept of childhood, which, in the nineteenth and twentieth centuries, sparked educational trends emphasizing instructional techniques that would allow the free development of the child. In modern times, the major rival to this concept is the idea that the child is born as a blank slate (*tabula rasa*) and is completely molded by the environment. In this theory of childhood, which can be traced to the eighteenth century, can be found the roots of modern behavioral psychology.

The book most closely identified with the origins of the concept of the child as a blank slate is English philosopher John Locke's *Some Thoughts Concerning Education* (1693). For Locke, the adult is primarily a product of his or her education in the world, and this education is a result of rewards and punishment received during childhood. Consequently, Locke argues, the most important factor in education is the development of correct habits, which depends on proper manipulation of rewards and punishment. Locke writes, "I grant, that good and evil, reward and punishment, are the only motives to a rational creature; these are the spur and reins, whereby all mankind are set on work and guided, and therefore they are to be made use of to children too."[51]

According to Locke, the most powerful reward for children is esteem and the most powerful punishment is disgrace (as opposed to corporal punishment). In a sense, Locke calls for the manipulation of parental love as a means of shaping the character of the child. He also expresses concern about children learning bad habits from other children, and he warns parents that sending their offspring to school might lead to such contagion.

Locke's solution to the influence that children exert on one another in school is to have teachers who are able both to teach subject matter and to shape proper habits. He advises parents to keep their children out of school until they find a school "wherein it is possible for the master to look after the manners of his scholars, and . . . show as great effects of his care of forming their minds to virtue, and their carriage to good breeding, as of forming their tongues to the learned languages."[52] In one sense, this echoes the traditional view that the teacher is responsible for the virtue of students. In another sense, however, Locke envisioned what we might call the modern concept of the teacher—a teacher who is given responsibility not only for imparting subjecting matter but also for consciously shaping character. For Locke, the child is viewed not as being either good or evil but as a person to be molded for the future.

Locke's concept of childhood, like Rousseau's, led to the rejection of traditional methods of instruction. Locke criticized what he called the ordinary method of instruction, which fills the mind with rules and precepts that are not understood and are quickly forgotten, and he considered memorization to be the poorest method of instruction. Locke advocated instead that the child learn through performance until the object of the lesson is mastered: "By repeating the same action, till it be grown habitual in them, the performance will not depend on memory, or reflection, the concomitant of prudence and age, and not of childhood; but will be natural in them."[53]

Locke's concept of childhood greatly influenced the development of public schools in the nineteenth and twentieth centuries. The concept of the child as a blank slate allowed educational leaders to believe they could create the good society through the proper molding of children. Nineteenth-century common school reformers such as Horace Mann specifically rejected the Calvinist view of the child born in sin for a concept of the child as a lump of clay that can be shaped for the future. This new concept allowed school reformers to dream of creating the perfect school–one that would produce the perfect political citizen, the perfect moral person, the perfect worker.

The romantic view that children are born good had the most influence on nineteenth- and twentieth-century dissenters against the controlling power of the public school. One model of education in the twentieth century, the "free school," called for opposing this power by encouraging the natural unfolding of the child. The romantic concept of childhood also played a role in the development of adolescent psychology and child study.

These concepts of childhood have never been as distinct in real life as they are in a historian's conceptualization, but they do provide a basis for understanding the effects of different concepts of childhood on the organization of education. The colonial view of childhood created an environment that was controlling and authoritarian. Major changes in education occurred with the rejection of the idea that the child is born in a state of sin and therefore must be controlled and made submissive. The viewpoint that the child is neither good nor evil and is a product of the environment allowed educators to view the school as a panacea for social, economic, and political problems.

CONCLUSION

What distinguishes education in pre-Revolutionary America from that in post-Revolutionary America is the concept of service to the broader needs of government and society. After the American Revolution, many Americans began to believe that a public system of education was needed to build nationalism, to shape the good citizen, and to reform society. In other words, education in the post-Revolutionary period was brought into the service of public policy.

Before the Revolution, education served mainly to prepare an individual to live a godly life and to confer status. The major goal of education was to ensure that the public knew how to read the Bible, religious tracts, and laws. Status was conferred by the classical education of the grammar school and college through the teaching of a particular cultural style and body of knowledge.

Although the colonists thought education was important, they did not believe the creation of an extensive and well-organized system of education was necessary. It was not until education was viewed as a government function, as opposed to a family function, that organized systems of schooling appeared. This occurred when government leaders began to see education as a useful tool for governing society. The closest any of the colonies came to creating a system of education was in the town schools in New England. However, even though these schools were established according to law, they were never organized into an educational system. The middle colonies contained a diversity of religious and private schools, and the southern colonies for the most part neglected the education of the general public.

The forces behind the changes that took place after the Revolution were in evidence in the pre-Revolutionary colonies. The academy movement stimulated thinking about education serving the practical needs of humanity as well as religious needs. Changing concepts of childhood made it possible for educators to dream of schools as institutions for creating the perfect society. And, more important, the general population began to realize the value of learning as a tool for gaining independence, not just for instilling subservience. For instance, Benjamin Franklin believed the rebellious spirit of the population was a result of the wide availability of libraries. In fact, the political tracts read by the colonists were instrumental in setting the stage for the American Revolution. As the history of schooling in the colonial period demonstrates, education can be brought into the service of either authority or independence.

NOTES

1. Quoted in Lawrence Cremin, *American Education: The Colonial Experience 1607–1783* (New York: Harper & Row, 1970), p. 15.
2. A good study of this faith in education is Henry Perkinson, *The Imperfect Panacea: American Faith in Education, 1865–1965* (New York: Random House, 1968).
3. One book that stresses this view of colonial education is Merle Curti, *The Social Ideas of American Educators* (Paterson, N.J.: Pageant Books, 1959). This interpretation of nineteenth-century education can be found in Michael Katz, *Class, Bureaucracy, and Schools: The Illusion of Educational Change in America* (New York: Praeger, 1971).
4. Lawrence Cremin, *The Wonderful World of Ellwood Patterson Cubberley* (New York: Teachers College Press, 1965).
5. Ellwood Cubberley, *Public Education in the United States: A Study and Interpretation of American Educational History* (Boston: Houghton Mifflin, 1934), p. 14.
6. Carl F. Kaestle, *Pillars of the Republic: Common Schools and American Society, 1780–1860* (New York: Hill and Wang, 1983).

7. Rush Welter, *Popular Education and Democratic Thought in America* (New York: Columbia University Press, 1962), p. 9.
8. Reprinted in Ellwood Cubberley, ed., *Readings in Public Education in the United States: A Collection of Sources and Readings to Illustrate the History of Educational Practice and Progress in the United States* (Cambridge, Mass.: Riverside Press, 1934), p. 16.
9. Ibid., pp. 18–19.
10. Curti, *Social Ideas*, pp. 23–24.
11. Paul Leicester Ford, ed., *The New England Primer* (New York: Teachers College Press, 1962).
12. All the quotes from *The New England Primer* are from the edition reprinted in ibid.
13. Quoted in Cremin, *American Education*, p. 186.
14. Ibid., pp. 58–79.
15. Ibid., p. 175.
16. Reprinted in Cubberley, *Readings in Public Education*, p. 13.
17. Ibid.
18. Cremin, *American Education*, pp. 220–221.
19. Ibid., p. 183.
20. Ibid., p. 259.
21. Ibid.
22. Quoted in ibid., p. 260.
23. Quoted in ibid., p. 261.
24. Ibid., p. 262.
25. Bernard Bailyn, *The Ideological Origins of the American Revolution* (Cambridge, Mass.: Harvard University Press, 1967), pp. vi–vii.
26. Robert Molesworth, *An Account of Denmark as It Was in the Year 1692* (Copenhagen: Rosenkilde and Bagger, 1976). None of the pages of the preface is numbered; all quotations are taken from the preface.
27. Ibid.
28. *Cato's Letters: Unabridged Reproduction of 6th Edition 1755*, Vols. I and II, Leonard Levy (New York: Da Capo Press, 1971).
29. Ibid.
30. Ibid., Vol. I, p. 96.
31. Ibid., Vol. II, pp. 306–309.
32. Ibid., p. 312.
33. Cremin, *American Education*, pp. 94–96.
34. Caroline Robbins, *The Eighteenth-Century Commonwealthman* (Cambridge, Mass.: Harvard University Press, 1959).
35. Brian Simon, *Studies in the History of Education, 1780–1870* (London: Lawrence & Wishart, 1960), pp. 34–35.
36. Robbins, *Eighteenth-Century Commonwealthman*, p. 350.
37. Theodore Sizer, ed., *The Age of the Academies* (New York: Teachers College Press, 1964), pp. 1–48.
38. Quoted in ibid., pp. 70–71.

39. L. Jesse Lemisch, ed., *Benjamin Franklin: The Autobiography and Other Writings* (New York: Signet, 1961), p. 72.
40. Ibid., p. 82.
41. Quoted in Sizer, *Age of the Academies,* p. 71.
42. Quoted in ibid.
43. Quoted in ibid., pp. 77–78.
44. Cremin, *American Education,* p. 480.
45. John Demos, *A Little Commonwealth: Family Life in Plymouth Colony* (New York: Oxford University Press, 1970), pp. 183–186.
46. Reprinted in ibid., p. 100.
47. Joseph F. Kett, *Rites of Passage: Adolescence in America, 1790 to the Present* (New York: Basic Books, 1977), pp. 1–38.
48. Ford, *New England Primer.* Pages are unnumbered in the reproduction of the original work contained herein.
49. Ibid.
50. Jean-Jacques Rousseau, *Emile* (New York: Dutton, 1911).
51. Peter Gay, ed., *John Locke on Education* (New York: Teachers College Press, 1964), p. 36.
52. Ibid., p. 48.
53. Ibid., p. 50.

CHAPTER 3

Nationalism, Moral Reform, and Charity in the New Republic

Following the American Revolution a variety of factors made education a central focus of efforts to stabilize the new political system and reform society. These factors contributed to the eventual creation of the common school system in the 1830s. For instance, immediately following the Revolution education was hailed as a method of building loyalty to the new government and unifying the people of the new republic. In addition, some people believed people should be educated before being allowed to practice political freedom. Also, there was a debate about how to educate citizens and leaders of the new government. In addition to these political concerns, there was a growing faith in the possibility of changing human character as a means of combating crime and poverty. Consequently, education increasingly became viewed as a means of saving society from crime and poverty by molding children's character.

Nationalism, which is still a concern of citizenship education, became an important issue after the American Revolution because of the feeling that America needed to be distinguished from its European origins. A search began for an American language, literature, and culture that would unify a nation whose diverse population encompassed a number of languages, religions, and cultures. The use of education as a means of creating a unified population became a major theme in the history of American education.

An important aspect of nationalism is patriotism—"love of country" or an emotional attachment to symbols of the country. The use of education during the post-Revolutionary period to promote feelings of patriotism was not unique to the United States. Leaders of many European countries, particularly Prussia, had realized the importance of encouraging feelings of patriotism as a means of unifying the citizenry and building military strength. The ultimate end of patriotism was to strengthen emotional ties to the country so that the common citizen would be willing to die in military service to the government.

Methods of teaching patriotism included studying a national literature and language, singing nationalistic songs, honoring the flag, and participating in patriotic exercises. In the United States, the most popular promoter of nationalism and patriotism was Noah Webster, often called the "Schoolmaster of America." Webster's spelling book, with its nationalistic themes, replaced *The New England Primer* in importance and use during the post-Revolutionary period.

Another theme that appeared in post-Revolutionary educational literature and that has been continually debated up to present times is how to establish a balance between freedom and order. On the one hand, the rhetoric of the American Revolution stressed the idea of freedom, but on the other hand, the strong religious and political feelings of many citizens of the new republic caused them to fear that uncontrolled freedom would lead to a decadent and chaotic society.

For many Americans, the balance of freedom and order was to be achieved through education. They argued that individuals could be allowed to be free if they were educated to be virtuous. In other words, freedom could be allowed if controls over behavior were internalized within the citizen. Stated in a different manner, freedom meant freedom to do good and act virtuously. Educational proposals by post-Revolutionary leaders such as Noah Webster emphasized the importance of educating citizens to be virtuous and thus to exercise their freedom in a correct manner.

A debate also took place about the type of knowledge needed by citizens of the new republic. Most writers on education realized the importance of an educated citizenry but varied in important ways on their definition of the nature of that education. Two major positions on this issue emerged during the late eighteenth and early nineteenth centuries.

One was that all citizens should be educated to read and write and that political opinions should be formed outside of educational institutions. This position was taken by Thomas Jefferson in his various writings on education. The other position was that educational institutions needed to teach basic principles of a republican form of government. This position was taken by the common school reformers (see Chapter 4).

The differences between these two positions are important. The first position relegates the shaping of political opinions to the free marketplace of ideas and places faith in the ability of individual citizens to form their own political beliefs, whereas the second position posits that it is necessary to have a single institution form correct political ideas. This particular argument entangled the schools in a continuing debate over who should define the political beliefs to be taught in the schools.

Also, educational writers in the post-Revolutionary period were concerned about the sources of leadership for a republican government. For Europeans, this issue was often answered by the existence of an aristocracy. In the new republic, however, educational institutions were frequently considered to be a means of selecting and educating future leaders, thus placing them in a pivotal role in the political and social process. Within this framework, education was given the task of consciously selecting talent. By the twentieth century, the selection process had broadened to encompass occupation as well as political concerns, so that selection became one of the most important social purposes of education.

Besides the political concerns sparked by the Revolution, Americans began to organize institutions for the moral reformation of society. It was believed that crime and poverty would end with the reformation of prisons and the establishment of charity schools. Central to this discussion was the acceptance of the idea that a person's character could be reformed. As I will discuss, faculty psychology contributed to the idea that society could be reformed by schools.

The developments set the stage for the evolution of the common school system in the 1830s and the multiplication of colleges in the early nineteenth century. The organization of the common school system in different states in the 1830s and 1840s provided the basis for the modern system of public schooling in the United States. This chapter will consider the important debates and institutional changes that foreshadowed the development of the common school system and the modern system of higher education.

In addition, the educational debates sparked by the revolution continue to the present. For instance, most governments use schools to teach patriotism. The problem is that nationalism and patriotism have been among the greatest sources of war in the twentieth century. While most people feel positive about their own government's schools teaching patriotism, they resent similar teachings in other countries. For instance, many citizens of the United States objected to the nationalistic and patriotic teachings of German school systems under Nazism and of Soviet schools under communism, while applauding the use of the Pledge of Allegiance and the singing of nationalistic songs in U.S. schools.

Also, the debates over freedom and order and methods of educating citizens are reflected in present-day discussions as to the social role of the school and who should determine the content of citizenship education. Can mass education be a means of maintaining social order? Can mass schooling reform society? Should schools simply provide the tools, such as reading, that will enable people to form their political opinions outside the context of a school? Or should they impose a political education on students? If the schools impose a poitical education, who should determine its content? These are important questions when considering the role of schooling in the political life of a country.

NOAH WEBSTER: NATIONALISM AND EDUCATION

Nationalism was a major theme in the work of Noah Webster. A prolific writer of political and social essays, he left as a legacy a standardized American dictionary of the English language, an American version of the Bible, and his famous spelling book. The wide use of Webster's speller and dictionary throughout the United States created a lasting mold for the American language.

Webster also made a political contribution to the development of the American common school system. Between 1815 and 1819 he served in the Massachusetts legislature and worked actively for a state school fund. One of his speeches to the legislature captures the flavor of what he believed would be the result of a system of common schools:

> I should rejoice to see a system adopted that should lay a foundation for a permanent fund for public schools, and to have more pains taken to discipline our youth in early life to sound maxims of moral, political, and religious duties. I believe more than is commonly believed may be done in this way towards correcting the vices and disorders of society.[1]

One historian has claimed that Webster's activities in the state legislature initiated the movement for common schools that culminated in Horace Mann's work in the 1830s.[2]

Born in Connecticut in 1758, Webster began his early career as a country schoolmaster. While teaching in 1779, he conceived the idea of developing a new system of instruction. In 1783, he completed one spelling book, the first of three volumes in a series titled *A Grammatical Institute of the English Language*. In 1784, he completed a grammar book, the second volume in the series, and a reader, which was the third. In 1785, he packed his bags and rode through the country as an itinerant lecturer, selling his instructional system.

Both his salesmanship and the content of his textbooks proved successful. One and a half million copies of the speller had been sold by 1801, 20 million by 1829, and 75 million by 1875. The speller became a model used by other spelling book authors. Its extreme popularity was demonstrated by the publication in 1863 of a Civil War edition in the South that was adapted "to the youth of the Southern Confederacy."[3]

Webster believed that, in addition to teaching reading and writing, his texts should produce good and patriotic Americans, develop an American language, and create a unified national spirit. As his biographer Harry Warfel states, "This unified series of textbooks effectually shaped the destiny of American education for a century. Imitators sprang up by the dozen, and each echoed Websterian nationalism. The word 'American' became indispensable in all textbook titles; all vied in patriotic eloquence."[4]

Webster believed that moral and political values had to be imposed on the child: "Good republicans . . . are formed by a singular machinery in the body politic, which takes the child as soon as he can speak, checks his natural independence and passions, makes him subordinate to superior age, to the laws of the state, to town and parochial institutions."[5]

One method used to instill proper political values was the Federal Catechism, which appeared in the early verions of Webster's spelling book. The inclusion of a catechism in a spelling book was not an original idea. *The New England Primer* contained one, but it was mainly religious in content. However, a catechism with political content was probably Webster's original idea. The use of a catechism required children to memorize questions and answers, which perpetuated an authoritarian method of instruction.

The content of Webster's Federal Catechism reflected his own concern—that the new republican government remain primarily a representative institution and not become democratic. For example, the Federal Catechism contains the following question and answer to be memorized by the reader:

> Q. What are the defects of democracy?
> A. In democracy, where the people all meet for the purpose of making laws, there are commonly tumults and disorders. A small city may sometimes be governed in this manner; but if the citizens are numerous, their assemblies make a crowd or mob, where debates cannot be carried on with coolness and candor, nor can arguments be heard: Therefore a pure democracy is generally a very bad government. It is often the most tyrannical government on earth; for a multitude is often rash, and will not hear reason.[6]

Webster's spelling books also contained a Moral Catechism to teach the moral values Webster considered necessary for maintaining order in a republican society. Like most Americans of this period, Webster equated public virtue with Christian morality. In other words, a good citizen is one who lives a Christian life. This attitude is similar in some ways to the goals of the early settlers in New England. The first part of the Moral Catechism illustrates the type of Christian morality people like Webster believed necessary in a republican society.

> Q. What is moral virtue?
> A. It is an honest upright conduct in all our dealings with men.
> Q. Can we always determine what is honest and just?
> A. Perhaps not in every instance, but in general it is not difficult.
> Q. What rules have we to direct us?
> A. God's word contained in the Bible has furnished all necessary rules to direct our conduct.
> Q. In what part of the Bible are these rules to be found?
> A. In almost every part; but the most important duties between men are summed up in the beginning of Matthew, in Christ's Sermon on the Mount.[7]

One aspect of Webster's concern with nationalism and virtue was the building of an emotional feeling of patriotism. In an essay entitled "On the Education of Youth in America," published in 1790, Webster writes, "It is an object of vast magnitude that systems of education should be adopted and pursued which may not only diffuse a knowledge of the sciences but may implant in the minds of the American youth the principle of virtue and of liberty and inspire them . . . with an inviolable attachment to their country."[8]

What he meant by an "inviolable attachment" is an emotional bond between citizen and government: Webster believed that "every class of people should know and love the laws" and that attachment to the law "may be formed by early impressions upon the mind." This emotional bond was to be forged by the creation of a national language and by the wide dissemination of the patriotic content of his textbooks. The following statement about Webster's method of selecting material for his readers illustrates his patriotic objectives: "In the choice of pieces, I have not been inattentive to the political interests of America. Several of those masterly addresses of Congress, written at the commencement of the late revolution, contain such noble, just and independent sentiments of liberty and patriotism, that I cannot help wishing to transfuse them into the breasts of the rising generation."[9]

Illustrative of his patriotic themes was the cover of his 1787 reader, which contained the words "Begin with the infant in the cradle; let the first word he lisps be Washington."[10] His readers contained Washington's Farewell Orders to the Army, patriotic poems, and (for the first time in a schoolbook) a history of the Revolutionary War.

For Webster, patriotism, nationalism, and virtue were the foci of educating the republican citizen. These educational values clearly emphasize representative as opposed to democratic government. Noah Webster's importance in the history of American education is twofold: He represented widely held opinions of his times, and he had a major effect on the education of children in the United States in the late eighteenth and nineteenth centuries.

THOMAS JEFFERSON: A NATURAL ARISTOCRACY

Thomas Jefferson's opinions on education in the new republic were quite different from those of his contemporaries and of later leaders of the common school movement. Unlike Benjamin Rush and Noah Webster, Jefferson did not believe that schooling should impose political values or mold the virtuous republican citizen. Rather, he believed that education should provide the average citizen with the tools of reading and writing and that political beliefs would be formed through the exercise of reason. For Jefferson, the most important means of political education was the reading of history and newspapers. In one of his more famous statements, he argues: "The basis of our government being the opinion of the people, the very first object should be to keep that right; and were it left to me to decide whether we should have a government without newspapers, or newspapers without a government, I should not hesitate a moment to prefer the latter."[11]

Jefferson was concerned with the education of future republican leadership. He believed that the new republic needed to identify its future leaders in the early years of their schooling and provide them with an education through college. This educated leadership would form a natural aristocracy.

Jefferson was born in 1743 in Shadwell, near Charlottesville, Virginia. His father was a Virginia magistrate and surveyor, and his mother was a member of one of the most prominent families in the colony. After graduating from the College of William and Mary, Jefferson was admitted to the Virginia bar in 1767. Between 1769 and 1775 he served as a member of the Virginia legislative assembly, and in 1776, as a member of the Continental Congress, Jefferson helped to draft the Declaration of Independence. As a strong proponent of individualistic democracy, he championed legislative proposals and constitutional amendments protecting freedom of speech and religion. In 1800 he was elected president of the United States.

One reason for Jefferson's opinion that democracy is possible was his belief in the existence of an inborn moral sense, which he refers to as "common sense." For this reason, his educational writings do not emphasize shaping and controlling students' moral behavior as a preparation for citizenship. Jefferson wrote to his friend Peter Carr in 1787 that the individual is "endowed with a sense of right and wrong. . . . This sense is as much a part of his nature as the sense of hearing, seeing, feeling; it is the true foundation of morality." Jefferson argues that this innate sense of right and wrong can be improved through exercise, like any other part of the body, and can be guided by reason. On the other hand, the study of moral rules can interfere with the proper functioning of this innate sense of morality. He writes, for example, "State a moral case to a ploughman and a professor. The former will decide it as well, and often better than the latter, because he has not been led astray by artificial rules."[12]

Jefferson's belief in reason and a moral sense did not cause him to reject the importance of knowledge and learning. In a letter to John Adams in 1814 he comments on his disgust with his recent reading of Plato's *Republic*. In simple terms, Plato argues that individuals are born with the world's knowledge and that the role of education is to reveal that inner knowledge to the individual. Jefferson complains in his letter that post-Revolutionary youths seemed to have a similar idea that they had acquired "all learning in their mother's womb and bring it into the world ready made." He goes on to attack the shallow education provided at academies, which committed "pupils to the theatre of the world, with just taste enough of learning to be alienated from industrious pursuits, and not enough to do service in the ranks of science." Jefferson then describes his dream for the establishment of a university that would teach every branch of science to its "highest degree."[13]

Jefferson's ideas on the role of education and knowledge in society reflect a belief in the possibility of improving the human condition: Individuals are born with reason and a moral sense, and education can improve the workings of these faculties and contribute to the increase of human knowledge. In his 1818 "Report of the Commissioners Appointed to Fix the Site of the University of Virginia," Jefferson likens this process to that of creating a new and better tree by grafting a cultivated tree onto a wild and uncultivated one. "Education, in like manner, engrafts a new man on the native stock, and improves what in his nature was vicious and perverse into qualities of virtue and social worth." In addition, he argues, each generation adds to the store of human knowledge, and this "constant accumulation must advance the knowledge and well-being of mankind, not *infinitely*, as some have said, but *indefinitely*, and to a term which no one can fix and foresee."[14]

Jefferson's belief that education can provide the tools and knowledge for the improvement of the exercise of morality and reason is evident in his most famous educational proposal, "A Bill for the More General Diffusion of

Knowledge," made to the Virginia legislature in 1779. This bill proposes that schools be established to provide tuition-free education for three years for all male and female children. In these schools, children were to be taught "reading, writing, and common arithmetick, and the books which shall be used therein for instructing the children to read shall be such as will at the same time make them acquainted with Grecian, Roman, English and American history."[15] This was to be the basic education of the citizens of the new republic.

Jefferson elaborates on the reasons for the content of this education in "Notes on the State of Virginia." He rejects the teaching of the Bible in reading instruction, stating "Instead, therefore, of putting the Bible and Testament into the hands of the children at an age when their judgments are not sufficiently matured for religious inquiries, their memories may here be stored with the most useful facts from Grecian, Roman, European, and American history." The development of morality, he argues, should be postponed until reason matures. The first elements of moral instruction should be for the purpose of teaching children "how to work out their own greatest happiness, by shewing them that it does not depend on the condition of life in which chance has placed them, but is always the result of a good conscience, good health, occupation, and freedom in all just pursuits."[16]

The most important part of moral instruction, according to Jefferson, is the study of history, which guides reason by providing the individual with knowledge about human actions. "History, by apprising them of the past, will enable them to judge of the future; it will avail them of the experience of other times and other nations; it will qualify them as judges of the actions and designs of men."[17]

For Jefferson, education contributes to the balance between freedom and order by providing all citizens with the basic tools of learning, a knowledge of history, and the ability to work out their own happiness and morality. He believed that knowledge, reason, and a developed moral sense would result in a natural order in a free society.

"A Bill for the More General Diffusion of Knowledge" also contains a plan for the selection and education of a natural aristocracy. The bill proposes the establishment of grammar schools in every county. An overseer of the reading-and-writing schools would choose "the boy of best genius in the school, of those whose parents are too poor to give them further education, and . . . send him forward to one of the grammar schools." After every one or two years in the Latin School, the best student of the group would be selected and given six more years of education. "By this means," Jefferson writes in "Notes on the State of Virginia," "twenty of the best geniuses will be raked from the rubbish annually, and instructed, at the public expence, so far as grammar schools go." Out of the selected group of grammar school graduates, half of the best would be sent at public expense for three years to the College of William and Mary.[18]

The talent selected through this three-tier system of education was to provide the leadership for the republic. According to Jefferson, the purpose of higher education is to "form statesmen, legislators and judges, on whom public prosperity and individual happiness are so much to depend." In addition, higher education should teach the principles and structure of government, promote the interests of agriculture and business, and advance the sciences.[19]

Jefferson's educational plan combines two ideas: preparing the citizen and preparing the political leader. Of the two goals, Jefferson believed the instruction of the citizen was the more important: "But of all the views of this law none is more important, none more legitimate, than that of rendering the people the safe, as they are the ultimate, guardians of their own liberty."[20]

From Jefferson's educational writings emerges the following portrait of the ideal citizen. Guided by a knowledge of history and the reading of newspapers, the individual would exercise reason and moral common sense to make political decisions. One of the most important decisions would be the selection of republican leadership. Ideally, the choice would be among members of the natural aristocracy that had been selected by the school system and given a university education. In the end, Jefferson compromised his belief in the free exercise of individual reason by proposing the censorship of political texts in the university training of the natural aristocracy. In this regard, Jefferson succumbed to the temptation of using education to teach what he believed were correct political doctrines. Even the major defender of the role of reason in a democratic society could not resist shaping the political education of future leaders. But even with this qualification of Jefferson's belief in the free exercise of reason, his doctrines provide a sharp contrast to those who believed that public schooling should educate "republican machines."

MORAL REFORM AND FACULTY PSYCHOLOGY

Americans in the early nineteenth century were taken with the idea that institutiions could perfect the good person and create the good society. This pattern of thinking made it possible for educational leaders to envision a system of common schooling that would lead to a moral and political reformation of society. The belief that institutional structures could be used to develop the good society was reflected in the expansion of charity schools in the early part of the nineteenth century and in the establishment of special institutions for delinquent youth.

Charity schools were the first to be based on the Lancasterian system of school organization and instruction, which revolutionized the concept of schooling. Before the introduction of the Lancasterian method, the main purpose of education was to develop the moral character of the child through memorization and recitation of didactic readings. *The New England Primer* is a good example of this type of instruction.

What was new about the institutional changes in the early part of the nineteenth century, and the Lancasterian system of instruction, was the idea that institutional arrangements were important to developing moral character. A belief developed that moral character could be shaped by the way students interacted in the school as well as through the learning of didactic material. In later years this would be referred to as the *process of socialization*.

In the early nineteenth century the belief in the importance of institutional arrangements in shaping moral character contributed to the already developing idea that schooling of the entire population was necessary for social and political order. As discussed earlier in this chapter, post-Revolutionary leaders viewed education as important in promoting nationalism and balancing freedom and order. These ideas, combined with a belief in the necessity of particular institutional arrangements, easily led to the conclusion that all children of the republic should be educated in a single common school system.

The acceptance of the notion of malleability of character provided the basis in the early nineteenth century for the belief that the good society could be created through schooling and other institutional changes. Of primary importance was the widespread belief in some form of faculty psychology. I showed in Chapter 2 how behavioral and romantic concepts of childhood had begun to develop in the eighteenth century. The behavioral concept of human psychology stressed the importance of the environment in shaping character, whereas the romantic concept stressed the unfolding of the inner nature of the individual.

Faculty psychology contained elements of both behaviorism and romanticism. The human mind was said to be divided into several different parts, such as intelligence and morality. These different faculties were natural components of the individual and could be influenced by the environment. For instance, Benjamin Rush, the leading American physician of the post-Revolutionary period and often called the father of American psychiatry, argued in 1786 that a moral faculty is a natural part of the human mind. Rush believed that the moral faculty had the function of "distinguishing and choosing good and evil." From this perspective, moral actions were dependent on the degree of development of the moral faculty. Rush argued that the moral faculties of some individuals were developed out of proportion to other faculties. He referred to these individuals as benevolent idiots and gave as an example an individual who "spent several hours of every day in devotion, in which he was so careful to be private that he was once found in the most improbable place in the world for that purpose, vz. in an oven." Rush also described individuals in whom all faculties except the moral faculty were highly developed. For instance, he cited the Duke of Sully, who was very learned, creative, and athletic but who "died in the flower of his age, in a common brothel, perfectly corrupted by his debaucheries, and expired with the glass in his hand, cursing and denying God."[21]

People adhered to many different forms of faculty psychology during the early part of the nineteenth century. For instance, Horace Mann, often called the "father of the common school," was a phrenologist, and his educational writings often refer to the different faculties of the mind (see Chapter 4 for a fuller discussion). In a report to the Massachusetts State Board of Education in

1848, for example, he likened an uneducated republic to an obscene giant "whose brain has been developed only in the region of the appetites and passions, and not in the organs of reason and conscience."[22]

One common characteristic of all varieties of faculty psychology was a belief that the virtuous functioning of the moral faculty is dependent on how it is cultivated. For instance, the prescription given by Rush for a well-functioning moral faculty included sunshine, a plain diet, water, and cleanliness. Rush also included with these physical remedies "mechanical means of promoting virtue," such as odors, eloquence from the pulpit, music, and solitude.[23]

Also, discipline and exercise of the various faculties of the mind were considered necessary for their proper development. This type of reasoning would often appear in educational reports. Yale College's famous report of 1828, which will be discussed in more detail later in this chapter, states, "In laying the foundation of a thorough education, it is necessary that all the important mental faculties be brought into exercise. . . . If the student exercises his reasoning powers only, he will be deficient in imagination and taste, in fervid and impressive eloquence."[24]

Faculty psychology in all its various forms reflected the growing belief in the perfectibility of the human being. This belief provided the intellectual basis for reform movements in the early part of the nineteenth century that produced modern systems of education and other institutions designed to improve human character. Of major importance was the idea of controlling the institutional environment affecting the individual as a means of achieving perfection.

CHARITY SCHOOLS, THE LANCASTERIAN SYSTEM, AND PRISONS

Charity schools and juvenile reformatories developed in the United States in the early part of the nineteenth century as part of a general attempt to reduce crime and poverty. Both institutions sought to perfect human character through some form of education. The beginnings of the idea that educational institutions can solve the problems of society can be seen in this early reform movement. From the early nineteenth century to present times, the school has continually been called on to solve the problems of poverty and crime.

The charity school movement is important because it was the first major attempt to use the school as a means of socializing children into an industrious way of life. Common school reformers of the 1830s and 1840s would use the same arguments for the ameliorating power of education as charity schools did. In addition, in some places charity schools provided the basic institutional structure for the development of common schools.

In general, charity schools and juvenile reformatories in the early nineteenth century sought to create good moral character by replacing a weak family structure and destroying criminal associations. An individual, it was believed, became a potential criminal when the family failed to provide adequate moral training and was eventually led astray through contact with a criminal community.

For instance, the failure of the family structure is emphasized in the petition for incorporation in 1805 of the organization that became the major promoter of the Lancasterian system—the New York Free School Society. The incorporation statement declares that the condition of the children of the poor "is deplorable indeed; reared up by parents who . . . are become either indifferent to the best interests of their offspring, or, through intemperate lives, are rendered unable to defray the expense of their instruction." The petition goes on to argue that the neglect of education had resulted in "ignorance and vice, and all those manifold evils resulting from every species of immorality."[25] This society, which was organized to provide education for the poor, within a short time dominated charity schooling in New York City. By the 1840s the schools of the New York Free School Society came under public control and became the core of the early system of public schools in New York City.

Like those involved with charity schools, reformers involved with juvenile reformatories linked waywardness with the failure of the family. The first reformatories, called houses of refuge, were founded in New York in 1824, in Boston in 1826, and in Philadelphia in 1828. The organization responsible for opening the New York House of Refuge was the New York Society for the Prevention of Pauperism, founded in 1815. In 1823 this organization changed its name to the Society for the Reformation of Juvenile Delinquents. Its report for 1822 states that children become wayward because no "moral standard of conduct has been placed before their eyes. No faithful parent has watched over them and restrained their vicious propensities."[26]

Arguing in the same manner, the Boston House of Refuge went so far as to advocate the use of its institution by any child who was considered to have an improper family life. Its 1829 report to the city of Boston argues that to avoid the evils arising from the neglect of family government, the city's laws should be extended so that any "parents, or guardians, or friends of children, who are unable to exercise any moral government, might place them in this institution."[27]

Thus the purpose of charity schools and reformatories was to correct the problems caused by the failure of parental government. In addition, they were to keep children and youth for exposure to immoral education by isolating them from criminal contacts. Members of the New York Free School Society believed that criminal associations were one of the major problems of raising children in a city. DeWitt Clinton, president of the New York Free School Society, issued this warning in 1809: "Great cities are, at all times, the nurseries and hotbeds of crimes . . . And the dreadful examples of vice which are presented to youth, and the alluring forms in which it is arrayed . . . cannot fail of augmenting the mass of moral depravity."[28]

The preceding arguments provided the rationale for the charity schools. In essence, they were supposed to eliminate crime and poverty by replacing the failed government of the family with the government of the school and by keeping children off the streets and out of contact with potential criminal associates. The argument that an important function of schooling is to keep children off the streets continued into the twentieth century.

Reformers involved in charity schools and juvenile reformatories believed the solution to crime and poverty to be education and provision of the proper institutional environment: Education was supposed to provide the tools by which an individual could function in a social role, and the institutional environment was supposed to teach an individual how to use these tools in a moral manner.

The charity school movement spread rapidly in the 1790s and the early 1800s. These schools, which provided the basic framework for the later development of public schools, were organized mainly by private associations such as the New York Free School Society. The existence of charity schools created a division between social classes—the poor attended chairity schools and the better-off attended other private and public institutions.

Although the stated intention of charity schools was to save the children of the poor from a life of crime and poverty, their creation also had important effects on existing private schools and, later, on the development of public schools. The best history of the early effects of the development of charity schools is Carl Kaestle's *Evolution of an Urban School System: New York City, 1750–1850*. Kaestle examined the registers of the private schools in New York City in the 1790s and found that they were not exclusive or limited to the education of the children of the wealthy. In fact, he argues, the private schools were common in several respects. First, they were the most common or prevalent system of education. Second, they all provided what was called a common system of education. And third, they were attended in common by children from a wide range of families with differing incomes and occupations.[29]

As Kaestle indicates, this last point is most important because school reformers at a later time would argue for the necessity of common public schools as a means of mixing the children of the rich and poor in the same classroom, in order to eliminate social-class divisions in education: "This third fact is the most important, for it is this sense of the word that was central to the ideology of the 'common school' reformers of the nineteenth century. The data . . . suggest that their reform, whether they knew it or not, was an attempt to restore the social mixing that had existed, at least in New York, before the creation of the free schools."[30] Private schools were attended by a variety of children from different social classes because tuition was adjusted according to the income of the parents. Furthermore, Kaestle found little difference between the percentage of children annually attending school in the 1790s and the percentage attending free public schools in the mid-1800s.

Kaestle also found that attempts in the 1790s to systematize the private schools in New York City failed and that these schools were unable to accommodate the influx of immigrants, particularly from Ireland and France. The result was that in the early nineteenth century private schools became, in Kaestle's words, "restricted more and more to the wealthy minority. Meanwhile, the city's public school system arose from the charity schools, which had played a traditional but numerically slight role in the colonial period.[31]

In addition to laying the foundation for later public schooling, charity schools provided the first organized educational opportunities for the increasing number of freed slaves settling in the North. Kaestle details these developments in *Pillars of the Republic: Common Schools and American Society, 1780–1860*. He states that a school for freed black slaves was opened in Philadelphia in 1770, in New York in 1787, and in Baltimore in 1792.[32]

The Lancasterian system, introduced into charity schools in the United States and England in the early nineteenth century, was revolutionary in its emphasis on the process of schooling as a means of developing moral character. It was considered ideally suited to charity schools because it was inexpensive and provided training in character development.

The New York Free School Society was mainly responsible for introducing and spreading the fame of the Lancasterian system in the United States. Most of DeWitt Clinton's dedicatory speech for the new Free School Society building in 1809 was devoted to praising the new instructional system. He was so enraptured with its potential that he stated, "I consider his [Joseph Lancaster's] system as creating a new era in education, as a blessing sent down from heaven to redeem the poor."[33] The system spread rapidly throughout the country, and its adoption was not limited to charity schools. Ellwood Cubberley found that the system was in use in the early nineteenth century from Massachusetts to Georgia and as far west as Detroit, Cincinnati, and Louisville. In 1822 the Pennsylvania state legislature, in an act reorganizing the second school District, required the use of the Lancasterian system.[34]

The popularity of the system in the United States eventually caused its English developer, Joseph Lancaster, to make his home here. He died in 1838 when he was run over by a horse and carriage after inspecting a New York Lancasterian school. At the time of his death, he had plans to push his system to a new height of educational efficiency. He had contracted with the New York Free School Society to run an experiment in which a system of instruction would be used that was supposed to teach forty children to read and spell accurately in four to six weeks.

Claims were made that civilization owed Joseph Lancaster a debt for coining the pregnant mottoes "A place for everything and everything it its place" and "Let every child at every moment have something to do and a motive for doing it."[35] These were the mottoes of a system designed to handle large numbers of pupils in an efficient, inexpensive manner. The system could supposedly handle as many as a thousand students at a time. Under the Lancasterian system, pupils were seated in rows and received their instruction from monitors, who received their instruction from the master, who sat at the end of the room. Monitors were selected from among the better students in the class, and they wore badges indicating their rank.

The discipline and orderliness required by the Lancasterian system were meant to provide the moral training. An engraving of a Lancasterian schoolroom in Pennsylvania illustrates how the training in orderliness was inherent in the system of classroom management. This particular room was designed to accommodate 450 students. The teacher sits at the head of the room on a raised platform. Beneath and in front of the teacher are three rows of monitors' desks placed directly in front of the pupils' desks. The pupils' desks are divided into three sections, each of which is divided into two parts, and each section is in line with one of the rows of monitors' desks. Arrows on the engraving indicate that a group of pupils would march to the front of the room and stand around the monitors' desks, where they would receive instruction from the monitors. When they finished, they would march to the rear part of their section and recite or receive further instruction from another monitor. While this group was marching to the rear, another group would be marching up to the front to take their places around the monitors. When finished, these pupils would march to the rear, and the group in the rear would move forward to the second part of their section to receive instruction from yet another monitor. Because each of the three sections had a group in front, one in the rear, and one in the middle working on different things, a total of nine different recitations could be carried on at one time.

Educators of the period made an analogy between the Lancasterian system and a factory. An unidentified French writer was quoted as saying, "It is a masterpiece which must produce a revolution in popular education. . . . It may be styled a manufactory of knowledge."[36] DeWitt Clinton described it as "a system which is, in education, what the neat finished machines for abridging labor and expense are in the mechanic arts."[37] Undoubtedly, the greatest selling point of the system was its cheapness. It provided a system for educating poor children inexpensively. Those promoting the system also believed that it provided character training for the child.

A student's submission to this factory system of education was supposed to lead to a sense of orderliness and obedience. The periodic movement of pupils and materials required order and discipline. Each student had an assigned place in the educational machine, and the machine was kept well oiled by a distribution of awards and punishments. Virtue was rewarded by a system of badges, the highest being the Order of Merit. Virtue and ability led to appointment to the rank of monitor. Lancaster developed a unique system of punishments. Children who talked frequently or were idle were punished by having a wooden log placed around their necks. Extreme offenders were placed in a sack or basket suspended from the roof of the school in full view of the rest of the pupils.

The constant activity, regimentation, and lockstep marching were supposed to imprint the virtues of orderliness and obedience indelibly on the student's mind. Clinton hailed Lancaster as the benefactor of the human race: "I contemplate the habits of order which it [the Lancasterian system] forms, the spirit of emulation which it excites, the rapid improvement which it produces, the purity of morals which it inculcates—when I behold the extraordinary union of celerity in instruction and economy of expense.[38]

The virtues of submission, order, and industriousness were considered necessary for functioning in the world of business. The Boston School Committee investigated the New York Lancasterian schools in 1828 and reported that the system kept students attentive and interested by permitting no moments of idleness. The committee praised the method and declared that "its effects on the habits, character, and intelligence of youth are highly beneficial; disposing their minds to industry, to readiness of attention, and to subordination, thereby creating in early life a love of order, preparation for business."[39]

The Lancasterian system was supposed to help the pauper child escape poverty and crime by imparting formal knowledge and instilling the virtues needed in the world of work. Within this framework of reasoning, the qualities of submission, order, and industriousness made the child moral by making him or her useful to and functional in society. In addition, the very act of attending school kept pupils off the streets and out of contact with the kind of learning believed to occur through contact with criminals.

Concern about the evil influence of the criminal community on the molding of human character was the basis for the establishment of houses of refuge for juvenile delinquents. At first, the New York Society for the Reformation of Juvenile Delinquents wanted only separate buildings within prisons for youthful offenders, but in 1824, after deciding this did not provide complete enough separation, it founded the New York House of Refuge.

Just as charity school reformers viewed cities as colleges of vice, promoters of juvenile reformatories viewed prisons as systems of criminal education. This attitude is clearly stated in the 1828 report of the New York House of Refuge, which called prisons "so many schools of vice . . . so many seminaries to impart lessons and maxims, calculated to banish legal restraints, moral consideration, pride of character, and self-regard.[40]

Like the charity schools, the juvenile reformatories sought to provide an institutional replacement for what was believed to be a failed family structure. The Lancasterian system was used in attempts to create an ideal family structure within the institutional setting of the reformatory. The ideal family government would separate the juvenile from evil and teach the habits of order and discipline. The Boston Prison Discipline Society's report in 1832 claims, "How much may parents, and all who have the care of youth, learn from the Houses of Refuge for Juvenile Delinquents." What could be learned, according to this report, was the morally rewarding effect on youth of "regular hours for solitude and sleep; regular hours for promoting cleanliness; regular hours for exercise and recreation; regular hours for obtaining knowledge human and divine; and regular hours for manual labor." The report goes on to state that the significance of the houses of refuge was their "unspeakably important lessons of instruction to the world, on these every day duties of parents and others."[41]

The houses of refuge emphasized regimentation and order. The New York House of Refuge instituted a rigorous schedule of Lancasterian instruction and labor. The first two hours of the morning were devoted to classroom instruction, and then there were four hours of labor in workshops. Then came lunch and a "little time . . . [for] recreation." In the afternoon, four hours were devoted to labor. Then came supper, followed by two more hours of Lancasterian instruction. Religious exercises were given in the early morning and before retirement at night.[42]

Both the New York and the Philadelphia houses of refuge followed similar schedules. In both systems, each child was placed in a separate cell at night. During the day, the children were not allowed to communicate while receiving instruction or performing work. Conversation was allowed only during free time.

In this manner, the juvenile offender was to be isolated for evil and trained in the habits of order, obedience, and industriousness. The 1833 annual report of the New York House of Refuge states that "obedience and industry are necessary to make good boys good men and useful citizens." The report goes on to hail its own success at being able "to implant principles of virtue and habits of industry, where the vilest and wickedest associations have pre-occupied the mind."[43] The education and training received by the inmates were intended to prepare them to fit into the social structure. Basic occupational skills were to be learned in the classrooms and workshops. The virtues instilled by the system were considered necessary in the world of work.

The development of charity schools, the Lancasterian system, and the houses of refuge reflected a growing faith in the power of schooling to solve the problems of society. They all contained within them, in varying degrees, institutional procedures that provided the individual with moral examples, habituated the student to moral conduct, and disassociated the pupil from evil influences. What is most important about these institutions is that they embodied the belief that education could end poverty and crime in society.

This belief in the ameliorating power of schooling became an essential part of the common school movement of the 1830s and 1840s. Charity schools provided a working model and, in some places, the basic institutional structure for the establishment of a common school system. In addition, they became a target of attack by some common school reformers who believed the existence of charity schools resulted in the separation of the children of the rich and the poor. This, it was believed, reinforced social-class differences. The hope of the common school was to overcome the problems of social class by mixing together all children in the same schoolhouse. A major result of this argument was the extension of the moral training provided in the charity schools to the children of all social classes.

INSTITUTIONAL CHANGE AND THE AMERICAN COLLEGE

Although the charity schools and houses of refuge served a different social stratum than did the colleges, similar arguments were given in support of a traditional collegiate life. *The Yale Report of 1828*, regarded as the standard for the maintenance of colleges in the nineteenth century, argued that it was necessary for the residential college to provide a family form of control over students, and it used faculty psychology to defend a traditional liberal arts curriculum against pleas for more practical studies and electives.

In the early nineteenth century, American colleges were established at an incredible rate in response to denominational rivalries, local boosterism, and public demand. Concerns about the nature of the college curriculum and the differences between public and private institutions were sparked by this growth. The resolution of these institutional issues was to have an important effect on the history of the college in the nineteenth century.

Nine colleges had been established in the colonies before the Revolutionary War. Between the Revolutionary War and the Civil War, approximately 250 colleges were established, and 182 of these survived into the twentieth century. The growth of the American college was highlighted in a striking comparison made in 1880 between American and British institutions of higher learning. It pointed out that England had four universities to serve a population of 23 million, while Ohio had thirty seven institutions of higher learning to serve a population of 3 million.[44]

The rapid expansion of American colleges created many institutional problems. A major issue was the nature of the college curriculum. In the early part of the nineteenth century, public demand for higher education placed pressure on colleges to achieve a balance between what Benjamin Franklin had referred to as the useful and the ornamental in learning. The traditional classical curriculum of Latin and Greek was still considered an ideal for the education of gentlemen. On the other hand, the usefulness of study of science and modern languages, along with a demand for education in practical subjects, created conflict over the nature of the college curriculum.

The increased number of institutions of higher education led to the inevitable problem of separating public and private control. Colonial colleges developed during a period when few distinctions were made between public and private schools. Public and private financing combined with public and private control to blur the status of colleges in relationship to government. This issue was finally resolved in *Dartmouth College v. Woodward* (1819), which affected not only the later history of colleges but also the development of American corporations.

The curriculum issues faced by colleges in the early nineteenth century reflected a general concern about the role of higher education in society and the proper education of the individual. As I discussed in Chapter 2, higher education during the early colonial period was primarily concerned with the education of ministers and public leaders. The classical curriculum of Latin and Greek was considered appropriate to serve these two social functions. The study of Latin was the traditional education for the ministry, and the study of Greek was part of the Renaissance ideal for the education of the gentleman ruler.

During their early years, all the colonial colleges reflected these social goals and educational ideas. This was certainly true of the early years of Harvard, as discussed in Chapter 2, and was true also of the College of William and Mary, established by royal charter in 1693 in Virginia to ensure a steady supply of Anglican clergymen. Yale and Princeton were established to serve religious purposes, but in a spirit of denominational rivalry. Yale was established in 1701 in reaction to what was believed to be the more liberal theological orientation of Harvard. In 1746 Princeton was established through support given by one branch of the Presbyterian church that had been affected by the religious Great Awakening of the eighteenth century. Baptists established the College of Rhode Island (later Brown University) in 1764; the Dutch Reformed church established Queen's College (later Rutgers University) in 1766; the Congregationalists founded Dartmouth in 1769; and King George III appealed for funds for the founding of what would later become the University of Pennsylvania and Columbia University.

The curriculum of colonial colleges did not remain static. Both science and the emphasis of the Enlightenment on reason found their way into the curriculum under the general label of natural philosophy. The works of Locke and Newton and Copernican theory began to appear in the readings at Yale in the eighteenth century. In 1734 Yale imported a telescope, a microscope, and a barometer. The growth in the influence of science is reflected in the curriculum changes made at Yale: In 1726 mathematics was required only in the fourth year, but by 1745 arithmetic was made an entrance requirement and mathematics was required in the second, third, and fourth years. At King's College (later Columbia University) in New York an attempt was made in 1754 to introduce a course of study in navigation, surveying, geography, and natural history that would teach "the knowledge . . . of every Thing useful for the Comfort, the Convenience and Elegance of Life . . . and everything that can contribute to . . . true Happiness."[45] These are only a few examples of the changes that began to take place in the college curriculum of the eighteenth century.

Richard Hofstadter argues in *Academic Freedom in the Age of the College* that the college boom of the early nineteenth century caused a major regression in the progress of the college curriculum and academic freedom. As discussed in Chapter 2 in regard to the development of academies, freedom of thought was considered an essential element in the development of science and the progress of society. Hofstadter writes, "During the last three or four decades of the eighteenth century the American colleges had achieved a notable degree of freedom, vitality, and public usefulness and seemed to have set their feet firmly on the path to further progress."[46]

On the other hand, he describes the opening decades of the nineteenth century as the great retrogression in collegiate education and academic freedom. Hofstadter argues that this retrogression occurred because colleges came to serve narrow religious interests. In the eighteenth century, the small number of colleges in existence had begun to move away from serving narrow sectarian interests, but the multiplication of colleges in the nineteenth century primarily reflected particular denominational concerns. Added to these religious concerns was local boosterism, which resulted, according to Hofstadter, in an intense denominational rivalry "to supply every locality with a cheap and indigenous institution that would make it possible for local boys who desired degrees to get them easily."[47]

In addition to the problems caused by the creation of a large number of colleges serving narrow sectarian interests, there was the problem of quality. Many of these institutions employed a limited number of faculty members, who were required to teach a maximum number of courses. Quality declined as, for example, the teaching of the classics was reduced to the teaching of grammar, so that the culture of antiquity was no longer conveyed.

Colleges started in the spirit of local boosterism often made little attempt to plan academic quality. Historian Frederick Rudolph describes the college-building mania: "Often when a college had a building, it had no students. If it had students, frequently it had no building. If it had either, then perhaps it had no money, perhaps no professors; if professors, then no president, if a president, then no professors." Rudolph portrays college building during this period as an activity that was undertaken with the same zeal as "canal-building, cotton-ginning, farming, and gold-mining."[48]

In the midst of the college boom, a search for a guiding standard was in progress. For many colleges, this standard came in the form of *The Yale Report of 1828*, which used faculty psychology to defend a traditional curriculum. In part, *The Yale Report* was a reaction to other proposed reforms in the college curriculum. Theodore Crane writes: "For decades after 1828 the Yale Report sustained traditionalists. Its assumptions seemed to reflect a realistic appraisal of the role played by American colleges and of the expectations of the public."[49] Rudolph argues that *The Yale Report* satisfied the established elites because it withstood demands for reforms that would have given American colleges a more practical and popular curriculum: "The religious, the very pious, the privileged—were the people who ran the colleges, people who also knew that the American college was running on a shoestring and that the old course of study, while the best, was also the cheapest."[50]

The Yale Report, like the charity schools and other reforms of the period, placed a great deal of importance on maintaining a family structure within an institutional setting. In defining the appropriate goal of a college, the report states its goal is "to LAY THE FOUNDATION of a SUPERIOR EDUCATION: and this is to be done, at a period of life when a substitute must be provided for *parental superintendence*." The report argues that students, when removed from the family, need to be protected against "untried scenes of temptation," and this protection would result from providing a substitute for parental control. These regulations "should approach as near to the character of parental control as the circumstances of the case will admit."[51]

To achieve this form of parental control, the report argues strongly for the necessity of a residential college: "The parental character of college government, requires that the students should be so collected together, as to constitute one family, that the intercourse between them and their instructors may be frequent and familiar."[52] To acomplish this objective, the report calls for the establishment of residence halls on college campuses.

Discussion took place during this period about the need to arrange the institutional environment of residence halls at colleges and academies. For example, in 1829 the Boston Prison Discipline Society gave full suport to the dormitory plans of an unnamed "important school in Massachusetts." These plans called for three stories of galleries along which individual rooms would face a large open space in the middle. Each room was to have a glass window. The master of the school could stand in the middle of the building and observe all the rooms. In this building, the society reported, the student would have time to read and reflect in his own room, and, more important, "the idle, profane and vicious youth is effectually prevented from corrupting his fellows, during those hours of darkness, in which there is the greatest danger."[53]

Within the residential environment of college life, students were to develop an intellectual culture—referred to in *The Yale Report* as "the *discipline* and the *furniture* of the mind"—through the study of a general curriculum. *The Yale Report* rejects the idea of colleges' providing practical and professional studies: "The great object of a collegiate education, preparatory to the study of a profession, is to give that expansion and balance of the mental powers, those liberal comprehensive views, and those fine proportions of character, which are not to be found in him whose ideas are always confined to one particular channel."[54]

Within the framework of the preceding statement, collegiate education was to provide a general background of knowledge and an exercise of mental powers so that the individual would be able to participate in a wide range of intellectual activities. In the words of the report, "Wherever he [the college graduate] goes, into whatever company he falls, he has those general views, on every topic of interest, which will enable him to understand, to digest, and to form a correct opinion, on the statements and discussions he hears."[55]

In addition to knowledge, a collegiate education was supposed to provide a balanced exercise of the different mental faculties. *The Yale Report* uses faculty psychology to explain the processes involved in achieving the goal of balanced mental training: "In laying the foundation of a thorough education, it is necessary that all the important mental faculties be brought into exercise." The report goes on to argue that if exercising any particular mental faculty were neglected, the mind would not reach full perfection. Full perfection was to be achieved through bringing each mental faculty to "the fair proportions which nature designed."[56]

The reasoning used in the report was that balanced mental faculties would result in a balanced character. The general studies offered by the college were to provide the exercise necessary for achieving a balance of mental faculties and character. As stated in the report, "In the course of instruction in this college, it has been an object to maintain such proportion between the different branches of literature and science, as to form in the student a proper balance of character."[57] Each subject-matter area would contribute to the exercise of a different part of the mind. For instance, the report claims that mathematics would teach demonstrative reasoning, physical sciences would teach inductive reasoning, ancient literature would provide finished models of taste, English reading would teach speaking and writing, philosophy would teach thinking, and rhetoric and oratory would teach the art of speaking.

The Yale Report has often been viewed as a conservative response to reforms proposed during the 1820s for electives and specialization in the college curriculum. Its attraction might have been the promise it offered of providing a general education that would confirm or confer social status. Implicit in the idea of education as developing a balanced character that could fit into any intellectual conversation or gathering was the assumption of easy movement between social classes. Receiving a general collegiate education might not have guaranteed access to any particular occupation, but it did promise to inculcate the culture and manners that might be useful in achieving any social advancement.

The Yale Report did seem to reflect general sentiments about the type of education required for the development of moral character. Similar arguments for parental government and for the training of mental faculties could be found in the charity school movement: Charity schools sought moral development through classroom management and instruction that replicated family government and exercised mental faculties, whereas *The Yale Report* extolled the use of residential colleges and a general curriculum to achieve a similar purpose. The differences, of course, were that charity schools wanted to uplift the children of the poor from a life of poverty and crime, whereas the colleges wanted to confer or confirm a social status. In either case, however, education was being used to shape the moral character of the individual for social purposes.

The Yale Report is important because it set the tone for collegiate education in the nineteenth century. The importance of the Dartmouth College case of 1819 lies in the fact that it began to define the lines between private and public education. In the seventeenth and eighteenth centuries, colleges, academies, reading-and-writing schools, and grammar schools were often established with little concern for distinctions between public and private education. As mentioned previously, most of these institutions received a combination of public and private money and were governed through a mixture of public and private control. Even a charity school organization—the New York Free School Society—received both public and private monies and was controlled by a private board of trustees, though eventually the schools established by this society came under complete public control.

The Dartmouth College case was the result of a dispute between Dartmouth president John Wheelock (son of Dartmouth's founder, Eleazor Wheelock) and an absentee board of trustees. To protect his power against the board of trustees, John Wheelock asked the New Hampshire state legislature to investigate the college. The board of trustees fired Wheelock, who immediately won the support of the state Republican party. The Republican governor charged the board of trustees with being a self-perpetuating group of aristocrats and worked with the state legislature to pass a bill that would change the name of the institution from Dartmouth College to Dartmouth University and, more important, bring the institution under state control.

The board of trustees immediately went to the Superior Court of New Hampshire to contest the state's action. Part of the state of New Hampshire's case rested on the fact that it had originally chartered the college. The question that quickly emerged in this case was whether Dartmouth was a public or a private corporation. On November 6, 1817, the superior court ruled that Dartmouth was a public corporation and subject to legislative control. On March 10, 1819, the case was heard before the U.S. Supreme Court.

The lawyer for the board of trustees was Dartmouth graduate Daniel Webster (class of 1801), who argued his case for five continuous hours. His eloquence, it was reported, brought Chief Justice John Marshall to tears. Webster presented his case in the form of an argument that asked, "Shall our state legislature be allowed to take that which is not their own, to turn it from its original use, and apply it to such ends or purposes as they, in their discretion shall see fit?"[58] Embodied in this question is the fundamental issue of the extent to which government power should be allowed to operate in the management of institutions. This question reaches beyond a consideration of educational institutions alone to encompass all institutions, including corporations.

PUBLIC VERSUS PRIVATE SCHOOLS

Certainly in colonial times there would have been little debate about the right of government to intervene in the affairs of institutions serving the public. Society was viewed as an integrated whole in which government had the responsibility to ensure correct actions by all its parts. However, the early nineteenth century was still influenced by the Revolutionary War, which had sought to limit the power of government, and by a rising capitalistic ideology that sought to eliminate all government involvement in the economic system. In fact, the major conflicts about expansion of the common school system in the 1830s and 1840s centered on the political issue of the extent to which government should be involved in the educational system. The significance of the Dartmouth College case was in delineating the line between government-controlled and private institutions.

Webter's famous statement before the Supreme Court—"It is, sir, as I have said, a small college, and yet there are those that love it"—may have influenced the Court's decision in favor of the board of trustees. The Supreme Court ruled that the charter granted by the New Hampshire legislature was a contract protected by the federal Constitution against alteration by the state.

The decision, written by Chief Justice Marshall, made a sharp distinction between private and public educational institutions. Recognition was given to the importance of education as a national concern and to the notion that this concern could be reflected in "an institution founded by government, and placed entirely under its immediate control, the officers of which would be public officers, amenable exclusively to government."[59] But, the argument continued, did this mean that all education should be entirely in the hands of government and every teacher a public employee? Did it mean that all donations for education became public property?

The Court's response to these questions was given in the form of a description of a corporation. Marshall's decision described a corporation chartered by a state as having immortality and individuality. These properties, given to a perpetual succession of persons or boards of trustees that acted as a single person, allowed a corporation to hold property and manage its own affairs. "It is chiefly for the purpose of clothing bodies of men, in succession," Marshall wrote, "with these qualities and capacities, that corporations were invented, and are in use."[60] Furthermore, the chief justice argued, a corporation did not participate in civil government unless that was the reason for its creation.

Therefore, according to the Court's decision, a corporation "is no more a state instrument than a natural person exercising the same powers would be."[61] This meant that a college chartered by the state had the same rights against government interference as did an individual. It also meant that if a state wished to promote education to serve its own purposes, it would need to create its own institutions and hire its own faculty. The same argument, of course, would apply to institutions for elementary and secondary education. Thus a sharp distinction was drawn between private and public institutions as a result of the Dartmouth College case, and a precedent was set that privately created educational institutions could not be forced to serve the purposes of government; this could be done only through institutions owned and operated by the government. Although court decisions in the twentieth century would allow for state regulation of private schools, the Dartmouth College case clearly drew the line between private and public schooling.

The college boom of the early nineteenth century was characterized by an emphasis on shaping individual character through a system of private, residential colleges. In the mid–nineteenth century, reform movements began to expand public colleges to serve public purposes. The most important factor in this reform movement was the Morrill Federal Land Grant Act of 1862.

CONCLUSION: CONTINUING ISSUES
IN AMERICAN EDUCATION

The debates about nationalism and civic education, the developing faith that
education can solve social problems, the expansion of urban charity schools,
and the growing distinctions between private and public institutions set the
stage for the common school movement of the 1830s and 1840s. In addition,
the educational issues of the period continue to be persistent problems in
American education.

The continuous nature of the educational issues of this period is reflected
in the writings of educational historians. As I discussed in Chapter 1, historians often reconstruct history from the perspective of the particular times in
which they lived.

One important issue is the degree to which political education should
attempt to control the future actions of citizens. As I noted in this chapter,
there is a major difference between the imposition of political values as
advocated by Noah Webster and the forming of political values by the reading
of newspapers as argued by Thomas Jefferson. This same argument is rele-
vant to issues of nationalism and patriotism. Should the schools build emotional attachments to symbols of the state through activities such as saluting
the flag and singing nationalistic songs? Or should patriotism be the expression of beliefs freely arrived at by the exercise of reason?

These questions are reflected in the writings of twentieth-century historians. Writing in the 1960s, when there was a concern about expanding
democratic rights to a broader range of citizens, Rush Welter states in *Popular
Education and Democratic Thought in America* that those hoping to find a democratic orientation in the Founding Fathers' views on education are often
disappointed. Welter notes that these early writings have a "tendency to
stress the conservative role of educational institutions in overcoming an
excess of popular liberty."[62]

The same interpretation of the period is given by Carl Kaestle in *Pillars of
the Republic*. Writing during the politically peaceful times of the late 1970s and
early 1980s, Kaestle found that the main concern of the post-Revolutionary
period was to balance freedom and order: "Political theorists and policy
makers were therefore concerned not only with protecting liberty, for which
the Revolution had been fought, but also with maintaining order, without
which all might be lost."[63] The purpose of education, according to Kaestle,
was to maintain the balance between order and freedom by producing virtuous, well-behaved citizens.

Kaestle places his interpretation in the broader framework of republicanism. According to him, during the post-Revolutionary period, *republicanism*
meant a combining of the concepts of virtue, balanced government, and
liberty. By *virtue*, "republican essayists meant discipline, sacrifice, simplicity,
and intelligence." Many of the early leaders believed in the natural virtue of
the landed yeoman—virtue that did not depend upon deliberate instruction.

However, the problem for these leaders was the increasing population of citizens who did not belong to the class of landed yeomen. For this group, natural virtue could not be assumed and deliberate instruction was needed.[64]

Kaestle indicates that educational proposals were motivated by factors other than fear of the disorder that would result from liberty. He argues that Revolutionary leaders were also captured by the idea of the perfectibility of humans and human institutions. They wanted to create a society that would be an alternative to the corrupt society of Europe and believed that education, by perfecting virtue, would contribute to achieving this utopian goal.

Kaestle does not draw a clear distinction between Jefferson's belief in individual reason and virtue and the more authoritarian ideas of leaders like Rush and Webster. On the other hand, in *The Social Ideas of American Educators*, Merle Curti considers educational leaders like Webster to represent a clearly conservative viewpoint on the organization of society. Writing in the radical economic and political climate of the 1930s, Curti states that Webster's spelling book contains a social philosophy "appropriate to a system which attached great value to acquiescence on the part of the poor in their poverty and at the same time promised ultimate success to those who would practice the virtues of frugality, industry, and submissiveness to moral teachings and to God's will."[65]

Curti concludes from his review of the moral maxims in Webster's speller that they were designed primarily to protect the property of the wealthy and that "other half-truths, equally fitting to a society in which some had more and others less, were read and re-read by American youth who learned their letters from the old 'blue-back.'"[66] In general, Curti finds that most post-Revolutionary educational practices and proposals continued, with only minor changes, the colonial class system of education.

Curti does think that Thomas Jefferson's ideas on education contrast sharply with others of the period. Curti argues that Jefferson displayed little sympathy for authoritarianism in education and that the ideas he advanced were hostile to the class character of existing educational practice. According to Curti, Jefferson's educational plan was a major step in the direction of breaking down class barriers in education. Specifically, he contends that Jefferson's proposal to select leaders from the masses through his three-tier system of education was the beginning of more democratic thinking about education: "Jefferson's quest for genius among the poor was far more democratic than anything that existed then, or was for a long time to exist."[67]

Nonetheless, Curti argues that Jeffersonian thought was limited by aristocratic pretensions. Without taking into account Jefferson's beliefs regarding the exercise of virtue and the role of history, Curti criticizes Jefferson for proposing a mainly literary education for the low and middle schools and argues that education of this type would be of little benefit "to common folk struggling on the less fertile soils and to frontiersmen with their peculiar problems."[68] He also criticizes Jefferson for displaying more interest in the organization of university studies than of schools for the common folk.

Despite these reservations, Curti hails Jefferson as the first American "to emphasize public education as an instrument for the realization of democracy and for the furthering of social reform."[69]

In Chapter 4, I will discuss various historical interpretations dealing with the use of education to end crime and poverty. Of course, this becomes one of the major themes in American schools. Also, it is one of the major areas of contention. Can education eliminate poverty and crime? Are attempts to end poverty and crime through education primarily efforts to impose a conservative agenda on the schools? Should changes in the economy, in contrast to education, be the means of eliminating crime and poverty?

The major tensions in these debates are between those who believe schooling should mold the virtuous citizen and those who believe schooling should provide the tools for the exercise of freedom. From the nineteenth century until the present, some have argued that a democratic society needs a school system that imposes morality, emphasizes patriotism, teaches respect for authority, and inculcates certain basic political values. At the same time, others have argued that schooling in a democratic society should provide the intellectual tools to all people that will enable them to select their own moral and political values. American educational philosophy has evolved as a blend of these two arguments.

NOTES

1. Quoted in Harry Warfel, *Noah Webster: Schoolmaster to America* (New York: Macmillan, 1936), p. 335.
2. Ibid., pp. 335–336.
3. Ibid., pp. 71–75.
4. Ibid., p. 93.
5. Quoted in ibid., p. 21.
6. "Noah Webster's Federal Catechism (1798)" in Sol Cohen, ed., *Education in the United States: A Documentary History* (New York: Random House, 1974), pp. 769–770.
7. "Noah Webster's Moral Catechism" in Cohen, *Education in the United States*, p. 771.
8. Noah Webster, "On the Education of Youth in America" in Fredrick Rudolph, ed., *Essays on Education in the Early Republic* (Cambridge: Harvard University Press, 1965).
9. Quoted in Warfel, *Noah Webster*, p. 86.
10. Quoted in ibid., p. 90.
11. Thomas Jefferson, "To Edward Carrington" in Gordon Lee, ed., *Crusade against Ignorance: Thomas Jefferson on Education* (New York: Teachers College Press, 1961), p. 102.

12. Thomas Jefferson, "To Peter Carr, with Enclosure" in Lee, *Crusade against Ignorance*, pp. 145–146.
13. Thomas Jefferson, "To John Adams" in Lee, *Crusade against Ignorance*, pp. 109–112.
14. Thomas Jefferson, "Report of the Commissioners Appointed to Fix the Site of the University of Virginia, &c." in Lee, *Crusade against Ignorance*, p. 119.
15. Thomas Jefferson, "A Bill for the More General Diffusion of Knowledge" in Lee, *Crusade against Ignorance*, pp. 83–92.
16. Thomas Jefferson, "Notes on the State of Virginia" in Lee, *Crusade against Ignorance*, p. 95.
17. Ibid., p. 96.
18. Ibid., p. 94.
19. Jefferson, "Report of the Commissioners" in Lee, *Crusade against Ignorance*, pp. 117–118.
20. Jefferson, "Notes" in Lee, *Crusade against Ignorance*, p. 96.
21. Benjamin Rush, "The Influence of Physical Causes upon the Moral Faculty" in Dagobert D. Runes, ed., *Selected Writings of Benjamin Rush* (New York: Philosophical Library, 1947), p. 186.
22. Horace Mann, "Twelfth Annual Report" in Lawrence Cremin, ed., *The Republic and the School: Horace Mann on the Education of Free Men* (New York: Teachers College Press, 1957), p. 92.
23. Benjamin Rush, "Influence of Physical Causes" in Runes, *Selected Writings*, pp. 198–202.
24. "The Yale Report (1828)" in Theodore Crane, ed., *The Colleges and the Public, 1787–1862* (New York: Teachers College Press, 1963), p. 86.
25. "Incorporation Statement of the New York Free School Society," reprinted in William O. Bourne, *History of the Public School Society of the City of New York* (New York: Wood, 1870), p. 3.
26. "1822 Report of the New York Society for the Prevention of Pauperism" in *Report of the Prison Discipline Society, Boston, 1828* (Boston: Press of T. R. Marvin, 1855), p. 174.
27. "1829 Boston House of Refuge Report to the City of Boston" in *Report of the Prison Discipline Society, Boston, 1829* (Boston: Press of T. R. Marvin, 1855), p. 246.
28. Quoted in Bourne, *History of the Public School Society*, p. 17.
29. Carl F. Kaestle, *The Evolution of an Urban School System: New York City, 1750–1850* (Cambridge, Mass.: Harvard University Press, 1973).
30. Ibid., p. 42.
31. Ibid., p. 187.
32. Carl F. Kaestle, *Pillars of the Republic: Common Schools and American Society, 1780–1860* (New York: Hill and Wang, 1983).
33. Quoted in Bourne, *History of the Public School Society*, p. 19.
34. Ellwood Cubberley, *Public Education in the United States: A Study and*

Interpretation of American Educational History (Boston: Houghton Mifflin, 1934), p. 129.

35. David Salmon, *Joseph Lancaster* (London: McKay, 1904), p. 9.
36. Quoted in George H. Martin, *The Evolution of the Massachusetts Public School System* (Englewood Cliffs, N.J.: Prentice-Hall, 1901), p. 138.
37. Quoted in Bourne, *History of the Public School Society*, p. 38.
38. Ibid., p. 19.
39. "Report on Monitorial Instruction to the Boston School Committee; Boston, 1828" in Ellwood Cubberley, ed., *Readings in Public Education in the United States: A Collection of Sources and Readings to Illustrate the History of Eduational Practice and Progress in the United States* (Cambridge, Mass.: Riverside Press, 1934), p. 137.
40. "1828 Report of the New York House of Refuge" in *Report of the Prison Discipline Society, Boston, 1828*, p. 174.
41. *Report of the Prison Discipline Society, Boston, 1832* (Boston: Press of T. R. Marvin, 1855), p. 570.
42. Ibid.
43. "1833 Report of the New York House of Refuge" in *Report of the Prison Discipline Society, Boston, 1833* (Boston: Press of T. R. Marvin, 1855), p. 694.
44. See Frederick Rudolph, *The American College and University* (New York: Knopf, 1962), pp. 48–49.
45. Quoted in ibid., pp. 31–32.
46. Richard Hofstadter, *Academic Freedom in the Age of the College* (New York: Columbia University Press, 1955), p. 209.
47. Ibid., p. 214.
48. Rudolph, *American College*, pp. 47–48.
49. Crane, *Colleges and the Public*, pp. 17–18.
50. Rudolph, *American College*, p. 135.
51. "Yale Report (1828)" in Crane, *Colleges and the Public*, p. 88.
52. Ibid.
53. *Report of the Prison Discipline Society, Boston, 1829*, p. 290.
54. "Yale Report (1828)" in Crane, *Colleges and the Public*, p. 90.
55. Ibid., p. 89.
56. Ibid., p. 86.
57. Ibid.
58. Quoted in Rudolph, *American College*, p. 209.
59. *Dartmouth College* v. *Woodward* (1819), quoted in Crane, *Colleges and the Public*, p. 70.
60. Ibid., p. 71.
61. Ibid.
62. Rush Welter, *Popular Education and Democratic Thought in America* (New York: Columbia University Press, 1962), p. 27.
63. Kaestle, *Pillars of the Republic*, p. 5.
64. Ibid.

65. Merle Curti, *The Social Ideas of American Educators* (Paterson, N.J.: Pageant Books, 1959), p. 32.
66. Ibid., p. 34.
67. Ibid., p. 41.
68. Ibid., p. 43.
69. Ibid., p. 44.

CHAPTER 4

The Ideology and Politics of the Common School

In educational history the 1830s and 1840s are known as the decades of the common school movement in the United States. It was during this historical period that the modern American school system began to take form. Obviously, schools and public school systems existed in the United States before the 1830s. What was different about the common school movement was the establishment and standardization of state systems of education designed to achieve specific public policies.

No other period in American educational history has stimulated as extensive a debate about its meaning and goals. In part, this debate reflects the importance of the common school movement to the American educational system. This chapter begins with a discussion of the various social and political groups that supported the common school movement, including the full-time educational reformers who devoted their lives to the common school ideal. Political, economic, and religious groups that opposed the establishment of the common school are considered next. Last, the meaning of the common school movement for the later development of the American school is explored.

Before the common school period, a variety of public and private school organizations existed. Massachusetts had laws requiring the provision of education and, as I discussed in Chapter 3, had established the first system of urban education in Boston in the 1790s. On the other hand, many states, such as New York and Pennsylvania, supported charity schools while a majority of children in those states attended private schools. Newer states had passed laws allowing for the development of schools but had not actively created organized systems of education. For instance, Ohio, after its admission to the Union in 1802, passed legislation in 1806 and 1816 allowing for the organization of schools supported by rents from lands and tuition. Beginning in 1821, Ohio law permitted the taxation of all property in a district for the support of schools. The state created a permanent school fund in 1827.

Although all these actions provided some support for education, they did not approximate the distinctive features of the common school movement. Probably the most important difference between the common school movement and previous educational developments in the United States was the concept underlying the common school movement of a school under state control teaching a common body of knowledge to students from different social backgrounds. This concept of schooling was to serve distinct social and political goals.

Three distinctive aspects of the common school movement made it different from past educational developments. The first was an emphasis on educating all children in a common schoolhouse. It was argued that if children from a variety of religious, social-class, and ethnic backgrounds were educated in common, there would be a decline in hostility and friction among social groups. In addition, if children educated in common were taught a common social and political ideology, a decrease in political conflict and social problems would result. Obviously, this aspect of the common school movement can be traced to late-eighteenth- and early-nineteenth-century educational advocates who wanted to teach nationalism as a means of promoting national unity and to those supporters of charity schools who wanted to use education as a means of eliminating poverty and crime. The idea of using education to solve social problems and build a political community became an essential concept in the common school movement. The term *common school* came to have a specific meaning: a school that was attended in common by all children and in which a common political and social ideology was taught.

The second important aspect of the common school movement was the idea of using schools as an instrument of government policy. Certainly, this aspect of education had existed in the past. Colonial schools were established to train a population that would understand and obey secular and religious laws. Writers after the Revolution advocated systems of schools to provide leaders and a responsible citizenry. What was different about the common school movement was the acceptance of the idea of a direct linkage between government educational policies and the solving and control of social, economic, and political problems. In this concept, the common school was to be a panacea for society's problems.

The third distinctive feature of the common school movement was the creation of state agencies to control local schools. In part, this was necessary if schools were to carry out government social, political, and economic policies. In the past, states like Massachusetts had passed laws requiring the establishment of schools in local communities or, in the cases of New York and Pennsylvania, had established state school funds for charity schools. In these situations, an official position had not been established to oversee the state educational system. In 1812 New York was the first American state to create the position of state superintendent of schools. In the 1820s some other states followed New York's lead and created the office of state superintendent of education, but it was during the 1830s that state supervision and organization of schools became a major educational reform. In part, this was the work of

the "father of the common schook," Horace Mann, who became the first
secretary of the Massachusetts Board of Education in 1837.

These three distinct features of the common school movement reflected
beliefs about the social and political role of education that had been gaining
increasing currency in the early nineteenth century. Probably the most important of these ideas was the belief that human nature can be formed, shaped,
and given direction by training within formally organized institutions. This
thinking was embodied in faculty psychology and in the charity schools. It
was a logical step for common school reformers to apply this reasoning to the
entire society and to argue that government-operated schools could create the
perfect society. Also, various groups, such as advocates of Lancasterian
schools and charity schools, believed that schooling could be a means of
economic and social improvement. They began to demand common schools,
but often for reasons quite different from those given by full-time common
school reformers. Although these differences existed within the common
school movement, the outcome of the movement's reforms was the beginning
of the modern American school system.

THE IDEOLOGY OF THE COMMON SCHOOL MOVEMENT

The creation of a popular ideology and justification for the common school
movement was mainly the work of a class of individuals who were able to
devote the majority of their time to the educational causes. These individuals
occupied newly created government positions that gave them the time and
authority to articulate the principles of the common school movement and
conduct a campaign to spread the common school ideology. The most prominent of these individuals were Horace Mann and Henry Barnard.

For the purpose of understanding the basic ideology of these full-time
common school reformers, this section concentrates on the life and ideas of
Horace Mann. It is important to understand that the popularly stated common school ideology did not necessarily reflect the reality of the changes
taking place in American education or reflect the positions held by all supporters of the common school. For instance, as mentioned briefly and as will be
discussed in a later section, the workingmen's parties supported the establishment of common schools for different reasons from those given in the
more popular rhetoric of the common school movement.

What is important about the ideoogy of the common school movement, as
stated by its major leaders, was that it established the basic framework, from
the nineteenth century to the present, for popular and official discussions
about the goals and purposes of public schooling in American life. Within
these early arguments for common schools can be found most of the hopes
and aspiratons that many Americans have had for the public schools. These
early justifications for public schooling not only claimed that schools could
solve the major social, economic, and political problems of society but also
argued that common schools were necessary for its very survival.

Two important mechanisms spreading the popular ideology of the common school were educational periodicals and newly created educational organizations. Between 1825 and 1850 more than sixty periodicals devoted to education were established. The most important of these journals were the *Massachusetts Common School Journal*, edited by Horace Mann; the *Connecticut Common School Journal*, edited by Henry Barnard; and the *Ohio Common School Director*, edited by Samuel Lewis. As historian Sally Wertheim states:

> One of the purposes of the journals was to build support for the common school movement in communities where the proper climate for acceptance of the idea of universal education did not exist. The periodicals represented leading educational ideas of the times, as perceived by their editors and publishers, and provided a forum for these educational leaders to advance their philosophies about education.[1]

According to Lawrence Cremin, the most important organizations for spreading the ideals of the common school were the American Lyceum, organized in 1825; the Western Literary Institute and College of Professional Teachers, founded in 1829; and the American Institute of Instruction, established in 1830. For common school reformers, Cremin claims, these organizations were an important "means of enunciating and pressing their demands."[2] They held countless lectures, public discussions, and conventions at which common school advocates were able to spread their ideas.

In many ways, the spread of the common school ideology was a fascinating example of the diffusion of ideas. But, it should be remembered, the spread of new ideas required a public that was willing to accept them. In many ways, the public had been made ready for the acceptance of the basic ideas of the common school movement by the educational writers of the post-Revolutionary period, such as Noah Webster and Thomas Jefferson, and by the arguments for social and moral reform made by the leaders of the charity school movement and the Lancasterian system. In addition, a belief in some form of faculty psychology made it possible for many Americans to accept the idea that the common school could be a panacea for the social, political, and economic problems of society.

Those who created and spread the ideology of the common school worked with as much fervor as leaders of religious crusades. And, in fact, there are striking parallels between the two types of campaigns. Both promised some form of salvation and moral reformation. In the case of the common school, the promise was the salvation of society.

In fact, the life and writings of Horace Mann can be characterized as a constant search for a means of social salvation. During his life he rejected Calvinism and adopted law as the means of social redemption, and after finding little hope in saving society through the establishment of proper laws, he turned to education. Mann was born in 1796 into a harsh Calvinistic environment in Franklin, Massachusetts. He claimed throughout his life that he abandoned Calvinism when, at the funeral of his twelve-year-old brother, who had died of drowning, the family's Calvinist minister used the occasion to warn other young people of the dangers of dying unconverted. Mann described this minister as one who expounded all the doctrines of total depravity, election, and reprobation and not only the eternity, but the extremity, of hell torments, unflinchingly and in their most terrible significance; while he rarely if ever descanted upon the joys of heaven and never, if ever, upon the essential and necessary happiness of a virtuous life.[3]

For Mann, phrenology and the common school became substitutes for his youthful experience with Calvinism. Calvinism had created for him a living hell that "spread a pall of blackness . . . beyond [which] . . . I could see the bottomless and seething lake filled with torments, and hear the wailing and agony of its victims."[4] In a series of letters to his sister in 1836, one year before becoming secretary of the Massachusetts Board of Education, he describes his rejection of this haunting vision of hell for a belief in good works in the present life. "My nature revolts at the idea of belonging to a universe in which there is to be never-ending anguish . . . while we are on earth, the burden of our duties is toward man.[5]

Mann entered the practice of law with the same fervor that would later characterize his involvement in common school reform. He was educated at Brown University and in 1823 was admitted to the bar and practice of law at Dedham, Massachusetts. Between 1827 and 1833 he served in the Massachusetts state legislature, where concerns with reforming society made him instrumental in enacting laws limiting the sale of alcohol and lottery tickets, establishing hospitals for the insane, and creating the Massachusetts State Board of Education.

While serving in the state legislature, he was surrounded by political and social events that affected his belief in the importance of common school reform and helped to shape his justification of the movement. A good way of understanding the social context of his decision to accept common school reform as the answer to society's problems is to read his description in his journal of events between the time he was asked to serve as secretary of the Board of Education and his acceptance of that position.

On May 18, 1837, Mann received a letter proposing his nomination to the newly created State Board of Education and urging him to lead the board as secretary. He wrote in his journal on that date that, could a person be successful in that office, "what a diffusion, what intensity, what perpetuity of blessings he would confer! How would his beneficial influence upon mankind widen and deepen as it descended forever!"[6] He did not communicate his acceptance of that position until the end of June. During that time, according to his journal entry for May 25, he read "Combe on the Constitution of Man." This was his basic text in phrenology, which provided him with the scientific hope that the mental faculties could be developed and shaped to create a moral and good individual and, consequently, a moral and just society. His continued involvement in general social reform was reflected by his attendance at meetings of the Massachusetts Temperance Society. This society believed that the ending of alcohol consumption would contribute to the elimination of poverty and crime and add stability to the family. Mann noted on May 25, after attending a meeting of the society, "The faith [temperance] is now in a forward state of realization; and what a triumph it will be! not like a Roman triumph that made hearts bleed, and nations weep, and reduced armies to captivity, but one that heals hearts, and wipes tears from a nation's eyes, and sets captivity free."[7]

Mann's fear of growing social disorder in the United States was heightened when, on May 30, someone tried to start a fire next to his hotel room. He says about the event, "Fortunately it was discoverd early, and extinguished. A gang of incendiaries infest the city. What a state of morals it reveals." Mann wondered how a group or individual could be driven to such an act. In the closing line of his description of the event, he touched on an important theme in the common school movement: The hope for eliminating this type of crime, as he argued in his later writings on education, was the training of the young child. Or, as he asks in his closing line, "When will society, like a mother, take care of *all* her children?"[8]

His fear of social disorder and religious conflict was further intensified when on Sunday, June 11, a riot took place between Catholics and Protestants in Boston. Tension between the two religious groups had been increasing in the United States with the immigration of large numbers of Irish. Irish Catholics generally were widely discriminated against in housing and employment. One of the more popular songs of the time was "No Irish Need Apply." In his descripton of the riot, Mann writes, "As I sit down to write, martial music is playing in the streets. A riot of almost unheard-of atrocity has raged for several hours this afternoon between the Irish population . . . and the enginemen and those who rallied to their assistance. . . . It is said lives are lost: it is certain that great bodily injury has been inflicted."[9] Mann goes on to reflect that the real problem was public opinion, which played a major role in the power of American government. The key to eliminating this type of riot, he felt, would be the proper education of public opinion.

Three days after the riot, Mann worried in his journal over whether or not to accept the leadership of the Board of Education. Finally, on June 30, after having reflected on phrenology, attended temperance meetings, experienced a firebombing, and observed a religious riot, he accepted the position. His journal for the date contains a statement of his belief in the ameliorating power of the school. With almost a religious passion, he states, "Henceforth, so long as I hold this office, I devote myself to the supremest welfare of mankind upon earth. . . . I have faith in the improvability of the race."[10]

Horace Mann believed that he was moving from the profession of law, which he felt had failed to save society, to a field of endeavor that promised universal salvation. A month after his acceptance he wrote to a friend that he had abandoned the practice of law for a higher calling. He explained that laws failed because they dealt with adults, whose character was already shaped, and the real hope was in molding the child: "Having found the present generation composed of materials almost unmalleable, I am about transferring my efforts to the next. Men are cast-iron; but children are wax. Strength expended upon the latter may be effectual, which would make no impression upon the former."[11]

Mann's hopes and dreams for the common school unfolded in the pages of the reports he wrote as secretary of the Massachusetts State Board of Education. The most important was *The Twelfth Annual Report*, written in 1848 after Mann resigned his educational post for a seat in the U.S. Congress. This report contained a summary of his ideas on the purposes of the common school.

In *The Twelfth Annual Report*, Mann returned to the reasoning he had used eleven years earlier when abandoning law for education. Again he argued that the hope for ridding society of evil actions was not in the law but in moral education. The increasing complexity of society, he felt, continually expanded the possibilities for moral transgression. He even dismissed as futile his earlier involvement in the passage of laws against the sale of alcohol, because "the government sees the evils that come from the use of intoxicating drinks, and prohibits their sale; but unprincipled men pander to depraved appetitites, and gather a harvest of dishonest profits."[12]

The answer to this steady expansion of crime, he maintained, was to educate the child. In language reflecting his ardent belief in the moral power of the school, he stated that there was one experiment society had not tried in its attempt to control crime: "It is an experiment which, even before its inception, offers the highest authority for its ultimate success. Its formula is intelligible to all; and it is as legible as though written in starry letters on an azure sky." This formula, and the key to the good society, he stated, was "best expressed in these few and simple words:—*Train up a child in the way he should go, and when he is old he will not depart from it.*'"[13] Mann claimed that all attempts to reform humanity had failed to realize the possibilities for shaping the character of children and youth.

In a broader sense, Mann put his hope in the schoolteacher, who, by educating children so that they would not transgress the law, would replace the police. This concept made schools the central institution for the control and maintenance of the social order. Also, it opened the door to the explosive political issue of whose morality would be taught in the public schools.

Mann walked a delicate tightrope in his advocacy of moral education in the schools. Given the temper of the times, moral education, which for most people meant a religious education, was considered an essential part of overall education. On the one hand, this meant that if Mann did not advocate a moral education with religious foundations, he faced the possibility of being called irreligious and of having the common school condemned as a secular institution without religious foundations. For most people during this period, the education of character had to be linked to religious doctrines; if not, it could be accused of being antireligious. On the other hand, if he did link moral education to religion, he had to make a choice about the religious tenets to which moral education should be linked. Given the fierce denominational rivalries of the time, any choice he made would create the possibility that the common school might be desroyed by competing religious groups.

Mann defended his position on this issue in *The Twelfth Annual Report* by arguing that the presence and use of the Bible in the schools provided instruction in the fundamental doctrines of Christianity without reference to denominational differences, and this provided the basis for all creeds: "Is it not, indeed, too plain, to require the formality of a syllogism, that if any man's creed is to be found in the Bible, and the Bible is in the schools, then that man's creed is in the schools? . . . If a certain system, called Christianity, were contained in . . . the Bible, then wherever the Bible might go, there the system of Christianity must be."[14]

In addition to the use of the Bible in the schools, Mann claimed that the laws of Massachusetts required the teaching of the basic moral doctrines of Christianity, which he listed as instruction in piety, justice, love of country, benevolence, sobriety, industry, frugality, chastity, moderation, and temperance. "Are not these virtues and graces," asked Mann, "part and parcel of Christianity?"[15] Within the framework of this reasoning, religious education in the common schools was to be based on a nonsectarian use of the Bible with the teaching of broad religious principles common to all Christian denominations.

Mann envisioned four destructive alternatives to this form of nonsectarian moral education. The first was to exclude all religious instruction from the schools. This, he argued, would make the schools "un-Christian," and the schools would receive no support from the general population. The second alternative was for the law to define and prescribe a system of religion for the schools, which, according to Mann, would involve the government in the establishment of religion and force a particular religion on all children. The third alternative was to give each religious sect with a majority in a community the power to define the religion of the schools. Mann strongly felt that this would result in the destruction of the common school by the heat of religious rivalries as all denominations fought for the inclusion of their doctrines. The last alternative was for the government to abandon all interference in the education of the young. As an advocate of the common school system, Mann quickly rejected this last possibility.

In the context of these arguments, the term *common* took on added meaning. Children in the common school were to receive a common moral education based on the general principles of the Bible and on common virtues, and such education was to eliminate crime and corruption in society.

Mann used the same type of reasoning in defining his goals for political education in the common schools. Like religious instruction, political instruction opened the door for groups with differing political ideas to fight over the content of political instruction. Mann stated in his *Twelfth Annual Report*, "It is obvious . . . that if the tempest of political strife were to be let loose upon our Common Schools, they would be overwhelmed with sudden ruin." His answer was to have schools teach only those articles of republican faith that were approved by "all sensible and judicious men, all patriots, and all genuine republicans." This political education, he proclaimed, would contain "articles in the creed of republicanism, which are accepted by all, believed in by all, and which form the common basis of our political faith."[16]

To avoid political controversy in the schoolroom, Mann proposed that the teacher avoid any discussion of or comment that touched on political disputes. However, "when the teacher, in the course of his lessons or lectures on the fundamental law, arrives at a controverted text, he is either to read it without comment or remark; or, at most, he is only to say that the passage is the subject of disputation, and that the schoolroom is neither the tribunal to adjudicate, nor the forum to discuss it."[17]

In this manner, Mann hoped to provide instruction in the fundamentals of politics without destroying the common school in the fury of political controversy.

Within the context of political education, the common in common school meant the teaching of a common political creed. The combination of moral and political instruction meant that the student leaving the common school would share with fellow students a set of moral and political beliefs; the result would be the creation of a society with a consensus of political and moral values.

For Mann, the inculcation of a common set of political beliefs would reduce the level of political violence in society as a whole. He hoped that a common school education would lead to political discussions based on a shared set of political beliefs. Thus, even though some disputes over political issues might arise, these disputes would take place in the context of a common political faith. Mann envisioned that political violence would be avoided because of the adherence to common articles of republican faith.

According to Mann, it was necessary to teach the importance of using the vote, as opposed to revolution and violence, to bring about political change. This was a particularly important issue during Mann's time because the extension of universal male suffrage had taken place in the 1820s. Before that time, the vote had been restricted by property requirements. In reference to the vote replacing political violence, Mann stated: "Had the obligations of the future citizen been sedulously inculcated upon all children of this Republic, would the patriot have had to mourn over so many instances, where the voter, not being able to accomplish his purpose by voting, has proceeded to accomplish it by violence."[18]

Mann wished to avoid not only political violence but also violence between social classes. Like Karl Marx in Europe, Mann was concerned with the creation of divisions between social classes caused by the growth of modern industry. *The Communist Manifesto* by Karl Marx and Friedrich Engels was published in 1848, the same year that Mann wrote his *Twelfth Annual Report* for the Massachusetts State Board of Education. Unlike Marx and Engels, Mann believed that the answer to social-class conflict was a common school education—not revolution by the working class.

Like Marx and Engels, however, Mann recognized that modern industrial development had created a major split between capital and labor and thus the intensification of class consciousness. Writing in the *Twelfth Annual Report* about industrial development in Massachusetts, he poses a warning question: "Are we not in danger of . . . those hideous evils which are always engendered between Capital and Labor, when all the capital is in the hands of one class and all the labor is thrown upon another?" He goes on to argue that if one class possesses all the wealth and education, and the other is poor and ignorant, then the latter will be "servile dependents and subjects of the former."[19]

"Now, surely," Mann writes with a great deal of conviction about the social power of the common school, "nothing but Universal Education can counter-work this tendency to the domination of capital and servility of labor." He believed that two alternatives existed through which common schooling could eliminate the problems between capital and labor. The first was to eliminate the friction caused by class consciousness. Mann admits that "a fellow-feeling for one's class or caste is the common instinct of hearts not wholly sunk in selfish regards for person, or for family." For Mann, the problem was not elimination of class consciousness but its expansion across social boundaries. Mann hoped that a common school education would spread feelings of class consciousness among all members of society: "The spread of education, by enlarging the cultivated class or caste, will open a wider area over which the social feelings will expand; and, if this education should be universal and complete, it would do more than all things else to obliterate factitious distinctions in society." In Mann's words, the expansion of class consciousness would "disarm the poor of their hostility towards the rich."[20]

The second way common schooling would eliminate the conflict between capital and labor was by increasing the general wealth of society. Mann felt that common schooling, by improving the general wealth of society, would be the answer to those reformers who were calling for a redistribution of property from the rich to the poor. His argument is one of the earliest considerations of schooling as capital investment and of teaching as the development of human capital. Within his framework of reasoning, education would produce wealth by training intelligence to develop new technology and methods of production. Investment in education is a form of capital investment because it leads to the production of new wealth, and teaching is a means of developing human capital because it provides the individual with the intellectual tools for improved labor.

In other words, according to Mann, common schooling would eliminate the problems of the unequal distribution of property by increasing the general wealth of society and, consequently, improving the economic conditions of the poor. It would prevent poverty by giving individuals the tools for enhancing their economic position in society. Therefore, as Mann states in one of his more famous passages in the *Twelfth Annual Report*, "Education, then, beyond all other devices of human origin, is the great equalizer of the conditions of men—the balance-wheel of the social machinery."[21]

Mann's arguments regarding the conflict between labor and capital added another meaning to the word *common*. Common schooling was to create a common social class by the extension of a common class consciousness among all members of society. Mixing the rich and poor within the same schoolhouse would cause social-class conflict to give way to a feeling of membership in a common social class and would thus provide society with a common set of political and moral values.

Mann uses arguments about education as capital investment to justify public financial support of the common school. One of the questions asked during the period was why those without children, or those who sent their children to private schools, should pay for the education of other people's children. Mann's answer is that the value of property is dependent on the work of previous generations and on the general level of prosperity of the community. He argues that property is held in trust by each generation, which through its labors increases its value. In other words, even a family without any children benefits from common schooling because common schooling increases the wealth of the entire community, which, in turn, increases the value of the family's property. Therefore, all members of society benefit economically from common schooling, whether or not they make any direct use of the schools.

With minor variations, Mann's statement of the goals and purposes of common schooling in his reports to the Massachusetts Board of Education were shared by the leading educational reformers of the time. This does not mean that they were shared by all members of society. In a sense, Mann's reports represented the official justification for the creation of a common system of education. Involved in this justification was the hope that all the social, economic, and political problems of society would be solved by putting together in a common school the children of all members of society and by teaching them a common set of political and moral beliefs.

But this utopian vision of the good society created by a system of common schooling has certain inherent problems. First was the real problem of agreement on a common set of political and moral values to be taught in the classroom. Such agreement concerning religious values never occurred, and, as a result, a private parochial system of education developed side by side with the common school. In the simplest terms, the common school never became common to all students. In addition, no proof existed that education would eliminate crime. In fact, one could argue that increased education simply meant improving the educational level of the criminal. Nor was there any real proof that a common school education could eliminate social, political, and economic unrest. It is possible, for instance, that social unrest is rooted in real economic and political problems that cannot be solved without dealing directly with the problems themselves. In this sense, the official ideology of the common school might be considered as essentially conservative because it did not call for any basic changes in the economic and political structure of society but placed its hope for social improvement on the education of the individual. In fact, the official ideology of the common school accepted the existing political and economic organization of society and held that any problems were the result of individual deviance or failure. Therefore, it was argued by common school reformers, the common school could create a utopian world by educating the individual to conform to the needs of existing political, social, and economic organizations.

Although there were obvious flaws in the reasoning of common school reformers, their faith in the power of the school continued into the twentieth century. The ideology of the common school became a standard part of the beliefs held by most Americans. Since the mid-1800s, the school has continually been seen as a means of eliminating poverty, crime, and social problems. In addition, the idea of education as capital investment and as a means of developing human capital became one of the major justifications for schooling in the twentieth century. Horace Mann and other common school reformers made a lasting contribution to the ongoing debate about the relationship between school and society.

WORKINGMEN AND THE STRUGGLE FOR A REPUBLICAN EDUCATION

The educational demands made by the workingmen's parties between 1827 and 1835 provide an example of how support of similar ideas and institutions by different groups and for different reasons can contribute to the advancement of an important social reform. Clearly, workingmen's parties wanted common schools, but for different reasons from those given by common school reformers. Nonetheless, the combined efforts of the workingmen's parties and the common school reformers gave the appearance of a popular struggle for the establishment of a common school system.

Although the political impact and social composition of workingmen's parties between 1827 and 1835 have been debated, there has been no dispute about the importance of education in the political campaigns of the workingmen's parties. Their educational arguments shared many of the characteristics of the ideology of common school reformers, particularly a general demand for free common public schooling to serve political and economic purposes. But the reasons given by workingmen's parties for the establishment of common schools were distinctly different from those given by Horace Mann and other common school reformers. The reformers stressed the necessity of teaching a common moral and political creed as a means of eliminating crime, poverty, and social unrest and providing for equal economic opportunity, whereas the workingmen's parties argued for the necessity of education as a means by which workers could protect themselves from economic and political exploitation. Common school reformers emphasized education as a mechanism of social control, while the workingmen's parties emphasized education as a mechanism for gaining political and economic power. Both groups agreed that a common education was necessary to eliminate distinctions between the rich and the poor and to promote equality of economic opportunity.

The workingmen's political movement began in Philadelphia in 1827 with a demand by the Mechanics Union of Trade Associations for worker influence on legislative action. In the spring of 1828 the Philadelphia Workingmen's Party nominated and campaigned for candidates to the state legislature. The organization of labor parties quickly spread through Pennsylvania, Delaware, Massachusetts, and New York. For most of these workingmen's parties, education became a central theme of their political campaigns.

Representative of the workingmen's parties' concern about education was the establishment in 1829 by the Philadelphia Mechanics Union of Trade Associations of a committee to investigate educational conditions in the city and state. The committee found that in all areas of the state except Philadelphia, Lancaster, and Pittsburgh little support for public instruction could be found. The committee also attacked the existence of charity schools. First, there was a concern that private individuals were using government money to provide education of questionable quality for the poor. In his excellent study "Education and the Working Class: The Expansion of Public Education during the Transition to Capitalism" historian William Russell quotes the committee as claiming that a large number of charity schools were "irresponsible institutions, established by individuals, from mere motives of private speculation or gain, who are destitute of character, and frequently, of the requisite attainments and abilities." In addition, the schools suffered from "ignorance, inattention and immorality." Criticisms were also raised that charity schools offered a limited curriculum and led to a loss of pride among parents.[22]

In general, the committee believed that government monies were being used primarily to support colleges and universities—a situation it argued was "exclusively for the benefit of the wealthy, who [were] thereby enabled to procure a liberal education for their children, upon lower terms than it could otherwise be afforded them." If this condition persisted, the committee reported, knowledge would be mostly in the hands of the privileged few and would "[consign] the multitude to comparative ignorance, and [secure] the balance of knowledge on the side of the rich and the rulers."[23] The answer to this situation was to make equal knowledge a common property of all groups in society.

In New York, a similar complaint was voiced about the private control of charity schools by the New York School Society (originally the New York Free School Society). The New York Workingmen's Party believed that the existence of charity schools and the lack of adequate funding of schooling were increasing social-class differences. The lack of education among workingmen, it was argued, kept them ignorant of their rights and allowed for exploitation by the privileged.

One of the most important points made in the arguments of the New York Workingmen's Party was that, in an industrial society, knowledge was power. Thus, keeping knowledge from the masses was considered one method of assuring the upper classes a monopoly on power. Russell explains the general view of the workingmen's parties: "Kept in ignorance, workers could be deprived of their rights, cheated in their daily business, and 'gulled and deceived' by 'designing schemers,' 'parasitic politicians,' 'greedy bank directors,' and 'heartless manufacturers.'"[24] In summary, workingmen's parties believed that the lack of a common school system was an attempt to deny them their rights and their share of economic and political power.

Workingmen's groups believed that common schooling was essential to the protection of their rights—that knowledge was necessary for the *equal* exercise of power in a democratic system of government. This argument is best expressed in an 1830 statement in the *Workingmen's Advocate*: "The right of self government implies a right to a *knowledge* necessary to the exercise of the right of self government. If all have an *equal* right to the first, all must consequently have an equal right to the second; therefore, *all* are entitled to *equal education*."[25]

In addition, access to knowledge meant protection of rights against what was considered the tyranny of the upper class. One statement in the *Workingmen's Advocate* in 1831 stresses that education was the only sure "defense against not only an infringement, but a total usurpation of the native rights of the people, by the monopolizing demagogues of the land."[26] An editorial in 1830 in the *Sentinel*, a workingmen's newspaper, wishfully claims that if the previous generation had been properly educated, it would not have been cheated and blinded by those currently wielding political and economic power.

Differences and similarities existed between the workingmen's parties' arguments for the necessity of education in a republic and those of the common school reformers like Horace Mann. Both groups agreed that education was necessary for the maintenance of a republican and democratic form of government, but the common school reformers emphasized political education as a means of making individuals worthy of democratic rights and as necessary for maintaining political harmony, whereas workingmen's groups emphasized the necessity of education for the equal sharing of power and the protection of rights. These differences suggest a different content in the political instruction to be offered in the schools. As a means of achieving his objectives, Mann wanted the basic principles of government and a common republican creed to be taught, while workingmen's groups called for the teaching of how to exercise power in the political system, the nature of political rights, and the protection of those rights as the means of achieving their goals.

With regard to crime and poverty, workingmen's groups and common school reformers shared an equal faith in the power of the school. In fact, in response to the issue of why a person without children should pay for the education of other people's children, workingmen's groups often advanced the argument that education increased the security of all people from criminal activities.

Common school reformers and workingmen's groups also shared a belief that equal education for all was necessary to reduce distinctions among economic classes, but again their reasons were different. The reason common school reformers wanted a common education was to reduce friction between capital and labor. Workingmen's groups wanted equal education as a means of ensuring that capital did not maintain a monopoly over knowledge and as a means of protecting their economic interests. As an editorial in the *Workingmen's Advocate* of 1834 states, education would provide workers with "a correct knowledge of their value as producers . . . [and of their] general interest as productive laborers." This knowledge, it was hoped, would destroy the causes of the dependency of workers on owners and the unjust accumulation of capital.[27]

Because knowledge was viewed as power and as a means by which capital maintained its grip over labor, it was logical for workingmen's groups to support equal education as a means of providing equal economic opportunity. The relationship between equality of educational opportunity and equality of economic opportunity has been stressed throughout the nineteenth and twentieth centuries.

The most extreme, but logical, linkage between equal education and equal economic opportunity was made by the New York Workingmen's Party in its state guardianship plan. The basic argument behind this plan was that equality of educational opportunity could not be achieved if one child went from school to an impoverished home life and another child went home to a life that was rich and offered many advantages. To achieve true equality of educational opportunity, the state guardianship plan argued, all children must be taken from their families and placed in state boarding schools, where they would receive equal treatment, equal clothes, equal food, and an equal education. Although the radicalism of this proposal split the party, it did highlight the extreme importance workingmen's groups gave to the connection between equality of educational opportunity and equality of economic opportunity.[28]

The question remains as to whether or not workingmen, as represented by these early labor parties, gained the type of education they wanted through the establishment of a common school system. As discussed in later chapters, tension existed in the nineteenth and twentieth centuries between organized labor and the public school system over the content of instruction. Labor often claimed that public school instruction was conservative and taught principles opposed to the organization of workers into unions. Whether or not this was the case does not detract from the very important effect workingmen's parties had on spreading ideas favoring common school education and winning support for the establishment of common schools. In fact, when one considers the dates of the activities of the workingmen's parties and the common school reformers, it is clear that the workingmen's parties paved the way for reformers such as Barnard and Mann.

The differences between the common school reformers and the workingmen's parties highlight the differences in meaning that can exist over commonly used words. One cannot assume that if all people say they favor education, they all favor the same thing. The word *education* has meant different things to different people. This is particularly true of the way the word was used in the different arguments given in support of the establishment of common schools.

THE WHIGS AND THE DEMOCRATS

The common school movement was born during a period of intense political change and rivalry. Of primary political importance in the 1820s was the ending of property qualifications for voting and the establishment of universal male suffrage. In addition, modern political parties were born in 1828, when the Jacksonian Democrats competed against the National Republican party (which died in the early 1830s and was replaced by the Whigs). The Whigs and the Democrats had almost equal shares of the nation's voters.

These political changes were related to the common school movement in several ways. First, universal suffrage created a concern with the education of the future voter. Many supporters of the common school movement stressed the importance of education in ensuring the maintenance of political order as democratic rights were extended. Second, political affiliation was the most important difference between groups advocating different forms of school organization. Most leaders of the common school movement were Whigs, who believed that government should intervene to maintain social order through a centrally managed school system designed to educate moral and responsible citizens. On the other hand, members of the Democratic party believed that social order would occur naturally, and therefore they believed in minimal government intervention and local control of the schools.

In their analysis of voting patterns in six states, Herbert Ershkowitz and William Shade found that between 1833 and 1843 the voting patterns of the members of each party were clearly different. By 1840, 80 to 100 percent of both Whigs and Democrats adhered to the point of view of their party. With regard to educational legislation, in most cases there were significant differences in party voting patterns.[29]

The differences between each party's political philosophy highlight important aspects of the common school and the continuing controversy over the political structure of schooling. Both political groups believed that education was a necessity but differed over the goals and structure of the educational system. In general, Whigs were concerned with morality, duty, and the reduction of social conflict and thus wanted an educational system that would shape moral character, teach social and political duties, and reduce conflict among social classes and political groups. Whigs believed these goals could best be achieved through centralized supervision by state governments. Democrats resisted the trend toward centralization of government control and talked mainly about rights and a society of conflicting interests.

In *The Concept of Jacksonian Democracy: New York as a Test Case*, Lee Benson describes the differences between these two political groups as positive versus negative liberalism. Within this framework, Whigs were advocates of a positive liberalism that called for government intervention to assure the workings of a free-market economy. Therefore, Whigs believed that government should provide money for education and for internal improvements to guarantee the establishment and functioning of institutions and economic organizations essential to the development of the country. For instance, Whigs argued that because private capital was not available for the development of canals and railroads essential for economic growth, the government should supply the needed capital. Benson quotes New York governor William Seward's 1839 message as a summary of the Whig position on internal improvements and education. Seward argued that government action and spending were necessary "to enlarge . . . national prosperity, while we equalize its enjoyments and direct it to the universal diffusion of knowledge."[30]

The Democrats represented negative liberalism and argued that government governed too much. They believed that the economy should function without any state intervention and that state monies should not be used to support a common school system. Benson states that John Bigelow, a leading writer for the Democrats in New York, "believed that the common school fund should be applied to the present crippling state debt and that thereafter the state should cease to propagate any science, art, trade, or religion among any class of people."[31]

In *The Political Culture of the American Whigs*, Daniel Howe argues that faculty psychology had the strongest influence on the moral philosophy of the Whigs, who believed that the balancing and regulating of the moral faculties were essential to the maintenance of social order. From this perspective, schools were necessary for ensuring harmony within the individual. Whigs believed that if moral faculties were left to themselves, the lower powers would escape control and wreck havoc. An unregulated faculty—whether pride, licentiousness, or some other appetite or emotion—was called a "passion." The good life entailed continual self-discipline as one sought to "suppress his passions" or "cultivate and improve his virtues."[32]

As Howe indicates, this philosophical perspective ruled out the idea of a laissez-faire society completely free of some form of regulation and "implied an active, purposeful central government, 'administering the affairs of the nation according to its best judgment for the good of the whole, and all parts of the whole.'"[33] According to this political ideology, the government should play an active role in maintaining the economy, regulating morality, and ensuring political and social order. Consequently, Whigs supported not only government funding of internal improvements (such as canals) but also the passage of laws to regulate morality. For instance, the temperance movement received strong support from Whigs.

For Whigs, schooling was the key to an ordered society. Howe summarizes the Whigs' political campaigns as being part of "a cultural struggle to impose on the United States the standards of morality we usually term Victorian. They were standards of self-control and restraint, which dovetailed well with the economic program of the party, for they emphasized thrift, sobriety, and public responsibility."[34] Whigs believed these values were necessary to bring discipline to voters.

The Whig idea that society requires a consciously arranged order and the Democratic free-market ideas reflected two different concepts of freedom. In turn, these differing concepts of freedom were reflected in attitudes about the political and social role of the school. For Whigs, true freedom occurred only when the balance of mental faculties within an individual ensured that passion did not reign over reason. In addition, Whigs contended, social conditions must be organized so that the individual was not tempted into activity that would disrupt the harmony of the mind. In other words, the Whig position was that true freedom was possible only if individuals received a proper education and social temptations were removed. This explains why many common school reformers were active in the temperance movement while working for greater centralization and uniformity in the school system.[35] Democrats, on the other hand, believed that true freedom was possible only in a society in which there was a minimum of government interference in the social order. Democrats viewed government attempts to order society as attempts to promote and protect the special privileges of the upper class.

Not all members of American society in the 1830s and 1840s complacently accepted the moral reform efforts of the Whigs. For example, Howe reports that many thought the Whigs' assumption of moral responsibility for others meddlesome. He tells the story of the burning of the church of Lyman Beecher, who was a Whig, temperance advocate, and minister.

> When Lyman Beecher's church on Hanover Street burned down, the volunteer fire companies, who hated his temperance crusading, refused to fight the flames. Instead, it is reported, they watched and sang: "While Beecher's church holds out to burn / The vilest sinner may return"—a parody of a hymn.[36]

The best study of the differences in educational philosophy between the Democrats and the Whigs was conducted by Carl Kaestle and Maris Vinovskis for their book *Education and Social Change in Nineteenth-Century Massachusetts*.[37] They studied the attempt in 1840 to abolish the Massachusetts State Board of Education and, of course, Horace Mann's position as its secretary. This action was considered a direct attack on the common school movement.

Kaestle and Vinovskis report that in the year preceding the attempt to abolish the board, a leading Massachusetts Democrat, Orestes Brownson, attacked the board for trying to "Prussianize" education by centralizing control over the schools. Brownson contended that the board was a vehicle for Whig ideas about education and maintained that control should remain at the local level.

In 1840 a legislative committee composed of three Whigs and two Democrats was established to investigate the work of the Board of Education. Surprisingly, given the majority of Whigs on the committee, its report attacked the board as an unnecessary expense and, to quote Kaestle and

Vinovskis, as "a danger to political and religious freedoms." The committee report argues: "District schools, in a republican goverment need no police regulations, no systems of state censorship, no checks of moral, religious, or political conservatism, to preserve either the morals, the religion, or the politics of the state. 'Let them ever be kept free and pure.'"[38] Obviously, this reasoning was almost the exact opposite of that given by Mann for establishing a common school system.

The committee's report provoked a series of other investigations that eventually led to a vote by the members of the state legislature on the abolition of the board. The attempt to abolish the board failed by a vote of 182 to 245. The legislative vote provided Kaestle and Vinovskis with data by which they could analyze the nature of the supporters and opponents of the common school system in Massachusetts.

Kaestle and Vinovskis classified the members of the legislature according to religion, occupation, the geographical area they represented, and party affiliation. They hoped to determine which factors were most important in determining support or nonsupport of the board. The assumption was made that a legislator's position on this issue reflected that individual's support or nonsupport of the common school movement.

After analyzing the data, Kaestle and Vinovskis concluded that party affiliation was the most important factor in determining a legislator's support or nonsupport of the board. They also found that religion was not an important factor in legislative action. Of course, the legislature did not include a large Catholic faction, so the rift between Catholics and Protestants was not represented in their findings. They did find that legislators from manufacturing areas tended to support the board, unlike those from rural areas.

The fact that party affiliation was the most important factor does not mean that all Whigs supported the existence of the board and that all Democrats stood in opposition. One-fifth of Whigs and one-third of Democrats did not follow the general voting pattern of their respective parties. But even with these defections from the positions of both political parties, political ideology was the most important factor in differentiating between supporters and nonsupporters of the Board of Education.

The differences between the political parties in Massachusetts reflected more general differences between the two political groups throughout the nation. According to Kaestle and Vinovskis, "the Whigs argued that positive government intervention was a necessary and useful means of improving the quality of public schools throughout the commonwealth." On the other hand, Democrats felt "that any increased state interference in local educational matters created the potential, if not the reality, of a centralized state school system that would dictate how children were to be educated."[39]

The struggle between Whigs and Democrats over the common school reflected a more general concern about how schools should be controlled and whose values should be taught in a school's curriculum. This debate, which has continued into the twentieth century, reflects in varying degrees the tension between those wanting popular control of the schools and little government intervention and those believing that government should work actively to ensure that the schools serve general social, political, and economic goals.

THE CATHOLIC ISSUE

The contradiction between the attempt to make schooling common to all children and the Protestant values that dominated common schools resulted in major disputes between Catholics and Protestants over the use of state educational funds. In large part, this conflict resulted from strong anti-Catholic feelings in the Protestant community. In the end, Catholics felt excluded from the common schools and found it necessary to establish their own system of independent parochial schools, which meant that the common schools never became common to all American children.

New York City was the scene of a major conflict over school funds in the 1840s, when Catholics demanded a share of the state educational funds that were being monopolized by the Public School Society (originally the New York Free School Society). Until this time, Catholics had been operating their own schools in an attempt to provide children of Catholic parents with an alternative to the Protestant-dominated schools of the Public School Society. Catholics objected to the use in the schools of the King James Version of the Bible and of textbooks that contained anti-Catholic statements.

The smoldering conflict between Catholics and Protestants in New York City erupted into a major conflict with the 1838 election of William Seward as governor of New York. Seward was a Whig and, like all good Whigs, was a strong advocate of government-sponsored internal improvements and increased state support of education. But his Whig philosophy had an important twist when it came to the issue of education. Although he believed that a centrally controlled and expanded system of education was necessary for the health of society, he also believed that state money for the support of Catholic schools was necessary to achieve this goal. It was this proposal that fanned the flames of conflict between Catholics and Protestants.

Seward indicated in his first message to the state legislature in 1839 that education would be an important part of his legislative agenda. He argued before the legislature that improved educational facilities were necessary for the development of responsible citizens and claimed that, during his administration, "improvement in our system of education will be wider and more enduring than the effects of any change of public policy."[40] As reflected in his other speeches and correspondence, one of his major concerns was to educate Catholic immigrants, particularly the Irish, for citizenship. He resisted the strong anti-Irish feeling that existed in the 1830s and 1840s and denounced American hatred of "foreigners."

Seward discovered, while visiting New York City, that large numbers of immigrant children were not attending school, and by 1840 he concluded that many of New York's Catholic children were not attending public schools because of their anti-Catholic atmosphere. His concern was that immigrant children might grow up to be adult illiterates who would become public burdens and never enter the mainstream of American life. He therefore proposed before the state legislature in 1840 that Catholic schools become part of the state school system while retaining their private charters and religious affiliation. As historian Vincent Lannie writes in *Public Money and Parochial Education*, "Seward urged the establishment of schools that would be acceptable to this minority group and staffed with teachers who spoke the same language and professed the same religious faith as their pupils. Such schools would be administered by Catholic officials but supported with public funds."[41]

Many Protestant Whigs were outraged by Seward's proposal and raised strong opposition to the plan. In a letter to a friend in 1840, Seward reasoned that any Whig who withheld support from him because of his proposal did not really support the "Whigism we derived from our forefathers of the Revolutionary Age nor is such the Whigism that I shall teach my children." He argued that it was necessary for the state to provide a moral and religious education to all children in order to maintain social stability and "if it cannot be otherwise conferred, may rightly be conferred by the employment for the purpose of teachers professing the same language and religious creed."[42]

The immediate response of the Catholic community in New York to Seward's proposal was to petition the Board of Aldermen of New York City for a portion of the common school fund. Historically, this petition was important because it enumerated Catholic complaints about the Protestant dominance of the public schools. First, the Catholic petitioners attacked the supposed nonsectarianism of the schools operated by the Public School Society. Of course, most common school reformers claimed that the schools could be nonsectarian if they taught the basic principles of Christianity. The petition cited a number of instances in which the reports of the Public School Society either called for religious instruction or demonstrated the existence of religious instruction in the schools. This religious instruction included the reading and study of the Bible, which the petition claimed made the school sectarian. The petitioners argued: "Even the reading of the Scriptures in those schools your petitioners cannot regard otherwise than as sectarian; because Protestants would certainly consider as such the introduction of the Catholic Scriptures, which are different from theirs, and the Catholics have the same ground of objection when the Protestant version is made use of."[43]

In addition, the petitioners complained of anti-Catholic statements in selections used for elementary reading lessons. They argued that historical and religious portions of the reading lessons were selected from Protestant writers who were prejudiced against Catholics. The petition stated: "The term 'Popery' is repeatedly found in them. This term is known and employed as one of insult and contempt towards the Catholic religion, and it passes into the minds of children with the feeling of which it is the outward expression."[44]

The petition recognized that the members of the Public School Society had tried to remove anti-Catholic sentiments from textbooks but, according to the petitioners, had failed because they were incompetent in their ability to identify anti-Catholic statements. As an example, the petition quoted the following passage from a textbook approved by the Public School Society:

Huss, John, a zealous reformer from Popery, who lived in Bohemia, towards the close of the fourteeth, and the beginning of the fifteenth centuries. He was bold and persevering; but at length, trusting himself to the deceitful Catholics, he was by them brought to trial, condemned as a heretic, and burnt at the stake.[45]

The petitioners argued that the anti-Catholic atmosphere of the schools operated by the Public School Society forced them to open their own schools for the education of the poor and that this amounted to a system of double taxation whereby they were taxed to support the schools operated by the Public School Society and to support an alternative school system. In the words of the petition, "The expense necessary for this [establishment of Catholic schools], was a second taxation, required not by the laws of the land, but by the no less imperious demands of their conscience."[46] Catholics' claims that they had to assume the burden of double taxation for the maintenance of Catholic schools continued into the twentieth century.

The petitioners recognized that public monies should not be used for the support of religion but claimed that this was precisely what was happening through public support of the Public School Society. The petitioners were willing to remove all religious instruction from their schools during school hours. To ensure that money was not used for religious instruction, they recommended that the organization of their schools and the control of the disbursement of money "shall be conducted, and made, by persons unconnected with the religion of your petitioners, even the Public School Society. . . . The public may then be assured that the money will not be applied to the support of the Catholic religion."[47]

Both Governor Seward's proposal and the Catholic petition brought a storm of protest from the Protestant community. The "great debate" began within a month of the presentation of the petition before the Board of Aldermen in the city's Common Council chambers. The Protestant community responded to the Catholic petition with the argument that if Catholics were willing to postpone religious instruction until after school hours, they should be willing to instruct the children attending the Public School Society schools after school hours. The Reverend Mr. Knox of the Dutch Reformed church claimed that the public schools were not "adverse to feelings of reverence for Catholic peculiarities." The Reverend Mr. Bangs of the Methodist church argued that all poor and wayward children should be forced to attend public schools. Bangs argued, in the words of Vincent Lannie: "This coercive action of the state would really be an act of compassion, since these vagrants would be snatched from the streets and their concomitant vices, and taught to become Christian gentlemen and competent citizens." And last, Gardner Spring of the Presbyterian church told the aldermen that he viewed the petition "with more alarm on account of the source from which it comes . . . if there was no alternative between infidelity and the dogmas of the Catholic Church, I would choose, sir . . . , to be an infidel tomorrow."[48]

The issue pitted Catholics against Protestants and forced realignments in the political parties. A Whig-nativist coalition developed in opposition to state support of Catholic schools and in favor of state support of public schools. Some Catholics remained in the Whig party and gave their support to Governor Seward. On the other hand, Democrats decided to support the Catholic school position and attracted a large following of independent Catholics. The actions of the Democratic party were consistent with the principle that schools should reflect the desires of the local community.

The school issue so inflamed public feelings that riots between anti-Catholics (a coalition of nativists and Irish Protestants) and Irish Catholics broke out during the 1842 election. The riot began in front of the city prison and quickly spread to attacks on unsuspecting Catholic individuals and homes. Some Catholics took refuge in a hotel, but it was also attacked by anti-Catholic mobs. Rioters even attacked the residence of Bishop Hughes behind St. Patrick's Cathedral.

Although emotions remained high, in 1842 the state legislature passed compromise legislation ending the existence of the Public School Society and turning over control of its schools to the public. In hopes of winning Catholic support for the public schools, the legislation established a central, elected school board that shared power with local boards at the ward level. It was hoped that in local wards that were primarily Catholic, ward control would result in the schools' reflecting Catholic sentiments. In the end, Catholics found this an unsatisfactory method of resolving their complaints.

New York City was not the only place where conflict erupted between Catholics and Protestants over the content of public schooling. In *Pillars of the Republic: Common Schools and American Society, 1780–1960*, Carl Kaestle details Protestant and Catholic conflicts around the country. For instance, in Philadelphia in 1843 the public school board ruled that Catholic children could read their own version of the Bible in public schools and be excused from other religious instruction. Protestants claimed that this was an attempt by Catholics to exclude the Bible from the schools. The result of this conflict was the Philadelphia Bible Riots, in which thirteen people died and a Catholic church was burned to the ground. Other conflicts of this type, though not of this intensity, occurred around the country.[49]

In the end, Catholics found it necessary to establish their own system of schooling, the organization of which emerged from the work of plenary councils held in Baltimore in 1852, 1866, and 1884. A major theme of these councils was that religious instruction should not be separated from other forms of instruction. At the First Plenary Council, church leaders told parents that they had a responsibility to "watch over the purity of their [children's] faith and morals with jealous vigilance." To avoid neglecting their children's upbringing, Catholic parents were urged to give their children a Christian education "based on religious principles, accompanied by religious practices and always subordinate to religious influence." The council urged that all possible sacrifices be made for the establishment of Catholic schools.[50]

The idea that religion must be an integral part of instruction ran counter to the increasingly secular quality of common school instruction in the mid-1800s and to the increasing importance of science. The Second Plenary Council meeting, in 1866, again emphasized the principle "that religious teaching and religious training should form part of every system of school education." In addition, concern was expressed about the large number of delinquent Catholic youths who were being sent to Protestant reformatories. The council admitted, "It is a melancholy fact, and a very humiliating avowal for us to make, that a very large proportion of the idle and vicious youth of our principal cities are the children of Catholic parents." It recommended the establishment of Catholic industrial schools to care for delinquent Catholic youths.[51]

The Third Plenary Council, in 1884, sent forth decrees for the establishment of a system of Catholic schools. The council warned that the continued trend toward secular education was resulting in the undermining of Christianity and argued that all religious groups were calling for a Christian education in the schools, reflecting a common concern with the preservation of religious faith. The council claimed it was not condemning the state "for not imparting religious instruction in the public schools as they are now organized; because they well know it does not lie within the province of the State to teach religion." In fact, it considered the creation of Catholic schools as beneficial to the state because such schools would create better citizens by educating better Christians. It declared: "Two objects therefore, dear brethren, we have in view, to multiply our schools, and to perfect them."[52]

To achieve the objective of ensuring a Catholic education, the council decreed that every church establish a parish school and that all Catholic parents send their children to Catholic schools. The following decrees of the Third Plenary Council established the ideals of Catholic education in the United States:

> I. That near every church a parish school, where one does not yet exist, is to be built and maintained in perpetuum within two years of the promulgation of this council, unless the bishop should decide that because of serious difficulties a delay may be granted. . . .
>   IV. That all Catholic parents are bound to send their children to the parish school, unless it is evident that a sufficient training in religion is given either in their own homes, or in other Catholic schools; or when because of sufficient reason, approved by the Bishop, with all due precautions and safeguards, it is licit to send them to other schools. What constitutes a Catholic school is left to the decision of the Bishop.[53]

The establishment of a Catholic school system suggests that the dream of creating a school system common to all children was impossible in a country settled by a wide variety of cultural and religious groups. It also demonstrates that some groups viewed the common school system as an attempt to impose a particular set of religious and cultural values on all American people. The Catholic rebellion against public school reformers gave proof to the argument that the common school reflected a primarily Protestant ideology. Beginning in the nineteenth century and continuing into the twentieth, many Catholics would refer to public schools as Protestant schools.

THE CONTINUING DEBATE ABOUT THE COMMON SCHOOL IDEAL

The conflicts over religion, the political control of common schools, and the differences between the goals of the workingmen's parties and Whig reformers are reflected in the differing historical interpretations of the common school era. Also, these differences in interpretation reflect modern concerns about the role of education in American society. On the one hand, there are those who see the common school period as a battle between liberals and conservatives for the establishment of a school system that would be of great benefit to all members of society. On the other hand, some historians argue that common schools were established to protect privileged economic and religious positions in society. These broad differences in historical interpretation contain elements of the debate that continues to this day about whose interests are served by the public schools. Therefore, understanding the differences in historical interpretation of the common school period is important to understanding both the common school reforms and the current debates about schooling.

The first major educational historian to portray the common school movement as a battle between liberals and conservatives over extending the benefits of schooling to all people was Ellwood Cubberley in his text first published in 1919, *Public Education in the United States: A Study and Interpretation of American Educational History*.[54] Cubberley describes liberals as good people who struggle for education for all people against avarice-minded conservatives.

Cubberley created a list of differing reasons for the support or nonsupport of common schools. The arguments he lists as being given in support of the common school movement include prevention and reduction of poverty and crime; increased work force productivity; elimination of "wrong ideas as to the distribution of wealth"; reduction of tensions among social classes; elimination of charity schools because they stigmatized a certain class in society; assimilation of immigrants; and preparation of the citizenry for the exercise of the right to vote. Of course, these arguments became the traditional arguments for the support of public schooling in the United States.

Cubberley also lists arguments for the expansion of state control over education. In one sense, these arguments can be viewed as part of the continuing debate about the rights of parents versus the rights of the state over the education of children. In Cubberley's words, the major arguments were as follows: "That a State which has the right to hang has the right to educate"; that "the taking over of education by the State is not based on considerations of economy, but is the exercise of the State's inherent right to self-preservation and improvement"; and finally, as a reflection of the common school emphasis on education serving government policies, "that only a system of state-controlled schools can be free to teach whatever the welfare of the State may demand."[55] Cubberley's list of the arguments favoring state control of education describes the actual political divisions that occurred during the 1830s and 1840s over the degree of government intervention in social and economic issues.

He lists the following as arguments given in opposition to the expansion of state power: "That taxes would be so increased that no state could long meet such a lavish drain" and "that there was a priestcraft in the scheme, the purpose being first to establish a State School, and then a State Church." Cubberley's list greatly oversimplifies the political debate about the extension of state control.[56]

Cubberley lists the arguments of those opposed to the social and economic reform arguments for the common school, which, according to his interpretations, centered around aristocratic ideas of social class: fear that common schools would destroy desirable social-class differences and educate people out of their proper place in society; fear that the industrious would be taxed to pay for the education of the indolent; fear that people without children would be forced to pay for the education of other people's children; fear that native-language instruction of non-English-speaking students would supplant English-language instruction in the schools; concerns of religious groups that the common school would hinder their advancement; and fear that private schools would be forced to close.

In general, Cubberley's interpretation is one that depicts the common school movement as the correct historical route to the development of an educational system that would benefit the majority of people by solving economic, political, and social problems. This vision of the common school movement received added support in Merle Curti's *Social Ideas of American Educators*, first published in 1935. Curti's history of education was written during the Depression, when there was a great deal of concern over the historical struggle between the haves and the have-nots.

For Curti, the common school movement was a major democratic movement designed to extend social benefits to the lower social classes in society. His description of the period is given in large part in chapters devoted to Horace Mann. He portrays Horace Mann as a great egalitarian and reformer. For Curti, Mann's primary motivation was a desire to ensure that all classes of society had equal access to knowledge. Curti states that Mann's "Social vision remained undimmed to the end, and all his work in the educational field was an effort to introduce into that field a more humane and democratic spirit."[57]

But, unlike Cubberley, Curti is highly critical of the conservative economic and social ideas held by Mann, an attitude that puts a critical edge on Curti's praise of the common school movement. Criticism of the social and economic opinions of common school reformers became an important factor in the revision of educational history that occurred in the 1960s.

The most dramatic revision came with the publication in 1968 of Michael Katz's *Irony of Early School Reform*, which deals with the decision in 1860 by Beverly, Massachusetts, voters to abolish their high school.[58] Katz used his discovery of resistance to the establishment of a high school in Beverly as a vehicle for providing a new interpretation of common school reforms. In the opening statement of his introdutory chapter, "Educational Reform: The Cloud of Sentiment and Historiography," he states: "For the most part historians have helped to perpetuate this essentially noble story, which portrays a rational, enlightened working class, led by idealistic and humanitarian intellectuals, triumphantly wresting free public education from . . . selfish, wealthy elite and from the bigoted proponents of orthodox religions."[59] This, of course, is the interpretation given to the period by Ellwood Cubberley.

But, Katz argues, one should immediately begin to question this historical interpretation when one considers that by the end of the nineteenth century most urban schools were "cold, rigid, and somewhat sterile bureaucracies." He goes on to ask, "Could a truly humanitarian urge to help realize widely diffused aspirations have turned so quickly into the dispassionate ethos of red tape and drill?"[60] In answering this question, Katz paints an entirely different picture of the evolution of the common school.

For Katz, the most important factors in explaining the common school movement are the social and economic changes associated with the bulding of factories, the increase in immigration, and the growth of cities. Within the context of these events, upper-class reformers were seeking to ensure that they would benefit from these changes by imposing a common school system that would train workers for the new factories, educate immigrants into acceptance of values supportive of the ruling elite, and provide order and stability among the expanding populations of the cities.

From this perspective, the rigid, bureaucratic schools that Katz claims existed by the end of the nineteenth century were not accidental but were the logical result of a school system designed to discipline a population to serve the needs of an urban and industrial society. The emphasis on attendance, disciplined study, and order was designed to socialize the student, particularly the immigrant child, to the requirements of the new factory systems. Learning to behave in school was a preparation for learning to work in the factory. Also, Katz argues, the bureaucratic structure of education, which evolved from common school reforms, was designed to ensure upper-class control of schooling. In his conclusion, Katz states that the common school movement was "a coalition of the social leaders, status-anxious parents, and status-hungry educators to impose educational innovation, each for their own reasons, upon a reluctant community."[61]

Katz's interpretation does not change the indentity of the leaders of the common school movement, but it does change their motivations. According to Katz, their actions were not the result of disinterested humanitarian impulses but were caused by a desire to protect their social positions and to provide the new industrial system with disciplined workers.

What became the most controversial aspect of this interpretation is the argument that common school reforms were imposed on an unwilling working class—an argument that posed an important challenge to traditional ways of viewing American schools. This interpretation suggests that the vast majority of people in the nineteenth century did not want the type of organization of schooling that became standard in the nineteenth and twentieth centuries. It is important to understand that this attitude did *not* reflect a general opposition among the populace to education and schooling but represented a rejection of common school reforms that sought to organize schools under central state control for the purposes of serving the social, political, and economic goals of government.

Katz's interpretation challenges not only Cubberley's benign view of the reformers but also interpretations that emphasize the importance of working-class support of the common school movement. Traditional labor history, beginning with the work of John R. Commons at the University of Wisconsin in 1918, stresses the key role of workingmen's parties in the late 1820s and 1830s in fighting for common school reforms. This interpretation places the American worker at the forefront of the battle for common schools. Of particular importance in this interpretation is the opposition of workers to the existence of charity schools, which they felt reinforced social-class distinctions. According to Commons's interpretation, members of the workingmen's parties supported the common school because it provided the children of the poor with equal educational opportunity by mixing the rich and poor. Equality of educational opportunity, it was believed, would provide the children of the poor and the working class with an equal opportunity to compete with the children of the more affluent classes.

Rush Welter emphasizes the role of workingmen's parties in *Popular Education and Democratic Thought in America* (1962), but his discussion minimizes their contribution to common school reform and stresses their contribution to later thinking about the democratic role of education. Welter, discussing the organized workingmen of the late 1820s and early 1830s, states, "Their numbers were few and their direct political influence was slight, but they first spelled out the educational perspective in which several generations of American democrats would see their society and their politics."[62]

A more complicated picture of common school reform emerges from Welter's interpretation of the workingmen's contribution to democratic educational theory: Although the workingmen's parties accepted the common school ideal of eliminating social-class distinctions and providing equality of opportunity, they also supported public schooling as a means of providing the working class with knowledge to protect itself against the interests and power of the privileged in society. This concept of political education in the common school, according to Welter, was different from the concept of education as a means of maintaining order in a free society. On the contrary, the workingmen's parties saw political education as a means of arming the working class against the authority and power of the upper class. In Welter's words, "In their [workingmen's] eyes political knowledge was useful, not because it supported the exercise of governmental authority, but because it provided an intellectual resource against authority."[63]

The importance of Welter's interpretation is his emphasis on the workingmen's support of school reform and his argument that the workingmen supported the common school for different reasons than did other members of society. Within the framework, the common school did not arise from a consensus of values about what the common school should accomplish but was a result of different social groups' each hoping that the common school would fulfill particular educational goals.

Although recognizing the role of the workingmen's parties in the struggle for public education, historians continue to emphasize the role of common schools in protecting the interests of certain groups in society. The scope of this interpretation was broadened in 1983 with the publication of Carl Kaestle's *Pillars of the Republic*. Kaestle argues that the common school movement was primarily designed to protect the ideology of an American Protestant culture. Most of the common school reformers, he states, were native-born Anglo-American Protestants, and their public philosophy "called for government action to provide schooling that would be more common, more equal, more dedicated to public policy, and therefore more effective in creating cultural and political values centering on Protestantism, republicanism, and capitalism."[64]

Kaestle identifies ten major propositions as constituting the American Protestant culture the common school was designed to protect. These ten propositions can be divided into four groups. The first group includes the belief in the fragility of the republican form of government, the importance of developing individual character to achieve social morality, and the role of personal effort in defining merit. This group of beliefs can be traced back to the early proponents of republican education, who believed that order could be maintained in a free republican society only through the education of responsible citizens. Kaestle argues that by the 1830s a certain confidence had developed that the experiment in republican government would survive, but there was still concern that action had to be taken to ensure its survival. In the common school movement, stress was placed on protecting the fragility of the republican form of government by providing a political education that taught a common set of political beliefs, emphasized the exercise of intelligence, and promoted a respect for laws. Or, as Kaestle states, the implication of native Protestant ideology was that "schooling should stress unity, obedience, restraint, self-sacrifice, and the careful exercise of intelligence."[65]

Also, as was discussed in Chapter 3, the belief that social morality was achieved through improving the quality of individual morality was a central theme of the charity school movement. As part of Protestant ideology and the common school movement, Kaestle argues, it resulted in a belief that a good moral education would produce a moral society. In addition, this aspect of Protestant ideology stressed that poverty could be eliminated if the children of the poor were taught that they could advance in society through their own individual effort.

The second group of factors in Kaestle's discussion is the role of women in society and the importance of the family and social environment in building character. According to Kaestle, Protestant ideology defined three central roles for women in middle-class families: to provide a sanctuary for the hardworking husband, to manage the household intelligently, and to nurture children. Of crucial importance was the role of women in child rearing, because this role involved education for the political and moral well-being of the nation. The arguments given for the importance of this social role for women provided a justification for recruiting women as teachers in common schools—an important aspect of common school reforms—because of their supposed skills in nurturing and developing morality. Another important factor, which will be discussed in more detail in Chapter 5, is the fact that women were cheaper to employ as teachers than men were.

As I noted in Chapter 3, during this period emphasis was also placed on the importance of the environment and family on the development of individual character. This was an important theme in faculty psychology and in the establishment of charity schools and houses of refuge. The stress on the importance of the family structure reinforced the importance of the domestic role of women.

In the third group of themes characterizing Protestant ideology, Kaestle includes a belief in the virtue of property and the availability of economic opportunity in the United States. Both Protestant ideology and the common school ideology contain the belief, according to Kaestle, that "property was to be respected because it taught virtue. Everyone should be taught to desire property and to respect property."[66] Related to this belief was a vision of America as the land of economic opportunity: The availability of property and education would make it possible for all people to achieve economic success.

The last group of themes Kaestle identifies includes a belief in the superiority of American Protestant culture, in the manifest destiny of American society, and in the necessity of unifying America's population. In the context of these beliefs, American Protestants believed that their religious values were the core of the American experiment with republicanism. As noted in Chapter 3, educational writers after the Revolutionary War, such as Noah Webster, equated Protestant-Christian values with republican values. Kaestle argues that this same theme appears in the Protestant ideology associated with the common school movement. Kaestle also argues that the belief in the superiority of Protestantism combined with a belief in America's unique destiny to "suggest to Americans that their nation was destined to reach the peak of human civilization."[67] The assumption of the superiority of Protestantism logically led to the belief that all people should be united by being educated into a Protestant culture.

These different interpretations highlight the complex factors involved in the common school movement. No single interpretation provides an adequate explanation. Rather, the common school appears to have been a result of a complicated set of often conflicting social and economic factors that included a humanitarian impulse to create the good society, a desire of the working class to enhance its political and economic position in society, a desire of manufacturers to have a disciplined and well-trained work force, a desire of the upper classes to protect their economic and social privileges, and a desire to maintain an American Protestant culture.

CONCLUSION

The common school movement provided the basic ideology and structure of the modern American school system. No single set of reasons or social forces brought it into existence. Rather, it was a product of a combination of political, economic, and social concerns that existed in the early part of the nineteenth century.

Politically, the success of the common school movement represents the victory of one political philosophy over another. Most individuals who supported and worked for a common school system believed that government should play an active role in ensuring the success of the economic and social system and that this was best achieved by centralizing and standardizing governmental processes. Many who opposed the development of the common school system believed that the government that governed best governed least, that the success of the economic and social system depended on the absence of government intervention, and that the free actions of the marketplace guaranteed the most equitable distribution of economic benefits. They opposed the centralizing tendencies of government and hoped to maximize popular control of the political process by maintaining local control.

In the 1830s these differences in political philosophy separated the Whigs from the Democrats: Most Whigs favored the centralization of control over education and the intervention of government, while most Democrats resisted the expansion of government power and fought to retain democratic localism. The tension and struggle between these two different political philosophies have continued into the twentieth century under different political labels and represent one of the major areas of disagreement in American political thought. By the middle of the twentieth century, conflict over this issue was expressed as a concern with centralization of educational control at the federal level—the Democratic party supported this trend because of the promise it held for a more just and equitable school system, whereas the Republican party resisted continued federal intervention and argued for local control and the benefits of the free marketplace. Throughout the history of the modern American school, differences in political pholosophies have had a major impact on the development and organization of education.

Culturally, the common school movement attempted to ensure that one set of cultural values remained dominant, as large groups of immigrants with differing religious and cultural values entered American life. During the early period of common school reforms, this primarily meant protecting a Protestant ideology against an influx of Irish Catholics. In the latter part of the nineteenth and early part of the twentieth centuries, Americanization programs for immigrants in the public schools served the same function.

The protection of a particular set of cultural and religious values was made possible by the way in which control of the school system was organized. The growth of centralized and bureaucratic control, as opposed to democratic localism, ensured that the dominant values of the school system would be Protestant and middle class. Beginning in the nineteenth century and continuing into the twentieth, the shifting patterns of control usually reflected the desire of one or more groups in society to ensure that the schools served particular political, social, and economic interests.

The development of the common school also reflected changing economic conditons. The early growth of industrialism placed a premium on education as preparation for work. From the standpoint of employers, common schooling could serve the useful function of socializing and training workers for the factory. From the workers' perspective, as reflected in the workingmen's parties, common schooling was a means of ensuring that employers did not maintain a monopoly over knowledge. Knowledge was power in the evolving modern industrial setting, and workers did not want to be kept from that source of power.

Also, the promise of Aemrican life was improved economic opportunity for all people. In fact, one could argue that the concept of equality of economic opportunity is a theme that has united all American people. For the worker, equality of economic opportunity was a means of improving one's personal economic condition. For the school reformer, such as Horace Mann, equality of econonmic opportunity was a means of reducing friction among social classes. For the employer, equality of economic opportunity was a means of ensuring a supply of the best possible workers by creating competition among workers in the labor market. For most members of society, the common school became the hope for providing and maintaining a society based on equality of economic opportunity.

Most social groups believed that the common school was the best means of controlling crime, social unrest, and political disruptions. In the early nineteenth century, workingmen, Protestants, Catholics, reformers, urban dwellers, and others shared a belief that the school was the key to social control and social stability. This belief became a standard fixture in the rhetoric surrounding the American school in the nineteenth and twentieth centuries.

In summary, by the middle of the nineteenth century most of the major themes of the modern American school had emerged. Persistent political divisions over schooling would occur, and dissent would continue in certain areas. Also, hope would continue that common schooling would bring forth the good society by improving economic conditions, providing equality of opportunity, eliminating crime, and maintaining political and social order.

NOTES

1. Sally Wertheim, "Educational Periodicals: Propaganda Sheets for the Ohio Common Schools" (Ph.D. dissertation, Case Western Reserve University, 1970), p. 1.
2. Lawrence Cremin, *The American Common School: An Historic Conception* (New York: Teachers College Press, 1951), p. 49.
3. Mary Peabody Mann, ed., *Life of Horace Mann* (Washington, D.C.: National Education Association, 1907), p. 13; Horace Mann's edited letters and journal are reprinted in this book.
4. Ibid., p. 14.
5. Ibid., pp. 49–50.
6. Ibid., p. 71.
7. Ibid., pp. 71–72.
8. Ibid., pp. 72–73.
9. Ibid., pp. 74–75.
10. Ibid., pp. 80–81.
11. Ibid., p. 83.
12. Edited copies of Horace Mann's reports can be found in Lawerence Cremin, ed., *The Republic and the School: Horace Mann on the Education of Free Men* (New York: Teachers College Press, 1957), p. 98.
13. Ibid., p. 100; italics in original.
14. Ibid., p. 106.
15. Ibid.
16. Ibid., pp. 94–97.
17. Ibid., p. 97.
18. Ibid., p. 93.
19. Ibid., p. 86.
20. Ibid., p. 87.
21. Ibid.
22. Quoted in William Russell, "Education and the Working Class: The Expansion of Public Education during the Transition to Capitalism" (Ph.D. dissertation, University of Cincinnati, 1981), pp. 274–275.
23. Quoted in ibid., pp. 276–277.
24. Ibid., p. 291.
25. Quoted in ibid., p. 294; italics in original.
26. Quoted in ibid., p. 295.
27. Quoted in ibid., p. 300.
28. Rush Welter, *Popular Education and Democratic Thought in America* (New York: Columbia University Press, 1962), pp. 51–52.

29. Herbert Ershkowitz and William G. Shade, "Consensus or Conflict? Political Behavior in the State Legislatures during the Jacksonian Era" in Edward Pessen, ed., *The Many-Faceted Jacksonian Era: New Interpretations* (Westport, Conn.: Greenwood Press, 1977), pp. 212–231.

30. Quoted in Lee Benson, *The Concept of Jacksonian Democracy: New York as a Test Case* (New York: Atheneum, 1966), p. 107.

31. Ibid.

32. Daniel Walker Howe, *The Political Culture of the American Whigs* (Chicago: University of Chicago Press, 1979), p. 29.

33. Ibid., pp. 29–30.

34. Ibid., p. 33.

35. Major L. Wilson, "What Whigs and Jacksonian Democrats Meant by Freedom" in Pessen, *Jacksonian Era*, pp. 192–212; Howe, *Political Culture*, pp. 23–43.

36. Howe, *Political Culture*, pp. 34–35.

37. Carl F. Kaestle and Maris Vinovskis, *Education and Social Change in Nineteenth-Century Massachusetts* (New York: Cambridge University Press, 1980).

38. Quoted in ibid., p. 215.

39. Ibid., p. 230.

40. Quoted in Vincent Lannie, *Public Money and Parochial Education: Bishop Hughes, Governor Seward, and the New York School Controversy* (Cleveland: Press of Case Western Reserve University, 1968), p. 16.

41. Ibid., p. 21.

42. Quoted in ibid., p. 24.

43. "To the Honorable the Board of Aldermen of the City of New York" in Neil McCluskey, ed., *Catholic Education in America: A Documentary History* (New York: Teachers College Press, 1964), pp. 70–71.

44. Ibid., p. 71.

45. Ibid., p. 72.

46. Ibid., p. 73.

47. Ibid., p. 76.

48. Quoted in Lannie, *Public Money*, pp. 85–87.

49. Carl F. Kaestle, *Pillars of the Republic: Common Schools and American Society, 1780–1860* (New York: Hill and Wang, 1983), pp. 167–172.

50. "First Plenary Council (1852)" in McCluskey, *Catholic Education in America*, pp. 78–81.

51. "Second Plenary Council (1866)" in McCluskey, *Catholic Education in America*, pp. 82–85.

52. "Third Plenary Council (1884)" in McCluskey, *Catholic Education in America*, pp. 86–92.

53. Ibid., p. 94.

54. Ellwood Cubberley, *Public Education in the United States: A Study and Interpretation of American Educational History* (Boston: Houghton Mifflin, 1934), pp. 164–165.

55. Ibid., pp. 165–166.
56. Ibid., p. 166.
57. Merle Curti, *The Social Ideas of American Educators* (Paterson, N.J.: Pageant Books, 1959), p. 138.
58. Michael B. Katz, *The Irony of Early School Reform* (Cambridge, Mass.: Harvard University Press, 1968).
59. Katz, *Irony*, p. 1.
60. Ibid., p. 2.
61. Ibid., p. 218.
62. Welter, *Popular Education*, p. 45.
63. Ibid., p. 48.
64. Kaestle, *Pillars of the Republic*, p. 103.
65. Ibid., p. 81.
66. Ibid., p. 90.
67. Ibid., p. 94.

Organizing the American School: The Nineteenth-Century Schoolmarm

The organization of the common school system focused on the development of elementary schools. It is important to understand that common school reform was primarily organizational and did not necessarily result in the expansion of educational opportunities. According to the statistical work reported by Carl Kaestle and Maris Vinovskis in *Education and Social Change in Nineteenth-Century Massachusetts*, the percentage of people under twenty years of age attending school in Massachusetts declined between 1840 and 1880. In addition, the amount of money spent per $1,000 of state valuation increased only slightly during this period. On the other hand, the average child in the same period increasingly received more days of instruction, and the length of the average school year in Massachusetts increased from 150 days in 1840 to 192 in 1880. Kaestle and Vinovskis examine the earlier work of economic historian Albert Fishlow and find that one of the primary effects of the common school reform was a shift of student population from private to public schools. Therefore, the primary result of common school reform in the middle of the nineteenth century was not the education of increasing percentages of children, but the creation of new forms of school organization.[1]

The real heroines of the common school movement were the schoolmarms. Actualization of the common school dream required three important steps that involved a complex relationship among a number of factors: the struggle of women for education and careers; the development of concepts of republican motherhood and of women as symbols of charity; the inclusion of sex-role differences in the organization of education; and the economic exploitation of women. The first, and probably most important, step was to create a stable, inexpensive teaching force that would uphold in the classroom the moral ideals of the common school movement. The creation of this teaching force began with the pioneering efforts of women educators, which resulted in the establishment of the first teacher training institutions. Common school reformers aided these efforts because they believed women would provide the schools with a stable, inexpensive, and moral teaching force.

Second, common school reformers believed that standardization of the organization of education was required to ensure that the schools taught a common moral and political philosophy. Of great importance was the function of supervision of instruction. In rural areas, the county superintendent became a major figure, riding from schoolhouse to schoolhouse checking on the quality of instruction and the adherence of teachers to a standard curriculum. In urban areas, city superintendents began to take over the functions of school committees in the supervision and evaluation of teachers and students. As larger schools replaced the one-room schoolhouse, two roles—principal teacher and assistant teacher—began to appear; the teaching functions of the principal teacher were slowly replaced with administrative duties. The emerging hierarchical system of supervision and administrative control made possible a uniform system of education.

An important factor in creating this hierarchical system was the subservient status of women. Hierarchical organization required a division of duties and subordination to authority. The emerging pattern in nineteenth-century education, which reflected more general social patterns, was for men to manage and women to teach. What was considered the natural subordination of women to men provided a social basis for creating a hierarchical educational system in which role expectations were the same as those in more general social situations. Thus, the function of women in the common school system was to be moral, nurturing, and loving teachers, guided and managed by men holding positions of authority as superintendents and principals.

The creation of a uniform common school system also required standardization of curriculum and instruction. Again, like the other organizational changes, this process was in only embryonic form in the decades before the Civil War. Of primary importance was the development of the graded school and graded textbook series. In addition, an early science of education developed around new methods of instruction. Also of major importance during these early years were Pestalozzian methods of instruction, which originated in Europe and upheld the ideal of woman as mother and teacher. Johann Pestalozzi's methods provided further justification for the subordinate role of women in teaching. In the most popular texts used during the development period of the common school, the McGuffey *Readers*, females are depicted as models of charity. The concept of charity justified the economic inequalities that were increasing with the expansion of industrialism. Combined with the other organizational changes, Pestalozzian techniques and McGuffey's *Readers* added the final touches to the portrait of the nineteenth-century schoolmarm as the inexpensive, moral, nurturing, stable, kind, charitable, and subordinate backbone of the common school system.

THE AMERICAN TEACHER

Early attempts to develop a professional teaching corps for the common schools involved a complex relationship among the struggle by women for education and careers, popular concepts of the role of women in the new republic, and the desire of common school reformers for a stable and moral teaching force. In addition, women were welcomed into the ranks of teaching by local school boards because they could be hired at lower wages than men. As a result, by the end of the Civil War women dominated the ranks of teaching and teacher education centered on the education of women.

Traditional histories of education identify the Reverend Samuel Hall's private school, established in 1823 in Concord, Vermont, as the first teacher training institution. However, a good argument can be made that the first teacher training institution in the United States was the Troy Female Seminary, officially opened by Emma Willard in 1821 but with earlier beginnings in 1814. Willard opened the seminary for the specific purpose of educating women for responsible motherhood and teaching. Her thoughts on the education of women can be traced to the American Revolution, when new ideas about the public role of women opened the door to new educational opportunities. These ideas provided women with the necessary leverage for increasing both their level of formal education and their opportunities as teachers and also provided later common school reformers with a justification for the increased utilization of women as teachers.

One effect of the American Revolution was to link the domestic responsibilities of women with broader public purposes. During colonial times, little consideration was given to the relationship between the domestic role of women and their role in the public sphere. Personal salvation and service to other members of the family were the major purposes of education for women during this period. As Mary Norton states in *Liberty's Daughters: The Revolutionary Experience of American Women, 1750–1800*,

> Prior to the Revolution, when the private realm of the household was seen as having little connection with the public world of politics and economics, women's secular role was viewed solely in its domestic setting. . . . [N]o one, male or female, wrote or thought about the possibility that women might affect the wider secular society through their individual or collective behavior.[2]

During and immediately after the Revolution, male and female writers began to link the domestic role of women with the development of republican citizens. Women, as mothers, were seen as having the responsibility for shaping the character of their sons as future republicans. This perception of the role of mothers logically led to the conclusion that women needed to be educated to assume the role of republican motherhood. In Norton's words:

> And so citizens of the republic set out to discover and define woman's public role. They found it not in the notion that women should directly participate in politics. . . . Rather, they located woman's public role in her domestic responsibilities, in her obligation to create a supportive home life for her husband, and particularly in her duty to raise republican sons who would love their country and preserve its virtuous character.[3]

The acceptance of the concept of republican motherhood allowed greater educational opportunities for women. Prior to the Revolution, the education of women was limited to reading and writing and, for some young girls, education at "adventure schools," which taught music, dancing, drawing, needlework, and handicrafts. After the Revolution, some academies began to open their doors to women, and schools began to be established for the specific purpose of educating young girls. These new educational opportunities for women included academic instruction in subjects such as geography, history, philosophy, and astronomy, which in the past had been taught only to boys. In addition, charity schools for girls were started during this period, and urban school systems—for instance, Boston's—began admitting girls.

One of the results of the expanding educational opportunities for women was that charity schools began to seek female graduates as teachers. This was different from colonial times, when women without any particular qualifications operated dame schools. After the Revolution, school authorities began to recruit young female academy graduates. In turn, educated women began to realize that teaching offered career possibilities. "Teaching," Norton argues, "was the first profession opened to women on a regular basis, and as such it attracted, albeit for only a few years of their lives, a large number of intellectually aware young women, many of them products of the republican academies."[4]

It was against this background that Emma Willard opened the Troy Female Seminary. In an address to the New York legislature in 1819, she declared the hopes of republican motherhood: "Who knows how great and good a race of men may yet arise from the forming hands of mothers, enlightened by the bounty of that beloved country,—to defend her liberties, to plan her future improvements and to raise her to unparalleled glory?"[5] In all her public statements, she supported the existence of a patriarchal family. She argued that women needed to be educated to be teachers both because of a shortage of male schoolmasters and in order to function as responsible mothers.

According to Anne Scott, as an encouragement for women to be self-supporting and educated, Willard provided "'instruction on credit' for any woman who would agree to become a teacher, the debt to be repaid from her later earnings." To facilitate this process, Willard maintained a teacher placement agency, which had difficulty meeting the demand for teachers. In Scott's words, "Someone commented that Emma Willard's signature on a letter of recommendation was the first form of teacher certification in this country."[6]

The curriculum at the Troy Female Seminary included a full range of academic subjects from Latin to geography. Furthermore, like other teacher educators in the early nineteenth century, Willard believed that development of character was the first aim of education and placed a great deal of emphasis on that and on moral virtues. As discussed later in this section, in the development of teacher institutes in the late 1830s, both she and Henry Barnard placed the same strong emphasis on education of character.

As Paul Mattingly demonstrates in *The Classless Profession: American Schoolmen in the Nineteenth Century*, the overriding concern of those interested in the reform of teaching in the 1830s and 1840s was the development of moral character.[7] As women began to be educated in larger numbers, school-men began to seek them out as teachers because of their belief in the inherent moral character of females. The teacher was to be a paragon of moral virtue whose influence would be felt and imitated by the students in the common school. If the schools were to reform and morally uplift society, it was reasoned, it was of fundamental importance that the teacher function as a model of morality. Consequently, along with education in the subject matter to be taught, a major goal of teacher training was to link methods of instruc-tion, classroom management, and the character of teachers to the develop-ment of students' moral character.

The emphasis on moral character had a lasting effect on the teaching profession. Through the nineteenth century and into the twentieth, teachers were expected to live exemplary lives, with their social activities constantly under public scrutiny. This is still true in some places. According to Willard Elsbree in *The American Teacher: Evolution of a Profession in a Democracy:* "The teacher's private life has always been open to public scrutiny like a goldfish in a glass bowl. Tradition has given teachers a place in society comparable to that accorded to ministers and the restrictions placed upon their conduct have been many and varied."[8] The control of the social life as teachers contributed to the low status of teaching as a profession.

The ideal characteristics of teachers for the common school are stated by Horace Mann in his *Fourth Annual Report* (1840) to the Massachusetts State Board of Education. First, he lists as a qualification for teaching a "perfect" knowledge of the subjects to be taught in the common schools. He complains that the major defect in existing schools' instruction is the teacher's lack of knowledge of the subject matter. The second qualification he lists is an aptitude for teaching, which he believed could be learned. He feared that inadequate or erroneous methods of teaching could destroy the moral charac-ter of students. As an example, he describes the custom in surveying in feudal Scotland of tying boys to landmarks and whipping them so they would retain a knowledge of the boundaries of the land and could be used as witnesses in any litigation. He states, "Though this might give them a vivid recollection of localities, yet it would hardly improve their ideas of justice. . . . But do not those, who have no aptness to teach, sometimes accomplish their objects by a kindred method?" A third essential qualification listed by Mann is the ability to manage and govern a schoolroom and to mold moral character. Mann believed that the primary source of moral instruction in the classroom was the moral character of the teacher. He lists "Good Behavior" and "Mor-als" as the fourth and fifth characteristics of a good teacher. With regard to good behavior, he states: "If, then, the manners of the teacher are to be imitated by his pupils—if he is the glass, at which they 'do dress themselves,' how strong is the necessity, that he should understand those nameless and innumerable practices, in regard to deportment, dress, conversation, and all personal habits, that constitute the difference between a gentleman and a clown."

Mann goes on to argue that one could accept eccentricities in a friend, "but it become quite a different thing, when the oddity, or eccentricity, is to be a pattern or model, from which fifty or a hundred children are to form their manners." In other words, a major requirement of a schoolteacher was to conform to accepted social customs.[9]

Under "Morals," Mann emphasizes the importance of having teachers "of pure tastes, of good manners, [and] of exemplary morals." He gave the responsibility for assuring the morality of teachers to local school committees or school boards. He writes that "the school committee are sentinels stationed at the door of every schoolhouse in the State, to see that no teacher ever crosses its threshold, who is not clothed, from the crown of his head to the sole of his foot, in garments of virtue."[10]

It was the nineteenth-century schoolmarm who was to fulfill the requirements of high morality and social conformity demanded by common school reformers. The reason women were recruited into teaching was candidly stated by the Boston board in 1841. Its annual report notes that within the previous year the number of male teachers in the system had declined by 33 while the number of female teachers had increased by 103. The report gives three reasons for supporting this trend. The first is a belief that women are better teachers of young children because of their natural child-rearing talents: "They [women] are endowed by nature with stronger parental impulses, and this makes the society of children delightful, and turns duty into pleasure."

Second, the report argues that because female minds are less distracted by worldly forces and because women have no other possibilities of employment, they can more easily concentrate on teaching:

> As a class, they never look forward, as young men almost invariably do, to a period of legal emancipation from parental control, when they are to break away from the domestic circle and go abroad into the world, to build up a fortune for themselves; and hence, the sphere of hope and of effort is narrower, and the whole forces of the mind are more readily concentrated upon present duties.

As statistics show, a major concern of the times was that men remained in teaching for only a short period of time. Because this created a great deal of instability in the teaching force, it was hoped that the narrow range of opportunities for women would keep them in teaching and thus provide a stabilizing influence.

The third reason for favoring women, the report argues, is because "they are also of purer morals." The report goes on to argue: "In the most notorious vices of the age, profanity, intemperance, fraud, &c., there are twenty men to one woman . . . on this account, therefore, females are infinitely more fit than males to be guides and exemplars of young children."[11]

The concern of educational leaders with creating a moral and nurturing teaching force complemented the notion of republican motherhood. The conjunction of these ideas provided justification for the increased use of women as teachers, while the social and economic conditions of teaching convinced school leaders of the wisdom of the idea. The compatibility of republican motherhood with the needs of common school systems received explicit attention in a famous report on education distributed in the United States in the late 1830s and the 1840s.

The author of that report was Calvin Stowe, a founder of the Western Literary Institute, one of the earliest associations for professional teachers in the United States. Stowe's wife, Harriet Beecher Stowe, the author of *Uncle Tom's Cabin*, provided a model of woman that extended her concerns beyond the domestic family into the arena of political and social issues. In his own public statements Calvin Stowe placed sharp limits on the proper role of women in the public sphere.

In 1836 Calvin Stowe departed for Europe to purchase books for the Lane Theological Seminary in Cincinnati, Ohio. Before he left, the state legislature passed a resolution requesting him to report on European systems of education. On his return in 1837, he presented his statement, "Report on Elementary Public Instruction in Europe," to the governor and state legislature. One important aspect of the report, discussed in more detail in the next section of this chapter, is his discussion of Pestalozzian educational methods as practiced in Prussia. The report received a great deal of attention and was widely circulated in the United States. The Ohio legislature printed 10,000 copies and distributed them to every school district in the state. Copies were also reprinted and distributed by the governments of Massachusetts, Michigan, North Carolina, Pennsylvania, and Virginia.

In the concluding section of his report, Stowe addresses the problem of recruiting and training teachers. First, he argues that, given the economic conditions in the United States, there is little hope of finding enough male teachers for all the schools. Therefore, the education of young children must be placed into the hands of women. Then, in one sentence, he ties together several strands of the arguments supporting women as teachers: "There is not the same variety of tempting employment for females as for men, they can be supported cheaper, and the Creator has given them peculiar qualifications for the education of the young."[12]

Stowe continues by alluding to the more advanced place of women in American society than in Europe and links this condition to American women's greater involvement in the public arena: "There is no country in the world where woman holds so high a rank, or exerts so great an influence, as here; wherefore, her responsibilities are the greater, and she is under obligations to render herself the more actively useful." He makes clear to his readers that although he supports a greater role for women in society, he believes that role should be limited. In reference to women of the period who were seeking political equality with men, he states,

> I think our fair countrywomen, notwithstanding the exhortations of Harriet Martineau, Fanny Wright, and some other ladies and gentlemen, will never seek distinction in our public assemblies for public discussion, or in our halls of legislation; but in their appropriate work of educating the young, of forming the opening mind to all that is good and great, the more they distinguish themselves the better.[13]

Stowe's statement illustrates how the emphasis on the domestic role of women could be used to severely limit the role of women in the public sphere.

A major reason for employing women was the lack of stability in the male teaching force. In the early nineteenth century, the typical pattern was for young men to enter teaching for a few years before continuing on to some other career. Consequently, the teaching force was young and inexperienced and had a high turnover rate, which made selection of teachers and control of their moral character difficult. Although the number of women teachers did increase (and by the end of the Civil War they dominated the ranks of teaching because the men had been called to military action), their teaching careers tended to be as short as those of men. In part, this was caused by continued low salaries.

Before the Civil War, the increase in the number of women in teaching varied from state to state, with females becoming a majority in the teaching force in some states. For example, in Connecticut 56 percent of the total teaching force was female by 1846, and the percentage increased to 71 in 1857. In 1862 the state superintendent in New Jersey reported that in 1852 there had been twice as many male teachers as female, but within ten years female teachers had come to outnumber male teachers. In Vermont 70 percent of the teaching force was female by 1850, and in Pennsylvania the proportion of female teachers increased from 28 percent in 1834 to 36 percent in 1856. The dramatic effect of the Civil War was felt in states such as Indiana, where the percentage of male teachers dropped from 80 percent in 1859 to 58 percent in 1864, and Ohio, where the number of male teachers declined from 52 percent in 1862 to 41 percent in 1864. New York reported a loss of 1,119 male teachers between 1862 and 1863, and in 1862 Iowa reported that the number of female teachers had exceeded the number of male teachers for the first time.[14]

The teaching force remained unstable despite the increased number of women in it because many women taught for only a few years before being married. This is seen in the ages of female teachers. Kaestle reports that in 1860 in southeastern Michigan, 77 percent of female teachers were between seventeen and twenty four years of age, and in Dane County, Wisconsin, 27 percent of female teachers were under 18.[15] Still, the caricature of the late-nineteenth-century teacher is the prudish, pedantic, spinster schoolmarm.

Statistics gathered by Elsbree indicate a continued problem for school leaders in the youth and inexperience of the teaching force: "The average age of teachers in Maine in 1866 was twenty-one and three quarters years; in Pennsylvania it was under twenty-four in 1856. In this latter state, of 7428 teachers in thirty-eight counties, 2328 or nearly one third of the total were under twenty-one years of age." In many cases, teachers remained in teaching only one year. It was reported that in Connecticut in 1858, two-thirds of the teachers were new to the system. New York reported in 1853 that of 20,000 teachers in the state, one-third would leave their positions and be replaced with new teachers. The *Pennsylvania School Report* for 1856 tabulated the amount of experience of teachers in thirty-four counties and found the following range of experience:

Those who have taught less than one year	1,793
Those who have taught between 1 and 3 years	2,035
Those who have taught between 3 and 6 years	1,058
Those who have taught over 6 years	1,124
Total	6,010[16]

Although the increased number of female teachers did not seem to fulfill the common school reformers' hopes of creating an experienced, stable teaching force, there was ample evidence that female teachers made education less expensive. In fact, from a look at the differences in salaries between male and female teachers in the nineteenth century, one could argue that the primary reason for the acceptance of women into the ranks of teaching was that they were inexpensive to employ. Table 1 in *The American Teacher*, originally compiled in 1920 by Warren Burgess, indicates not only the differences between the salaries of men and women but also the differences between the salaries of rural and urban teachers. The figures give some indication of the economic position of teachers during this period. In his compilation, Burgess estimated that the weekly wage of a common laborer was $4.86 in 1841 and $7.98 in 1864, while artisans earned an average of $8.28 in 1841 and $12.66 in 1864. This means that male urban teachers earned more during this period than either common laborers or artisans. On the other hand, urban and rural female teachers and rural male teachers earned less than common laborers.

Burgess's statistics were supported by a survey conducted by Horace Mann for the *Common School Journal* in 1843, in which Mann claims to have ascertained the wages of "journeymen, shoemakers, carpenters, blacksmiths, painters, carriage-makers, wheelwrights, harness-makers, cabinet and pianoforte makers and some others." He reports that all these occupations paid more than teaching and that the salaries of some were from 50 to 100 percent higher than the average salary of teachers.[17]

In addition to indicating why school boards increasingly hired female teachers, Burgess's figures provide some explanation for the high turnover in teaching. Compared with laborers and artisans, it would appear that perhaps only urban male schoolteachers earned enough to support a family and that both urban and rural female teachers earned barely a subsistence wage. For women, marriage would most certainly have been an attractive economic alternative to the income earned as a teacher, and for male rural teachers, other occupations certainly would have appeared to be economically more attractive.

The problem of stability in the rural teaching force was compounded by the practice of supplementing salaries with the custom of "boarding 'round." Before the Civil War, it was the practice in most rural areas for teachers to spend a week or more in the home of each child attending their schools. This meant that rural teachers had to pack their belongings and move frequently during the school year. Students' families provided food and housing as part of their contribution to the teacher's salary. In 1862 Vermont reported that 68 percent of its teachers boarded around, and in 1846 Connecticut reported that 84 percent of its teachers engaged in this practice.[18]

The practice of boarding around was not conducive to maintaining a stable teaching force. It is hard to imagine that many people would want to spend their lives moving from house to house. Also, this practice certainly was more suited to the young and inexperienced than to the older person.

In addition to the utilization of women in teaching, common school reformers hoped to improve teaching through the establishment of teacher institutes and normal schools, both of which introduced the novel idea that methods of instruction could be taught and learned. In a broader sense, this marked the beginning of the study of pedagogy and the investigation of various methods of instruction. Also, normal schools opened a new arena for the education of women. Female students dominated the classes in normal schools, and in turn normal schools contributed to the increase in the number of female teachers.

Before the Civil War, the most important type of teacher training organization was the teacher institute. The idea of teacher institutes was developed by Emma Willard and Henry Barnard in Connecticut in 1839. This uniquely American experiment in teacher education spread rapidly throughout the country. The typical teacher institute met once or twice a year for two to four weeks. At first, teachers paid the cost of the institute, but later, private citizens and the government covered the expenses. The primary objective of the institutes was to provide a brief course in the theory and practice of teaching.

As Paul Mattingly argues, the institutes were conducted very much like religious revivals. Concepts of methods of instruction were vague, and the greatest emphasis was placed on elevating the moral character of the teachers. Of course, the stress on moral character was in keeping with the general tone of common school reform. Mattingly states, "For this generation of professional educators this institution [the teacher institute] made explicit, more than any other educational agency, how determined schoolmen were to equate professionalization with 'awakening' of moral character rather than with the training in communicable skills and the standard techniques of teaching."[19]

Mattingly underlines a distinctive feature of the concern with development of moral character. Those involved with teacher training were interested in producing not moral crusaders who would engage in open public conflict over moral and social issues but teachers who would limit their moral campaigns to shaping student character. In other words, teacher education did not encourage or train teachers to confront directly the products of "weak moral character," such as corrupt political structures, economic injustice, or actual criminal activities.

This approach to the education of teachers safely removed discussions of moral character from the political arena. Like the education of common school students, the stress in teacher education was on motives, not consequences. As Mattingly states, "Out of a political necessity to avoid controversial issues in the act of instruction, schoolmen developed their own rituals of moral inquiry and proper maneuvers. The moral sphere dealt primarily with motives which were treated both as aspirations and as embryonic consequences."[20] The result was a passive quality to the moral training of teachers and students, as opposed to a preparation for them to take active public positions on moral issues. What was important to common school reformers was ensuring that training for both teachers and students would stifle all desire to do anything morally incorrect.

This approach to the training of moral character was in keeping with general social attitudes about women. The majority of students at teacher training institutions in the nineteenth century were women. It would not have been in keeping with the temper of the times if these institutions had trained women to become public crusaders, because active political and social endeavors were not considered a proper part of the social role of women in the nineteenth century. As stated earlier, the proper role for women was to connect with the public sphere by nurturing moral character in the family and the school. Thus, both in the common school and in teacher training institutions, there was little discussion of the major social, economic, and political problems confronting society. Discussion was limited to individual motives and desires.

Ironically, although the nineteenth-century schoolmarm was given responsibility for the morality of society, she was limited in political and social activities. This limitation had consequences for the development of both the profession of teaching and the concept of citizenship in the schools. A passive type of morality, not socially active moral behavior, was expected of teachers. They were expected to prevent social problems but not to engage actively in solving existing problems. Students were also included in this concept of passive citizenship. They were to learn not to break the law, but they were not taught how to deal actively with injustice.

The result was that teachers in the nineteenth century were expected to live exemplary moral lives and avoid active participation in political, social, and economic issues. These expectations would change (as discussed in Chapter 11) when female teachers organized to improve the economic rewards of their profession. By the middle part of the twentieth century, their union activity had resulted in active teacher participation in political and social campaigns.

Although teacher institutes were the primary means of teacher education before the Civil War, by the end of the nineteenth century formally organized teacher training institutions became more important. The establishment of Emma Willard's Troy Female Seminary, with its emphasis on academic education and the education of moral character, was quickly followed in the 1820s and 1830s by other experiments in teacher education institutions. The most important of these experiments was the first state normal school, opened in

Lexington, Massachusetts, in July 1839. Soon after, normal schools were established at Barre, Massachusetts, in September of the same year, and at Bridgewater, Massachusetts, the following year.

Normal schools were supposedly modeled on Prussian institutions, but the term *normal* was of French derivation. The early normal schools prepared teachers to teach in what would later be considered the elementary school grades. The ordinary practice was for normal school students, who were mostly female, to graduate from elementary or common schools and directly enter normal schools. As the pattern developed in the nineteenth century and clearer distinctions were made between elementary and secondary education, important differences emerged in teacher education for the two levels. Teachers in secondary institutions, high schools, and academies tended to be graduates of colleges and universities, whereas elementary school teachers tended to be graduates of normal schools. These differences contributed to the justification for paying secondary school teachers more than elementary school teachers. This difference in salaries has continued into the twentieth century.

The low salaries of normal school graduates as compared with those of secondary school teachers also reflected the primarily female composition of normal schools. In 1856 the four normal schools in Massachusetts reported a student population of 332, 290 of whom were girls. Between 1862 and 1886 the Oswego State Normal and Training School in New York had 1,245 female graduates and 128 male graduates.[21] The same enrollment pattern existed at the Bridgewater Normal School in Massachusetts, from which, between 1854 and 1904, 2,075 females graduated, compared with 546 males.[22]

Although normal schools became a major source of female education in the nineteenth century, they provided a very abbreviated form of education. After graduation from elementary schools but before being sent back to elementary schools as teachers, normal school students received a one- or two-year course that included a review of material that had been learned and was to be taught in the elementary school grades and instruction in classroom management and methods of teaching. Overriding this formal curriculum was the concern with moral character. As Mattingly states, "In a sense, the nineteenth-century normal school always determined as its first priority the creation of a common, moral purpose out of the diverse needs and interests of school teachers."[23] In considering the development of the normal school, it is important to remember that a majority of teachers in the nineteenth century were not graduates of normal schools. In some places, even in 1900 and even in reform-minded Massachusetts, only a bare majority of teachers had attended normal schools.

These early attempts to create a professional corps of teachers in the United States linked the educational concerns of common school reformers with the desires of women for further education and for careers. Women, as republican mothers and vessels of virtue, were considered the ideal teachers for a system of schooling that emphasized moral development. However, the second-class citizenship of women and the low salaries in teaching contributed to the generally low status of teaching as a profession in the nineteenth and early twentieth centuries. Indeed, even the earliest professional teacher training, with its limited preparation for elementary school instruction, its mainly female student population, and its emphasis on moral exhortation, further contributed to the low-status professional image of teaching.

THE MATERNAL MODEL OF INSTRUCTION

Given the attitudes about morality and women in the early and middle nineteenth century, it is not surprising that the first widespread theory of instruction was based on the concepts of maternal love and the cultivation of the moral faculty. Like the belief in the importance of the role of republican motherhood, the educational theories of Johann Pestalozzi gave to the mother and the household the main responsibility for the salvation of society. Pestalozzi's concept of maternal instruction in the home became his model for instruction in the school.

Any discussion of educational ideas must give recognition to the difference between theory and practice. Usually there is a time lag between the development of a theory and its impact on practice. For instance, Barbara Finkelstein, in her study of elementary school classrooms in the nineteenth century, found that the majority of teachers had students recite, work at their desks, or listen to verbal instruction by the teacher: "North and south, east and west, in rural schools as well as urban schools, teachers assigned lessons, asked questions and created standards of achievement designed to compel students to assimilate knowledge and practice in a particular fashion." Finkelstein argues that teachers during this period were of two major types: the "intellectual overseer," who stressed memorization and punished failures in assignments, and the "drillmaster," who had the students repeat material in unison.[24]

Many common school reformers hoped that those types of classroom practices would be replaced by what they considered the more humane educational methods of Pestalozzi. The major impact of Pestalozzian theory was its emphasis on relating instruction in the early years to objects in the real world, on learning by doing, and on the importance of activity, as opposed to sitting at a desk. By the end of the nineteenth century, these Pestalozzian practices had become an important part of progressive instructional theory, and by the twentieth century they were an important part of elementary classroom practice.

A maternal and moral model of instruction complemented the goals of common school reformers and the growing role of women in education. In addition, one of the major intellectual revolutions that accompanied the development of teacher training was the idea that people could be taught how to teach. This meant that the process of teaching was open to study and inquiry and that methods of instruction could be developed and imparted to future teachers. Joseph Lancaster and his monitorial system (see Chapter 3) provided the first systematic method of classroom management; Johann Pestalozzi popularized the first systematic method of instruction.

The development of a system of instruction involved the formulation of theories of learning or, to state it another way, an attempt to match the laws of the mind to the process of learning. Most early attempts in the United States to teach methods of instruction disregarded theories of the mind and systematized only traditional instructional techniques. For instance, in a letter to Henry Barnard in 1841, Cyrus Peirce, the head of the first normal school, in Lexington, Massachusetts, describes the method of instruction he imparted to future teachers as involving four different methods of recitation: "I have four different methods of recitation. 1st, by question and answer; 2d, by conversation; 3d, by calling on one, two, three more or less, to give an analysis of the whole subject contained in the lesson; and 4th, by requiring written analyses."[25] Peirce considered these methods to be "the best way of teaching the same things effectually to others." This explication of the methods of instruction incorporated traditional school recitations.

In contrast, by 1861, when the Oswego State Normal and Training School was established in Oswego, New York, Pestalozzian ideas were considered the basis for relating the development and functioning of the mind to learning in the classroom. In fact, the Oswego State Normal and Training School launched the Oswego movement, which helped to spread Pestalozzian concepts throughout the United States.

Johann Pestalozzi (1746–1827) was born in Zurich, Switzerland, and in 1781, after dabbling in journalism and education, he wrote his classic, popular description of domestic education, *Leonard and Gertrude*. His ideas on education quickly spread throughout the Western world. Many American visitors to Prussia in the early nineteenth century were impressed by the use of Pestalozzian methods in the schools. The English Home and Colonial Institution, organized in 1836, became a forum for the dissemination of Pestalozzian ideas in England, the United States, and Canada. This organization had developed from the work of Charles Mayo, who, beginning in 1818, adapted Pestalozzian ideas to English infant schools.

Pestalozzi's theories of maternal education paralleled in time and content the development of concepts of republican motherhood in the United States. *Leonard and Gertrude* is the story of the moral and social reform that occurs as a result of the extension of maternal influence and education from the home to the public sphere. The story is set in the small village of Bonnal. The main characters are Leonard, an alcoholic husband, and Gertrude, a brave and pious wife. It is a tale of moral struggle between the forces of evil and idleness and the forces of maternal love and nurturing. The opening lines of the tale describe the social conditions that could be remedied if education were based on maternal values. The reader is told that "his [Leonard's] trade would have enabled him to support his family of a wife and seven children, if he could have resisted the temptation to frequent the tavern, where there were always idle loafers to entice him in, and induce the good-natured, easygoing man to squander his earnings in drink and gambling."[26]

The struggle by women to redeem their men from the pitfalls of demon rum and gambling became a classic tale by the end of the nineteenth century. In Pestalozzi's story, Leonard and the village are redeemed because domestic relationships are maintained by Gertrude's becoming a public model. To symbolize the connection between the domestic role of women and the public sphere, Pestalozzi has three male leaders of the village visit Gertrude's home and study her system of household management. Their analysis of Gertrude's actions provides the basis for the development of a pedagogical theory.

In the story, the visit by the three village leaders occurs just as the family is completing breakfast. After the children wash the dishes, they immediately engage in a variety of tasks, including spinning and gardening. What is most impressive for the visitors is Gertrude's ability to integrate instruction into the activities of the household. A trademark of the Pestalozzian method is the use of common objects in instruction and the development of the child's powers of observation, as opposed to abstract teaching that has little connection to the realities of life. For instance, *The New England Primer* (see Chapter 2) taught numbers without any reference to real objects, whereas Gertrude gives instruction in arithmetic by having her children count the number of steps from one end of the room to the other, and two of the rows of five panes each, in one of the windows, gave her an opportunity to unfold the decimal relations of numbers. She also made them count their threads while spining, as well as the number of turns on the reel when they wound the yarn into skeins.[27]

Shortly after departing from Gertrude's home, one of the visitors dashes back and proclaims that he will be the schoolmaster of Bonnal. The next day, after returning to observe Gertrude's family further, the village leaders ask Gertrude to help the newly self-appointed schoolmaster. "Then they explained to her that they regarded the proper education of the youthful population as the only means of elevating the condition of the corrupt village; and full of emotion, Gertrude promised them she would do anything in her power to forward the good cause."[28]

Pestalozzi later declared that "maternal love is the first agent in education."[29] In *How Gertrude Teaches Her Children*, written between 1799 and 1804 while Pestalozzi was a schoolmaster, he draws a direct connection between maternal love and individual moral development. He argues that people must love and trust other people before they are able to love and trust God and that the germ of love and trust is developed in the mother's nurturing of the child. The mother's lack of response to the irregular desires of the infant teaches the first lessons in obedience; in addition, the infant learns to be grateful for the mother's actions. The combination of trust, gratitude, love, and obedience forms the early beginnings of a conscience.

According to Pestalozzi, the development of conscience and moral feelings that is learned from interaction with the mother depends on the art of instruction. He argues that society does not provide the child with moral instruction, because such instruction is a distortion of nature. It is the responsibility of the teacher to arrange the world encountered by the child so that the early beginnings of moral ideas will be developed.

Like all aspects of Pestalozzian instruction, the development of morality depends on the education of the senses: "The first instruction of the child should never be the business of the head or of reason; it should always be the business of the senses, or the heart, of the mother." What he declares as the second law of instruction is to move slowly from the exercise of the senses to the exercise of reason. In accord with the general attitudes of the time, he associates the senses, or heart, with women and reason with men. "It is for a long time the business of the heart," Pestalozzi states with regard to instruction, "before it is the business of the reason. It is for a long time the business of the woman before it begins to be the business of the man."[30]

Pestalozzi always declared that he was trying to psychologize the education of humanity, by which he meant adapting methods of instruction to human development and the laws of the mind. He was greatly influenced by Jean-Jacques Rousseau's *Emile* (see Chapter 2), in which the inability of children to reason until the age of adolescence is stressed. Before that time, Rousseau argues, the child should not be given verbal instruction but should learn from experience and nature. Pestalozzi emphasizes that the young child should receive no verbal instruction and that learning should be a result of experience. In addition, he accentuates the importance of educating the senses. From the education of the senses, one is to move to an understanding of ideas and eventually to a knowledge of God and morality.

The concentration on the education of the senses, the use of objects in instruction, and the replacement of corporal discipline with control through love revolutionized methods of instruction. Certainly a major contrast exists between the type of instruction of young children provided by the recitation of *The New England Primer* and Pestalozzi's statement that the best general methods of instruction "are speech, the arts of drawing, writing, reckoning and measuring."[31]

Americans returning from visits to Europe in the early nineteenth century helped to acquaint fellow Americans with Pestalozzian methods of instruction. One of the earliest visitors was John Griscom, who was active in social and educational reform in New York. His visit to Europe in 1818 included tours of hospitals, schools, prisons, and charitable institutions. *A Year in Europe*, the story of his trip, includes glowing reports of Lancasterian schools in England and Pestalozzian schools in Prussia. After the publication of this book, Griscom became actively involved in social and educational reform by serving, among other positions, as chairman of the committee that established the New York House of Refuge and as a leader in the establishment of a monitorial high school in New York in 1825.

On his trip, Griscom visited Pestalozzi at the educational institution he had established at Yverdun in 1805. Griscom was warmly greeted by Pestalozzi and was given a tour of the school, which at that time had ninety boys from a variety of European countries. In the classroom visited by Griscom, the teacher did not use books but relied solely on the use of objects. Griscom claimed that the constant interaction between students and the instructor made it too difficult to write a detailed account of the type of instruction provided in the classroom. His more general description states:

> We saw the exercises of arithmetic, writing, drawing, mathematics, lessons in music. . . . To teach a school, in the way practiced here, without book, almost entirely by verbal instructions, is extremely laborious. The teacher must be constantly with the child, always talking, questioning, explaining, and repeating. The pupils, however, by this process, are brought into very close intimacy with the instructor.[32]

In general, Griscom was most impressed by the moral aspects of the Pestalozzian methods: "But the greatest recommendation of the Pestalozzian . . . plan of education, is the moral charm which is diffused throughout all its operations."[33] He felt that children educated under this method would become more moral and intelligent members of society.

Many Americans learned about Pestalozzian methods of instruction while visiting schools in Prussia, where Pestalozzi became very popular in the nineteenth century. Another visitor was Calvin Stowe, whose widely circulated "Report on Elementary Public Instruction in Europe" is discussed in the previous section. Stowe included in his report a description of a classroom in a Berlin school using Pestalozzian methods. Like Griscom, Stowe was struck by the amount of verbal exchange between the teacher and the students. The use of objects for instruction and the education of the senses are very evident in Stowe's description:

> He [the teacher] first directs their [students'] attention to the different objects in the school-room, their position, form, color, size, materials of which they are made of, &c., and requires precise and accurate descriptions. He then requires them to notice the various objects that meet their eye on the way to their respective homes; and a description of these objects and the circumstances under which they saw them, will form the subject of the next morning's lesson. Then the house in which they live; the shop in which their father works; the garden in which they walk, &c., will be the subject of the successive lessons; and in this way for six months or a year, the children are taught to study things, to use their own power of observation, and speak with readiness and accuracy, before books are put into their hands at all.[34]

After giving a detailed description of the structure of Prussian schools, Stowe strongly recommends the system as moral and practical. He argues that it educates all faculties of the mind and demonstrates to the student the practical value of knowledge. In addition, he claims it elevates the moral condition of all children.

The model of mother as teacher has a profound impact on textbooks, classroom equipment, and methods of teaching. Just as Gertrude used the objects of her household for purposes of instruction, by the late nineteenth century textbooks and teachers began to use real objects to illustrate lessons. For example, map work became important in the study of history and geography, the counting of objects became a method of learning arithmetic, and the study of nature became a source of scientific understanding for young children. In *How Teachers Taught: Constancy and Change in American Classrooms, 1890–1980,* Larry Cuban includes a set of three photographs depicting elementary school classrooms in Washington, D.C., in 1900. In two of the photographs, students are shown working alone at individual desks. In the third, students are gathered around a table at the head of the classroom examining, with the teacher, models of parts of the body. On the blackboard is a drawing of the heart, and leaning against the wall is a full-sized drawing of the human body with its inner parts illustrated. Although a direct connection cannot be made between the work of Pestalozzi and the student activity depicted in this classroom, Pestalozzi's work and the spread of his ideas must be given some credit for the illustrations, objects, and teaching activities shown in that photograph.[35]

THE EVOLUTION OF THE BUREAUCRATIC MODEL

David Tyack states in *The One Best System: A History of American Urban Education* that as the organization of American schools developed, "the employment of women appears to correlate highly with the pace of bureaucratization."[36] This correlation can be explained by the relationship between the values inherent in bureaucratic organizations and the attributes ascribed by nineteenth-century society to males and females.

By the late nineteenth century, the following elements made up the bureaucratic organization of the typical school system:

1. A hierarchy with a superintendent at the top and orders flowing from the top to the bottom of the organization
2. Clearly defined differences in roles of superintendent, principals, assistant principals, and teachers
3. Graded schools in which students progressively moved from one grade to another
4. A graded course of study for the entire school system to assure uniformity in teaching in all grades in the system
5. An emphasis on rational planning, order, regularity, and punctuality

Tyack cites a number of other causes for the adoption of a bureaucratic organization. He argues that "the pressure of numbers was a main reason for the bureaucratization that gradually replaced the older decentralized village pattern of schooling."[37] According to Tyack, this pressure forced school leaders to seek some method of achieving system and efficiency in school systems that had grown up haphazardly. In addition, many nineteenth-century school leaders believed that bureaucratic organization taught students values necessary for functioning in an industrial society. Tyack quotes a statement made in 1871 by William T. Harris, a superintendent of schools and U.S. commissioner of education: "The first requisite of the school is *Order:* each pupil must be taught first and foremost to conform his behavior to a general standard." Harris claimed that modern industrial society required "conformity to the time of the train, to the starting of work in the manufactory," and therefore "the pupil must have his lessons ready at the appointed time, must rise at the tap of the bell, move to the line, return; in short, go through all the evolutions with equal precision."[38]

In more general terms, it appears natural that school people would turn to bureaucratic organization as a model for the most advanced system of school organization. In the minds of nineteenth-century educators, it also seemed logical to socialize a student for the type of organization that was developing in business and industry. For instance, one of the major requirements of the developing industrial organization was regularity of attendance by the work force. The factory system as it was developing could not operate unless every worker was assigned a specific task, had his or her tasks coordinated, and was on the job at a specific time.

Just as regular attendance and punctuality became important for factories, these behaviors were considered important by school people for the management of educational systems and as values to be taught to schoolchildren in preparing them to function in society. Nothing more clearly demonstrates this relationship between the requirements of organization and the desire to teach organizational values than the mania that developed among nineteenth-century educators over student attendance and punctuality. Because of the need for organization and the desire to teach industrial values, tardiness to class became a major student offense.

Although the motivation of protecting middle-class values and status, the increasing size of school systems, and the desire to teach bureaucratic values are all important explanations for the adoption by schools of a bureaucratic model, the increased feminization of the teaching force is what made it possible to link social roles outside the school with roles within the educational bureaucracy.

The feminization of teaching and the development of bureaucratic organization involved two interrelated nineteenth-century social beliefs. First, it was widely believed that women were naturally subordinate to men. Thus it was natural, as bureaucratic school systems evolved, that men managed and women taught. Second, a theme that ran through Pestalozzian methods of instruction and the arguments for having women instruct young children was the attribution of rational activity to males and emotional activity to females— men were responsible for the head, women for the heart.

The importance of the subordination of women to men in the evolution of bureaucratic school systems is demonstrated by the history of the graded school. One of the major organizational changes in the schools in the nine-

teenth century, considered important for introducing efficiency and uniformity of instruction, was the separation of students into separate classrooms
by age. Before this development, students had been taught in ungraded
classrooms in which teachers were responsible for simultaneously teaching a
variety of subjects to students at different levels of knowledge. For example,
Ellwood Cubberley includes in *Public Education in the United States* a sketch of a
Providence, Rhode Island, grammar school in 1840, where each floor seated
228 students in a single room and was conducted as a single school.[39] A
master teacher and assistant teachers combined their efforts to teach the
entire group within this large, ungraded classroom. In 1823, Boston schools
were being built with rooms that seated 300 pupils, on the premise that three
large groups would be taught by one master teacher and two assistant
teachers. And, of course, monitorial schools (see Chapter 4) were conducted
in large, ungraded groups.

The major inspiration for the creation of graded schools came from
accounts of visitors to Prussia of school organization in that country. After
visiting Prussia in 1843, Horace Mann wrote in his *Seventh Annual Report* that
"the first element of superiority in a Prussian school, and one whose influence extends throughout the whole subsequent course of instruction, consists
in the proper classification of the scholars." Mann went on to describe how
schoolhouses were constructed so that each group of students, divided by age
and attainment, could be housed in a single classroom. The ungraded large
classroom, Mann argues, created the difficulty for the teacher of trying to
teach a variety of subjects at one time. On the other hand, he says,

> All these difficulties are at once avoided by a suitable classification, by such a
> classification as enables the teacher to address his instructions at the same
> time to all children who are before him, and to accompany them to the
> playground at recess or intermission without leaving any behind who might
> be disposed to take advantage of his absence.[40]

When the first school based on the Prussian method of classification was
built in the United States, it incorporated not only graded classrooms but also
what Tyack refers to as the "pedagogical harem" of a male principal and
female teachers. The establishment of the first graded school, the Quincy
School, is credited to John Philbrick, who became its first principal. Philbrick
had worked hard to convince the Boston School Board of the wisdom of
applying Horace Mann's ideas on pupil classification.

When the Quincy School was opened in 1848, its radical design attracted
national attention. Rather than the usual school construction of the period—
large rooms accommodating hundreds of students—the Quincy School contained a greater number of schoolrooms, each of which could hold fifty-six
students. What was considered its greatest improvement was the provision of
a separate room for each teacher and a desk for each student. The Boston
School Committee adopted specific requirements that each classroom be
twenty-eight square feet. By 1855 the committee had every building in the city
divided into small classrooms. By 1866 the Quincy plan became a model for

school construction in San Francisco, New Orleans, Cincinnati, New Haven, and Louisville. The Quincy plan tended to be more popular in urban areas, while many rural areas retained one-room schoolhouses. In 1920 there were still 200,000 one-room schoolhouses.[41]

Philbrick's description of the relationship between the staffing of the school and the unique design of the building indicates how perceived differences in sex roles fit the new concept of school organization. After stating that all scholars in a single classroom would attend to the same lesson, Philbrick specifies the following type of arrangement among staff members: "Let the Principal or Superintendent have the general supervision and control of the whole, and let him have one male assistant or sub-principal, and ten female assistants, one for each room."[42]

The very architecture of the Quincy School established the sex-role and authority differences in the new system of graded schools. The Quincy School had four floors; the first three contained classrooms and the top floor was a large assembly hall. More important, with regard to symbols of authority, a separate office for the principal was included in the design. According to Ellwood Cubberley, in the twentieth century the design for the Quincy School became the standard for urban elementary schools throughout the country.[43]

The adoption of this plan for elementary school organization based on the classification of students and the self-contained classroom is inextricably linked with the system of staffing that placed the male principal in charge of "pedagogical harem." This pattern of administrative control within the school had been evolving in the early nineteenth century as schools became larger. Originally, a teacher would be designated as head teacher and given the responsibility of observing assistant teachers and reporting directly to the board of education. The head teacher was also referred to as the principal teacher. As the size of schools increased, the duties of the principal teacher became more administrative and less involved with direct classroom instruction. One important duty of the principal became the supervision of other teachers in the school. The Cincinnati school report for 1858 cited by Willard Elsbree illustrates the evolution of the position of principal: "The most efficient agency in the improvement of the schools has been the constant and active supervision of the Principals over the labors of their Assistants." The report notes that this was a recent phenomenon. "They [the principals] were, till within the last two years, only teachers of the highest classes of their respective schools." However, with the assignment of new responsibilities, changes had been made in room arrangements to reflect the new role of the principal. The Cincinnati report describes how "By a regulation of your Board . . . .the Principals . . . have some recitation rooms assigned to them, where they keep records, examine classes, and transact the general business of their schools."[44]

As this pattern of graded elementary schools spread into other American cities, the grade system became more clearly defined. Once the general category of elementary students was established, it was necessary to determine how many levels of classification should exist in a school. The average duration of common school education at the time the Quincy School was built was seven to nine years. A survey of forty-five cities conducted by the U.S. commissioner of education in 1870 indicated that by that time, the majority of elementary schools classified students into eight separate grades. The eight-year elementary school remained the standard until the junior high school was developed in the early twentieth century.[45]

The development of the eight-year elementary school and its accompanying "pedagogical harem" was part of the more general growth of hierarchical bureaucratic organization in education. As previously mentioned, these organizational developments reflected not only differences between sex roles, but also differences in characteristics attributed to each sex. Studies of organizational forms conducted in the latter part of the twentieth century show that a hierarchical bureaucracy embodies characteristics most often associated with males. Sociologist Rosabeth Kanter argues that this form of organization specifies that the ideal manager is one who is rational and objective. In the nineteenth and early twentieth centuries, these characteristics have most often been ascribed to males. Kanter states:

> This "masculine ethic" elevates the traits assumed to belong to men with educational advantages to necessities for effective organizations: a tough-minded approach to problems; analytical abilities to abstract and plan; a capacity to set aside personal, emotional considerations in the interests of task accomplishment; and a cognitive superiority in problem-solving and decision-making.[46]

In other words, organizational forms specify certain characteristics for leadership, and if these characteristics are associated by society with a particular gender, then sex bias is built into the organizational model. According to Kanter, it has been assumed in the nineteenth and twentieth centuries that women are governed by emotions and are prone to "petty" concerns with interpersonal relationships and responsibilities. In terms of the managerial requirements of a hierarchical bureaucracy, this means that women do not make good managers and that their role in this type of organization is to be supportive of male leaders.

The evolution of the graded elementary school supports Kanter's analysis. Women were considered to be more effective in the education of young children because of their emotional nature and nurturing qualities, characteristics not ascribed to men. Men, on the other hand, were not considered ideal for teaching young children because of their supposed lack of emotional qualities and their reliance on the use of reason. The graded school with a single male principal in power and subordinate female teachers in self-contained classrooms fit nicely into these social stereotypes. From the perspective of nineteenth-century society, the rational male should govern the school and provide limits and order to the emotional nature of the female schoolteacher.

Within the framework of Kanter's analysis, an important, but not the only, reason for the development of hierarchical bureaucracy in education is that it was compatible with the hiring of large numbers of female teachers to fill the lower ranks of the hierarchy. For instance, the role of school superintendent, an important element in the school bureaucracy as it developed in the nineteenth century, evolved with a clear understanding by most participants that the role would be filled by males who would control a primarily female work force. In *The One Best System,* Tyack quotes statements that illustrate the existence of this attitude. He cites an 1878 article in *Harper's* that states that "women teachers are often preferred by superintendents because they are more willing to comply with established regulations and less likely to ride headstrong hobbies" and a nineteenth-century superintendent of the Denver school system who claimed that when teachers have advice to give to their superiors, "it is to be given as the good daughter talks with the father."[47]

The development of the role of superintendent was important in the evolution of a hierarchical educational organization. The primary reason for creating the position was to have a person work full-time at supervising classroom instruction and assuring uniformity in the curriculum. As discussed in Chapter 5, an important common school reform was the creation of the office of state superintendent, whose purpose was to organize a uniform system of common schools. Direct classroom supervision evolved along with the positions of city and country superintendents. The creation of these local positions paralleled the establishment of the office of state superintendent. In addition, they were associated with the district system of organizing schools.

In the nineteenth century, the district system became the most widespread method of organizing state systems of education, but by the twentieth century, it became an obstacle to providing equal educational opportunity. The creation of the district system allowed wealthy school districts to exist side by side with poor school districts. Thus it was often difficult to accomplish the common school dream of mixing the rich and the poor in the same schoolhouse.

The idea of the school district originated with the Massachusetts Law of 1789, which affirmed the Old Deluder Satan Law of 1647 (see Chapter 2) and authorized towns to establish boundaries for school support and attendance; these would be called *districts*. Later laws, in 1800, 1817, and 1827, gave members of a school district the right to hold meetings, choose officers, collect school taxes, select schoolbooks, and hire teachers. The New England states of Maine, Vermont, New Hampshire, Rhode Island, and Connecticut instituted the district system early in the nineteenth century. The idea spread to New York in 1812 and westward to Ohio in 1821, Illinois in 1825, Tennessee in 1830, Indiana in 1833, Michigan in 1837, and Kentucky and Iowa in 1838.

Depending on the exact political organization of the state, the development of local supervision was associated with the development of the role of district or county superintendent. Willard Elsbree provides colorful examples of the work of these early superintendents. A Bucks County, Pennsylvania, school superintendent states in his report in 1856, "In one school, where I had drawn the map of Pennsylvania on the black board, the same diagram had remained for a year, the board never having been used in the interim." In another situation, the county superintendent describes how "not a scholar in the school could tell me in what country he lived, and when I held up Holbrook's five inch globe, the oceans on which were painted blue, and asked what it was, a large boy, at least seventeen years of age, replied, 'a bird's egg!'" The activities of the Bucks County superintendent reflect the primary duty of these early superintendents, which was to supervise instruction. For instance, the state superintendent of New York reported that "the schools of the state were visited during the year 1854 by the several town and city superintendents 22,082 times."[48]

The evolution of the office of city school superintendent paralleled the establishment of district and county offices. Buffalo, New York, was the first city to establish the position, in 1837, and was quickly followed by Louisville, St. Louis, Providence, Springfield, Cleveland, Rochester, and New Orleans. One of the major functions of the early city school superintendents was to write a uniform course of study for their school systems. This course of study naturally paralleled the establishment of graded schools. For instance, Tyack reports that William Wells, superintendent of the Chicago schools from 1856 to 1864, published *A Graded Course of Instruction with Instructions to Teachers* in 1862 based on his efforts to institute a citywide uniform system of instruction related to the classification of students by grade. Wells's graded course of study specified topics to be covered in each grade as well as appropriate methods of instruction. Tyack describes the contents of this course of study: "Children began with the alphabet at the age of five, learned to count to 100 and do simple addition in the next grade, and proceeded in the next years to learn about the mysteries of Roman numerals, the hanging gardens of Babylon, the Crusades, and the Trojan War." According to Tyack, Wells's course of study was adopted by many cities as an official curriculum.[49]

The graded school, the uniform course of study, the district system, and the positions of principal and of city, district, county, and state superintendent were all elements in the early development of a hierarchical, bureaucratic organization for the administration of American education. In the twentieth century the bureaucratic organization of the schools became more clearly defined as the professionalization of school administration developed. Many factors contributed to the development of this type of organization, including the real problems created by the increased size of schools and school districts, the common school ideal of a uniform curriculum for all children, the desire of the middle class and native groups to protect their values and power, and the need for socialization of students for an industrial workplace. The creation of a hierarchy was facilitated by the use of female teachers. In Lotus Coffman's 1911 study of teachers, he argues that the increasing number of women in the teaching force was

> due in part to the changed character of the management of the public schools, to the specialization of labor within the school, to the narrowing of the intellectual range or versatility required of teachers, and to the willingness of women to work for less than men. . . . [A]ll of the graded school positions have been preempted by women; men still survive in public school work as "managing" or executive officers.[50]

McGUFFEY'S *READERS* AND THE SPIRIT
OF CAPITALISM

The popularity and importance of William McGuffey's *Readers* in the latter half of the nineteenth century can be compared to the role of *The New England Primer* during colonial times and Noah Webster's *Spelling Book* in the first half of the nineteenth century. *The New England Primer* prepared readers for submission to the authority of the family, the Bible, and the government, and Webster's *Spelling Book* taught republican values designed to maintain order in a free society. McGuffey's *Readers* contain numerous moral lessons designed to teach appropriate behavior in a developing industrial society with increasing concentrations of wealth and expanding social divisions between the rich and the poor. Within this context, the readers provide an example of the actual meaning given to attempts to reduce social-class tensions by mixing the rich and the poor in the common school.

The growth in popularity of McGuffey's *Readers* paralleled the development of the common school. Ironically, even as the nineteenth-century schoolmarm took over the schoolroom, girls occupied little space in the new reading series. Females are seldom-discussed characters in these moral tales dealing with social behavior in a developing industrial society. If the McGuffey *Readers* were our sole source for understanding human conduct in the latter half of the nineteenth century, we would have the impression that the only role for women in the development of a capitalistic and industrial society was to serve as models of charity. The concept of charity is important because it justifies the concentration of wealth by making the rich the stewards of wealth for the poor. Even in their role as models of charity, however, girls were less frequently portrayed than boys were. As depicted in the moral tales in McGuffey's *Readers*, girls were almost invisible in the school relationships of developing capitalism.

The McGuffey *Readers* were written in the heart of what was considered the West in the 1830s. William Holmes McGuffey was born in 1800 near Washington, Pennsylvania, and was raised on a homestead in Trumbell County, Ohio. In 1825, after a period of education and teaching in the schools of the frontier, McGuffey accepted a teaching post at Miami University in Oxford, Ohio, near the booming city of Cincinnati. Through his work as an educator, McGuffey became an active member of the Western Literary Institute and College of Professional Teachers and a friend of Calvin and Harriet Beecher Stowe at the Lane Seminary in Cincinnati. As a result of his educational contacts in Cincinnati, the Cincinnati publishing firm of Truman and Smith asked McGuffey in 1834 or early 1835 to prepare a series of textbooks.

The McGuffey *Readers* were prepared specifically for use in the developing common school systems. The series, first published between 1836 and 1838, contains a primer, a speller, and four readers. A fifth reader was added in 1844. The series was revised between 1841 and 1849 and again in 1853, 1857, and 1879. The changes in 1857 and 1879 were primarily in gradation of material and in binding. Sales figures for the series are indicative of its use and popularity. Between 1836 and 1920, approximately 122 million copies were sold, with the strongest sales, as indicated by the following figures, occurring between 1870 and 1890.[51]

1836–1850	7,000,000
1850–1870	40,000,000
1870–1890	60,000,000
1890–1920	15,000,000

The content of the McGuffey *Readers* varies in length and difficulty, from short and simple stories in the first, second, and third readers to selected literary writings by a variety of authors in the fourth and fifth readers. Each story and poem in the less advanced readers is preceded by a spelling list and by definitions of words used in the selection and is followed by several related questions.

The goal of the stories in the McGuffey *Readers* is to teach reading and, like the general goal of the common school, to impart moral lessons. An analysis of the content of the stories in the 1843 edition of *McGuffey's Newly Revised Eclectic Second Reader* reveals the range of moral values, the importance given to certain moral themes, and the different expectations for boys and for girls in dealing with moral issues.[52]

McGuffey's Newly Revised Eclectic Second Reader contains 104 readings of one to three pages. Some of the readings are religious selections such as the Lord's Prayer, the Story of Joseph, and the Child's Prayer. There are also a number of historical sketches, poems, and tales about animals and birds. Some stories, like "Story of the Coat" and "Store of Buttons," are designed to convey information about objects. Of course, many of these writings about history, nature, and objects are designed to teach a particular moral lesson.

The largest group of writings in the second reader, about 35 percent of the 104 selections, deals directly with problems of moral character. Given the primacy of moral education in the common school movement, this emphasis is not surprising. Of these didactic stories, twenty-nine center on the character of boys and only eight on the character of girls.

There are several ways to explain the neglect of girls in these didactic tales. One could assume that it reflects the subordinate, secondary role of women in society. In other words, McGuffey's attitude toward females reflects the more general vision men had of women's place in society. Another explanation could be that the female character was considered to have few moral defects. This explanation is supported by one of the major reasons given for recruiting women into teaching, namely, the purity of their moral character. In fact, in the stories in the second reader, the range of moral problems for girls is very narrow as compared with that for boys. In two of the stories dealing with girls, "Mary and Her Father" and "The Little Letter Writer," the theme is learning and the value of education. In another story, "The Greedy Girl," the moral problem is gluttony, which is illustrated by a little girl who eats so much that she constantly gets sick. Untidiness is the central theme in "A Place for Every Thing," a story about a girl who constantly loses things and learns from another girl to put everything in its proper place.

One could conclude from these stories that in the nineteenth century the central problems in the character of girls were considered to be overeating, a lack of appreciation for learning, and untidiness. The other four stories dealing with girls do not present problems of character, but models of charity. In "The Kind Little Girl," the central female character shares with animals and hungry people; in "A Dialogue on Dress," a girl refuses new clothes so that she can save to buy clothes for the poor; in "The Two White Doves," a girl and boy give their doves to a sick child; and in "The Last Two Apples," a girl gives the last apples to her siblings. Thus, in half the stories dealing with female character, girls are presented as acting charitably in certain situations.

The theme of charity is also important in the stories dealing with boys. As was mentioned previously, this was an important theme in the developing social relationships of capitalism. The range of character problems exhibited by boys in the McGuffey *Readers* is much greater than that associated with girls. In the twenty-nine stories dealing with boys, the themes include relationship to nature, value of learning, gluttony, mercy, pranks, charity, industriousness, honesty, courage, envy, alcoholism, insolence, and thrift.

Interestingly, the most frequent theme in *McGuffey's Newly Revised Eclectic Second Reader*, one that appears in six of the stories, is a boy's relationship to nature. This probably reflects the importance of the expanding West and the role of nature in nineteenth-century life. In the second story of the reader (the first of which deals with the importance of reading), a boy is depicted reflecting on the loveliness of the sun and the goodness of God. In contrast to the boys who love nature are the boys in "The Bird Set Free," who rob birds' nests.

The second most frequent theme, which appears in five of the stories about male character, is charity, and the third most frequent theme is the value of education. To understand the importance of charity, consideration must be given to the general social and political messages in all the McGuffey *Readers*. This analysis is done by Richard Mosier in *Making the American Mind: Social and Moral Ideas in the McGuffey Readers*. As the title suggests, Mosier approaches his analysis from the perspective that the wide use of the McGuffey *Readers* had a profound impact on average Americans by shaping their attitudes toward political, social, and economic institutions.

In general, Mosier argues that the political messages found in the pages of the McGuffey *Readers* are conservative and express a distrust of popular participation in government. Within this conservative framework, the primary purpose of government is the protection of property. Mosier contends that most of the political ideas in the readers express the values of the Whig Party as opposed to the Democratic party of the early nineteenth century. This, of course, means that the books agree with the political values of the leadership of the common school movement.

The fear of spreading democracy, or suffrage, is expressed in the McGuffey *Readers'* support of the common school system. In Mosier's words, "The antidote for these new forms of demagoguery and radicalism [Jacksonian democracy] was religion and education, the fire engines of Church and State, to which conservatives turned in their darkest hours." He argues that the purpose of education, as reflected in the readers and in conservative political thought, was

> for education . . . [to] be linked particularly with a call to return to the stern moral code of the Puritan fathers . . . [when] the objects of education were considered largely in terms of religious and moral culture. . . . [T]he McGuffey readers voiced their fear for the corrupting influences of the new age that had come upon them, and hinted that in the metaphysical subtleties of the great New England theologians lay the appropriate foundations for state, school, church, and society.[53]

The treatment of economic issues in the McGuffey *Readers*, Mosier maintains, is premised on the Calvinistic concept that wealth is an outward sign of inner salvation. This economic argument allowed for an acceptance of a society that was experiencing increasing concentrations of wealth and an expanding social distance between the rich and the poor. Wealth was a sign of God's blessing, and poverty was a sign of God's disapproval. Within this economic argument, for the poor to gain wealth they had to be godly and industrious, and for the rich to continue receiving the blessings of God they had to use their wealth in a godly fashion.

Therefore, charity was a means for the rich to remain worthy of their wealth in the eyes of God and a justification for a concentration of wealth in their hands. Mosier states about the contents of the McGuffey *Readers*, "Those who are wealthy are reminded that they are so by the grace of God, and that this grace and concession implies a responsibility toward the poor. . . . Many are the lessons that praise the charitable activities of the merchant, and many are those that show the kindness of the rich to the poor."[54] This conceptual framework gave the wealthy a stewardship over the riches of the earth and the destiny of the poor.

Within the context of this gospel of wealth, the poor were placed in a paradoxical situation. On the one hand, the existence of the poor was considered inevitable and, therefore, an acceptable part of the social order. On the other hand, some argued that poverty existed because the poor did not have the virtues of the rich and that the poor could escape poverty by being industrious, thrifty, and moral. As Mosier summarizes the dominant attitude in the McGuffey *Readers*: "It was argued that the poor would always be with us, that the best for them was charity and benevolence, but that no one need be poor. There are, argued the apostles of acquisition, numerous avenues to success that stand open for the sober, the frugal, the thrifty, and the energetic."[55]

The best examples of this gospel of wealth are two successive stories in the 1843 edition of *McGuffey's Newly Revised Eclectic Second Reader*, having the descriptive titles "The Rich Boy" and "The Poor Boy." The reader is informed in the first story that the rich boy knows "that God gives a great deal of money to some persons, in order that they may assist those who are poor." In keeping with the idea that the rich are elected by God, the rich boy is portrayed as being humble, kind to servants, and "careful not to make a noise in the house, or break anything, or put it out of its place, or tear his clothes."

The reader is also told that this model of virtue "likes to go with his parents to visit poor people, in their cottages, and gives them all the money he can spare. He often says: 'If I were a man, and had plenty of money, I think no person who lived near me should be very poor.'" The story ends with the rich boy dreaming of how he would use his future wealth:

> I would build a great many pretty cottages for poor people to live in, and every cottage should have a garden and a field, in order that the people might have vegetables, and might keep a cow, and a pig, and some chickens; they should not pay me much rent. I would give clothes to the boys and girls who had not money to buy clothes with, and they should all learn to read and write, and be very good.[56]

Certainly, a child reading "The Rich Boy" would easily conclude that God is just and that the rich boy deserves to inherit his parents' wealth.

In a similar fashion, the reader of "The Poor Boy" might conclude that poverty is good because of its effects on moral character. The poor boy is portrayed as industrious, helpful, moral, and eager to learn. The story opens, "The good boy whose parents are poor, rises early in the morning; and all day long, does as much as he can, to help his father and mother." It goes on to explain that the poor boy studies hard so that when he grows up, he can read the Bible and find gainful employment.

The story makes a clear distinction between the poor boy who is good and poor boys who are bad. In the story, the poor boy hurries home from his lessons to help his parents. On the way, the reader is told, "he often sees naughty boys in the streets, who fight, and steal, and do many bad things; and he hears them swear, and call names, and tell lies; but he does not like to be with them, for fear they should make him as bad as they are; and lest any body who sees him with them, should think that he too is naughty." Unlike the rich boy wanting to help the poor, he dreams of earning his own living. The poor boy likes his food of bread and bacon and does not envy the rich little boys and girls "riding on pretty horses, or in coaches." At the end of the story, the poor boy states his acceptance of his social position: "I have often been told, and I have read, that it is God who makes some poor, and others rich;—that the rich have many troubles which we know nothing of; and that the poor, if they are but good, may be very happy: indeed, I think that when I am good, nobody can be happier than I am."[57]

In summary, the two stories provide a justification for economic inequality and a rationale for accepting one's position in life. After reading the stories, poor boys might have been pleased to learn that they could be happy if they were good and that they were free of the burdens and responsibilities of the wealthy. Rich boys might have been pleased to learn that their good fortune was a blessing from God that required them only to adopt paternalistic attitudes toward the poor.

The economic arguments embodied in the McGuffey *Readers* provide another means of understanding the goals of the common school. One of the basic reasons given for the establishment of a common school system, as I discussed in Chapter 3, was that it would reduce antagonisms between the rich and the poor. In addition, consciousness of one's particular social class was to be changed into a consciousness of belonging to the more general social class of humanity.

Because McGuffey's *Readers* were written for the common schools and were among the most popular texts during the time the common school system was growing, it can be assumed that they offer an important perspective on how the reduction of tension between the rich and the poor would take place. In other words, the readers provided part of the real content of the more general educational rhetoric. From this perspective, one might conclude that the common school was supposed to solve the problem of social-class tension by educating children to accept their positions in society and the existing economic arrangements. The poor were educated to accept the existence of the rich—to learn that the rich would take care of them and that they were free of the responsibilities that accompanied wealth. Indeed, the poor were taught that their happiness depended on behaving in a manner that would not antagonize the wealthy. For their own good and, obviously, for the good of the wealthy, the poor were taught to be free of envy, thrifty, industrious, and moral.

From the standpoint of the rich, social-class tensions would be reduced by learning humility and charity toward the poor. They were not to disdain the poor, but were to learn to love them. Therefore, educating the rich in the common school was meant to reduce social-class antagonisms in two ways: first, by disarming the rich of negative feelings about the poor, and second, by teaching the rich to perform acts of charity as a means of disarming the poor of hostility.

The McGuffey *Readers'* concerns with mortality and with developing virtuous character made them an ideal companion for the growth of the common school and the industrial society. In the readers, the concept of republican motherhood is enlarged to include behaviors considered important in a society of increasing economic and social tensions. In the early nineteenth century, men and women considered the traits of motherhood to be ideal as methods for educating good republicans.

In the latter half of the century, it was easy to extend the nurturing qualities of motherhood to include acts of charity. Furthermore, charity, as discussed earlier, was an essential concept for justifying inequalities in the distribution of wealth. Therefore, females, particularly women teachers, became symbols of the virtues needed to maintain order in a republican society and of the kindness and acts of charity required to maintain order in a capitalistic society.

CONCLUSION

The organization of the common school in the middle of the nineteenth century established certain patterns of development that would begin to change and take on new direction by the late nineteenth and early twentieth centuries, when women began to rebel against their subservient status in the educational hierarchy and to seek a greater voice in educational policy through unionization and participation in the administration of the schools. These changes occurred as schools modeled themselves on industry and became more bureaucratic.

The schools developed an expanded economic role in the increasingly urban and industrial society of the late nineteenth century, and as this happened, the high school joined the elementary school as an institution at which attendance was considered essential for all people. Pedagogy—the science of education—changed during this period to meet the needs of the corporate model of the school and the new economic role of schooling. But even with all these changes, the schoolmarm remained the backbone of the educational system. As models of republican motherhood and sisters of charity, they continued to toil in the factories of education.

NOTES

1. Carl F. Kaestle and Maris Vinovskis, *Education and Social Change in Nineteenth-Century Massachusetts* (New York: Cambridge University Press, 1980), pp. 9–46.
2. Mary Beth Norton, *Liberty's Daughters: The Revolutionary Experience of American Women, 1750–1800* (Boston: Little, Brown, 1980) p. 297.
3. Ibid., pp. 297–298.
4. Ibid., p. 293.
5. Quoted in Anne Firor Scott, "The Ever Widening Circle: The Diffusion of Feminist Values from the Troy Female Seminary, 1822–1872," *History of Education Quarterly*, Vol. 19, No. 1 (Spring 1979), p. 7.
6. Ibid., p. 8.
7. Paul H. Mattingly, *The Classless Profession: American Schoolmen in the Nineteenth Century* (New York: New York University Press, 1975).
8. Willard Elsbree, *The American Teacher: Evolution of a Profession in a Democracy* (New York: American Book Compoany, 1939), p. 296.
9. Horace Mann, "Fourth Annual Report (1840)" in Lawrence Cremin, ed., *The Republic and the School: Horace Mann on the Education of Free Men* (New York: Teachers College Press, 1957), p. 47.
10. Ibid., pp. 50–52.
11. Quoted in Elsbree, *American Teacher*, p. 201.
12. Calvin Stowe, "Report on Elementary Public Instruction in Europe" in Edgar Knight, ed., *Reports on European Education* (New York: McGraw-Hill, 1930), p. 311.
13. Ibid.
14. Elsbree, *American Teacher*, pp. 202–208.
15. Carl F. Kaestle, *Pillars of the Republic: Common Schools and American Society, 1780–1860* (New York: Hill and Wang, 1983), p. 126.
16. Elsbree, *American Teacher*, pp. 293–294.

17. Quoted in ibid., pp. 280–281.
18. Elsbree, *American Teacher*, p. 288.
19. Mattingly, *Classless Profession*, pp. 62–63.
20. Ibid., p. 57.
21. Ned Dearborn, *The Oswego Movement in American Education* (New York: Teachers College Press, 1925), p. 32.
22. Mattingly, *Classless Profession*, pp. 154–155.
23. Ibid., p. 135.
24. Quoted in Larry Cuban, *How Teachers Taught: Constancy and Change in American Classrooms, 1890–1980* (White Plains, N.Y.: Longman, 1984), p. 19.
25. "Cyrus Peirce to Henry Barnard" in Merle Borrowman, ed., *Teacher Education in America: A Documentary History* (New York: Teachers College Press, 1965), pp. 60–61.
26. Johann Pestalozzi, *Leonard and Gertrude*, trans. Eva Channing (Lexington, Mass.; Heath, 1901), p. 11.
27. Ibid., pp. 130–131.
28. Ibid., p. 135.
29. Johann Pestalozzi, "How a Child Is Led to God through Maternal Love" in J. A. Green, ed., *Pestalozzi's Educational Writings* (London: Edward Arnold, 1916), p. 266.
30. Johann Pestalozzi, *How Gertrude Teaches Her Children: An Attempt to Help Mothers to Teach Their Own Children and an Account of the Method*, trans. Lucy Holland and Francis Turner (Syracuse, N.Y.: Bardeen, 1898), p. 294.
31. Ibid., p. 317.
32. John Griscom, "A Year in Europe" in Knight, *Reports*, p. 60.
33. Ibid., p. 55.
34. Stowe, "Report on Elementary Public Instruction" in Knight, *Reports*, p. 277.
35. Cuban, *How Teachers Taught*, pp. 20–21.
36. David Tyack, *The One Best System: A History of American Urban Education* (Cambridge, Mass.: Harvard University Press, 1974), p. 61.
37. Ibid., pp. 38–39.
38. Quoted in ibid., p. 43.
39. Ellwood Cubberley, *Public Education in the United States: A Study and Interpretation of American Educational History* (Boston: Houghton Mifflin, 1934), p. 308.
40. Horace Mann, "Seventh Annual Report to the Masschusetts State Board of Education, 1843" in Ellwood Cubberley, ed., *Readings in Public Education in the United States: A Collection of Sources and Readings to Illustrate the History of Educational Practice and Progress in the United States* (Boston: Houghton Mifflin, 1934), pp. 287–288.
41. William Cutler, "Cathedral of Culture: The Schoolhouse in American Educational Thought and Practice since 1820," *History of Education Quarterly*, Vol. 29, No. 1 (Spring 1989), pp. 1–40.
42. Quoted in Tyack, *One Best System*, p. 45.

43. Cubberley, *Public Education,* p. 312.
44. Quoted in Elsbree, *American Teacher,* pp. 174–175.
45. Tyack, *One Best System,* p. 45; Cubberley, *Public Education,* pp. 306–315.
46. Rosabeth Kanter, "Women and the Structure of Organization: Exploration in Theory and Behavior" in Marcia Millman and Rosabeth Kanter, eds., *Another Voice* (Garden City, N.Y.: Doubleday Anchor, 1975), p. 43.
47. Quoted in Tyack, *One Best System,* p. 60.
48. Quoted in Elsbree, *American Teacher,* p. 49.
49. Tyack, *One Best System,* pp. 45–46.
50. Quoted in ibid., p. 61.
51. Richard Mosier, *Making the American Mind: Social and Moral Ideas in the McGuffey Readers* (New York: Russell & Russell, 1965), pp. 167–170; Harvey C. Minnich, *William Holmes McGuffey and His Readers* (New York: American Book Company, 1936), pp. 30–89.
52. William H. McGuffey, *McGuffey's Newly Revised Eclectic Second Reader* (Cincinnati: Winthrop B. Smith, 1843).
53. Mosier, *Making the American Mind,* p. 31.
54. Ibid., p. 161.
55. Ibid., p. 162.
56. McGuffey, *McGuffey's,* pp. 47–48.
57. Ibid., pp. 48–50.

Education as Deculturalization: Native Americans and Puerto Ricans

When the U.S. government conquered the Native American tribes and Puerto Rico, it instituted educational policies designed to strip these groups of their native cultures. Deculturalization is the educational process of eliminating cultures. In the case of Native Amerians and Puerto Ricans, the United States attempted deculturalization as part of a process of winning the loyalty of these conquered people to the U.S. government. As part of the deculturalization process, federal and state governments institute programs of Americanization designed to replace native cultures with the dominant white culture of the United States.

In engaging in the act of conquest and the process of deculturalization, the U.S. government reflected a belief held by many Americans in the superiority of the dominant white culture and political institutions of the United States. I would argue that most conquering nations justify their actions by claiming cultural and political superiority. In the case of the United States in the nineteenth century, feelings of superiority were embedded in beliefs about the "manifest destiny" of the nation.

Manifest destiny was a belief that ultimately the United States would expand its borders to the Pacific Ocean. Manifest destiny was justified by a belief in the superiority of U.S. culture, political institutions, and morality. Conquered Indian tribes were considered by whites to be culturally and morally inferior. Consequently, educational programs established by the federal government were designed to deculturalize the tribes and then "civilize" them. Deculturalization included attempts to destroy Native American cultures, languages, and religon. In the conquered lands of northern Mexico and Puerto Rico, similar educational policies of deculturalization were introduced

130

to eliminate the Hispanic traditions. Of particular importance was the attempt to substitute English for Spanish as the dominant language.

Also, federal leaders were concerned with winning the loyalty of these conquered people to the U.S. government. Consequently, deculturalization was accompanied by Amerianization programs. Conquered Indians and Puerto Ricans were exposed to educational programs that emphasized patriotism and loyalty to the U.S. government. As tribal governments fell, Indian schools raised the U.S. flag and forced students to pledge their loyalty to the conquering nation. The same pattern of Americanization occurred after the capture of Puerto Rico. Forced allegiance to the flag was accompanied by patriotic exercises and celebrations of U.S. national holidays and heroes.

In a broader framework, deculturalization and Americanization could be considered logical educational policies for any conquering nation. Any country interested in controlling another would want to gain the allegiance of the conquered peoples. Indeed, the conquerors would want the conquered to feel emotional ties to the conquerors' government and society. In addition, conquerors would want the conquered to emulate the conquerors' culture. With Native Americans and Puerto Ricans, federal and state officials attempted to gain emulation by using textbooks which reflected the dominant white culture of the United States and which contained no reference to Hispanic or Indian cultures. If conquered peoples could be forced to emulate the dominate culture of the United States, it was believed, they would rush to embrace their conquerors rather than resist subjugation.

I will examine the process of deculturalization and Americanization by tracing the history of Indian education in the United States from the early nineteenth century to the middle of the twentieth century. The educational history of Puerto Rico provides a good example of the methods and problems faced by a conquering nation as it tries to subjugate the local population. I will trace Puerto Rican educational history from the time of the U.S. conquest in 1898 to the gaining of commonwealth status in the 1950s. In Chapter 13, I will continue these stories as part of the unfolding of the great civil rights movement of the 1950s and 1960s.

NATIVE AMERICANS*

Motivated by a combination of altruism and greed for land, U.S. government officials in the nineteenth century engaged in two of the world's most massive educational campaigns to replace, within one generation, native languages and cultures with the English language and European culture. The first attempt at cultural change occurred in the 1830s with the removal of Native Americans fom the southeastern part of the United States to Indian Territory.

---

* I would like to thank the librarians and staff at the Huntington Free Library of the National Museum of the American Indian for their help in finding material on the education of Native Americans.

The second attempt occurred in the latter part of the nineteenth century, when Native American children were removed from their families and tribes and placed in nonreservation boarding schools.

These efforts at cultural change were part of several distinct phases in the federal government's educational policies for Native Americans that paralleled changes in land policies and demands by white settlers for the removal or extermination of Indians. In addition, government policies were influenced by shifting images of the Native American which ranged from "noble savage" to "depraved aborigine." On the other hand, Native Americans, as a conquered people, were forced to work out their ideas on education in the context of federal policies. For Native Americans, one of the central educational problems was the protection of their languages and culture.

In the first phase of educational policies, from the end of the Revolutionary War to the 1820s, the federal government purchased Indian lands and provided missionary schools to assimilate Indians to European culture. The second phase, from roughly the 1830s to the Civil War, involved the removal of Indians in the southeastern part of the country to Indian Territory west of the Mississippi. Essentially, the land removal policies of the 1830s move most Indians out of Tennessee, Georgia, Florida, Alabama, Mississippi, and Louisiana. During this phase, the federal government supported schools in Indian Territory (what is now Oklahoma) with the hope that Native Americans would be "civilized" in one generation. This approach to education and land issues broke down during the Indian Wars that followed the end of the nineteenth century. Federal policy during this period was designed to destroy native languages and customs and build allegiance to the U.S. government by removing children from their families at an early age and placing them in boarding schools where the use of native languages and customs was forbidden. In the third phase, during the 1920s and 1930s, federal leaders rejected the idea of destroying native languages and cultures and supported day schools, community schools, and restoration of native cultures. This phase ended in the 1940s and 1950s, when the federal government adopted termination policies designed to eliminate Indian tribes and integrate Native Americans into the dominant European culture. This phase ended in the 1960s and 1970s, as American Indians organized and demanded more control of the policies affecting their lives.

Native Americans' own educational policies were developed in the context of federal policies. During the first phase, between the American Revolution and the 1820s, several tribes, particularly the Cherokees and the Choctaws, developed their own school systems with funding from the federal government. But in the 1830s, these tribes, along with the Seminoles, Creeks, and Chickasaws, were removed to Indian Territory, where they established their own governments and school systems. These school systems, Indian leaders hoped, would contribute to the political and economic development of Indian nations and contribute to their independence. But these hopes were dashed in the late 1890s and early twentieth century as the federal government adopted policies designed to destroy the Indian nations in Indian

Territory. This process occurred at the same time that western Indians were being conquered and placed in reservations. During this phase of conquest, Indians could only hope to resist federal policies. During the third phase, during the 1920s and 1930s, Indians responded favorably and aided attempts to resurrect and maintain Native American languages and cultures. This phase provided opportunities for Indians to organize and eventually resist the termination policies of the 1940s and 1950s and campaign for self-determination in the 1960s and 1970s.

This chapter will focus on Native American educational developments from the American Revolution to the 1930s. The period from the 1940s to the present will be covered in later chapters. Because of my own Choctaw heritage, I will use the history of that tribe as an example of Native American education in the nineteenth century.

THE AMERICAN BOARD AND
THE CIVILIZATION FUND

Following the American Revolution, leaders of the newly established government decided that the best policy for acquisition of Indian lands was by purchase and the signing of treaties as opposed to outright conquest. In 1783, George Washington outlined his Indian policies in a letter to James Duane, who headed a select committee on Indian affairs in the Continental Congress. Washington argued that purchase of Indian lands was preferable to the high expense of a war. In Washington's mind, the country was large enough to accommodate both European and Indian populations. In his letter, Washington states, "As the Country, is large enough to contain us all; and as we are disposed to be kind to them and to partake of their trade, we will . . . establish a boundary line between them and us."[1]

Part of Washington's concern, and the concern of many other American leaders prior to the Civil War, was that the advance of European civilization in the United States was destroying most of the Native American population. Of course, this concern did not reflect a desire to limit the expansion of the European population, but it did reflect a concern about protecting Native Americans from what were considered the worst aspects of European civilization—gambling, alcohol, fraud and stealing, and depraved sexual activities.

From this perspective, the logical solution was to protect the Indians by making them Christians and farmers. By instilling Christian morality and the value of hard work, it was hoped, Indians could resist some of the corrupting influences of white settlers. Consequently, federal policies in the nineteenth century supported missionary and manual labor schools. No one raised the issue of separation of church and state when the federal government provided direct financial support for missionary schools.

The two events that established the pattern of federal support of religious schools among Indians was the creation of the American Board of Commissioners for Foreign Missionaries (American Board) in 1810 and the passage of the Civilization Fund Act in 1819. In essence, the American Board provided the missionary teachers and the Civilization Fund Act provided the money. Of course, there were other religious groups providing missionaries, particularly—much to the chagrin of Protestant churches—the Catholic church. And, of course, there were other sources of financial support, such as donations from local church congregations.

The architect of the Civilization Fund Act and the later removal of the southeastern tribes to Indian Territory was Thomas L. McKenney, who served as superintendent of Indian trade from 1816 to 1822 and superintendent of Indian affairs from 1824 to 1830. From McKenney's perspective it was only a matter of time before the southeastern Indians would be pushed from their homes. He believed that the only hope for Native Americans' survival was an educational plan that would "civilize" them. His interest in educating Indians was sparked by the work of a Presbyterian missionary, Cyrus Kingsbury, among the Cherokee Indians. Kingsbury introduced schools based on the Lancasterian system of education, which was being used in many of the charity and public schools of the Northeast.[2] Of course, one of the central features of the missionary educational program was the teaching of morals along with reading, writing, and arithmetic. In this situation, being civilized meant adopting the moral code of European civilization. Interestingly, most southeastern tribes welcomed the educational program but not the moral and religious instruction.[3]

The wording of the Civilization Fund Act reflets Thomas L. McKenney's concern about the disappearance of Native Americans. The Act states as its goal: "providing against the further decline and final extinction of the Indian tribes . . . and . . . introducing among them the habits and arts of civilization."[4] Under the act, the President was given the power to hire teachers to instruct Indians in agricultural methods and reading, writing, and arithmetic. The first Indian tribe to establish an extensive school system under the provision of the Civilization Fund Act was the Choctaws.

Similar to McKenney, the Choctaws believed that education was vital to their survival as it would enhance their ability to resist the incursions of white settlers and to deal with the federal government. While McKenney favored removal of the southern tribes, the Choctaws believed that education was essential to protect against the confiscation of their traditional lands. These attitudes are reflected, in part, in a letter written by Choctaw leader David Folsom in 1819. In the letter, Folsom apologized for his poor English and the fact that he had attended school for only six months. But, he said, with the decline of hunting, education was vital to the survival of the Choctaw Nation. He stated: "I have been talking to my people, and have advised them for the best, turn their attention to industry and farming, and lay our hunting aside. And here is one point of great work, is just come to hand, before us which is the establishment of a school; and the Choctaws appear to be well pleased."[5]

Therefore, part of the Choctaw Nation welcomed Cyrus Kingsbury as he shifted his attention from the Cherokees to the Choctaws. In August 1819,

Kingsbury met with the ruling council of the Choctaw Nation to discuss the development of schools. The council voted to provide annuities of $3,000 a year and donated $1,800 and eight cows to support the establishment of missionary schools. Kingsbury, aided by Choctaw leaders John Pitchlynn and David Folsom, opened a mission school in 1821.

It is important to understand that the Choctaws, like other southeastern tribes, welcomed missionary schools and provided them with financial support. In addition, Choctaws were particularly pleased at the idea of developing a written language. With the aid of the Folsom family, missionary teacher Cyrus Byington prepared a Choctaw grammar book, speller, and dictionary. Portions of the Bible and hymns were translated into Choctaw. Later, after their removal to Indian Territory, both the Cherokees and Choctaws produced bilingual newspapers and operated bilingual classrooms.[6]

The operation of one of these missionary schools was described by an English traveler, Adam Hodgson, in a surviving 1820 report. There were eighty students in the school visited by Hodgson, seventy of them boarding with the missionary family. Fifty of these students had spoken only Choctaw when beginning their schooling. The students awoke at daybreak and did chores around the mission. They gathered at seven o'clock for reading, prayers, and breakfast. Then they attended school, where they again prayed and read a chapter of the Bible. After being examined on the chapter studied the previous day, they were instructed in reading, writing, and arithmetic. At the end of school, the boys were engaged in agricultural tasks and the girls learned sewing and other domestic arts.[7]

While Hodgson was visiting the school, David Folsom arrived to talk to the students. Folsom, who had traveled sixty miles for the occasion, translated for the students from English to Choctaw a letter he had received from some friends from the North. He then spoke to the students at great length in Choctaw.[8] This use of native languages in the classroom was in sharp contrast to federal policies in the late nineteenth century, which banned the use of native languages in Indian schools.

The missionary schools established in the Choctaw Nation were typical of the manual labor schools established by missionaries among other Indians. The goal of the manual labor schools was to instill in Indian children the work habits and moral values of the European settlers and to teach the skills necessary to operate farms along the model of white settlers. In other words, the schools were designed to change patterns of living among Indians and to replace their traditional economies. Therefore, the manual labor schools divided their time between instruction in "letters, labor and mechanic arts, and morals and Christianity" and "a practical use of the tools for the artisan and the implements of the farmer."[9]

While the Choctaws and Cherokees embraced missionary education, there was little they could do to stop the inevitable takeover of their lands by the federal government. During the 1830s, what were known as the Five Civilized Tribes—Choctaws, Cherokees, Seminoles, Creeks, and Chickasaws—were removed from their homes in what is now Florida, Georgia, Alabama, Mississippi, Louisiana, and Tennessee and sent on the infamous "trail of tears" to Indian Territory.

The superintendent of Indian Affairs and designer of the removal plan, Thomas McKenney, justified the removal as being a major educational project for the civilizing of Indians. In an 1829 letter and speech to The Indian Board for the Emigration, Preservation and Improvement of the Aborigines of America in New York City, McKenney outlined the purposes of his policies. A central part of McKenney's argument was that Native Americans could not be civilized as long as they remained in immediate contact with white settlers and traders. The purpose of removing the Indian tribes to a newly created Indian Territory was to isolate them and then educate them. In a letter to the New York group, McKenney asks, "Now can any one doubt, who knows the present unhappy depressed condition of our Indians, that this removal, and this system, would not lift them in a single generation to a level with ourselves?" To those who might doubt this policy, McKenney replies, "To such, I would put the questions:

> Does not the present wretched condition of these people demand the adoption of some effort to save them? And if something is not attempted, is it not plain that while we are reasoning in the forum, the enemy, having scaled the walls, is within the city, devastating and whelming it in ruins? My own opinion is . . . that the crisis has arrived in which they are to be *saved* or *lost!*[10]

One reason McKenney gave for isolating Indians from whites was a sense of moral despair among Indians that he believed was caused by the superiority of white settlers. This sense of inferiority to whites, McKenney argued, caused Indians to give up any attempts to become civilized.[11] In addition, the first contact with white traders often resulted in alcoholism and introduction to the vices of white civilization. These factors, according to McKenney, had resulted in the disappearance of most of the Indian population that had once inhabited Maine, Massachusetts, Rhode Island, Connecticut, Pennsylvania, New Jersey, Maryland, Virginia, and North and South Carolina. For instance, according to McKenney's calculations, there remained only forty-seven members of the once numerous Powhatan Indians, who had occupied Virginia. And, as he pointed out to his audience, it would be hard to find descendants of the Indians who had once inhabited the present site of New York City.[12]

In McKenney's words, the solution was "to give them a country, and to secure it to them by the most ample and solemn sanctions . . . in exchange for theirs."[13] Once they were placed in Indian Territory, according to McKenney, schools and churches would be established to enlighten the next generation. In closing his address, McKenney states, "unless the Indians can be prevailed on to remove, and place themselves under the redeeming influences which you are ready, in their behalf [referring to the proposed missionary work in Indian Territory of some members of the audience], to see faithfully applied, *they must perish.*"[14]

When the Indian removal act was passed by Congress in 1830, the Choctaws were the first tribe to agree to the plan by signing the Treaty of Dancing Rabbit Creek on May 30, 1830. The Treaty of Dancing Rabbit Creek illustrates some of the internal dynamics taking place in Indian tribes and the often underhanded methods of federal officials. During the late eighteenth and early nineteenth centuries, many mixed-bloods (individuals with both European and Indian ancestry) rose to prominence in Indian tribes because of their ability to speak both their own Indian language and English. Often, those mixed-bloods were the major advocates of establishing schools and adopting the agricultural methods of the white settlers.

At the time of the signing of the Treaty of Dancing Rabbit Creek, a mixed-blood Choctaw, Greenwood Leflore, was chief of the Western district of the Choctaw Nation. Leflore's father traveled from French Canada to the French province of Louisiana establishing trading posts. He had married a mixed-blood Choctaw, and Greenwood was born on June 3, 1800. In 1822, he was made chief. As a mixed-blood chief, he tried to suppress numerous tribal customs and prohibited the use of charms by medicine men. He advocated Christianity and the expansion of education.

His support and signing of the Treaty of Dancing Rabbit Creek led to his eventual ouster as Chief of the Western Division of the Choctaw Nation. Indeed, he was strongly criticized for accepting 1,000 acres of land, the military title of colonel, and tuition for his daughter's education from the federal government for signing the treaty. When he was accused of taking a bribe for signing the treaty, he supposedly said, "Which is worse, for a great government to offer a bribe or a poor Indian to take one?"[15]

Under the Treaty of Dancing Rabbit Creek the Choctaws ceded their lands in Alabama and Mississippi for land in Indian Territory. Under the Treaty, the Choctaws were to operate their own government under the protection of the U.S. government. The treaty specifically stated, "no Territory or State shall ever have a right to pass laws for the government of the Choctaw Nation of Red People and their descendants; and . . . no part of the land granted them shall ever be embraced in any Territory or State."[16]

The removal of tribes to Indian Territory raised the issue of the legal status of tribal governments and, as part of the operation of government, tribal school systems. This issue was clarified in a U.S. Supreme Court ruling in 1831 involving the extension of the laws of the state of Georgia over the Cherokee Nation. The Cherokees argued that this was illegal because they were a foreign nation. The question, as posed in the decision of the Court, was: "Is the Cherokee nation a foreign state in the sense in which that term is used in the constitution?"[17] The Court argued that in the section of the Constitution dealing with the regulation of commerce a distinction is made among foreign nations, states, and Indian tribes. Consequently, Indian tribes are not foreign countries, but they are political entities that are distinct from states. In the words of the Court, Indian tribes are "domestic dependent nations. . . they are in a state of pupilage. Their relation to the United States

resembles that of a ward to his guardian."[18] Consequently, provisions granting control to the tribal governments under the supervision of the federal
government and guaranteeing the right to the land in Indian Territory were
included in the treaties signed by the other four civilized tribes.

Of course, many Indians did not want to be removed to Indian Territory.
The Treaty of Dancing Rabbit Creek guaranteed that Choctaws who did not
wish to go to Indian Territory would be allotted land in Mississippi. To the
amazement of federal officials, thousands of Choctaws decided against removal and sought their allotment of land, which, of course, very few received. In the case of the Cherokees, many tribal members went into hiding
and struggled to avoid being removed to Indian Territory.[19]

A great deal has been written about the suffering of the Indian tribes on
the "trail of tears" to Indian Territory. One has to imagine the enormity of the
task of moving entire nations of Indians from the South to the West. In many
cases, it was a forced trek under the supervision of the military. The removal
was made worse by the lack of roads, swollen rivers, and some of the worst
blizzards in recorded history. In addition, cholera epidemics accompanied
many of the tribes as they struggled to reach Indian Territory. Indian removal
involved the most extensive forced movement of people in modern history.[20]

Once settled in Indian Territory, the Five Civilized Tribes quickly engaged
in the business of organizing governments and establishing school systems.
In the case of the Choctaws, Greenwood Leflore remained in Mississippi,
expanding his grant of land to 15,000 acres and purchasing many slaves.[21]
Leflore's ownership of slaves was typical of some of the wealthier Choctaws
who migrated to Indian Territory. After the Civil War the issue of freed slaves
became an important area of contention between the Choctaw Nation and the
federal government. As I will discuss later, the Choctaws eventually established a segregated school system for the children of the freed slaves.

Like some of the other tribes, the Choctaws organized a republican form
of government with elections, a court system, and police, and they developed
a successful economy. Except during the chaos following the Civil War, the
Choctaws prospered. The Civil War presented a problem for the tribe because
of its ownership of slaves and its support of the Confederacy. But even with
the economic and political problems following the war, the Choctaws proved
so successful that many whites tried to gain citizenship in the Choctaw
Nation. The tribe earned income from coal mines, land sold to the federal
government, taxes on cattle shipped through from Texas, and a number of
other ventures. To limit the number of whites seeking to become citizens
through marriage so that they could participate in Choctaw prosperity, the
tribal government passed a marriage law in 1875 that provided that no white
man could marry into the tribe unless he had a certificate of good character
signed by at least ten Choctaw citizens. In addition, the law required the
white person to take the following oath of allegiance to the Choctaw Nation:

> I do solemnly swear that I will honor, defend, and submit to the constitutions
> and laws of the Choctaw Nation, and will neither claim nor seek from the
> United States government or from the Judicial tribunals, thereof any protec-

tion privilege or redress incompatible with the same, as guaranteed to the Choctaw Nation by the treaty stipulations entered into between them so help me God.[22]

The educational system established by the Choctaws was based on a selective program under which the best students were sent to academies and the best graduates of the academies were sent east to attend college. In 1842, the ruling council of the Choctaw Nation provided for the establishment of a comprehensive system of schools. A compulsory attendance law was enacted by the Choctaw Nation in 1889.

The schools were developed in cooperation with the missionaries. In this regard, Superintendent of Indian Affairs Thomas McKenney's dream of establishing schools in Indian Territory became a reality. The Spencer Academy (the author's uncle, Pat Spring, died in the fire that burned down the academy in 1896) was opened in 1844 and the Armstrong Academy in 1846. By 1848, the Choctaws had nine boarding schools paid for by tribal funds. In addition, a system of day or neighborhood schools was organized, and by 1860 these schools enrolled five hundred students. And, after the Civil War, the Choctaws established a system of segregated schools for the children of freed slaves.[23]

In addition, an adult literacy program was developed by missionaries through a system of Saturday and Sunday schools. Whole families would camp near a school or church to receive instruction in arithmetic, reading, and writing. Instruction was bilingual in both Choctaw and English. While there were not many texts in Choctaw, missionaries did translate many portions of the Bible, hymn books, moral lectures, and other religious tracts into Choctaw.[24]

While some of the teachers were white missionaries, most of them were Choctaws who had been educated in tribal schools. The teachers were examined in the common school subjects and the Choctaw constitution. The teachers followed a course of study modeled on that of neighboring states and taught in English, using the *Choctaw Definer* to help children translate from Choctaw into English.

The Spencer Academy for boys and the New Hope Academy for girls were the leading schools. The children who attended these schools were selected by district trustees until 1890 and after that by county judges. Selection was based on "promptness in attendance and their capacity to learn fast."[25] Only one student could be selected from any particular family.

In 1885, the tribal council removed the two academies from missionary management and placed them under the control of a board of trustees. In 1890, a school law was enacted that required male teachers at the Spencer Academy to be college graduates and to have the ability to teach Greek, Latin, French, and German and female teachers at the New Hope Academy to have graduated from a college or normal school and to be able to teach two modern languages besides English. The faculty of both schools included both white and Choctaw instructors.

School reports issued by the Choctaw Nation indicate that large numbers of Choctaws did attend school. The actual population of Choctaws in Indian Territory in 1890, the first year a federal census was taken, was 10,017. In addition, there was a population of 4,406 African Americans.[26] A school report in 1869 indicates that there were 1,847 students in Choctaw day schools and 22 students attending colleges in what were referred to as "the States." The tuition and board for the college students was paid for by tribal funds. A school report of 1875 listed 1,118 students in day schools, 60 students at the Spencer Academy, 50 students at the New Hope Academy, and 10 students away at various colleges. By 1893, there were 3,819 in day schools, 490 in academies and boarding schools, and 40 attending college.[27]

The success of the Choctaw educational system was paralleled by that of the Cherokee Nation. The Cherokees were given land just north of the Choctaw Nation. The Cherokees displayed a great deal more resistance to removal than the Choctaws. In fact, the final stage of removal in 1838 required the U.S. Army to assemble and march the Cherokees at bayonet point. Of the 11,500 that marched on this final phase of the trail of tears, 4,000 died of illness and exposure.[28]

Similarly to the Choctaws, the Cherokees had developed a system of schools prior to removal to the West. A Cherokee, Sequoyah, developed a written language for the tribe based on the use of eighty-five symbols. His work was published by missionaries in 1821 and used in the tribal newspaper. According to Jon Reyhner and Jeanne Eder's history of Indian education, Sequoyah believed that his writing system would help to preserve Cherokee culture.[29]

In 1841, after removal, the Cherokee National Council organized a national system of schools with eleven schools in eight districts, and in 1851 it opened academies for males and females. By the 1850s, the majority of teachers in these schools were Cherokee. Reyhner and Eder write, "By 1852 the Cherokee Nation has a better common school system than the neighboring states of Arkansas and Missouri."[30]

The success of the Choctaw and Cherokee school systems was highlighted in a congressional report released in 1969. The report noted that "In the 1800s, for example, the Choctaw Indians of Mississippi and Oklahoma [Indian Territory] operated about 200 schools and academies and sent numerous graduates to eastern colleges."[31] The report went on to praise the Cherokee schools. In the words of the report, "Using bilingual teachers and Cherokee texts, the Cherokees, during the same period, controlled a school system which produced a tribe almost *100% literate* [emphasis is mine]."[32] The report concluded—"*Anthropologists have determined that as a result of this school system, the literacy level in English of western Oklahoma Cherokees was higher than the white populations of either Texas or Arkansas.*"[33]

Inevitably, the expansion of white settlers to the west brought an end to the nations of the Five Civilized Tribes. In 1887, Congress passed the Dawes Act, which was designed to break up tribal control of land by granting allotments to individuals as opposed to tribal organizations. In 1893, Congress established the Dawes Commission to deal specifically with the tribes living in Indian Territory. In 1894, the Dawes Commission issued its report calling for an end to the tribal governments of the Five Civilized Tribes.

The report of the Dawes Commission recognized that "the United States is under treaty obligations not to interfere in their [the Five Civilized Tribes'] internal policy . . . and has guaranteed to them self-government and absolute exclusion of white citizens from any abode among them."[34] But, the commission argued, the authors of the original treaties had not dreamed of the present growth of the country and the possibility that white settlers would be demanding land in Indian Territory. In addition, the commission attacked the tribal governments as being corrupt and economically exploiting their condition by leasing land to white settlers and entering into contracts for development of natural resources. The leasing and contracting policies of the tribes resulted in large numbers of whites living in Indian Territory.

The Dawes Commission used the educational conditions of whites and African Americans as another justification for eliminating tribal governments. Under the system of tribal governments, one had to be a citizen of a tribe to attend schools operated by the tribal governments. As a result, the Dawes Commission report indicates, "there are thousands of white children in this territory who are almost wholly without the means of education, and are consequently growing up with no fitting preparation for useful citizenship."[35] With regard to African Americans, the Dawes Commission criticized the adoption procedures of the tribes. While recognizing that the Choctaws and Cherokees had adopted their freed slaves, the report complained that the two tribes had never given them the promised forty acres. The Chicksaws were criticized for treating their former slaves as aliens. With regard to education, the report states, "In the Cherokee tribe the schools provided for the freedman are of very inferior and inefficient character, and . . . their children are growing up in deplorable ignorance."[36]

In 1899, the U.S. government began the process of taking over the tribal educational systems with the appointment of John D. Benedict as superintendent of schools for Indian Territory. Benedict attacked the tribal schools for emphasizing cultural issues and not emphasizing vocational education. He was particularly critical of the selective system that sent some children to academies and colleges.

The Choctaws reacted immediately to these criticisms by passing a resolution that embodied the pride and hope of the tribe in its school system. The resolution reads, "it would be a wrong against modest pride to wrest from the Choctaws and Chickasaws their schools, their higher edifice. Our present school system is the work of many years of earnest effort and steady improvement; and to take from us an institution cherished in its growth to close attachment would be at least unfair." The resolution proudly contains the statement "Our management of the schools has proved satisfactory as is attested by results."[37]

In 1901, the Choctaw school system passed out of tribal control and the boarding schools were turned into vocational schools for training full-bloods.

In 1906, Congress passed a law dealing with the final issues in dissolving the tribal governments, and in 1907 Oklahoma was admitted as a new state. With these acts, the nations of the Five Civilized Tribes ceased to exist as separate political entities.

In addition, the nature of citizenship changed for these tribes. While living under tribal governments in Indian territory, Indians maintained citizenship within their particular nation. On March 3, 1901, Congress granted U.S. citizenship to all Indians living in Indian Territory. Citizenship was not granted to other Indians until 1924, when an act of Congress proclaimed: "That all non-citizen Indians born within the territorial limits of the United States be, and they are hereby, declared to be citizens of the United States."[38]

In 1969, a congressional report complained of the decline in educational achievement after the Five Civilized Tribes lost control of their school systems. The report states, "Now, after almost 70 years of Federal and State controlled education, the Cherokees have the following educational record: 40 percent of adult Cherokees are functionally illiterate in English; only 39 percent have completed the eighth grade; the median educational level of the tribe's adult population is only 5.5 years; dropout rates of Indian students are often as high as 75 percent."[39] The report cited one statistic as an example of the tragic decline of education in what had once been Indian Territory: "The statistical data speak for themselves: 87 percent dropout by the 6th grade at an all-Indian public elementary school near Ponca, Okla."[40]

RESERVATIONS AND BOARDING SCHOOLS

As white settlers moved into western lands in the latter part of the nineteenth century, leaders in the U.S. government were forced to reconsider their relationships to tribes and their attempts to "civilize" Indians. First, there was the problem of land on which to settle displaced tribes. Unlike in the 1820s and 1830s, there was a realization that white settlement would eventually cover most of the continent. In 1858, Commissioner of Indian Affairs Charles E. Mix, in his annual report, declared that the U.S. government had made several serious errors in dealing with the southeastern tribes, including "the assignment to them of too great an extent of country, to be held in common."[41] Holding large tracts of land in common, according to Commissioner Mix, limited the attempts to civilize the Indian because it prevented Indians from learning the value of separate and independent property.

Reservations and allotment programs were the responses to the land issue. The reservation system combined with education was considered by the U.S. government as the best method of dealing with what Commissioner of Indian Affairs Luke Lea called the "wilder tribes."[42] In the *Annual Report of the Commissioner of Indian Affairs* in 1850, Commissioner Lea argued that certain Indian tribes, specifically the Sioux and Chippewas, had an "insatiable passion for war" and that it was "necessary that they be placed in positions where they can be controlled."[43] Once concentrated in reservations where they could be controlled, the tribes would be compelled to remain until they proved themselves to be civilized. Under this system, the federal government was to supply agricultural implements to aid in this process of civilization.

Provisions for manual labor schools on reservations were specified in Commissioner Mix's report of 1858. Mix argued that reservation sites should be selected that would minimize contact with whites and provide opportunities for Indians to learn agricultural skills. To aid in the process of preparing Indians for agriculture, manual labor schools were to be established that would teach basic skills in reading, writing, arithmetic, and agricultural skills. Of particular importance, according to Commissioner Mix, was the role of manual labor schools in molding the character of future generations of Indians in what he called "habits of industry." To carry out this enterprise, Commissioner Mix recommended that a military force should remain in the vicinity of the reservations "to aid in controlling the Indians."[44]

Adding to the problem for government officials, western Indians displayed a great deal more resistance to white incursions onto their lands. This resulted in Indian wars across the plains of the West during the latter half of the nineteenth century. In 1867, Congress created an Indian Peace Commission to deal with the warring tribes. The Indian Peace Commission advocated different methods for the education and civilization of Indians. The Peace Commission placed emphasis on the role of education in converting Indians to civilization. Nathaniel Taylor, Chairman of the Peace Commission, told Crow Indians at Fort Laramie: "Upon the reservations you select, we . . . will send you teachers for your children."[45] According to Jon Reyhner and Jeanne Eder, this promise was embodied in the Treaty of Fort Laramie with the Sioux and their allies.[46]

The members of the Peace Commission were not entirely satisfied with the traditional attempts to educate Indians, particularly with regard to language. The Indian Peace Commission report of 1868 states that differences in language were a major source of the continuing friction between whites and Indians. Therefore, according to the report, an emphasis on the teaching of English would be a major step in reducing hostilities and civilizing Native Americans. In the words of the report: "Through sameness of language is produced sameness of sentiment and thought; customs and habits are moulded and assimilated in the same way, and thus in process of time the differences producing trouble would have been gradually obliterated."[47]

Replacing the use of native languages with English, destroying Indian customs, and teaching allegiance to the U.S. government became the major educational policies of the U.S. government toward Indians during the latter part of the nineteenth century. An important part of these educational policies was the boarding school, which was designed to remove children from their families at an early age and thereby isolate them from the language and customs of their parents and tribes. These boarding schools were quite different from those operated by the Choctaws in Indian Territory, which were somewhat elite institutions within their educational system and were not designed to destroy Indian customs and languages.

In *A History of Indian Education,* Jon Reyhner and Jeanne Eder demonstrate the connections between the establishment of boarding schools for Indians and the history of black education in the South. The first off-reservation boarding school was the Carlisle Indian School, established in Carlisle, Pennsylvania, in 1879. The founder of the school, Richard Pratt, had commanded an African-American cavalry in Indian Territory between 1867 and 1875. According to Reyhner and Eder, Pratt's interest in founding a boarding school was sparked when he took seventeen adult Indian prisoners of war to Hampton Institute.[48] As I will discuss in Chapter 7, Hampton Institute played a major role in the development of African-American education in the South. Booker T. Washington was educated at Hampton and used it as a model when he established Tuskegee Normal and Industrial Institute in 1881. As I will discuss in more detail in Chapter 7, the primary purpose of Hampton was to prepare freed slaves to be teachers who could instill work values in other freed slaves. In the words of historian James Anderson, "The primary aim [of Hampton] was to work the prospective teachers long and hard so that they would embody, accept, and preach an ethic of hard toil or the 'dignity of labor.'"[49]

Pratt not only wanted to instill the work ethic in Indian children but also, as he told a Baptist group, immerse "Indians in our civilization and when we get them under [hold] them there until they are thoroughly soaked."[50] The slogan for the Carlisle Indian School reflected the emphasis on changing the cultural patterns of Indians: "To civilize the Indian, get him into civilization. To keep him civilized, let him stay."[51]

Pratt's educational philosophy embodied the principles behind the allotment movement of the latter part of the nineteenth century. The allotment program, which was applied to the Five Civilized Tribes with the breakup of Indian Territory, was designed to distribute commonly held tribal property to individual Indians. It was assumed that individual ownership would instill the capitalistic values of white civilization in Indians. In fact, tribal ownership was viewed as a form of socialism that was antithetical to the values of white American society. Also, the allotment program was another method of dealing with the Indian land problem. In the *Annual Report of the Commissioner of Indian Affairs* in 1881, Commissioner of Indian Affairs Hiram Price criticized previous attempts to civilize Indians because they did not teach the necessity of labor. This could be accomplished, Price argued, only when individual Indians were made responsible for their own economic welfare. This could be done, he contended, by allotting Indians "a certain number of acres of land which they may call their own."[52]

Pratt attacked the tribal way of life as socialistic and contrary to the values of "civilization." Reflecting the values of economic individualism, Pratt complained about missionary groups who *did not* "advocate the disintegration of the tribes and the giving to individual Indians rights and opportunities among civilized people."[53] He wrote to the Commissioner of Indian Affairs in 1890, "Pandering to the tribe and its socialism as most of our Government and mission plans do is the principal reason why the Indians have not advanced more and are not advancing as rapidly as they ought."[54]

Between the founding of the Carlisle Indian School in 1879 and 1905, twenty-five nonreservation boarding schools were opened throughout the country.[55] It is important to emphasize the *nonreservation* location of the boarding schools because of the educational philosophy that Indian children should be removed from family and tribal influences.

An important issue for both nonreservation boarding schools and schools on reservations was the teaching of English. As discussed previously, the attitude of many white educators in the latter part of the nineteenth century was that elimination of tribal languages and the learning of English would lead to the absorption and practice of white values by Indians. In the *Annual Report of the Commissioner of Indian Affairs* in 1887, Commissioner J. D. C. Adkins ordered the exclusive use of English at all Indian schools. Atkins pointed out that this policy was consistent with the requirement that only English be taught in public schools in territories acquired by the United States from Mexico, Spain, and Russia. And, comparing the conquest of Indians to the German occupation of the French provinces of Alsace and Lorraine, where it was required that German rather than French be used in the schools, Atkins declared, "No unity or community of feeling can be established among different peoples unless they are brought to speak the same language, and thus become imbued with like ideas of duty."[56]

Also, in an attempt to build a sense of community with the white population, it was hoped that Indian children would transfer their allegiance from their tribal governments to the federal government. Consequently, in 1889, Commissioner of Indian Affairs Thomas J. Morgan issued "instructions to Indian Agents in Regard to Inculcation of Patriotism in Indian Schools," which required that an American flag be flown in front of every Indian school. The instructions state, "the 'Stars and Stripes' should be a familiar object, and students should be taught to reverence the flag as a symbol of their nation's power and protection."[57] In addition, the instructions required the teaching of American history and the principles of the U.S. government. There was no suggestion in the instructions that the history of Native Americans and their governments be taught in the schools. Also, the instructions called for the teaching of patriotic songs and the public recitation of "patriotic selections."[58]

In one of the more interesting uses of celebrating national holidays as a method of building support for government policies, Commissioner Morgan's instructions required that schools inculcate in students allegiance to government policies designed to break up tribal lands. After a sentence requiring the celebration of Washington's birthday, Decoration Day, the Fourth of July, Thanksgiving, and Christmas, the instructions state: "It will also be well to observe the anniversary of the day upon which the 'Dawes bill' for giving to Indians allotments of land in severalty become a law, viz, February 8, 1887, and to use that occasion to impress upon Indian youth the enlarged scope and opportunity given them by this law and the new obligations which it imposes."[59]

In 1889, Commissioner Morgan wrote a bulletin on "Indian Education" which outlines the goals and policies of Indian schools. The bulletin was distributed by the U.S. Bureau of Education with an introduction written by the Commissioner of Education, William T. Harris. In the introduction, Harris praised what he called "the new education for our American Indians," particularly the effort "to obtain control of the Indian at an early age, and to seclude him as much as possible from the tribal influences."[60] Harris singled out the boarding school as an important step in changing the character of American Indians. Harris argued that it was necessary to save the American Indian, but, he wrote, "We cannot save him and his patriarchal or tribal institution both together. To save him we must take him up into our civilization."[61]

Commissioner Morgan opened the bulletin with a statement of general principles of education for what he identified as a Native American population of 250,000 with a school population of 50,000. These general principles called for systematizing the system of Indian education, increasing its availability to Indian children, and making it compulsory for all Native American children to attend school. In addition, Indian education was to place special stress on vocational training for jobs and on teaching English. With regard to instruction in English, the bulletin states, "only English should be allowed to be spoken, and only English-speaking teachers should be employed in schools supported wholly or in part by the Government."[62] Also, the general principles stressed the importance of teaching allegiance to the U.S. government. As an added note, Morgan stressed the importance of bringing together the members of many different tribes in boarding schools as a means of reducing antagonisms between them.

After outlining the general principles of Indian education, Morgan turned to the issue of the high school. Morgan noted that the government at that time was not supporting high schools for American Indians but only non-reservation boarding schools, reservation boarding schools, and day schools. Morgan favored the introduction of high schools for Indians as a means of breaking "the shackles of . . . tribal provincialism."[63] In advocating high schools, Morgan stressed the character-training qualities of a secondary education. He states, "the whole course of training [high school] should be fairly saturated with moral ideas, fear of God, and respect for the rights of others; love of truth and fidelity to duty; personal purity, philanthropy, and patriotism."[64]

Similar to the goals he gave for a high school education, he argued that grammar schools should stress systematic habits, "fervent patriotism," and the duties of citizens. Morgan stressed the character-training aspects of grammar schools, which he felt should develop an independent economic person as compared to an Indian who is dependent on communal tribal living. Reflecting the reality of how Indian schools were conducted, Morgan states that in grammar school: "No pains should be spared to teach them that their future must depend chiefly upon their own exertions, character, and endeavors. . . . In the sweat of their faces must they eat bread."[65]

Morgan also advocated early childhood education as a method of counteracting the influence of the Indian home. Similarly to the boarding school, early childhood education would help to strip away the influences of Indian culture and language. Morgan states, "Children should be taken at as early an age as possible, before camp life has made an indelible stamp upon them."[66]

With hindsight, one might consider this plan of Indian education as one of the great endeavors to destroy cultures and languages and replace them with another culture and language. The key to the process was the removal of children from the influences of family and tribe and their placement in educational institutions where they would not be allowed to speak their native languages or practice native customs. As part of this educational effort, there was a concerted effort through a forced program of patriotism to have Indians switch their loyalties from their tribal governments to the federal government.*

The conditions in boarding schools lived up to Morgan's previously quoted edict: "In the sweat of their faces must they eat bread." During the 1920s, a variety of investigators of Indian schools were horrified by the conditions they found. At the Rice Boarding School in Arizona, Red Cross investigators found that children were fed "bread, black coffee, and syrup for breakfast; bread and boiled potatoes for dinners; more bread and boiled potatoes for supper."[67] In addition to a poor diet, overcrowded conditions contributed to the spread of tuberculosis and trachoma.

Using a paramilitary form of organization, boarding schools were supported by the labor of the students. As early as the fifth grade, boys and girls attended classes for half the day and worked for the other half. As part of the plan to teach agricultural methods, children raised crops and tended farm animals. The paramilitary organization was reflected in the constant drilling of students. The children were given little time for recreation. They were awakened at five in the morning and marched to the dining room, then marched back to the dormitories and classrooms. At the Albuquerque Indian School students marched in uniforms with dummy rifles. For punishment children were flogged with ropes, and some boarding schools contained their own jails. In the 1920s, anthropologist Oliver La Farge called the Indian schools "penal institutions—where little children were sentenced to hard labor for a term of years to expiate the crime of being born of their mothers."[68]

THE "MERIAM REPORT"

The publication of the "Meriam report" in 1928 began the process that ended this massive educational effort to change the language and culture of an entire people. The report was based on investigations conducted in 1926 by the Institute for Government Research at John Hopkins University at the request of the Secretary of Interior, Hubert Work. The report was known by the name of the principal investigator, Louis Meriam, and it was published as *The Problem of Indian Administration.*[69]

---

*The emphasis on patriotism is also reflected in the fact that the first rule of Indian school service was: "1. There shall be a flagstaff at each school, and in suitable weather the flag of the United States shall be hoisted each morning and taken down at sunset." Department of the Interior, United States Indian Service, *Rules for the Indian School Service 1913* (Washington, D.C.: U.S. Government Printing Office, 1913), p. 3.

The report states that the most fundamental need in Indian education was a change in government attitude. The report accurately states that education in "the past has proceeded largely on the theory that it is necessary to remove the Indian child as far as possible from his home environment."[70] Completely reversing this educational philosophy, the report states that "the modern point of view in education and social work lays stress on upbringing in the natural setting of home and family life."[71]

The report went on to argue that the routine and discipline of Indian schools destroyed initiative and independence. In addition, the report criticizes the provision of only half a day of schooling and of working students at heavy labor at a young age. In particular, the report was critical of boarding schools and the isolation of children from their families and communities.[72]

Ironically—at least from the standpoint of the previous history of Indian education—federal policy after the issuance of the Meriam report stressed community day schools and the support of native cultures. The report argues that community day schools would serve the purpose of integrating education with reservation life. During the 1930s, Indian education placed stress on community schools and the rebuilding of the cultural life of American Indians. As I will discuss in a later chapter, these policies changed dramatically in the 1950s and 1960s with attempts to terminate tribes and with Indian participation in the civil rights movement.[73] In the end, the legacy of the allotment program and the educational efforts of the latter part of the nineteenth century was increasing illiteracy among the Five Civilized Tribes of the Indian Territory and the destruction of family life and Indian customs on the reservations. For the rest of the century, American Indians would attempt to rebuild what the federal government had destroyed.

PUERTO RICANS

Educational policy regarding Puerto Rico followed a pattern similar to that for Native Americans. The policy was based on a desire to win the loyalty of a conquered people and stabilize control of Puerto Rico as part of a broader strategy for maintaining U.S. influence in the Caribbean and Central America. Puerto Rico, Guantanamo Bay, Cuba, and the Panama Canal Zone were the linchpins of this strategy.[74] The use of education as part of the colonization of Puerto Rico was explicitly stated in 1902 in the annual report of the second commissioner of education, Samuel Lindsay: "Colonization carried forward by the armies of war is vastly more costly than that carried forward by the armies of peace, whose outpost and garrisons are the public schools of the advancing nation."[75]

Consequently, U.S. educational policy in Puerto Rico emphasized building loyalty to the U.S. flag and institutions, as well as deculturalization. The patriotic emphasis was similar to the Americanization programs directed at Native Americans. And, just as U.S. and state educational policies attempted to strip Indians of their languages and cultures, U.S. educational policy in

Puerto Rico attempted to replace Spanish with English as the majority language and introduce children to the dominant U.S. culture.

Puerto Rico became a colony of the United States in 1898 at the conclusion of the Spanish-American War. The war represented the final demise of Spanish empire in the Americas. The events leading up to the Spanish-American War were primarily centered in Cuba where, prior to the outbreak of the war, a liberation army composed of Cuban rebels revolted against Spanish rule and economic domination by foreign sugar and tobacco industries. The liberation army marched through the countryside torching plantations and plunging Cuba into economic chaos. The Spanish response was brutal: 200,000 Spanish troops were sent to Cuba to stop the liberation army, and the infamous concentration camp order was issued. The concentration camp order moved women, children, and men from villages into garrison towns as a method of cutting off all support to the rebel army. Citizens were executed or their property confiscated if they were found traveling outside garrison towns without a passport.

The U.S. government was interested in the rebellion from several perspectives. First, there was an interest in reducing Spanish influence in the Americas. Within this context, the government was sympathetic to the liberation army's goal of ousting the Spanish. Second, the government was interested in protecting American-owned sugar and tobacco plantations. This meant economic stabilization. For this purpose, the U.S. government wanted the establishment of a stable democratic government that would protect the property interests of foreign investors. As a result of this concern, the U.S. government was not interested in the liberation army ruling Cuba at the conclusion of the war. Third, the U.S. government was interested in establishing military bases in the Caribbean. But, because of the politics surrounding the U.S. entry into the war, Puerto Rico became a colony of the United States rather than Cuba. Consequently, for military purposes, Guantánamo Bay, Cuba, was retained by the United States and military bases were established in Puerto Rico.

The event that sparked a congressional declaration of war was the sinking of the battleship *Maine* in Havana harbor on February 15, 1898. The immediate reaction was to claim that the sinking had been caused by the Spanish, but a later investigation found that a coal fire on the ship had caused a powder magazine to explode. Even though the Spanish might not have been responsible for the sinking, "Remember the *Maine*" became the rallying call for the war.

As a result of the rebel war and the sinking of the *Maine*, President William McKinley asked Congress for a joint resolution authorizing intervention in Cuba. The resolution passed by Congress called on the Spanish to abandon all claims to governing Cuba and to remove all its forces from the island. An important part of the resolution stated that the United States had no intention of exercising sovereignty over Cuba.

Spain, of course, considered the resolution a declaration of war. And the war quickly escalated to global proportions. On one side of the world, the U.S. Navy sailed into Manila in the Philippines. On the other side of the world, American troops joined the Liberation Army to oust the Spanish from Cuba. On October 18, 1898, U.S. forces, which had invaded Puerto Rico less than three months previously, raised the U.S. flag in San Juan and declared the end of Spanish rule and the beginning of U.S. dominion.

While events in Cuba were the main cause for the United States initiating the conflict, the final treaty focused on other Spanish territorial possessions. The U.S. Congress had already declared its intention not to rule Cuba; consequently, the United States demanded that Spain secede Puerto Rico, the island of Guam in the Central Pacific, and the Philippines. With the signing of the treaty on December 10, 1898, the U.S. military gained strategic bases in the Caribbean, the Pacific, and the Far East. In 1901, before relinquishing Cuba, the U.S. Congress passed legislation dictating that Cuba sell or lease lands for naval stations to the United States. This paved the way for the United States to establish a naval base at Guantánamo Bay, Cuba.[76]

THE AMERICANIZATION OF PUERTO RICO

When considering U.S. educational policy in Puerto Rico, it is important to understand that the citizens of Puerto Rico did not ask to become part of the United States. In fact, the goal of the independence movement in Puerto Rico throughout the nineteenth century was independence from Spain, not cession to the United States. Similar to its actions in Cuba, Spain attempted to crush any attempts to gain liberation from its rule. Typical of the independence movement was the Puerto Rican Revolutionary Committee, which, in 1863, marched under the banner "Liberty or Death. Long Live Free Puerto Rico."

In addition, in 1897, the year before the outbreak of the Spanish-American War, Spain declared Puerto Rico an autonomous state. The residents of the now former colony of Spain quickly established a constitutional republican form of government; however, Spain still appointed the governor, who had restricted power. The newly independent government assumed power in July 1898, just before the landing of U.S. troops.

Therefore, after a long struggle for an independence that was quickly snatched away by an invading U.S. military, Puerto Rican citizens did not welcome subjugation by the U.S. government. In fact, Puerto Rican resistance to U.S. control, while not as strong as it was in the early twentieth century, continues to this day.

The anger among Puerto Ricans was heightened by the fact that the United States immediately placed them under the control of a military government operated by the War Department. Within less than a year, Puerto Rico went from being an autonomous state to being ruled by a military dictatorship.

The strong Puerto Rican independence movement contributed to a wave of resistance to the educational policies designed for Americanization and deculturalization. A list of these policies were compiled by Aida Negron De Montilla in her book *Americanization in Puerto Rico and the Public-School System 1900–1930*. I provide here a summary of the list followed by an explanation of how these policies evolved.

In examining this list, the reader should consider the items in the broad context of how a nation can use schools to impose its will on a conquered people. This is a case study in both an attempt to dominate through education and resistance to that domination. Some of the items in the list are presented as "attempts" because of the high level of resistance to these plans by the Puerto Rican people.

Summary List of Americanization Policies in Public Schools in Puerto Rico

1. Required celebration of U.S. patriotic holidays, such as the Fourth of July, which had not been celebrated prior to conquest
2. Patriotic exercises designed to create allegiance to the United States, such as pledging allegiance to the U.S. flag and studying important historical figures of U.S. history
3. Replacing local textbooks and curricula with ones reflecting the way of life in the United States
4. Attempts to expel teachers and students who engaged in anti–United States activities
5. Attempts to use teachers from the United States as opposed to local teachers
6. Introduction of organizations, such as the Boy Scouts of America, to promote allegiance to the United States
7. Attempts to replace Spanish with English as the language of instruction[77]

The first U.S. commissioner of education in Puerto Rico, Martin Grove Brumbaugh, captured the general thrust of these policies when he wrote in a preface to a history book, "President McKinley declared to the writer that it was his desire 'to put the conscience of the American people in the islands of the sea.' "[78] Brumbaugh was appointed in 1900, when military rule was replaced with a colonial government established by Congress under the Foraker Act. With the passage of the Foraker Act, which was in effect between 1900 and 1917, the President was given the power to appoint a commissioner of education for Puerto Rico.

While the military was in control, the educational system was organized along the lines of a U.S. model. In addition, the War Department created a commission to recommend educational policies for the island. The commission's report became a guide for Brumbaugh and the next six commissioners of education. The report outlined the basic methods of Americanization. It recommended that Puerto Rico have "the same system of education and the same character of books" as the United States, that teachers be "Americans," and that students be instructed in the English language.[79]

The commission's attitude about the power of education was similar to those who believed that Native Americans could be Americanized in one generation. At times, the language of the report gives the school an almost mystical power. "Put an American schoolhouse in every valley and upon every hilltop in Porto [sic] Rico," the report states, "and in these places . . . American schoolteachers, and the cloud of ignorance will disappear as the fog flies before the morning sun."[80]

While the report stressed Americanization, it cannot be considered simply a cynical statement by a conquering power. In fact, the commission found that only 10 percent of the population was literate. Both the commission's report and the later actions by the commissioners of education was undertaken in the spirit of trying to help the Puerto Rican people. The problem was the assumption that U.S. institutions, customs, and beliefs were the best in the world and that they should be imposed. The attempt to help was accompanied by an attitude of moral and cultural superiority.

During his short tenure (1900–1901), Brumbaugh began the process of Americanization. In a letter to school supervisors, he stated, "No school has done its duty unless it has impressed devout patriotism upon the hearts and minds of all the children."[81] He recruited teachers from the United States. Most of these teachers spoke only English, which meant that by default their instruction was not bilingual. Every school on the island was given an American flag, with most of them being donated by the Lafayette Post, Army of the Republic, New York City. The raising of the U.S. flag was used to signal the commencement of classes. Patriotic exercises were organized in the school with children being taught U.S. national songs such as "America," "Hail, Columbia," and "The Star-Spangled Banner."[82]

Therefore, within only four years of being an autonomous nation, Puerto Rican children were being educated to shift their allegiance from Puerto Rico to another country. The introduction of George Washington's birthday as a school holiday was part of this process. Schools were told to impress on students Washington's "noble traits and broad statesmanship." Exercises were organized which consisted of singing U.S. patriotic songs and reading Washington's speeches. In San Juan, 25,000 students were involved in the celebration. In Brumbaugh's words, "These exercises have done much to Americanize the island, much more than any other single agency."[83]

Letters were sent to teachers instructing them to celebrate, on June 14, 1901, the creation of the U.S. flag. Teachers were instructed to engage students in a celebration of the flag beginning with a flag salute followed by the singing of the U.S. national anthem. After this opening exercise, teachers were instructed to have students give speeches, recitations, and patriotic readings and to sing patriotic songs and march to band music.

Learning English was considered an important part of the Americanization process. In any language are embedded the customs and values of a particular culture. Similarly to American Indians, Puerto Ricans were taught English to build patriotism. In his annual report, Brumbaugh states, "The first English many of them knew was that of our national songs."[84] While many teachers from the United States were not capable of conducting bilingual instruction, Brumbaugh believed that Spanish should be taught along with

English. But, Brumbaugh believed, teachers from the United States should be placed in kindergarten and elementary schools to begin English instruction as early as possible.

During Brumbaugh's tenure Puerto Rican resistance to U.S. educational policies began to appear in the magazine *La Educación Moderna* in a 1900 article, "English in the Schools." The article attacked "the spirit of . . . supremacy with which the English language is being imposed."[85]

The second commissioner of education, Samuel Lindsay (1902–1904) introduced more policies designed to educate Puerto Rican children into the U.S. way of life. An important part of his program was sending Puerto Rican teachers and students to the United States to learn the English language and U.S. culture. These trips were designed to prepare Puerto Rican teachers to teach about the United States when they returned to the classroom.[86] Combined with the patriotic celebrations initiated during Brumbaugh's tenure, the program of study abroad was intended to inculcate the values of the dominant society in the United States.

Lindsay also began to tighten policies regarding the teaching of English. First, he included an examination in English as part of the general examination for gaining a teacher's certificate.[87] Readers should consider the impact of this requirement in the context of their own country. Imagine if you were a teacher and suddenly, within four years of conquest, you were being examined on your knowledge of the language of the conquering country!

The language issue was taken one step further by Lindsay's successor, Roland Falkner. Falkner's impact on language policies extended far beyond his term, from 1904 to 1907. Falkner ordered that all instruction past the first grade be conducted in English. Of course, the major problem he encountered was that most Puerto Rican teachers did not know enough English to conduct instruction in that language. Consequently, as an incentive to improve their English skills, Falkner ordered that teachers be classified according to their scores on the English examination. In addition, the government provided English instruction for Puerto Rican teachers. Of course, it was impossible to convert an entire school system from one language to another in a short time, and therefore the results of the language policy were very spotty.

In addition, the journal *La Educación Moderna* launched an attack on the language policies. One Puerto Rican teacher complained in the journal that the instruction given by American teachers and that given by Puerto Rican teachers in English was having a disastrous effect on the students. The newspaper *La Democracia* editorialized that nothing could be done about the situation until the Department of Education was controlled by Puerto Ricans.[88]

While the language issue continued as a source of friction between Puerto Rican teachers and U.S. authorities, the next commissioner of education, Edwin Dexter (1907–1912), tried to increase the significance of patriotic celebrations in the schools. Although the Fourth of July was not a date in the school calendar, Dexter dressed a group of schoolchildren in red, white, and blue and marched them through the streets of San Juan under a large patriotic banner. Also, Dexter considered the celebration of Washington's and Lincoln's birthdays and Memorial Day to be an important means of teaching English because all events were conducted in that language. Adding to these activities, Dexter introduced military drill into the schools.[89]

In 1912, Puerto Rican teachers organized the Teachers Association to resist the policies of the commissioner of education. A teacher's magazine, *La Educación Moderna*, heralded the event: "Day after day we have worked for the defense of our mother tongue and at last today we see our efforts and publicity crowned with success by the meeting of the Teachers Association."[90]

During the term of Commissioner of Education Edward Bainter (1912–1915), the Teachers Association started a campaign to resume teaching in Spanish. The organization passed a resolution calling for the teaching of arithmetic in Spanish. In 1914, the organization requested that Spanish be used as the language of instruction in the first four years of grammar school with English being taught as a subject.

In 1915, resistance to the imposition of English sparked a student strike at Central High School in San Juan. The strike occurred when a student, Francisco Grovas, was expelled for collecting signatures to support legislation that would require Spanish to be the language of instruction in the Puerto Rican schools. This caused Commissioner of Education Paul Miller (1915–1921) to proclaim that any student participating in a strike would be suspended from school indefinitely.[91]

The strike at Central High School reflected a rising wave of nationalism and calls for independence. By 1915, Puerto Ricans were divided over the issues of independence and U.S. citizenship. The debate over citizenship was sparked by the introduction of legislation into the U.S. Congress to grant citizenship to Puerto Ricans. Speaking before the House of Representatives in 1916, Puerto Rican leader Muñoz Rivera requested that Congress let the Puerto Rican people vote as to whether or not they wanted U.S. citizenship. Ignoring this plea, Congress passed the Jones Act, which was signed into law by President Woodrow Wilson in 1917.[92]

The Jones Act obligated Puerto Ricans to serve in the U.S. military while denying them the right to vote in national elections. Similarly to the Native Americans in Indian Territory, who were granted citizenship in 1901 as part of the process of abolishing tribal governments, many Puerto Ricans did not welcome this grant of citizenship.

Despite the imposition of citizenship, students and other groups continued to campaign for independence. One dramatic outbreak of nationalism occurred in 1921 during graduation exercises at Central High School when a student orator waved a Puerto Rican flag and cheered for independence. Commissioner Miller responded by ordering the removal of "the enemy flag" from the auditorium. Students responded that if the flag were removed they would leave the ceremonies.[93]

Tensions increased in the 1920s with the appointment of the first Puerto Rican to the post of commissioner of education. As commissioner from 1921 to 1930, Juan B. Huyke imposed Americanization programs with a vengeance. Appointed because he favored assimilation to the United States in contrast to independence, Huyke called the independence movement unfortunate and stated his belief that it would shortly disappear from the minds of Puerto Ricans. He considered Puerto Rico to be "as much a part of the United States as is Ohio or Kentucky."[94] Defining Americanism as patriotism "He that does not want to be a teacher of Americanism would do well not to follow me in my work."[95]

Committed to Americanization, Huyke resisted attempts to return to Spanish as the language of instruction. Huyke required that all high school seniors pass an oral English examination before they could graduate. School newspapers written in Spanish were banned. English became the required language at teachers' meetings, and teachers were asked to use English in informal discussion with students. School rankings were based on students' performance on English examinations. Student clubs were established to promote the speaking of English. Teachers who were unable or unwilling to use English in instruction were asked to resign.[96]

Similarly to his predecessors, Huyke linked the ability to speak English to the learning of patriotism. This was exemplified by the creation of a School Society for the Promotion and Study of English Language for all eighth-, ninth-, and tenth-graders in Puerto Rico. Supporting patriotism and English, society members were required to wear small American flags in their buttonholes and speak only English. For the celebration of American Education Week in 1921, Huyke recommended as a topic for a speech "American Patriotism—wear the flag in your heart as well as in your buttonhole."[97] In the monthly publication of the Department of Education of Puerto Rico, *Puerto Rico School Review*, Huyke summarized the attitudes about the role of the school in the colonialization of Puerto Rico: "Our schools are agencies of Americanism. They must implant the spirit of America within the hearts of our children."[98]

Resistance to Huyke's policies came from the Puerto Rican Teachers Association and students. The Teachers Association protested the lack of material on Puerto Rico in the curriculum and the failure to recognize Puerto Rican holidays and celebrations in the school calendar. They complained about the fact that out of the seventeen high school principals in Puerto Rico, only five were Puerto Rican. And, of course, they protested the English-language policies. Protest marches by university students were branded by Huyke as "aggressively anti-American" and students were expelled. Professors were warned to stop their support of the protests or resign their positions.[99]

Increasing protests over school policies eventually resulted in the Padin Reform of 1934, which restricted English-language instruction to high school and made content instruction in the upper elementary grades in Spanish. But textbooks remained in English. During the 1930s, President Franklin D. Roosevelt urged a bilingual policy with a stress on the importance of learning English. In Roosevelt's words, "But bilingualism will be achieved . . . only if the teaching of English . . . is entered into at once with vigor, purposefulness, and devotion, and with the understanding that English is the official language of our country.''[100]

In 1946, the Teachers Association was able to pressure the Puerto Rican legislature into passing a bill requiring that instruction in public schools be given in Spanish. President Harry Truman vetoed the bill. From the perspective of many Puerto Ricans, the language issue could be resolved only by giving the island more political autonomy. On October 30, 1950, President Truman signed the Puerto Rican Commonwealth Bill, which provided for a plebiscite to determine whether Puerto Rico should remain a colony or become a commonwealth. In 1951, Puerto Ricans voted for commonwealth status despite protests by those urging Puerto Rican independence. Commonwealth status gave Puerto Ricans greater control of their school systems, and consequently Spanish was restored in the schools.[101]

CONCLUSION: METHODS OF DECULTURALIZATION AND AMERICANIZATION

The educational policies following the conquest of Native American tribes, Mexico, and Puerto Rico provide a guide to methods of deculturalization and Americanization. In many instances, these methods were not very effective. Despite the educational programs of the schools, all three groups maintained their cultural traditions. In part, the limited success of deculturalization might have been a result of resistance to these programs. Native Americans and Puerto Ricans struggled to pass on their traditions and languages to their children and resisted attempts at deculturalization.

It could be that deculturalization programs are self-defeating. When parents and children resist attempts to strip them of their cultural heritage, they might also resist other educational programs. In other words, deculturalization programs might turn both parents and children against all educational programs offered by schools. For instance, consider the dramatic decline in literacy among the Five Civilized Tribes after their schools were taken over by the state of Oklahoma. Under tribal leadership, the schools reflected native culture. Under the control of the state of Oklahoma, deculturalization programs resulted in a dramatic decline in literacy among the next generation of Indians.

On the other hand, Americanization programs might have been more effective. Native Americans and Puerto Ricans served in the military and fought in World War II and later wars. On the other hand, many Native Americans and Puerto Ricans still cling to nationalist sentiments. At the time of my father's death, the Great Seal of the Choctaw Nation—which is now on the Oklahoma state flag—hung prominently on his living room wall. Born in 1903 in Indian Territory, my father at birth had citizenship in both the Choctaw Nation and the United States. Symbolically, this dual citizenship represents the divided loyalty still felt by many Native Americans and Puerto Ricans.

Therefore, the educational programs for deculturalization and Americanization had mixed results. In general, deculturalization programs have used the following educational methods.

Methods of Deculturalization

1. Segregation and isolation.
2. Forced change of language.
3. Content of curriculum reflects culture of dominant group.
4. Content of textbooks reflects culture of dominant group.
5. Dominated groups are not allowed to express their culture and religion.
6. Use of teachers from dominant group.

The first method of deculturalization, segregation and isolation, was used with Native Americans. Indians sent to Indian Territory were isolated in the hope that missionary teachers would "civilize" them in one generation. Indian children sent to boarding schools were isolated from the cultural traditions of their tribe as they were "civilized."

Forcing a dominated group to abandon its own language is an important part of deculturalization. Culture and values are embedded in language. Educational policymakers in the nineteenth and early twentieth centuries believed that substituting English for Native American languages and for Spanish was the key to deculturalization. But the language issue created the greatest resistance by dominated groups. In fact, the attempt to change the languages of the groups under consideration may have been the major cause of the limited effectiveness of deculturalization programs.

Using a curriculum and textbooks that reflect the culture of the dominating group was a typical practice of state school systems and federal educational programs. Native Americans and Puerto Ricans attended schools where the curriculum and textbooks reflected the culture of the dominant white culture of the United States. The hope was that these groups would emulate the culture reflected in the curriculum and textbooks.

In boarding schools, Native American children were not allowed to practice their cultural traditions or their native religions. In Puerto Rican schools, the cultural bias of the curriculum and textbooks left little room for Puerto Rican culture. In both cases, the result might have been to alienate the children from the school.

And last, the use of teachers who represented the dominant culture was considered an important means of deculturalization. Missionary teachers and teachers from the Bureau of Indian Affairs were supposed to represent "civilization" to Native American children. Teachers brought from the United States to Puerto Rico were supposed to be cultural role models.

All of these methods of deculturalization were accompanied by programs of Americanization. Basically, these programs were designed to create emotional attachments to symbols of the U.S. government. In the case of Native Americans and Puerto Ricans, Americanization programs were supposed to change the loyalty of these people from their tribal governments or, in the case of Puerto Rico, from their nationalistic traditions to the U.S. government. The basic program for creating these emotional attachments included:

1. Flag ceremonies (one of the first methods used with Indian tribes and Puerto Ricans)
2. Replacement of local heroes with U.S. national heroes in school celebrations
3. Patriotic celebrations
4. Focusing the study of history on the traditions of the dominant white culture of the United States

The attempts at deculturalization were eventually countered in the 1950s and 1960s by the great civil rights movement. The strong resistance to deculturalization during the great civil rights movement highlights the difficulty, if not impossibility, of deculturalization through educational institutions.

NOTES

1. "George Washington to James Duane, September 7, 1783" in Francis Paul Prucha, ed., *Documents of United States Indian Policy*, 2nd ed. (Lincoln: University of Nebraska Press, 1990), pp. 1–2.
2. Samuel J. Wells, "Federal Indian Policy: From Accommodation to Removal" in Carolyn Keller Reeves, ed., *The Choctaw before Removal* (Jackson: University of Mississippi Press, 1985), pp. 195–197.
3. Jon Reyhner and Jeanne Eder, *A History of Indian Education* (Billings, Mont.: Eastern Montana College, 1989).
4. "Civilization Fund Act, March 3, 1819," in Prucha, *Documents of United States Indian Policy*, p. 33.
5. Angie Debo, *The Rise and Fall of the Choctaw Republic* (Norman: University of Oklahoma Press, 1961), p. 42.
6. Ibid., p. 43.
7. Ibid., pp. 43–44.
8. Ibid., p. 44.
9. Quoted in Evelyn C. Adams, *American Indian: Government Schools and Economic Progress* (New York: Arno Press, 1971), p. 36.
10. "Thomas McKenney to J. Evarts" in *Documents and Proceedings Relating to the Formation and Progress of a Board in the City of New York for the Emigration, Preservation, and Improvement of the Aborigines of America July 22, 1829* (New York: Vanderpool & Cole, Printers, 1829), p. 18.
11. Ibid., p. 14.
12. "Address" in *Documents and Proceedings*, pp. 28–39.
13. Ibid., p. 41.
14. Ibid., p. 43.
15. R. Halliburton, Jr., "Chief Greenwood Leflore and His Malmaison Plantation" in Samuel J. Wells and Roseanna Tubby, eds., *After Removal: The*

Choctaw in Mississippi (Jackson: University of Mississippi Press, 1986), p. 58.

16. Debo, *Rise and Fall*, p. 55.
17. "Cherokee Nation v. Georgia 1831" in Prucha, *Documents of United States Indian Policy*, p. 58.
18. Ibid., p. 59.
19. Grant Foreman, *Indian Removal: The Emigration of the Five Civilized Tribes of Indians* (Norman: University of Oklahoma Press, 1972), pp. 19–56, 229–294.
20. The best book about the deprivations of the Indians during the removal process is Foreman, *Indian Removal*.
21. Halliburton, "Chief Greenwood Leflore," p. 58.
22. Quoted in Debo, *Rise and Fall*, p. 180.
23. Ibid., pp. 60–61, 101–109.
24. Ibid., p. 62.
25. Ibid., p. 238.
26. Ibid., p. 222.
27. Ibid., pp. 240–242.
28. Foreman, *Indian Removal*, pp. 229–314.
29. Reyhner and Eder, *History of Indian Education*, p. 31.
30. Ibid., p. 34.
31. *Indian Education: A National Tragedy—A National Challenge 1969 Report of the Committee on Labor and Public Welfare U.S. Senate, 91st Congress, 1st Session* (Washington, D.C.: U.S. Government Printing Office, 1969), p. 25.
32. Ibid.
33. Ibid.
34. "Report of the Dawes Commission, November 20, 1894" in Prucha, *Documents of United States Indian Policy*, p. 191.
35. Ibid., p. 194.
36. Ibid., p. 195.
37. Quoted in Debo, *Rise and Fall*, pp. 285–286.
38. "Indian Citizenship Act June 2, 1924" in *Documents of United States Indian Policy*, p. 218.
39. *Indian Education: A National Tragedy*, p. 25.
40. Ibid., p. 29.
41. "Indian Commissioner Mix on Reservation Policy," in Ibid., p. 92.
42. "Indian Commissioner Lea on Reservation Policy," in Ibid., p. 82.
43. Ibid.
44. "Indian Commissioner Mix," p. 95.
45. Reyhner and Eder, *History of Indian Education*, p. 38.
46. Ibid., p. 39.
47. "Report of the Indian Peace Commission January 7, 1868" in *Documents of United States Indian Policy*, p. 107.
48. Reyhner and Eder, *History of Indian Education*, pp. 79–80.
49. James D. Anderson, *The Education of Blacks in the South 1860–1935* (Chapel Hill: University of North Carolina Press, 1988), p. 34.

50. Quoted in Reyhner and Eder, *History of Indian Education*, p. 80.
51. Ibid.
52. "Indian Commissioner Price on Civilizing Indians October 24, 1881" in *Documents of United States Indian Policy*, p. 155.
53. Quoted in Reyhner and Eder, *History of Indian Education*, p. 81.
54. Ibid.
55. Ibid., p. 86.
56. "Use of English in the Indian Schools September 21, 1887" in *Documents of United States Indian Policy*, p. 175.
57. "Inculcation of Patriotism in Indian Schools December 10, 1889" in *Documents of United States Indian Policy*, p. 181.
58. Ibid., pp. 180–181.
59. Ibid., p. 181.
60. General T. J. Morgan, "Indian Education," Bureau of Education, Bulletin No. 1, 1889 (Washington, D.C.: U.S. Government Printing Office, 1890), p. 4.
61. Ibid., p. 5.
62. Ibid., p. 9.
63. Ibid., p. 12.
64. Ibid.
65. Ibid., p. 16.
66. Ibid., p. 17.
67. Margaret Szasz, *Education and the American Indian: The Road to Self-Determination, 1928–1973* (Albuquerque: University of New Mexico Press, 1974), p. 19.
68. Quoted in ibid., p. 22.
69. Lewis Meriam, *The Problem of Indian Administration* (Baltimore: The Johns Hopkins Press, 1928).
70. Ibid., p. 346.
71. Ibid.
72. Ibid., pp. 346–403.
73. See Szasz *Education and the American Indian*, pp. 37–106; Reyhner and Eder, *History of Indian Education*, pp. 102–109.
74. Ivan Musicant, *The Banana Wars: A History of United States Military Intervention in Latin America from the Spanish-American War to the Invasion of Panama* (New York: Macmillan, 1990), p. 2.
75. As quoted in Aida Negron De Montilla, *Americanization in Puerto Rico and the Public-School System 1900–1930* (Rio Piedras: Editorial Edil, 1971), p. 62.
76. Ibid., pp. 6–79.
77. Negron De Montilla, pp. XI–XII.
78. Ibid., p. 37.
79. Ibid., pp. 35–36.
80. Ibid., p. 36.
81. Ibid., p. 51.
82. Ibid., pp. 47–48.

83. Ibid., p. 49.
84. Ibid., p. 48.
85. Ibid., p. 58.
86. Ibid., pp. 63–64.
87. Ibid., p. 71.
88. Ibid., pp. 105–106.
89. Ibid., pp. 121–123.
90. Ibid., p. 135.
91. Ibid., pp. 140, 170.
92. Ibid., p. 163.
93. Ibid., pp. 172–173.
94. Ibid., p. 178.
95. Ibid., p. 180.
96. Ibid., pp. 260–261.
97. Ibid., p. 183.
98. Ibid., p. 181.
99. Ibid., p. 187.
100. Catherine Walsh, *Pedagogy and the Struggle for Voice: Issues of Language, Power, and Schooling for Puerto Ricans* (New York: Bergin & Garvey, 1991), p. 20.
101. Ibid., pp. 20–21.

CHAPTER 7

Education and Segregation: Asians, African Americans, and Mexican Americans

Segregation in public schools in the United States was directly related to maintaining an inexpensive source of labor. For instance, in the late nineteenth and early twentieth centuries Japanese, Chinese, and Korean immigrants worked at low wages on the railroads, in factories, and on farms, while at the same time their children were being segregated from European American children in California schools. In the South, segregated education was justified as providing an inexpensive source of workers for industrialization and the maintenance of agriculture. With the great immigration of inexpensive Mexican farm workers to the United States in the early twentieth century, segregated schools were created to ensure that their children would also become farm workers.

This relationship between segregated schools and economic exploitation was based on several factors. One was that segregated schools provided an inferior education compared to schools serving European Americans. This made it difficult for economically exploited groups to use education as a means of economic advancement. The second factor was that many segregated students were taught to believe they were inferior, and, therefore, many accepted an inferior economic status. Of course, there were many segregated students who resisted the brand of inferiority and, later in life, fought school segregation. The third factor was that segregated education tended to emphasize the inculcation of habits and values required for menial employment. And, last, segregated education tended to reinforce many European Americans' belief in their own superiority to Asians, African Americans, and Mexican Americans. This feeling of superiority helped to justify the economic exploitation. Believing in their own racial superiority, many European Americans could continue to pay low wages and to accept the squalid living conditions of these groups without feeling a sense of guilt. European

Americans could say to themselves, "This is the only way these people know how to live. They should be grateful for what I give them."

ASIANS

The treatment of Asians in California in the late nineteenth and early twentieth centuries provides the best example of the relationship between segregated education and economic exploitation. At one time or another, Japanese, Chinese, Mexican Americans, Indians, and blacks were forced into segregated schools. In each case, a relationship existed between segregation and some form of economic exploitation. For instance, by the 1880s, 75,000 Chinese were living in California and working on railroads and farms and in factories. According to Charles Wollenberg in *All Deliberate Speed: Segregation and Exclusion in California Schools, 1855–1975*, as California's largest nonwhite minority, the Chinese were "regarded as 'yellow barbarians' and potential economic rivals."[1] Whites were concerned about keeping Chinese workers confined to particular occupations and, at the same time, feared that the Chinese might move into other occupations and take jobs away from them. During the 1870s a movement arose in San Francisco, which had the largest concentration of Chinese, to deport all Chinese from the country.

Reflecting the general anti-Chinese sentiment, the San Francisco school system refused to admit Chinese children. In 1884, when a Chinese couple tried to enroll their child in the school system, the San Francisco Board of Supervisors responded with the following statement: "Guard well the doors of our public schools that they [the Chinese] do not enter. For however stern it might sound, it is but the enforcement of the law of self-preservation, the inculcation of the doctrine of true humanity and an integral part of the iron rule of right by which we hope presently to prove that we can justly and practically defend ourselves from this invasion of Mongolian barbarism."[2]

The California courts ruled in favor of admitting the Chinese child, but the San Francisco school district responded to the court decision by asking the California assembly to allow separate facilities for "Mongolians." During the same period, the San Francisco schools rushed to establish a separate school for the Chinese. Sacramento followed San Francisco's example and established a segregated school for Chinese in 1893. The rigid policy of segregation broke down by 1905, when the board of education had to let Chinese youths attend the regular city high school.

The establishment of segregated schools for Japanese children in California caused an international incident. Japanese immigrants did not enter California in large numbers until the early twentieth century. Although California employers saw Japan as a cheap source of Asian labor, antioriental hysteria greeted the Japanese, as it had the Chinese. While native whites worried about job competition and the resulting low wages, Japanese entered the country with expectations of becoming permanent citizens and with high educational standards. The Japanese, like the Chinese, were caught between American companies wanting to use cheap oriental labor and American workers who did not want the competition. In either case, arguments of racial inferiority and "yellow menace" were used to justify either exclusion from the United States or economic exploitation.

The resolution that segregated Japanese children in the San Francisco school district stated that segregation was "not only for the purpose of relieving the congestion at present prevailing in our schools, but also for the higher end that our children should not be placed in any position where their youthful impression may be affected by association with pupils of the 'Mongolian race.'"[3] In 1906 the San Francisco Board of Education established a separate school for Chinese, Japanese, and Korean children. A majority of the Japanese parents boycotted the school, and the Japanese community then tried to win public opinion in Japan to its side as a means of forcing favorable action from the U.S. government. Editorials began to appear in Tokyo newspapers claiming that segregation was an insult to the nation, and in October 1906 the American ambassador to Japan warned the U.S. government of the developing international situation. The result was that President Theodore Roosevelt threatened the San Francisco school system with federal action if segregation did not end. However, the involvement of the federal government did not end segregation for the Japanese in other areas; they continued to face various exclusionary laws and legal actions through World War II.

The history of education in California provides an example of the varieties of segregation that have occurred in public schools, whereas the history of education in the South offers an example of the most extensive form of school segregation resulting from economic exploitation, racial prejudice, and the desire by majority whites to create a permanent underclass of workers.

AFRICAN AMERICANS

The history of African-American education highlights both the denial of education as a means of continuing economic exploitation and the use of segregated education as a means of assuring an inexpensive source of labor. In addition, the history of African-American education illustrates attempts by dominated groups to acquire an education that would help in gaining economic and political equality.

Before the Civil War, slaves in the South were denied an education by law. Resistance to educating slaves was rooted in a fear that education would give them access to ideas that would cause rebellions and threaten the very institution of slavery. Between 1800 and 1835, southern states passed laws making it a crime to educate slaves. Of course, education can provide training either for obedience or for the seizing of political and economic power. According to Henry Bullock in *A History of Negro Education in the South: From 1619 to the Present*, there was a "general fear that literacy would expose the slaves to abolition literature."[4]

Some slaves were given a limited education as a means of increasing their economic worth. In some cases this meant training them for skill occupations. Owners sent slaves away for training as carpenters and mechanics, and many of these educated slaves provided services essential to the operation of plantations. However, this education was narrowly limited to training for particular occupations and did not offer any instruction that might threaten the order of the slave society. Of course, any education nonetheless has the potential to provide tools that lead to demands for freedom.

Despite laws forbidding educating slaves, by the outbreak of the Civil War in 1860, 5 percent of slaves had learned how to read, sometimes literally at the risk of life or limb. Individual slaves would sneak books and teach themselves while hiding from their masters. Sometimes self-taught slaves would pass on their skills and knowledge to other slaves. In *The Education of Blacks in the South 1860–1935,* James Anderson quotes the former slave Ferebe Rogers about the educational work of her ex-slave husband during the years of slavery: "On his dyin' bed he said he been de death o' many a nigger 'cause he taught so many to read and write."[5]

In the North prior to the Civil War, freed slaves encountered strong resistance to their attempts to gain an education that was equal to that of European Americans. This struggle is illustrated by Stanley Schultz in *The Culture Factory: Boston Public Schools, 1789–1860.*[6] It was in the context of a newly developing urban educational system that African Americans in Boston began their struggle for a quality education. Boston organized the first comprehensive system of urban schools after the passage of the Massachusetts Education Act of 1789. This law required towns to provide elementary schools for six months of the year and grammar schools in communities with more than two hundred families. According to Schultz, the black population in Boston in 1790 was 766 out of a total population of 18,038. At the beginning of the nineteenth century no law or tradition excluded black children from the public schools. Some were enrolled in public schools, while others attended private ones.[7]

However, very few black children actually attended school. The low attendance rate, Schultz argues, was a result of the poor economic conditions of the black population and the hostile reception given black children in the public schools. Partly as a result of prejudice in the existing public schools, in 1798 a group of black parents asked the city for a separate system of schools for their children. The Boston School Committee rejected this request with the reasoning that if it provided separate schools for blacks, it would also need to provide separate schools for other ethnic groups. The black parents then requested and received financial help from white philanthropists and opened a school that survived for only a few months. In 1800 a group of thirty-six blacks again asked the Boston School Committee to establish a separate school for their children. Again the answer was no. Two years later the black community opened another separate private school.[8]

Finally, the school committee accepted the idea of supporting a segregated school. In 1806, a permanent black school was established with funds from white philanthropists and the school committee. In 1812, the school committee voted permanent funds for the school and established direct control over it.[9]

The Boston School Committee's decision created a complex situation. First, the committee supported and controlled a segregated school, although no law in existence required segregation. In theory at least, black children were free to attend public schools other than the one established for them. Second, the black community supported the segregated school as an alternative to the prejudice existing in the other schools. And last, the school was supported by a combination of private and public monies. Private contributions to the school became a major factor when Abiel Smith died in 1815 and left the entire income for his shares in New England turnpikes and bridges and from the U.S. bonds he had owned to the support of black schools. The school committee assumed trusteeship of the estate, which meant that it controlled both the school and the majority of private funds supporting the school.[10]

By the 1820s some people in the black community began to question their earlier request for segregated schools. One major problem was the quality of teachers hired by the school committee for the black schools. Other complaints began to appear as well. In 1833 a subcommittee issued a report on the conditions of the schools. The major conclusion of this report was that black schools were inferior to other schools in both the quality of education and the physical conditions. The report argued that "a classroom better than a basement room in the African Church could be found. After all, Black parents paid taxes which helped to support white schools. They deserved a more equal return on their share of the city's income."[11]

The most important conclusion of the report was that segregated education was not benefiting either race. The school committee did not deal with this repudiation of the original reasons for establishing segregated schools, concentrating instead on building a new school. This activity did not, however, answer the concerns of the black community, which was beginning to believe that only integrated education would provide equal educational opportunity.

Concerns about the quality of education in segregated schools were heightened by the writings of a local black abolitionist, David Walker. Walker was born in North Carolina in 1879 of a free mother and a slave. According to North Carolina law, Walker was thus born free. He moved to Boston in the early 1820s and became a contributor to and local agent for the nation's first black newspaper, *Freedom's Journal*, published in New York.

Walker argued in his writings that four principal factors were responsible for the poor situation of blacks in the nation. Slavery, the use of religion to justify slavery and prejudice, and the African colonization movement designed to send free blacks back to Africa were three of the factors. The fourth factor was education. Walker argued that white Americans were trying to keep black Americans from receiving any significant amount of education. As proof, he cited the laws in the South that made it illegal to educate slaves. In the North, according to Walker, the inferior education blacks received in the schools was designed to keep them at a low level of education: "Most of the coloured people when they speak of the education of one among us who can write a neat hand, and who perhaps knows nothing but to scribble and puff pretty fair on a small scrap of paper, immaterial whether his words are grammatical, or spell correctly, or not; if it only looks beautiful, they say he has as good an education as any white man."[12]

After studying the conditions of the Boston schools, Walker reached the conclusion that segregated education in the city was a conspiracy by whites to keep blacks in a state of ignorance. Walker claimed that the school committee forbade the teaching of grammar to black children. Although this was not true, Schultz does point out that black children received a poorer education than white children did and that the New Testament was the basic text used in black schools.

Walker's arguments added fuel to the fire. Demands by the black community for integrated education intensified, and for almost two decades more the black community struggled with the school committee to end segregated education. Part of the issue was the loss of control of black schools by the black community. This was one of the problems causing the lines between public and private education to be unclear. Originally, the black community had sought segregated schools as an alternative to the prejudice black children experienced in existing schools and had been able to exercise control over its early private educational endeavors. Over the years, however, the school committee had gained complete control, so that any complaints the black community had about its schools had be to resolved by the committee. The black community might have found segregated schools satisfactory if it could have exercised control over its schools and if it had received the same financial support as the white community did for its schools.

In 1849 the protests over segregated schools finally reached the Massachusetts Supreme Judicial Court when Benjamin Roberts sued the city for excluding his five-year-old daughter from the schools. In this particular case, his daughter had to pass five white primary schools before reaching the black school, so Roberts tried to enroll her in one of the closer white schools. He lost the case on a decision by the court that the school system had provided equal schools for black children. This was one of the first separate-but-equal rulings in American judicial history.

The issue of segregation in Massachusetts schools was finally resolved in 1855, when the governor signed into law a requirement that no child be denied admission to a public school on the basis of race or religious opinions. In September of that year the Boston public schools were integrated without any violent hostilities.

The story of African-American education in Boston illustrates the struggle to gain a quality education. A similar struggle occurred in the South after the Civil War as former slaves attempted to advance themselves in the economy of the South. But the struggle in the South met strong resistance from whites who wanted either to deny education to all blacks or to limit education in segregated schools to preparation for the lowest rungs of the southern economy.

SEGREGATED SCHOOLS IN THE SOUTH

After the Civil War, former slaves struggled to establish schools, and in many cases they were assisted by teachers from the North. In Reconstruction conventions following the Civil War, blacks fought for the establishment of state school systems. In the words of W. E. B. DuBois, "Public education for all at public expense was, in the South, a Negro idea."[13] In the early 1870s, black children were enrolled in school systems at percentages higher than those for whites, but by the 1800s this situation began to change as whites exerted greater control over the state political systems and passed discriminatory laws. By the 1890s, as a consequence of sharecropping and other forms of economic exploitation and discriminatory laws, many blacks found themselves living in conditions that were close to slavery.

During and immediately after the Civil War, former slaves took the initiative in establishing schools. The first of these efforts was made by a black teacher, Mary Peake, who organized a school in 1861 at Fortress Monroe, Virginia.[14] The role of freed slaves in establishing schools was recorded by the first national superintendent of schools for the Freedman's Bureau, John W. Alvord. Based on his travels through the South in 1865, Alvord's first general report for the Freedman's Bureau in 1866 described former slaves' efforts at self-education. Everywhere in the South, he found ex-slaves studying elementary textbooks. He describes a school in North Carolina organized by two freed slaves with 150 students in attendance. An illustration in *Harper's Weekly* in 1866 showed a large classroom full of freed slaves and a black teacher in the Zion School in Charleston, South Carolina. The administrators and teachers of the school were all African Americans, and the average daily attendance was 720 students.[15]

By the middle of the 1870s differing ideas on education were struggling for dominance in the South. Because of their need for children as farm laborers, planters resisted most attempts to expand educational opportunities for black children. On the other hand, former slaves were struggling for an education that would improve their economic and political positions in southern society. In contrast to these two positions, there were groups of white southerners who believed that the expansion of education was necessary for the industrialization of the South. These white southerners supported schooling for African Americans as a means of teaching them industrial habits and keeping them on the lowest rungs of southern society. For those southerners who supported industrialization, blacks represented a potential source of cheap labor who, unlike northern workers, would not form unions.

Within the black community in the 1890s, divisions developed over how to pursue the struggle for education. This division is most often associated with two major black leaders—Booker T. Washington and W. E. B. Du Bois.

Washington accepted compromise with white demands and the establishment of segregated industrial education; De Bois maintained that no compromise with white demands should be made and that black education should be concerned with educating the future leaders of the black community. To a certain extent, however, the preceding statements oversimplify both their positions. Their hopes for schooling were interwoven with their hopes for their race, the realities of southern society, and their political strategies. In the history of schooling, Washington is most often associated with the establishment of segregated schools, whereas Du Bois was instrumental in the founding in 1909 of the National Association for the Advancement of Colored People (NAACP), which has led the successful struggle against school segregation in the United States.

The speech that most clearly outlined the southern compromise and the role of blacks in the developing industrial order was given by Washington at the International Exposition in Atlanta in 1895. Washington tried to convince his all-white audience of the economic value of African Americans to the new industrial South by beginning his speech with a story about a ship lost at sea whose crew was dying of thirst. The ship encountered a friendly vessel, which signaled for the crew to cast down their buckets in the surrounding water. After receiving the signal four times, the captain finally cast down his bucket to find fresh water from the mouth of the Amazon River. This, Washington told his audience, was what the South needed to do to build its industrial might: cast down its buckets and use black workers. Washington continued his speech by outlining the advantages of black workers for the South. Of primary importance was that the South would not need to rely on foreign workers. "To those of the white race," Washington exclaimed, "who look to the incoming of those of foreign birth and strange tongue and habits for the prosperity of the South, were I permitted I would repeat what I say to my own race, 'Cast down your bucket where you are.'"[16] Washington continued by extolling the virtues of black workers and their faithfulness during the years of slavery. He claimed that blacks could show a devotion that no foreign workers would ever display and called for an interlacing of the interests of black and white southerners.

Then, in one sentence that would become famous in both the South and the North, Washington presented the compromise he saw as necessary for winning white southerners to his argument: "In all things that are purely social we can be as separate as the fingers, yet one as the hand in all things essential to mutual progress." Here was the great compromise—acceptance by blacks of social segregation for the opportunity to participate in the new industrial order of the South. As Washington explained in the conclusion of his speech, he believed that once the economic value of blacks had been established, social acceptance would follow. "No race," he argued, "that has anything to contribute to the markets of the world is long in any degree ostracized." In Washington's mind, "the opportunity to earn a dollar in a factory just now is worth infinitely more than the opportunity to spend a dollar in an opera-house."[17]

Washington believed that African Americans would be able to prove themselves economically by receiving the right form of education. Before that speech, Washington had received recognition throughout the South for his establishment of the Tuskegee Institute. The Tuskegee idea originated in Washington's educational experiences at the Hampton Institute. Washington had been born to slavery and after the Civil War attended Hampton, which had been established by General Samuel Armstrong, whose missionary parents had organized an industrial school for natives in Hawaii.

Washington was strongly influenced by General Armstrong's vision of the role of education in adjusting former slaves to their new place in the southern social order. Armstrong believed that the purpose of education was adjusting African Americans to a subordinate position in southern society. He also believed that blacks should be denied the right to vote and that they should be segregated, in short that they should not be granted the same civil equality as whites.[18]

As part of the process of adjusting African Americans to permanent subordination in society, Armstrong argued that the primary purpose of educating African Americans was the development of "proper" work habits and moral behavior. This argument was based on a belief that "savages" were mentally capable but lacked a developed morality. Historian Anderson quotes Armstrong: "Most savage people are not like 'dumb driven cattle;' yet their life is little better than that of brutes because the moral nature is dormant."[19]

As Armstrong envisioned the process, Hampton graduates would become teachers who would educate the rest of the African-American population in the moral and work habits taught at Hampton. Taking its cue from attitudes regarding the education of Native Americans, Hampton was to be the agent for civilizing freed slaves. With Hampton teachers spread across the South, Armstrong believed, African Americans would be "civilized" and brought to accept their subordinate place in society.

The key to the civilizing process advocated by Armstrong and incorporated into Hampton's educational program was hard work. Armstrong believed that hard work was the first principle of civilized life. It was through hard work, according to Armstrong, that people learned the right moral habits. He believed that African Americans needed to be educated in the value of hard work if they were to assume their proper place in southern society.

Consequently, the curriculum at Hampton emphasized hard manual labor as part of teacher training. In addition, Armstrong believed that classical studies only developed vanity in black students and should not be part of the teacher training curriculum for black students. Therefore, rather than studying the traditional liberal arts, Hampton male students worked in a sawmill, on the school farm, as dishwashers and busboys in the kitchen, as waiters in the dining room, and as houseboys in the living quarters. Hampton female students sewed, cooked, scrubbed, and plowed fields on the school's farm.[20]

Of course, according to many southern whites, the type of work performed by Hampton students was the type of work all African Americans should perform. In the context of Armstrong's larger philosophy, the occupational training at Hampton reflected the subordinated roles African Americans would play in the new economic order. By learning the habits and moral values associated with doing these tasks, Hampton graduates, Armstrong believed, would teach other African Americans the habits and values required to make these tasks lifelong occupations.

Therefore, when General Armstrong and Booker T. Washington used the term "industrial education," they primarily meant the development of good work and moral habits as opposed to learning a particular vocational skill. For instance, historian James Anderson in his history of black education reproduces photographs of prospective female teachers at Hampton plowing and tilling a farm field. Obviously, these future teachers were not being educated to be farmers. But they were learning the work habits that Armstrong wanted his graduates to pass on to their students.

It was Armstrong's philosophy of education that guided Washington in the establishment of Tuskegee. Washington scorned the traditional forms of education brought south by northern teachers. He felt that traditional education was useless and left the student with false promises for a better life. In his autobiography, *Up from Slavery,* he tells the story of mothers who taught their daughters the skill of laundering. "Later," Washington says, "these girls entered the public schools and remained there perhaps six or eight years. When the public-school course was finally finished, they wanted more costly dresses, more costly hats and shoes." Washington summarizes the effects of a traditional public school education: "In a word, while their wants had been increased, their ability to supply their wants had not been increased in the same degree. On the other hand, their six or eight years of book education had weaned them away from the occupation of their mothers." In another situation, Washington criticizes a young man fresh out of high school who "sitting down in a one-room cabin, with grease on his clothing, filth all round him, and weeds in the yard and garden, engaged in studying French grammar."[21] Washington's message was heard throughout the North and South. It was particularly welcomed by those trying to organize the southern school system. The idea of segregated industrial education that stressed proper moral and work habits also received support from major educational conferences and private foundations. It was this support that made segregated education a permanent fixture in southern states until the 1950s and 1960s. In Henry Bulluck's words:

> The industrial curriculum to which many Negro children were exposed, supposedly designed to meet their needs, reflected the life that accompanied their status at that time. They had always farmed. The curriculum aimed to make them better farmers. Negro women had a virtual monopoly on laundering, and Negro men had [worked] largely as mechanics. The industrial curriculum was designed to change this only in so far that Negroes were trained to perform these services better.[22]

As James Anderson tells the story, segregated industrial education as the model for black southern education received support from both southern industrialists and northern philanthropists. For instance, steel magnate and philanthropist Andrew Carnegie gave the first major endowment to Tuskegee because he believed that educating black workers was necessary to maintain the United States' position in the world economy. Carnegie stressed the importance of maintaining proper work habits among the black southern population. In comparing the black work force in South Africa to that in the United States, Carnegie wrote, "We should be in the position in which South Africa is today but for the faithful, placable, peaceful, industrious, lovable colored man; for industriousness and peaceful he is compared with any other body of colored men on the earth."[23]

Indeed, southern industrialists welcomed the idea of segregated industrial education because it promised cheap labor and the avoidance of labor unions. One of the things Washington argued in his Atlanta speech was that the industrialists in the South had to choose between immigrant labor and black labor, and that the problem with immigrant laborers was that they formed labor unions. For instance, southern railroad magnate and Tuskegee supporter William H. Baldwin, Jr., argued that for the South to compete in international markets it would have to reject the high wages demanded by white labor unions and rely upon the labor of African Americans.[24]

Despite the fact that some southern industrialists and educational leaders supported segregated industrial education for blacks, actual government financial support declined rapidly after the 1870s. In his classic study *The Education of the Negro in the American Social Order*, Horace Mann Bond collected information on school expenditures from a variety of southern states. For instance, a table illustrating spending in Alabama shows that in 1875–1876 expenditure per capita was actually higher for blacks than for whites. This relationship existed until the 1880s. By 1900 the situation had so far reversed that the per capita expenditure for whites was four to five times higher than that for blacks. Bond found similar statistics throughout the South.[25]

Therefore, by 1900, African Americans in the South faced a segregated public school system that made few expenditures for the education of their children. The major resistance to increased school expenditures for black students came from planters, who considered education a direct threat to their use of black children as agricultural laborers. As I will discuss in the next section of this chapter, the concerns of southern planters were similar to those expressed by farmers in Texas and California regarding the education of the children of Mexican-American farm workers. Southern planters foresaw the possibility that schooling would cause African Americans either to leave menial agricultural work or to demand higher wages. In addition, planters depended on the use of child labor and, consequently, opposed compulsory education laws. Some planters forced schools to begin their school year in December, after the harvest. In addition, they fought efforts to increase state financing of schools.[26]

By 1875, according to James Anderson, the planters' efforts resulted in halting the expansion of schools for African Americans in the South. Between 1880 and 1900, Anderson writes, "the number of black children of school age increased 25 percent, but the proportion attending public school fell."[27]

Consequently, by 1900 the dream of education for African Americans in the South was shattered as the majority of public expenditures went to support white segregated schools and large numbers of black children were kept working in the fields. In 1900, 49.3 percent of African-American boys between the ages of ten and fifteen were working, while 30.6 percent of the girls in the same age category were employed. The majority of these children, 404,225 out of 516,276, were employed as unskilled farm labor.[28] In the end, the segregation of public schools resulted in the denial of education to large numbers of black children.

RESISTING SEGREGATION

The major resistance to school segregation came from the NAACP, which has struggled for integrated education from its founding in 1909 to the present time. W. E. B. Du Bois, a founder of the NAACP and editor of the magazine *Crisis*, became the leading opponent of Washington's southern compromise. Du Bois was born in Great Barrington, Massachusetts, earned a Ph.D. at Harvard, studied in Europe, and became one of America's leading sociologists. However, like most blacks in the late nineteenth and early twentieth centuries, he had difficulty finding a university teaching position. Some of his most famous studies were done while he taught at Atlanta University; *The Philadelphia Negro: A Social Study* was written with the support of the University of Pennsylvania but without an appointment to its faculty. One of his major public statements attacking the arguments of Booker T. Washington is *The Souls of Black Folk*, published in 1903.

In *The Souls of Black Folk*, Du Bois claims that Washington's compromise resulted in disaster for black people in the south: "Mr. Washington distinctly asks that black people give up, at least for the present, three things—First, political power, Second, insistence on civil rights, Third, higher education of Negro youth,—and concentrate all their energies on industrial education, the accumulation of wealth, and the conciliation of the South." The result, Du Bois argues, was the "disfranchisement of the Negro," the "legal creation of a distinct status of civil inferiority for the Negro," and the "steady withdrawal of aid from institutions for the higher education of the Negro."[29]

Du Bois envisioned a different type of education for blacks, one that would provide leaders to protect the social and political rights of the black community and make the black population aware of the necessity for constant struggle. He also wanted to develop an Afro-American culture that would blend the African background of former slaves with American culture. In part, this was to be accomplished by the education of black leaders.

What Du Bois hoped to accomplish through education is well described in his story of John. In the story, a southern black community raises money to send John to the North for an education. The community's hope is that he will return to teach in the local black school. After receiving his education in the North, John does return to teach. He goes to the house of the local white judge and, after making the mistake of knocking at the front door instead of the rear door, is ushered into the judge's dining room. The judge greets John with his philosophy of education: "In this country the Negro must remain subordinate, and can never expect to be [the] equal of white men." The judge describes two different ways in which blacks might be educated in the South. The first, which the judge favors, is to "teach the darkies to be faithful servants and laborers as your fathers were." The second way, the one supported by Du Bois and most feared by white Southerners, is described by the judge as putting "fool ideas of rising and equality into these folks' heads, and . . . [making] them discontent and unhappy."[30]

What was most important for Du Bois was to educate blacks to be discontented with their social position in the South. Unhappiness—not happiness—was his goal. Du Bois describes John, before his meeting with the judge, standing on a bluff with his younger sister and looking out over an expanse of water:

> Long they stood together, peering over the gray unresting water.
> "John," she said, "does it make everyone—unhappy when they study and learn lots of things?"
> He paused and smiled, "I am afraid it does," he said.
> "And, John, are you glad you studied?"
> "Yes," came the answer, slowly and positively.
> She watched the flickering lights upon the sea, and said thoughtfully, "I wish I was unhappy,—and—and," putting both arms about his neck, "I think I am, a little, John."[31]

Du Bois's ideal of an educated black citizenry struggling against oppression became a reality even within a segregated society and educational system. Certainly, the combination of segregated education and the lack of funding of schools serving African Americans hindered the social and economic advancement of blacks. It took more than a half century for the NAACP to win its battle against segregated education in the South. During that period of legal struggle, segregated schooling was a major factor in condemning blacks to an inferior status in society.

THE SECOND CRUSADE

The first crusade for black education in the South took place during and after the Civil War, while the second crusade occurred from 1910 to the 1930s. The second crusade involved the expansion of segregated schools for African-American children paid for by a combination of personal donations of time and money by black citizens, donations by private foundations, and government money. It was through these efforts that by the 1930s common schools were finally established for black children. What is important to note about the second crusade is that black southern citizens had to pay directly from their own income to build schools for their children, while, at the same time, they paid local and state taxes, which went primarily to support white segregated schools.

One of the important private foundations supporting the second crusade was the Anna T. Jeanes Fund. The Jeanes Fund paid up to 84 percent of the salaries for teacher supervisors and elementary industrial education. The majority of the time of the Jeanes teachers, as they were popularly called, was spent in raising money for the construction of schoolhouses and the purchase of equipment. According to James Anderson, between 1913 and 1928 Jeanes teachers raised approximately $5 million. In this respect, Jeanes teachers played an important role in helping African Americans raise the money for black education that was being denied them by state and local governments dominated by white citizens.

The Julius Rosenwald Fund, named after its founder, Julius Rosenwald, the president of Sears, Roebuck and Company, led the campaign in building schools for black children. The first Rosenwald school was completed in 1914 in Lee County, Alabama. The construction of this one-teacher schoolhouse cost $942. Indicative of how the costs were being shared, impoverished local black residents donated $282 in cash and free labor. Local white citizens gave $360. The Rosenwald Fund gave $300.[32]

Between the building of the first Rosenwald school in 1914 and 1932, 4,977 rural black schools were constructed that could accommodate 663,615 students. The total expenditure for building these schools in 883 counties in fifteen southern states was $28,408,520. James Anderson provides the following breakdown for the financial sources of this massive building program: Rosenwald Fund—15.36 percent; rural black people—16.64 percent; white donations—4.27 percent; and public tax funds—63.73 percent.[33]

According to historian Anderson, the public tax funds used to build the Rosenwald schools came primarily from black citizens. In fact, he argues that the majority of school taxes collected from black citizens went to the support of schools for white children. Anderson writes, "During the period 1900 to 1920, every southern state sharply increased its tax appropriations for building schoolhouses, but virtually none of this money went for black schools."[34] Booker T. Washington complained, "The money [taxes] is actually being taken from the colored people and given to white schools."[35]

In reality, because of the source of funding, many of these public black schools were owned by local black citizens. One analysis of school expenditures in the South concluded that blacks owned 43.9 percent, or 1,816, of a total of 4,137 schools. Many of the schools identified as being in the public domain were paid for through the voluntary contributions of black citizens.[36]

Therefore, the second crusade for black education in the South involved a great deal of self-help from the black community. It was through the struggles and sacrifices of the black community that by the 1930s African-American children in the South had a viable system of education. Of course, the major drawback to this system was segregation and unequal financial support by state and local governments. Overcoming segregated education would require, as I will discuss in Chapter 13, another period of activism by black citizens in the 1940s, 1950s, and 1960s.

MEXICAN AMERICANS

As the Five Civilized Tribes were being removed from the southeast to Indian Territory, U.S. settlers in northern Mexico were waging a war that culminated in 1837 with the Mexican government accepting the loss of part of its land and recognizing the newly created independent nation of Texas. Many citizens believed in the manifest destiny of the United States to extend its territorial reach from the Atlantic to the Pacific. While the Five Civilized Tribes located on land just north of Texas organized their governments, the U.S. settlers controlling the nation of Texas formed a government and debated whether or not they should remain independent or allow themselves to be annexed by the United States.

The idea of manifest destiny contained sentiments of superiority that would haunt the relationships between "Anglos" and Mexican Americans. In the minds of some white citizens, the United States was destined to rule the continent because of its Protestant culture and republican form of government. In the minds of these citizens, Mexico stood for Catholicism and feudalism. In addition, the Mexican peoples were of Spanish and Indian descent. Many of the Northern European people who settled the United States looked with scorn on the people of Spain and also, as I described in the previous chapter, wanted to rid the continent of Indian cultures.

The attitude of racial, religious, and cultural superiority which provided motivation for the United States to take over Mexican land and which fueled hostilities between the two countries throughout the nineteenth and early twentieth centuries was reflected in the treatment both of the Mexicans who remained after the U.S. conquest and of later Mexican immigrants. Segregated schools, housing, and discrimination in employment became the Mexican-American heritage. Reflecting the attitude of the Mexican government toward the anti-Mexican feelings in the United States, the president of Mexico, General Porfirio Díaz, was reported to have remarked in the latter part of the nineteenth century: "Poor Mexico! So far from God and so close to the United States."[37]

The evolution of discriminatory attitudes and practices toward Mexican Americans occurred in two stages. The first stage involved the treatment of the Mexicans who remained after conquest. The second stage occurred in the late nineteenth and early twentieth centuries, when U.S. farmers encouraged the immigration of farm laborers from Mexico and political and economic conditions in Mexico caused many Mexicans to seek residence in the United States.

In *Anglos and Mexicans in the Making of Texas, 1836–1986*, David Monejano argues that a victor has the choice of either eradicating the conquered population or assimilating them to its own culture.[38] Both things occurred after the United States completed its conquest of Mexican territory. After the Texas government agreed in 1849 to be annexed to the United States, President James Polk sent a small army to the Rio Grande under the leadership of General Zachary Taylor to protect the Texas border. Taylor's presence sparked a military reaction by Mexico which resulted in the U.S. Congress declaring war on May 13, 1846. Later in the century, former President Ulysses S. Grant wrote about the declaration of war and the subsequent military campaigns as "the most unjust war ever waged by a stronger against a weaker nation . . . an instance of a republic following the bad example of European monarchies."[39]

The United States did not confine its military actions to Texas. Within one month after the congressional declaration of war, President Polk ordered a war party under the command of Colonel Stephen Kearny to travel from Fort Leavenworth, Kansas, and occupy the Mexican city of Santa Fe, New Mexico. After entering Mexican territory, Kearny issues a proclamation that "The undersigned enters New Mexico with a large military force for the purpose of seeking union with, and ameliorating the condition of the inhabitants."[40] Kearny promised, without authorization from President Polk, that all Mexican citizens in New Mexico would be given U.S. citizenship, and he convinced many local officials to take an oath of allegiance to the U.S. government. The Mexican governor fled Santa Fe, and Kearny entered the city on August 17, 1846, without encountering any significant resistance.

One month later, on September 25, 1846, Kearny left Santa Fe for the Mexican province of California. A year before Kearny's departure from Santa Fe, a small military force under the command of Captain John C. Fremont had arrived at Fort Sutter, California. Aided by the presence of Fremont's force, a group of American settlers declared—similarly to events that occurred in Texas on July 4, 1846—that California was the Bear Flag Republic. The leaders of the new nation created a flag featuring a single star and a crude grizzly. At the celebration for the new republic, Fremont announced that he planned to conquer all of California. Military historian General John Eisenhower writes regarding Fremont's proclamation: "This pronouncement was remarkable because it was made at a time when Fremont had no knowledge of whether or not Mexico and the United States were at war."[41] On December 12, 1846, Kearny arrived in San Diego to complete the final conquest of California.

The expanding war eventually led to the occupation of Mexico City by U.S. military forces on September 14, 1847. The war ended on May 30, 1848, when the Mexican congress ratified the Treaty of Guadalupe Hidalgo, which ceded to the United States Mexican territory from Texas to California. One of the important provisions of the treaty was that all Mexican citizens remaining in the conquered territories would be granted U.S. citizenship.

Besides creating a lasting resentment toward and suspicion of the U.S. government by the Mexican government, the acquisition of Mexican lands presented the problem of what to do with the conquered Mexican citizens.

The bestowal of U.S. citizenship on former Mexican citizens did not resolve the problem of the negative feelings of Anglos toward those who could not be called Mexican Americans.

As I previously mentioned, David Montejano identified two patterns in the treatment of the conquered Mexican Americans in Texas in the nineteenth century. The pattern of extermination and ejection occurred in central and southeastern Texas with the uprooting of entire communities. Mexican Americans were physically driven out of Austin in 1853 and 1855 and out of the counties of Matagorda and Colorado in 1856. A large part of the Mexican population of San Antonio was driven out by 1856.[42]

The ejection of the Mexican population was justified by racist attitudes. Frederick Law Olmsted recorded many of these attitudes while traveling through Texas in 1855 and 1856 as a reporter for *The New York Times*. Olmsted overheard newly arrived settlers complaining that Mexicans "think themselves as good as white men" and that they were "vermin to be exterminated."[43] He found a general feeling among Anglo settlers that "white folks and Mexicans" were never meant to live together. He quoted a newspaper article published in Matagorda county that began: "The people of Matagorda county have held a meeting and ordered every Mexican to leave the county."[44] The article went on to justify the expulsion by calling the Mexicans in the area "lower class" and contending that the Mexicans were likely to take black women as wives and steal horses.

One of the important consequences of this negative action against Mexicans was to make it easier for American settlers to gain land in the area. In this case, racism served as a justification for economic exploitation. While the Mexican population declined in these areas after the war, it rose again during the early twentieth century. The same racist arguments were then used to justify paying Mexican farm workers lower wages and establishing a segregated system of schooling.

In the southern part of Texas, a different pattern developed for the treatment of the conquered Mexican population. Montejano calls this pattern a peace structure which involved two major components. One component involved bringing the Mexicans under the authority of Anglos in political matters, while the other involved an accommodation between the Mexican and Anglo elites.[45] This accommodation served as a basis for the creation of large cattle ranches. Anglo cattle raisers gained access to large tracts of land either by marrying into elite Mexican families or through direct purchase. In this accommodation, Anglos made a distinction between what they identified as the Castilian elite, who controlled vast amounts of land, and the average Mexican, who was identified as a peon. In the minds of Anglos, this division involved a racial distinction. Peons, as compared to the Castilian elite, were considered racially inferior because of their Indian ancestry. The Castilian elite were accepted because of their supposed lack of Indian heritage and Spanish ancestry. In other words, Anglos held the same racist attitudes toward peons as they did toward Indians.[46]

These racist attitudes permeated the life of the cattle ranches established in southern Texas during what is referred to as the cowboy era in Texas history. By the 1860s, the railroad was extended to Kansas. This made it possible to raise cattle in Texas, drive them on foot to Kansas, and then ship them east. Between 1866 and 1880 more than 4 million cattle were marched north out of Texas. The term "cowboy" was coined to describe the workers who took the herds north. The cattle drives would follow either the Chisholm Trail or the Western Trail north from southern Texas through Indian territory to Kansas.[47] The taxes levied on the drives by the Choctaws in Indian territory helped to support their school system.

On the cattle ranches of the cowboy era, the authority structure created a division between Mexican and Anglo cowboys. The Anglo cowboys, of course, exercised authority over the Mexican ones. In addition, facilities were segregated. Anglo cowboys ate in the ranch dining room and refused to eat with the Mexicans; Mexican cowboys camped with the herds and consumed their rations at their campsites.[48] This segregation established a pattern for later forms of segregation.

Similar to the treatment of the Indians, a major concern of the conquered Mexican population was the mandate that English was to be spoken in the schools. In 1856, two years after the Texas legislature established public schools, a law was passed requiring the teaching of English as a subject. In 1870, at the height of the cowboy era, the Texas legislature passed a school law requiring English to be the language of instruction in all public schools.[49] The same attempt to eradicate Spanish occurred in the conquered territory of California. The California Bureau of Instruction mandated in 1855 that all school classes be conducted in English. In *The Decline of the Californios: A Social History of the Spanish-Speaking California 1846–1890*, Leonard Pitt writes about the English-only requirement in public schools: "This linguistic purism went hand in hand with the nativist sentiments expressed in that year's legislature, including the suspension of the publication of state laws in Spanish."[50]

In general, Mexican Americans in the last half of the nineteenth century tried to escape the anti-Mexican attitudes of public school authorities by attending either Catholic schools or nonsectarian private schools. In California, some members of the Mexican community were interested in providing a bilingual education for their children. They wanted their children to improve their ability to read and write Spanish and become acquainted with the cultural traditions of Mexico and Spain, while at the same time learning to speak English. In some places, such as Santa Barbara, California, local Mexican leaders were able to bypass the state requirement on teaching in English and were able to maintain a bilingual public school. But in most places bilingual instruction could be had only through schools operated by the Catholic church.[51]

In Texas, a bilingual education could be had in parochial schools and, in south Texas, in private schools established by the Mexican community. These private Mexican schools tried to maintain both the Spanish language and

Mexican culture. The three major purposes of these Mexican schools were to impart Mexican ideals, teach Mexican traditions and history, and maintain racial pride among the students.[52] Because of the language issue, Mexican-American students were discouraged by local school authorities from attending the first public school opened in El Paso in 1883. Consequently, Mexican Americans opened their own Mexican Preparatory School in 1887. Similarly to California, some Texas communities did not enforce the English-only rule. The first public school opened in Brownsville in 1875 was attended primarily by Mexican-American children. Since most of these children did not speak or understand English, the English-only rule was not enforced until the fourth grade.[53]

The patterns of discrimination and segregation established in the nineteenth century were accentuated during the great immigration of Mexicans into the United States during the early twentieth century. Between 1900 and 1909, 23,991 Mexicans immigrated to the United States. Between 1910 and 1919 this figure increased dramatically to 173,663, and between 1920 and 1929 the number rose to 487,775.[54]

One of the keys to understanding the continuing patterns of racism and segregation is the fact that the immigration of Mexicans was encouraged by U.S. farmers because Mexicans were an inexpensive source of labor in the booming agricultural regions of Texas and California. By the 1890s, the era of the cowboy was drawing to a close. Railroads had penetrated Texas, making the cattle drives across Indian Territory unnecessary. In addition, because of a variety of economic changes, the cattle industry itself was in a decline. Consequently, many Texans turned to farming. As the twentieth century unfolded, the expansion of the railroad made it possible to ship agricultural goods from California to the East. Similarly to Texans, California farmers needed cheap labor. For some farmers, Mexicans were ideal laborers. As one Texas cotton grower put it: "They are docile and law-biding. They are the sweetest people in this position that I ever saw."[55]

Anglo attitudes about the education of the children of immigrant Mexicans involved two conflicting positions. On the one hand, farmers did not want Mexican children to go to school because school attendance meant that they were not available for farm work. On the other hand, many public officials wanted Mexican children in school so that they could be "Americanized." In addition, many Mexican families were reluctant to send their children to school because of the loss of the children's contribution to the family income.

These conflicting positions represent the two methods by which education can be used as a method of social control. One is to deny a population the knowledge necessary to protect its political and economic rights and to economically advance in society. Farmers wanted to keep Mexican laborers ignorant as a means of assuring a continued inexpensive source of labor. As one Texas farmer stated, "Educating the Mexicans is educating them away from the job, away from the dirt." Reflecting the values of the farmers in his district, one Texas school superintendent explained, "You have doubtless heard that ignorance is bliss; it seems that is so when one has to transplant onions. . . . So you see it is up to the white population to keep the Mexican on his knees in an onion patch or in new ground. This does not mix very well with education."[56] A school principal in Colorado stated, "never try to enforce compulsory attendance laws on the Mexicans. . . . The banks and the company will swear that the labor is needed and that the families need the money."[57]

Therefore, according to Guadalupe San Miguel Jr. in *"Let All of Them Take Heed": Mexican Americans and the Campaign for Educational Equality in Texas, 1910–1981,* one of the most discriminatory acts against the children of Mexicans was the nonenforcement of compulsory school laws.[58] A survey of one Texas county in 1921 found only 30.7 percent of Mexican school-age children in school. In another Texas county in the 1920s, school authorities admitted that they enforced school attendance on Anglo children, but not on Mexican children. San Miguel Jr. quotes one school authority from this period: "The whites come all right except one whose parents don't appreciate education. We don't enforce the attendance on the whites because we would have to on the Mexicans."[59] One school superintendent explained that he always asked the local school board if they wanted the Mexican children in school. Any enforcement of the compulsory education law against the wishes of the school board, he admitted, would probably cost him his job.[60]

Those Mexican children who did attend school faced segregation and an education designed, in a manner similar to the programs applied to Indians, to rid them of their native language and customs. School segregation for Mexican children spread rapidly throughout Texas and California. The typical pattern was for a community with a large Mexican school population to erect a separate school for Mexican children. For instance, in 1891 the Corpus Christi, Texas, school board denied admission of Mexican children to their "Anglo schools" and built a separate school.

In *Chicano Education in the Era of Segregation,* Gilbert Gonzalez finds that the typical attitude in California schools was reflected in the April 1921 minutes of the Ontario, California, Board of Education: "Mr. Hill made the recommendation that the board select two new school sites; one in the southeastern part of the town for a Mexican school; the other near the Central School."[61] Gonzalez reports that a survey conducted in the mid-1930s found that 85 percent of the district investigated in the Southwest were segregated.[62] In *All Deliberate Speed: Segregation and Exclusion in California Schools, 1855–1975,* Charles Wollenberg quotes a California educator writing in 1920: "One of the first demands made from a community in which there is a large Mexican population is for a separate school."[63] A Los Angeles school official admitted that pressure from white citizens resulted in certain neighborhood schools being built to contain the majority of Mexican students.[64]

Besides outright racist attitudes toward Mexican Americans, school segregation was justified by the same argument used to justify isolating southeastern Indians in Indian Territory. Educators argued that the segregation of Mexican children would provide the opportunity to, in Gonzalez's words,

"Americanize the child in a controlled linguistic and cultural environment, and . . . to train Mexicans for occupations considered open to, and appropriate for, them."[65]

Segregation also served the purpose, according to Montejano, of maintaining white supremacy. Anglo and Mexican children both knew that segregation was intended to separate the superior from the inferior. In addition, Mexican schools were in poorer physical condition, the Mexican children used books discarded by Anglo schools, and Mexican teams could not participate in Anglo athletic leagues. The sense of inferiority learned in the segregated educational system was reinforced in adult life by the refusal of Anglo restaurants to serve Mexicans and segregated housing.[66]

Those Mexican children attending segregated schools were put through a deculturalization program. Similarly to that for the Indians who were isolated in Indian Territory and boarding schools, the deculturalization program was designed to strip away Mexican values and culture and replace the use of Spanish with English. The term most frequently used in the early twentieth century for the process of deculturalization was "Americanization." The Americanization process for Mexicans should not be confused with the Americanization programs encountered in schools by children of European immigrants. As Gilbert Gonzalez argues, the Americanization of Mexicans, as opposed to Europeans, took place in segregated school systems. In addition, the assimilation of Mexicans was made difficult by the nature of the rural economy, which locked Mexicans into segregated farm work. Anglos also showed greater disdain for Mexican culture than they did for European cultures.[67]

An important element in the Americanization of Mexican schoolchildren, as it was for Indians, was eliminating the speaking of their native language. Educators argued that learning English was essential to assimilation and the creation of a unified nation. In addition, language was considered related to values and culture. Changing languages, it was assumed, would cause a cultural revolution among Mexican Americans. Typical of this attitude was a Texas school superintendent, who was quoted by Gonzalez as saying that "a Mexican child 'is foreign in his thinking and attitudes' until he learns to 'think and talk in English.'"[68]

In 1918, Texas passed legislation with stricter requirements for the use of English in public schools. The legislation made it a criminal offense to use any language but English in the schools. In addition, the legislation required that all school personnel, including teachers, principals, custodians, and school board members, use only English when conducting school business.[69]

Similarly to their attitudes regarding Indian culture and values, many Anglos believed that Mexican culture and values discouraged the exercise of economic entrepreneurship and cooperation required in an advanced corporate society. As I discussed in the previous section, it was believed by many whites that the communal lifestyle of Indians hindered their advancement in U.S. society. On the other hand, Mexicans were criticized as having a fatalistic acceptance of the human condition, being self-pitying, and being unable to work with others in large organizations. Also, many Anglos felt that Mexicans were too attached to their families and to small organizations such as local clubs.[70]

The attempted deculturalization of Mexicans did not always extend to superficial cultural aspects such as food, music, and dance. Those advocating cultural democracy felt that these cultural traditions could be maintained while attempts were made to socialize Mexican children into an entrepreneurial spirit, or what was called an "achievement concept."[71]

It is again important to stress that most Mexican children did not encounter these deculturalization programs simply because of a combination of lack of enforcement of compulsory education laws and the necessity for children to help support their families. In addition, there were reports of Mexican children dropping out of school because of the anti-Mexican bias of the curriculum. This was particularly true in Texas, where in history instruction stress was placed on the Texas defeat of Mexico.[72]

In addition, many children of migrant farm workers received little opportunity to attend school. In fact, in some areas of California, state laws on school attendance were routinely violated by local school boards to ensure the availability of children for farm work. In 1928, with support from the state, the Fresno County, California, superintendent of school opened a special migratory school. Children attended between 7:30 A.M. and 12:30 P.M. and then joined their parents in the fields. This five-hour school day was in clear violation of state law on the number of hours of attendance, but the California government never enforced this requirement on the migratory schools, and the five-hour day became typical for schools serving migrant children. In some parts of California, migrant children were completely denied an education. In the 1930s, public schools in Ventura County, California, displayed signs reading "No Migratory Children Wanted Here."[73]

Of course, many in the Mexican-American community protested against this denial of education to their children, the existence of school segregation, and the attempts at deculturalization. In 1929, representatives from a variety of Mexican-American organizations met in Corpus Christi, Texas, to form the League of United Latin American Citizens (LULAC). This organization was primarily composed of middle-class Mexican Americans, as opposed to Mexican farm laborers and migratory workers. In fact, membership was restricted to U.S. citizens.[74]

LULAC adopted a code that reflected the desire of middle-class Mexican Americans to integrate the culture of Mexico with that of the United States. The code attempted to balance a respect for U.S. citizenship with a maintenance of cultural traditions. On the one hand, the code asked members to "Respect your citizenship, conserve it; honor your country, maintain its traditions in the minds of your children, incorporate yourself in the culture and civilization." On the other hand, the code told its members to "Love the men of your race, take pride in your origins and keep it immaculate; respect your glorious past and help to vindicate your people."[75]

Clearly, LULAC was committed to a vision of the United States that was multicultural and multilingual. In contrast to the public schools, which were trying to eradicate Mexican culture and the use of Spanish, LULAC favored bilingualism and instruction in the cultural traditions of the United States and Mexico. The LULAC code called upon its members to "Study the past of your people, or the country to which you owe your citizenship; learn to handle with purity the two most essential languages, English and Spanish."[76]

As an organization, LULAC was dedicated to fighting discrimination against Mexican Americans, particularly in the form of school segregation. In fact, one of the founders of LULAC, J. Luz Saenz, argued that discrimination and the lack of equal educational opportunities were hindering integration of Mexicans into U.S. society. In summarizing the position of LULAC, Saenz stated, "As long as they do not educate us with all the guarantees and opportunities for free participation in all . . . activities . . . as long as they wish to raise up on high the standard of SUPREMACY OF RACES ON ACCOUNT OF COLOR . . . so much will they put off our conversion . . . [to] full citizens."[77]

LULAC's first challenge to school segregation occurred in 1928 with the filing of a complaint against the Charlotte, Texas, Independent School District. In this case, a child of unknown racial background adopted by a Mexican family was refused admission to the local Anglo elementary school and was assigned to the Mexican school. Her father argued that because of her unknown racial background she should be put into the Anglo school. The state admitted that the local school district did not have the right to segregate Mexican children. On the other hand, local school officials justified the segregation of Mexican children because they required special instruction in English. After determining that the child spoke fluent English, the state school superintendent ordered the local school district to enroll the student in the Anglo school. While this potentially opened the doors of Anglo schools to Mexican children who spoke fluent English, it did little to end segregation.[78]

LULAC's second case involving school segregation occurred in 1930 when the Del Rio, Texas, Independent School District proposed a bond election to construct and improve school buildings. Included in the proposal were improvements for the Mexican school. Mexican-American parents in the district complained that the proposal continued the practice of segregating their children from other students. The local superintendent defended segregation as necessary because Mexican students had irregular attendance records and special language problems. The court accepted the arguments of local school authorities that segregation was necessary for educational reasons. On the other hand, the court did state that it was unconstitutional to segregate students on the basis of national origin. This decision presented LULAC with the difficult problem of countering the educational justifications used for segregation. At a special 1931 session, LULAC members called for scientific studies of arguments that segregation is necessary for instruction.[79]

While LULAC focused most of their efforts on school segregation, there was a concern about what was perceived to be the anti-Mexican bias of textbooks. In 1939, the state president of LULAC, Ezequiel Salinas, attacked the racism and distortions of Mexicans in history textbooks. Significant changes in the racial content of textbooks did not, however, occur until the full impact of the civil rights movement hit the publishing industry in the 1960s.[80]

While LULAC was struggling to end segregation in Texas, Mexican-American organizations in California were attacking the same problem. By the 1930s, Mexican children were the most segregated group in the state. The California situation was somewhat different from that of Texas, because of a 1935 state law allowing for the segregation of Chinese, Japanese, "Mongolians," and Indians. While Indians born in the United States were exempt from this law, the state did allow segregation of "descendants of the original American Indians of the United States." According to Charles Wollenberg, "In this torturous and indirect fashion, the 1935 law seemed to allow for segregation of Mexican 'Indians,' but not of Mexican 'whites.'"[81]

As I will discuss in Chapter 13, the struggle to end segregation played a major role in the great civil rights movement of the post–World War II period. The efforts of both the NAACP and LULAC finally resulted in the end of legal segregation of African-American and Mexican-American students. While the great civil rights movement brought the end of segregation, it also opened the door to feelings of racial and cultural pride. From World War II to the 1990s, Native Americans, Puerto Ricans, African Americans, and Mexican Americans have demanded that public schools recognize their distinct cultures and incorporate these cultures into curricula and textbooks.

NOTES

1. Charles M. Wollenberg, *All Deliberate Speed: Segregation and Exclusion in California Schools, 1855–1975* (Berkeley: University of California Press, 1976), p. 30.
2. Quoted in ibid., pp. 28–29.
3. Quoted in ibid., p. 53.
4. Henry Allen Bullock, *A History of Negro Education in the South: From 1619 to the Present* (New York: Praeger, 1970), p. 11.
5. James Anderson, *The Education of Blacks in the South 1860–1935* (Chapel Hill: University of North Carolina Press, 1988), p. 17.
6. Stanley Schultz, *The Culture Factory: Boston Public Schools, 1789–1860* (New York: Oxford University Press, 1973).
7. Ibid.
8. Ibid.
9. Ibid.
10. Ibid.
11. Ibid., p. 169.
12. Quoted in ibid., p. 173.
13. Quoted in Anderson, *Education of Blacks*, p. 6.
14. Ibid., p. 7.

15. Ibid., pp. 6–8.
16. Booker T. Washington, "Up from Slavery" in John Hope Franklin, ed., *Three Negro Classics* (New York: Avon Books, 1965), p. 147.
17. Ibid., p. 149.
18. Ibid., p. 36.
19. Anderson, p. 40.
20. Ibid., p. 55.
21. Washington, "Up from Slavery," pp. 77, 94.
22. Bullock, *History of Negro Education*, p. 88.
23. Quoted in Anderson, *Education of Blacks*, p. 91.
24. Ibid., pp. 90–91.
25. Horace Mann Bond, *The Education of the Negro in the American Social Order* (New York: Octagon Books, 1966), p. 153.
26. Ibid., pp. 22–23.
27. Ibid., p. 23.
28. Ibid., p. 149.
29. W. E. B. Du Bois, "The Souls of Black Folk" in Franklin, *Three Negro Classics*, pp. 246–247.
30. Ibid., p. 373.
31. Ibid., p. 372.
32. Ibid., p. 153.
33. Ibid.
34. Anderson, p. 156.
35. Quoted in ibid.
36. Ibid.
37. Quoted in John S. D. Eisenhower's *So Far from God: The U.S. War with Mexico 1846–1848* (New York: Anchor Books, 1989), p. xv.
38. David Montejano, *Anglos and Mexicans in the Making of Texas, 1836–1986* (Austin: University of Texas Press, 1987), p. 25.
39. Eisenhower, *So Far from God*, p. xvii.
40. Ibid., p. 208.
41. Ibid., p. 214.
42. Montejano, *Anglos and Mexicans*, pp. 28–29.
43. Ibid., p. 29.
44. Ibid., p. 28.
45. Ibid., p. 34.
46. Ibid., p. 84.
47. Ibid., pp. 53–56.
48. Ibid., pp. 83–84.
49. Guadalupe San Miguel Jr., *"Let All of Them Take Heed": Mexican Americans and the Campaign for Educational Equality in Texas, 1910–1981* (Austin: University of Texas Press, 1987), pp. 6–7.
50. Leonard Pitt, *The Decline of the Californios: A Social History of the Spanish-Speaking California 1846–1890* (Berkeley: University of California Press, 1968), p. 226.
51. Ibid., pp. 225–226.

52. San Miguel, *"Let All of Them Take Heed,"* p. 10.
53. Ibid., p. 11.
54. Montejano, *Anglos and Mexicans,* p. 180.
55. Quoted in ibid., p. 188.
56. Quoted in ibid., p. 193.
57. Gilbert Gonzalez, *Chicano Education in the Era of Segregation* (Philadelphia: Balch Institute Press, 1990), p. 108.
58. San Miguel, *"Let All of Them Take Heed,"* p. 47.
59. Ibid., pp. 48–49.
60. Ibid., p. 50.
61. Gonzalez, *Chicano Education,* p. 21.
62. Ibid., p. 22.
63. Charles M. Wollenberg, *All Deliberate Speed: Segregation and Exclusion in California Schools, 1855–1975* (Berkeley: University of California Press, 1976), p. 111.
64. Ibid., p. 112.
65. Ibid., p. 22.
66. Montejano, *Anglos and Mexicans,* pp. 230–231.
67. Gonzalez, *Chicano Education,* pp. 35–36.
68. Ibid., p. 41.
69. San Miguel, *"Let All of Them Take Heed,"* p. 33.
70. Gonzalez, *Chicano Education,* pp. 133–134.
71. Ibid., pp. 134–135.
72. Montejano, *Anglos and Mexicans,* p. 231.
73. Gonzalez, *Chicano Education,* p. 105.
74. Mario T. Garcia, *Mexican Americans: Leadership, Ideology, and Identity 1930–1960* (New Haven: Yale University Press, 1989), pp. 25–62.
75. Ibid., p. 30.
76. Ibid.
77. Quoted in San Miguel, *"Let All of Them Take Heed,"* p. 72.
78. Ibid., pp. 76–78.
79. Ibid., pp. 79–80.
80. For a study of changes in the racial composition of textbooks, see Joel Spring, *Images of American Life: A History of Ideological Management in Schools, Movies, Radio, and Television* (Albany: State University of New York Press, 1992), pp. 205–214.
81. Wollenberg, *All Deliberate Speed,* p. 118.

CHAPTER 8

Schooling and the New Corporate Order

In the last two decades of the nineteenth century, American society and the educational system were transformed by the impact of urbanization, industrialization, and immigration. As the concentration of population shifted from rural to urban areas, large factories and business organizations began to dominate the economic system. From a country that had been largely agricultural and centered in rural areas and small towns, there emerged a nation learning to adapt to the complex patterns of living required by urban life, large corporate organizations, and unions. Adding to the complexity of the situation were large numbers of immigrants from southern and eastern Europe who served as inexpensive labor for the new industrial plants and filled the ghettos in expanding urban areas. These new immigrants frightened older immigrant groups and created concern among industrial leaders, who feared that they were bringing in radical ideologies and creating unrest among American labor.

The American educational system changed by taking on broader social and economic functions. In urban areas, schools expanded their social functions by adding school nurses and health programs, introducing showers, providing after-school and community activities, and attaching playgrounds to school buildings. Educators tried to change the school curriculum to solve the perceived social problems caused by the loss of the values of a small-town, rural society. Special Americanization programs were instituted for the new waves of immigrants.

Of profound importance to the future of American education was the decision to organize the school system to improve human capital as a means of economic growth. In fact, the development of human capital as a means of solving problems in the labor market became a major educational goal of the twentieth century. It resulted in the acceptance of vocational education as a legitimate part of the educational system and the establishment of the comprehensive high school designed to provide students with differing curricula to meet their various interests in a complex and specialized society. In the twentieth century, the high school became an institution serving the majority of youths.

Complementing the goal of developing human capital was the evolution of the science of education, an important part of which was the measurement of intelligence, interests, and abilities. It was with tools of measurement that schools attempted objectively to match the student with an educational program and future occupation. Vocational guidance developed at the same time as another means of helping students select a course of study and a future job. Vocational education, the comprehensive high school, the junior high school, and vocational guidance were all viewed as means of adapting the educational system to the new economic order.

Also, the political structure of schooling changed as corporate models of organization became popular. The modern school bureaucracy emerged as educators emulated factories and businesses. As this process occurred, educational administration became professionalized and new concepts of educational control emerged. In addition, teachers modeled their teaching on forms of industrial organization and initiated the first teachers' unions.

As these changes took place, questions were raised about which groups in society were receiving the most educational benefits. Some historians claim that these changes benefited all of society, whereas others argue that corporations attempted to organize the school system to meet their own economic needs. The issue of political power has been of primary importance in this debate.

EXTENDING THE SOCIAL ROLE OF THE SCHOOL

In the late nineteenth century, immigration and industrialization expanded urban areas and created a host of social problems. Crowded ghettos, inadequate urban services, and a population primarily rural in origin contributed to unsanitary living conditions and the spread of disease. Added to these conditions was a belief held by many Americans that a sense of community was being lost with the growth of urban America and that this loss would cause the urban population to suffer alienation, a breakdown in traditional forms of social control, and, as a consequence, increased crime and poverty. A fear also arose that the new immigrants would destroy traditional American values and create a strong following for radical economic and political ideas.

The school was considered a logical institution to prevent these problems by providing social services, teaching new behaviors, and creating a community center. Nurses, health facilities, and showers were added to schools in order to control the spread of disease, and special instructional programs were introduced to educate children about sanitary conditions. Americanization programs were offered as a means of assimilating children of immigrants into American life and preventing the spread of radical ideologies. Playgrounds were attached to schools to provide after-school activities for children that, it was hoped, would reduce juvenile delinquency. To curb the sense of alienation caused by urban living, auditoriums and special facilities for adults were provided by schools to serve as centers for community activities.

All these educational changes expanded the social functions of the school. Of course, ending poverty and crime had been a traditional goal of the school since the early nineteenth century, but common school reformers at that time had seen those goals being achieved through instruction in the classroom. The changes in the late nineteenth century made the school more than a center of instruction by turning it into a major social agency.

John Dewey, the great educational philosopher of the period, explained the new social functions of the school to educators who gathered in 1902 for the annual convention of the National Education Association. He told school people from around the country that education must provide a "means for bringing people and their ideas and beliefs together, in such ways as will lessen friction and instability, and introduce deeper sympathy and wider understanding." Using the schools as social centers, he argued, would morally uplift the quality of urban living by replacing brothels, saloons, and dance halls as centers of recreation. More important, he considered the school to be a potential clearinghouse of ideas that would interpret to the new urban industrial worker the meaning of his or her place in the modern world. Through an exchange of ideas and the establishment of relationships with a variety of people, an understanding of others and the bonds of an interdependent society would develop. The school as social center, Dewey told his audience, "must interpret to [the worker] the intellectual and social meaning of the work in which he is engaged: that is, must reveal its relations to the life and work of the world." For Dewey, therefore, the new role of the school was to serve as an agency providing social services and a community center that would solve the problem of alienation in an urban industrial society.[1]

A major educational movement that combined the expansion of the social role of the school with an emphasis on improving urban living was the movement to establish public kindergartens. Kindergartens had originally served upper-class families, but by the 1880s and 1890s they were considered a primary educational method of dealing with the problems of urban poverty. In a broader context, one could argue that early childhood education, as represented by the kindergarten movement, originated in concerns with urban problems.

The concept of kindergarten as introduced in the United States in the 1860s and 1870s by Carl Schurz and Elizabeth Peabody was almost mystical in nature. The original kindergarten was opened in Germany in 1840 by Friedrich Froebel (1782–1852) as a method of early childhood education that was to lead the child from a world concentrated on self to a society of children. As the name implies, the kindergarten was conceived as a garden of children to be cultivated in the same manner as plants. Like Johann Pestalozzi, Froebel advocated a model maternal teacher whose method "should be passive and protective, not directive and interfering." Froebel believed that the divine spirit existed in all humans and that it was the key to social harmony. By cultivating the garden of children, the kindergarten teacher was to bring forth their divine spirits and create a sense of unity among all humans.[2]

The first public school kindergarten in the United States was opened in St. Louis, Missouri, in 1873 for the specific purpose of dealing with urban poverty: In his excellent history of the St. Louis school system, *The Public and the Schools: Shaping the St. Louis System, 1838–1920,* Selwyn Troen describes how that system's famous superintendent, William Torrey Harris, analyzed the distribution of children in the city according to the locality of "haunts of vice and iniquity" and decided that the only way of saving slum children from corruption was to get them into school at an early age. Harris first requested that the school board lower the minimum age of school attendance. After being refused by the school board, he recommended the establishment of kindergartens as a permanent part of the school system. Harris claimed that kindergartens were necessary because traditional socializing agencies like the family, church, and community had collapsed:

> Living in narrow, filthy alleys, poorly clad and without habits of cleanliness, "the divine sense of shame," which Plato makes to be the foundation of civilization, is very little developed. Self respect is the basis of character and virtue; cleanliness of person and clothing is a sine qua non for its growth in the child. The child who passes his years in the misery of the crowded tenement house or alley, becomes early familiar with all manner of corruption and immorality.[3]

Within this context, the kindergarten was to be a substitute for the habits of living and moral training formerly taught by the family organization that supposedly had been lost in the slums of the new urban areas.

The curriculum established for the kindergarten in the St. Louis school system was intended to redeem the slum child by, in Troen's words, bridging "the 'nurture' of the family with the established program of the district school." A major effort of the kindergarten program was to teach virtues and manners considered necessary for community living. Emphasis was placed on teaching moral habits, cleanliness, politeness, obedience, regularity, and self-control. Thus, the kindergarten was to be not only a substitute for the socialization that supposedly was no longer offered by the family, but also a preparation for the habits required by the school.[4]

This same relationship between urban reform and the kindergarten is found by Marvin Lazerson in his brilliant history of the Boston school system, *Origins of the Urban School: Public Education in Massachusetts, 1870–1915.* According to Lazerson, the first director of Boston's kindergartens, Laura Fisher, saw them as being directly concerned with elevating the home life of the urban poor. In an article published in 1904, she states, "The mere fact that the children of the slums were kept off the streets, and that they were made clean and happy by kind and motherly young women; that the child thus being cared for enabled the mother to go about her work in or outside the home— all this appealed to the heart of America, and America gave freely to make these kindergartens possible."[5]

A major goal of the early kindergarten movement was to teach children habits that would reform the home. In other words, the early kindergarten was viewed as a method of educating the parents, particularly the mother. An early example of this thinking can be seen in Lucy Wheelock's tale "A Lily's Mission," in which two slum children bring a flower home to their dingy apartment. The mother has failed to keep the house clean; the father is out drinking. Overjoyed at seeing the flower, the mother places it on a windowsill, only to discover that dirt prevents any sunlight from shining through the window to the flower. With the window clean, the sunlight reveals the filth of the apartment, which is then quickly cleaned. The mother washes and dresses, and the father, overcome by his new environment upon his return home, vows to give up the bottle.[6]

The concept of parental education introduced by the kindergarten movement extended the role of the school in a new direction that gave the kindergarten a social role far beyond anything originally intended by Froebel. As a new educational institution, the kindergarten was to compensate for the supposed loss of socialization within the slum family, to protect the young child from the influences of the street, to provide preparation for entrance into regular elementary school classes, and to educate the parents, particularly the mother.

These extended social goals resulted in the kindergarten losing its original emphasis on creative play and self-expression. In place of these activities, the kindergarten stressed creating order and discipline in the child's life as compensation for family life and as preparation for school. Lazerson found that as the kindergarten evolved in Massachusetts in the twentieth century, it became less involved in parental education and that, in the end, discipline, order, and protection from the urban environment became its primary objectives.

The play movement, and the resulting changes it led to in the school, was another product of the desire among educational reformers to protect children from the harmful effects of city life and to provide a mechanism for controlling the process of socialization. One major goal of this movement was to reduce juvenile crime by providing parks and playgrounds. This approach to curing urban social problems began with the development of small sandlots for children in the 1880s and reached a high point with the establishment of the Chicago park system in 1904. Between 1885 and 1895, sandlots were constructed in congested areas of Boston, Chicago, Philadelphia, and New York City. These play areas were designed for children under twelve years of age and usually included a kindergarten program. One student of the movement reports that the dominant motive for establishing sandlots was "to keep children off the street and out of mischief and vice."[7]

A major result of the play movement is that the school became responsible for the after-school play of urban children. For instance, in 1895 the chairman of the Advisory Committee on Small Parks of New York City asked the police to indicate on a map the areas of high rates of juvenile crime. After the committee found that all areas with newly founded parks had a decreasing crime rate, it attempted to speed the development of parks by having the city adopt the following law: "Hereafter no schoolhouse shall be constructed in the City of New York without an open-air playground attached to or used in connection with the same."

In addition to protecting children from bad influences in the streets, play was to protect individuals from the nervous strain of urban living. In 1917 Henry S. Curtis, an organizer of the Playground and Recreation Association and former supervisor of the playgrounds of the District of Columbia, summarized the following reasons for the widespread movement to establish playgrounds and parks in the United States. In urban areas, children confined to schools and adults trapped in factories and businesses needed fresh air and the opportunity to exercise their bodies in order to avoid "the rapid increase of insanity and the growing instability of the nervous system." But, according to Curtis, "it has not been these reasons that have weighed most strongly with the people that have promoted the movement." Rather, he stated, the dominant motive and major concern of the leaders of the play movement was the fact that there was "little for the children to do in the cities, and that in this time of idleness the devil has found much for idle hands to do. . . . The home seems to be disappearing, and crime, despite increasingly effective police and probation system, is increasing everywhere."[8]

Like the kindergarten, the playground was to replace the socializing influence of family life supposedly lost in the growth of urban America. In addition to providing recreation and physical activity, the playground was to teach good habits, such as cleanliness, and contribute to the general health of the community. The development of small parks included the construction of elaborate recreational and bathing facilities. For example, in 1898 Boston created a bath department as part of its city administration. This department had control of the city beaches, the floating baths, and the municipal bathhouses. The floating baths were platforms supporting a row of dressing rooms around an open area of water. In 1899 Boston had fourteen floating baths, two swimming pools, and seven shower baths. In New York, floating baths were started in 1876, and by 1899 a total of fifteen had been built. A campaign was waged in New York in the 1890s to increase the number of shower baths available because they were more usable during the winter than the floating baths were.

It was logical that this aspect of the playground movement would also become a school activity. The first reported school bath was a shower opened in a Boston school in 1889. Cremin reports in *The Transformation of the School* that "the teachers of New York, for example, found themselves giving hundreds of baths each week. The syllabi said nothing about baths, and teachers themselves wondered whether bathing was their charge. But there were the children and there were the lice."[9] The addition of the shower room to the public school symbolized the expansion of the school as a social agency.

The playground movement was more than just an attempt to reduce urban crime and supplement the socializing influence of the family. The leaders of the movement believed that directed play was necessary for producing the types of adults required by corporate industry. An important concept in this argument is that of directed play as opposed to free play. The early leaders of the play movement did not want to establish playgrounds and parks where adults and children would come to play without guidance; rather, they believed that the state should interfere and direct play toward social ends. Play movement leaders like Joseph Lee and Henry Curtis wanted organized play to produce future workers who would be cooperative, good citizens. Therefore, playground games and activities were organized to produce a sense of team spirit, habits of cooperation, and a willingness to play by the rules. In other words, play was viewed as another method of social control.[10]

The establishment of summer, or vacation, school was another means of extending the influence of the school over children's lives. Cambridge, Massachusetts, was one of the first reported cities to propose a vacation school, or summer school. In 1872 its school committee reported the need for a vacation school because summer was "a time of idleness, often of crime, with many who are left to roam the streets, with no friendly hand to guide them, save that of the police." The superintendent of the same school district was still asking for a summer school as an inexpensive form of police control when he wrote in his school report in 1897, "The value of these schools consists not so much in what shall be learned during the few weeks they are in session, as in the fact that no boy or girl shall be left with unoccupied time. Idleness is an opportunity for evil-doing. . . . These schools will cost money. Reform schools also cost money."[11]

Summer schools were established in rapid succession in urban areas. Boston established them in 1885; New York, in 1894; Cleveland, in 1897; and Chicago, in 1898. The Chicago vacation schools were considered models. They were opened in the most densely populated parts of the city, and enrollment was limited to a first-come, first-served basis. The principal of the system reported that they were received with such enthusiasm that at "one of the schools it was found necessary to call in the police to remove the parents who crowded the halls of the building, insisting that their children must be accepted." In another area, fifty children were held up on their way to school, and their cards of admission were taken from them."[12]

The school as an expanding social agency also became involved in providing school nurses and lunch programs. Much of this work was the result of the settlement house movement, which sought to reform conditions among the poor. Workers in the settlement house movement campaigned for a broader view of the social functions of the school and were responsible in the late nineteenth and early twentieth centuries for the first citywide lunch program in New York schools, the first school physician (in 1897), and the first experiments in providing school nurses in Chicago.[13]

Kindergartens, playgrounds, showers, lunches, and nurses were recognized as giving broader social meaning and uses to the public school. In a book published in 1910, Clarence A. Perry's Wider Use of the School Plant, the author begins by noting, "The children who went to school back in the eighties skipped out of the school house door at half past three and scampered down the street shouting with glee. . . . Within a couple of decades all this has changed." He found that in 1910 public school buildings were "open not only days but evenings. . . . Children go to them Saturdays as well as Mondays, and in some places the school rooms are not left unvisited even on Sundays."[14]

Another important factor in the wider use of the school was the concern with loss of community. The use of the school as a social center was viewed as one means of reestablishing within an urban context a sense of community that had been lost with the passing of rural and small-town life. It was believed that the neighborhood school could be a means of organizing urban populations into a corporate body of specialized tasks and lifestyles cemented together by common allegiances. An example of this attitude is provided by J. K. Paulding, a New York writer who argued in 1898 that democracy could function only with the existence of a spirit of democratic fraternalism resulting from the unification of individual aspirations into a common way of life. He argued that the school, by opening its doors a little wider and becoming a social center, could bring in neighborhood life and create the necessary spirit of democratic fraternalism. An article by H. E. Scudder in the *Atlantic Monthly* in 1896 suggested that the school could attract more people by improving the beauty of its buildings, attaching a public library, organizing a museum and conservatory, and using its walls as a public art gallery. The author states, "The common schoolhouse is in reality the most obvious center of national unity."[15]

During the 1890s, social centers developed rapidly throughout the country. New York organized its after-school recreational activities into social centers in 1897. The University Settlement in New York organized clubs in twenty-one school buildings for the specific purposes of reducing individual selfishness and promoting a spirit of social cooperation. In Chicago, social centers were established in the fieldhouses of the park system, and neighborhood groups engaged in a variety of activities, including community orchestras and choral clubs. A local women's club in Milwaukee persuaded that city in 1907 to open school buildings for local evening meetings. When the Russell Sage Foundation surveyed the social center movement in 1913, it found that among 788 school superintendents contacted around the country, 330 reported the use of their schools as social centers. By 1920 the movement had spread to 667 school districts.[16]

Changes in school architecture reflected the growing commitment to the concept of the school as social center. One school superintendent complained to his colleagues in 1897 that it was difficult to open schools to adults because in most buildings access to assembly rooms was "gained only by climbing flights of stairs, always with embarrassment and often with risk of accident from fire or other causes." His suggestion, which was incorporated into later school plans, was to construct assembly rooms on the ground floor, with easy access from the street.[17]

Classroom furniture also had to be changed to meet the multiple needs of the school and the adult social center. Demands were made to replace school desks bolted to the floor with flat-top desks that could be rearranged for use in club and recreational activities. By 1910, schools such as Washington Irving High School in New York were being designed specifically to function as social centers. The lobby of the school contained a neighborhood art gallery, and the auditorium provided facilities for neighborhood drama groups. Office space was set aside in the school to accommodate the staffs of local clubs and associations.

One leader of the social center movement, Edward J. Ward, believed that schools could be a means of reforming urban politics by reducing political tensions. Ward advocated the establishment of social centers in schoolhouses as centers for political discussion. He envisioned the day when voting districts would be the same as school districts and the ballot box would be placed in the schoolhouse. When this occurs, he wrote, "the schoolhouse . . . becomes, for all its possible wider uses, the real social center; and the way is clear and the means are at hand for supplying the fundamental and supreme lack in the machinery of democracy." The social center, he believed, was the key to developing political cooperation [18]

As the school social center idea spread throughout the United States, it took on a variety of forms. In Chicago the park fieldhouses served the function of bringing the community together on a social basis, and schoolhouses were used to promote political cooperation. In 1914 the Russell Sage Foundation reported that 142 political meetings had been held in Chicago school buildings during a municipal election. The civic clubs of Los Angeles fought to have polling booths and political meetings in school buildings instead of in "livery stables and small, dingy, out-of-the-way and hard-to-find places." They believed that locating the polling booth in the school would protect it from tampering by corrupt political forces.[19]

The social center was also seen as a means of helping immigrants adjust to urban living. For instance, the Women's Municipal League of Boston worked for the opening of social centers in the local schools as part of its more general civic work to improve the lives of immigrants. The president of the league wrote in 1912 that social centers were opened because "it is our endeavor to make our city a true home for the people, it is not enough that we should merely make it a house. . . . We must also ensure that there shall be within it recreation, enjoyment, and happiness for all."[20]

In one sense, kindergartens, social centers, playgrounds, and the wider use of the school plant were intended to handle the problems created by the new immigrants from southern and eastern Europe and can be considered one aspect of the more general attempt to Americanize immigrants. These new uses of the school were justified as necessary for replacing the declining influence of the family and at the same time were considered necessary as a means of socializing immigrant children to the American way of life.

The term *Americanization* was used to refer to more than just the use of the school as a social agency. It also encompassed classroom instruction designed to teach immigrant children and adults the English language and American customs. As social institutions, American schools in the late nineteenth and early twentieth centuries were faced with massive pressure from immigrant populations. This created major problems in classroom space and instruction. Investigators for the U.S. Senate Immigration Commission in 1908 found that there were more than sixty nationalities in thirty-seven cities and that 58 percent of all students had foreign-born parents. For particular cities, the percentages of students with foreign-born parents were as follows: New York, 72 percent; Chicago, 67 percent; Boston, 64 percent; Cleveland, 60 percent; and San Francisco, 58 percent.[21]

One response of schools to the immigrant population was to offer adult night school classes in English, government, and naturalization. By offering this activity, the schools were serving a direct need, not trying to compensate for the supposed failure of another institution. Adult night school classes further opened the door of the schoolhouse to the community and contributed to the claim that the school was becoming the social center of urban America.

In both the adult courses and the accommodation of immigrant children during regular school hours, a tension existed between the wish to protect immigrant culture and the push for Americanization. There is little doubt that most immigrant groups flocked to the schools, but on their arrival there, they often found a great deal of hostility toward their language and customs. Immigrant children found their names being Anglicized and were frequently told not to speak the language of their parents and to forget their native customs. In these situations, Americanization meant cultural imperialism and the building of a national spirit that was suspicious of foreign countries and ways of living.

One important aspect of Americanization was a fear of radical political ideas. Many national leaders argued that ideas about socialism and communism were being brought to this country by immigrant groups. One hundred percent Americanism came to mean opposition to radical economic and political ideologies. For example, in 1917 Cleveland's superintendent of schools recommended the firing of "any teacher 'whose sympathies are proved to be with our country's enemies' (it was not necessary, he said, to express disloyalty in words, since teachers influenced pupils merely by the convictions and fundamental desires of the . . . heart)."[22]

Therefore, Americanization gave a new meaning to the citizenship training provided by the public schools. Horace Mann had argued that the school should teach a consensus of political and social values. The concept of Americanization changed the political goals of the school to include teaching against radical ideas, particularly socialism and communism. As the social center of the new urban America, the school became a bastion of Americanism and antiradicalism.

One suspects that when educators talked about the collapse of the family and community, they meant either that the style of family and community life was not to their liking or that they wanted the school to take over the social functions of those institutions. Certainly, many immigrant groups maintained strong family structures and community life in urban America, but for those Americans who believed that immigrants were threatening the traditional American way of life, immigrant families and communities were considered to be deviant and in need of change.

Within the context of the preceding argument, the movement to expand the school as a social agency could have had several meanings. It could have meant that traditional institutions were indeed collapsing and the social order of the school needed to expand to replace those institutions. Or it could have meant that the immigrant forms of family and community were unacceptable and the school needed to destroy those forms by taking over their functions. The expanded social role of the school could also have been the result of a desire to exert more rational control over the social order by having government institutions assume greater social functions.

Whatever the reason, by the early twentieth century the school had in fact expanded its functions into areas undreamed of in the early part of the previous century. Kindergartens, playgrounds, school showers, nurses, social centers, and Americanization programs turned the school into a central social agency of urban America. The one theme that ran through all these new school programs was the desire to maintain discipline and order in urban life. Within this framework, the school became a major agency for social control.

THE CHANGING CLASSROOM—
HERBART, DEWEY, AND THORNDIKE

In studying history, one must be careful that statements about what should be are not confused with reality. Nowhere is this more important than in studying the history of classroom practices. Although there is evidence that new theories of instruction advocated in the late nineteenth and early twentieth centuries by the Herbartians, John Dewey, William James, and Edward Thorndike did have an impact on classroom practices, there is no evidence that this impact occurred in any consistent or organized pattern. After closing their classroom doors, teachers still tended to teach using a variety of personal instructional methods. Keeping the preceding caution in mind, in this section we will examine the evolution of classroom practices by discussing the environment of the classroom and new theories of instruction.

In New York City, school architect C. B. J. Snyder designed what would become the standardized classroom plan in the first half of the twentieth century: rows of desks bolted to the floor and facing the blackboard, with "48 permanent desks for grades 1 through 4; 45 desks for grades 5 and 6; and 40 for grades 7 and 8."[23] In his book *How Teachers Taught: Constancy and Change in American Classrooms, 1890–1980,* Larry Cuban estimates that in the period from 1920 to 1940, 79 percent of the desks in secondary schools were also bolted to the floor. Movable furniture was allowed in special classes and in kindergarten, but fixed desks were maintained in large classes to avoid noise and confusion. In more progressive school systems, such as that of Denver, Colorado, only 19 percent of desks in secondary schools were stationary; no figures are available for Denver elementary schools. On the other hand, in

1920 in Washington, D.C., almost two-thirds of elementary school desks were bolted to the floor. By 1929 only 200 desks had been replaced by portable ones, but in 1930 a five-year program was initiated that replaced 7,000 stationary desks. In Washington, D.C., high schools, one-third of desks were bolted to the floor.[24]

The example of these three cities suggests that the majority of classrooms allowed for little student movement. The number of students in a class was another important factor in determining pedagogical method. Small classes allowed for greater experimentation and flexibility, whereas large classes tended to require an emphasis on order and discipline. In other words, large classes often dictated the use of pedagogical methods that exerted control over students.

In New York City around the time of World War I, elementary school sizes averaged about 50 students. By 1930 this figure had declined to 38 students, but this number varied from school to school, with at least 17 percent of elementary classes having 45 or more students. In Denver in 1923, 60 percent of all elementary school classes had 30 to 40 students, 13 percent had more than 40, and 27 percent had fewer than 30. By 1934 the effects of the Depression had increased class sizes: Only 3 percent had fewer than 30 students, 33 percent had more than 40, and 64 percent had between 30 and 40 students. High school classes averaged between 30 and 40 students. Washington, D. C., had a segregated school system, and class size varied with the racial composition of the school. In 1922 the average elementary school class size for whites was 34.3 students, while for blacks it was 37.3. By 1932 these figures had declined to 30.8 whites and 36.1 blacks per classroom. Hidden in these figures is a great deal of variation. In 1927–1928, 29 percent of both black and white elementary classrooms had more than 40 students. Averages are not given for secondary schools.[25]

These statistics on class size and the organization of classrooms suggest that the majority of classroom teachers would have had difficulty adopting pedagogical techniques requiring a great deal of mobile student activity. On the other hand, some classrooms did exist in which such student activity was possible.

An educational approach known as the Herbartian movement was strongest in the United States in the 1880s and 1890s and owed its origins to the work of German psychologist Johann Herbart (1776–1841). The major contribution of the Herbartian movement was the class lesson plan suitable for any type of class size or organization. Undoubtedly, the lesson plan became a fixed feature of American education because it allowed for bureaucratic control over the teacher. More simply stated, the lesson plan became a means by which the school principal or supervisor could quickly check on teacher activity. Also, the lesson plan as it developed reflected a conceptualization of education that placed an emphasis on order and planning. To a certain extent, it fit the requirements of large classes with fixed environments.

Herbartians, of course, believed in more than just lesson plans, but in the final analysis the public school classroom reduced Herbartian ideas to a concern with detailed planning of classroom practices. Charles De Garmo, a leading American exponent of Herbart, argues in a book published in 1895 that Herbart added an essential ingredient to the pedagogy of Johann Pestalozzi. According to De Garmo, Herbart accepted the Pestalozzian ideas of learning through the senses and with objects but thought that Pestalozzian pedagogy lacked a clear idea of how knowledge is assimilated into the mind. In the chapter "What Pestalozzi Left for Herbart to Do," De Garmo states that the Pestalozzian method "does not show how mental assimilation can best take place, or how the resulting acquisition can be made most efficiently to influence the emotional and volitional side of our nature. Perception is . . . the first stage in cognition, but its equally important correlative is apperception, or mental assimilation."[26]

In Herbartian thought, the key to mental assimilation and to the organization of the lesson plan is interest. One could argue that the doctrine of interest set the stage for child-centered education. In the simplest terms, the doctrine of interest states that knowledge is best assimilated if it is of interest to the student. Interests can arise from knowledge or from social contacts. Interests related to knowledge include speculative, empirical, and aesthetic interests; interests arising from contact with others include sympathetic, social, and religious interests.

According to the Herbartians, the best method of instruction is to present material that is related to a previous interest of the student. Therefore, it is important to coordinate subject matter properly and to organize lessons based on the stages of development of student interests. For instance, Herbart argued that the natural interests of the child dictate the teaching of Greek before the teaching of Latin.

The Herbartian lesson plan follows five steps: (1) preparation, (2) presentation, (3) comparison and abstraction, (4) generalization or definition, and (5) application. Preparation involves reminding the student of previous knowledge and interests that relate to the material being presented. Presentation is organized so that the material is related to previous interests and knowledge. Comparison and abstraction show the relationships between the new material and things already known by the students. Generalization attempts to make up a single definition that expresses the central idea of the lesson. Application applies the generalization to some other experiences.

Willard Elsbree states, "Without question, these five simply stated steps exercised more influence on teaching practice in America between 1890 and 1905 than all other psychological discoveries and philosophical creations combined."[27] Although the Herbartian lesson plan underwent significant change over time, the idea of a formally organized daily lesson became a fixed feature of American education. An educational environment of large classes and bolted-down desks was not antithetical to the lesson plan. Daily lesson plans also suited an environment based on hierarchical control, order, and discipline.

In contrast, the pedagogical theories of John Dewey (1859–1952) found little acceptance in the standard American classroom. In fact, when Dewey was organizing his famous Laboratory School at the University of Chicago in 1896, one problem he encountered was finding tables suitable for the work of groups of children, in place of individual desks designed to be permanently fixed to the floor. In practice, Dewey's methods emphasized student interests, student activity, group work, and cooperation—methods premised on the idea that the school had to serve a new social function in a world of increasing urban life and large corporations.

When Dewey founded the Laboratory School, he wanted to develop methods that would demonstrate to the student the social value of knowledge and the interdependence of society. One method Dewey hoped would achieve these objectives was the development of social imagination through cooperative group activities. Dewey defined *social imagination* as "the habit of mentally constructing some actual scene of human interaction, and of consulting that for instruction as to what to do." One of his early educational experiments took place in the 1890s, in a high school ethics class, where Dewey wanted the students to view ethics in relation to real problems as opposed to abstract principles. Dewey presented the students with an actual case of human misery and asked them to use social imagination to work out the problem of charity. Social imagination is the ability to relate isolated ideas to the actual conditions that have given them their original meaning. Dewey argued that this method aided a student in forming "the habit of realizing for himself and in himself the nature of the practical situations in which he will find himself placed."[28]

This method of teaching ethics is based on another important principle. Dewey believed that ideas, values, and social institutions originate in the material circumstances of human life. He rejected the notion that they are of divine origin or reflect some type of ideal. One problem, he thought, is that a belief in ideal forms causes civilization to become trapped by ideas and institutions that are no longer practical. According to Dewey, ideas, values, and institutions should change as the needs of society change. The term *pragmatism,* which is often associated with this school of philosophy, means in its simplest form that humans should adopt those ideas, values, and institutions that best work in a particular social situation.

One can understand why many religious groups in the twentieth century reacted negatively to Dewey's ideas. Most religious groups believe that human action should be guided by the word of God and that legitimate values are of divine origin, whereas Dewey's philosophy relies on the ability of individuals to interpret their own experience instead of relying on the word of God.

Dewey believed it was unnecessary for students to become aware of the relationship between knowledge and social experience and to be given an opportunity to act on ideas. It was his conviction that the product of social imagination is merely information until acted on. When acted on, it becomes judgment. "The child," Dewey stated, "cannot get power of judgment excepting as he is continually exercised in forming and testing judgment." Therefore, as Dewey saw it, the school must avoid the teaching of abstract ideas; rather, it must provide actual conditions out of which ideas grow, and the child must be given an opportunity within the school to test moral and social judgments. In other words, according to Dewey, the school had to become a community of real social relationships.[29]

An often quoted statement by Dewey is that the school is a community with a real social life. Dewey wanted to utilize this community and make it a part of the learning process. He believed that the learning process should be part of an active solution to a social problem because this provides the best basis for helping the student to see the social value of knowledge. For instance, counting was introduced at the Laboratory School by having nursery school children set the table for the midmorning snack. The children quickly learned to count by matching the number of utensils to the number of students.

Dewey, like others of his generation, believed that modern urban industrial life was not providing the social context for teaching children habits of order, industry, and cooperation. He hoped students would learn such habits while working in the school community. In 1899 Dewey explored these issues in "The School and Society," a series of lectures given in response to criticism of the work at the Laboratory School. In the lectures, he stressed that the march of industrialism had destroyed a form of household and community life that had given the child "training in habits of order and of industry, and in the idea of responsibility, of obligation to do something, to produce something, in the world." In the past, he argued, these habits had been learned because most occupations centered around the household. Dewey reminded his audience in industrial Chicago that "those of us who are here today need go back only one, two, or at most three generations to find a time when the household was practically the center . . . [of] all the typical forms of industrial occupation."[30]

It was Dewey's contention that at one time the child experienced and participated in the total industrial process of the community. From these community experiences the child learned moral habits, industry, and social cooperation. "But it is useless to bemoan the departure of the good old days of children's modesty, reverence, and implicit obedience," Dewey stated. The problem was to retain the advantages of the present and at the same time introduce "into the school something representing the other side of life—occupations which exact personal responsibilities and which train the child in relation to the physical realities of life."[31]

The work that went on in the Laboratory School was designed to create social interaction among pupils that would foster efficient learning and good social habits. The activity of the younger members of the school centered around household occupations. Work directed toward a common productive end, Dewey believed, created an atmosphere of community. Children between the ages of four and five were given the responsibility of preparing their own midmorning meals. They discussed their home life and were led to explore marketing, mail service, and other related occupations. The children played at making a dry-goods store that provided them with the opportunity to develop habits of industry, responsibility, and social cooperation. As a requirement of completing their projects, they also learned to read, write, and do arithmetic.

As the children progressed, they were led to ever-widening circles of activity. At age six, the children were introduced to farm activities. They built a farmhouse and barn of blocks and explored the problems of climate and farm production. At age seven, they began to study the historical development of civilization—a theme that persisted throughout the rest of their stay at the Dewey school. Activity was always associated with their studies; for example, the children began their study of history by investigating occupations and engaging in activities such as weaving and building smelters.

The study of history at the Laboratory School reflected Dewey's ideas about social imagination and community. Children were to develop social imagination by learning to relate ideas, inventions, and institutions to the social conditions that gave birth to them. This process was also supposed to make the pupil aware of interdependence within society: "A society is a number of people held together because they are working along common lines, in a common spirit, and with references to common ends."[32] Dewey felt that a community had existed in America's past because the individual had been aware of the total industrial process, and this awareness joined people into a community through a sense of working together.

Dewey believed that modern urban industrial society had destroyed this sense of community and common goals and that the school had to actively foster its growth. The function of social imagination, learned in the cooperative work of the school, was to help students relate their work to the total industrial process and to become aware of sharing common social purposes.

Facing his audience of critics in industrial Chicago in 1899, Dewey stated, "How many of the employed are today mere appendages to the machines which they operate! This . . . is certainly due in large part to the fact that the worker has had no opportunity to develop his imagination and his sympathetic insight as to the social and scientific values found in his work."[33] In 1902 Dewey argued before the National Educational Association that the school should be the center around which a genuine community life is maintained in urban America: "It must interpret to [the worker] the intellectual and social meaning of the work in which he is engaged: that is, must reveal its relations to the life and work of the world."[34]

As other educators translated Dewey's ideas into classroom practice, many of his concerns about social imagination and the historical roots of occupations were lost. For many, Dewey stood for group activity, learning by doing, relating material to the interests of the child, and doing projects. Statements by Dewey such as "the true center of correlation on the school subjects is . . . the child's own social activities" were used to justify a variety of group and social activities within the school. Often these methods placed an emphasis on group conformity that went beyond anything Dewey intended. For instance, Dewey believed that motives and choices grow out of social situations; he did not believe, as many other educators were to argue, that individual motives and goals should conform to the wishes of the group. Dewey wanted to free individual action, not submerge it in the mediocre standard of group consensus.

In 1906 Colin Scott, one popularizer of group activity in the classroom, organized the Social Education Association. The reason Scott wanted to organize classrooms into working groups is that that is how modern society is organized, and thus he considered working groups the most efficient form of social organization. He argued that the traditional classroom atmosphere ran counter to modern social organization and that the classroom should initiate group projects as preparation for entering a society of cooperative groups.

Through the Social Education Association, Scott promoted the use of self-organized group activity in the classroom as a means of preparing students for life in a cooperative society. The association's charter states: "The fundamental purpose of education should be to prepare the child for a useful life of social service as an active and creative member of the social organism." Scott's principle of self-organized group activity was to allow children the opportunity to choose their own goals, organize their own groups, and organize their own work.[35]

One example of this method related by Scott is a class in which the students were asked, "If you had time given to you for something that you enjoy doing, and that you think worthwhile, what should you choose to do?" Three boys immediately decided on printing. They formed a printing group and began publishing material for the class. In other examples given by Scott, history classes were divided into the Senate and the House of Representatives, selected students to be government printers, and studied history as a series of legislative bills and debates.[36]

With the spread of Dewey's work and the activities of the Social Education Association, the idea of socialized classroom activity became popular. Articles in educational journals and books on group classroom activities appeared in large numbers. The topics ranged from socializing arithmetic drills to teaching cooking with self-organized groups. Following the lead of education professors like Michael V. O'Shea at the University of Wisconsin and Irving King at the University of Iowa, courses in social education began to be offered in teacher training programs.

At Teachers College, Columbia University, William Heard Kilpatrick used his classes in educational theory to teach a form of group learning called the *project method*. His article on the method was first printed in 1918 and became so popular and widely used that it went through seven printings by 1922. The heart of the project method is what Kilpatrick called the "socially purposeful act"—an activity directed toward a socially useful end. As an example, Kilpatrick cited the situation of a girl making a dress. The act of making a dress could be considered a project if the girl was motivated by a social purpose and if she actually planned and made the dress. According to Kilpatrick, the purposeful act is the basic unit of the worthy life and democracy: "A man who habitually so regulates his life with reference to worthy social aims meets at once the demands for practical efficiency and of moral responsibility. Such a one presents the ideal of democratic citizenship." Within the classroom, children were prepared for a purposeful life by pursuing projects that grew out of social situations.[37]

Kilpatrick's project method also reflects the tendency in many social education proposals of the 1920s to stress social conformity. He considered development of moral character to be one of the important results of the project method and defined *moral character* as "the disposition to determine one's conduct and attitudes with reference to the welfare of the group." In the classroom, the inculcation of this disposition was a function of group acceptance or rejection: "There are few satisfactions so gratifying and few annoyances so distressing as the approval and disapproval of our comrades. . . . When the teacher merely coerces and the other pupils side with their comrade . . . conformity may be but outward. But when all concerned take part in deciding what is just . . . conformity is not merely outward." According to Kilpatrick, moral character is developed when the individual is conditioned always to respond to the desires of the group.[38]

The project method, group activity, socialized learning, child-centered education, and the educating of social imagination were ideas that received a wide audience in the educational community. In many ways, these methods of instruction seemed suitable for preparing students for a world of highly organized living in cities and corporations. Undoubtedly, most teachers trained in the first half of the twentieth century received some exposure to these methods. The actual use of the methods depended on the teacher, the school district, the number of students in a class, and the environment of the classroom.

Although large classes with bolted-down desks might not have been suitable for socializing methods of instruction, they were ideally organized for the pedagogical methods advocated by William James and Edward Thorndike. James (1842–1910), a leading Harvard philosopher and psychologist, condensed his two-volume work published in 1890, *Principles of Psychology*, into a one-volume text for teachers, *Talks to Teachers on Psychology: And to Students on Some of Life's Ideals,* published in 1899. Thorndike (1874–1949) studied under James at Harvard and incorporated many of James's ideas into his own work. Thorndike can be considered the father of educational psychology. His major work, *Educational Psychology,* published in 1913, set the tone for the field for several decades.

Both James and Thorndike were associated with the development of *stimulus-response,* or behavioral, concepts of learning. In James's classic example of learning in the opening section of *Principles of Psychology,* a baby is pictured reaching for a candle flame, a reflex action caused by the stimulation of the fire. The baby's fingers are burned, and it learns not to reach for the flame. James contends that in any future stimulation by the fire of a candle, the baby's nervous system would respond with memories of pain, inhibiting the original grasping reflex and causing the hand to be withdrawn.[39]

For James, this simple learning situation initiates the development of habits in the baby. James considered the building of habits to be the most important function of education because through controlled development of habit, social order could be maintained: "Habit is thus the enormous fly-wheel of society, its most precious conservative agent. It alone is what keeps us all within bounds of ordinance, and saves the children of fortune from the envious uprisings of the poor. It alone prevents the hardest and most repulsive walks of life from being deserted by those brought up to tread therein."[40]

James extended the concept of habit into the thought process. As he envisioned it, the mind contains a steady stream of consciousness, and when confronted with a choice, the individual selects an action out of that stream of thought. Of course, the individual is conditioned to attend to particular ideas in the stream of consciousness in particular situations. That is, James believed that choices are determined by previous stimulus-response learning. This reasoning about human action was problematic for James because it seems to deny free will. If all actions and choices are determined by previous learning, then there is no free will and no individual responsibility for one's actions. This issue has been a central problem in behaviorism since the time of James's original study. James argued his way out of the dilemma by claiming that individuals have the power to make the effort to attend to particular things in the stream of consciousness.

Although James never advocated specific classroom practices, his psychological theories suggest that correct habits can be built through exercise and drill. Edward Thorndike made these two classroom practices part of his pedagogical theory when he translated stimulus-response learning into what he called *connectionism*. Connectionism refers to the connection, or relationship, between stimulus and response. Thorndike argued that all changes in the human intellect are the result of certain fundamental laws that affect these connections.

What Thorndike called *fundamental laws of change* became his basic methods of instruction. In general, they are mechanical methods that had been traditional classroom practices. In some ways, Thorndike simply justified the traditional by making it sound scientific. For instance, his first fundamental law, the Law of Exercise, states that "other things being equal, the oftener or more emphatically a given response is connected with a certain situation, the more likely it is to be made to that situation in the future." He gives as an example a child responding "six" to the question "How many are four and two?" Supposedly, if the child repeats the answer to the question enough times, they will be permanently connected in the mind. Thorndike states this law more briefly: "Other things being equal, exercise strengthens the bond between situation and response."[41]

Thorndike's second law of learning, the Law of Effect, states: "The greater the satisfyingness of the state of affairs which accompanies or follows a given response to a certain situation, the more likely that response is to be made to that situation in the future." For instance, in the example of the child responding "six" to the question "How many are four and two?" the correct answer would be strengthened if the child were rewarded with candy or a smile.[42]

Thorndike viewed teaching as a science concerned with the control of human behavior: "Using psychological terms, the art of teaching may be defined as the art of giving and withholding stimuli with the result of producing and preventing certain responses." The power of the teacher was in his or her control of the stimuli. Thorndike divided stimuli into two categories: "under direct control" and "under indirect control." Stimuli under direct control include the use of love and tact by gestures, facial expressions, and speech. Stimuli under indirect control are the physical conditions of the school and classroom.[43]

Thorndike's dream was to turn all teaching into a scientific profession in which all educators would be guided by the scientific method and spirit. As scientific professionals, educators would be concerned with controlling the learning of students and with scientific measurement of results. In Thorndike's world, the scientifically constructed test is at the heart of the educational process: "Testing the results of teaching and study is for the teacher what verification of theories is to the scientist. . . . It is the chief means of fitting teaching to the previous experience and individual capacities of pupils."[44]

Like Dewey, Thorndike had a social vision that is directly related to the educational methods he advocated. At the center of his social vision is the concept of tests and measurement. He believed that the ideal social organization is one in which people are scientifically selected for their social roles through testing. According to Thorndike, human classification through tests and measurement would produce a more efficient society by matching individual talents with social needs. This theory made psychologists and schools the major determiners of the distribution of human resources.

Thorndike's social ideals had important implications for the meaning of democracy and equality of opportunity (see Chapter 10). What is important to understand at this point is the central importance of measurement in Thorndike's social philosophy, based on his role in the development of intelligence tests.

Thorndike believed that intelligence is determined by nature and that it can be measured by tests. He defined intelligence as the number of connections the mind can make between stimuli and responses: A "person whose intellect is greater or higher or better than that of another person differs from him in the last analysis in having, not a new sort of physiological process, but simply a larger number of connections of the ordinary sort." This definition of intelligence allows for measurement of the number of connections and, consequently, for the quantification of intelligence.[45]

The idea that intelligence is primarily a product of nature, as opposed to environment, had major implications for social policy. Thorndike stood squarely on the nature side of the nature-nurture debate. Regarding measurement of intelligence, he states, "What is essential to the hypothesis is that by original nature, men differ in respect of the number of connections or associations with ideas which they can form, so that despite identical outside environments, some of them would have many more than others."[46] Psychologists who believed that nature is the primary determiner of intelligence also believed that intelligence can be inherited (see Chapter 9), which usually led to the conclusion that racial differences exist regarding intelligence. For instance, a common belief of the period was that northern Europeans had naturally superior intelligence compared to southern Europeans.

The classroom environment of bolted-down desks and large numbers of students was more conducive to Thorndike's stimulus-response, drill, reward, and measurement methods of instruction than to the types of group activity and socialized forms of instruction advocated by the social educators. One can easily imagine that a teacher trained in both traditions, when faced with a controlled and structured classroom environment, would tend to adopt Thorndike's scientific methods. One also can imagine that, under these conditions, many teachers accepted the doctrines of classroom control as preached by William Bagley in his popular book *Classroom Management*.

Classroom Management became a standard teacher training text during the first quarter of the century and was reprinted thirty times between 1907 and 1927. Bagley believed that the primary role of the school is to build good industrial habits of the type needed on the assembly line. Bagley's ideal teacher is one who would "rigidly 'hew to the line' in all of those initial stages of habit building," and in his ideal school everything is reduced to rigid routine. Bagley states that the expert observer could immediately gauge the efficiency of the teacher by "the manner in which lines pass to and from the room."[47]

Because Bagley could find no arguments against pupils keeping step while walking, he advocates the Lancasterian method of lockstep marches. He also insists that students be given drills in packing their desks in a certain order, in going to assigned places at the blackboard, in leaving the room, and in marching through the cloakroom to collect coats. To reduce the problem of children interrupting class activities, he states that "regular habits should be speedily established with regard to the bodily functions." He recommends that lines of children pass through the lavatories at recess time before they are allowed on the playground. Bagley urges teachers to train their students to give physical attention on command: "In general, the command, Attention! should be stimulus for the habitual adjustment of the body in a certain definite posture." He recommends as the ideal posture "head erect, eyes turned toward the teacher, hands or arms folded (preferably the former), feet flat on the floor, instant cessation of all . . . school work or activity."[48]

Many teachers faced with large classes and wanting to maintain order probably followed Bagley's recommendations. As the most popular system of classroom management, it complemented Thorndike's instructional methods more than those of the social educators. But what teachers actually did in their classrooms demonstrated a great deal of variation. In his analysis of classroom activity in the New York schools between 1920 and 1940, Larry Cuban found that in elementary schools most (41 percent) group instruction was a mix of teacher and student-centered instruction. Strictly teacher-centered instruction occurred 27 percent of the time, and student-centered instruction occurred 32 percent of the time. He found similar variation of proportion for classroom activities and high school instruction. He found more student-centered instruction during this period in Denver than in New York, whereas patterns in Washington, D.C., were closer to those in New York.

Cuban's general conclusion about teaching during this period is that teachers used a variety of methods depending on the conditions they encountered and their own personal philosophies. The problem was that many of these approaches to instruction contradicted one another. It was difficult to reconcile the doctrines of John Dewey with those of Edward Thorndike, for example, or the demands for efficiency with those for child-centered education. Cuban argues that teachers were beset with contradictory "impulses to be efficient, scientific, child-centered, and authoritative," and the result was that "teachers constructed patchwork compromises to contain these competing, often contradictory, impulses but (and here I can only speculate) at a cost of leaving within many a vague uneasiness over the aims of teaching, classroom discipline, and relations with students that seldom [went] away."[49]

CONCLUSION

The variety and contradictory nature of classroom practices highlight a major problem in understanding the functioning of the American educational system. At times, there has been little relationship between the expressed goals of education and actual educational practices. In part, this was caused by the variety of social forces acting on the school. Elites and educational leaders might have wanted the school to expand as a social agency to provide order and discipline and training and control of future workers, but these desires were often countered by students and parents, who wanted to use the schools as a means of gaining upward mobility and greater political power, and by teachers, who had other social objectives. Therefore, although the educational system may have been structured to exert social control, that goal may have been modified by other social forces.

NOTES

1. John Dewey, "The School as Social Center," *National Education Association Proceedings* (1902): 373–383.
2. Friedrich Froebel, *Pedagogics of the Kindergarten,* trans. Josephine Jarvis (Englewood Cliffs, N.J.: Prentice-Hall, 1899), pp. 1–15.
3. Quoted in Selwyn K. Troen, *The Public and the Schools: Shaping the St. Louis System, 1838–1920* (Columbia: University of Missouri Press, 1975), p. 101.
4. Ibid., p. 104.
5. Quoted in Marvin Lazerson, *Origins of the Urban School: Public Education in Massachusetts, 1870–1915* (Cambridge, Mass.: Harvard University Press, 1971), p. 50.

6. Ibid., p. 55.
7. Clarence E. Rainwater, *The Play Movement in the United States* (Chicago: University of Chicago Press, 1922), p. 52.
8. Henry S. Curtis, *The Play Movement and Its Significance* (New York: Macmillan, 1917), pp. 1–10.
9. Cremin, *Transformation of the School, Progression in American Education, 1876–1957* (New York: Random House, 1961), p. 71.
10. Paul C. Violas, *The Training of the Urban Working Class: A History of Twentieth Century American Education* (Skokie, Ill.: Rand McNally, 1978), pp. 67–92.
11. Sadie American, "The Movement for Vacation Schools," *American Journal of Sociology* (November 1898), pp. 310–312.
12. O. J. Milliken, "Chicago Vacation Schools," *American Journal of Sociology* (November 1898), pp. 291–295.
13. Cremin, *Transformation of the School*, p. 64.
14. Clarence Arthur Perry, *Wider Use of the School Plant* (New York: Russell Sage Foundation, 1910), pp. 3–4.
15. J. K. Paulding, "The Public School as a Centre of Community Life," *Educational Review* (February 1898), p. 148; H. E. Scudder, "The Schoolhouse as a Centre," *Atlantic Monthly* (January 1896), pp. 103–109.
16. Clarence Arthur Perry, *The Social Centers of 1912–13* (New York: Russell Sage Foundation, 1913), and *School Centre Gazette, 1919–1920* (New York: Russell Sage Foundation, 1920).
17. A. Gove, "Public Schoolhouses and Their Uses as Centers of Instruction and Recreation for the Community," *Education* (March 1897), pp. 407–411.
18. Edward J. Ward, *The Social Center* (New York: Appleton, 1913), p. 18.
19. Clarence Arthur Perry, *The School as a Factor in Neighborhood Development* (New York: Russell Sage Foundation, 1914).
20. T. Bowlker, "Woman's Home-Making Function Applied to the Municipality," *American City*, Vol. 6, (1912), pp. 863–869.
21. David Tyack, *One Best System, A History of Urban Education* (Cambridge: Harvard University Press, 1974), p. 230.
22. Ibid., p. 234.
23. Larry Cuban, *How Teachers Taught: Constancy and Change in American Classrooms, 1890–1980* (White Plains, N.Y.: Longman, 1984), p. 49.
24. Ibid., pp. 49, 71–72, 86–89.
25. Ibid., pp. 50, 71, 87.
26. Charles De Garmo, *Herbart and the Herbartians* (New York: Scribner's, 1895), p. 7.
27. Willard Elsbree, *The American Teacher: Evolution of a Profession in a Democracy* (New York: American Book Company, 1939), p. 407.
28. John Dewey, "Teaching Ethics in the High School," *Educational Review* (November 1893), p. 316.
29. John Dewey, "Ethical Principles Underlying Education," *The Third Yearbook of the National Herbart Society* (Chicago: National Herbartian Society, 1897), p. 31.

30. John Dewey, "The School and Society" in Martin Dworkin, ed., *Dewey on Education: Selections* (New York: Teachers College Press, 1959), p. 36.
31. Ibid., p. 37.
32. Ibid., p. 39.
33. Ibid., p. 46.
34. John Dewey, "School as Social Center," p. 381.
35. "Social Education as Association," leaflet included in bound edition of *Social Education Quarterly*, Vol. 1.
36. Colin A. Scott, *Social Education* (Boston: Ginn, 1908), pp. 102–146.
37. William Heard Kilpatrick, *The Project Method* (New York: Teachers College Press, 1918), p. 6.
38. Ibid., p. 14.
39. William James, *Principles of Psychology* (1890; reprint, New York: Dover, 1950), Vol. 1, pp. 24–26.
40. Ibid., p. 121.
41. Edward Thorndike, "Education, A First Book" in Geraldine Joncich, ed., *Psychology and the Science of Education: Selected Writings of Edward L. Thorndike* (New York: Teachers College Press, 1962), p. 79.
42. Ibid.
43. Edward Thorndike, "The Principles of Teaching Based on Psychology" in Joncich, *Psychology*, pp. 60–61.
44. Ibid., pp. 65–66.
45. Edward Thorndike, "The Measurement of Intelligence" in Joncich, *Psychology*, p. 104.
46. Ibid., pp. 105–106.
47. William Chandler Bagley, *Classroom Management* (New York: Macmillan, 1925), pp. 18–40.
48. Ibid.
49. Cuban, *How Teachers Taught*, pp. 103–104.

Education and Human Capital

A major argument used by Horace Mann in support of the organization of a common school system was that it would promote economic development. This justification for public schooling became extremely important in the late nineteenth and twentieth centuries as vocational education and vocational guidance were introduced on a large scale and the high school developed as an institution to serve all youth. In fact, one could argue that schooling as a means of developing human capital has become the most important goal of the educational system in the twentieth century.

This chapter explores the early concepts surrounding the relationship between education and human capital by discussing the development of vocational education, vocational guidance, and the high school. In considering the history of these aspects of education, three important factors must be taken into account. First, the school was used to select individuals for particular occupations. The institution that most clearly embodied this goal was the high school, which developed a differentiated curriculum based on the future occupational destination of the student. Together with vocational guidance, the modern high school was viewed as one of the primary means of sorting individuals to meet the needs of the labor market.

Second, it was argued in the nineteenth and twentieth centuries that education improved the skills of individuals and made them more productive on the job and that, in turn, increased productivity resulting from increased education enhanced economic growth. Within the context of this argument, increased investment in education would increase the economic wealth of society.

And third, pressure was placed on schools by students, particularly in high schools, to provide an education that would be useful in getting a job. Student demand for credentials sometimes forced high schools to change their curricula to meet the needs of the labor market. Therefore, schools were caught between the demands of industry owners to provide an education that would improve the quality of the work force and the demands of students for an education that would be useful in acquiring a job. These combined pressures contributed to the demise of the classical high school curriculum.

THE HIGH SCHOOL

In the early part of the twentieth century, a complex set of social, economic, and educational conditions shaped the modern high school for service to a broader range of the population. Traditionally, the nineteenth-century high school was portrayed as an elite institution serving only a minority of youth. More recent studies suggest that larger numbers attended high schools than had been thought. Maris Vinovskis found that in one county in Massachusetts in the 1860s at least one out of every five children attended high school when a school was located in their vicinity. When combining attendance at public and private secondary schools, he found that 19 percent of youths had some form of high school training. In one medium-sized town, one-third of eligible youths received some high school education.[1]

Also recent studies demonstrate that nineteenth-century high schools served a broader range of the population than had previously been thought. This more diversified student population put pressure on high schools to develop a curriculum that would prepare students for the labor market. David Labaree, in his history of the Central High School of Philadelphia between 1838 and 1939, found that parental and student pressure on the school forced it to become an institution that provided credentials for getting a job. When the school opened, it was dedicated to providing a moral and civic education along with practical skills. Within a short time, however, pressure from students and parents forced the school to focus on training that provided for success in the job market.[2]

It was this emphasis on education to serve economic and social needs that shaped the development of the modern high school. By the late nineteenth century, high schools began to adopt a differentiated curriculum to serve different vocational aspirations. For those with vocational aspirations that required a college diploma, high schools began to provide a specifically college preparatory curriculum. For those who wanted a high school education for employment immediately after graduation, a more general curriculum was offered. In addition, many high schools began to adopt vocational education programs.

The modern high school also embodied a greater concern with the social development of youth. In concrete terms, this meant the addition of high school activities such as clubs, student government, assemblies, organized athletics, and other social events. These social activities were also justified by their contribution to the workings of the economic system. It was through these activities that American youth were to learn how to cooperate in an industrial society based on large-scale corporations and unions.

The increasing importance of the high school in the twentieth century is best reflected in the changing patterns of school attendance. In 1890, 202,963 students attended 2,526 public high schools. Ten years later, in 1900, these figures had more than doubled to 519,251 students in 6,005 public high schools. In 1912 the enrollment level reached 1,105,360. These dramatic increases continued; by 1920, 28 percent of American youths, or 2,200,389 students, between the ages of fourteen and seventeen were in high school. It was during the 1920s that the high school truly became an institution serving the masses. By 1930, 47 percent of youths between the ages of fourteen and seventeen, or 4,399,422 students, were in high school, and during the Depression years of the 1930s the American high school began to serve the majority of youths—enrollments increased to 6,545,991 in 1940, representing two-thirds of the population between the ages of fourteen and seventeen.[3]

Although the preceding figures clearly indicate that the high school as an institution serving the majority of youths was a product of the twentieth century, important stages in its development occurred during the nineteenth century. The first American high school, the Boston English Classical School, established in 1821, was inspired by the academies founded in the eighteenth and early nineteenth centuries. Like the academies, the high school sought to provide a more practical course of studies than those being offered in traditional grammar schools.

The establishment of the Boston English Classical School was a direct result of the concerns of parents in Boston about sending their children out of town to private academies. The committee that recommended the establishment of the school complained that "many children are separated from their parents and sent to private academies in this vicinity, to acquire that instruction which cannot be obtained at the public seminaries. Thus, many parents, who contribute largely to the support of these institutions, are subjected to heavy expense for the same object out of town."

The "public seminaries" referred to in this complaint were the grammar schools, which according to this committee were not meeting the needs of some parents in Boston. In fact, the committee indirectly compared the type of education provided in the publicly supported grammar school with that provided in the private academy when it stated: "A parent who wishes to give a child an education that shall fit him for an active life, and shall serve as a foundation for eminence in his profession, whether Mercantile or Mechanical, is under the necessity of giving him a different education from any which our public schools can now furnish." Three years after its opening, the Boston English Classical School changed its name to English High School. It offered a course of studies ranging from navigation and bookkeeping to moral and political philosophy.[4]

In 1827 the Massachusetts legislature passed a law that further stimulated the growth of high schools within the commonwealth. The law did not use the term *high school* but required every town of more than five hundred households to have a master to teach American history, bookkeeping, geometry, surveying, and algebra; in addition, every community with more than four thousand people was required to have an instructor in Latin, Greek, history, rhetoric, and logic. Most of the twenty-six schools established by 1840 as a result of this law were called high schools.

The number of high schools grew slowly during the nineteenth century. State authorization was instituted in Pennsylvania in 1836 and in New York in 1853. The general legal status of high schools was uncertain until the famous Kalamazoo decision of 1874, which was interpreted as supporting the general development of the public high school. The case resulted from a Michigan law of 1859 authorizing school districts with more than 100 children to establish high school departments if so mandated by the vote of the people. In the Kalamazoo case, *Charles E. Stuart and Others v. School District No. 1 of the Village of Kalamazoo and Others* (1874), the plaintiffs claimed that the high school in their area was illegal because a vote had never been taken and that no authority existed in the state to create free high schools through taxation levied on the people. In his written decision, Justice Thomas M. Cooley of the Supreme Court of Michigan dismissed the issue of the public vote by noting many irregularities in municipal administration and by arguing that the public showed its approval through its support of the institution.

Of course, the major issue was taxation for support of the high school. This complaint by the plaintiffs raised the whole issue of public taxation for support of higher education. Judge Cooley expressed surprise at the questioning of this idea: "We supposed it had always been understood in this state that education, not merely in the rudiments, but in an enlarged sense, was regarded as an important practical advantage to be supplied at their option to rich and poor alike." Cooley went on to argue that the provision in the state constitution for the establishment of free schools implied the establishment of high schools. He stated that "beginning in 1817 and continuing until after the adoption of the present constitution," state policy had been moving clearly "in the direction of free schools in which education, and at their option the elements of a classical education, might be brought within the reach of all the children of the state." This interpretation meant that the provision in the state constitution for free schools included high schools and gave constitutional legitimacy to their development. Other state courts followed Michigan's lead, with the result that general support grew for the development of public high schools.[5]

According to Edward Krug, the most "significant expression in the decision was the one including 'the elements of a classical education.'"[6] A classical education was still considered a prerequisite for college admission. As Judge Cooley portrayed the system, the high school was made part of an organizational ladder extending from the early grades to college. The inclusion of classical education made the high school both an institution providing practical education and an institution preparing students for college.

Although the Kalamazoo decision laid the groundwork for the inclusion of high schools in the general interpretation of state constitutional provisions for free schooling, some confusion developed over the purposes of a high school education and the relationship between high schools and colleges. In

1892, at the beginning of the period of rapid expansion of the high school, the National Education Association formed the Committee of Ten on Secondary School Studies under the leadership of Harvard President Charles Eliot. The initial concern of the committee was to create uniform requirements for admission to colleges. Many high school educators found it difficult to organize a course of study when different colleges had different requirements for admission. Of course, any decision about the organization of studies had to consider the general purposes of a high school education.

The importance of the Committee of Ten's final report was that it established a general framework for discussion of the goals of secondary education. In many ways, the report of the committee reflected the crossroad between an educational system designed to provide everyone with a common education and an educational system organized to provide everyone with a specific education based on a future social destination.

One of the major questions facing the Committee of Ten was whether or not different courses of study should be offered to students ending their education at the secondary level and those planning to go on to college. In other words, should preparation for life differ from preparation for college? This seemingly innocuous question had important implications for the role of education in a democratic society. Because more children of wealthy families tended to go to college than those of poor families, a difference in curriculum for the college- and non-college-bound student had the potential of creating a class system of education.

The response of the Committee of Ten to this issue was to recommend against any differences in the courses of study for the two groups of students. Debate immediately following the issuance of the report in 1894 gave clear recognition to the social implications of the decision against separate curricula for college- and non-college-bound high school students. For example, at the first official presentation of the report, Francis Parker stated, "One unanimous conclusion of all the conferences [that produced the report], a conclusion without a single dissenting voice, or vote, is worth all the cost and all the pains that were necessary to produce the report. That conclusion is that there should be no such thing as class education." He went on to argue that an attempt was under way to reduce city schools to charity schools and to provide the poor with only a partial education. In the context of rejecting a class-based education, Parker stated, "There is no reason why one child should study Latin and another be limited to the '3 R's.'"[7]

While attempting to avoid class-based education, the Committee of Ten tried to balance individual interests and needs with the educational programs that did not differentiate between college- and non-college-bound students. It was hoped that this balance could be achieved by high schools offering four different courses of study of equal value for college admission. Only one of the proposed courses of study, Classical, required both Latin and Greek. The Latin-Scientific program required only Latin, the Modern Language sequence required neither Latin nor Greek, and the English course of study made Latin an option. The four courses of study proposed by the Committee of Ten marked the beginning of a decline in the importance given to classical studies in college admission requirements.

Ironically, the major criticism of the report of the Committee of Ten was that it was elitist because it did not propose a special course of study for non-college-bound students. This debate highlights one of the complex issues in the relationship between education and a democratic society. For instance, one can argue that providing an education that meets individual needs and interests is democratic because it places the individual at the center of educational decisions. But it can also be claimed that such an education is undemocratic because it results in people receiving an education that locks them into their social class.

Central to all of these discussions were the differences between the rich and the poor. Some argued that the poor needed a practical education that would prepare them for the realities of their future lives—this would constitute the meeting of individual needs and interests. Of course, meeting those needs in this fashion limited the educational opportunities of the poor and provided the rich with a superior education as measured by the social and cultural power it conferred.

The debate over the meaning of education in a democratic society was fundamental to the organization of the American high school. The most influential position taken on this issue was that of educators and civic leaders concerned with social efficiency. In *The Shaping of the American High School*, Edward Krug, the great historian of the American high school, identifies social efficiency as the most predominant school of thought in influencing the development of the high school. As a doctrine, social efficiency was one aspect of the argument for the development of human capital. Educators and civic leaders interested in social efficiency wanted education to produce individuals who were trained for a specific role in society and who were willing to work cooperatively in that role.

Social efficiency doctrines had broad implications for education. First, the argument suggested that school curricula should be organized to meet the future social needs of the students. Second, it was believed that school activities should be designed to teach cooperation as preparation for future social activities. Third, social efficiency arguments proposed differentiated curricula based on the future social destination of the student.

A leading early-twentieth-century educator, William C. Bagley, claimed in 1905 that "social efficiency is the standard by which the forces of education must select the experiences that are impressed upon the individual. Every subject of instruction, every item of knowledge, every form of reaction, every detail of habit, must be measured by this yardstick." Although Bagley's statement illustrates the range of application of the idea of social efficiency, an article by Arthur Call in 1909 reveals how educators committed to social efficiency believed they held a revolutionary position in contrast to a traditional position on academic education. Call states that the primary aim of education is "not to promote academic training, [but] to enable the pupils by means of free, fair and genial social intercourse, under the leadership of friendly and large-spirited men and women, to obtain practice in real life, to become socially and serviceably efficient." In this case, "socially and serviceably efficient" means an ability to perform a job well and to get along with others.[8]

The educational doctrines of social efficiency were part of a more general reconceptualization of the American economic system. In the early nineteenth century, most of the population was rural and involved in agriculture, and industrial development was in its early stages. For most Americans, the doctrines of laissez-faire capitalism, with their stress on economic individualism, seemed to best explain the ideal workings of the economic system. Within this social vision, the economic system worked best when individuals were allowed to pursue their own individual interests within a free marketplace. Of course, as represented by the earlier discussion in this book of Whigs and Democrats, differences arose about the degree of government intervention and freedom to be allowed in the marketplace.

Laissez-faire doctrines have continued up to the present in the United States but have been tempered and, in some cases, have been challenged by a differing view of the economic system that resulted from the development of urban areas, large corporations, and large unions. This new view of the economic system can roughly be called twentieth-century liberalism; it was this economic vision that produced social efficiency–minded educators and that had the major impact on the shaping of the high school in the twentieth century.

The proponents of twentieth-century liberalism and socially efficient education accepted the growth of large-scale organizations in a modern corporate society but felt that certain changes needed to occur to ensure efficient operation of the new economic system. Of primary importance was ending traditional ideas about economic individualism and the pursuit of self-interest. It was argued that the new large-scale organizations required cooperation, not competition. What this meant for public schools was that students needed to be taught to work together and that the stress of competition needed to be reduced. During the early part of the twentieth century these ideas resulted in an emphasis in the schools on group activities, sharing, and working together. Some educators saw the students sitting at an individual desk and working alone as a symbol of economic individualism and competition and sought to replace that scenario with groups of students working together around a table.

Social efficiency doctrines and the new economic thought stressed the importance of specialization and expertise in the new large-scale organizations. Specialization, it was reasoned, increased efficiency by allowing each person to concentrate on a single individual task. This was the model of the assembly line and modern bureaucracy, where individual tasks were coordinated through the organization. For educators, specialization meant education of the student for a particular occupation. Under the doctrines of social efficiency, the ideal was to socialize students for cooperation in large-scale organizations where each individual would be performing a specialized task.

ι

A second important aspect of twentieth-century liberalism was the acceptance of the idea of government intervention to ensure the fair operation of the economic system. At one level, this meant the establishment of government regulatory agencies to supervise various industries, such as transportation, and government attempts to break up and regulate monopolies. At another level, this meant an attempt by the school to ensure equality of opportunity in the labor market by objectively selecting students for different educational programs.

All of these aspects of twentieth-century liberalism were important elements in the doctrine of social efficiency. Cooperation, specialization, and equality of opportunity were the key concepts around which the modern high school was organized. Of course, these doctrines of social efficiency ran counter to the traditional academic thrust of the high school.

The battle between the older academic concepts of the high school and the new doctrines of social efficiency was waged in the popular presses in the early part of the twentieth century. For instance, in 1912 the *Saturday Evening Post* published two articles opposing the academic tradition in the high school. One article, by William Mearns, carries the opinionated title "Our Medieval High Schools: Shall We Educate Children for the Twelfth or the Twentieth Century?" The author argues that "culture" had come to dominate the high school, which he stereotyped as an institution wherein "it is clean hands and a pure collar . . . it is knowledge of Hegelian philosophy; it is Greek; it is Latin; it is a five-foot shelf of books; it is twenty thousand a year; it is a sight of truth and a draught of wisdom; it is a frock coat and pearl gloves." In contrast to what he labeled the medieval concept of high schools, he argues that the modern high school should become a democratic institution in which the only studies offered would provide for "efficient service to the community about it."[9]

The other *Saturday Evening Post* article, "The High School and the Boy," by William Lewis, argues that "the high school's largest service is the best possible training for economic efficiency, good citizenship, and full and complete living for all its pupils." The author thought this could best be accomplished by eliminating the dissection of literary masterpieces, providing a wide range of mathematics (but not algebra), and offering foreign languages only as electives. In a later book, *Democracy's High School*, Lewis calls for an education "in citizenship and in right social thinking."[10]

Related to the concept of social efficiency were attitudes about the social development of adolescents. Within the context of psychological thought in the early twentieth century, adolescence was the most important age for developing the sense of cooperation and social service required by modern society. The most influential psychologist in this area was G. Stanley Hall (1844–1924), founder of the child study movement in the 1890s and pioneer in the field of adolescent and developmental psychology.

In his classic work *Adolescence*, published in 1904, Hall states, "The whole future of life depends on how the new powers [of adolescence] now given suddenly and in profusion are husbanded." According to Hall's theory of recapitulation, each stage of individual development parallels a stage of social evolution. Childhood, the years between four and eight, corresponds to a cultural epoch when hunting and fishing were the main activities of humanity. From eleven to twelve, according to Hall, the child recapitulates the life of savagery. During puberty, the new flood of passions develops the social person: "The social instincts undergo sudden unfoldment and the new life of love awakens."[11]

Hall's theories supported other contemporary beliefs that adolescent interests and abilities must be harnessed and directed to some socially useful function. This meant the establishment of institutions such as the high school to capture and channel the sexual-social drives of the adolescent. Hall argues that the utilization of adolescent drives should be the criterion by which institutions are evaluated. He believed that the proper socialization of adolescents is the panacea for most social problems: The "womb, cradle, nursery, home, family, relatives, school, church and state are only a series of larger cradles or placenta, as the soul . . . builds itself larger missions, the only test and virtue of which is their service in bringing the youth to ever fuller maturity."[12]

The image of adolescence projected by Hall's psychology and represented in the popular press of the time was of a romantic stage of life during which the developing sexual-social drives could lead the adolescent to either a life of decadence or a life of social service. The romantic and poetic impulses of youth, it was believed, could be captured and directed toward socially useful projects such as helping the poor, the community, or the nation. Boy Scouts, Girl Scouts, the YWCA, YMCA, and other youth organizations were justified by their ability to channel the sexual-social drives of the teenager for the good of society. On the other hand, when youths of the 1920s adopted the style of the Jazz Age, the popular press warned of the imminent collapse of civilization. In other words, youth represented either a promising future or a collapsing civilization.

The role played by youths in shaping the psyche of the twentieth century had important consequences for the development of the high school, which became the primary social institution for capturing and channeling the sexual-social drives of teenagers. As discussed in more detail later in this section, students' social life or extracurricular activities became an important aspect of high school culture in America. Given the importance Americans placed on the development of youths for the future of the nation, in the twentieth century the high school came to symbolize the promise of American life.

As the role of youths increased in the public mind and social efficiency educators continued their attack on academics in the high school, the National Education Association organized a commission in 1913 whose report eventually established the basic framework for the modern high school. This group, the Commission on the Reorganization of Secondary Education, issued its final report in 1918 as the now famous *Cardinal Principles of Secondary Education*. The report, which reflects the strong influence of social efficiency rhetoric, attempted to shape the high school to meet the needs of the modern corporate state. Its final recommendation calls for the creation of a comprehensive high school that would include a wide variety of curricula designed to meet the needs of different types of students. The comprehensive high school became the standard for secondary education for more than half a century.[13]

Unlike the report of the Committee of Ten, *Cardinal Principles of Secondary Education* calls for a broad program of various courses of study: "Differentiation should be, in the broad sense of the term, vocational . . . such as agricultural, business, clerical, industrial, fine-arts, and household-arts curriculums." One of the major questions facing the commission was whether or not a differentiated curriculum should require the establishment of separate schools to teach the different curricula; for instance, separate academic and vocational schools.[14]

The commission's answer to this question provided the framework for the organization of the comprehensive high school. The commission argued for comprehensive schools in which all students would come together because this would aid "the pupil through a wide variety of contacts and experiences to obtain a basis for intelligent choice of his educational and vocational career" and would ensure the choice of a curriculum best suited to the student's need. According to the commission, specialized schools might introduce distracting influences, such as location, athletic teams, and friendships. These influences, rather than consideration of curriculum, might determine which school the student attended. The comprehensive high school, in the opinion of the commission, would eliminate those factors from consideration—everyone would attend the same school regardless of his or her choice of course of study.[15]

The commission also used the rhetoric of social efficiency to justify the comprehensive high school, which, the commission argued, allowed for what it called the two components of democracy—specialization and unification. The commission's report states: "The purpose of democracy is so to organize society that each member may develop his personality primarily through activities designed for the well-being of his fellow members and of society as a whole." The specialized and differentiated curriculum of the comprehensive high school was to train each student to perform a specific task that would benefit society. Within the context of this argument, democracy was viewed mainly as a means of social organization that would allow each individual to do what she or he is best able to do for the good of the social whole. Education was supposed to fit the individual into a social position that would enable him or her to make a maximum contribution to society. The report stated in bold type that "education in a democracy . . . should develop in each individual the knowledge, interests, ideals, habits, and powers whereby he will find his place and use that place to shape both himself and society toward ever nobler ends."[16]

According to the report, the second component of democracy, or social efficiency, is unification. This democratic ideal shaped the social organization of the modern high school. The report defined *unification* as that part of the ideal of democracy that brought people together and gave them "common ideas, common ideals, and common modes of thought, feeling, and action that made for cooperation, social cohesion, and social solidarity." Although educators in the nineteenth century stressed the importance of schooling in building social cohesion, their primary focus was on the early grades. *Cardinal Principles*, however, gave the major responsibility for socialization to the high school: "In this process the secondary school must play an important part because the elementary school with its immature pupils cannot alone develop the common knowledge, common ideals, and common interests essential to American democracy."[17]

The major problem in providing social cohesion was the fact that different students pursued different courses of study. To compensate for the separation caused by the differentiated curriculum, the commission proposed three means of creating a sense of unity. The first, which was directed at the immigrant, emphasized the need for teaching the "mother tongue" and social studies. The other two were organizational techniques, one was "social mingling of pupils through the organization and administration of the school," and the other, directly related to this proposal, was "participation of pupils in common activities . . . such as athletic games, social activities, and the government of the school."[18]

Thus, the twentieth-century solution to building unification and cooperation through education was to provide extracurricular activities in the high school. The various elements of school life that were included in the term *extracurricular activities* were in existence long before the issuance of *Cardinal Principles*, but during the 1920s extracurricular activities developed into an educational cult. Courses in organizing extracurricular activities were offered in teacher training institutions, and textbooks and books of readings on the topic were published. In 1926, the *Twenty-Fifth Yearbook of the National Society for the Study of Education* was devoted to the topic. As in any educational movement, certain figures emerged as leaders. One in particular was Elbert K. Fretwell of Teachers College, who organized summer courses for school administrators on preparation of extracurricular programs. Between 1923 and 1927 Fretwell flooded *Teachers College Record* with long bibliographies of material on assemblies, clubs, student government, and homerooms.[19]

It would be a mistake, however, to assume that extracurricular activities entered the high school only because they served some broader social purposes. In fact, most high schools already had some form of extracurricular activities, but it was in the 1920s that educators tried to use these activities for specific educational purposes. Thomas Gutowski's history of extracurricular activities in Chicago reveals that activities entered high schools because of student demand and the desire of school authorities to maintain order. The concern with controlling students' behavior was a result of the vandalism and disorder accompanying the growth of the high school population. In the late nineteenth century, principals found themselves battling lunchroom rowdiness and chaos in the halls. Locks were first introduced on schoolroom doors in 1888. Student government was also introduced as a means of maintaining order in schools; school authorities often saw it as a means of using students to control other students. Athletic teams and clubs were often initiated by students and then brought under school authority as a means of controlling their activities. Therefore, by the 1920s a wide variety of activities had been added to the functions of the school. These extracurricular activities became the central focus of educators in the 1920s for the socializing of youth for the needs of the modern corporate society.[20]

It was a student government that was the central feature of all extracurricular activities programs. The important place student government assumed in the public schools resulted from activities by urban reform groups in the 1890s in New York City, which saw it as a method of preparing the children of immigrants for participation in democratic government. In 1904, Richard Welling organized the National Self-Government Committee, which campaigned vigorously into the 1940s for student government in public schools and colleges. Before organizing the student government campaign, Welling claimed he realized that education was the key to civic reform. In 1903, he lamented that merely "telling the voters that their taxes were too high did not lead to action at the polls." The best method of encouraging political involvement, he decided, was to give citizens an opportunity to practice the intelligent use of political rights. Having reached this conclusion, he contacted Charles Eliot, then president of the National Education Association, and asked permission to address the organization's annual convention. Before the convention, he made a ringing appeal for student government as a means of curing corrupt government. He told gathered educators, "The New generation must be imbued with a new spirit of civic patriotism . . . you must teach the machinery of government by means of some form of applied civics."[21]

Student governments were instituted by American schools at a phenomenal rate, and by the middle of the twentieth century very few high schools were without some form of student government. Throughout this course of development, no serious suggestion was ever made that students be given real power. The purpose of student government was to provide applied civics, not to run the school. A typical attitude was that taken by William McAndrew, onetime superintendent of the New York City public schools. Writing in 1897 on a proposed student government plan, he stated, "I believe the plan of delegating any of the executive powers of that officer [principal] to those so irresponsible as students would be unwise."[22] There was general agreement, at least among educators during this period, that, as one writer stated, "any plan that gives pupils full control of the government of a school, a school city, or a school democracy, without the advice and aid of teachers will necessarily lead to an ignominious failure."[23]

The other organizations making up extracurricular activities were justified as contributing to the unification of the school and the preparation of students for participation in a cooperative democracy. In most plans, student governments or student associations were to work with the faculty in the administration of additional extracurricular activities, which usually included the student newspaper, clubs, athletics, and assemblies. One principal stated in 1917 that an organized program of this nature would "assist in making the spirit of democracy, 'all of each and each for all' to pervade the school."[24]

The school newspaper was justified as a means of teaching both English and teamwork and of creating a spirit of unity within the school. Publication of a paper, like any school club activity, was considered a means of teaching people to work cooperatively. The school newspaper was to contribute to a feeling of unity by providing each student with news about school events. Some supporters of school newspapers considered the creation of unity or school spirit to be the most important function of this activity. One supporter wrote: "The Press Association . . . meets an important demand. It is a unifying organization, and is therefore a wholesome factor if properly directed. Its purpose is to edit a school paper through which a school spirit may be awakened and nourished."[25] Through reading the paper, the student was to gain a sense of the unity of school life and a feeling of loyalty. To a certain extent, the paper was to be a public relations method of building a good image of the school in the student's eyes. As one writer put it, "The school paper . . . will create school patriotism and an increased interest in all the activities of the school, educational, athletic, and social."[26]

Clubs in high school programs ranged across a variety of areas. Most high schools and academies in the nineteenth century had some social organizations—usually literary and debating societies—but in the twentieth century a much broader choice of club activities was offered and was justified with claims that the clubs would teach participation in cooperative activities. After the 1918 publication of *Cardinal Principles,* which suggested that one of the purposes of education was the development of meaningful leisure-time activities, the argument frequently appeared that clubs served to prepare students for worthy use of leisure time. For example, one article in 1921 on club activities stated: "A school's service to the future makers of America does not end with preparing them for working hours which occupy only a third of the day. It must also provide specifically for the worthy use of leisure."[27]

The argument was made that athletics could contribute to training for participation in a democratic community in two ways. First, as part of a general health program, it would ensure individual physical efficiency. In language common to human capital theories, *Cardinal Principles* stressed good health as a means of assuring the maximum development of human resources. Second, athletics taught the student how to cooperate and work with a team. This orientation was one reason for the rapid growth of football in the public schools. As a team game, football fostered the coordination and cooperation believed to be needed in a corporate organization. A Seattle high school principal told the National Education Association in 1915, "In the boy's mind, the football team is not only an aggregation of individuals organized to play, but a social instrument with common needs, working along common lines, and embodying a common purpose."[28] The spirit generated by athletic games between schools was considered another means of uniting students and was also considered an important public relations method. The problem, as seen by one professor of physical education in 1914, was maintaining a balance between the development of the individual and the entertainment of spectators. His confidence that this could be achieved is expressed in his statement that fifteen years earlier, high school athletics had been "accustomed to playing a game unrestrained and without cooperation. All sorts of tricks were used to win a contest, such as importing players, choosing biased officials, and resorting to unfair tactics in general. . . . Today our athletes from the high schools represent the best sportsmanship possible."[29] The success of football in uniting the community and generating spirit eventually unbalanced the two purposes. In 1923 a high school teacher complained, "Rivalry between certain schools has become so intense that players meet in a spirit of hatred and revenge, and special policing is necessary to guard against outbreaks of hostility between rival rooters."[30]

According to *Cardinal Principles*, the activity that was most important in contributing to school unity was the assembly, because it brought together students who were otherwise separated by grades, courses of studies, and ability groups. A statement in 1925 by an associate superintendent of schools in Pittsburgh, Pennsylvania, illustrates this point of view: "Students are divided into classes according to their academic advancement, further divided by their curricula. . . . Blocking the pathway to unity is an almost infinite variety of individual differences. The assembly is the one agency at hand capable of checking these tendencies."[31] Assemblies became one of the great events in American high schools. Books, programs, and articles with suggestions for auditorium exercises flooded the educational market. Band concerts, vocational talks, drama productions, class projects, and patriotic celebrations all became part of the public school paraphernalia. The importance of the assembly as school unifier continued through the 1920s. This is exemplified by the opening words of a book entitled *Assemblies for Junior and Senior High Schools*, published in 1929: "Junior and senior high schools daily accept the challenge to prepare students for life in a democracy. . . . Specialized organization and complex activities necessitate unification through athletics, the school newspaper, and the assembly. Because of its frequency and provision for universal participation, the assembly may be considered the foremost integrating factor."[32]

The desire to create a cooperative and unified spirit was one of the major factors in the organization of the comprehensive high school. *The Fifth Yearbook of the Department of Secondary-School Principals*, published in 1921, states with regard to extracurricular activities, "What we wish the state to be the school must be. The character of our citizens is determined by the character of our pupils and the development of character in this broadest sense must be the goal of education."[33]

The comprehensive high school became a mixture of planned social activities and a variety of curricula, all of which were attempts to prepare a new generation for a society based on large organizations and occupational specialization. In this context, the development of human capital meant selection and training for a specialized task and socialization for a society based on cooperation.

VOCATIONAL EDUCATION, VOCATIONAL GUIDANCE, AND THE JUNIOR HIGH SCHOOL

Vocational education, vocational guidance, and the junior high school were important elements in the development of the comprehensive high school and key parts of the attempt to organize the educational system to develop human capital. By emphasizing training for specific occupations in publicly-supported institutions, vocational education represented a revolution in the role of schooling. Vocational education made the development of human capital through training an important part of the educational system. Vocational guidance became the institutional mechanism for matching students and educational programs with the needs of the labor market. Together, vocational education and vocational guidance assumed the function of promoting industrial efficiency through proper selection and training of labor power. Early junior high schools experimented with ideas about vocational guidance and preparation for the corporate world and thus contributed to the development of the comprehensive high school.

A recent history of vocational education by Harvey Kantor argues that vocational education never fully succeeded in training workers for industrial occupations. What vocational education did accomplish was to make preparation for jobs the major function of American high schools. In addition, it predisposed educators and other public leaders to think of education as a cure for economic problems. This thinking about the role of public schools has persisted throughout the twentieth century.[34]

The early development of vocational education has often been associated with the manual training movement. In 1880 Calvin Woodward founded the Manual Training School at Washington University in St. Louis. The idea of manual training was not to teach a trade but to provide the student with manual activities that would complement a liberal education. In most cases, the emphasis in manual training was on metal- and woodworking and drafting.

Woodward described manual training in an address to the National Teachers Association in 1883 as being "for all children as an element in general education." He argued that a truly liberal education prepared the child for all activities, both mental and physical. Although he supported manual training as part of a liberal education, he also claimed that it would provide opportunities for better occupational choices, elevate the quality of work, and solve labor problems. The way it would end labor problems was by giving future workers the skills to adapt to industrial changes. The exposure to manual labor would make the student aware of the variety of occupations requiring educated labor and, in Woodward's words, "bring into the manual occupations a new element, a fairly educated class, which will greatly increase their value, at the same time it gives them new dignity."[35]

Before 1900, little support existed for public education that would train students for specific occupations. A major factor in changing attitudes about specific job training was concern about the position of the United States in world markets relative to other industrialized countries, such as Germany. This concern was made explicit in a series of reports in the early twentieth century urging the development of vocational education. The 1905 *Report of the Committee on Industrial Education of the National Association of Manufacturers* states, "Technical and trade education for youth is a national necessity, and the . . . nation must train its youth in the arts of production and distribution." Germany was both feared for its activities in world markets and admired for its educational system, which included vocational and trade schools. For many, copying the German vocational system of education was necessary for improving America's position in international trade. For example, the 1905 report states: "The German technical and trade schools are at once the admiration and fear of all countries. In the world's race for commercial supremacy we must copy and improve upon the German method of education."[36]

In its 1912 report, the Committee on Industrial Education directly related concerns about developing human capital to fears of foreign competition. The report argues that two types of capital exist in the world. One type includes land, machinery, and money, and "the other kind is human capital—the character, brains and muscle of the people. . . . This capital we have not developed; we have overlooked the whole question of its complete and efficient development." The failure to develop this human capital, according to the report, was leading to great industrial waste. The report warns: "We should act at once because of the stress of foreign competition. We are twenty-five years behind most of the nations that we recognize as competitors. We must come nearer to the level of international competition."[37]

Discussions about vocational education included arguments that traditional secondary education was not suited to a majority of students and that academic training for those students needed to be replaced with vocational training. It was this type of argument that the writers of the *Cardinal Principles* feared would result in a class-based education, and they accepted this argument as justifying a differentiated curriculum in a comprehensive high school. For example, the 1912 *Report of the Committee on Industrial Education* crudely divides children into "abstract-minded and imaginative," "concrete, or hand-minded," and "the great intermediate class, comprising all degrees of efficiency." It states that although traditional academic education fulfilled the needs of the abstract-minded, the intermediate class required an academic education with "highly developed, practical and extended courses of pre-vocational and manual training." The report claims that concrete-minded students were "one half of the youth of the land, that our present educational system has been horrible, unmindful, uninformed and inconsiderate." Using a German model, the report recommends the establishment of continuation schools for children who left school and went to work, as a means of improving the quality of this type of worker.[38]

The real development and expansion of vocational education came with the passage by the U.S. Congress of the Smith-Hughes Act in 1917. The fact that this action took place at the federal level is indicative of the consideration given to vocational education as part of America's economic and foreign policy. This act symbolizes the increasing tendency in the twentieth century to define a national interest in education that would be used to justify federal intervention.

The most important document in the early vocational education movement, the recommendations of which were incorporated into the Smith-Hughes Act, is the 1914 report of the Commission on National Aid to Vocational Education, established by the U.S. Congress. Historically, the document is important because it outlined all the major arguments for vocational education and resulted in the passage of the Smith-Hughes Act. The report opens with a general plea for vocational education as a means of reducing waste in the use of human resources. It also argues that vocational education is justified from a purely educational point of view because it meets the individual needs of students; provides equal opportunity for all to prepare for their life work; develops a better teaching process—learning by doing; and introduces the idea of utility into education. The report also claims that vocational education would reduce the discontent of workers: "Industrial and social unrest is due in large measure to a lack of a system of practical education fitting workers for their calling."[39]

The report of this congressional commission elaborates on the necessity for vocational education as a means of developing human capital through addressing problems in natural resources and the traditional dependence of American industry on foreign labor. The report argues that as America's natural resources were being depleted, foreign countries were finding new sources of supply. "We cannot continue to draw indefinitely on Europe for cheap labor, nor will cheap labor in the immediate future meet the urgent need in American industry for the more intelligent service necessary if we are to satisfy the rising demand for a better product from our domestic as well as our foreign markets." Vocational educational was advocated as an important answer to the economic problems facing the United States.[40]

Like other reports of this period, that of the Commission on National Aid to Vocational Education claims that vocational education would meet the individual needs of students. In making this claim, the report gives a particular meaning to the term *equality of opportunity*. The report states:

1. Vocational Training Is Needed To Democratize The Education of The Country:
(a) By recognizing different tastes and abilities and by giving an equal opportunity to all to prepare for their life work.[41]

During the common school period in the nineteenth century, equality of opportunity meant giving everyone the same education so that they could compete on equal terms in the labor market. In the context of the reasoning of this report, equality of opportunity meant giving students different types of education based on the individual's future occupation. This change in meaning of equality of opportunity had important implications for the general organization of the educational system and was one of the major shifts in educational ideology to take place between the nineteenth and twentieth centuries.

The commission's report resulted in the passage of the Smith-Hughes Act. This legislation contained a very narrow definition of vocational education, which, according to Marvin Lazerson and W. Norton Grubb in their introduction to their *American Education and Vocationalism: A Documentary History, 1870–1970*, resulted in "strengthening and legitimizing the evolving dual system of education." The legislation defined vocational education as dealing with specific occupational skills. The alternative, according to Lazerson and Grubb, was a broad concept of vocational education that would have prepared the individual for a wide variety of occupations and made individuals competent to change their skills to keep up with changes in technology. The Smith-Hughes Act reinforced a dual system of education—a differentiated curriculum—by clearly separating vocational training from academic training and providing federal money to accomplish that task.[42]

The legislation established a federal Board for Vocational Education, whose tasks were to advise local communities and states, administer vocational education funds, and publish research. This act recognized three types of vocational education: vocational schools providing all-day training, part-time schools for young workers, and evening schools for adult workers. The money provided by the legislation was to motivate action by states and communities but was not meant to cover the full cost of vocational programs.[43]

Federal expenditures in 1917–1918 represented 27 percent of money spent nationally on vocational education, and in 1925–1926 it represented 24 percent. The Smith-Hughes legislation did not result in a rapid growth in the number of students in full-time vocational education courses. In 1912–1913, 6.9 percent of high school students were in vocational programs, and in 1924 the figure was only 6.7 percent.[44]

The campaign for vocational education led to more general consequences for American schooling. This campaign reinforced arguments for elective courses and differentiation of the curriculum. More important, according to Krug, it contributed "to a widespread bias against the so-called academic side of school work, particularly for the alleged 'masses.' This bias flowed from the attempt to promote industrial education by disparaging the work of what were referred to as the 'literary' schools."[45] By distinguishing between the "abstract minded" and the "concrete minded," the vocational education movement opened the door for a class-based education, which assumed that the majority of the children of workers would best be served by vocational programs.

Vocational guidance was the other important aspect of selection and training of students based on the development of human capital. Its purpose was to reduce inefficiency in the distribution of human resources. Vocational guidance developed in a number of cities during the early days of the twentieth century. The movement was inspired by the drive for industrial efficiency and, like other movements in education, contained utopian hopes for the general reform of the social system. For example, Eli Weaver, the pioneer of vocational guidance in New York City, envisioned the establishment of a central government vocational bureau that would function as a commodity-exchange market. He made this proposal after organizing, between 1906 and 1910, committees of teachers in the New York high schools to work with students in planning the students' careers. The function of the central bureau would be to determine the types of training and character needed in available occupations. The bureau would also conduct surveys of the labor market to determine labor shortages and surpluses. This information would be used to encourage or discourage training in particular occupations depending on the needs of the labor market. Within the schools, vocational guidance and educational programs would be based on information supplied by the bureau. Also, the bureau would place high school graduates in appropriate occupations. Weaver claimed that the guidance agency would "facilitate the exchange of labor between the workers and employers as the exchange of other commodities is now assisted through the standardizing operations of other exchanges."[46]

In addition, vocational guidance was conceived of as a means of changing the general pattern of industrial development. One way of doing this was to keep workers out of certain types of industry. J. Adams Puffer, principal of the Lyman School for Boys and director of the Beacon Vocation Bureau in Boston, argues in a book published in 1913 that vocational guidance should channel youth into constructive, not neutral or destructive, occupations. Puffer labels liquor, patent medicines, unwholesome foods, and vicious amusements as destructive occupations. Neutral occupations were harmless but did not contribute to the efficiency of the social order. According to Puffer, "If each teacher in the United States, each year, guided into constructive work one single boy or girl who would otherwise have followed some neutral or destructive occupation, that alone would probably wipe out the whole of both non-constructive groups."[47]

There was a tendency in the early stages of the guidance movement to view the client as raw material for the industrial machine and to assume the responsibility for shaping good industrial character. For instance, as reported in 1913, as part of the guidance program at the De Kalb Township High School in Illinois, the principal would quote business maxims such as "It is none of my business what you do at night, but if dissipation affects what you do the next day, and you do half as much as I demand, you will last half as long as you hoped." Frank Parsons, founder of the first vocational bureau in Boston in 1908 and often called the "father of vocational guidance," would use an interview and a self-analysis sheet to determine what personality adjustments would be necessary for his clients. During the course of an interview, Parsons would make his own character appraisal by watching the manners and habits of his subject. This appraisal would be followed by a take-home questionnaire. The instructions on the questionnaire told the client: "Look in the glass. Watch yourself. Get your friends to . . . tell you confidentially what they think of your appearance, manners, voice. . . . Get your family and friends to help you recognize your defects." Following these instructions, the individual would answer questions ranging from issues of self-reliance and industriousness to queries such as "Do you wear your finger-nails in mourning and your linen overtime?"[48]

Although these aspects of general reform were present in the early vocational guidance movement, its main thrust remained that of promoting industrial efficiency. The role of the vocational guidance counselor as it emerged from these more general social goals was part labor specialist, part educator, and part psychologist. As labor specialist, the guidance counselor needed an understanding of the job market and its requirements. At the founding meeting of the Vocational Educational Association in 1913, Frederick G. Bonser of Teachers College demanded that a professional education be developed that would train the vocational counselor to know the "relationship between present and probable supply and demand, the relative wages, and the changes in methods, devices, and organization affecting the workers." Bonser emphasized the importance of studying the physical and mental requirements of occupations."[49]

As psychologist, the early guidance counselor used a variety of tests to determine occupational abilities. The earliest were developed by Harvard psychologist Hugo Munsterberg, who pioneered vocational aptitude testing when he designed tests to determine which Boston streetcar motormen would be least likely to have accidents. In historical terms, Munsterberg believed he was bringing together two major movements in American life: scientific management and vocational guidance. In the same way that scientific management studied industrial organization, Munsterberg wanted to study the job performance and aptitudes of the individual worker. His tests of Boston streetcar motormen were designed to measure powers of sustained attention as a means of determining the likelihood of an accident. Working later with the American Telephone and Telegraph Company, Munsterberg developed tests of memory, attention, and dexterity for job applicants."[50]

Tests of the type developed by Munsterberg were quickly adapted to the purposes of vocational guidance. For instance, Jesse B. Davis, a Michigan high school principal and early vocational guidance leader, inspired by Hugo Munsterberg's streetcar and telephone tests, worked with the Michigan State

Telephone Company in 1912 and 1913 to develop aptitude tests for telephone operators. These tests included measurements of ability to remember numbers, of speed, and of motor accuracy.

In the schools, vocational guidance became educational guidance and evaluation of individual interests and abilities. The Grand Rapids Central High School in Michigan became an early model for vocational guidance. The first meeting of the Vocational Guidance Association, in 1913, was held in Grand Rapids, and the principal of the school, Jesse B. Davis, was elected the first secretary of the association. The following year he was elected its president. Davis believed that the major function of education was to guide students into their proper place in the corporate structure and socialize them for that structure through the social life of the school. The social life of Central High School was organized into a pyramid of activities; the base of the pyramid included clubs, athletics, and student government and, in ascending order to the top of the pyramid, a Boys and Girls Leadership Club, a student council, an advisory council, and at the top, the principal. Davis believed that this school organization reflected the realities of an organized industrial system. He compared his position as principal to that of a general manager: "The ideals upon which honest living and sound business stand, are the ideals of the public schools."[51]

While these industrial traits were being learned in the social life of the school, classwork was organized to help students to find a job. Topics in English composition were assigned in progressive steps designed to lead to self-understanding and career choice. In the ninth grade, high school students analyzed their own character and habits. In the eleventh grade, each student chose a career and investigated the type of preparation he or she would need. In the twelfth grade, students made "a special study of the vocation with respect to its social obligations, its peculiar opportunities for human service, and responsibilities [to] the community." Davis believed that people should enter an occupation with the idea that "it was the best means by which, they, with their ability, might serve their fellow man."[52]

More typical of the developing role of the counselor was the one suggested by Meyer Bloomfield, Frank Parsons' successor as director of the Boston Vocation Bureau. In an article in Charles Johnston's 1914 anthology *The Modern High School*, Bloomfield states that the "vocational-guidance movement has . . . made clear one of the most important and generally neglected services which a school can render, and that is educational guidance."[53] Educational guidance was defined as helping students select educational programs that matched their interests, abilities, and future occupations. Within this framework, the curriculum was to be subservient to the occupational goals of the students. Ideally, the school counselor would match a student to an occupation and then to a course of study that would prepare the student for his or her vocation.

One of the main arguments for the establishment of the first junior high schools was that they would facilitate the vocational guidance of students and the differentiation of the curriculum. As Edward Krug states in *The Shaping of the American High School*, the junior high school "put forward as advantageous features . . . the advancement of practical subjects, the provision for early differentiation, and the fostering of socialized aims." A survey of New York City junior high schools conducted between 1911 and 1913 listed as opportunities offered by the junior high "(a) an opportunity to offer different courses of study; (b) an opportunity to adapt the instruction to the two sexes and to the requirements of high schools and vocational schools; (c) an opportunity to classify pupils according to ability."[54]

This survey of New York junior high schools appeared at a time when the New York schools were considering expanding their intermediate schools or junior highs to include the ninth grade as well as the seventh and eighth grades. New York had established its first seventh- and eighth-grade intermediate schools in 1905 and began adding the ninth grade in 1915.

In 1910 differentiation of the curriculum was one of the major features of the first junior high school to receive national attention. Superintendent Frank Bunker of the Berkeley, California, school system wrote in support of his nationally publicized three-year intermediate school, "To force all children in the seventh and eighth grades . . . to take the same work is clearly wrong."[55]

Within the new junior high schools, guidance personnel were to have the role of aiding seventh- and eighth-grade students to choose a course of study. A report on the Rochester, New York, junior high schools stated that they provided "vocational counselors, teachers with shortened teaching programs, [who] confer with pupils and visit homes to consult with parents."[56] In other school systems, the principal often functioned as counselor. For instance, the Los Angeles school system opened its first junior high in 1911; in this school, pupils chose, with the aid of the principal, among six courses of study.

Another response to the guidance problem was to institute the advisory, or homeroom, period. This special period was eventually utilized as both a center for social activity in the school and a part of the guidance program. One highly publicized example was the Ben Blewett Junior High School in St. Louis. Beginning in the seventh grade, each child at the Ben Blewett School spent 150 to 200 hours a year in advisory periods. In the course of the seventh-grade advisory periods, the student made a choice of a future career. In the eighth grade each student was programmed into one of three different courses of study depending on vocational choice. Principal Philip Cox, who organized the school in 1917, stated that a guiding principle was the "responsibility [of the school] to each child as an individual, and to society, whose agent it is for leading the children as individuals and as groups toward the goal of social efficiency."[57]

In the same way that arguments were made for developing unity and cooperation in the comprehensive high school, it was argued that socialization was an important goal of the junior high school. One enthusiastic supporter of the junior high school idea wrote in the May 1919 issue of *Educational Review* that a new spirit would pervade the junior high school.

"This spirit will be the spirit of cooperation, the spirit of service and of sacrifice for the common good." As in the comprehensive high school, the vehicle for the new social spirit was to be extracurricular activities. A 1922 survey of the nine years of development of New York junior high schools showed 387 clubs and 68 other after-school activities in operation. The clubs ranged from 83 centering around physical training to 31 devoted to history projects.[58]

The focus for socialization in junior high schools was clubs. Because clubs were centered around specific activities, they helped to guide students' developing interests. This, of course, was the justification used for providing vocational guidance at the junior high school level. The organizational center for club activities and guidance in most junior high schools was the homeroom period. Like most educational innovations of the time, the homeroom developed its own supporting rationale. One basic argument given for the homeroom was that the junior high school student tended to be lost and confused by departmental teaching. The homeroom was to provide a "home" where the student could seek direction and advice. The principal of Garfield Junior High in Richmond, Indiana, wrote, "The work of teacher-advisers or home-room teachers, as they are sometimes called—is to unify the school life of the pupil."[59]

The wedding of vocational guidance and socialization in the junior high school provided the complete educational program for the development of human capital. Differentiation would prepare the student for a particular place in society, and socialization would teach the student to cooperate and work for the good of the entire organization. One example of this combination was evident at the Ben Blewett Junior High School. Its principal claimed that teachers could differ with him on anything except "the two fundamental principles for which the school stands." The first principle was a differentiated curriculum, and the second was that "the school cannot be a preparation for adult social life except as it reproduces within itself situations typical of social life."[60]

One of the major debates about the junior high school was the degree of differentiation that should be undertaken with early adolescents. This was one of the issues considered by the Commission on the Reorganization of Secondary Education in *Cardinal Principles*. The commission concluded that the junior high school years should be a period of vocational exploration and prevocational counseling and that differentiation based on vocational choice should be delayed until high school. In general, this became the accepted pattern for junior high education in the 1920s.

In summary, vocational education, vocational guidance, and the junior high school were all justified by appeals to the need for development of human capital. National concerns about international economic competition provided support for educational innovations designed to train and socialize students for the new corporate world. Like those instituted in the comprehensive high school, these innovations directly linked public schools to the needs of the economic system.

PUBLIC BENEFIT OR CORPORATE GREED?

Whether or not the expanded role of the school, changes in classroom practices, and the development of the comprehensive high school, vocational education, and vocational guidance reflected corporate greed or public demands is widely debated by historians. Were schools simply institutions for maintaining social order and ensuring a climate that protected new corporate wealth? Or were schools primarily serving public interests? In a broad perspective, one could answer yes to both questions. The historical evidence seems to support both positions.

At one end of the scale, historians have described the major educational changes occurring in the late nineteenth and early twentieth centuries as simply responses to the problems caused by the collapse of traditional institutions and the influx of immigrants unfamiliar with American democratic ways of living. At the other end of the scale, the argument has been made, the schools were brought under the control of the new corporate elite to serve its social and economic interests. In the middle of this debate has been the claim that immigrants and workers helped to define their own educational future through rational economic choices.

One early interpretation of this period is that given by Ellwood Cubberley, who was both a chronicler of the period and a participant in many of its educational changes, in *Public Education in the United States: A Study and Interpretation of American Educational History.* First published in 1919, Cubberley's work reflects the attitudes of many educators about social and economic conditions in the late nineteenth and early twentieth centuries and the thinking of some educational reformers of that period. His interpretation is that the schools had to change to meet the threat posed to democratic institutions by immigrants from southern and eastern Europe and to instill the social values lost with the passing of small-town rural life.

Cubberley portrays the immigrants from southern and eastern Europe as being politically, socially, and educationally backward as compared with earlier immigrants from northern and western Europe. He states that these newer immigrants were "largely illiterate, docile, often lacking in initiative, and almost wholly without the Anglo-Saxon conceptions of righteousness, liberty, law, order, public decency, and government, [and] their coming has served to dilute tremendously our national stock and to weaken and corrupt our political life." He includes in this category Italians immigrating after 1870; Poles, Bohemians, Hungarians, Slovaks, and Austrians arriving after 1880; and Jews, Russians, Japanese, Koreans, and residents of the Balkans. According to Cubberley, these immigrant groups were a threat to the American way of life.[61]

Cubberley argues that in the past the assimilation of immigrant groups had been easier because most spoke English (except for the Germans), had common values, and were free "of a priesthood bent on holding nationalities together for religious ends." On the other hand, the assimilation of newer groups had been retarded because of their large numbers, their settlement in urban areas, and various language and religious differences. Cubberley argues that these conditions made it necessary for the schools consciously to institute Americanization programs "to so assimilate the foreign-born that they come to have our conceptions of law and order and government, and come to act in harmony with the spirit and purpose of our American national ideals."[62]

After detailing the technological and industrial changes after the Civil War and the growth of urbanization in America, Cubberley goes on to maintain that the influence of the home and church had been seriously weakened, and, consequently, traditional values of courtesy, respect, obedience, and honesty were not as widely taught to children as in the past. In addition, the homogeneous community of the American past was dissolving, so that it no longer exercised restraint over individual actions; and the nature of employment had also changed to meet the growing requirements of specialization in the factory system.

Cubberley argues that, against the background of these changes, the school changed to meet the needs of society: "As modern city-life conditions have come more and more to surround both boys and girls, depriving them of the training and education which earlier farm and village life once gave, the school has been called to take upon itself the task of giving training in those industrial experiences and social activities which once formed so important a part of the education of American youths." Also, he claims, the growth of divisions among social classes as a result of industrialization required the schools to build a new social consciousness and unity.[63]

Therefore, Cubberley's interpretation of the educational changes of the late nineteenth and early twentieth centuries is that the school changed simply to solve social and economic problems. Within this framework, the school is seen as a mere captive of social conditions. There is little or no discussion by Cubberley of the school as a political institution shaped by the competition of various interest groups in society.

Lawrence Cremin, in his 1961 landmark study, *The Transformation of the School: Progressivism in American Education, 1876–1957*, uses the same interpretative framework, but without the attitude of Anglo-Saxon superiority found in Cubberley's description of the new immigrants. Cremin places all major educational changes of the late nineteenth and the twentieth centuries under the label of progressivism and states that this movement began as "a many-sided effort to use the schools to improve the lives of individuals." Cremin lists as elements in this "many-sided effort" the expansion of the social functions of the school "to include direct concern for health, vocation, and the quality of family and community life"; the use of principles of psychology and the social sciences in classroom instruction; and the attempt to have instruction meet the needs of "different kinds and classes of children."[64]

Like Cubberley, Cremin does not deal with political conflicts or with the issue of whose interests were being served by the changes in educational institutions. His basic assumption is that the school was a benign institution and that most educational changes were the result of attempts to improve the quality of life for all people.

Unlike Cubberley, however, Cremin presents a broader view of the educational community's reaction to the new immigration. He identifies one school of thought, which he associates with Cubberley, as believing that Americanization meant Anglicization. Cremin argues that others believed that the promise of national unity was in the creation of a new nationality that would result from a melting together of the old and new immigrants. Still another group believed that cultural pluralism was possible, allowing ethnic identity to be maintained in the framework of shared American values. Cremin also provides an in-depth and scholarly interpretation of the school's response to industrialization and urbanization.

Many scholars have opposed the view that most educational change in the late nineteenth and early twentieth centuries was primarily a product of altruism. One set of interpretations argues that the political and administrative structure of education changed to ensure elite and corporate control of the educational system and to produce cooperative and docile workers. Another set of interpretations portrays the educational change of the period as a result of the dynamic interplay between the demands of industry and the demands of workers. This interpretative framework makes historical change a product of conflict—not the manipulation of passive workers by powerful business leaders.

The earliest historical study to span both interpretative frameworks is Merle Curti's *Social Ideas of American Educators*. Unlike Cubberley, who views industrial evolution as a matter of technological triumph, Curti discusses the major clashes and wars between workers and capitalists in the late nineteenth century. Curti contends that the majority of educational changes that occurred at that time were designed to serve the interests of the owners of industrial enterprises. For instance, he argues that vocational education and manual training were attempts to control and counteract radicalism among American workers: "An increasing number of educators advocated manual training and industrial education as the best specific means of counteracting radicalism on the part of the working masses." According to Curti, vocational education, the differentiated curriculum of the comprehensive high school, and other educational reforms were designed specifically to improve the industrial efficiency of America for competition in world markets. Even the values of cooperation and interdependence that were to be taught in the classroom are considered by Curti to be attempts to deny the inevitable conflict between labor and capital. Curti maintains that the values of most leading educators were economically conservative: "Hardly an annual meeting of the National Education Association was concluded without an appeal on the part of educators for the help of the teacher in quelling strikes and checking the spread of socialism and anarchism." The educators who were developing moral training for the schools, he states, "turned . . . increasingly to the social sciences as means by which schools might inculcate respect for law and order, and suspicion for the doctrines of socialism and anarchism."[65]

Although Curti paints a picture of the public schools as institutions enlisted by the power of organized wealth to train and select workers and inculcate values supportive of their control, he does recognize the efforts of organized labor to influence educational policy. Of special importance, from Curti's viewpoint, was the founding of the Chicago Federation of Teachers—the predecessor of the American Federation of Teachers—in the early twentieth century by classroom teacher Margaret Haley. Curti sympathetically relates Haley's belief that "public school teachers must recognize the fact that their struggle to maintain the efficiency of the schools through better conditions for themselves was part of the same great struggle which manual workers had been making for humanity through their efforts to secure living conditions for themselves and their children." Haley fought against the tendency to turn schools into factories and children into future factory workers (see Chapter 10). To a certain extent, Curti views militant teachers as being allied with organized labor against school administrators, who were allied with business interests.[66]

Another school of historical interpretation places the idea that business controlled and used the school in the broader conceptual framework of the rise of the corporate liberal state. Clarence Karier, Paul Violas, and Joel Spring's *Roots of Crisis: American Education in the Twentieth Century*, Joel Spring's *Education and the Rise of the Corporate State*, and Clarence Karier's *Shaping the American Educational State* advance the idea that schools in the late nineteenth and early twentieth centuries were shaped as instruments of the corporate liberal state for maintaining social control. Karier states some believed that the corporate liberal state "could be used as a positive vehicle to reconcile the competing interest of capital, labor and the public welfare. They further surmised that such conflicting interest could be reconciled by effectively rationalizing and stabilizing an ever expanding economy of production and consumption of goods and services."[67] In other words, the government was to intervene in the economy and social system to maintain balance and rational order. The public schools were seen as in important instrument used by the government to aid in the rationalization and minimization of conflict by selecting and training students for their future positions in the economy and by imbuing the population with a sense of cooperation and national spirit.

According to this interpretation, the corporate liberal state was operated by expert managers using scientific methods, which in the case of the public schools meant psychologists armed with tests to measure intelligence, abilities, and interests. Within this interpretive context, the expanded social functions of the school, the socialized classroom with its emphasis on cooperation, vocational education, vocational guidance, testing, and a differentiated curriculum were all instruments to be used to provide rationality and order in society.

This group of historians emphasizes the concept of social control—a concept born during the late nineteenth and early twentieth centuries and used by the architects of corporate liberalism to justify their actions. This idea is most clearly stated by sociologist Edward Ross in a series of articles that appeared in the *American Journal of Sociology* between 1896 and 1898. In these articles, Ross defines social control as the means of maintaining social order and he divides the means of control into external and internal forms. External forms of control involve direct confrontation between individuals and the police or government. Internal forms of control, which Ross considers more democratic and to be most relied upon, involve psychic control—control of the conscience of individuals. In America's past, Ross argues, internal forms of control were established through the community, family, and church. The problem for the future, he maintains, was that these traditional instruments of internal control were collapsing with the growth of industrialization and urbanization.

Ross suggests that these traditional instruments of social control be replaced with new forms, such as mass media, propaganda, and education, and argues that reliance on education as a means of control was becoming characteristic of American society as the school began to take the place of the church and family: "The ebb of religion is only half a fact. The other half is the high tide of education. While the priest is leaving the civil service, the schoolmaster is coming in. As the state shakes itself loose from the church, it reaches out for the school."[68]

Within the framework of the corporate liberal state, education, through the utilization of social science, was seen as the ideal mechanism for engineering social control for the benefit of all. The traditional forms of social control exercised through the church, family, and community were considered inadequate for modern society because they could not be scientifically managed, whereas the school could be used as an instrument of rational planning. Ross believed that modern civilization was learning this important lesson. He argues that the advantage of the school over the home as a means of control was in the fact that a public official was substituted for a parent: "Copy the child will, and the advantage of giving him his teacher instead of his father to imitate, is that the former is a picked person, while the latter is not." In the school, the child learned "the habit of obedience to an external law which is given by a good school discipline." In rather interesting language, Ross refers to education in the context of social control as collecting "little plastic lumps of human dough from private households and shap[ing] them on the social kneadingboard."[69]

In summary, those who argue within the framework of the corporate liberal state interpret educational changes in the late nineteenth and early twentieth centuries as an attempt to scientifically engineer a specialized and cooperative society. According to these educational historians, the major problem in this effort is that science and claims of objective social engineering were only masks for values that were racist and designed to control the majority of people. On the other hand, some argue that controllers of the liberal corporate state were merely trying to engineer a society that would protect their interests and that educators, the schools, social science, psychologists, and other engineers of the human mind were merely servants of power.

A variation on the theme of the corporate liberal state is used by David Tyack in his well-written, scholarly study *The One Best System: A History of American Urban Education.* An important element in Tyack's history is the development of modern urban educational bureaucracies and power structures. Like Merle Curti, Tyack concludes that education was controlled by business and corporate elites, and like Karier, Violas, and Spring, he believes that an alliance existed between the new corporate leaders and the intellectuals who served as their instruments of power. Regarding the campaign from 1890 to 1920 to reform urban education, Tyack states: "At that time an interlocking directorate of urban elites—largely business and professional men, university presidents and professors, and some 'progressive' superintendents—joined forces to centralize the control of schools."[70]

Using the corporate model developed by the historians of the corporate liberal state, Tyack argues that the administration of schools during this period was patterned after that of the modern corporation and factory. He calls these centralizers of organizational control and power "administrative progressives," in contradistinction to the political progressives who had organized the corporate liberal state.

A major problem with both Tyack's interpretation and that of the historians of the corporate liberal state is that they treat the worker, the immigrant, and the average citizen as pawns in a power game played by a ruling elite of businesspeople and intellectuals. According to this view of history, the masses of humanity were merely objects of decisions made by conspiratorial seekers of control; thus the average citizen is depicted as not wanting or caring about the educational reforms of the period and as not having an effect on the system.

A strong attack on this idea is made by historian Julia Wrigley in *Class Politics and Public Schools: Chicago, 1900–1950.* One of her main concerns is the lack of attention given by historians of the liberal corporate state to the impact of conflict between labor and capital on the shaping of the schools: "In their readiness to call attention to the successes of the social elite in dominating and socializing those below . . . [historians of the liberal corporate state] have given little weight to the social conflicts that have occurred over the creation and shaping of public institutions."[71]

Wrigley argues that attention must be given to the double-edged character of education: On the one hand, it can be used to promote docility, and, on the other hand, it can heighten criticism of the system. She finds that Chicago business leaders resisted increased spending for education because of a fear of an "overeducated" work force, but when faced with the prospect of increased school attendance by working-class children, they began to demand a differentiated curriculum that emphasized character development and vocational training. In contrast, Wrigley states, organized labor promoted increased education for working-class children and supported a broad liberal education for all children.

Wrigley's book highlights the continual struggle between business and organized labor. The picture she presents is one of constant attempts by both groups to promote educational policies that matched their own economic interests. Business struggled to maintain a school system that was inexpensive and produced students trained and socialized to meet the requirements of the labor market, whereas organized labor struggled to force business to spend more on education that would produce students capable of protecting their economic, political, and social rights. For Wrigley, the educational institutions of the twentieth century are not a product of elite imposition but were shaped by this social struggle.

Another approach to interpreting history is to consider social change as a product of interaction between different social groups. William Reese's *Power and the Promise of School Reform: Grassroots Movements During the Progressive Era* stresses that many of the changes in the social functions of schools in the late nineteenth and early twentieth centuries were a product of local groups putting pressure on the business leaders and professionals who were gaining control of local school systems. His study focuses on the history of three communities: Milwaukee, Wisconsin; Toledo, Ohio; and Rochester, New York. Within these communities, Reese portrays a combination of parents' associations, women's organizations, labor unions, and other groups struggling to have the schools meet the needs of the local community. Out of this struggle came the use of the schoolhouse as a social center, the establishment of playgrounds, the provision of health facilities in schools, and the creation of summer schools.

The important issue raised by Reese is whether or not school reform was imposed on a passive population. Reese's research certainly disproves this interpretation. But the arguments regarding the use of these reforms as instruments of social control by a dominant elite are also valid. Reese recognizes that these different groups fought for the control of schools and of the school reform movement. He summarizes this situation in the following words:

> To a banker on the Milwaukee board of education in 1910, school organization represented business ethics, and teachers were hired to instill proper values into incipient workers. To members of middle-class women's organizations, however, schools were humanitarian institutions that sponsored free breakfasts for the hungry and safe playgrounds for guttersnipes. Political radicals and progressive trade unionists, on the other hand, often saw schools as evolving democratic forms that nevertheless required vigilance and continual protection from the serpentine arms of manufacturers and capitalists.[72]

Reese's interpretation provides a method of interpreting the politics of education in the twentieth century. Within this interpretative framework, the school is seen by a variety of opposing groups as an institution that can serve their particular purposes. By the 1980s and 1990s, one can see this particular theme in the struggles over educational policy that is taking place between the Democratic and Republican parties.[73]

With regard to the early twentieth century, there would appear to be some contradiction between the idea of elites using school reform as an instrument of social control and more populist groups supporting similar reform to benefit the working class. These seemingly contradictory sets of interpretations can be resolved by the argument that both the haves and have-nots shared a similar vision of the best organization for society.

This is an argument I originally made in my book *Education and the Rise of the Corporate State.*[74] I would argue that by the early twentieth century many groups in society shared a vision that social problems could be resolved through the expansion of the activities of social institutions including the public schools. For instance, on the one hand, leaders of industry could support school health programs, vacation schools, and playgrounds because they believed that these programs would produce better workers and reduce the expansion of labor unions. On the other hand, unions and socialists could support these programs because they believed they served the interests of the working class. In both situations, these differing groups shared a common vision of how to achieve their particular goals.

THE MEANING OF EQUALITY OF OPPORTUNITY

One of the dominant themes in schooling in the twentieth century is equality of opportunity. The differentiated curricula of the junior and senior high schools and vocational guidance were to provide equal opportunity from the perspective of improving human capital. Within this context, equality of opportunity took on special and complex meanings. First, equality of opportunity was considered good for society because it increased industrial efficiency by matching individual talents to specific occupational requirements. Everyone was to be given an equal chance to rise or fall on the social ladder according to individual abilities. This meant that everyone would be given an equal chance to run the social race—*not* that everyone would have equal income or social status. Second, equality of opportunity was considered good for the individual because it allowed a person to find the best place in the economic system in which to develop personal interests and abilities.

A major change occurred between the nineteenth and twentieth centuries in the school's role in providing equality of opportunity. In the early days of the common school movement, education was to provide equality of opportunity by giving everyone a common or equal education, after which the social race would begin, with everyone competing for places in the social and economic structure. In the twentieth century, the provision for equality of opportunity was made a part of the school system through vocational guidance and a differentiated curriculum. No longer did students receive an equal, or common, education; rather, they received different educations based on individual differences. The race for social positions was no longer to be a function of the marketplace but of the scientific selection process in the school.

A major argument for making the provision for equality of opportunity a function of the school instead of the marketplace was that the marketplace was unfair because of the influence exerted by wealth and family background. It was believed that the school would be more objective about selecting people for their economic and social places through the use of scientific instruments of selection.

Therefore, the science of education, particularly measurement, was considered the key to the efficient use of human resources. Scientific measurement of intelligence, abilities, and interests was to serve as an objective means of providing equality of opportunity. This concept of equality of opportunity gave the expert and the school a major role in determining an individual's place in society. In essence, scientific measurement, combined with a differentiated curriculum, was to develop human capital by objectively controlling the provision of equality of opportunity.

A major problem with this concept of equality of opportunity, as is reflected in the history of segregated education, was that the supposed objectivity of scientific measurement and public schools was often a mask for social-class and racial discrimination. Once the schools tried to determine a person's place in the social and economic system, they were open to charges of discriminating against particular social or racial groups. As a result, a major theme in the history of schooling in the twentieth century has been discrimination against minority groups and certain social classes. The use of schooling to increase economic efficiency through the development of human capital opened the door for education to become a central focus of social controversy in the twentieth century. Interwoven with the theme of human capital has been the politics of education. As is demonstrated by the history of education in the South, the group or groups that control the schools have a major influence in determining the outcomes of attempts to provide equality of opportunity.

NOTES

1. Maris A. Vinovskis, "Have We Underestimated the Extent of Antebellum High School Attendance?" *History of Education Quarterly*, Vol. 28, No. 4 (Winter 1988), pp. 551–567.
2. David F. Labaree, *The Making of an American High School: The Credentials Market and the Central High School of Philadelphia, 1838–1939* (New Haven, Conn.: Yale University Press, 1988).
3. Edward Krug, *The Shaping of the American High School: Vol. 1* (New York: Harper & Row, 1964), pp. 169–170, 284; and *The Shaping of the American High School: Vol. 2, 1920–1941* (Madison: University of Wisconsin Press, 1972), pp. 42, 218–219.

4. Edward Krug, *Salient Dates in American Education: 1635–1964* (New York: Harper & Row, 1966), pp. 46–50.

5. Ibid., pp. 91–95.

6. Ibid., p. 93.

7. Quoted in Krug, *Shaping,* Vol. 1, p. 68.

8. Quoted in ibid., pp. 274–275.

9. Quoted in ibid., p. 280.

10. Quoted in ibid., p. 281.

11. G. Stanley Hall, *Adolescence* (Englewood Cliffs, N.J.: Prentice-Hall, 1904), Vol. 1, p. xv; G. Stanley Hall, "Childhood and Adolescence" in Charles Strickland and Charles Burgess, eds., *Health, Growth, and Heredity* (New York: Teachers College Press, 1965), p. 108.

12. G. Stanley Hall, *Adolescence* (Englewood Cliffs, N.J.: Prentice-Hall, 1904), Vol. 2, p. 125.

13. Commission on the Reorganization of Secondary Education, National Education Association, *Cardinal Principles of Secondary Education,* Bureau of Education Bulletin (Washington, D.C.: U.S. Government Printing Office, 1918). The remainder of the discussion of *Cardinal Principles,* the comprehensive high school, and extracurricular activities is taken from Joel Spring, *Education and the Rise of the Corporate State* (Boston: Beacon Press, 1972), pp. 108–125.

14. Commission on the Reorganization of Secondary Education, *Cardinal Principles,* p. 109.

15. Ibid., pp. 109–110.

16. Ibid., p. 110.

17. Ibid.

18. Ibid., p. 111.

19. For instance, Elbert K. Fretwell, "Extra-Curricular Activities of Secondary Schools," *Teachers College Record* (January 1923; January 1924; May 1926; June 1926; June 1927).

20. Thomas W. Gutowski, "Student Initiative and the Origins of the High School Extracurriculum: Chicago, 1880–1915," *History of Education Quarterly,* Vol. 28, No. 1 (Spring 1988), pp. 49–72.

21. Richard Welling, *As the Twig Is Bent* (New York: G. P. Putman's Sons, 1942), p. 91; and *Self Government Miscellanies.*

22. William A. McAndrew, *School Review* (September 1897), pp. 456–460.

23. Walter L. Phillips, "Pupil Co-operation in Self-Goverment," *Education* (April 1902), p. 543.

24. Edward Rynearson, "Supervised Student Activities in the School Program," *First Yearbook, National Association of Secondary School Principals* (Cicero, Ill.: National Association of Secondary School Principals, 1917), pp. 47–50.

25. D. E. Cloyd, "Student Organizations in City High Schools," *Education* (September 1910), pp. 17–20.

26. Frank K. Phillips, "The School Paper," *Industrial Arts Magazine* (July 1917), pp. 268–271, reprinted in Joseph Roemer and Charles F. Allen,

eds., *Readings in Extra-Curricular Activities* (New York: Teacher's College Press, 1929), pp. 462–467.

27. Mary A. Sheehan, "Clubs—A Regular Social Activity," *High School Journal* (October 1921), pp. 132–135, reprinted in Roemer and Allen, *Readings,* p. 304.
28. V. K. Froula, "Extra-Curricular Activities: Their Relation to the Curricular Work of the School," *National Education Association Proceedings* (1915), pp. 738–739.
29. James Naismith, "High School Athletics and Gymnastics as an Expression of the Corporate Life of the High School" in Charles H. Johnston, ed., *The Modern High School* (New York: Scribner's Sons, 1914), p. 440.
30. C. M. Howe, "The High-School Teacher and Athletics," *School Review* (December 1923), pp. 781–782.
31. Charles R. Foster, *Extra-Curricular Activities in the High School* (Richmond, Va.: 1925), pp. 108–109.
32. Eileen H. Galvin and M. Eugenia Walker, *Assemblies for Junior and Senior High Schools* (New York: Professional & Technical Press, 1929), p. 1.
33. Francis H. J. Paul, "The Growth of Character Through Participation in Extra-Curricular Activities," *The Fifth Yearbook of the Department of Secondary-School Principals* (Cicero, Ill.: National Association of Secondary School Principals, 1921), Vol. 2, pp. 54–60.
34. Harvey R. Kantor, *Learning to Earn: School, Work, and Vocational Reform in California, 1880–1930* (Madison: University of Wisconsin Press, 1988).
35. Calvin Woodward, "The Fruits of Manual Training" in Marvin Lazerson and W. Norton Grubb, eds., *American Education and Vocationalism: A Documentary History, 1870–1970* (New York: Teachers College Press, 1974), pp. 60–66.
36. National Association of Manufacturers, "Reports of the Committee on Industrial Education (1905, 1912)" in Lazerson and Grubb, *American Education,* p. 91.
37. Ibid., pp. 92–96.
38. Ibid., pp. 97–100.
39. U.S. Congress, House, 63rd Cong., 2nd Sess., 1914, "Report: Commission on National Aid to Vocational Education" in Lazerson and Grubb, *American Education,* pp. 116–132.
40. Ibid.
41. Ibid.
42. Lazerson and Grubb, *American Education,* pp. 30–31.
43. Ibid.
44. Ibid.
45. Krug, *Shaping,* Vol. 1, pp. 243–244.
46. Eli W. Weaver, *Wage-Earning Occupations of Boys and Girls* (New York: Student's Aid Committee of the High School Teachers' Assoc., 1912). The remainder of the discussion of the history of vocational guidance and the junior high school is taken from Spring, *Education and the Rise of the Corporate State,* pp. 91–108.

47. J. Adams Puffer, *Vocational Guidance* (Chicago: Rand McNally, 1913), p. 274.
48. Frank Parsons, *Choosing a Vocation* (Boston: Houghton Mifflin, 1909), pp. 32–44.
49. Frederick G. Bonser, "Necessity of Professional Training for Vocational Counseling" in *Vocational Guidance: Papers Presented at the Organization Meeting of the Vocational Association, Grand Rapids, Michigan, October 21–24, 1913,* U.S. Bureau of Education Bulletin no. 14 (1914), p. 38.
50. Hugo Munsterberg, *Psychology and Industrial Efficiency* (Cambridge, Mass.: Harvard University Press, 1913), pp. 36–55.
51. Jesse B. Davis, *Vocational and Moral Guidance* (Boston: 1914), pp. 46–123.
52. Jesse B. Davis, "Vocational and Moral Guidance in the High School," *Religious Education* (February 1913), p. 646.
53. Meyer Bloomfield, "Vocational Guidance in the High School" in Johnston, *The Modern High School*, p. 612.
54. Krug, *Shaping*, Vol. 1, pp. 327–335.
55. Quoted in ibid., p. 328.
56. Quoted in *Report of the Committee to Make a Survey of the Junior High Schools of the City of New York* (1924), p. 236.
57. Philip Cox, "The Ben Blewett Junior High School: An Experiment in Democracy," *School Review* (May 1919), pp. 345–359.
58. Thomas W. Gosling, "Educational Reconstruction in the Junior High School," *Educational Review* (May 1919), pp. 384–385.
59. N. C. Hieronimus, "The Teacher-Adviser in the Junior High School," *Educational Administration and Supervision* (February 1917), p. 91.
60. Cox, "Ben Blewett Junior High School," p. 346.
61. Ellwood Cubberley, *Public Education in the United States: A Study and Interpretation of American Educational History* (Boston: Houghton Mifflin, 1934), pp. 485–486.
62. Ibid., pp. 488–489.
63. Ibid., pp. 502–504.
64. Lawrence Cremin, *The Transformation of the School: Progressivism in American Education, 1876–1957* (New York: Vintage Books, 1961), pp. viii–ix.
65. Merle Curti, *The Social Ideas of American Educators* (Paterson, N.J.: Pageant Books, 1959), pp. 218–222.
66. Ibid., p. 242.
67. Clarence Karier, *Shaping the American Educational State, 1900 to Present* (New York: Free Press, 1975), p. xix.
68. Edward A. Ross, *Social Control* (New York: Macmillan, 1906), p. 175.
69. Ibid., p. 168.
70. David Tyack, *The One Best System: A History of American Urban Education* (Cambridge, Mass.: Harvard University Press, 1974), p. 7.
71. Julia Wrigley, *Class Politics and Public Schools: Chicago, 1900–1950* (New Brunswick, N.J.: Rutgers University Press, 1982), p. 13.

72. William J. Reese, *Power and the Promise of School Reform: Grassroots Movements During the Progressive Era* (Boston: Routledge & Kegan Paul, 1986), p. xx.
73. I use this interpretative framework in Joel Spring, *Conflict of Interests: The Politics of American Education* (White Plains, N.Y.: Longman, 1988).
74. Joel Spring, *Education and the Rise of the Corporate State* (Boston: Beacon Press, 1972).

CHAPTER 10

Meritocracy: The Experts Take Charge

A new elite emerged in the late nineteenth century that was composed of public administrators, efficiency experts, professional managers, and social scientists who were captivated by the vision of a scientifically managed society. This vision of social organization placed the expert in charge. Throughout the country, political reform groups sought to replace the politician in government with a public servant or bureaucrat. The new professional administrators were to bring expert knowledge and skills to the management of organizations. It was claimed that the politician served only special interests, whereas the professional administrator or public servant served the general public. Of course, the creation of government bureaucracies has serious implications for the meaning of democracy.

For the public schools, the vision of scientific management included a professionally trained corps of administrators who would assume greater control of the schools as the governing power of school boards diminished. "Keep the schools out of politics!" became the war cry of the new professional educators. In practice, these changes resulted in small school boards that were composed of community elites and had limited functions. These school boards relinquished many of their traditional functions to the new professional administrators.

Schools were also given an important role in the vision of a scientifically controlled society because they were considered the central social institution for the selection and training of human capital. In the schools, the measurement expert became the manager of human resources. Psychologists marched into the schools armed with batteries of tests to measure students for their future places in society.

Within the schools, psychologists and professional administrators joined hands to preach a new version of equality of opportunity. No longer were the schools to play a passive role in the provision of equality of opportunity, simply providing an equal education and letting social position be determined by competition in the marketplace. The new breed of scientific managers distrusted the free interaction of the marketplace, because uncontrollable factors such as family wealth or poverty could cause a mismatch between individual abilities and occupational requirements. The free marketplace was considered both unfair and inefficient in the distribution of human resources.

During the earlier part of the nineteenth century, it was thought that the school would provide equality of opportunity by offering an equal education that would allow for equal competition among individuals after they completed their education. The major hope was that the school would make it possible for children of poor families to compete on equal terms with children from rich families. The newer version of equality of opportunity, which emerged in the 1920s and 1930s, combined the hope of providing the opportunity for equal competition between children of the rich and of the poor with a desire to create an efficient society in which interests and abilities matched social position.

The new school leaders hoped to replace the alleged unfairness and inefficiency inherent in free-market competition with the supposedly scientific objectivity and fairness of the scientifically managed public school. Instead of leaving social selection to the uncertainties of the marketplace, it was hoped that social selection—the provision of equality of opportunity—would become a function of scientific management and measurement in educational institutions. The new tools for providing equality of opportunity were the junior and comprehensive high schools, with their differentiated curricula, and the new tests being developed within the expanding field of psychology.

Behind the claims of fairness and scientific objectivity lurked important questions about the meaning of democracy in a scientifically managed society. First, there was the problem of reconciling governance by expertise with governance by the will of the majority. Second, there was the problem of values. Claims of fairness and scientific objectivity lose meaning when the role of individual values is considered. Decisions about the management of organizations, the use and contents of tests, and the abilities and attitudes that should be taught were based on individual values, not scientific principles. Consequently, claims of scientific objectivity often masked personal prejudices and self-interest. For instance, tests often relegated certain racial groups to an inferior position in society and, at the same time, through claims as to the importance of scientific measurement, ensured the social prestige and importance of the new test makers.

The source of the new elite of professional managers and social scientists and the citadel of hope for the scientific understanding and management of society were the new universities. By the end of the nineteenth century, colleges and universities began to change from institutions that simply conferred a liberal education and prepared students for the professions into institutions that were to be centers for the creation of new knowledge through research and training grounds for the scientific management of society. Spurred by the increasing importance of science and the model of the German university, American higher education underwent a major transformation with the creation of graduate education and the new vision of the social role of the college and university.

The attempts to use the school to manage society scientifically and the professionalization of school management are explored in this chapter. First, the professionalization of school administration and the changing political structure of American education are considered. Second, the early history of tests and measurement and the philosophical problems that emerged in that field, and third, the development of special classrooms are discussed. Last, the new role of higher education and the development of graduate schools of education are described.

MERITOCRACY AND EFFICIENT MANAGEMENT

Meritocracy is a concept of society based on the idea that each individual's social and occupational position is determined by individual merit, not political or economic influence. Scientific management of both human capital and organizations is a central idea in the meritocracy concept. For the schools, meritocracy was both a social goal and a method of internal organization. To achieve meritocracy as a social goal, the schools were to create a society based on merit by objectively selecting and preparing students for their ideal places in the social order. As a method of internal organization, meritocracy meant the creation of an administrative structure in which the positions held by professionals depended on their training and abilities as opposed to their political influence and power.

The attempt to create a meritocracy in the organization of the schools was concurrent with the establishment of small school boards. In fact, several related changes in the administrative and political structure of American schools occurred at the same time as the concept of meritocracy gained prominence. Of major importance was the establishment of small school boards and the resultant increase in the number of duties and, consequently, the power of school administrators. As this occurred, school administrators adopted techniques of scientific business management for use in the administration of the schools.

Three important sets of ideas were used to justify these political and administrative changes. The first was the concept that the school should be kept out of politics. In most cases, this meant putting the major power and control of the schools into the hands of administrators serving the interests of the children, not into the hands of politicians serving special interests. This argument justified the increasing power of school administrators in relation to boards of education.

The second set of ideas centered on the concept of democratic elitism and was used to justify the creation of small school boards. What is meant here by *elitism* is control of the schools by local civic elites composed primarily of people who exercise power over local public policy without, in most cases, holding offices in government. They usually work through informal networks and civic organizations such as a local chamber of commerce or service club.

The civic elites involved in school administration in the early twentieth century viewed themselves not as conspiratorial groups working behind the scenes for their own self-interest, but as enlightened leaders working for the good of the entire community. One recent study of the occupations of civic elites found that over 50 percent were bankers, industrialists, and heads of local businesses, while the remainder included heads of local utilities, newspaper people, civic association executives, clergy, university administrators, and professionals (lawyers, doctors, and the like).[1]

In the rhetoric of democratic elitism, only the "best"—the elite—should determine important public matters, because they have proven themselves successful and possess superior knowledge of public affairs. For instance, it was argued that a factory worker would have less ability than a banker to make correct decisions about the public interest regarding schooling. Following this line of reasoning, reformers argued that the schools should be governed only by the "best" members of the community and, therefore, that school board elections should be instructed so that only the "best" could be elected.

The third set of ideas dealt with the proper relationship between the school board and the school administration. As the rhetoric of school administration developed in the early twentieth century, it became common to argue that the proper role of the administrators was to administer that policy *without interference from the board of education.* These distinctions between roles helped to increase and justify the power of school administrators.

These changes in the administration and political control of the schools and their accompanying justifications were caused by a complex and interwoven set of historical changes. No single factor explains all the changes, but all the factors were closely related. The establishment of small school boards sometimes resulted from the fear of local elite groups that their control over the schools would be lost to the political machines gaining ascendancy in urban politics at that time. In this case, local elites sought the restructuring of school board elections to ensure that their own control over the system would continue. In other cases, new elites composed of professionals viewed small school boards as a means of wresting power from the control of traditional elites.

The reduction in size of school boards was one factor that contributed to increasing administrative power. As school boards declined in power and ability to function in the schools, their traditional activities were passed on to the school administration. Also, the growth in size of school districts, particularly urban ones, required more administration and coordination. In turn, school administrators welcomed these changes because they increased their power, status, and income. School administrators championed ideas such as keeping the schools out of politics and maintaining clear lines between the functions of the school board and those of the administration. Administrators willingly adopted the principles of scientific management because it gave them status comparable to that of members of the business community.

The close relationship between local elites and school administrators became an important factor in the politics of education in the twentieth century. This relationship can be traced in the history of early school board reforms. One historical study of these changes is Joseph M. Cronin's *Control of Urban Schools: Perspectives on the Power of Educational Reformers.* Cronin argues that the major concern of reformers in urban schools in the 1890s was to reduce the power of local ward bosses, whose influence encompassed the appointment of teacher and members of the board of education. Within the context of this argument, the influence of ward bosses was a threat to the power of middle- and upper-class reformers.[2]

The way to destroy the influence that ward bosses had over urban schools was to centralize control, reduce the size of school boards, and make elections nonpartisan and at large. Middle- and upper-class reformers also hoped that the social composition of boards of education would change by eliminating the participation of workers and small-business people. In other words, these changes were intended to ensure the power of the groups campaigning for them.

For example, a pamphlet published by the Voter's League of Pittsburgh for the 1911 fall election deplored the fact that school boards contained only a small number of "men prominent throughout the city in business life . . . in professional occupations . . . holding positions as managers, secretaries, auditors, superintendents and foremen." The pamphlet argued that a person's occupation was a strong indication of her or his qualifications for the school board: "Employment as ordinary laborer and in the lowest class of mill work would naturally lead to the conclusion that such men did not have sufficient education or business training to act as school directors." Included on the list of those the reform group thought should not be on school boards were "small shopkeepers, clerks, workmen at any trades, who by lack of educational advantages and business training, could not, no matter how honest, be expected to administer properly the affairs of an educational system."[3]

The city of Cincinnati provides an example of how local elites consolidated their control after changing the procedures for the election to the board of education. In Cincinnati and throughout Ohio, the reform movement was headed by John Withrow, who was associated through marriage with the leaders of finance and business in the Cincinnati community. After the death of his first wife in the 1890s, Withrow, a struggling physician, married the daughter of local utilities magnate General Andrew Hickenlooper. After the marriage, Withrow's financial and social position changed from that of a physician of moderate income living in modest surroundings in the downtown area of Cincinnati to that of a socially prominent physician living in a mansion and financed by his new father-in-law. His fortunate marriage allowed him the leisure to devote considerable time to educational reforms and also gave him the opportunity to meet informally and establish relationships with leading members of the Cincinnati community. He worked with James N. Gamble, a founder of Procter & Gamble, a company that would exert major influence over the schools throughout the twentieth century.[4]

What is important about Withrow's activities is that after he had successfully worked for legislation to implement school board reforms, he created an organization of civic leaders for the purpose of maintaining control of the school system. This model was followed in many cities around the country. Initially, Withrow worked for the passage of a small-school-board bill in 1913 that reduced the size of urban school boards from roughly thirty to forty members to seven. In addition, elections were made citywide as opposed to election by district, and all school board elections were made nonpartisan.

It is important to understand how these changes in procedure for election of school board members affected the social composition of the board. When elections took place on a citywide basis, citizens who wanted to get onto the school board needed enough money and organizational backing to campaign throughout the city, whereas under the previously used method of election by district, candidates needed to campaign only within a small geographical area. Election by district had allowed candidates with limited financial resources and organizational backing to campaign door to door within a small district and talk to friends and neighbors. After elections were made citywide, it became more difficult for clerks, workingpeople, or small shopkeepers to be elected.

Making school board elections nonpartisan eliminated political parties from the nomination and campaign process. With the elimination of participation by organized political parties, the business and financial community became the major group with financial resources and organizational skills. Thus, the reduction in school board size also reduced the opportunity for average citizens to be represented in school affairs. The combination of these reforms almost guaranteed that school boards would represent the views and values of the financial, business, and professional communities.[5]

After passage of the small-school-board legislation in 1913, Withrow was concerned with consolidating the power of upper-class reformers over the school boards. What was required was the creation of an organization to fill the vacuum left by the establishment of nonpartisan elections. Shortly after the passage of the legislation, Withrow wrote to his friend Frank Dyer, superintendent of the Boston schools and former superintendent of the Cincinnati schools: "The small school board bill has passed and I am hoping to be set free from further cares and worries in connection with public education. I can't, however, help being anxious about getting the proper board under the new laws." What he wanted from Dyer was advice about establishing an organization that would ensure a "proper board." Withrow continues his letter to Dyer:

> Therefore I write you to send me the method of formation of the Boston school council or association, or whatever they call that organization that they have there, as I am told, entirely apart from the legally elected board. I am wanting here to start a federated education council . . . to make nominations for the school board and express opinions on the fitness of all nominations made from any other source.

It is clear from Withrow's letter that he viewed this form of organization as a method for circumventing the nonpartisan sections of the 1913 small-school-board bill. Withrow states in his letter to Dyer: "Now that the new law forbids any political party, by primary or convention, from naming candidates for the board of education, these candidates are to be nominated by petition only. What I want to know is, is there a similar or substantially similar committee or council or federation in Boston?"[6]

No record exists of Dyer's response to Withrow's letter. What Withrow did in Cincinnati in 1913 was to form the Citizen Council on Public Education, composed of representatives of the leading civic organizations in the community. The Citizen Council used a nominating committee to select school board candidates and a campaign committee to ensure their election. In 1921 the nominating and campaign committees were merged, and the original organization was absorbed under the banner of the Citizens School Committee.

The Citizens School Committee informally controlled elections to the school board from the 1920s until the time of the desegregation controversies of the late 1960s. As was stated by former acting superintendent of the Cincinnati public schools Robert Curry, whose career in the Cincinnati schools spanned the half century from 1925 to 1975, "Until the 1960s, the Board members, with few exceptions, had been nominated by the Citizens School Committee and had not been opposed by other candidates." During those years, most board members held their positions for long periods of time. Of the 49 Cincinnati school board members elected between 1914 and 1964, 18 were from the business and financial community, 10 were lawyers, 3 were physicians, 3 were religious leaders, and 4 were former educators (including retired superintendent Frank Dyer, who served on the board between 1920 and 1931); the occupations of the remaining 11 members are unknown. Clearly, the social composition of the board of education in Cincinnati in the first half of the twentieth century did not represent the social composition of the community.[7]

Similar patterns of shifting control occurred in other communities. Sol Cohen shows in *Progressives and Urban School Reform* how reform movements in New York City combined destruction of ward control of the schools with anti-Catholic sentiments. In the 1894 New York mayoral election, a reform mayor was elected who fought for centralization of control and removal of schools from the power of the politicians. Under the traditional New York ward system, the mayor appointed twenty-one commissioners of common schools, and they in turn appointed five trustees for each ward. The ward trustees appointed all teachers and janitors, nominated principals and vice principals, and furnished school supplies. This system provided opportunity for graft, but it also created a situation wherein the trustee had to be sensitive to local needs and desires. As Cohen states, "The reformers' battle cry, 'Take the schools out of politics,' not only meant take the schools out of the hands of Tammany Hall, it also meant take the schools out of the hands of the Roman Catholic Church."[8]

Some debate has taken place among historians about whether these school board reforms were a product of upper-class desires to assume control of the schools or of the vying for power of one group of community leaders against another. David Plank and Paul Peterson argue in their article "Does

Urban Reform Imply Class Conflict? The Case of Atlanta's School" that "while the reformers in Atlanta were members of the middle and upper classes . . . the Atlanta school reforms were carried out not over the objections of working class politicians but rather at the expense of the city's most prestigious civic leaders."[9]

The actual reforms that took place in Atlanta were slightly different from those in other cities. The Atlanta school board had traditionally been elected on a citywide basis, which meant, according to Plank and Peterson, that the city's social elite had always been in control. The actual reforms instituted in the late 1890s involved a reduction in school board membership from seventeen to seven and in the number of board committees from ten to two. These reductions meant less participation by board members in the functioning of the schools and, consequently, increased power for the school administrators. This shift in power was evidenced by increased responsibilities for the superintendent and by the hiring of an additional full-time assistant superintendent.

Where Plank and Peterson locate the sources of these reforms suggests an interesting hypothesis about the influence of reformers on the adoption of business management techniques by school administrators. Plank and Peterson argue that in Atlanta, the reforms were a product primarily of the activities of middle-class professionals who were concerned with modernization. In this context, school board reforms were designed not to wrest power from the working class but to introduce modern administrative techniques while retaining power within one faction of the urban elite.

Whether the goal of school board reforms was to empower one elite group over another or to allow elites to wrest power from politicians representing the working class, the end result was that school boards did come to be dominated by civic elites. In 1916 Scott Nearing, a professor of economics at the University of Pennsylvania, wrote to the superintendents of 131 school systems in cities with populations over 40,000 according to the 1910 census to get information about the social composition of their boards of education.

One important discovery by Nearing was the low representation of women on boards of education. He found that in large cities (with populations over 500,000), 12 percent of board members were women. In cities with populations of 100,000 to 500,000, 8 percent were women, and in cities of under 100,000, 5 percent were women. In general, Nearing found that 75 percent of all board members from reporting cities were business or professional people and that business people composed more than 50 percent of the total number of board members.[10]

In 1927 George Counts published a similar study of 1,654 school boards, half of which were rural. Like Nearing, Counts found women excluded from control; only 10.2 percent of board members were women, and they were mainly on urban school boards. He found that urban school boards were dominated by proprietors, professionals, and business executives and that farmers were in the majority on rural school boards. One cause of this situation, Counts noted, was the argument that developed in the twentieth century that it was necessary for professional and business leaders to control school boards.[11]

Accompanying the rise of elite school boards was the introduction of modern business techniques into the management of the schools. The earliest study of this phenomenon, one that is critical of this direction in twentieth-century American education, is Raymond E. Callahan's *Education and the Cult of Efficiency.* Callahan portrays the school administrator in the early twentieth century as capitulating to a business-person mentality because of both public pressure and the rewards that could be gained by adopting a status equal to that of members of the business community. He suggests that school administrators had abandoned the scholarly role of educational philosopher and curriculum leader for that of school administrator as business person.[12] Although more recent studies suggest that school administrators had traditionally viewed their role in business terms,[13] all agree that school administration became professionalized around concepts of scientific management borrowed from the business community.

Scientific management, or Taylorism, exploded on the American scene in the early part of the twentieth century under the leadership of time-and-motion-study pioneer Frederick W. Taylor. Taylor believed that the basic problems of American industry stemmed from unsystematic organization and control of work. He argued that scientific study could determine the proper method of doing every job. The problem in the past, he maintained, was that workers in factories and business organizations had been allowed to follow their own decisions or rules of thumb for the completion of a task. Scientific management promised to replace the unsystematic actions of workers with a planned and controlled work environment.

One principle of Taylorism that had important consequences for the organization of schools is hierarchical organization, with management directing the actions of workers. In Taylor's words, in the past, "almost all of the work and the greater part of the responsibility were thrown upon the men."[14] Under Taylorism, management assumed more duties by reducing workers' responsibilities and need for decision making. An organization was envisioned in which decisions would be made at the top, based on scientific studies, and would flow to the bottom.

Taylorism complemented the social efficiency thinking of educators because it mandated that workers be scientifically selected and trained for their particular jobs and that cooperation between management and workers occur "so as to insure all of the work being done in accordance with principles of the science which has been developed." The principles of hierarchical management, scientific study and control of the elements in the organization, selection and training of individuals for places within the organization, and cost-effectiveness became the focus for the professionalization of public school administration. Public school leaders jumped on the scientific management bandwagon with a vengeance. For instance, well-known efficiency expert Harrington Emerson was asked to speak at the 1911 meeting of the High School Teachers Association of New York City on the topic "Efficiency in the

High Schools through the Application of the Principles of Scientific Management." After telling his audience that it needed to have high ideals, good counsel, discipline, and common sense, he presented the practical side of the administrative efficiency movement. He stated that the most important element in practical methods or principles was standardization: planning, standard records, standard conditions, standardized operations, standard instructions, and standard schedules.[15]

Across the country, school administrators applied themselves to their newly acquired roles by trying to establish uniform procedures and lines of control. *Standardization* became the magic word. Administrators were preoccupied with standardizing student forms, evaluations of teachers and students, attendance records, personnel records, and hiring procedures. Cost-effectiveness also became an important part of this process as administrators worried about cost-effectiveness in the classroom, the ordering of supplies, the purchase of insurance, building maintenance, and office management. For many superintendents, the dollar became the major educational criterion. For instance, Frank Spaulding, a nationally renowned superintendent of the period, conducted studies of the economic value of different parts of the curriculum. Using a complex and vague formula, Spaulding reported in 1920 on the comparative worth of high school subjects. He argued that educational administrators needed to determine the cost and educational value of the subjects taught so that scientific decisions could be made about the cost efficiency of the curriculum. For example, he determined "that 5.9 pupil-recitations in Greek are of the same value as 23.8 pupil-recitations in French; that 12 pupil-recitations in science are equivalent in value to 19.2 pupil-recitations in English." Based on these calculations and a concern with cost-effectiveness, Spaulding argued that "when the obligations of the present year expire, we ought to purchase no more Greek instruction at the rate of 5.9 pupil-recitations for a dollar. The price must go down, or we shall invest in something else."[16]

Business values affected thinking about both administration and the value of education. Between 1900 and 1924, school administration rapidly professionalized around these values of cost-effectiveness and scientific management. An important factor in professionalization was specialized training, and one measure of this factor was the increase in the number of graduate courses in educational administration. In 1910, when principles of scientific management began to sweep the nation, Columbia University's Teachers College conferred 13 graduate degrees in administration and supervision out of a total of 73. In 1916, the institution granted 316 graduate degrees, of which 95 were in administration and supervision. By 1924, not only had the number of degrees jumped to 939, but 390 of these were in administration and supervision.[17]

More revealing is the actual content of the education of professional administrators. One content analysis of textbooks in educational administration conducted in the early 1930s (which means that the texts analyzed had been written in the 1920s or earlier) found "over four-fifths of eight thousand pages are devoted to the purely executive, organizational, and legal aspects of administration." These texts lacked critical analysis of educational problems, educational philosophy, or educational issues in a social context. The focus of training for school administrators was not scholarship and learning, but principles of management.[18]

A shared belief developed among the community of educational administrators that their major concern should be management. A survey of professors of administration and superintendents of city schools conducted in the early 1930s found that school finance was considered the most important topic in a school administrator's education, followed in descending order by business administration, organization and administration of supervision, organization and supervision of the curriculum, administration of teaching personnel, public relations and publicity, and organization of schools and the school system. The list continued through issues of school housing, school law, and school records, without any mention of instruction or discussion of broader concerns about the role of education in society, the nature of learning, or issues in educational policy.[19]

A survey of doctoral dissertations on educational administration written between 1910 and 1933 reveals the major topics of research to be the following: 55 dissertations out of 290 were on fiscal administration, followed by business administration (34), pupil personnel (29), personnel management (29), and legal provisions (24). The remainder of the dissertation topics ranged from buildings and equipment to educational organization. Many of them dealt with topics such as "school plumbing, the school janitor, fire insurance and the cafeteria."[20]

The professionalization of educational administration around principles of scientific management, cost-effectiveness, and a business mentality did not escape criticism. Jesse Newlon, a school administrator and president of the National Education Association, warned his colleagues at the association's 1925 meeting of the danger of superintendents' functioning only as business managers. Callahan states that "he told his audience of administrators that they must be 'students of the social sciences, of all that is included in the fields of history, sociology, economics, psychology, political science . . . ' The educational leader, [Newlon] said, 'must be a reader and a student.'"[21]

In his history of the professionalization of educational administration, Callahan bemoans the fact that educational administration took the route of business rather than that of scholarship. From another perspective, in *The One Best System: A History of American Urban Education*, David Tyack labels this new breed of school executive as the "administrative progressive[s]" who "(1) were a movement with identifiable actors and coalitions; (2) had a common ideology and platform; and (3) gained substantive power over urban education."[22]

Tyack stresses that an interlocking set of interests, values, and purposes existed among civic elites, reform groups, and the new breed of administrative progressives. From Tyack's perspective, the actions of this informal network shaped the modern school system. Therefore, educational reform took place from the top down.

Within Tyack's framework, it is logical that the new forms of school boards dominated by civic elites appointed administrators who reflected their business values and interests. Of course, it cannot be determined whether the administrative progressives adopted these values in response to the civic elites or, given the spirit of the period, whether they actually had a common culture. Whatever the reason, between 1890 and the Depression years of the 1930s, business dominated in the control of the schools and business values dominated the management of the schools. Tyack states, "Educational administrators drew elaborate comparisons between the roles of business leaders and superintendents." He gives as an example Professor Franklin Bobbit of the University of Chicago, who in 1916 contrasted a manufacturing company of 1,200 people with a school system of similar size. After comparing citizens to stockholders and superintendents to corporate managers, Bobbit concluded, "When it is asserted that educational management must in its general outlines be different from good business management, it can be shown from such a parallel study that there is absolutely no validity to the contention." Bobbitt's comparison was used verbatim by the U.S. commissioner of education.[23]

An almost symbiotic relationship developed between the new breed of school administrators and the elite school boards. The smaller school boards required increased administrative assistance and welcomed a sharing of business values. In turn, the administrative progressives depended on elite school boards for their appointments as school superintendents. For instance, in Cincinnati a system of mutual support was established between the Citizens School Committee (the organization of civic leaders that had gained control of school board elections) and the superintendent. In the 1921 school board election, Superintendent Ralph Condon actively campaigned for the candidates of the Citizens School Committee. When a resolution was introduced at the September 26, 1921, board meeting condemning his actions, Condon responded: "I want to repeat . . . that it was my duty . . . to advocate election of candidates who represented the non-partisan control of education, for, to my mind, there is no greater issue involved in the administration of education than this: Keep the schools out of politics; keep politics out of the schools." In this context, keeping the schools out of politics simply meant keeping the schools within the control of the local civic elite.[24]

With the professionalization and increase in duties of educational administrators and the decrease in functions of boards of education, clear definitions of proper roles developed. In the rhetoric of the times, school boards were to establish general education policies and administrators were to administer those policies without interference from the boards. In part, self-interest and self-protection prompted school administrators to support these clear distinctions in roles. They wanted freedom from the school board and the resultant increase in power.

For example, in a report to the board of education made in 1923, after a trip across the country to inspect other school systems, Superintendent Condon of Cincinnati gave expression to this ideal relationship between school board and administrators. In his report, he identified characteristics he believed made one school system superior to another: "The best schools are likely to be found where there is the clearest recognition of what constitutes executive and administrative responsibility, with the Superintendent and his staff in charge of the administration of educational policies clearly and distinctly responsible to the Board of Education . . . but unhampered in the execution of educational plans and policies which have been approved." Condon told the board that where he had seen this relationship between the board and superintendent, there was "peace, harmony, good understanding . . . and good results. Where this relationship did not exist there was controversy, misunderstanding and a general level of distrust."[25]

The concerns of the new educational administrators and elite school boards matched the general educational rhetoric about social efficiency and the development of human capital. In one sense, the administrative progressives became the new social engineers, organizing and directing a school system that would produce measured and standardized workers for the labor market, much the same as factories standardized products. The business attitudes and cost consciousness of the school administrators pleased the business people who dominated the boards of education. These professional and business people were happy to relinquish functions to an administration that promised to provide more education at less expense and to graduate students who would meet the occupational requirements of American business. Of course, this was not the entire story—other political forces also played a role in shaping American schools (see Chapter 11).

MEASUREMENT AND DEMOCRACY

"Great will be our good fortune," wrote Robert Yerkes, head of the U.S. Army psychology team, "if the lesson in human engineering which the war has taught is carried over directly and effectively into our civil institutions and activities." The decisive point in the development of the science of measurement was World War I and the organization of the modern American army. Psychologists involved in constructing intelligence tests for the classification of army personnel, which later became models for tests used in the public schools, considered the army the ideal form of modern social organization because it embodied what was considered the proper classification of labor power. Expressing great hope for the future, Yerkes stated, "Before the war mental engineering was a dream; today it exists and its effective development is amply assured."[26]

The vision of a society in which social organization would be a product of scientific measurement raised basic questions about the meaning of democracy. The fundamental problem for social scientists was to resolve the conflict between a belief that only those of high intelligence should rule and the concept of a democratic society in which people with low intelligence are allowed to vote. In addition, during the post–World War I period, most psychologists believed that intelligence is inherited and can be controlled through selective breeding. For many, this meant that eugenics and the elimination of defective forms of intelligence were the major hopes for the improvement of civilization.

For many psychologists, the concept that intelligence is inherited also meant that intelligence levels vary among different ethnic groups. A major result of the army tests developed during World War I was allegedly proof that ethnic groups from southern and eastern Europe had lower levels of intelligence than those from northern Europe. This finding led many psychologists to argue that the new wave of immigration from southern and eastern Europe was reducing the general level of intelligence of the American people. These findings played a major role in the passage of legislation restricting immigration into the United States.

Psychologists saw the schools as playing a major role in achieving a society in which intelligence would rule and students would be scientifically selected and educated for their proper places in the social organism. It was hoped that testing in the schools would enable schools to fulfill the dream of providing fair and objective equality of opportunity through scientific selection. Tests were considered the key to a socially efficient society.

Henry Herbert Goddard captured this vision in a lecture given in 1920: "[It] is not so much a question of the absolute numbers of persons of high and low intelligence as it is whether each grade of intelligence is assigned a part, in the whole organization, that is within its capacity." Goddard went on to suggest that humans could learn from the busy bee how to achieve "the perfect organization of the hive." "Perhaps," he stated, "it would be wiser for us to emulate the bee's social organization more and his supposed industry less."[27]

The most significant analysis of the implications of this testing is made by historian Clarence Karier in *Shaping the American Educational State: 1900 to the Present*. Karier's book is both an analysis of the movement and an anthology of original articles. Karier argues that the use of intelligence testing as a means of establishing a meritocracy became another method of justifying social-class differences and racial discrimination. Now the wealth of the rich could be justified on the grounds of innate levels of intelligence. Indeed, psychologists at the time argued that the rich deserved to be rich because they were more intelligent than the poor. In Karier's words: "The hierarchical social class system was effectively maintained then as it is today, not so much by the sheer force of power and violence, but by the ideological beliefs of people within the system." One method of getting people to accept their position in society was to convince them that the particular position they held reflected their individual merit. The measurement of intelligence was one method of convincing a person of his or her particular social worth. Karier states, "There is, perhaps, no stronger social class stabilizer, if not tranquilizer, within a hierarchically ordered social class system than the belief, on the part of the lower class, that their place in life is really not arbitrarily determined by privilege, status, wealth and power, but is a consequence of merit, fairly derived."[28]

The army intelligence tests were developed by a team of psychologists who met at Henry Herbert Goddard's Vineland Institute in New Jersey. Goddard founded the Vineland Institute in the late 1880s as a training school for the feebleminded. He later translated and introduced into the United States the writings and intelligence tests of French psychologist Alfred Binet, who, at the request of the French minister of public instruction, had developed tests to separate mentally retarded children from normal children. Binet's intelligence test became a model for the development of intelligence tests in the United States.

In the 1890s, Goddard argued that many of the social problems of urban and industrial society would be solved through classification of intelligence and institutionalization of individuals with lower levels of intelligence. He believed that the major problem in modern society was that people of lower intelligence, who were suitable for agricultural and rural societies, had migrated to urban areas, where they were unable to deal with the complexities of living. He contended that this situation was responsible for the increase in urban crime. For Goddard, the social importance of intelligence testing was its ability to identify persons of lower intelligence before they committed crimes and were institutionalized.

As was mentioned previously, lurking behind the early discussions of intelligence were assumptions about the relative intelligence of different ethnic groups and social classes. Because the definition of the term *intelligence* was often vague, psychologists tended to build their own personal prejudices into tests. For instance, underlying Binet's test was a definition of intelligence that was both vague and relative. On the one hand, Binet defined native intelligence as "judgment, other wise called good sense, practical sense, initiative, the faculty of adapting one's self to circumstances"; on the other hand, he claimed that intelligence is relative to the individual's social situation. Thus "an attorney's son who is reduced by his intelligence to the condition of a menial employee is a moron . . . likewise a peasant, normal in ordinary surroundings of the fields, may be considered a moron in the city." While admitting that important differences in language ability between social classes might affect test results, he stated that social-class differences added validity to the test: "That this difference exists one might suspect, because our personal investigations, as well as those of many others, have demonstrated that children of the poorer class are shorter, weigh less, have smaller heads and slighter muscular force, than a child of the upper class; they less often reach the high school; they are more often behind in their studies."[29]

Early test writers never distinguished between native intelligence and character. For example, Goddard argued that the scores achieved on intelligence tests indicated how well an individual could control his or her emotions; in other words, level of intelligence indicated type of character—the wise person is also the good person. Edward L. Thorndike went so far as to suggest that ability to do well on tests gives evidence of justice and compassion. He purposely tried to make his intelligence tests difficult and long, so they would demonstrate the "ability to stick to a long and, at the end, somewhat distasteful task." A report from one institution of higher learning using the Thorndike test in the early 1920s states, "Two or three students fainted under the three-hour strain, and the faculty became indignant at this alleged imposition of hardship."[30]

The team of psychologists gathered at Vineland in 1917 had little time to debate the meaning of the word *intelligence.* Working with amazing speed, the group completed its work by June 10 and, after trying out the tests in army camps, sent a copy of the examiner's guide to the printer on July 7. Two forms of the test were developed—the Alpha, for literate soldiers, and the Beta, for illiterate soldiers. By the end of World War I, the tests had been given to 1,726,966 members of the army.

After the 1918 armistice, the government flooded the market with unused test booklets, which educators immediately utilized. Guy M. Whipple, a leading psychologist at that time, reported in 1922 that the army Alpha test was most widely used in colleges both because it was the first test constructed by a team of well-known psychologists to be tried on large numbers of men in the army and because "the test blanks were procurable for several months after the armistice at prices far below [those at which] other tests could be produced."[31]

The results of the army tests raised some important questions in the minds of psychologists about immigration and the functioning of democracy. Analysis of the tests yielded the startling conclusion that the average mental age of Americans was thirteen. This finding caused Goddard to ask, in a book published shortly after World War I bearing the suggestive title *Human Efficiency and Levels of Intelligence,* "What about democracy, can we hope to have a successful democracy where the average mentality is thirteen?" According to Goddard, the ideal would be for the top 4 percent of the population in intelligence to rule the other 96 percent. The problem, however, was the lack of confidence among the masses in those with higher intelligence. In Goddard's words: "Here is the root of our social troubles and here is found the explanation of everything from local labor troubles to Bolshevism. Intelligence has made the fundamental error of assuming that it alone is sufficient to inspire confidence."[32]

According to Goddard, once confidence was established, those with little intelligence would elect those with a great deal of intelligence: "Intelligence can only inspire confidence when it is appreciated. And how can unintelligence comprehend intelligence?" Goddard then argued that although the morons and imbeciles at the Vineland Training School did not elect the superintendent, "they would do so if given a chance because they know that the one purpose of that group of officials is to make the children happy."[33]

Goddard argued that those with intelligence must devote themselves to the welfare of the masses. In his words, "Whenever the four million choose to devote their superior intelligence to understanding the lower mental levels and to the problem of the comfort and happiness of the other ninety-six million, they will be elected the rulers of the realm and then will come perfect government—Aristocracy in Democracy.[34]

This vision of the ideal meritocracy—rulership by an aristocracy of intelligence—was Goddard's solution to reconciling a belief in a meritocracy based on intelligence with the concept of democracy.

Building the confidence of the masses in those with intelligence is an important element in maintaining a meritocratic society of experts. Building this type of confidence was also a self-serving endeavor for psychologists, because it required that people respect the ability of psychologists to manage human resources. Thorndike captures the spirit of this reasoning in a 1920 article in *Harper's* magazine, "The Psychology of the Half-Educated Man." Thorndike portrays the "half-educated" person as one with just enough knowledge to think he or she can act independently of the expert. In Thorndike's words: "Such a man is likely to try (and fail) to understand the specialist instead of obeying him. He does not 'know his place' intellectually."[35]

For Thorndike, the person who tries to act independently of expert opinion is a public danger and at the mercy of clever charlatans. The rural society of the past, Thorndike reasoned, could rely on the common sense of individuals, but modern complex society depends on the rule of experts: "Wherever there is the expert . . . should we not let him be our guide? Should we not, in fact, let him do our thinking for us in that field?"

Out of this discussion of the half-educated person emerged a startling description of the educated person. "The educated man," Thorndike proclaimed, "should know when not to think, and where to buy the thinking he needs." This is another important element in reconciling meritocracy with democracy—the masses must be made confident so they will elect the most intelligent, and they must be educated not to think but to buy the thinking they need. In such a society, the role of the school is to select individuals for their places in the meritocracy and to provide an education that prepares individuals to live in a society ruled by merit and intelligence.

In addition to raising concerns about the functioning of democracy, the army intelligence tests fueled the flames of prejudice against immigrants from southern and eastern Europe. A major study of the test results was published by Carl Brigham in 1923 as "A Study of American Intelligence." Although he later disavowed the racist conclusions of his study, in the mid-1920s Brigham developed the Scholastic Aptitude Test (SAT), which was destined to dominate the field of college entrance examinations. Brigham divided the ethnic stock of America into Nordic, Alpine, Mediterranean, and Negro categories. Nordic stock originated in countries such as Sweden, Norway, and England; Alpine stock came from countries such as Romania, Austria, and Hungary; and Mediterranean stock came from areas such as Italy, Greece, and Spain. According to Brigham's analysis of the Alpha and Beta tests, Nordic groups were intellectually superior to Alpine and Mediterranean groups, Alpines were superior to Mediterraneans, and Mediterraneans were superior to Negroes.[36]

Brigham was concerned that the intermixture of these ethnic groups would cause a decline in the general level of American intelligence: "We must now frankly admit the undesirable results which would ensue from a cross between the Nordic in this country with the Alpine Slav, with the degenerated hybrid Mediterranean, or with the negro, or from the promiscuous intermingling of all four types." After examining immigration patterns in the nineteenth and twentieth centuries, he warned, "According to all evidence available, then, American intelligence is declining, and [this decline] will proceed with an accelerating rate as the racial admixture becomes more and more extensive." The only hope for stopping this downward spiral of American intelligence, he maintained, was restrictive and highly selective immigration laws and "the prevention of the continued propagation of defective strains in the present population."

Thus, as the use of tests spread through the schools, serving to separate students into different curriculum groups, the tests also served the purpose of reinforcing ethnic and social-class differences. For educators who adhered to the arguments of the psychologists, it appeared natural to channel children from lower economic and social groups into vocational education and those from upper social groups into college preparatory courses. In fact, the allegedly scientific nature of the tests gave an air of objectivity to ethnic and social-class bias.

The widespread adoption of intelligence tests in the 1920s created a major debate over whether nature or nurture exerted the greatest influence on level of intelligence. An important defense of nature was given by Lewis M. Terman (1877–1956), an original member of the army team of psychologists who had gained fame for his revision of the original Binet test, which is now known as the Stanford-Binet test. Terman also developed the intelligence quotient (IQ) scale, which assigns normal intelligence a value of 100. Terman accepted the existence of ethnic differences in intelligence, and in an article in *World's Work* in 1922 he claimed that "the immigrants who have recently come to us in such large numbers from Southern and Southeastern Europe are distinctly inferior mentally to the Nordic and Alpine strains we received from Scandinavia, Germany, Great Britain, and France."[37]

The major educational debates about nature versus nurture occurred within the National Society for the Study of Education. In the society's 1928 yearbook, Terman considers the importance of this debate in relation to the future goals of education: "If the differences found are due in the main to controllable factors of environment and training, then theoretically, at least, they can be wiped out by appropriate educational procedures—procedures which it would then become our duty to provide."[38] However, the majority of studies reported in the yearbooks reached the opposite conclusion; they found that the number of days of attendance, amount spent on education, and preschool education were less important factors in predicting achievement than was measured native intelligence.

Faced with what he considered to be overwhelming evidence for the dominant role of native intelligence, Terman did not reject the importance of schooling but argued that emphasis should be placed on nonacademic goals. He argued that even though intelligence test scores were not influenced by schooling, mass education should not be rejected, nor should it be concluded "that we might as well discard our alphabet, nail up our schools, and retreat to the jungle." For Terman, the question was not whether the school should be abandoned, but what form education should take. He thought that the studies of the relationship among schooling and intelligence and educational achievement suggested that schools placed too much emphasis on mastery of subjects, because mastery depends not on length of schooling, cost, or other factors, but on a factor that is independent of schooling: intelligence. He argued that the school, viewed in this context, should "place more emphasis than we now do upon the ethical and social ends of education, and care more than we now do about making the school a wholesome place to live.[39]

Ironically, at the same time that measurement people were giving the school a central role in the distribution of human resources, they were also promulgating a doctrine of native intelligence that undercut the ameliorative role of the school. What this means is that the early measurement movement reinforced social-class and ethnic differences by claiming they reflected differences in intelligence, but at the same time, it discounted the role of the school in doing anything about these differences. In the eyes of the leaders of the measurement movement, the role of the school was to build correct social attitudes, select individuals for their places in society, and educate them for those places. For Terman, Thorndike, Goddard, and others, improvement in the population could be achieved only through sterilization, restrictive immigration, and selective breeding.

SPECIAL CLASSROOMS AND
BUREAUCRATIC ORDER

The title of this section is a variation of the title "Bureaucratic Order and Special Children: Urban Schools, 1890s–1940s" used by Joseph Tropea in his study of the development of special classes for children with handicaps and behavior problems. Tropea's basic argument is that special classes were created by school administrators in the late nineteenth and early twentieth centuries to handle students who in previous times would not have been in school. In the context of this argument, compulsory attendance laws forced school people to deal with *all* children, including problem children. Because of this requirement, compulsory attendance laws were considered by some teachers and principals as a threat to the order of classrooms and schools.

Therefore, the creation of special classes paralleled the enforcement of compulsory attendance laws. For instance, before the passage of such laws in Pennsylvania and Maryland, neither Philadelphia nor Baltimore had special classes for "exceptional children," but after passage of the compulsory attendance law in Pennsylvania in 1897 and in Maryland in 1902, both cities instituted special classes. It should be noted that teachers resisted the enforcement of the laws because it meant that they would have to deal with problem children. Tropea quotes the superintendent of the Baltimore schools after passage of the 1902 law: "When the school attendance law goes into operation in January, some special provision will need to be made for . . . boys who are unmanageable in the regular schools."[40]

In most cities, this "special provision" meant the creation of special classes for students labeled as "disciplinary" and "backward." Since the concern was with maintaining classroom order, the majority of students placed in these special classes were male. In Tropea's words, "Compulsory attendance laws did not eliminate exclusionary practices; they merely changed the form of exclusion to in-school segregation."[41]

During the 1920s, special classes began to assume a broader range of labels. For instance, in 1922 Baltimore had special classes for "Open Air," "Crippled," "Deaf," "Subnormal," and "Disciplinary." Enrollment in "Subnormal" classes in the Baltimore schools expanded rapidly from 56 students in 1921 to 1,179 students in 1925. After 1925, enrollments in "Disciplinary" and "Subnormal" classes declined and were balanced by increased enrollments in new classes called "Vocational," "Prevocational," and "Mentally Handicapped." Mentally and physically handicapped students remained excluded from regular classrooms until the 1970s, when lobbying by groups representing the interests of the handicapped, plus federal legislation, forced schools to mainstream handicapped children into regular classes. Tropea summarizes his study: "Since rules of law [compulsory attendance laws] and classroom order appeared incompatible, administrators had to mediate between legislative mandates and expectations of teaching authority. The conflict between compliance with the law and satisfaction of teachers' concerns for order was resolved through the special classroom."[42]

THE UNIVERSITY AND MERITOCRACY

In the minds of those who envisioned a scientifically managed society, the university was at the pinnacle. The role of graduate schools in the evolving world of public education was to provide the research and educate the leaders for the scientific management of the system. In the twentieth century, schools of education were expanded to include graduate studies and educational research in addition to teacher training programs. These new graduate schools of education became centers of professional control.

Although German and English universities were important models for the development of American high education, the university in America became a unique institution devoted to a concept of service. This concept of social service is part of the general ideology of placing the expert in charge and of service to society. In an article published in 1906, Lyman Abbot, a clergyman and editor of *Outlook* magazine, explores this role of the American university. Abbot argues that the English universities emphasized culture and the education of aristocrats, whereas the German universities focused on scholarship and the education of scholars. American universities emphasized service to society and education for a life of social service.[43]

The idea of the institution of higher education as a center of expert service for society represents a sharp break with traditional goals. As described in Chapter 3, colleges in the nineteenth century focused on liberal education as provider of the discipline and furniture of the mind. By the end of the nineteenth century, the role of higher education had shifted dramatically to that of servicing the needs of the corporate state. Several important events occurred as these changes evolved in the goals of higher education. First, the passage of the Morrill Land Grant Act of 1862 was the beginning of federal government involvement supportive of a broad social role for higher education. Second, large numbers of American students went to Germany in the latter half of the nineteenth century and returned with the idea of organizing graduate schools patterned after German universities. Third, modern industry began to depend on research to maintain a competitive edge in the marketplace. Over time, industry and government increasingly used universities as centers for research and development.

In the twentieth century, this new role for higher education generated a persistent tension between the earlier concept of providing a liberal education and the emerging concept of servicing industrial and government needs and conducting research. In addition, the concept of academic freedom, which allowed escape from the narrow and restrictive thought of the nineteenth-century college, came into conflict with the new emphasis on service to society.

The 1862 Morrill Act establishing land grant colleges was the culmination of many years of work by reformers in higher education to achieve a greater service orientation in institutions of higher education. Henry Tappan (1805–1881), foremost among these early reformers as a critic of *The Yale Report* and as president of the University of Michigan between 1852 and 1863, tried to give new direction to higher education. In his 1852 inaugural address at Michigan, he embraced the model of the German university and proclaimed the university to be a major center for the creation and expansion of national wealth: "In demanding the highest institutions of learning, . . . [we are] creating not only, important and indispensable commodities in trade, but providing also, the very springs of all industry and trade, of all civilization and human improvement, of all national wealth, power and greatness."[44]

Tappan argued that the university's pursuit of science would lay the groundwork for the future prosperity of business and industry. As he told his audience, "A people aiming at large increases of wealth by agriculture, manufactures, and commerce, of all others should aim to found and foster the noblest institutions of learning. . . . They of all others require men of science." He said a university should encompass all areas of knowledge, including knowledge of the objective world and knowledge about oneself. Following what he called the Prussian model, Tappan proposed the establishment of a scientific course of study that would parallel the classical curriculum. Tappan tried to convince his audience that he was not discrediting classical learning by proposing a scientific course of study, but attempting to provide an education suited to differing individual interests and tastes. He argued that both the classical and the scientific curricula were equally good and equally responsive to a student's needs, and, in an example indicating the direction in which he wanted the university to move, he stated, "A farmer may find Chemistry very closely connected with his calling but what can he do with Latin and Greek and the higher mathematics?"[45]

The Morrill Act was passed against a backdrop of arguments that the role of higher education was to provide an education suited to one's place in life and that science played an important role in industrial and agricultural advancement. The sponsor of the legislation was Representative Justin Morrill of Vermont, who had first tried to get federal aid for higher education in 1859. Along with Tappan, many other national leaders had been calling for more practical forms of higher education similar to that proposed in the Morrill Act. Of particular importance was Jonathan Baldwin Turner's 1851 plan for an industrial university, eventually endorsed by the Illinois state legislature. Turner divided society into two classes and argued that traditional liberal education served the interests of the upper class, but not those of the industrial class. He wanted a university to be established with a dual curriculum to serve both classes. He warned that a system of higher education that served only one class created the possibility "that they should form a ruling caste or class by themselves, and wield their power more or less for their own exclusive interests and the interests of their friends."[46]

The Morrill Act of 1862 specifically dealt with the issue of educating the industrial classes. The legislation stated that the money derived from lands granted under the act would be used "to teach such branches of learning as are related to agriculture and the mechanic arts, in such manner as the legislatures of the States may respectively prescribe, in order to promote the liberal and practical education of the industrial classes in the several pursuits and professions in life." The Morrill Act gave to each state 30,000 acres of public land per each senator and representative the state sent to Congress. Because the Civil War was in progress at the time, the teaching of military tactics was included in the legislation. The major effect of the legislation was to create a rapid expansion after the war of higher education designed to aid the agricultural and industrial sectors.

The emphasis on providing higher education to serve the agricultural and industrial sectors was only one aspect of the changes occurring in higher education. The other major changes resulted from the influence of the German universities and their emphasis on science, research, and academic freedom. The authors of *The Yale Report* of 1828 did not incorporate into their document any goals related to higher education as producer of new knowledge, but the universities in the latter part of the nineteenth century had become centers of research aimed at discovering new knowledge to improve society and the economic system.

In the latter half of the nineteenth century, many outstanding American students made pilgrimages to study at German universities. Before 1850, roughly 200 American students had made the trip, but after the Civil War the numbers increased rapidly, and during the decade of the 1880s almost 2,000 made the journey. Many of these students earned their doctorates in Germany and returned to hold important positions in universities.

Students returned from Germany with ideas about the importance of science and research. In Germany, and later in the United States, scholars began to apply scientific methods of research to every field of knowledge, including economics, history, and theology. German research began to take on the characteristics of specialization, objectivity, and the use of heavily documented evidence.

The German concept of science emphasized the pursuit of truth for its own sake, not merely for utilitarian purposes. Although this concept of research did take hold in the United States, it was often in conflict with demands for research to produce useful products. This tension has existed in science and other fields of research up through the twentieth century.

The idea of the university as a center for research in the pursuit of truth changed the concept of teaching. In the American college of the nineteenth century, teaching involved students' learning traditional forms of knowledge, often by recitation or through the explication of texts. In the German universities, these methods were replaced with lectures on the results of research. In addition, the research seminar and laboratory were used to train students to conduct research under the supervision of a professor.

The German idea of the university became the model for the American graduate school. Specialized learning, the research seminar, and an emphasis on research became hallmarks of the graduate school concept. These changes in higher education gave new meaning to the role and status of the college professor. No longer did professors simply educate the future generation; now they were experts producing new knowledge and often serving as consultants to business, industry, government, and educational institutions.

With its new sense of social importance, the American professorate became dissatisfied with traditional methods of college governance, which placed strictures on the actions of faculty in and out of the classroom. Of major importance in justifying increased freedom of and control by the faculties was the German concept of academic freedom. German academics believed that the pursuit of truth required absolute freedom of inquiry, so that any avenue of investigation could be followed. In Germany, academic freedom included the concepts of *Lernfreiheit* and *Lehrfreiheit*.

Lernfreiheit refers to the right of German students to determine their field of studies, follow any sequence of courses, govern their own private lives, and assume primary responsibility for final examinations. This concept of academic freedom for the student found little support in American higher education, except for freedom of choice through an elective system. On the other hand, *Lehrfreiheit* became an important part of academic life in the United States. Based on the idea that the pursuit of truth requires freedom to conduct research, the ideal of *Lehrfreiheit* gave university professors freedom to lecture and report on their research as well as to conduct any type of research. In Germany, freedom of teaching and inquiry became a distinctive feature of the academic profession, one not shared with other members of society. In fact, a distinction was made between freedom within the university and freedom outside the university. Within the university, the academic profession was expected to make bold statements about society and its field inquiry work.

In the United States, the concept of academic freedom underwent considerable modification, in part because American institutions of higher learning were governed by boards of trustees that often represented important economic and political interests outside the universities. At time, these boards of trustees prevented the independence of the faculty.

What evolved in the United States was a concept of academic freedom in which professors were not expected, as they were in Germany, to attempt to win students to their point of view. In Germany, academic freedom included the idea that faculty members had the freedom to teach whatever they wanted and the right to persuade students to accept their personal opinions and interpretations of a field of knowledge. For the American professorate, the tradition that developed was one of objectively presenting a variety of points of view on a controversial topic and refraining from commenting on issues outside the professor's area of expertise.

Ideas about academic freedom and the new role of the university were introduced into older American institutions. For instance, in his 1869 inaugural address as president of Harvard University, Charles Eliot, who later headed the Committee of Ten and served as president of the National Education Association, told his audience: "A university must be indigenous; it must be rich; and above all, it must be free. The winnowing breeze of freedom must blow through all its chambers. It takes a hurricane to blow wheat away. An atmosphere of intellectual freedom is the native air of literature and science." While recognizing the importance of freedom in the university, Eliot prescribed faculty actions befitting the particular notion of academic freedom that evolved in the United States. "It is not the function of the teacher," Eliot stated in his inaugural address,"to settle philosophical and political controversies for the pupil, or even to recommend to him any one set of opinions as better than any other. Exposition, not imposition, of opinions is the professor's part."[47]

A factor that restrained academic freedom in the United States was the underwriting of new American universities by industrial barons. During the latter half of the nineteenth century, the model of the German university found its home in these newly established schools. In 1865 Ezra Cornell, having earned a fortune in the telegraph business and public lands, endowed Cornell University, which was to serve the industrial classes and be a model research institution. In 1867 Johns Hopkins, who had gained a considerable fortune through commerce, endowed Johns Hopkins University. The primary purpose of this university was to function as a graduate school. New England industrialist Jonas Clark's endowment of Clark University in 1887 allowed G.

Stanley Hall to turn it into a major center for graduate studies. A railroad empire provided the money for Leland Stanford to found Stanford University in 1885, and oil money allowed John D. Rockefeller to establish the University of Chicago in 1890. The Armour Institute was funded by the meat-packing industry, and the Carnegie Institute by the steel industry.

These are only a few of the major institutions of higher learning that were backed by large-scale corporate wealth and that adapted the German model of the university to research in service to industry and government. In the words of David Noble in *America by Design: Science, Technology, and the Rise of Corporate Capitalism,* "The growing need within industries for scientific research, and the drive toward cooperation with educational institutions to secure it, paralleled the development of research with the universities." Noble argues that these new universities, like the public schools, were given the task of educating individuals to meet the needs of the industrial system: "While the primary mission of the university within the industrial system was the 'efficient production of human material' according to 'industrial specifications'—which made not only the building of universities, but education itself an industry—the role of universities as centers of research for industry was also a vital one." Within the context of Noble's argument, the "efficient production of human material" refers to the education of scientists, managers, and engineers and the training of economists, psychologists, and sociologists to aid in industrial production.[48]

An inevitable tension developed between the interests of corporate wealth that came to dominate American higher education and the increasing independence and prestige of the American professorate. In the late nineteenth and early twentieth centuries, many professors were threatened because of their political views. For example, in 1894 Richard Ely, director of the University of Wisconsin School of Economics, Politics and History, was accused by the Board of Regents of believing in strikes and boycotts. Ely was charged with threatening to boycott a local firm in support of an employee strike and with expressing the same prounion sentiments in his writings. The regents eventually exonerated Professor Ely and issued what has been called the Wisconsin Magna Charta, which contains the famous lines "Whatever may be the limitations which trammel inquiry elsewhere we believe the great State University of Wisconsin should ever encourage that continual and fearless sifting and winnowing by which alone the truth can be found."[49]

At Stanford University, Professor Edward Ross, educated in Ely's seminars at the University of Wisconsin, defended socialist Eugene V. Debs and wrote a pamphlet in favor of free silver that was used by the Democratic party. Mrs. Leland Stanford was upset by Ross's actions and wrote a letter to the president of Stanford complaining that Ross was playing "into the hands of the lowest and vilest elements of socialism."[50] In May 1900, Ross spoke at a meeting of organized labor to protect immigration of Chinese labor. This action struck home for the Stanfords because Chinese labor had been widely used in their railroad empire. Again Mrs. Stanford reacted and this time forced Ross's resignation. Ross defended himself in his resignation letter, declaring: "I had no choice but to go straight ahead. The scientist's business is to know some things clear to the bottom, and if he hides what he knows, he loses his virtue."[51] Ross expressed the moral imperative of academic freedom—the constant quest for truth regardless of the difficulties. Of course, this quest was sometimes hindered by self-interested trustees and by faculty members interested in personal security and gain.

Ross's resignation led to an investigation by the American Economic Association. This action established a precedent for the protection of academic freedom that eventually led to the organization of the American Association of University Professors (AAUP) in 1915. As in previous defenses of academic freedom, the AAUP rested its case for academic freedom on the requirements of science. Of course, underlying the argument that freedom is necessary for research was a defense of the new independent status of the American professorate as a leader of technological, scientific, and social change.

In this atmosphere of research, science, and the new role of universities, graduate schools of education blossomed. Several factors complicated the development of colleges and departments of education in American universities. First, a tradition existed of training elementary school teachers in two-year normal schools. Second, the standards for admission to normal schools were low—in most cases not even a high school diploma was required. Finally, many secondary school teachers who were educated at colleges had not received any professional training.

In the late 1800s, several factors began to change this nineteenth-century pattern of teacher training. First, the requirements for admission to normal schools were tightened. In 1895, 14 percent of a sample of fifty-one normal schools required a high school diploma for admission. By 1905, the percentage had increased to 22 percent. The Department of Normal Schools of the National Education Association passed a resolution in 1908 in favor of requiring a high school diploma for admission to normal schools. By the 1930s, most normal schools required a high school diploma.

Second, the four-year teachers college began to replace the normal school. It was argued that the two-year normal school course did not provide the teacher with a broad enough liberal education. This transition occurred rapidly during the 1920s. In 1920, there were 137 state normal schools and 46 teachers colleges in the United States. By 1933, the number of normal schools had decreased to 30 and the number of teachers colleges had increased to 146.

Last, as part of the more general trend toward establishing graduate schools, colleges and universities began to add departments and colleges of education. The first permanent chair of education in the United States was established at the University of Iowa in 1873, and the University of Iowa created the College of Normal Instruction in 1878. The University of Michigan opened the Department of the Science and Art of Teaching in 1879; in 1881 the Department of Pedagogy was opened at the University of Wisconsin; in 1887 Teachers College at Columbia University was founded. By 1899, departments or chairs of education had been established at 244 American universities.

Working in the midst of these changes in the organization of professional training in education and as a professor of education at Stanford University, Ellwood Cubberley viewed the rapidly proliferating graduate schools of education as producers of and leaders in the new scientific study of education. Writing about the first quarter of the twentieth century, he states, "Within this period of time entirely new means of attacking educational problems have been developed through the application of statistical procedures, the use of standardized tests, and the devising of scales for the measurement of the intelligence of school children." He goes on to argue that the development of the scientific study of education allowed for the evaluation of educational results in quantitative terms.[52]

Like their colleagues in other divisions of the university, faculties in graduate schools of education tried to increase their status through conducting research and applying the scientific method to problems in education. As noted earlier, graduate schools of education enhanced the status of practitioners by conferring graduate degrees. In turn, graduate students in education, seeking improved employment by gaining advanced degrees, created an avalanche of often useless educational research.

Although graduate schools of education became important for conferring status in the world of the public schools, they often struggled for status among other university disciplines. Theodore Sizer and Arthur Powell argue that the low status of the education faculty on university campuses was a result of the type of recruiting that occurred when education faculties rapidly expanded in the early part of the twentieth century. They contend that most of the positions were filled by people who had received their basic training through their work in the field of education. Thus, colleges of education were staffed with former school administrators and teachers who primarily taught and wrote about their personal experiences. In most cases, the study of education was not grounded in theory, but reflected the professors' individual experiences. Sizer and Powell paint an uncomplimentary picture of the professor of education as he or she emerged in the early twentieth century: a "gentle, unintellectual, saccharine, and well-meaning . . . bumbling doctor of undiagnosable ills, harmless if morosely defensive. He is either a mechanic . . . or he is the flatulent promoter of irrelevant trivia."[53]

Even though graduate schools of education struggled for status on university campuses, their power was soon felt in the education world. In *Managers of Virtue: Public School Leadership in America, 1820–1980*, David Tyack and Elisabeth Hansot depict the leading professors in the new graduate schools as important members of what they call the "educational trust." They argue that the alliance of these faculty members with school administrators, elite school boards, and big business produced the major changes in education during the early twentieth century.

A major source of power for some of these faculty members and graduate schools derived from the education and placement of school administrators. On a national level, the most powerful faculties were at Teachers College at Columbia University, the University of Chicago, and Stanford University.

Tyack and Hansot describe the leading faculty in school administration at these institutions as the "placement barons." Citing Robert Rose's 1969 dissertation, "Career Sponsorship in the School Superintendency," they report that George Strayer, Paul Mort, and Nicolaus Engelhardt at Teachers College established an "old boys' network"—that is, faculty members were known to board members and other school administrators around the country. They quote one of Rose's informants as saying "All of them had the knack of conveying the feeling that they were definitely aware of you as a person, had an affinity for you, and were concerned with being helpful to you in your future career. . . . They took pride in talking about 'their boys.'" The power of the "placement barons" at Teachers College is reflected in the 1939 roster of the American Association of School Administrators; Tyack and Hansot report that according to this roster, "287 superintendents held Teachers College M.A.'s and 32 had doctorates, a far greater proportion than that represented by any other university."[54]

Tyack and Hansot also reported that at the University of Chicago, Professor William C. Reavis's endorsement of students prompted students to establish a Reavis Club. In California, Ellwood Cubberley, the educational historian whose more traditional historical interpretations have been cited in this text, endorsed and was a mentor to most of the administrators in California in the early twentieth century. Cubberley was often referred to as "Dad Cubberley" and reportedly was admired and emulated throughout the state.

While Teachers College, Stanford, and the University of Chicago were powerful on a national level, many state universities came to dominate local areas. According to Tyack and Hansot, at institutions such as Ohio State University, for instance, professors of administration knew most school superintendents by their first names and exerted influence over boards of education in the region. It was also the case that many of the faculty members at these "local" institutions had been trained at "national" institutions—this created an informal national alliance of educational faculties.

In addition to their power to recommend school administrators and influence their opinions, important faculty members earned a great deal of money by consulting with local school districts. The magic words of the new progressive administrators were *research* and *study*, and for university people this meant extra income. Tyack and Hansot quote a comment made by one graduate of Teachers College: "Once when Strayer and Engelhardt came out [from] a meeting . . . they expressed disappointment that they were not getting some consulting work in this state. I told them I couldn't see why I shouldn't be making that money as well as they."[55]

CONCLUSION

Graduate schools of education were one important link in the educational power structure that came to dominate public schools in the early part of the twentieth century. They joined hands in their quest to create a well-ordered, scientifically managed society with the new breed of school administrators using business management techniques, elite school board members, faculties in graduate schools of education, and experts in measurement. Their common vision of a meritocracy organized around the school was one that promoted their own self-interest. It probably is not inaccurate to assume that when Henry Herbert Goddard divided American society into 4 million who should be leaders and 96 million who should be followers, he considered himself a member of the 4 million. A scientifically managed meritocracy would guarantee most of the members of this alliance positions of power and privilege.

The major flaw in this alliance was the potential for conflicts of interest among its members. As will be described in Chapter 11, the greatest tension in the alliance was between the business people, who wanted the system to be inexpensive, and the school administrators and professors of education, who wanted to ensure the continued growth of their educational empire. Also, the vision of meritocracy excluded many groups, particularly minority groups, from positions of affluence and power, and this created another level of tension between the educational alliance and those who suffered discrimination and exclusion. Furthermore, any failure of the schools to meet national goals made them vulnerable to criticism.

Eventually, the alliance collapsed under the economic pressures of the Depression of the 1930s, when educators resisted the desire of business elements to reduce financial support to the public schools. In addition, professional educators, who as a group included school administrators and professors of education, came under attack after World War II for supposedly having "weakened" the academic training offered by the schools, thus making it difficult for the United States to compete with the Soviet Union in developing military weapons for the Cold War. Finally, the very idea of a meritocracy based on the sorting function of the school came under severe attack by the civil rights movement in the 1950s and 1960s.

The dream of a scientifically managed society collapsed under the tensions created by the self-interest of the movement's leaders, who used the mantle of science to legitimize and protect their economic and social power. However, the educational structures they created in their quest for meritocracy have lasted up to the present time, and even though the dream of equality of opportunity through schooling has been seriously questioned, management of human capital is still one of the primary goals of education.

NOTES

1. David Kirby, T. Robert Harris, and Robert Crain, *Political Strategies in Northern School Desegregation* (Lexington, Mass.: Lexington Books, 1973), p. 116.
2. Joseph M. Cronin, *The Control of Urban Schools: Perspectives on the Power of Educational Reformers* (New York: Free Press, 1973).

3. Quoted in Samuel P. Hays, "The Politics of Reform in Municipal Govern-ment in the Progressive Era," *Pacific Northwest Quarterly* (October 1961), p. 163.

4. Margaret Withrow Farny, *Sevenmile Harvest: The Life of John Withrow, 1854–1931* (Caldwell, N.J.: Progress Publishing, 1942), pp. 57–172.

5. The conservative effect of nonpartisan elections is analyzed in Willis D. Hawley, *Nonpartisan Elections and the Case for Party Politics* (New York: Wiley, 1973).

6. Quoted in Farny, *Sevenmile Harvest*, p. 174.

7. Robert P. Curry, *Fifty Years in the Cincinnati Public School, 1925–1975* (Cincinnati: Cincinnati Historical Society, n.d.); Paul Erwin, *Cincinnatians Promote City Schools, 1913–1963* (Cincinnati: Citizens School Committee, 1964).

8. Sol Cohen, *Progressives and Urban School Reform* (New York: Teachers College Press, 1964), pp. 16–55.

9. David N. Plank and Paul E. Peterson, "Does Urban Reform Imply Class Conflict? The Case of Atlanta's Schools," *History of Education Quarterly*, Vol. 23 (Summer 1983), p. 152. This article was reprinted as Chapter 6 in Paul E. Peterson, *The Politics of School Reform 1870–1940* (Chicago: University of Chicago Press, 1985).

10. Scott Nearing, "Who's Who in Our Boards of Education?" *School and Society*, Vol. 5 (January 20, 1917), pp. 89–90.

11. George S. Counts, *The Social Composition of Boards of Education: A Study in the Social Control of Public Education* (Chicago: University of Chicago Press, 1927).

12. Raymond E. Callahan, *Education and the Cult of Efficiency* (Chicago: University of Chicago Press, 1962).

13. See, e.g., Barbara Berman, "Business Efficiency, American Schooling and the Public School Superintendency: A Reconsideration of the Callahan Thesis," *History of Education Quarterly* (Fall 1983), pp. 297–319.

14. Quoted in Callahan, *Cult of Efficiency*, p. 27.

15. Ibid., pp. 27, 55–57.

16. Quoted in ibid., p. 73.

17. Ibid., p. 214.

18. Ibid., p. 200.

19. Ibid., p. 201.

20. Ibid., p. 202.

21. Ibid., p. 203.

22. David Tyack, *The One Best System: A History of American Urban Education* (Cambridge, Mass.: Harvard University Press, 1974), p. 128.

23. Ibid., p. 144.

24. *Cincinnati Board of Education Proceedings*, September 26, 1921, pp. 5–7.

25. *Cincinnati Board of Education Proceedings*, January 8, 1923, pp. 16–19.

26. Quoted in Joel Spring, "Psychologists and the War: The Meaning of Intelligence in the Alpha and Beta Tests," *History of Education Quarterly*, Vol. 12 (Spring 1972), p. 3.

27. Henry Herbert Goddard, *Human Efficiency and Levels of Intelligence* (Princeton, N.J.: Princeton University Press, 1920), pp. 35, 62.

28. Clarence J. Karier, ed., *Shaping the American Educational State: 1900 to the Present* (New York: Free Press, 1975), p. 138.

29. Alfred Binet and Theodore Simon, *The Development of Intelligence in Children* (Baltimore: Williams and Wilkins, 1916), p. 318.

30. Guy M. Whipple, "Intelligence Tests in Colleges and Universities," *National Society for the Study of Education Yearbook*, Vol. 21 (1922), p. 260.

31. Ibid., p. 254.

32. Goddard, "Human Efficiency" in Karier, *Shaping the American Educational State*, pp. 165–170.

33. Ibid.

34. Ibid.

35. Edward L. Thorndike, "The Psychology of the Half-Educated Man" in Karier, *Shaping the American Educational State*, pp. 238–244.

36. Carl C. Brigham, "A Study of American Intelligence" in Karier, *Shaping the American Educational State*, pp. 207–215.

37. Lewis M. Terman, "Were We Born That Way?" in Karier, *Shaping the American Educational State*, pp. 197–207.

38. Quoted in Edgar Gumbert and Joel Spring, *The Superschool and the Superstate* (New York: Wiley, 1974), p. 101.

39. Ibid., pp. 104–105.

40. Joseph L. Tropea, "Bureaucratic Order and Special Children: Urban Schools, 1890s–1940s," *History of Education Quarterly*, Vol. 27, no. 1 (Spring 1987), p. 32.

41. Ibid., p. 34.

42. Ibid., p. 52.

43. Frederick Rudolph, *The American College and University* (New York: Knopf, 1962), pp. 356–357.

44. Henry Philip Tappan, "Inaugural Discourse" in Theodore Rawson Crame, ed., *The Colleges and the Public, 1787–1862* (New York: Teachers College Press, 1963), p. 150.

45. Ibid., p. 165.

46. Jonathan Baldwin Turner, "Plan for an Industrial University for the State of Illinois (1851)" in Crane, *Colleges and the Public*, pp. 172–190.

47. Quoted in Walter Metzger, *Academic Freedom in the Age of the University* (New York: Columbia University Press, 1955), p. 126.

48. David F. Nobel, *America by Design: Science, Technology, and the Rise of Corporate Capitalism* (New York: Knopf, 1977), pp. 131, 147.

49. Quoted in Metzger, *Academic Freedom*, p. 153.

50. Ibid., pp. 164–165.

51. Edward Ross, "Statement Regarding Forced Resignation from Stanford University, November 13, 1900" in Karier, *Shaping the American Educational State*, pp. 25–28.

52. Ellwood Cubberley, *Public Education in the United States: A Study and Interpretation of American Educational History* (Boston: Houghton Mifflin, 1934), p. 689.
53. Arthur G. Powell and Theodore Sizer, "Changing Conception of the Professor of Education" in James Cornelius, ed., *To Be a Phoenix: The Education Professorate* (Bloomington, Ind.: Phi Delta Kappa, 1969), p. 61.
54. David Tyack and Elisabeth Hansot, *Managers of Virtue: Public School Leadership in America, 1820–1980* (New York: Basic Books, 1982), pp. 140–142.
55. Quoted in ibid., p. 143.

CHAPTER 11

The Politics of Education

The political structure of American education emerged in the twentieth century as a complex set of alliances, multiple levels of power, and continual struggles among various educational factions and public groups. The politics of education can best be described as the politics of professionalism; professional educators fought for power with one another and with political and other community leaders.

Alliances between school boards and school administrators in the early twentieth century created strong tensions between political leaders and professional administrators. The cry "Keep the schools out of politics" was used by professional school administrators in their attempt to consolidate their power over the educational system. A major result was the creation of lasting tensions between politicians and school officials. By the Depression years of the 1930s, this tension erupted into a full-scale debate over whether the public schools or the federal government should have responsibility for youth programs. In the climate of the Cold War following World War II, politicians blamed the professional educators for having "weakened" the public school curriculum and made the school allegedly inferior to those in the Soviet Union. Extensive federal involvement in education during the 1950s was in part a result of a feeling that political actions were required to save the schools from the anti-intellectual clutches of the professional educators.

In attempting to protect their power from politicians, administrative progressives established alliances with business elites. At one level, this alliance developed smoothly because both groups advocated scientific management and hierarchical control. Business communities were pleased with school administrators who promised efficient, cost-effective school systems.

At another level, an almost inevitable conflict developed between the cost consciousness of the business community and the desire of the administrative progressives to protect and expand their educational empires. The economic pressures of the Depression split the close alliance that had existed between educators and the business community, and by the 1950s, business had

280

joined with politicians to declare that professional educators had made the schools the weakest link in America's defense against communism. Criticism of this type has continued into the 1980s, with schools being blamed for America's difficulties in international competition with Japan and West Germany.

The politics of educational professionalism involved both links between the profession and outside political interests and struggles for power within the profession. The reforms of administrative progressives resulted in teachers occupying the lowest rung of the administrative hierarchy and becoming objects of the new techniques of scientific management. Low pay coupled with resentment of administrative reforms resulted in the creation of militant teachers' organizations.

Some teachers believed their major hope was in organizing unions similar to other unions and joining forces with organized labor. In some cases, this created a situation in which teachers were allied with local trade unionists in a struggle for more pay, better working conditions, and a greater voice in educational policy making. These struggles pitted teachers against administrators interested in protecting their own power and a business community interested in keeping teacher salaries at a low level. Actions such as this led to the establishment of the American Federation of Teachers (AFT), which for many years pioneered the use of union tactics in education.

Teachers also tried to gain control of the National Education Association (NEA) and turn it into an organization with a primary interest in teacher welfare. Teachers lost this battle against school administrators in the early twentieth century but finally captured control in the 1960s and 1970s and turned the NEA into the largest teachers' union. By the 1980s, the NEA and the AFT had become important factors in national politics. Both groups attempted to establish alliances with politicians to gain legislation favorable to their interests.

While these struggles were being waged and alliances were being formed, the federal government began to play an increasing role in education. The role of the federal government in education must be understood in the context of the development of national educational policies. Because education is a power given to the states by the Constitution, a political body that could enforce a national educational policy did not exist. But even with the absence of national control, a great deal of similarity could be found among public schools throughout the United States. This was due mainly to the existence of national professional groups that shared information and ideas and issued policy statements. In addition, superintendents and other school administrators moved from community to community, instituting similar educational programs. Colleges of education across the country tended to use the same methods for training teachers and administrators. Also, textbooks were published for a national market. Therefore, despite local control of education, American schools became increasingly alike.

Before the 1940s, the most important organization for establishing national educational policy was the NEA. Although the organization lacked real political power, it was influential because its membership of professional educators held strategic positions in school systems around the country. Through official policy statements and informal contacts, the NEA exerted a great deal of national influence until the 1940s and 1950s. As the power of the NEA over national educational policy declined, the organization underwent dramatic change, and in the 1960s and 1970s it emerged as more powerful than the AFT, the other of the two teachers' unions.

Before the Depression, the primary influence of the federal government on national educational policy was through its support of vocational education, as mandated by the 1917 Smith-Hughes Act. The Smith-Hughes Act was a response to concern over the United State's role in international trade (see Chapter 9). In this case, the federal government intervened in educational policy to protect an identified national interest. Federal intervention in education increased during the Depression, when unemployed youths became a national problem. In the 1940s and 1950s, the Cold War created a framework for massive federal intervention, and as a result, the federal government replaced the NEA as the major source of national educational policy.

The second major cause of the increased role of the federal government was the civil rights movement of the 1950s and 1960s, which attempted to rectify the discriminatory actions of local school administrators and community elites. Factors contributing to racially segregated education were testing, differentiated curricula, laws in southern states requiring segregation, and school attendance zones in areas outside the South. The nature of control of local schools forced minority groups to bypass local government and seek redress and protection from the federal government.

In summary, the political world of education in the early twentieth century included alliances between school administrators and local business elites, alliances between some urban teachers and trade unions, an alliance between school administrators and college professors to keep the NEA from serving as a teacher welfare organization, and a growing grass-roots movement to end segregation in the schools. National educational policy was formulated in the hallways of the NEA and was spread through the informal networks of school administrators and college professors.

In this chapter, these political developments are covered up to World War II. At that time, inherent tensions began to break down many of these alliances, organizational changes started to take place, and the federal government emerged as the major source of national educational policy.

THE POLITICS OF PROFESSIONALISM: TEACHERS VERSUS ADMINISTRATORS

By the late nineteenth century, low wages, lack of retirement funds, and the scientific management plans of administrative progressives caused some teachers to seek aid through mutual organization. Low salaries and a lack of retirement funds had been persistent problems throughout the nineteenth century. In many ways, because of the number of women who entered teaching after the Civil War, these problems were directly related to other feminist issues of the period. Viewed from this perspective, the early attempts to organize teachers can be considered primarily a women's movement.

The scientific management reforms of administrative progressives contributed to an increased sense of powerlessness among many teachers. Scientific management institutionalized and provided justification for the traditional educational harem of female schoolteachers ruled by male administrators. Within the hierarchical structure of the new corporate model, teachers were at the bottom of the chain of command. Orders flowed from the top of the administrative structure to the bottom. Teachers became objects of scientific management, having no power or organizational means of directly influencing educational policy. Consequently, one reason teachers began to organize was to gain influence on educational policy.

Many of the early struggles of teachers' organizations focused both on wages and working conditions and on administrative reforms. This was particularly true of the Chicago Teachers' Federation. Organized by Margaret Haley and Catherine Goggin in 1897, this organization was the forerunner of the American Federation of Teachers, established in 1916, and it struggled for many years against the reforms of administrative progressives.

The issue of merit pay versus seniority as a means of determining pay scales was a major issue for teachers during this period and has continued to be so throughout the twentieth century. Obviously, administrative progressives tended to favor pay scales based on some scientific determination of teacher quality, and merit pay fit neatly into the concept of meritocracy. On the other hand, teachers tended to favor pay scales based on seniority. They believed pay scales based on a supposedly scientific determination of teacher quality only gave administrators more power and control, and they considered arguments for scientific assessment of teacher quality to be no more than justifications for administrators rewarding favored teachers.

An excellent study of the development of teachers' organizations is Wayne Urban's *Why Teachers Organized*. He argues that teachers organized for two major reasons: to improve wages and working conditions and to secure seniority. In Urban's words, "First, teachers organized to pursue material improvements, salaries, pensions, tenure, and other benefits and policies which helped raise teaching in the cities to the status of a career for women who practiced it." In other words, the struggle for increased economic benefits made it possible for women to consider teaching a lifelong career, not just an interim occupation before marriage. In addition, Urban states, "Through the pursuit of salary scales and other policies, teachers sought to institutionalize experience, or seniority, as the criterion of success in teaching."[1]

Urban uses the history of teachers' organizations in Atlanta, Chicago, and New York to support his interpretation. Although these three cities differ in size and location, the teachers' organizations in each shared similar goals and concerns. One common theme was resistance to administrative reforms. This was particularly true in the Chicago Teachers' Federation and the teachers' associations organized in New York City. These organizations resisted not only scientific management but also centralization of power in small school boards, which they considered elitist and anti-immigrant. Consequently, teachers' organizations in these cities struggled against both administrative progressives and urban elites. The resistance to elite takeover of the schools was an important factor in causing some teachers to associate with organized labor in what was viewed as a common struggle against corporate managers and control by the rich.

From Urban's perspective, these conflicts resulted in differing interpretations of the meaning of *professionalism:* "Teachers sought to preserve their existing employment conditions and therefore labeled attacks on them 'unprofessional,' while administrative reformers labeled their innovations attempts to 'professionalize' the teaching force."[2] Thus, for some teachers the word *professional* meant greater teacher control of educational policy, and for administrators it meant improving the quality of the teaching force through scientific management. Administrators thought teachers were acting in an unprofessional manner if they resisted administrative control.

Most teachers' associations in the early part of the twentieth century, in contrast to those in New York and Chicago, tended to be politically conservative and did not join the organized labor movement. An example was the Atlanta Public School Teacher's Association (APSTA), which was formed in 1905. This organization, Urban argues, was more typical of most teachers' associations: "The Atlanta teachers' reluctance to formally affiliate with labor and their hesitancy to link their own salary battles to political reforms like women's suffrage were representative of the caution which characterized teachers' associations in most cities."[3]

The goals adopted by APSTA when it was organized remained consistent throughout its first fifteen years of existence: improving salaries and working conditions, general promotion of teachers' rights and interests, and providing a means of social contact for teachers. According to Urban, "From 1905 to 1919, the association devoted itself to pursuing higher salaries."[4]

Clearly unlike the Chicago and New York teachers' associations, APSTA avoided taking positions on educational policy issues and forming alliances with organized labor. The organization even avoided involvement in educational policy issues such as promotion of students and grading policies. On the other hand, the association responded rapidly to issues involving wages. For instance, in 1915 the Atlanta Board of Education adopted a merit system of pay in response to pressure exerted by APSTA.

The fight in Atlanta over merit pay illustrates the conservative nature of many of the reforms resulting from the work of administrative progressives. In this case, merit pay was a means of reducing the payroll by $15,000. The savings would come from the anticipated reduction in the salaries of high-seniority teachers considered undeserving of merit increases. To battle against merit pay, the teachers' association became directly involved in school board elections in 1918 and proposed a slate of school board candidates who

opposed the policies of the dominant elite. In 1919, in an attempt to strength-
en its general political power, APSTA joined the AFT.

Atlanta demonstrates the tensions that developed among teachers, school
board members, and school administrators. In this case, the arguments of
scientific management through merit pay clearly worked in the interests of
those concerned with keeping down the costs of public education. To conservative interests, merit provided a "scientific" means of justifying reductions
in teachers' salaries. For school administrators, merit pay strengthened their
positions within the educational system by giving them more control over
teachers and expanding their range of activity. This situation led naturally to a
sharp division of interests between school administrators and teachers, and
between teachers and the local power elite.

The lack of a radical political ideology distinguished APSTA and most
other teachers' associations from those in New York and Chicago. Although
APSTA recognized the differences between their own economic interests and
those of the administrators and power elite, it did not conclude that they
reflected a more general difference between the economic interests of capital
and labor. Organized labor, on the other hand, did articulate its position that
the goals of scientific management would turn the worker into a well-con-
trolled, poorly paid employee. From the perspective of organized labor, the
differences between teachers and school boards reflected the more general
differences between the interests of the worker and the capitalist, and the
desire of elite school boards and school administrators was to deny children
of workers a quality public school education through the device of reducing costs.

Although most teachers' associations did not make this radical ideological
analysis, the Chicago Federation of Teachers (CFT) did ally itself with organized labor because it believed that workers and teachers shared a set of
interests. The ideological position taken by the CFT is important because the
efforts of this group were primarily responsible for the formation of the AFT.
Also, the political battles of the CFT clearly illustrate the differing economic
interests of those who supported and those who rejected the reforms of
administrative progressives.

One of the finest studies of the political struggles of the CFT is Julia
Wrigley's *Class Politics and Public Schools: Chicago, 1900–1950*. Wrigley's book
portrays a sweeping battle in which organized labor and teachers were on one
side and conservative business interests and school administrators on the
other. The struggle she depicts involved issues of educational policy in
addition to those of wages and working conditions. According to Wrigley,
these differences were linked to the opposed interests of capital and labor.

In part, the more radical position of the CFT is explained by its association
in 1902 with the Chicago Federation of Labor (CFL). It is impossible to know
whether the CFT would have independently maintained a radical perspective. Certainly, its linkage of educational issues with more general political
and economic problems made the CFT the most radical teachers' organization
in the United States in the early twentieth century. The motivation for the

CFT to join the CFL in 1902 was a letter from the president of the CFL that declared, "The time has come for the workingmen of Chicago to take a stand for their children's sake, and demand justice for the teachers and the children so that both may not be crushed by the power of corporate greed."[5] When the CFT aligned itself with the CFL, it told the many teachers who hesitated to take such a bold step that the children of working-class people were more interested in education than was any other group in Chicago. In political terms, the leadership of the CFT saw workers as representing the largest group of organized voters concerned with schooling.

From this perspective, affiliation with organized labor meant increased political power for teachers. Later, this theme was stressed by the teachers' union as the reason for its superiority over the NEA. Even with fewer members than nonaffiliated organizations, labor-affiliated teachers' associations claimed they were in a better bargaining position because they were backed by the money and large membership of organized labor.

Concerns about gaining political power and winning the allegiance of a large block of organized voters spurred the CFT to link its efforts to the women's suffrage movement. Margaret Haley's description of Catherine Goggin, cofounder with Haley of the CFT, captures the spirit of the relationship between the teachers' unions and the women's suffrage movement: "[Goggin] brought home to the teachers in her unique, forceful way the revelation of their disadvantage as nonvoters. I remember the effect it had on the audience of teachers when she said, 'Why shouldn't the City Council give our money to the firemen and policemen? Haven't they got votes?' There was no doubt but that this incident converted many a teacher to the cause of woman's suffrage."[6]

Organized labor took definite positions on educational policies that in turn were reflected in the policies of the CFT. For instance, in 1913 the Chicago Federation of Labor and the Illinois Federation of Labor opposed the Cooley bill, a plan for vocational education that would have established a dual school system. Commercial and business groups supported the plan because they wanted the schools to train students to meet their employee needs.

Wrigley reports that the Commercial Club, an organization for the purpose of long-range business planning, hired Edwin Cooley, for whom the legislation was named, to study European systems of vocational education. One objective of the Commercial Club was complete reorganization of the schools as a means of increasing the supply of skilled workers. Cooley was clearly impressed with the vocational schools in Germany. On his return from Europe in 1906, he gave a speech, "Public School Education in Morals," that, according to Wrigley, linked vocational education with the building of morality. He argued that vocational education was necessary because working-class students were not interested in academic subjects. His arguments took on a racist tone when he stated, "In dealing with the moral, intellectual, and social conditions of the inferior races, the statesmen of to-day tries to approach them from a practical point of view and to induce them or to compel them to form habits of industry." He continued, "Slavery was wrong, but whatever else it did or did not do, it compelled the acquisition of habits of industry in the slave and marked a step in advance over the previous condition of savagery."[7]

Cooley believed three major virtues should be taught in the schools: industry, punctuality, and obedience. He suggested that punctuality was more important than spelling and that the insistence by the schools "on this virtue is doing much to suppress a certain kind of selfishness and waste that seems to be inseparable from the man or woman who refuses to conform to time regulations." According to Cooley, obedience might be in disfavor in a democracy, but it is the basis for all civilization.[8]

The specific vocational plan developed by Cooley and the Commercial Club called for regular common schooling for all children up to the age of fourteen, after which children would choose between going to work or entering an academic program. Under the Cooley bill, vocational continuation schools would be established for children who went to work; the children would be released form work activities to attend these schools. The dualism in this program is clear: It separated children who attended full-time academic programs from those who worked and attended part-time vocational schools.

From the first discussions about the Cooley bill, organized labor charged that the true purpose of the legislation was to produce docile workers. At both the local and the state levels, organized labor maintained that children of workers did not necessarily leave school voluntarily but often were forced by economic conditions to work. Organized labor argued that working-class children were being punished by receiving an inferior form of education and that all children should be guaranteed a general education until the age of sixteen. Organized labor rejected the model of German education, because this type of education helped to maintain a class-oriented society. In general, labor argued that employers wanted children to experience a dreary education as preparation for dreary working conditions.

The position of organized labor and the CFT on the Cooley bill exemplifies the economic and political concerns interjected into debates about educational policy. In the end, the Cooley bill was defeated. This defeat was interpreted as proof of the power of organized labor and as evidence for why teachers should join hands with labor organizations.

Progressive administrative reforms were introduced into the Chicago school system during the superintendency (1900–1909) of Edwin Cooley, the same man who authored the Cooley bill. During his administration, Cooley placed the hiring and firing of teachers at the superintendent's level, increased the power of the superintendent's office, tightened the organizational structure of the schools, tied teachers' salaries to examinations and outside course work, and developed an allegedly scientific method of evaluating teachers for promotion. When the Chicago school system began to adopt these administrative methods of scientific management, the CFT joined with other organized labor groups in denouncing the methods as simply a new system to control workers.

The CFT denounced progressive administrative reforms in general, claiming they reduced democratic control of the schools and turned them into institutions to primarily serve the needs of employers. More specifically, teachers were enraged at the idea of promotion based on an efficiency rating. They argued that the proposed secrecy of the evaluation system led to favoritism and to violation of teachers' democratic rights.

CFT activism in opposition to scientific management resulted in the appointment by the Chicago Board of Education of Ella Flagg Young as superintendent of schools in 1909. Young was one of the first women in the United States to hold the position of superintendent in a large city. She believed in democratic control of the schools and had excellent rapport with the CFT. It can be argued that her appointment by a conservative school board was an attempt to decrease militancy among teachers. In fact, however, after her appointment, she established teachers' councils as a method of increasing teachers' participation in and control of the educational system. Young's first major disagreement with the school board was over the issue of vocational education. She opposed the Cooley bill because, in Wrigley's words, "she did not believe 'in training the young to belong to a lower industrial class.'" Young's comments led a local newspaper to claim that she was stirring up class antagonisms. After her attack on the Cooley bill, she began to lose favor in the eyes of school board members. She also resisted board demands that teachers' union members be demoted. In 1913 Young was forced to resign her position.[9]

Young's perspective on the nature of teachers' organizations is historically important. At first, she had worried about the affiliation of teachers with organized labor and the general militancy of the CFT, but she claimed these reservations were removed with the unfolding of teacher militancy. At the 1916 convention of the NEA, President of the Chicago Board of Education Jacob Loeb delivered a speech attacking the CFT to which Young replied "I was not large enough in the beginning to see, I had not the insight to see, that these women were realizing that they had not the freedom, the power, which people should have who are to train the minds of the children." As for the CFT's affiliation with organized labor, Young said she at first thought it was a mistake but later accepted it because it increased the political power of teachers. She argued before the convention: "They [the teachers] found that in order to get anything done they must have voting power behind them. And they found that people, the men, in their own station and rank in life, the college-bred men, were not ready to do anything for them; therefore they were compelled to go in with those who had felt the oppression and the grind of the power of riches." Young concluded her speech by arguing that the cause of disagreements between the teachers and the board of education was "class antagonism."[10]

Young's speech reflects the atmosphere and the language in use during the first decades of the 1900s. In the latter part of the twentieth century, it became unusual for educational leaders to refer to class antagonisms and the power of the rich. In fact, since the 1970s, teachers' unions have tended to adopt a much more conservative approach to social and political issues.

The American Federation of Teachers was formed in 1916 at a meeting of three Chicago Teachers' organizations (the CFT, the Chicago Federation of Men's Teachers, and the Chicago Federation of Women High School Teachers) in Gary, Indiana. The membership quickly expanded to include locals from Indiana, New York, Pennsylvania, and Washington, D.C. The American Federation of Labor (AFL) quickly welcomed the AFT into its membership. At the presentation ceremony accepting the AFT into the AFL, Samuel Gompers, president of the AFL, welcomed the new union with the hope that it "may bring light and hope in the lives of American educators, and give and receive mutual sympathy and support which can be properly exerted for the betterment of all who toil and give service—Aye, for all humanity."[11]

Until the 1970s, the AFT was considered the radical alternative to the National Education Association. Certainly, the CFT exemplified the more radical wing of the teachers' movement. Whether radical, like the CFT, or more conservative, like APSTA, all groups involved in the movement to organize teachers shared certain themes. Wages and working conditions were central to the concerns of teachers. Throughout the nineteenth century, low wages had discouraged long-term employment in teaching. The reforms instituted by progressive administrators and school boards had not included increasing teacher salaries as a central focus of concern. In fact, many school boards wanted to keep down the cost of education and opposed salary increases. Certainly, these economic conditions contributed to a feeling among teachers that they needed to organize for increased wages. In addition, teachers were motivated to oppose the attempts of administrators to gain greater control and administrative use of the principles of scientific management.

The movement to establish teachers' organizations added a new dimension to the politics of education in the twentieth century. It created an organizational forum for the expression of tension generated by the reforms of administrative progressives and the continuing problems of low teacher salaries. These new organizations created a political struggle both within the educational establishment and against conservative groups wanting to maintain low teacher salaries and impose a conservative ideology in the schools. The importance of teachers' unions in the politics of education increased in the 1960s, when the unions accepted the use of strikes, and the NEA became a militant teachers' organization.

THE RISE OF THE NATIONAL EDUCATION ASSOCIATION

The National Education Association was formed in 1857 by ten state teachers' organizations with the common objective of upgrading the teaching profession. By the 1890s, the NEA had become the major leader in formulating educational policies and the center of development of educational policy. The original name of the group, National Teachers' Association, was changed in 1870 to National Education Association. Although the professed goal of the organization was to improve teaching, teachers had a difficult time gaining power within the organization. Nothing better exemplifies the early attitudes of the NEA than the fact that women were excluded during the first year of the organization's existence.

By the 1870s, the NEA had developed into an umbrella organization with four policymaking divisions named after their particular areas of concern—Normal Schools, Higher Education, Superintendence, and Elementary Education. As the NEA evolved, more divisions were added to encompass most areas in education. From about 1890 to the 1950s, general educational policy was formulated through formal and informal contacts within these divisions. In the 1950s, the federal government began to assume the leadership role in national educational policy.

Particularly within the NEA's Department of Superintendence, powerful cliques formed and became part of what David Tyack calls the "educational trust." Their contacts within the NEA and other organizations allowed administrative progressives to spread their reforms—which, as was discussed earlier, were from the top down.

Attempts were made within the organization in the early twentieth century to get the leadership of the NEA to concentrate on teacher welfare issues. Margaret Haley, who had helped to organize the CFT, was a leader in this attempt. As David Tyack and Elisabeth Hansot state in *Managers of Virtue: Public School Leadership in America, 1820–1980*, "Margaret Haley was the main leader among those female militants who challenged the male old guard in the NEA and sought to force them to attend to the concerns of the women teachers who made up the vast majority of the profession." According to Tyack and Hansot, the first signs of Haley's militancy appeared at the 1901 NEA convention, at the conclusion of William T. Harris's remarks on the flourishing condition of public education and the advisability of the rich giving money to the schools. Haley jumped up and attacked the idea of big-business support, arguing that low teacher salaries were the important issue. Harris responded with words reflecting the sexism within the organization and the elitist mentality of its leaders: "Pay no attention to what that teacher down there has said, for I take it she is a grade teacher, just out of her school room at the end of the year, worn out, tired, and hysterical. . . . It was a mistake to hold NEA meetings at this time of year . . . and if there are any more hysterical outbursts, after this I shall insist that these meeting be held at some other time of the year."[12]

Haley envisioned an organization controlled by and operated for the benefit of teachers. She argued that her opponents wanted central control by a small group that was part of a "conspiracy to make a despotism of our entire school system."[13] Greater control by teachers could be achieved only through a reorganization to distribute increased power to the rank-and-file teacher, but the actual reorganization resulted in decreased teacher power. Improvements brought about by teacher activism were the establishment of the Department of Classroom Teachers within the NEA in 1912 and greater attention by the leadership to teacher welfare issues.

By 1917 the NEA had become large enough to warrant hiring its first full-time secretary and moving its headquarters to Washington, D.C. Once it was located in Washington, the NEA's leaders believed, World War I would offer an excellent opportunity for strengthening relations with the federal government and increasing membership. The decision to work with the federal government was the first step in the forging of close ties between the NEA and educational bureaucrats in the government. As part of the war effort and its desire to work with the federal government, the NEA established the Commission on the National Emergency to publicize its war work in the schools and to develop new ideas about the role of government in education. Several of the commission's ideas became realities several decades later. Federal aid to education is one important and highly debated idea that emerged from the commission. Another proposal called for the creation of a separate department of education in the federal government.

The drive during World War I to increase NEA membership not only was successful but, ironically, contributed to the demise of teacher power in the NEA. Between 1917 and 1920, NEA membership increased from 8,000 to 50,000. In the campaign to bring in more members, the NEA leadership organized discussions of a national program for improving teacher salaries and gaining greater support for the schools and called for greater participation by teachers in the administration of the schools. The massive increase in membership led to a reorganization that virtually eliminated teacher power in the NEA for the next five decades.

Prior to its reorganization, NEA conventions were conducted like town meetings, with each member in attendance allowed one vote. Thus, teachers in the city in which the NEA held its convention could attend en masse and cast more votes than the sum of those cast by delegates from other cities. For instance, at the 1918 and 1919 NEA conventions, attendance by local teachers was large enough to defeat plans for reorganization.

The leadership of the NEA proposed a representative form of governance under which each state association would elect delegates to the convention. The plan was to limit voting rights to these elected delegates. Although the leadership argued that more orderly meetings would result, activist teachers did not accept this argument because they felt the reorganization was a threat to teacher power within the NEA. This threat was a reality. In *Why Teachers Organized*, Wayne Urban demonstrates the effect of reorganization on teacher power. He cites as an example the 167 voting delegates from Illinois in the 1920s; of these, 135 were "county and city superintendents, college presidents and professors, or elementary- and high-school principals." Of the remaining delegates, only fourteen were elementary school teachers.[14]

Until the 1920 convention, activist teachers were able to defeat reorganization plans by packing the convention with local teachers. These efforts were defeated in 1920, when the convention was held in Salt Lake City, Utah. In a conservative state like Utah, teachers listened to their administrators and bowed to authority. At the convention, teachers voted in town meeting style to eliminate that voting format in favor of voting by delegates. In addition, state superintendents and NEA state officers were made ex officio delegates. Consequently, the NEA became an organization dominated by administrators, with little power given to teachers.

Urban argues that the takeover of the NEA by administrators was part of the general increase in school administrators' power during the 1920s. He concludes, "The defeat of teachers' power in the NEA was one case among many where teachers lost to the new educational executives. The consequence of reorganization was a large-membership, administrator-dominated NEA which retained that character until the early 1970s."[15]

The NEA continued as a powerful force in the development of educational policy until the rise of federal government power in the 1950s. In the 1950s, when the public schools came under attack and professional educators were blamed for the anti-intellectual state of the schools, the NEA was considered a major source of the problem. And, of course, the 1920 reorganization only increased the tension existing between teachers and administrators. This tension was not eased until the 1960s and 1970s, when the NEA was reorganized into a militant teachers' union.

THE POLITICAL CHANGES OF THE DEPRESSION YEARS

The economic depression of the 1930s caused several major political shifts in the educational world. First, the economic crisis began to split the alliances among local school administrators, school board, and local elites. Many school administrators and school boards wanted to maintain educational programs in the face of demands by other local leaders to reduce educational spending. Second, the economic pressures of the Depression led some leading educators to advocate use of the schools to bring about a radical transformation of society. This created the image that radicals were taking over the schools, which contributed to right-wing arguments in the 1940s and 1950s that public schools had come under the influence of communism. Last, the federal government introduced new programs to solve the problem of youth unemployment. This expanded the role of the federal government in education and set the stage for later intervention in the 1940s and 1950s. In addition, it created tension between professional educators and the federal government as to each group's role in control of youth.

Jeffrey Mirel's prizewinning essay "The Politics of Educational Retrenchment in Detroit, 1929–1935" is an excellent study of educational politics during the Depression. According to Mirel's study, the Detroit school board resisted demands by the conservative business and financial community to reduce educational spending. Obviously, school administrators supported the position of the school board. What is interesting about this situation is that school board membership was drawn from the same elite group that was demanding reductions in spending.

Mirel points out that the Depression hit the Detroit public schools after a decade of growth and reform. The city's educational program had been expanded to include junior high schools, vocational education, and manual training. Reforms in the administration of the schools paralleled those in other school systems around the country. In addition, the Detroit school system became heavily indebted for construction of new school buildings to accommodate an increasing student population. Between 1920 and 1930, the student population of the school system increased from 122,690 to 250,994, and the number of administrators and teachers increased from 3,750 to 7,525. In 1916 the school board had been reorganized to reduce its membership from twenty-one members elected by ward to seven members elected at large. In Mirel's words, "Where the old Board had had a sizable number of clerks and tradesmen, the new Board was composed entirely of important businessmen, professionals, and, in the case of Laura Osborn, the wife of a prominent attorney."[16]

When the Depression hit Detroit, school revenues plummeted from $17,885,000 in 1930–1931 to $12,875,000 in 1932–1933. Furthermore, the student population increased, and debts continued from the school-building boom of the 1920s. Faced with these conditions, members of the business and financial community began to call for reductions in teacher salaries and educational programs. The school board accepted the idea of salary reductions but resisted cutbacks in educational programs.

A major demand by the business community was to eliminate "fads and frills" in the schools. In particular, vocational education and kindergarten were singled out as areas that could be eliminated. The board's resistance to these cuts indicates a dedication by board members to the use of the schools to improve the workings of the economic system. In Mirel's words: "Recent scholarship has specifically identified kindergartens, manual training, home economics and athletics as programs designed to shape proper roles and attitudes for future workers and managers. The Detroit school board's [action] to save programs and cut salaries is consistent with that model."[17] The split between school board members and the business community indicates an emerging division at the time between those wanting to solve the problems of the Depression by reducing government spending and those wanting to use the government to protect the economic system.

Other factors complicated these political divisions. On issues other than those involving money, the school board and the business community remained in agreement. For instance, the school board joined with the business community to resist demands by communist groups to hold weekend rallies in the schools. On the other hand, labor groups and socialists supported the school board's resistance to program cuts. This did not mean that the school board and the socialists had a common ideology, but that both groups were interested, for different reasons, in protecting social institutions.

David Tyack, Robert Lowe, and Elisabeth Hansot, in *Public Schools in Hard Times: The Great Depression and Recent Years*, stress the tensions that arose between school people and the business community during the Depression. They argue that as the Depression worsened and the public became more critical of business interests, "school leaders attacked their former allies. In part, their new-found hostility stemmed from a common belief that industrial and commercial leaders were spearheading a campaign to cut school taxes." The educational retrenchment proposals of the U.S. Chamber of Commerce exemplify the growing tension between the business community and public educators. In 1932, all members of the U.S. Chamber of Commerce received letters from the manager of the organization's finance committee asking for consideration of a range of possible educational cutbacks in their communities. This letter proposed retrenchment through "the elimination of evening classes and kindergartens, the shortening of the school day, an increase in the size of classes, and the imposition of tuition for high school attendance."[18]

Responding to calls for retrenchment by the U.S. Chamber of Commerce and other business organizations, in 1933 the NEA established the Joint Commission on the Emergency in Education (JCEE). The JCEE and many school administrators believed public relations was the key to fighting retrenchment. The JCEE used the public relations model as a two-pronged attempt to unite all educators in resisting attempts at retrenchment and to provide publicity to persuade the public to support the schools. The superintendent of the Pasadena, California, public schools commented about the onset of the Depression: "The immediate response of the friends of public education was to turn to the public relations agent, the professional public opinion builder, the fashion setter in a desperate and dramatic appeal to rebuild the faith of the American people in public education and to restore the support of public education."[19]

In their quest for better public relations, the JCEE and Phi Delta Kappa, the honorary education fraternity, analyzed public criticisms of the schools as reported in the popular press. They found the top five criticisms to be as follows: "soft pedagogy, lack of contact with life, overemphasis on vocations, severe discipline and overwork, and neglect of character."[20] These findings were distributed as a mimeographed booklet, "Evaluating the School Program," for the purpose of responding to proposals for cutbacks made by the U.S. Chamber of Commerce.

The arguments between the JCEE and the U.S. Chamber of Commerce illustrate the tensions occurring at the national level between professional educators and the business community. As relations grew more strained, more members of the education community began to issue radical critiques of the economic system and to propose using the school as a means of social reconstruction. Although the average local school administrator was not very influenced by these more radical arguments, the business community did express concern that radical educators were taking over the schools. The emerging educational philosophy of social reconstructionism contributed to the collapse of relations between professional educators and the business community.

Social reconstruction was born in a speech, "Dare Progressive Education Be Progressive?" given by George Counts at the 1932 annual meeting of the Progressive Education Association. A version of the speech was later distributed under the title "Dare the Schools Build a New Social Order?" In his speech, Counts attacked the organization of capitalism as being "cruel and inhuman" and "wasteful and inefficient." He argued that concepts of competition and rugged individualism had become outmoded with the development of science and technology and called for a new economic system that would free people from poverty.[21]

During the 1920s, Counts had criticized business control of boards of education. According to Counts, a major requirement of using the schools to build a new social order was to find a group of leaders whose interests focused on the needs of society and its children. He proposed that teachers assume leadership of the reconstruction of society because their primary allegiance was to children, not to private economic interests. In Counts's vision, teachers would lead children down the path of social reconstruction by openly admitting that all teaching was indoctrination. Once this was out in the open, the teacher could rationally select which principles would be indoctrinated into the child.

Counts recognized that teachers would need to choose between indoctrinating children into a conservative or a progressive economic philosophy and that doing so would require teachers to "combine education with political statesmanship." In *The Progressive Educator and the Depression: The Radical Years*, C. A. Bowers quotes Counts's statement: "I am not over sanguine, but a society lacking leadership as our does, might even accept the guidance of teachers." Counts went on to exhort teachers to reach for power: "If democracy is to survive, it must seek a new economic foundation . . . natural resources and all important forms of capital will have to be collectively owned."[22]

Members of the NEA quickly picked up the challenge of using the schools to build a new social order. At the 1932 convention in Atlantic City, New Jersey, the NEA Committee on Social-Economic Goals for America issued a report in which direct reference is made to the importance of Counts's "Dare the School Build a New Social Order?" The report, which urges the NEA to assume leadership in constructing the new social order, states, "The NEA is saying, and I hope saying more or less militantly, that a social order can be built in which a social collapse such as the present one will be impossible."[23] The committee's resolution was accepted without major debate by the convention. Although the NEA never assumed militant and radical leadership during the 1930s, the very act of approving the report indicated growing militancy among educators and the association's split from the business community.

A journal called *Social Frontier*, founded in 1934, eventually became the focal point of social reconstructionist writings. Three major themes emerged from the journal's editorial writing: (1) capitalism has failed to fully use science and technology for the benefit of humanity; (2) in the capitalistic system, the profit motive has a negative effect on individual morality; and (3) the current economic order in the United States creates economic insecurity for large groups of people.[24]

It would be difficult to measure the impact of the social reconstructionist movement on American education. The actual number of subscribers to *Social Frontier* was only 3,751, and, in fact, during the Depression years the public schools never did assume a leadership role in the rebuilding of society. Nonetheless, the social reconstructionist movement did contribute to the image that educational leaders were among the more liberal elements in society. This image only helped to widen the gap between the community of professional educators and the business community.

Federal government involvement in education created another arena of political struggle. One important factor in this struggle was President Franklin D. Roosevelt's dislike and distrust of professional educators. The antagonism between the federal government and professional educators continued through the 1950s. Adding to the conflict was the NEA's demand for federal money without federal control. One important consequence of this political friction was that, except for its funding of a few programs, the federal government gave little aid to the public schools. The majority of federal attention was directed to the problem of youth and youth unemployment. Two of the most important programs to emerge from this concern were the National Youth Administration (NYA) and the Civilian Conservation Corps (CCC), which will be discussed later in this section.

Both these programs were products of general anxiety about the effect on youths of the Depression. This anxiety can be understood by examining the romantic concept of youth that developed in the twentieth century. Early in the twentieth century, thinking about youth concentrated on the relationship between sexual drives and socialization. Many educators during this period argued that institutions such as the high school needed to direct the sexual-social drives of youths to social service (see Chapter 9).

During the 1920s, youths were increasingly displaced from the labor market and attended school in greater numbers. This, plus all the previously mentioned factors, contributed to the development of a unique cultural style that came to be known as the Jazz Age, or Flapper Era. New forms of dress, music, dance, codes of conduct, and technology emerged. The flapper, jazz, modern dance, a new morality, and the automobile all became part of youth culture. Youth fads of the 1920s centered on the consumption of new products of technology. The automobile provided a form of mobility that had never before existed.

Those concerned with the youth problem often traced the supposed decline of morality, as well as youth's free spirit and rebellion against authority, to the automobile. Lengthy articles and discussions on the automobile and morality appeared in popular magazines. In 1926 the headmaster of the Lawrence School lamented the maelstrom his students would be entering. When he was eighteen, he said, life had been less difficult because there had been no "prohibition," "ubiquitous automobile," "cheap theater," "absence of parental control," and "emancipation of womanhood."[25]

Many Americans agreed during the 1920s that youth was being led down the path to Hell—a place or condition of hedonistic pleasure and liberated sexuality. In 1926 *Forum* magazine published two articles by members of the younger generation under the title "Has Youth Deteriorated?" The affirmative response to this question in one article reflects concern that unrepressed sexuality leads to chaotic and uncivilized disorder. Young people, one of the youthful authors states, "rush in an impetuous, juvenile stampede, not knowing what lies ahead. They have hurled aside all conventions; accepted standards are 'nil'. . . . 'Liberate the Libido' has become, through them our national motto." To the author of the negative response, it is important that "beauty and idealism, the two eternal heritages of Youth, are still alive. It is a generation which is constituting the leaven in the rapid development of a new and saner morality." Both articles refer to youth as "us" and stress that the central concern of youth appears to be sexual standards. As one of the young writers states,

> This tremendous interest in the younger generation is nothing more or less than a preoccupation with the nature of that generation's sex life. What people really want to know about us, if they are honest enough to admit it, is whether or not we are perverted, whether we are loose, whether we are what they call immoral; and their curiosity has never been completely satisfied.[26]

When *Literary Digest* conducted a national survey on the younger generation in 1922, it found an overriding concern with the decline of sexual morality. The survey questioned high school principals, college presidents and deans, editors of college newspapers, and editors of religious weeklies across the country. The editor of *Moody Bible Institute Monthly* responded to the survey with a declaration that in both manners and morals, society "is undergoing not a revolution, but a devolution. That is to say, I am not so impressed by its suddenness or totalness as by its steady, uninterrupted degeneration." From a college newspaper editor at the University of Pennsylvania came the opinion that "the modern dance has done much to break down standards of morals." Describing life on his campus, the editor complains, "To the girl of to-day petting parties, cigaret-smoking, and in many cases drinking, are accepted as ordinary parts of existence. . . . She dresses in the lightest and most flimsy of fabrics. Her dancing is often of the most passionate nature." A respondent from the Phi Kappa Psi House at Northwestern University in Evanston, Illinois, sums up the general mood of the survey: "One outstanding reflection on the young set today is the reckless pursuit of pleasure."[27]

To those who believed that social order depends on properly directing social-sexual instincts, the new morality of the 1920s represented a direct threat to the foundations of civilization. However, the frivolous style of life associated with youth in the 1920s came to an abrupt end when the Depression struck. Unemployed youths now became a central issue. Like the other marginal groups—such as blacks—youths were the last hired and first fired. Lacking the seasoned skills of older workers, young people found it increasingly difficult to obtain jobs during a time of high unemployment. According to the 1940 Census, by the end of the Depression, 35 percent of the unemployed were under age twenty-five, whereas only 22 percent of the total employable population fell within that age range.

In 1935, in response to the crises of the Depression, the American Council on Education established the American Youth Commission to investigate the problems of youth in America. In 1937 the chairman of the council offered the following picture: Defining *youths* as individuals between the ages of sixteen and twenty-four; he describes a mythical town of Youngsville, which has a population of 200 youths. Within this town, 76 youths have regular jobs, 40 go to school or college, 5 go to school part-time, 28 are married women, and 51 are out of work and out of school. Half of those out of work receive federal aid. Youngsville is also experiencing a major decline in personal health. According to the statistics of the Youth Commission, 1 out of 4 young people in America at the time had syphilis or gonorrhea, and 5 percent were, would be, or had been in an asylum. Added to these problems was the highest crime rate in the country.[28]

One striking characteristic of youths during the Depression was their reported lack of idealism and rebelliousness. Unlike in the past, marginality in the 1930s was accompanied not by affluence but by a desire for economic security. When Howard Bell of the American Youth Commission surveyed the young people of Maryland in the 1930s as a representative sample of all American youth, he found that 57.7 percent of the youths surveyed named lack of economic security as the major problem for young people in America. Concerns about economic security were accompanied by a realization that youth was a special group in society. Bell found "that only one-fourth of the youth believed that there was no youth problem."[29]

A second important condition affecting youths during the Depression was the cultural and social climate of the period. *McCall's Magazine* assigned Maxine Davis to travel around the country and report on the state of youth. Traveling for four months and covering 10,000 miles through the cities and along the back roads of America, she produced not only articles but also a book in which she labeled the youth of the Depression the "lost generation." Among the "lost generation," she reports, "we never found revolt. We found nothing but a meek acceptance of the fate meted out to them, and belief in a benign future based on nothing but wishful thinking." The major problem among the lost generation was lack of economic security. The collective nature of the lost generation, Davis argued, was a product of the psychopathic period in which these young people had grown up.

> Boys and girls who came of voting age in 1935 were born in 1914. Their earliest memories are of mob murder and war hysteria. Their next, the cynical reaction to war's sentimentality and war's futility. Their adolescence was divided between the crass materialism of the jazz 1920's and the shock of economic collapse. In effect they went to high school in limousines and washed dishes in college.[30]

In the context of these attitudes about youth, the federal government launched the National Youth Administration (NYA) and the Civilian Conservation Corps (CCC). Of the two programs, the CCC was the more important in terms of future developments because it became a model for youth corps–type programs. The major goal of the NYA, which was started in 1935, was to relieve youth unemployment by providing economic incentives for returning to school. In a very crass way, the schools were considered to be custodial institutions that could take the pressure off unemployment rates. During the first year of its existence, the program provided $6 a month for high school students, $15 a month for college students whose parents were on relief, and other financial aids to older youths who were out of school. In addition, institutions were asked to develop special work projects for students receiving NYA aid. Many institutions organized beautification and landscaping projects.

The first CCC camp opened in 1933 amid great hopes that outdoor group living would solve unemployment problems and implant a spirit of democratic cooperation among the participants, who lived a semimilitary life with reveilles, inspections, and physical training. Some of the leaders of the CCC came from the army and the Forest Service. These leaders believed that a productive adult could be created through hard work, clean living, and discipline. Educators in the camps played a subordinate role to both the camp administrators and the camp's organizational goals.

Participants in the CCC would usually rise at 6:00 A.M. After breakfast and perhaps physical exercise, they would work at planting trees, building bridges, clearing trails, fighting fires, and other types of forestry activities. At the end of the day, members of the CCC could take classes. Attendance at the courses was voluntary, and the subject matter was determined by the participants. In general, the courses were devoted to remedial training, vocational education, or general instruction.

In *The Shaping of the American High School: 1920–1941*, Edward Krug argues that the CCC set the stage for a battle between professional educators and members of the federal government over who should control American youth. Although there was no winner of this battle, the consequence was increased strain between the federal government and the educational community. According to Krug, the cause of the problem was that since World War I, educators had placed hopes in the development of a total youth program. The CCC had the potential to be such a program, but it was under the control of the federal government, not the educational establishment. In Krug's words: "It seemed to educators at this point that the country was ready for the total youth program envisioned since the end of the War. Now, with victory in their grasp, the ideologues of social efficiency faced the loss of all this to the extraschool agencies of the New Deal."[31]

The war of educators against the NYA and the CCC was highlighted by the publication of *The Civilian Conservation Corps, The National Youth Administration and the Public Schools* by the Educational Policies Commission in 1941, after the beginning of World War II. The Educational Policies Commission had been organized in 1932 by the Department of Superintendence of the NEA and the Commission on the Social Studies in the Schools. The book recommends that during periods of unemployment, the federal government provide money for public works but not for the purpose of training, and also that federal funds be used under state and local control. The report argues that the CCC and the NYA should be abolished as soon as emergency defense work was completed and all their functions were transferred to state and local governments. The book criticizes the federal programs for high costs per enrollee in comparison with the cost of educating a public school student.

Although this book represented a declaration of total war against the New Deal programs, World War II was responsible for their actual demise. Congress, in a desire to eliminate nonwar spending, eliminated appropriations for the CCC in 1942 and the NYA in 1943. In one sense, the war solved the problem of unemployed youths, but the CCC model would remain for years in legislators' minds. Even during the war, government officials searched for some form of total youth program similar to the CCC (see Chapter 12).

CONCLUSION

As World War II arrived on the scene, the political factions within the world of education were in disarray. Teachers had been organizing for almost half a century for the purpose of improving salaries and working conditions and increasing their power in the educational bureaucracies that had been established by administrative progressives. The strain between teachers and educational administrators would smolder until the 1960s and 1970s, when teachers' associations would step up their militant activities for better wages and increased teacher power.

The split between local elites and school administrators and between professional educators and the federal government was a major factor in educational politics through the 1950s. During the 1940s and 1950s, professional educators were continually criticized for making the public schools academically weak in comparison with those in the Soviet Union. After World War II, anticommunism and the cold war became issues in the debates between local groups and professional educators and between professional educators and the federal government. The displacement of the NEA's national policy role by the power of the federal government took on increasing importance. The CCC and the NYA symbolized the growing presence of the federal government in education and the rift between federal policymakers and professional educators. The Depression set the stage for the next round of political battles in education, which were fought at the conclusion of World War II.

NOTES

1. Wayne Urban, *Why Teachers Organized* (Detroit: Wayne State University Press, 1982), p. 22.
2. Ibid., p. 41.
3. Ibid., p. 45.
4. Ibid., p. 53.

5. Quoted in Julia Wrigley, *Class Politics and Public Schools: Chicago, 1900–1950* (New Brunswick, N.J.: Rutgers University Press, 1982), p. 34.
6. Quoted in ibid., pp. 34–35.
7. Quoted in ibid., p. 67.
8. Ibid.
9. Ibid., p. 124.
10. Quoted in ibid., p. 127.
11. Quoted in William Edward Eaton, *The American Federation of Teachers, 1916–1961* (Carbondale: Southern Illinois University Press, 1975), p. 17.
12. Quoted in David Tyack and Elisabeth Hansot, *Managers of Virtue: Public School Leadership in America, 1820–1980* (New York: Basic Books, 1982), pp. 186–187.
13. Quoted in ibid., p. 186.
14. Urban, *Why Teachers Organized*, p. 127.
15. Ibid., p. 133.
16. Jeffrey Mirel, "The Politics of Educational Retrenchment in Detroit, 1929–1935." *History of Education Quarterly*, Vol. 24 (Fall 1984), p. 325.
17. Ibid., p. 350.
18. David Tyack, Robert Lowe, and Elisabeth Hansot, *Public Schools in Hard Times: The Great Depression and Recent Years* (Cambridge, Mass.: Harvard University Press, 1984), pp. 22, 58.
19. Quoted in ibid., p. 74.
20. Quoted in ibid., p. 75.
21. C. A. Bowers, *The Progressive Educator and the Depression: The Radical Years* (New York: Random House, 1969), p. 15.
22. Quoted in ibid., p. 19.
23. Quoted in ibid., p. 23.
24. Ibid., p. 24.
25. Quoted in Mather A. Abbott, "The New Generation." *The Nation* (8 December 1926), p. 587.
26. Anne Temple, "Reaping the Whirlwind." *Forum*, No. 74 (July 1926), pp. 21–26; Regina Malone, "The Fabulous Monster," *Forum*, No. 74 (July 1926), pp. 26–30.
27. "The Case against the Younger Generation," *Literary Digest* (June 17, 1922), pp. 40–51.
28. "Outlook for Youth in America: Report on Panel Discussion," *Progressive Education*, No. 14 (December 1937), p. 595.
29. Howard Bell, *Youth Tell Their Story* (Washington, D.C.: American Council on Education, 1938).
30. Maxine Davis, *The Lost Generation* (New York: Macmillan, 1936), p. 4.
31. Edward A. Krug, *The Shaping of the American High School: Vol. 2, 1920–1941* (Madison: University of Wisconsin Press, 1972), p. 325.

Big Bird: Movies, Radio, and Television Join Schools as Public Educators

When he was helping to plan the first television production of *Sesame Street* in the 1960s, Lloyd Morrisett advanced the argument that television could be the third educator along with the public schools and the family. In fact, as I will discuss later in this chapter, Morrisett believed that television could be a better educator than the school or family because it did not punish the child.

The idea that mass media might be a substitute for the public school was not a new idea in the 1960s. Earlier in the century many educators believed the development of movies and radio represented a major challenge to the supremacy of public schools as an influence on the minds of children and as a source of a common culture and shared values. Educators were quick to criticize the impact of these new forms of mass media on both national culture and children. Leaders of the movie and broadcast industries responded to this criticism by consciously shaping the ideological content of the ideas they disseminated to the public. In the 1930s, the movie and broadcasting industries joined the school as educators of the public.

This chapter begins with an analysis of the censorship debate over movies. Out of this debate emerged the idea that an important goal of censorship was the shaping of movies to teach the public moral, social, and political lessons. Next I discuss the educational community's criticism of the impact of movies on children and the connections between educators and the film industry. The final section on movies analyzes the 1930 movie code, which was a response to these criticisms. In the next section, on radio, I explore the debate between major broadcasters and educators over who should determine national culture. At the center of this debate was whether radio should be nonprofit and controlled by educators or commercial and controlled by owners of capital.

The following section deals with the radio censorship codes that developed as a result of criticism of children's radio programs. These radio codes emphasized the use of heroes to shape the morality of children. Therefore, many children's programs were designed to teach moral lessons by having the good heroes triumph over the evil villains. By the 1950s, a similar set of codes governed television broadcasting. And in the 1960s, the idea of using entertainment as a medium for education took hold with the creation of the Children's Television Workshop and the first production of *Sesame Street*.

THE CENSORSHIP DEBATE

In 1922 Will Hays, president of the newly formed Motion Picture Producers and Distributors of America (MPPDA), appearing at the annual meeting of the National Education Association (NEA), stated his organization's commitment to the goals of "establishing and maintaining the highest possible moral and artistic standards in motion picture production, and developing the educational as well as the entertainment value and the general usefulness of the motion picture." Hays concluded the speech with the promise "We accept the challenge in the righteous demand of the American mother that the entertainment and amusement of . . . youth shall be worthy of their value as a potent factor in the country's future."[1]

Hays's appearance before the NEA illustrates the complex combination of political pressures and interrelationships between educators and the entertainment world that has had an effect on the content of movies, radio, television, and public schools. One reason the MPPDA was formed was to counter demands for increased government censorship of movies. As the largest and most influential educational organization, the MPPDA considered it essential to win the NEA to its side in its public relations campaign against government censorship.[2]

Hays devoted part of his speech to warning educators about the evils of government censorship of movies. He told the delegates to the convention, "I am against political censorship, of course, because political censorship will not do what is hoped for it in the last analysis." What Hayes offered the educators as an alternative to political censorship was censorship by the industry at the point of production. In his words, "But there is one place and one place only where the evils can be eliminated . . . and that is at the point where and when pictures are made." Hays promised his audience that "Right is right and wrong is wrong, and men know right from wrong. The corrections can be made, real evil can and must be kept out, the highest standards of art, taste, and morals can be achieved, and it is primarily the duty of the producers to do it."[3]

By the 1930s, a combination of pressures from religious organizations, fear of government censorship and antitrust action, and the desire to attract middle-class families to movie houses resulted in the MPPDA enforcing a self-regulatory code that shaped the moral, social, and political content of American films. The values contained in the movie code were very close to those being taught in American schools. Youngsters during this period might attend school during weekday hours and attend movies at night and on weekends. Whether sitting in rows in schoolrooms or in movie houses, children received a consciously constructed vision of the workings of the world.

The debate over censorship of movies centered on the question of whether mass media in the twentieth century should be controlled for the purpose of avoiding negative influences on audiences or for the purpose of teaching audiences moral and political lessons. For those advocating government censorship of movies, the primary concern was the removal of objectionable material from films. On the other hand, those advocating self-censorship tended to argue that the content of films should be controlled for the purpose of teaching social lessons. From an economic standpoint, the movie industry favored self-censorship and self-regulation. Government censorship created economic problems because films constantly had to be edited after production to meet the requirements of local and state censorship. The movie industry's commitment to self-censorship led to an acceptance of the idea that films should consciously teach moral and political lessons.

The spread of government censorship of films, in contrast to self-censorship by the film industry, was justified by arguments that the government had an obligation to maintain social order and that movies had the potential of inciting criminal acts. Between the enactment of the first municipal censorship law in Chicago in 1906 and the 1930s, a wave of municipal and state laws dealing with the content of movies spread across the country. New York, Ohio, Pennsylvania, Virginia, and Kansas were a few of the states that adopted licensing laws. It is estimated that between 1922 and 1927, forty-eight bills dealing with movie censorship were introduced into state legislatures and that before the 1950s there existed at one time or another ninety municipal censorship boards. The most important of these boards were located in Chicago, Detroit, Memphis, Atlanta, and Boston.[4]

Defenders of government censorship stressed the obligation of government to maintain social order and compared censorship to other government controls over the distribution of ideas such as public schools. Ellis Oberholtzer, secretary of the Pennsylvania State Board of Motion Picture Censors, wrote in 1921 in comparing state censorship to public schools,

> The efforts which are made to convert the unlikeliest of young human beings at school into useful citizens are many. From the care of their teeth and the public feeding of them when they are hungry up to the old purely educational processes developed to the nth degree, our social efficiency has been tried and proved. . . . I for one fail to see, therefore, how by any fair system of reasoning we can be held to be without some duty to inquire into the course of the film man with his 15,000 or more picture houses set in every nook and corner of the land at the door of each inhabitant.

Oberholtzer placed censorship into the general category of government responsibility for the actions of citizens: "The misbehavior of this citizen [the one influenced by movies]," Oberholtzer concluded, ". . . is not beyond our concern."[5]

The advocates of self-regulation, as opposed to government censorship, explicitly argued that self-regulation should ensure that movie audiences were taught moral and social lessons. They criticized government censorship because it only removed negative scenes without controlling the general theme of a film. One of the earliest arguments for self-censorship was given by John Collier, a cofounder of the privately operated National Board of Review or, as it was sometimes called, the National Board of Censorship.

The National Board of Review was organized after New York City police, under orders from the mayor and chief of police, closed 550 movie houses on Christmas Day 1908 for violating Sunday closing laws. The closings were part of a larger crusade against vice. In reaction to such police actions, theater owners organized the National Board of Review in the hope that self-censorship would stop future vice raids. The majority of the executive committee of the National Board of Review were wealthy Protestant males, including Andrew Carnegie, Samuel Gompers, presidents of major universities, and "representatives from the Federal Council of Churches, the YMCA, the New York School Board, the Society for the Prevention of Crime headed by the most powerful vice crusader in the city, the Reverend Charles Parkhurst, and the moralistic Postal Inspector, Anthony Comstock."[6]

Cofounder John Collier presented the guiding philosophy of the National Board of Review in a series of magazine articles in *The Survey*. As Collier explained, the board's censorship code emphasized the importance of movies teaching moral lessons. In this sense, the censors wanted the movies to be uplifting by teaching the public moral lessons, in a manner similar to that of schools. The organization's code stressed the importance of movies depicting good winning out over evil. The code states, "The results of the crime [as shown in movies] should be in the long run disastrous to the criminal so that the impression is that crime will inevitably find one out. The result (punishment) should always take a reasonable proportion of the film." In addition, emphasis was to be given to the role of government in maintaining a moral society. "As a general rule," the code argues, "it is preferable to have retribution come through the hands of authorized officers of the law, rather than through revenge or other unlawful or extra-legal means." Of course, the board expressed a great deal of interest in the portrayal of sexual relationships. The board's standards would "not allow the extended display of personal allurements, the exposure of alleged physical charms and passionate, protracted embraces" and it would "also disapprove the showing of men turning lightly from woman to woman, or women turning lightly from man to man in intimate sexual relationships."[7]

Following Collier's line of reasoning, the major defense of voluntary self-censorship was that movies were an art form that had the responsibility to teach the public moral and social lessons. Since it was in the economic interest of the movie industry to support self-censorship as opposed to government censorship, this argument became the standard defense of the industry against government censorship. To justify its self-censorship code, the MP-PDA used the argument that films were a form of social art. When the

National Board of Review was undermined with the passage of a New York State law requiring the licensing of movies in 1921, the MPPDA assumed leadership in advocating self-censorship.[8]

The formation of the MPPDA reflected the growing concentration of the movie industry. In the 1920s, the "Big Eight" film companies that formed the MPPDA made 90 percent of American films, as compared to the sixty firms in operation in the United States in 1912. The Big Eight were Paramount, Twentieth Century–Fox, Loews (MGM), Universal, Warner Brothers, Columbia, United Artists, and Radio-Keith-Orpheum (RKO).[9] The concentration of the movie industry caused studio owners to fear government antitrust action as well as government censorship.

The concentration of the industry in the MPPDA made it possible for the Hays Office, as it was called, to exercise a "dictatorship of virtue" over the content of American films. The exercise of this power occurred when movies were becoming a major part of the leisure-time activities for most Americans. Money spent on movies was the largest portion of the recreation budget for the average American family during the 1920s. Large cities averaged one movie seat for every five to seven people in the population. Also, the composition of movie audiences had changed. In 1912 only 25 percent of the movie audiences were clerical workers and 5 percent were from the business classes, but during the 1920s the audiences changed from being mainly working class and immigrant to including the middle class.[10]

Shortly after taking office, Hays launched a major public relations campaign designed to stop attempts at increased government censorship, to hold off possible antitrust action, and to improve the image of movies for the growing middle-class audiences. He organized a public relations office, a public information department, and a title registration bureau. Hays used the public relations department as a vehicle for establishing ties with groups that could potentially attack the industry and that could be used to improve the industry's moral and social image. At the first meeting, in June 1922, Hays appointed Lee Hanmer of the Russell Sage Foundation to chair the Committee on Public Relations, which included representatives from the Camp Fire Girls, the Boy Scouts, the General Federation of Women's Clubs, the International Federation of Catholic Alumnae, the Young Men's Christian Association, and the National Education Association.[11]

The public relations campaign of the MPPDA increasingly included educational leaders, who served to improve the image of the movie industry and provided justification for self-censorship. But this relationship was not without problems for the movie industry. As will be discussed in the next section, educators provided research that popularized the idea that movies had a detrimental effect on the health and morality of children and youth.

EDUCATORS AND THE MOVIES

When Will Hays first appeared before the National Education Association in July 1922, it was only one month after the forming of the Public Relations

Committee and six months after he accepted the leadership of the MPPDA. His pledge to accept the challenge "of the American mother" for worthy entertainment for American youth was given to an audience that had mixed feelings about the educational value of movies. On the one hand, many educators considered movie houses a major competition to schools for control of the minds of children. On the other hand, educators recognized the importance of using movies for instructional purposes. As the relationship between the movie industry and the educational establishment evolved in the 1920s and 1930s, the two groups found ways to serve each other's needs. The movie industry welcomed the claim made by educators that schools could improve movies through the education of future audiences, because such education would provide another argument against government censorship. This claim led to the establishment of movie appreciation courses in high schools, which, besides providing an argument against government censorship, benefited the movie industry by creating an audience for certain types of movies. In addition, the movie industry used educators for public relations purposes and for the sale of classroom films. Educators benefited by financial support from the movie industry, the development of classroom films, and justification of the importance of the school in educating movie audiences.

The ambivalent attitudes of educators toward the movie industry were evident in early discussions about educational films. Alfred Saunders, the manager of the education department of Colonial Picture Corporation, spoke in 1914 to the NEA on "Motion Pictures as an Aid to Education." As one of the first representatives of the movie industry to speak to the NEA, Saunders was concerned primarily with selling films to public schools. After his review of available movie projectors and films suitable for schools and a claim that "every school that is equipped with a projecting machine may cover the cost of it by allowing the parents to attend exhibitions in the evening," a discussion erupted among the gathered educators about the values of movies.[12]

Educators complained, as they later would about radio and television, that movies were in competition with the schools for the minds of children. In the NEA discussion in 1914, Peter Olesen, superintendent of schools from Cloquet, Minnesota, stated: "In less than twenty years, the motion picture business has secured a hold on the minds of people which is almost equal to that of the school and the daily press." Olesen warned that movies might be having a stronger hold on the mind of the child than the schools: "I believe that one reason why it is hard to interest some children in school today is that their minds have been filled and their imagination thrilled with too vivid motion pictures, and, when these children come to school, they are disappointed because the teacher cannot make the subject as interesting as a motion-picture show."[13]

The educators' fears about the effect of movies on children were reinforced in the 1920s and 1930s by an extensive set of research monographs called the Payne Studies, which are considered by the early historian of the MPPDA Raymond Moley to be one of the major contributing factors to the final enforcement of the movie code.[14] The Payne Studies were organized in 1928 under the leadership of W. W. Charters, director of the Bureau of

Educational Research at Ohio State University. The idea for the studies came from Reverend William Short, organizer of the Motion Picture Research Council in 1927 and a longtime critic of the movies. In 1928 he brought together a group of educators, psychologists, and sociologists to discuss possible research studies on the effect of movies on children. After the meeting, Short received financial support from a private foundation, the Payne Fund, for creation of a Committee on Educational Research and for a series of research studies.[15]

Twelve research studies were completed under the sponsorship of the Payne Fund. The studies were done by a formidable array of social scientists and educators and published in a series of volumes by the Macmillan Company.[16] In addition, W. W. Charters published a final summary volume in 1933. A popular summary of the studies was written under the auspices of the Payne Fund by Henry James Forman and published in 1935 under the title *Our Movie Made Children*. The popularity of Forman's book was reflected in the fact that it was reprinted seven times between 1933 and 1935.[17]

Touching on parental fears, one of the Payne studies concluded that movies had a detrimental effect on the health of children by disturbing sleep patterns. In cooperation with the Bureau of Juvenile Research in Columbus, Ohio, researchers wired the beds of children in a state institution to measure the amount of movement during sleep. The children were divided into different groups to measure the effect of movies and other conditions on restlessness during sleep. One group of children was made to drink coffee at 8:30 P.M. Another group underwent sleep deprivation, being kept up until midnight and then awakened early in the morning, until complaints by the matrons of the institution ended this part of the experiment. Another group of children was taken to the movies before going to bed. The research findings concluded that movie attendance caused as much disturbance during sleep as drinking two cups of coffee at 8:30 P.M. On the basis of this study, W. W. Charters warned, "Thus it appears that movies selected unwisely and indulged in intemperately will have a detrimental effect upon the health of children."[18]

Charters described the sleep studies as one link in a chain of negative effects of movies on children. The other links involved the content and attitudes of movies. Researchers found that movies had a significant effect on the conduct and attitudes of children. One study compared the behavior of children who attended movies four to five times a week with those from similar economic and social backgrounds who went to movies twice a month. It was found that those who attended more frequently had lower deportment grades in school, did more poorly on school subjects, and were rated lower in reputation by their teachers. A study of children living in congested areas of New York City arrived at a similar conclusion about the effects of movies on behavior.

Another Payne study focused on the effect of movies on the emotional responses of children. In this experiment, children seated in the balcony and rear seats of a movie theater in Columbus, Ohio, were wired to galvanometers. These devices measured their responses to scenes depicting dangerous situations and containing sexual material. The study found that scenes of danger created the greatest reaction in nine-year-olds, the degree of reaction declining with age, and that, not surprisingly, teenagers had a greater reaction to sex scenes than young children did. The reaction to scenes of danger was considered as causing unnecessary fright in young children, and the reaction to sex scenes was considered unhealthy for teenagers.

Adding to the concern about the emotional reaction of teenagers to movies was the important study by Herbert Blumer, associate professor of Sociology at the University of Chicago, using the autobiographies of 1,800 college and high school students, office workers, and factory workers. This study was important from two standpoints. First, I think the study demonstrates the important role of movies in bringing about the sexual revolution of the twentieth century. Second, it added significantly to fears that movies were having a detrimental effect on the population. Blumer asked his 1,800 participants to keep journals on the effect of movies on their lives. One of the major conclusions Blumer reached after reading the journals was the important role of movies in teaching lovemaking. Blumer wrote, "They [the journals] force upon one the realization that motion pictures provide, as many have termed it, 'liberal education in the art of loving.'"[19] Typical of the journal entries was that of a male college sophomore who recounted, "She would make me go with her to see [a movie] . . . and then when we returned home she made me make love to her as she had seen the other two on the screen." Another college male wrote, "The technique of making love to a girl received considerable of my attention, and it was directly through the movies that I learned to kiss a girl on her ears, neck, and cheeks, as well as on the mouth." The journal of one female high school sophomore was typical of other journals by girls of her age: "I have learned quite a bit about lovemaking from the movies."[20] In addition to teaching teenagers about lovemaking, Blumer concluded that movies were taking over the fantasy world of youth. He claimed that 66 percent of 458 journals written by high school students provided evidence that movies were linked to daydreaming.

In general, the Payne Studies presented a very negative portrait of the effects of movies on children. They were said to disturb children's sleep patterns, heighten emotional feelings, influence social attitudes, cause daydreaming, teach lovemaking, and flood the mind with ideas and facts that were retained over long periods of time. In addition, movie attendance was linked to poor grades, misbehavior in school, and juvenile delinquency.

Of particular importance for heightening public concern about the effects of movies was the supposed link between movie attendance and delinquency. Henry Forman presented this argument in graphic detail in his popularized version of the Payne Studies. Forman wrote, "A number of adolescent and youthful criminals give circumstantial accounts of their path to, and arrival at, criminality, and, rightly or wrongly, but very positively, they blame the movies for their downfall." Forman stated that girl inmates in an institution for sex delinquents attributed "to the movies a leading place in stimulating cravings for an easy life, for luxury, for cabarets, road-houses and wild parties, for having men make love to them and, ultimately, for their particular delinquency." Citing one of the Payne Studies, Forman stated, "[in] a high-delinquency area and a region where most of the youth is of foreign-born parentage, the movie enters into innumerable patterns of their lives and constitutes, in effect, an institution of informal education, socially uncontrolled and wholly unsupervised." Forman wanted to impress the reader with the evils of the movie house. Quoting the words of one Dr. Wesley Mitchell, Forman expressed the sentiment "Motion pictures are one of the most powerful influences in the 'making of mind' at the present time. They affect great masses of people during the impressionable years of childhood and youth."[21]

A major recommendation of the Payne Studies was the creation of movie appreciation courses in public schools. In fact, a volume written for the Payne series by Edgar Dale, research associate at the Bureau of Educational Research of Ohio State University, was *How to Appreciate Motion Pictures: A Manual of Motion-Picture Criticism Prepared for High School Students*.[22] In preparing this manual, Dale worked with members of the National Council of Teachers of English and with William Lewin, chairman of the council's committee on photoplay appreciation.[23] In 1934 the National Council of Teachers of English published Lewin's manual for the teaching of movie appreciation in high schools.[24] In addition, Dale received help from Paramount studios and the MPPDA.

Dale's volume opens with a chapter explaining to the high school reader how a movie appreciation course will provide standards for judging films and increasing enjoyment by introducing students to techniques in film production. In keeping with the idea that the content of films can be controlled through the education of audiences, Dale concludes Chapter 2: "By shopping for your movies you will raise the whole level of motion pictures that are produced. Poor pictures will no longer be made, and there will be many more good ones."[25] After instructing the student on the various aspects of filmmaking, Dale ends the volume on the same theme: "You have the power to influence the future of motion pictures."[26]

At the time that William Lewin worked with Edgar Dale on the movie appreciation textbook for the Payne Studies, he organized a film study group at Central High School in Newark, New Jersey.[27] Lewin's previously mentioned book, *Photoplay Appreciation in American High Schools*, was written as part of his work for the Committee on Photoplay Appreciation of the National Council of Teachers of English. In the volume, Lewin notes that during his tenure as teacher in the Newark schools, the supervisor of English for the school system pioneered the use of study guides for movies. This use of study guides became an important part of movie appreciation courses. Also, the study guides were supported by the industry because, as will be described later in this section, they were a form of advertising. In 1930 and 1931 Lewin had conducted studies of movie selection by high school students and educators. In an article for the National Council of Teachers in 1931 he reported his findings and suggested the establishment of a committee of educators to rate movies. Subsequently, the president of the National Council of Teachers of English asked Lewin to organize a photoplay appreciation committee. Edgar Dale was made a member of the committee, and, in cooperation with the National Council of Teachers of English and the Payne Fund, his textbook was distributed to high schools throughout the country.[28]

The Committee on Photoplay Appreciation chaired by William Lewin gathered statistics on adolescent movie selection and attendance and conducted an experiment—involving sixty-eight groups of students in sixteen states and the District of Columbia—comparing students receiving instruction in movie appreciation with those receiving no instruction. The study claimed that movie appreciation classes caused children and youth to select movies that had a positive effect on their conduct. Only 14 percent of the students who did not receive movie appreciation courses could name movies that affected their conduct, whereas 26 percent of those taking movie appreciation courses could name movies that affected their conduct. While the percentage of those whose conduct was affected by movies was relatively low, the committee used the figures to demonstrate the importance of movie appreciation training. As examples of the important influence of movies on conduct, the committee quoted an eleventh-grade girl in Memphis: "After seeing [the movie] *Sign of the Cross*, I went to church on a weeknight." In reference to the same movie, a twelfth-grade girl in Los Angeles wrote, "It made me glad I was a Christian: it made me stronger in my faith; it made me hold to my religion." Regarding the movie *Twenty Years in Sing Sing*, an eleventh-grade boy in Newark wrote, "It took away my tendency, more or less, from crime." And a boy in St. Cloud, Minnesota, stated about the same film, "It influenced me to be careful of my actions, as it is difficult to escape the arm of the law."[29]

Certainly, the movie industry must have been pleased that the National Council of Teachers of English was advocating movie attendance as part of the general education of youth and was motivating students to attend more movies. Rather than movie attendance being viewed in a negative light, it was being presented by the council as an extension of the work of the school. In the general conclusion of Lewin's study, an eleventh-grade student was quoted: "Before this experiment [the movie appreciation course], I went to movies just to kill time; movies weren't even a favorite hobby of mine. I didn't realize that there could be both educational and enjoyable pictures. . . . I've learned to select the better pictures. I think now I'll go to more pictures and appreciate them more."[30]

The Committee on Photoplay Appreciation concluded that movie appreciation courses combined with movie attendance had a positive effect on the character and education of students. In the words of the committee, "Class instruction excels in developing appreciation of high ideals of character in screen portrayals, the greatest gain being in appreciation of honesty, with large gains registered also for bravery, devotion, and self-sacrifice. . . . Movie influence on instructed pupils . . . is generally in the direction of higher ideals."[31] As will be discussed in the next section, uplifting the ideals of the movie viewer was precisely the goal of the movie code adopted by the MPPDA in the 1930s.

In a finding that must have pleased the movie industry, the National Council of Teachers of English concluded that movie attendance increased the reading of books used in writing screenplays. This conclusion provided justification for cooperation between the National Council of Teachers of English and the MPPDA in the writing and distribution of study guides to the public schools. In 1933, after the experiment of the Committee on Photoplay Appreciation, the council established a central reviewing committee for films, which during that year produced study guides for the films *Emperor Jones*, *Little Women*, and *Alice in Wonderland*. In 1934 the work was transferred from the National Council of Teachers of English to the National Education Association's Department of Secondary Education. In 1934 and 1935, study guides were distributed to public schools for *Great Expectations*, *Treasure Island*, *Little Women*, *David Copperfield*, *Dog of Flanders*, and *Les Misérables*.[32]

The movie industry and, supposedly, public school teachers were ecstatic about the distribution of these guides. For the movie industry it meant increased attendance at particular movies, free publicity, and good public relations. By 1937, study guides and information about movies were being sent to teachers of English, history, geography, and the sciences, to be used for directing students to see movies that illustrated material used in the classroom instruction. It was estimated that by 1937, three million students were receiving instruction in movie appreciation.

An example of the importance of study guides to the motion picture industry was outlined in an article in the May 16, 1936, *Motion Picture Herald* on the marketing of *Romeo and Juliet*. According to the article, the MPPDA directed its marketing campaign to sixteen national social, community, and educational groups with an estimated membership of 36,211,395. Based on an average admission of twenty-five cents, it was estimated that the potential admission grosses of this group were about $9 million. As part of the campaign, the Department of Secondary Education of the National Education Association prepared a study guide which was expected to be used in every high school English class in the United States. In describing the relationship between the movie industry and the schools in the marketing of films, the article states, "Half a million copies of this study guide will be made available for use as text material in schools and to be taken home to be read by all the family. All of this has a definite relation to the box office potentialities." In addition to the study guides, exhibits about the movie were shown in a school, library, or museum in fifty major cities in the United States. According to *The Motion Picture Herald*, these efforts made the film the number one box office success for September 1936 and one of the top ten box office successes in 1937 and 1938.[33]

These developments in the relationship between the movie industry and educators were reviewed by Will Hays when he appeared before the annual meeting of the NEA in 1939, seventeen years after his initial appearance.[34] In his speech, Hays recognized the similar responsibilities of educators and movie producers in the distribution of ideas in society. "That educators and motion picture producers have certain specialized and mutual interest in the motion picture as a purveyor of ideas and motivator of activities," Hays told the convention, "even the layman has come to realize." Hays described the importance of the movie code for making films educational and morally uplifting. In Hays's words, the code required that in films, "crime, wrong doing, evil, or sin shall not be made attractive; that correct standards of life shall be presented; that law, natural or human, shall not be ridiculed, or sympathy created for its violation."[35] It was the standards of this code, Hays maintained, that made it possible to bring together the worlds of the movies and the schools as purveyors of ideas.

THE PRODUCTION CODE: CREATING A POLITICAL AND MORAL CONSCIENCE

Intense economic pressures placed on the movie industry by religious organizations, particularly the Catholic church, by educators, and by other concerned groups resulted in the enforcement of the production code Hays proudly referred to in his 1939 speech before the NEA. Like other proposals for self-censorship, the production code was designed to shape movies so that they taught audiences moral, political, and social lessons. With the enforcement of the code in the 1930s, the movie industry joined the schools as an institution that consciously attempted to form the public mind.

Hays's first efforts at censorship occurred after a storm of protests by religious groups in 1923 at a possible movie production of the best-selling novel by Homer Croy, *West of the Water Tower*, which dealt with illegitimacy and a dissolute clergyman. In addition to the protest of religious groups about the portrayal of the clergyman, the National Congress of Parents and Teachers feared that a movie based on the novel would increase book sales. Despite these objections, the movie was produced and released. As a result of continued protests, Hays was able to convince the members of the MPPDA to require that all books and plays to be used for movies be reviewed by his office.[36] In 1927 Hays expanded the efforts at self-censorship by the adoption of a list of "Don'ts and Be Carefuls." In 1930 this list was replaced by a more extensive "Code to Govern the Making of Talking, Synchronized and Silent Pictures." The enforcement of the 1930 code was completed by a 1934 agreement that no movies would be released that were not approved by the Production Code Administration.

The actual writing and enforcement of the code was dominated by representatives of the Catholic church. This representation was a reflection of the militancy of the Catholic church regarding the content of movies and the ability of the church to ban movies to its parishioners and hinder export to predominantly Catholic countries. The two authors of the code were a Catholic publisher of *The Motion Picture Herald*, Martin Quigley, and a Catholic priest, Daniel Lord, S.J., professor of Dramatics at the University of St. Louis.

In 1936 the code received the official blessing of the Catholic church when it was endorsed by the Pope.[37]

The 1930 code was premised on the idea that entertainment should provide audiences with moral, social, and political lessons. It was designed to shape the content of movie scripts and filming techniques and, at the same time, eliminate objectionable scenes and dialogue. Quigley argued in his book *Decency in Motion Pictures*, published after his participation in the writing of the code, that the motion picture should be a form of entertainment that establishes ideals for audiences. He rejected the argument that art should be free to follow its own development. With regard to youth, Quigley maintained, art should provide guiding ideals for living in the world. Quigley rejected government censorship of movies because it turned decisions about morality over to the democratic process. Since morality, at least from Quigley's point of view, was determined by God, it should not be influenced by the whims of democratic decision making. Therefore, he maintained, self-regulation of the production of movies was preferable to government censorship.[38]

The code written by Quigley and Lord and approved by the MPPDA argues that traditional forms of art appeal in different ways to different social classes and groups of people. In the words of the code, "Music has its grades for different classes; so has literature and drama." On the other hand, movies appeal "at once to every class—immature, developed, undeveloped, law abiding, criminal." In addition, the mobility and ease of distribution of movies make it possible to reach "places unpenetrated by other forms of art." Therefore, the code states, "it is difficult to produce films intended for only certain classes of people."[39]

The argument that movies, unlike traditional art forms, could not be restricted to certain classes of people was a major reason given by the code for the necessity of censorship. As the code states, "The exhibitor's theatres are built for the masses, for the cultivated and the rude, the mature and the immature, the self-respecting and the criminal. Films, unlike books and music, can with difficulty be confined to certain selected groups." Included in this argument was an important distinction between modern mass media and traditional forms of public communication. Specifically, the code compares movies to books, newspapers, and plays. The code argues that books depend on words and the imagination of the reader, while movies depend on the vividness of presentation of visual and sound effects. Consequently, films have a greater potential for influencing mass behavior and therefore cannot be given as wide a latitude in content as books. In comparing movies with newspapers, the code states that newspapers simply describe events while movies try to give them the reality of life.

The code stresses the importance of the social role of entertainment and art. It states that entertainment can be morally uplifting or morally degrading. As examples, the code describes baseball and golf as being morally uplifting and cockfighting and bullfighting as being degrading. In the words of the code, "correct entertainment raises the whole standard of the nation. Wrong entertainment lowers the whole living conditions and moral ideas of a race."

A similar argument is used regarding the social role of art. Significantly, the code calls movies "the art of the multitudes." As with the topic of entertainment, the code stresses that art can be morally uplifting or degrading. The code mentions great painting and music as examples of morally uplifting art and indecent books and unclean paintings as examples of degenerate art.

After presenting a justification for self-censorship of the industry, the code states the guiding principles for the production of movies. It is these principles that shaped the content of movies from the 1930s to the 1960s. The guidelines of the code can be divided into the categories of (A) religious, (B) moral, (C) offensive to certain individuals, (D) crimes against the law, and (E) political. The religious category is concerned with movie situations that might be offensive to organized religious groups. The moral concerns are with the portrayal of good and evil as well as specific sexual situations. The category "offensive to certain individuals" referred to movie scenes that might spark racial tensions or might be found objectionable by some people or organized groups because of personal tastes and beliefs. Elimination of movie scenes depicting crimes against the law reflected the feelings expressed by educators and religious leaders that movies were teaching people how to be criminals and making criminal actions acceptable. The political restrictions of the code dealt with attitudes toward the law, the justice system, the U.S. political system, and foreign countries.

In writing the 1930 code, Lord and Quigley followed the general restrictions of the 1927 list of "Don'ts and Be Carefuls." The major complaint of religious groups about the 1927 list had been its lack of detail and enforcement. Therefore, as background to the 1930 code, I am presenting the 1927 list and dividing it into the categories of (A) religious, (B) moral, (C) offensive to certain individuals, (D) crimes against the law, and (E) political. In addition, the 1927 list is separated into things that "shall not appear in movies" and those things requiring "special care."[40]

Don'ts and Be Carefuls, 1927
Shall Not Appear in Movies
A. *Religious*
1. Pointed profanity . . . this includes the words "God," "Lord," "Jesus," "Christ" . . .
2. Ridicule of the clergy
B. *Moral*
1. Children's sex organs
2. Any licentious or suggestive nudity . . .
3. Any inference of sex perversion
4. White slavery
5. Sex hygiene and venereal diseases
C. *Offensive to Certain Individuals*
1. Miscegenation (sex relations between the white and black races)
2. Scenes of actual childbirth . . .
D. *Crimes against the Law*
1. The illegal traffic drugs
E. *Political*
1. Willful offense to any nation, race, or creed

Special Care
A. *Moral*
1. The sale of women, or a woman selling her virtue
2. First-night scenes
3. Man and woman in bed together
4. Deliberate seduction of girls
5. The institution of marriage
6. Excessive or lustful kissing . . .
B. *Offensive to Certain Individuals*
1. Brutality and possible gruesomeness
2. Actual hangings or electrocutions as legal punishment for crime
3. Apparent cruelty to children and animals
4. Branding of people and animals
5. Surgical operations
C. *Crimes against the Law*
1. Sympathy for criminals
2. The use of firearms
3. Theft, robbery, safecracking, and dynamiting of trains, mines, buildings, etc. (having in mind the effect which a too-detailed description of these may have upon the moron)
4. Technique of committing murder by whatever method
5. Methods of smuggling
6. Rape or attempted rape
D. *Political*
1. The use of the flag
2. International relations (avoiding picturizing in an unfavorable light another country's religion, history, institutions, prominent people, and citizenry)
3. Attitude toward public characters and institutions
4. Sedition
5. Titles or scenes having to do with law enforcement or law-enforcing officers

The 1930 code gives as the first general principle "No picture shall be produced which will lower the moral standards of those who see it. Hence the sympathy of the audience shall never be thrown to the side of crime, wrongdoing, evil or sin." Envisioned in the formulation of the first general principle of the 1930 code is a moral world where good always triumphs over evil and good people are always justly rewarded. It is a movie-made world where cowboys in white hats always beat the bandits in black hats. The code states that movies must avoid scenes that might make evil attractive to audiences. The problem, according to the code, is when "evil is made to appear attractive or alluring and good is made to appear unattractive." Distinguishing between sympathy for a crime or sin as opposed to sympathy for the plight of a sinner, the code warns against the sympathy of the audience being "thrown on the side of crime, wrong-doing, evil, sin."

In support of the creation of a moral universe in movies where a triumphal good holds sway over a hated evil, the second general principle of the 1930 codes states, "Correct standards of life, subject only to the requirements of drama and entertainment, shall be presented." While the code doesn't give a specific definition of "correct standards of life," it does state that the plots and characters in movies should develop the right ideals and moral standards. This is to be accomplished by movies giving audiences a moral model for living. In the words of the code, "if motion pictures consistently hold up for admiration high types of characters and present stories that will affect lives for the better, they can become the most powerful natural force for the improvement of mankind."

The third general principle of the 1930 code protects the image of laws and governments. This principle states, "Law, natural or human, shall not be ridiculed, nor shall sympathy be created for its violation." Natural laws are defined by the code as the principles of justice dictated by a person's conscience. With regard to human law, the code specifies that audience support should always be developed for government laws. The code warns against movies that are sympathetic to the commission of a crime as opposed to favoring the law. In addition, the code states, "The courts of the land should not be presented as unjust." While individual courts officials might be portrayed in movies as unjust, the code warns, "the court system of the country must not suffer as a result of this presentation."

Following the three general principles is a list of particular applications, which are only slightly different from the 1927 "Don'ts and Be Carefuls." The main differences are (1) the addition of warnings about the portrayal of the "use of liquor in American life," "undressing scenes," "indecent exposure," "dancing costumes," and "obscenity in word" and (2) the additional statement "The treatment of bedrooms must be governed by good taste and delicacy." When applied at the beginning of production of a movie, the 1930 code created for an unsuspecting audience a particular moral and political vision of the world.

A Production Code Administration was established on July 1, 1934, with Joseph Breen as its leader. Producers submitted screenplays and movies to Breen's office, which, in turn, issued lists of corrections. In retrospect, many of the items censored by Breen's office seem petty, but they are understandable in the context of the Production Code Administration's goal of protecting the industry from criticism and protecting the morality of the nation. For instance, Joseph Breen wrote to Jack Warner, president of Warner Brothers Studios, criticized parts of the classic *Casablanca* starring Humphrey Bogart and Ingrid Bergman because they suggested loose sexual mores and the lack of seriousness of marriage bonds. As part of the criticism, Breen wrote, "The following lines seem unacceptably suggestive: 'It used to take a villa in Cannes . . . and a string of pearls [in reference to seduction]. Now all I ask is an exit visa' and 'How extravagant you are throwing away women like that. Some day they may be rationed.'" A major concern was the suggestion in the plot that, while married, Ilsa (Ingrid Bergman) had had a love affair with Rick (Humphrey Bogart) in Paris. Breen wrote to Warner, "a suggestion of a sexual affair [between Ilsa and Rick] . . . would be unacceptable if it came through in the finished picture. We believe this could possibly be corrected by replacing

Chapter 12

the fade-out . . . with a dissolve, and shooting the succeeding scene without any sign of a bed."[41]

The 1930 movie code's distinction between movies and books is high-lighted by the censorship of novels adapted to the screen. The reader will recall that the introduction to the code called for the censorship of movies, as opposed to books, because books appealed to only certain groups in society while all groups attended movies. Thus, what was acceptable in book form was not acceptable in the form of a movie. Of course, this meant that for the cooperative effort between the movie industry and educators to develop study guides and exhibits of great "classics" brought to the screen, the screen adaptations had to meet the requirements of the Production Code Adminis-tration. As movies were the "art of the multitudes," Breen's office was not going to allow the portrayal on the screen of novels that might threaten sexual morality, the family, and marriage.

For instance, Leo Tolstoy's great novel *Anna Karenina*, which centers on an adulterous relationship, became a major problem for the Production Code Administration. After much discussion, MGM agreed with the Breen office to change the plot of the novel in the movie so that the "'matrimonial bond' would be 'positively defended.'" Breen's office wanted Karenina to affirm frequently "the sanctity and inviolability of marriage as a sacrament and as a civil contract." Minor characters in the novel were given greater preeminence in the movie as a means of highlighting the value of marriage. A happily married young couple and another couple who were reluctant to divorce, all minor characters in the novel, were made more important in the movie. Karenina was never to be portrayed in the movie as being happy with her lover. The censorship office and the producers agreed to eliminate any men-tion of Karenina's illegitimate child which appears in the novel. After freely changing the novel's plot, Breen's office demanded certain changes and deletions in the script. For example, Breen wanted to delete the following speech by Anna Karenina: "Am I ashamed of anything I've done? Wouldn't I do the same again tomorrow? Who cares what people say so long as I love you and you—change." Breen also wanted changes in the filming whereby adultery would not be accentuated. Breen's office recommended that scenes not be played in Anna's bedroom but be filmed in the living room or boudoir.[42]

Such censorship of plots, lines, and settings by the Breen office would, according to the movie code, create films that were morally uplifting and ensure that good always triumphed over evil. In addition, Breen's office looked carefully for any scenes that might portray the law or the legal system in a negative light. For instance, Breen wrote to Jack Warner of Warner Brothers regarding the film *The Maltese Falcon*: "Spade's speech about the district attorney should be rewritten to get away from characterizing most district attorneys as men who will do anything to further their careers. This is important."[43]

The movie code not only extended protection to courts, district attorneys, and the entire legal system, it also protected lawyers. The Production Code

Administration suggested that if a movie presented "the wrong kind of lawyer" then the producer should balance the picture with the "right kind of lawyer." A statement from the Production Code Administration read, "We, never, in our experience, have approved a picture wherein it was indicated, in the final summation, that unethical or dishonest lawyers are sympathetic characters, or that there is any approval, in the end of the story, of these unethical practices."[44]

In summary, fears of government censorship, a desire to maintain good public relations and attract families to movies, complaints by educators about the effect of movies on children and youth, and pressures from religious organizations forced the movie industry to adopt a censorship code that shaped the moral, social, and political content of movies. After 1934, movie audiences were presented with a moral world where good always won out over evil, collective action resulted in mob violence, and good triumphed because of individual action. Regarding political action, audiences saw a world where government was benign and the good citizen did not try to change basic political processes but reformed government by getting rid of corrupt politicians. In addition, at least until the propaganda films of World War II, movies presented an uncritical and superficial view of the nations of the world.

SHOULD COMMERCIAL RADIO OR EDUCATORS DETERMINE NATIONAL CULTURE?

"British vs. American Radio Slant, Debate Theme in 40,000 Schools" head-lined a front-page story in 1933 in *Variety*, the theatrical trade weekly. The pro industry weekly reported that radio circles believed the selection of the theme for high school debates around the country was part of an "anti-radio"—a term *Variety* used when referring to opponents of commercial radio—propaganda campaign against the American system of broadcasting. This campaign was being waged by educators, religious groups, and nonprofit organizations that wanted the federal government to license more education-al and nonprofit radio stations. The central issue in the high school debate was whether or not radio should be privately owned and financially sup-ported by advertising or, like the British system, operated by the government and supported by some form of taxation. With the profits of advertising determining the content of programming, these educators worried that com-mercial radio might be destroying American national culture. With an esti-mated one hundred persons expected at each debate, the major radio networks feared that a possible four million people might hear the question discussed. "Many, perhaps most, of these people," *Variety* lamented, "have been unaware of the existence of the question."[45]

In the 1930s, commercial radio networks operated under a constant fear that government action might take away their domination of the airwaves. They were particularly concerned about educators who were fighting mad about the loss of radio licenses as a result of government favoritism toward commercial radio and as a result of actions taken under the Radio Act of 1927, which created the Federal Radio Commission (FRC). Meeting in 1928, the FRC decided to eliminate interference between radio stations by adopting a new allocation plan for the distribution of licenses. Under this plan, radio stations with the greatest financial resources, most expensive equipment, and most varied programming were given preference in the issuance of licenses. This meant that commercial broadcasters were favored over educational broadcasters.[46] Writing in the mid-1930s for the proeducational broadcasting group the National Advisory Council on Radio in Education, a professor of education at Adelphi College, S. E. Frost, determined that between 1921 and 1936 there were 202 licenses granted by the government to educational organizations. As of January 1, 1937, there were only thirty-eight licenses held by educational institutions. In addition to government favoritism of large networks, many licenses were lost as a result of inactivity and financial failure.[47]

The first major network, the National Broadcasting Corporation (NBC), was organized in 1926 under the combined ownership of the Radio Corporation of America, General Electric, and the Westinghouse Corporation. American Telephone and Telegraph backed out of participation when an agreement was signed that NBC would continue to use its telephone wires as its broadcast network. Until 1943, NBC operated a red network and a blue network. Under government pressure, it sold the blue network, which became the American Broadcasting Company (ABC). The Columbia Broadcasting System (CBS) was formed in 1928 under the leadership of William Paley, with Paramount-Publix, the movie giant, holding a 49 percent partnership. Then, providing some competition with these broadcasting giants, the Mutual Broadcasting System was formed in 1934.[48]

Commercial networks were nervous about the national high school debate theme because a vocal coalition of educators, religious organizations, and other interested groups were demanding that 25 percent of the broadcasting licenses be given to nonprofit institutions. Leading this movement was the National Committee on Education by Radio. Formed in 1930 and funded by the Payne Foundation, the committee had representatives from nine major national educational organizations, including the National Education Association, the National Catholic Association, the American Council on Education, the National Association of State Universities, and the National Council of State Superintendents.[49]

Like the advocates of self-censorship of movies, who wanted entertainment to be a vehicle for moral and civil lessons, the members of the National Committee on Education by Radio were concerned primarily about radio programming serving as an instrument for building a national culture. When they met in May 1934 in the midst of efforts to get Congress to grant 25 percent of broadcast licenses to nonprofit stations, the committee selected as its topic "The Use of Radio as a Cultural Agency in a Democracy." At the meeting, John H. MacCracken, associate director of the American Council of Education, argued that radio would never have an important role in ordinary

classroom instruction. Instead, he argued, the phonograph record was a more flexible means of conveying a lesson requiring the dramatization of the human voice.[50] In general, the conference members believed that the most important educational role for radio was to build a national culture outside of school and provide adult education.

The general tenor of the conference was reflected in the question posed for the first morning session of the conference: "A National Culture—By-Product or Objective of National Planning?" The topic was first discussed by Jerome Davis, a member of the executive committee of the American Sociological Society and a faculty member of the Yale Divinity School. After reviewing the rise of commercial radio and the decline of educational radio, Davis argued that radio of the 1930s was distributing negative cultural values through advertising. "Children," Davis told the gathered educators, "are told that when they drink Cocomalt they are cooperating with Buck Rogers and heroine Wilma. . . . I am not questioning the quality of Cocomalt, but the outrageous ethics and educational effects of this advertising on the child mind." On the other hand, Davis argued, if it were possible to plan programs "for the younger generation on an educational instead of a profit basis, the dramatic adventures of historical figures in American life—those who have really contributed something to the welfare of the nation and the world—could be told." Davis lashed out against programming driven by profits and the quality of music and programs on commercial radio, and he concluded with a demand that commercial radio be required to devote at least 20 percent of its programming to educational programs.[51]

Joy Elmer Morgan, editor of the *Journal of the National Education Association*, chair of the National Committee on Education by Radio, and later president of the NEA, echoed Davis's sentiments when warning the audience, "You will discover that the advertising agency is taking the place of the mother, the father, the teacher, the pastor, the priest, in determining the attitudes of children."[52]

Morgan made a sweeping attack on the effects of radio and movies on American culture. Based on a pursuit of profits, these two media, Morgan argued, were spreading a form of entertainment that was the negation of culture and positive values. In fact, Morgan maintained, the only things keeping the country going were the culture and values from the period prior to the advent of these forms of mass entertainment. In Morgan's words, "America today is operating on a momentum which was acquired in the days before radio. It is operating on a momentum which the people acquired before the motion picture began teaching crime and gambling and the cheap and flippant attitude toward the verities of life." Speaking as editor of the NEA *Journal*, Morgan worried about what would happen to the United States when the generation being raised in the age of commercial media reached adulthood. The problem, as Morgan saw it, was the pursuit of profits by movies and radio determining national culture. "No one knows what will happen," Morgan told the sympathetic audience, "when this country comes into the hands of those who have been exposed to the propaganda of the

money changers and to the debasing material which they have broadcast into the lives of the people."[53]

Morgan discussed the differences between public schooling as a creator of mass culture, and commercial radio and movies, when answering the session's question on whether or not culture was a by-product or objective of national planning. Morgan listed three requirements for the building of a culture. The first was freedom of speech, the second was the idea of progress, and the third was planning. Freedom of thought, Morgan argued, provided the opportunity for the creation of new ideas in science and in social and political thought. Without advances in these areas, culture remained static.

Reflecting the belief that the public schools were in competition with commercial radio and movies for the determination of national culture, Morgan related the idea of progress to the development of the common school system in the United States. Morgan argued that it had been Horace Mann's belief in the possibility of progress through the improvability of humans that had led to his crusade for common schools. And it was the common school of the 1890s, Morgan claimed, that had made possible the rapid advances in American civilization in the 1890s and early twentieth century. In Morgan's words, "The first great development of the common school came during the 1890's and when that generation which was in the schools in the '90's came onto the scene of action, America had a period of the most rapid advance which has ever been known in any civilization."[54]

Morgan also related planning to the development of the common school. From her perspective, planning, accompanied by freedom of thought and a belief in progress, made possible the advance of civilization. "The common school," Morgan stated, ". . . is an example of far-sighted planning. It does not expect to make a profit today or at the end of the month or even at the end of the year."[55] The common school exists to serve society, and therefore its use can be planned.

Therefore, within this conceptualization of the development of culture, public schools advance culture while movies and radio destroy culture. Morgan argued that radio and movies hindered the advancement of civilization because profits took precedence over freedom of thought, the idea of progress, and socially meaningful planning. Morgan's answer for making radio an important contributor to the advancement of culture was to eliminate private ownership of broadcasting, to have listeners' interests determine program content, and to promote the cultural use of radio over commercial uses.

In addition, Morgan argued, children needed to be protected against commercial exploitation. "We should look upon the effort to go over the heads of parents, the church, and the school, to the child mind with something of the horror that we would look at the poisoning of a spring or well."[56]

The afternoon session tackled the question "On Whom Rests the Responsibility for the Cultural Use of Radio?" It was followed the next morning by reports from various committees discussing the questions posed on the first day of the conference. Of particular interest in this follow-up discussion were

the comments of William G. Carr, research director of the National Education Association, regarding the similar problems posed by movies and radio. Carr called for studies of the effects of radio that would be similar to those of the Payne Studies on movies. Carr stated, "We have in radio a problem somewhat similar to that of the motion pictures. Both are growing privately owned businesses with great possibilities for constructive or destructive educational effects." A set of findings on the effect of radio, he believed, would arouse public interest.

The last session on the afternoon of the second day was devoted to discussing the adoption of the "Report of Committee on Fundamental Principles Which Should Underlie American Radio Policy." The report contained a summary of the opinions regarding national radio policy held by representatives from the major educational organizations attending the conference. The report, like discussions of self-censorship in the movie industry, stressed the importance of using radio as a means of social control. In fact, it stressed the importance of conscious control for this purpose. The opening to the final report of the conference states, "Radio broadcasting—this great, new agency—should be so guided and controlled as to insure to this nation the greatest possible social values." And, the report on, "The social welfare of the nation should be the conscious, decisive, primary objective, not merely a possible by-product incidental to the greatest net returns to advertisers and broadcasters."

To achieve this conscious control of the social values promoted by radio, the report recommended that listeners' needs and desires take precedence over commercial interests; that minority groups gain access to radio; that the "impressionable, defenseless minds of children and youth must be protected against insidious, degenerative influences"; and that controversial issues and America's best culture be broadcast over radio. With regard to the issue of ownership, the report made a general statement that "The government should cease incurring expense for the protection of channels for the benefit of private monopoly without insuring commendable programs satisfactory to citizen listeners."

The broadcasters countered this attack by launching a campaign to prove that commercial radio brought educational programs to the American home. "Strategy of commercial broadcasters," *Variety* noted in May 1934, "will be to demonstrate as completely as possible that adequate opportunity is afforded under present setup for nonprofit programs." Like the movie industry, broadcasters took their campaign directly to the educators. "The first shot in the defensive campaign was fired several weeks ago," *Variety* reported, "when Merlin H. Aylesworth, NBC head, told the National Education Association convention that 'education gets a 50–50 break over our networks.'"[57]

The title of Aylesworth's speech before the NEA, "Radio as a Means of Public Enlightenment," appeared to have been chosen to counter the claims by educators that commercial radio was destroying American culture. As president of NBC, Aylesworth told the educators gathered at their annual meeting that radio had joined with the church, the home, and the school as a

source of public enlightenment. The American broadcasting system, he claimed, provided the greatest variety of programming of any system in the world. He claimed that 20 percent of broadcasting on commercial radio was educational, while 30 percent was of "educational value." These figures were used to claim that 50 percent of network radio was devoted to educational programming. In giving examples of educational programs, he referred only to NBC's "Music Appreciation Hour," which he stated was heard weekly in 50,000 schools by six million children. Educators in the audience must have wondered what programs constituted the rest of the 50 percent of educational programming.[58]

The most articulate defense of the broadcasting industry was presented to the FCC by CBS President William Paley. As with Aylesworth's speech before the NEA, the title of Paley's address, "Radio as a Cultural Force," suggested an attempted rebuttal of the arguments expressed at the May meeting of the National Committee on Education by Radio. Paley justified the American broadcasting system in the context of a market economy. Since radio is operated as a business, he argued, broadcasters must provide programs that attract listeners. Therefore, the first problem for the networks was to win an audience and then hold that audience. In addition, he argued, radio, unlike newspapers, cannot be geared to a specific audience. It must have universal appeal. To achieve these goals, Paley maintained, radio programs had to appeal to the emotions and self-interest of listeners along with appealing to their intellect.

Paley then went on to ask whether educational and religious leaders should determine what the best programming for listeners is or whether that should be determined by the selections of individual listeners. The arguments presented by the members of the Committee on Education by Radio suggested that a group of intellectual and moral leaders should decide what is best for the public and that radio should be turned into a form of public education. Paley, on the other hand, justified the American broadcasting system through claims that it was democratic because it was based on listener selection. In this situation, arguments for democracy were used to defend a broadcasting system that was primarily controlled by two networks and whose content was influenced by government officials, corporate needs, and the bias of advertisers. Paley stated, "We cannot assuredly, calmly broadcast programs we think people ought to listen to, if they know what is good for them; and then go on happily unconcerned as to whether they listen or not."[59]

Paley also attacked the format of educational radio as being undemocratic and based on aristocratic assumptions. Quoting from an article he had written for the *Annals of the American Academy of Political and Social Science,* he argued that the common school system had created independent and critical thinkers. Paley stated that American democratic education prepared citizens for direct application of the humanities and arts as opposed to the aristocratic concept of learning for learning's sake. In his words, "Experience has taught us that one of the quickest ways to bore the American audience is to deal with

art for art's sake, or to deify culture and education because they are worthy gods."[60]

The FCC sided with the radio industry and reported to Congress that commercial radio was providing adequate educational programming. What was needed, the commission argued, was cooperation between broadcasters and the educational community. For this purpose they created the Federal Radio Education Committee, which became another platform for the debate over the role of education in the American broadcasting system.

Obviously, the creation of the Federal Radio Education Committee as an alternative to the 25 percent allotment plan was favored by the broadcasting industry but not by the members of the Committee for Education by Radio. The goal of the Federal Radio Education Committee was to establish cooperation between educators and commercial broadcasters and to support studies on the educational use of radio. This action created no threat to the broadcasting industry and, in fact, provided a means for commercial broadcasters to prove that they were serving the public interest. Educators did gain federal assistance in the development of education by radio, but they lost at this time in their efforts to create an educational network. Public broadcasting was eventually to be realized with the passage of the Public Broadcasting Act of 1967.

CRIME AND GORE ON CHILDREN'S RADIO

In December 1934, Thomas Rishworth, the director of radio station KSIP in St. Paul, Minnesota, made the mistake of challenging the local Parent-Teacher Association (PTA) to stop its "glib" criticism of children's radio programs and offer constructive advice. He said that he was tired of hearing the Minnesota PTA complain that radio broadcasts were disturbing children with blood-and-gore tales, causing them to toss and turn in their sleep, and making them miss meals when their favorite programs were being aired.[61]

One week later, representatives of the PTA and Boy Scouts and other community members met with Rishworth to discuss the problems of children's radio. Besides the previously mentioned complaints, John Donahue, a probation officer in St. Paul, stood up at the meeting and warned that radio programs like *Jack Armstrong* were causing law-breaking tendencies among the community's children through their portrayal of likable villains.[62]

Contrary to Rishworth's original intentions, the meeting ended with a call for boycotts of advertisers of children's programs and strict censorship of radio listening by parents. Even the trade newspaper, *Variety*, was caught by surprise by the outcome of the meeting. *Variety* tended to take the side of the networks. Its original article on the story gave the impression that Rishworth would easily be able to handle the critics of children's radio. After the critics announced a boycott of advertisers, *Variety*, in an article titled "Air Reformers after Coin," claimed that the real goal of critics in St. Paul was to make money in the radio business. Without naming the group, the newspaper stated that one of the groups represented at the meeting with Rishworth was trying to peddle its own scripts to commercial sponsors.[63]

The interaction between Rishworth and the local PTA exemplified the protests against children's radio that were occurring across the country. Complaints about children's radio began to appear in popular magazines in the early 1930s. Typical of these articles was a 1933 editorial in *Parents Magazine* written in response to the many complaints received in its offices about children's programs. The editorial was accompanied by a cartoon depicting a frightened young girl sitting on the floor next to a radio spewing forth the words "Scram! Don't Shoot! Kidnapped! They're Going to Kill Me! Help! Murder! Bang! Bang! Kill Him! Police!" The editorial stated that the majority of complaints it received were about the high pitch of fear and emotional excitement radio caused in young children. The editor urged parents to write to sponsors to protest the quality of children's programs.[64]

Parental protests were voiced through local PTAs and women's clubs. For example, in February 1933 the Central Council of the PTA of Rochester, New York, issued a public statement which, according to *Variety*, declared "the crime ideas [in radio programs] harmful to moral fibre of children and the bloodcurdling situations tend to excite youngsters in a manner to interfere with their sleep." The PTA sent protests to local stations with hints of a boycott of advertisers.[65] A few months later the California PTA issued a list of "bad" radio programs and called for unofficial censorship of programs broadcast between 5:00 P.M. and 8:00 P.M., which were considered the prime hours for children to listen to radio. The California PTA expressed its concern about "all programs emphasizing killing, robbing, impossible or dangerous situations."[66]

The actions of PTA groups began to have some effect on network broadcasting. In February 1933, NBC announced that in response to mounting mass complaints that children were trying to mimic the action of criminals appearing on radio programs, it would begin to "blue-pencil" radio scripts that had criminal themes.[67] Advertisers began to show concern. *Variety* announced in August 1933 that "Commercials are yielding to the agitation of PTA associations." The advertising agency for Jell-O was supposedly leading the way by shifting from sponsorship of horror programs to a radio version of *The Wizard of Oz*. Members of other advertising agencies expressed surprise that the protests hadn't started sooner and believed that horror on radio was overdone.[68]

The other major organization protesting the content of children's radio was the National Council of Women, composed of twenty-eight national women's organizations. The head of the council's Women's National Radio Committee, Mrs. Harold V. Milligan, laced her attack against children's radio with strong feminist language. In a 1935 letter to *Variety*, she described her committee as the first coordinated effort by women to register their complaints against radio, which, in her words, is "man-made" and "man regulated."[69] The following year, at a national radio conference, she declared, "Women vote, and they have influence on public opinion, yet big business does very little to indicate its willingness to earn the respect of millions of women who are serious about the one problem—children's programs on the radio."[70]

Like the PTA, the Women's National Radio Committee was concerned about the blood and gore in children's programming. In addition, the organization was concerned about the effects of advertising. In describing the growth of women's interest in radio, Milligan stated, ". . . there sprang into being . . . a consciousness on the part of women that radio was a guest in the American home. . . [we] were grateful for the stimulating experience . . . but we were dubious of the growing tendencies of the American advertiser to inflict programs that we did not think were worthy of our children's attention." To capture the child's attention, she argued, the advertiser believed that it had to make programs highly stimulating. Also, she complained, advertisers were exploiting children as consumers.[71]

Modeling themselves after the movie industry, the radio networks reacted to these pressures by trying to include complaining organizations in a public relations campaign. The fact that the radio industry was borrowing methods form Will Hays's Motion Picture Producers and Distributors Association was boldly stated in a headline in *Variety:* "Radio Wants Clubwoman Good Will: Offer Transmitters to Gals with Messages—Will Hays Started It." The article dealt with CBS Chicago affiliate WBBM offering free air time to local women's clubs, the DAR, and the PTA. The *Variety* article states, "Following the plan laid down by Will H. Hays of the picture industry in organizing public opinion, stations are giving attention to the problem of building up goodwill."[72]

By 1935 the FCC began to respond to the complaints of the PTAs and women's clubs. On April 3, 1935, *Variety* announced, "Deluged with bleats from educators and parents, Commish [FCC] is agreed that if broadcasters do not move on their own to cook up more satisfactory entertainment for children the government must apply the whip." The FCC admitted that under its "anticensorship" clause it could not directly control the content of children's radio, but it could threaten stations with the possibility of taking away licenses by stringently applying the public service requirement and by rigidly enforcing technical rules. In addition to feeling pressure from public groups, the FCC also was receiving pressure from the White House and Congress to do something about "Goosepimple Kid Shows." In the words of *Variety*, "Kids' programs of blood-and-thunder type appear doomed under new drive."[73]

By May 1935, the FCC cleanup was in full swing. Its efforts at cleaning up radio extended beyond just children's radio. Again the FCC could not openly declare its attempts at censorship, but it let radio stations know that it was concerned about the following types of programming and advertising:

1. Lotteries
2. Fortune tellers
3. Racing tips

    4. Blood and thunder kids' programs
    5. Birth control compounds
    6. Fat-removing compounds[74]

In June 1935 the FCC instructed its field personnel to report radio broadcasts that violated what *Variety* called "Radio's 10 Commandments." Besides advertising and objectionable religious and medical programs, *Variety* claimed that the FCC included in its Ten Commandments "attacks on government officials or governmental departments."[75]

The broadcasting industry's response to public and government pressure paralleled that of the movie industry. The networks announced the institution of self-censorship codes, and in early June 1935 the Philco Corporation announced the establishment of a Radio Institute of the Audible Arts that was to be modeled on the Hays organization in the movie industry. The stated purpose of the organization was to hold off government censorship of radio by recommending programs and by acting as a clearinghouse for information. The institute compiled a mailing list of 5,000 women's clubs, PTAs, and other interested groups.[76]

The most widely publicized response was CBS's announcement in May 1935 of a self-censorship code designed to "clean up" broadcasting.[77] This was not a surprise move on the part of CBS. Previously, in his annual report to board members in 1933, CBS President William Paley had argued against government censorship of network programming and advocated voluntary censorship.[78] Also, CBS had already adopted a number of standards to guide programming. In 1928 and 1929 it had issued guidelines for dealing with controversial public issues, and in 1931 it had banned attacks on religious groups. Some standards regarding advertising had also been established in the early 1930s.[79]

NBC reacted to the announcement of CBS's code by claiming that it had adopted a similar code in 1934.[80] But NBC did not pull together its broadcast standards into a single booklet for public distribution until 1939. Before 1939, NBC claimed that its broadcast standards were stated in personal letters to advertisers.[81]

The public was informed of the code by William Paley in a broadcast over the Columbia network on May 14, 1935. Paley began the broadcast by reminding listeners of how radio now permeated the lives of most Americans. "You hear the voices of Columbia," Paley said, "for many hours each day. These voices are familiar in your home, perhaps in your workshop, and even in your automobile and the restaurants and theaters you visit." In words that suggested the possible changes in social relationships caused by radio, Paley continued, "These voices are frequently more familiar comrades, than some of your closest personal friends." After painting a picture of the intimate relationship between the listener and broadcaster, Paley described the general outlines of the new broadcasting code.[82]

The files at the CBS library indicate that the self-censorship code was issued as part of a well-orchestrated public relations campaign. In its official announcement, CBS described the formation of an Advisory Committee on

Children's Programs as the final step in creating the administrative machinery to control the content of advertising, to limit the length of advertising announcements, and to bring "children's programs up to a level generally approved by parents and authorities on child health and child psychology." In addition, CBS announced that the work of its newly formed Advisory Committee would be aided by the Child Study Association. The announcement quoted William Paley regarding the formation of the Advisory Committee: "The vivid reality of radio presentations affords an opportunity both to entertain and to help the child of which we hope to take the fullest advantage."[83]

The policies announced by CBS dealt directly with the two major complaints about American broadcasting: advertising and children's radio. Of central importance to the future of children's radio programs was the emphasis in the code on creating moral and social heroes to guide youth. The code was premised on the notion of the importance of hero worship in a child's life. Radio programs such as *Superman*, *The Lone Ranger*, and *Tom Mix* exemplified this type of hero-based children's drama. Like the movie code, CBS's code emphasized the importance of not teaching children antisocial behavior by presenting criminals and crime in a positive light. In addition, the code reflected the complaints of women's clubs about the quality of advertising on children's programs.

The code distributed by CBS in 1935 opens with a statement that links the necessity of self-censorship directly to corporate profits. The code states: "It is incumbent upon the broadcaster constantly to examine general policy so as to assure steady progress in building and holding radio's audience. Such watchfulness serves the interests of the audience, of the advertiser, and of the broadcasting companies alike."[84] Without mentioning pressures from public groups and government officials, the code refers to the current concern of the broadcasting industry with children's programs and "unpleasant discussions of bodily functions, bodily symptoms, other matters which similarly infringe on good taste."[85] This last item referred to the advertising of such items as laxatives.

The section on children's programs begins with a discussion of the varieties of viewpoints among parents and authorities as to which programs are suitable for children and the attempt by commercial sponsors to provide appropriate programs. But even with these considerations, the code argues, it is necessary to eliminate instances of poor judgment. The code disclaims any attempt by CBS to be "arbiter of what is proper for children to hear." But, the code states, CBS "does have an editorial responsibility to the community, in the interpretation of public wish and sentiment, which cannot be waived."[86] Using this justification, the code provides the following list of themes and dramatic treatments that would not be allowed on children's programs:

1. The exalting, as modern heroes, of gangsters, criminals and racketeers will not be allowed.
2. Disrespect for either parental or other proper authority must not be glorified or encouraged.

3. Cruelty, greed, and selfishness must not be presented as worthy motivations.
4. Programs that arouse harmful nervous reactions in the child must not be presented.
5. Conceit, smugness, or an unwarranted sense of superiority over others less fortunate may not be presented.
6. Recklessness and abandon must not be falsely identified with a healthy spirit of adventure.
7. Unfair exploitation of others for personal gain must not be made praiseworthy.
8. Dishonesty and deceit are not to be made appealing or attractive to the child.[87]

After stating these prohibitions, the code presents an argument for centering children's radio around hero worship. The code argues that radio programs for children of elementary school age should provide entertainment of a moral nature. The code notes that children's literature continues to provide "heroes worthy of the child's ready impulse to hero worship, and of his imitative urge to pattern himself after the hero model." Literature of this nature, the code notes, "succeeds in inspiring the child to socially useful and laudable ideals such as generosity, industry, kindness and respect for authority . . . it serves, in effect, as a useful adjunct to that education which the growing and impressionable child is absorbing during every moment of its waking day."[88]

As mentioned, by 1934 NBC claimed it was using a similar code and in 1939 it officially released its code. Its censorship of children's programs actually began in 1933, when NBC announced that listeners' complaints about the effects of crime shows on youth were causing it to "blue-pencil" scripts with crime themes. Officials at NBC expressed concern that letters indicated that children were trying to mimic criminals and crime situations.[89]

Like the CBS code, NBC's code linked self-censorship to protection of markets. The code argued that enforcing self-censorship would avoid the broadcast of anything that "might in any way divert part of an audience from one network or station to another." The first section of NBC's code banned from the network advertisements dealing with speculative finances, personal hygiene, weight-reducing agents, fortune-tellers, professions, cemeteries, alcoholic beverages, and firearms. The second section of the code was devoted to children's programs and the last section to general standards that would govern all programs.[90]

The NBC code stressed that all children's programs should stress law and order, adult authority, good morals, and clean living. As in the CBS code, heroes were to play a function in shaping children's morality. The code states, "The hero or heroine and other sympathetic characters must be portrayed as intelligent and morally courageous . . . and disrespect for law must be avoided as traits in any character that may be presented in the light of a hero to the child listener." In addition, the code states that programs' themes should emphasize mutual respect, fair play, and honorable behavior. Adventure stories were singled out because of their potential to upset children emotionally. Prohibited from adventure programs were torture, horror, superstition, kidnapping, "morbid suspense," and extreme violence.

Children's programs were also to be covered by eleven "Basic Program Standards" that were to be applied to all NBC programs. Three of these standards dealt with items that might offend religious groups, such as irreverent reference to God, material offensive to religious views, and sacrilegious material. Included in the standard regarding material offensive to religious groups was a ban on statements offensive to racial groups. The standards also discouraged the introduction of murder and suicide into programs and prohibited descriptions of "antisocial" practices and insobriety. One standard reserved the use of "flash" to special news programs, and another warned against false statements. Except in factual news statements, there were to be no references to people featured in criminal and sensational news stories. And, reflecting broadcasting's concern about offending important people, one standard reads, "Figures of national prominence as well as the peoples of all nations shall be presented with fairness and consideration."[91]

CHILDREN'S TELEVISION WORKSHOP AND
SESAME STREET

The actions within the movie and broadcasting industries in the 1930s set the pattern for later years. A combination of government and advocacy group pressures continued to shape the ideas disseminated by movies and the broadcasting industries. During World War II the federal government made a concerted effort to shape the content of radio and movies for the war effort. Immediately following the war, public schools, movies, and broadcasting were affected by the "Red scare" with suspected communists being purged. These agencies for the dissemination of ideas to the public were "cleansed" to meet the requirements of the Cold War. By the 1960s, less attention was paid to movies as television became a dominant media form. As with radio, the ideas and values distributed to the public by television were influenced by both the government and advocacy groups.[92]

As they did with movies, educators complained about the negative effects of television on children's learning. This criticism received public support in the 1960s from the head of the FCC, Newton Minow. In a speech at the 1961 meeting of the National Association of Broadcasters, Minow declared that television was a vast "wasteland." He opened the speech with praise for the potential of television and a denial that he intended to use government powers to censor broadcasting. After soothing his audience with these words, Minow launched his attack. He invited the broadcasters to sit with their eyes glued to their television sets from the time stations went on the air until the stations signed off. "I can assure that you will observe," he told them in words that were to be echoed around the country, "a vast wasteland." This wasteland is, he stated, "a procession of game shows, violence, audience participation shows, formula comedies about totally unbelievable families, blood and thunder, mayhem, violence, sadism, murder, Western bad men, Western good men, private eyes, gangsters, more violence, screaming, cajoling, and offending. And most of all, boredom. True, you will see a few things you will enjoy. But they will be very, very few."[93]

Minow's speech sparked the interest of many Americans and eventually culminated in the forming of the Carnegie Commission on Educational Television. In 1967, President Lyndon Johnson accepted the recommendations of the Carnegie Commission of Educational Television. A major recommendation, which was eventually approved by Congress, was for the creation of the Corporation for Public Broadcasting. To a certain extent, the legislation envisioned commercial television producing programs for low culture and public television producing programs for high culture. Also, the legislation reflected the concerns of educators in the 1930s about the effect of broadcasting on national culture.[94]

The Carnegie Commission's recommendation for children's television included the use of television as a means of social reform. The commission's proposal for children's programming contained two revolutionary ideas about the educational use of television. First was the idea that television could be used as an informal means of education. This proposal harkened back to the debates during the early days of movies when it was proposed that censorship be used to turn entertainment movies into a form of public education. In the words of the Carnegie Commission, "Important as this can be for adults, the informal educational potential of Public Television is greatest of all for children."[95]

Second, the commission proposed that television should focus on preparing preschool children for formal education. This proposal was very much in line with the development in the 1960s of Head Start programs, which were to prepare "disadvantaged" children for kindergarten or the first grade. Under this proposal, television would informally educate preschool children as well as focusing on the education of the "disadvantaged." "Public Television programs," the report states, "should give great attention to the informal educational needs of preschool children, particularly to interest and help children whose intellectual and cultural preparation might otherwise be less than adequate."[96]

The proposal was based on an idea gaining increasing popularity in the 1960s that preschool education significantly improved the achievement of children in school and that it could break the cycle of poverty. At a dinner party in March 1966, one of the supervisors of the Carnegie Corporation's grants, Lloyd Morrisett, proposed the idea of television as a form of preschool education to television producer Joan Cooney. Funded by the corporation, in October 1966 Cooney completed a feasibility study on the use of television to educate preschool children.[97]

Lloyd Morrisett hoped that television could solve the problem of the slow spread of kindergarten and nursery schools around the United States. Believing that preschool education was important for the cognitive development of children, he worried that preschools "would slowly, if at all, reach many of the children who needed them, particularly underprivileged children for whom preschool facilities might not be available." The answer to this problem, he felt, was in the ability of television to reach large numbers of children.[98]

As Morrisett conceptualized the project, television should become one partner in the general education of children. Within this framework, television was the third educator along with the family and the school. "The real answer to problems of early education," Morrisett wrote, "is for the total culture of childhood, including television as an important element, to work in harmony with the family and later the school."[99]

Again, a proposal of the Carnegie Corporation received federal money. During the two years between the feasibility study and the establishment of the Children's Television Workshop, 48.8 percent of the $8 million spent on the project came from federal sources. The majority of the federal money came through the U.S. Office of Education. The importance of the informal relationships between the government and foundations is illustrated by a story told in Ellen Condliffe Lagemann's history of the Carnegie Corporation. Lagemann describes a trip by Joan Cooney, now an employee of the corporation, and Barbara Finberg, a corporation program officer concentrating on early childhood education, to Washington to see the U.S. Commissioner of Education. According to Lagemann, Commissioner Harold Howe II was "well acquainted with many people at the Carnegie Corporation, including Morrisett . . . [and he was] quickly interested in the idea of a children's series. 'Let's do it,' Cooney remembered him saying at the end of their meeting."[100] Commissioner Howe became a major proponent of preschool education through television. In 1968, the Children's Television Workshop was organized, and on November 10, 1969, the first production of *Sesame Street* was broadcast.

The organization of the Children's Television Workshop required cooperation between educators and television producers. As Joan Cooney described the process, the informal network of the Carnegie Corporation was used to select an educational advisor for the Workshop. Cooney had met many academics selected by the corporation while doing the feasibility study. In addition, Lloyd Morrisett, in Cooney's words, "through his position at Carnegie, knew personally most of the leading people in the field of educational psychology." As their first choice, they decided to ask Gerald Lesser, Bigelow Professor of Education and Developmental Psychology at Harvard, to be their chief advisor and chairman of the Board of Advisors.[101]

Lesser was the guiding hand in the development of the educational goals for the first major production of the Children's Television Workshop, *Sesame Street*. Lesser rejected the attitude held by many educators that education could solve most of the world's problems. He wrote, "Educators cannot remedy the injustices to minorities in our society or create new life styles or new communities to replace deteriorating ones. Yet they sometimes act as if they think they can."[102] The belief that education could have only a limited role in social reform tempered the original focus on helping children of the poor.

While Lesser saw a limited role for education in social reform, he did believe that something drastic had to be done about the educational problems in the United States. Writing about the "fifty billion dollars" that was spent on a "massive educational superstructure which holds captive over fifty million children," he complained, "[that] we are failing to educate our children, either disastrously or to a degree no worse than the failures of other social and political institutions, is almost beyond dispute."[103]

Lesser believed that television could be a means of rescuing the entire educational system. In fact, he argued that television had certain ingredients that made it somewhat superior to the public schools. Public schooling, he maintained, depended on control of the student by others, public humiliation, and the continuous threat of failure. Television learning contained none of these elements. In front of the television, Lesser argued, the child learns without fear of a public or teacher, there is no threat of humiliation, and the child can control the learning process by the flip of a switch.

Consequently, Lesser believed that television was an ideal educator. It was nonpunitive, and it provided a shelter from the emotional stresses of society. "We may regret the conditions in our society that make sanctuaries necessary and must guard against a child's permanent retreat into them," Lesser wrote, "but sanctuaries are needed, and television is one of the few shelters children have."[104]

Also, Lesser believed television was a superior educator because it could be entertaining. He argued that traditional thinkers separated the idea of entertainment and education. In fact, many believed that entertainment would contaminate education. Lesser referred to this as a "lunatic" view of education. Like the early censors who wanted entertainment movies to be educational, Lesser believed that television would be an ideal vehicle for educating through entertainment.[105]

Besides lauding the potential educational value of television, Lesser was impressed by the statistics on television viewing. Using calculations made in 1967, Lesser estimated that in homes with preschool children the television was on fifty-four hours per week and that, on average, a high school graduate had spent 12,000 hours in school and 15,000 hours watching television. In fact, a high school graduate had spent more time watching television than was spent at any other activity.[106]

Given all of the above factors, Lesser believed that television could be the savior of the entire educational system while at the same time he doubted the ability of education to cause massive social reform. Consequently, he felt the Children's Television Workshop should not limit its focus to the education of children of the poor. In part, the desire for success influenced the decision to create a program for all children. In Lesser's words, "To succeed, a national television series must attract as large a national audience as possible, including children from all social classes and cultural groups and from all geographic regions."[107]

Producing a program for all children caused a dilemma regarding the desire to reduce the educational gap between the children of the rich and the poor. Obviously, the attempt to reach all children restricted the ability of program to narrow the gap. In fact, as Lesser admitted, the program could increase the gap. Lesser wrote, "We hoped that poor children would learn as much and that the gap would not be widened, despite the fact that almost all comparisons of educational progress show middle-class children proceeding more rapidly."[108] The solution offered to this dilemma was to make the series appealing to children of the poor and to encourage viewing in poor families.

Therefore, while *Sesame Street* was supposed to appeal to a national audience, concerns with educating the children of the poor directly influenced the overall goals of the program. Even though Lesser felt negatively about public schooling, he argued that the only realistic goal was to emphasize an education that would prepare children to enter school. This decision tied the program directly to the needs of formal schooling.

Because of his negative feelings about formal schooling, Lesser added a somewhat cynical note to how the program could prepare children. "Since one major premise was the preparation of disadvantaged children for school," Lesser argued, "the most useful ammunition we could give the child was the ability to "read" the teacher, to pick up the small covert clues in the teacher's behavior that would allow him to guess what the teacher wants to hear."[109] Therefore, from Lesser's perspective, *Sesame Street* could help children by teaching them the implicit rules of schooling so that the child could conform to the behavioral expectations of teachers. Lesser's cynical proposal was overruled by the staff of the Children's Television Workshop.

The emphasis on preparation for school and concerns about children of the poor determined the basic shape of *Sesame Street*. The staff decided that poor parents wanted their children to achieve in the basic subjects of reading, writing, and arithmetic. The major complaint of these parents, the staff felt, was the failure of the school to teach these subjects. Therefore, the staff concluded that the program should focus on preparation for learning these subjects in school.

According to Lesser, teaching the alphabet was the most controversial decision regarding preparation for school. This decision created "howls of repugnance . . . over . . . use of the new technology to teach what appears to be an arbitrary and useless skill."[110] But, it was argued, the alphabet was essential for early reading. What television could accomplish, in the framework of Lesser's belief that learning can be entertaining, was to make memorization of the alphabet a form of entertainment.

During its early years, *Sesame Street* did score a major success in reaching children of the poor. During the first broadcast year, it was estimated that almost 50 percent of the potential preschool audience watched the program, including children in day care and other prekindergarten programs serving children of the poor. It was found that the program was watched by 91 percent of the at-home children in low-income Bedford-Stuyvesant and Harlem sections of New York City. Eighty-eight percent of low-income families interviewed in Chicago tuned their sets to *Sesame Street*.[111]

One reason for the success of the program was the campaign, particularly in low-income urban areas, to create an awareness of the program. To create an awareness of the program, *Sesame Street* clubs were established, people went door-to-door to alert families to the program, a *Sesame Street Magazine* was distributed, and announcements were made through libraries, schools, and community organizations. In Chicago, 120 mothers in low-income areas conducted *Sesame Street* viewing sessions. A similar project was conducted in the Mexican-American section of Los Angeles. The Children's Television Workshop ran a Neighborhood Youth Corps Project which involved adolescents from poor families in teaching preschool children. Of course, the project focused on the viewing of *Sesame Street*. During the first broadcast year, 240 adolescents worked in viewing centers with 1,500 children. The following year the numbers increased to 1,200 adolescents helping 15,000 children of the poor in thirteen different cities. By 1972, there were 10,000 tutors helping 100,000 preschool children in viewing centers.[112]

In a broader framework, the publicity campaign helped to legitimize television as the third educator that could be considered equal to the role of formal schooling and the family. Again, it is important to note that the *Sesame Street* concept was different from instructional television designed for the classroom. Now education moved into the home in the format of an entertainment program. In addition, it truly nationalized the educational process. From coast to coast, children were watching the same program. The program created a mass culture among preschool children.

The use of television as a third educator seemed to contradict all the charges that television viewing was a passive and mind-numbing experiencing. Lesser argued that a great deal of learning takes place through modeling. According to Lesser, children do not need to interact to learn; they can model themselves after television characters. In fact, modeling fit Lesser's concept of a nonpunitive form of education. "The child," Lesser wrote, "imitates the model without being induced or compelled to do so. . . . By watching televised models, children learn both socially desirable and undesirable behaviors."[113] Television, Lesser argued, can provide models that show what behaviors are possible and what consequences might result from an action.

In addition to modeling behavior, Lesser believed television could create myths to guide children's actions. In this context, television was supposed to educate the public in the same manner as movies censored by the 1930 code. In Lesser's words, television could provide "a vision of the world as it might be." These myths were to be created by the presentation of what Lesser called simple goodness. He believed that children did not learn from preaching. Considering television's role in presenting life's tensions and deprivations,

Lesser reasoned, "Surely it can create others that help them toward a more humane vision of life."[114]

The argument for creating myths made ideological management dependent on creating unrealistic images of goodness. As in previous movie and broadcasting codes, good had to win out over evil. This reasoning spilled over into decisions about portraying normal urban life on *Sesame Street*. In the end, the decision was made to present urban life as "a vision of the world as it might be" and not in its reality.

Lesser believed that little could be gained by showing the child living in an urban ghetto the harsh realities of life. As planning of the program evolved, there was a drift toward presenting the sweeter side of life. In giving only the positive side of life, the staff realized that they might be accused of presenting a sugar-coated world.[115]

The decision to present a distorted view of urban living is exemplified by Lesser's description of a program designed to show children how an urban bus driver and passengers act on a trip around the city. "Now, we all know that a bus driver is often not out best example of someone who is courteous and civil," Lesser wrote. "But on *Sesame Street*'s bus trip, the driver responds to his passengers' hellos and thank-yous, tells a child who cannot locate his money, 'That's all right you can pay me tomorrow,' and upon seeing a young woman running after his bus just as it has left the curb, actually stops to let her on."[116]

This depiction of an urban bus trip was a major misrepresentation of most urban transportation systems. In fact, Lesser himself referred to it as an "outrageous misrepresentation." But he justified the decision as presenting a model of behavior that would guide children to a better world. In justifying the presentation of an urban transportation system in this idealized fashion, Lesser stated, "We wanted to show the child what the world is like when people treat each other with decency and consideration. Our act of faith . . . was that young children will learn such attitudes if we take the trouble to show them some examples, even if *we stretch familiar reality a bit in order to do so* [emphasis is mine]."[117]

The desire to create positive myths and to help children of the poor influenced the decision to present strong male-identification figures. The staff reasoned that poor children lacked positive male role models and that public schooling was dominated by female role models. Therefore, they decided to "show men on *Sesame Street* in warm, nurturing relationships with young children." The result was an attack on the program for the lack of strong female characters. Newspaper columnist Ellen Goodman complained that "The females that do live on *Sesame Street* can be divided into three groups: teacher, simp, and mother. . . . Oh yes, a cow." As time went on, the program introduced positive female roles. But the early emphasis was on strong male roles.[118]

Sesame Street was harmoniously integrated. Of course, this presentation sugar-coated the harsh realities of racial conflict in American society. Lesser noted that one of the charges made against the program was that it taught "minority-group children to accept quietly middle-class America's corrupt demands to subjugate themselves." Multiracial groups worked and played harmoniously on *Sesame Street* at the same time that whites and African Americans clashed on the streets.[119]

The production of *Sesame Street* opened the door to a new era in public education and to the influence of national educational policy on the world of television. *Sesame Street* extended organized education to the out-of-school student while joining the government's war on poverty. This new era in television was highlighted by the Children's Television Workshop's production of *The Electric Company* and *3-2-1 Contact*.

Edward Palmer, the Director of Research for the Children's Television Workshop, called *The Electric Company* and *3-2-1 Contact* "home-and-school hybrids." Like *Sesame Street*, they were expected to attract out-of-school viewers. In addition, they could be viewed in school. Consequently, these programs brought together the worlds of home television viewing and formal classroom instruction. Also, like *Sesame Street*, the programs reflected federal educational policy. Or, in the words of Palmer, "Both series further illustrate how television can be tied to needs of children in which our whole society has a stake."[120]

The production of *The Electric Company* was directly tied to the Nixon administration's concern with the teaching of basic skills. Its first broadcast in 1971 was intended to reach seven- to ten-year olds who might be having difficulty reading. It was also used in first-grade classrooms as an introduction to reading. It was estimated that half the viewers were in school settings, while the other half viewed the program in out-of-school settings. After one year, 34 percent of the nation's elementary schools were using the program. Using closed-circuit television systems, some elementary schools made the program available to teachers throughout the school day. Nixon's commissioner of education, Sidney Marland, called *Sesame Street* and *The Electric Company* "the best educational investment ever made."[121]

3-2-1 Contact was directly related to the career education goals of the Nixon administration. As I will discuss in Chapter 15, the Nixon administration believed that it could reduce campus unrest and solve labor market problems by relating all academic subjects to career education. In addition, there was continuing pressure to educate more scientists and technical workers. As Palmer indicates, the program was a direct reflection of these national policy objectives. Palmer wrote, "The series was created in the late 1970s because the U.S. had fallen behind as a nation in preparing large enough numbers of children well enough to fill the demand for specialists in science and technology in the workplace." The program was designed to attract children to science and technology before they entered the ninth and tenth grades.[122]

The argument that television should be used to influence career choices continued into the 1980s. Ernest Boyer, president of the Carnegie Foundation for the Advancement of Teaching argued in 1983 that teenagers were confused about life's choices. "Public television," he stated, "better than the high school vocational counseling programs, could show teenagers what it is like to work at various occupations." Boyer's statement reflected the fact that the productions of the Children's Television Workshop and the Corporation for Public Broadcasting had convinced educational leaders that television could be the third educator.

CONCLUSION

The government officials, educators, and foundation leaders responsible for the development of the Corporation for Public Broadcasting and the Children's Television Workshop conceded to commercial television the determination of mass culture. In contrast to the 1930s, little was said in the 1960s about audience's choices turning commercial broadcasts into a form of democratic culture. There seemed to be a general acceptance of the fact that commercial programming was shaped by a combination of influences by advocacy groups, government officials, advertisers, industry standards, and the production process. If commercial television shaped mass culture, then mass culture was indirectly shaped by these influences on commercial broadcasting. From this perspective, public television was given influence over high culture, while commercial television was allotted low culture.

The division of this influence on national culture was made primarily by an interconnected set of ideological managers. Of major importance among these managers were private foundations, whose influence expanded after World War II through the funding of research, policy commissions, and educational and broadcasting programs.

This web of educators, foundations, and intellectuals extended into the federal government. Funds, policies, and personnel moved along the threads of this web among government bureaucracies, foundations, educational institutions, and the Corporation for Public Broadcasting. It is difficult to determine the boundaries of influence of the different parts of the web.

The Children's Television Workshop is an example of the interconnections in the web. It received funding from foundations, the U.S. Office of Education, and the Corporation for Public Broadcasting. The advisers and staff were drawn from educational institutions, foundations, the U.S. Office of Education, and the world of broadcasting. The result of this web was to make the Children's Television Workshop an instrument of federal educational policies.

The Children's Television Workshop continued the pattern of trying to shape public morality by presenting the world as harmonious and good. Like the movie and broadcasting codes of the 1930s, programs such as *Sesame Street* created a tension between the projected image of the world and reality. On the one hand, this tension might have created a cynical feeling about these images of morality, which might have led to a rejection of these forms of projected morality. On the other hand, these images might actually have provided a standard as to what the world should be like.

Therefore, the creation of the Corporation for Public Broadcasting and the Children's Television Workshop added a new dimension to ideological management in the United States. Corporations, foundations, educators, and government officials joined hands to make television an instrument of federal educational policies and a molder of high culture. Along with the family and the school, public television, by instructing out-of-school children, became the third educational institution. While commercial television was given influence over mass culture, public television assumed the leadership of high culture.

NOTES

1. Will Hays, "Improvement of Moving Pictures," *Annual Proceedings of the National Education Association, Vol. 60, 1922* (Washington, D.C.: National Education Association, 1922), pp. 252–257.
2. An analysis of the public relations campaign can be found in a report by the Department of Research and Education, Federal Council of the Churches of Christ in America, *The Public Relations of the Motion Picture Industry* (New York: Federal Council of Churches, 1931).
3. Ibid., p. 255. A history of the development of the MPPDA can be found in Raymond Moley, *The Hays Office* (Indianapolis: Bobbs Merrill, 1945).
4. For surveys of state and municipal censorship boards, see Thomas Leary and J. Roger Noall, "Note: Entertainment: Public Pressures and the Law—Official and Unofficial Control of the Content and Distribution of Motion Pictures and Magazines," *Harvard Law Review*, Vol. 71 (1957), pp. 326–367, and Randall, *Censorship of the Movies: The Social and Political Control of a Mass Medium* (Madison: University of Wisconsin Press, 1965), pp. 15–18, 88–89.
5. Ellis Oberholtzer, "What Are the 'Movies' Making of Our Children?" *World's Work*, Vol. 4 (January 1921), pp. 249–263.
6. Lary May, *Screening Out the Past: The Birth of Mass Culture and the Motion Picture Industry* (New York: Oxford University Press, 1980), pp. 53–55.
7. John Collier, "Censorship and the National Board," *The Survey*, Vol. 35 (October 1915), pp. 9–14.
8. Richard Randall, *Censorship of the Movies*, p. 16.
9. May, *Screening Out the Past*, pp. 169–177.
10. Ibid., pp. 164–165.
11. Moley, *Hayes Office*, pp. 135–137.
12. Alfred H. Saunders, "Motion Pictures as an Aid to Education," *Annual Proceedings of the National Education Association, Vol. 52, 1914* (Ann Arbor, Mich.: National Education Association, 1914), pp. 743–745.

13. "Discussion," *Annual Proceedings of the National Education Association, Vol. 52, 1914* (Ann Arbor, Mich.: National Education Association, 1914), p. 747.

14. Moley, *Hays Office,* pp. 77–78.

15. See W. W. Charters, "Chairman's Preface" in *Motion Pictures and Youth: A Summary* (New York: Macmillan, 1933), pp. v–vii.

16. The following is a list of authors and research titles sponsored by the Payne Fund. Many of the researchers were famous within their disciplines, which added to the prestige of the studies: (1) P. W. Holaday, Indianapolis Public Schools, and George Stoddard, Director, Iowa Child Welfare Research Station, "Getting Ideas from the Movies"; (2) Ruth C. Peterson and L. L. Thurstone, Department of Psychology, University of Chicago, "Motion Pictures and the Social Attitudes of Children"; (3) Frank Shuttleworth and Mark May, Institute of Human Relations, Yale University, "The Social Conduct and Attitudes of Movie Fans"; (4) W. S. Dysinger and Christian Ruckmick, Department of Psychology, State University of Iowa, "The Emotional Responses of Children to the Motion Picture Situation"; (5) Charles Peters, Professor of Education, Pennsylvania State College, "Motion Pictures and Standards of Morality"; (6) Samuel Renshaw, Vernon L. Miller, and Dorothy Marquis, Department of Psychology, Ohio State University, "Children's Sleep"; (7) Herbert Blumer, Department of Sociology, University of Chicago, "Movies and Conduct"; (8) Edgar Dale, Research Associate, Bureau of Educational Research, Ohio State University, "The Content of Motion Pictures"; (9) Edgar Dale, "Children's Attendance at Motion Pictures"; (10) Herbert Blumer and Philip Hauser, Department of Sociology, University of Chicago, "Movies, Delinquency, and Crime"; (11) Paul Cressey and Frederick Thrasher, New York University, "Boys, Movies, and City Streets"; (12) Edgar Dale, Research Associate, Bureau of Educational Research, Ohio State University, "How to Appreciate Motion Pictures."

17. Henry James Forman, *Our Movie Made Children* (New York: Macmillan, 1935).

18. Charters, "Chairman's Preface," p. viii.

19. Herbert Blumer, *Movies and Conduct* (New York: Macmillan, 1933), p. 50.

20. Ibid., pp. 45–49.

21. Forman, *Our Movie Made Children,* pp. 280–282.

22. Edgar Dale, *How to Appreciate Motion Pictures: A Manual of Motion-Picture Criticism Prepared for High-School Students* (New York: Macmillan, 1933).

23. Ibid., p. vii.

24. William Lewin, *Photoplay Appreciation in American High Schools* (New York: Appleton-Century, 1934).

25. Dale, *How to Appreciate,* pp. 16–25.

26. Ibid., p. 231.

27. Ibid., p. 227.

28. Lewin, *Photoplay Appreciation,* pp. v–vii, 69.

29. Ibid., pp. 30–33.

30. Ibid., p. 51.

31. Ibid., pp. 94–95.

32. Moley, *Hays Office*, pp. 148–149.

33. The article is quoted in ibid., pp. 151–153.

34. Will H. Hays, "The Motion Picture in Education," *Annual Proceedings of the National Education Association, Vol. 127, 1939* (Washington, D.C.: National Education Association, 1939), pp. 80–86.

35. Ibid., p. 80.

36. Moley, *Hayes Office*, pp. 57–58.

37. Ibid., pp. 87–88.

38. Martin Quigley, *Decency in Motion Pictures* (New York: Macmillan, 1937).

39. Reprints of the 1930 movie code can be found in Moley, *Hays Office*, pp. 241–248, and Gerald Mast, ed., *The Movies in Our Midst* (Chicago,: University of Chicago Press, 1982), pp. 321–333.

40. A reprint of the 1927 code can be found in Moley, *Hays Office*, pp. 240–241.

41. Reprinted in Gerald Gardner, *The Censorship Papers: Movie Censorship Letters from the Hays Office 1934–1968* (New York: Dodd, Mead, 1987), pp. 2–3.

42. Moley, *Hays Office*, pp. 101–102.

43. Gardner, *The Censorship Papers*, pp. 38–39.

44. Moley, *Hays Office*, p. 115.

45. "British vs. American Radio Slant, Debate Theme in 40,000 Schools," *Variety*, Vol. 111, No. 12 (August 29, 1933), p. 1.

46. See Philip T. Rosen, *The Modern Stentors: Radio Broadcasters and the Federal Government, 1920–1934* (Westport, Conn.: Greenwood Press, 1980), pp. 128–133; and Erik Barnouw, *A Tower of Babel: A History of Broadcasting in the United States to 1933* (New York: Oxford University Press, 1966), pp. 172–179.

47. S. E. Frost, *Education's Own Stations: The History of Broadcast Licenses Issued to Educational Institutions* (Chicago: University of Chicago Press, 1937), pp. 1–5.

48. Ibid.

49. The other members were the National University Extension Association, the Jesuit Educational Association, the Association of Land-Grant Colleges and Universities, and the Association of College and University Broadcasting Stations.

50. Tracy F. Tyler, ed., *Radio as a Cultural Agency: Proceedings of a National Conference on the Use of Radio as a Cultural Agency in a Democracy* (Washington, D.C.: The National Committee on Education by Radio, 1934), p. 125.

51. Ibid., pp. 3–10.

52. Joy Elmer Morgan, "A National Culture–By-Product or Objective of National Planning?" in ibid., p. 29.

53. Ibid., p. 30.
54. Ibid., p. 27.
55. Ibid., p. 30.
56. Ibid., p. 32.
57. "Fight Pedagogs' 25% Raid: Radio Answers Uplift Group," *Variety*, Vol. 115, No. 9 (August 14, 1934), p. 31.
58. Merlin H. Aylesworth, "Radio as a Means of Public Enlightenment," *Annual Proceedings of the National Education Association, Vol. 72, 1934*, pp. 99–102.
59. William Paley, "Radio as a Cultural Force: These notes on the economic and social philosophy of America's radio industry, as represented by the policies and practices of the Columbia Broadcasting System, Inc., were embodied in a talk on October 17, 1934, before the Federal Communications Commission, in its inquiry into proposals to allot fixed percentages of the nation's radio facilities to non-commercial broadcasting," CBS Reference Library, New York City, pp. 8–9.
60. Ibid., p. 13.
61. *Variety*, Vol. 117, No. 1 (December 18, 1934), p. 34.
62. "St. Paul Meet on Kid Programs Calls Radio Villains Likeable; Suggest Boycott, Probation" *Variety*, Vol. 117, No. 2 (December 25, 1934), p. 29.
63. "Air Reformers after Coin," *Variety*, Vol. 117, No. 7 (January 29, 1935), pp. 1, 66.
64. Clara Savage Littledale, "Better Radio Programs for Children," *Parents Magazine*, Vol. 18, No. 13 (May 8, 1933), p. 1.
65. "Boycott MDSE in Air Protest?" *Variety*, Vol. 109, No. 12 (February 28, 1933), p. 47.
66. "Cal. Teachers List 'Bad' Programs," *Variety*, Vol. 110, No. 8 (May 2, 1933), p. 34.
67. "Squawks Force NBC Move for Less Horror," *Variety*, Vol. 109, No. 12 (February 26, 1933), p. 45.
68. "Now Agree Too Much Horror for Kids, Junior Programs Turning to Fantasy," *Variety*, Vol. 111, No. 8 (August 1, 1933), p. 41.
69. "Women's Radio Committee Clarifies," *Variety*, Vol. 118, No. 10 (May 22, 1935), p. 36.
70. "Mrs. Harold Milligan" in C. S. Marsh, ed., *Educational Broadcasting 1937* (Chicago: University of Chicago Press, 1938), p. 259.
71. Ibid., pp. 258–259.
72. "Radio Wants Clubwoman Good Will: Offer Transmitters to Gals with Messages—Will Hays Started It," *Variety*, Vol. 112, No. 6 (October 17, 1933), p. 37.
73. "Dime Novel Air Stuff Out: Protests Chafe FCC into Action," *Variety*, Vol. 118, no. 3 (April 3, 1935), pp. 1, 58.
74. "Stations Must Be Mind-Readers: FCC Will Not Divulge Policies," *Variety*, Vol. 118, No. 8 (May 8, 1935), p. 51.

75. "Radio's 10 Commandments," *Variety*, Vol. 118, No. 12 (June 5, 1935), p. 31.
76. "Talk a Radio 'Hays Org.,'" *Variety*, Vol. 118, No. 13 (June 12, 1935), p. 43.
77. "CBS' Clean-up Pledges," *Variety*, Vol. 118, No. 10 (May 22, 1935), p. 37.
78. "Paley in Annual Report Deprecates 'Straightjacket' for Broadcasting; Air Voluntarily Censors Programs," *Variety*, Vol. 113, No. 12 (March 6, 1934), p. 44.
79. "Summary of CBS Policies Relating to Program Material and Advertising Copy," prepared by CBS Research Department, October 1940, CBS Reference Library, New York City.
80. "NBC Slant on CBS Policy" in ibid., p. 37.
81. "Sponsor Rights Defined," *Variety*, Vol. 134, No. 4 (April 5, 1939), p. 23.
82. "Statement by William S. Paley Over the Columbia Network, Tuesday, May 14, 1935," CBS Reference Library, New York City.
83. Ibid., p. 2.
84. "New Policies: A Statement to the Public, to Advertisers and to Advertising Agencies," May 15, 1935, CBS Reference Library, New York City, p. 3.
85. Ibid., p. 3.
86. Ibid., p. 4.
87. Ibid., p. 5.
88. Ibid., p. 6.
89. "Squawks Force NBC Move for Less Horror," *Variety*, Vol. 109, No. 12 (February 26, 1933), p. 45.
90. "NBC's Tentative Program Code," *Variety*, Vol. 134, No. 4 (April 5, 1934), p. 24.
91. Ibid.
92. For a study of the role of the federal government in coordinating movies and radio for the war effort, see Allan M. Winkler, *The Politics of Propaganda: The Office of War Information 1942–1945* (New Haven, Conn.: Yale University Press, 1978). For a study of the effect of the Cold War on the movie industry, see Larry Ceplair and Steven Englund, *The Inquisition in Hollywood: Politics in the Film Community, 1930–1960* (Berkeley: University of California Press, 1979). The red scare in the broadcasting industry is discussed by Erik Barnouw in *The Golden Web: A History of Broadcasting in the United States 1933–1953* (New York: Oxford University Press, 1968), pp. 253–305. Kathryn Montgomery's *Target Prime Time: Advocacy Groups and the Struggle over Entertainment Television* (New York: Oxford University Press, 1989) provides a history and analysis of the effect of advocacy groups on the ideological content of entertainment television.
93. As quoted in James L. Baughman, *Television's Guardians: The FCC and the Politics of Programming, 1958–1967* (Knoxville: University of Tennessee Press, 1985), p. 61.

94. See Joel Spring, *Images of American Life: A History of Ideological Management in Schools, Movies, Radio, and Television* (Albany: State University of New York Press, 1992), pp. 231–251.

95. Ibid., p. 95.

96. Ibid., p. 95.

97. Ellen Condliffe Lagemann, *The Politics of Knowledge: The Carnegie Corporation Philanthropy, and Public Policy* (Middleton, Conn.: Wesleyan University Press, 1989), p. 232.

98. Lloyd Morrisett, "Introduction" in Gerald S. Lesser, *Children and Television: Lessons from "Sesame Street,"* (New York: Vintage, 1975), p. xxi.

99. Ibid., p. xxvi.

100. Lagemann, *The Politics of Knowledge,* p. 233.

101. Joan Cooney, "Foreword" in Lesser, *Children and Television,* p. xvii.

102. Lesser, *Children and Television,* p. 7.

103. Ibid., pp. 8–9.

104. Ibid., p. 23.

105. Ibid., pp. 89–90.

106. Ibid., p. 19.

107. Ibid., p. 80.

108. Ibid., pp. 80–81.

109. Ibid., p. 60.

110. Ibid., p. 47.

111. Ibid., p. 204.

112. Ibid., pp. 208–211.

113. Ibid., pp. 24–25.

114. Ibid., pp. 254–255.

115. Ibid., p. 95.

116. Ibid., p. 95.

117. Ibid., p. 95.

118. Ibid., p. 199.

119. Ibid., p. 200.

120. Edward L. Palmer, *Television & America's Children: A Crisis of Neglect* (New York: Oxford University Press, 1988), p. 103.

121. Ibid., p. 104.

122. Ibid., pp. 106–108.

CHAPTER 13

The Great Civil Rights Movement

The great civil rights movement of the 1950s, 1960s, and 1970s received its strength from the accumulated grievances of dominated cultural and racial groups. Led by the National Association for the Advancement of Colored People (NAACP), as I discussed in Chapter 7, African Americans pressed their case for the end of segregation in schools and public facilities and an equal opportunity to participate in the American economic system. The actions of African Americans made other groups more militant in their quest for equality of opportunity.

Native Americans, as I discussed in Chapter 6, rebelled against the attempts at deculturalization and loss of tribal rights and in the 1950s and 1960s began to campaign for self-determination, particularly in the area of education. Mexican Americans, as I discussed in Chapter 7, continued to fight against segregation and for preservation of Mexican culture and the Spanish language in the schools. By the 1960s, Puerto Ricans joined Mexican Americans in supporting bilingual education.

The great civil rights movement touched all aspects of schooling. First, of course, was the issue of segregation. Court orders requiring desegregation ranged from forced busing to achieve racial balance to voluntary segregation through magnet schools. Magnet schools created a revolution in American education as school systems established specialized schools, such as schools for creative arts or science, designed to attract students of all races. Magnet schools were strengthened by the campaign to create specialized schools reflecting dominated cultures. The great civil rights movement also affected the publishing industry as minority cultures demanded equal representation in textbooks.

Also, the great civil rights movement opened the door to demands that the public schools reflect minority cultures. African Americans, Native Americans, Mexican Americans, and Puerto Ricans demanded that their unique cultures be recognized and be given a place in the school curriculum. These demands gave impetus to the movement for multicultural education in the 1980s and 1990s.

346

SCHOOL DESEGREGATION

The desegregation of American schools was the result of over a half century of struggle by the black community. Since its founding in the early part of the twentieth century, the NAACP had struggled to end discriminatory practices against minority groups. The school desegregation issue was finally decided by the U.S. Supreme Court in 1954 in *Brown v. Board of Education of Topeka*. The decision did not bring immediate results, because resistance to court-ordered desegregation arose. The frustration caused by the slow pace of school integration and the continuation of other forms of discrimination contributed to the growth of a massive civil rights movement in the late 1950s and early 1960s. The response of national political leaders to the civil rights movement was the enactment of strong civil rights legislation.

It is important to remember that school desegregation and civil rights legislation were not the products of a benign government but were the result of tremendous struggle and public demonstrations. Politically, African Americans were forced by their lack of power at local and state levels to seek redress for their grievances from the federal government. National leaders tried to avoid dealing with civil rights issues but were finally forced by public demonstrations to take action. With regard to schooling, federal action resulted in greater federal control of local schools and a feeling among school board members that local control of education was rapidly disappearing.

The key legal issue in the struggle for desegregation was the interpretation of the Fourteenth Amendment to the Constitution. This constitutional amendment was ratified in 1868, shortly after the close of the Civil War. One of its purposes was to extend the basic guarantees of the Bill of Rights into the areas under state and local government control. The most important and controversial section of the Fourteenth Amendment states, "No State shall make or enforce any law which shall abridge the privileges or immunities of citizens . . . nor . . . deprive any person of life, liberty, or property, without due process of law; nor deny to any person within its jurisdiction the equal protection of the laws."

A major test of the meaning of the Fourteenth Amendment with regard to segregation occurred in 1895 in a Supreme Court case involving Homer Plessy, who was one-eighth black and seven-eights white and had been arrested for refusing to ride in the "colored" coach of a train, as required by Louisiana law. The Supreme Court ruled that segregation did not create a badge of inferiority if segregated facilities were equal and the law was reasonable. In establishing the "separate but equal doctrine," the Supreme Court failed to clearly define what constitutes equal facilities and what is reasonable.

The overturning of the separate but equal doctrine and a broader application of the Fourteenth Amendment came in 1954 in the historic and controversial Supreme Court decision *Brown v. Board of Education of Topeka*. In 1953, *Brown* was one of five school segregation suits to reach the Supreme Court. It became the first case simply because the five cases were heard in alphabetical order. The Brown case began in 1951, when Oliver Brown and twelve other parents represented by NAACP lawyers brought suit to void a Kansas law that permitted but did not require local segregation of the schools. In this particular case, Oliver Brown's daughter was denied the right to attend a white elementary school within five blocks of her home and forced to cross railroad tracks and travel twenty-one blocks to attend an all-black school. The federal district court in Kansas ruled against Oliver Brown, using the argument that the segregated schools named in the suit were substantially equal and thus fell within the separate but equal doctrine.

In preparing its brief for the Supreme Court, the NAACP defined two important objectives: to show that the climate of the times required an end to segregation laws and to show that the separate but equal doctrine contained a contradiction in terms—that is, that separate facilities were inherently unequal. Evidence from recent findings in the social sciences presented by the NAACP to prove that separate facilities were inherently unequal provided the basis for overturning the separate but equal doctrine. It also caused a storm of protest alleging that the Supreme Court was basing decisions on nonlegal arguments. Throughout the South, it was widely believed that the Court was being persuaded by communist-oriented social scientists. Billboards appeared on highways demanding the impeachment of Chief Justice Earl Warren for his role in subverting the Constitution.

The Supreme Court argued in the Brown decision, "In the field of public education the doctrine of 'separate but equal' has no place. Separate educational facilities are inherently unequal." To support this argument, the Supreme Court wrote one of the most controversial single sentences ever to appear in a Court decision: "Whatever may have been the extent of psychological knowledge at the time of *Plessy v. Ferguson* this finding is amply supported by modern authority."[1]

Two social scientists, Kenneth Clark and Gunnar Myrdal, had a major influence on the Court's decision. Clark, a social psychologist at the City College of New York, acted as general social science consultant to the NAACP. His central argument, and the one given in the NAACP brief to the Court, was that officially sanctioned segregation by a state or local government organization caused personality damage to the children of both dominated and dominant groups. Dominated-group children became aware of their inferior status and often reacted with feelings of inferiority and a sense of personal humiliation. This created internal conflict between the need for a sense of personal worth and the lack of respect provided by the majority group. As a means of coping with this conflict, Clark argued, certain patterns of behavior develop that are related to the socioeconomic class of the dominated child. "Some children," the argument states, "usually of the lower socio-economic classes, may react by overt aggressions and hostility directed toward their own group or members of the dominant group. Antisocial and delinquent behavior may often be interpreted as reactions to these racial frustrations."[2]

Clark and the NAACP claimed before the Supreme Court that segregation caused behavioral patterns that led to crime and violence among lower-class blacks. For middle- and upper-class dominated-group children, they claimed, racial segregation was likely to result in either withdrawal and submissive behavior or rigid conformity to middle-class values and standards. Racial segregation was believed to cause a lowering of morale and depression in the level of educational aspirations for all dominated-group children. For dominant-group children, they stated, "confusion, conflict, moral cynicism, and disrespect for authority may arise . . . as a consequence of being taught the moral, religious and democratic principles of the brotherhood of man . . . by the same persons and institutions who, in their support of racial segregation . . . seem to be acting in a prejudiced and discriminatory manner."[3]

Another major influence on the Court's decision was Gunnar Myrdal's book *An American Dilemma*. Myrdal, a Swedish social scientist, was invited in 1937 by the Carnegie Corporation to do a study of the social conditions of blacks in the United States. The major thesis of the resulting book is that Americans were facing a major moral dilemma between the ideals of American democracy and the actions regarding race relations. He defines the "American Dilemma" as the conflict between "the valuations preserved on the general plane . . . of the 'American Creed'" and "the valuation on specific planes of individual and group living." This dilemma, Myrdal argues, has a direct effect on behavioral patterns. People who act in conflict with their belief in the American Creed need to find a means of defending their behavior to themselves and others. This is accomplished by twisting and mutilating social reality and by producing emotionally loaded rationalizations for particular behavior. As a result of this distortion of social reality, firmly entrenched popular beliefs developed concerning blacks, which the study states are "bluntly false and which can only be understood when we remember the opportunistic ad hoc purposes they serve."[4] The purpose of the study was to undercut these false belief systems and help to end the American Dilemma by providing a true picture of social reality and a careful depiction of the actual conditions of American black people.

In 1955 the Supreme Court issued its enforcement decree for the desegregation of schools. One problem facing the Court was the lack of machinery for supervising and ensuring the desegregation of vast numbers of segregated school districts. The Court resolved this problem by relying on federal district courts to determine the equitable principles for desegregation. Federal judges were often part of the social fabric of their local communities and resisted attempts at speedy desegregation. Consequently, integration occurred at a slow pace until additional civil rights legislation was passed in the 1960s and the mounting frustrations in the black community fed the flames of a militant civil rights movement.

The evolution of the mass media in the 1950s was an important factor in the civil rights movement because it became possible to turn local problems into national issues. Thus, even though presidents had traditionally shown a great deal of deference to the important white southern political structure, the emergence of the mass media as a powerful force allowed both the federal government and civil rights groups to put unprecedented pressure on southern political leaders, forcing them to comply with national civil rights legislation. In fact, enforcement of the Supreme Court school desegregation ruling depended in large part on civil rights groups making effective use of television. In one sense, the struggle that took place was a struggle between public images. Concern over America's international image grew as pictures of racial injustice flashed around the world, and the president's public image was often threatened when examples of racial injustice were shown to millions of television viewers and the question was asked, What is our president doing about this situation?

The most dramatic technique used by civil rights groups was nonviolent confrontation. The massive nonviolent response of black people in the South confronted with an array of cattle prods, clubs, and fire hoses wielded by cursing southern law enforcement units provided dramatic and shocking television viewing for the nation. The Congress on Racial Equality (CORE), the Student Nonviolent Coordinating Committee (SNCC), and the Southern Christian Leadership Conference (SCLC), led by the Reverend Martin Luther King, Jr., provided the national drama and the final push for national civil rights legislation.

The introduction of nonviolent confrontation into the civil rights movement came from the Christian student movement of the 1930s, which, under the leadership of the Fellowship for Reconciliation, was committed to use of the Gandhian technique of *satyagraha* (nonviolent direct action) in solving racial and industrial problems in the United States. CORE, a major organization in the civil rights movement, was organized at the University of Chicago in 1942. The two basic doctrines of the early CORE movement were commitment to racial integration and the use of Christian nonviolent techniques.

CORE did not rise to national prominence until the late 1950s, when another Christian leader, Dr. Martin Luther King, Jr., made nonviolent confrontation the central drama of the civil rights movement. King was born in 1929 in Atlanta, Georgia, into a family of Baptist ministers. His maternal grandfather founded the Ebenezer Baptist Church, and his father made the church into one of the largest and most prestigious Baptist churches in Atlanta. In 1944, King entered Atlanta's Morehouse College, where he claimed to have been influenced by his reading of Henry David Thoreau's *Essay on Civil Disobedience*. He later wrote about the essay, "Fascinated by the idea of refusing to cooperate with an evil system, I was so deeply moved that I reread the work several times. This was my first intellectual contact with the theory of non-violent resistance."[5]

In 1948, King entered the Crozier Theological Seminary in Chester, Pennsylvania, where for the first time he became acquainted with pacifism through a lecture by A. J. Muste. King wrote that at the time he considered Muste's pacifist doctrine impractical in a world confronted by the armies of totalitarian nations. Of more importance to King's intellectual development was his exposure to the social gospel philosophy of Walter Rauschenbusch, which actively involved the church in social reform as a means of creating a kingdom of God on earth. Although he rejected the optimistic elements in the social gospel, King argued that any concern with the souls of humans required a concern with social and economic conditions.

King also studied the lectures and works of Mohandas K. Gandhi. The Indian leader's work convinced King that the Christian doctrine of love could be a force for social change. King wrote, "Gandhi was probably the first person in history to lift the love ethic of Jesus above mere interaction between individuals to a powerful and effective social force on a large scale." Like the early members of CORE, King became convinced that nonviolent resistance "was the only morally and practically sound method open to oppressed people in their struggle for freedom."[6]

The incident that launched Martin Luther King's civil rights activities and provided scope for his Ghandhian form of the social gospel occurred on December 1, 1955. On that date, Rosa Parks, who had worked a regular day as a seamstress in one of the leading department stores in Montgomery, Alabama, boarded a bus and took the first seat behind the section reserved for whites. Later during the journey home, several white passengers boarded the bus. The driver ordered Rosa Parks and three other black passengers to stand so that the white passengers could have seats. Rosa Parks refused and was arrested. The black ministers in the community quickly organized in response to this incident, and on December 5 the Montgomery bus boycott began.

The bus boycott lasted for over a year and finally ended on December 21, 1956, when, after a Supreme Court decision against segregation on buses, the Montgomery transit system was officially integrated. King emerged from the struggle a national hero among dominated groups. In 1957 he organized the Southern Christian Leadership Conference, which became the central organization in the civil rights struggle.

After SCLC was formed, boycotts and nonviolent demonstrations began to occur throughout the South. On May 17, 1957, Martin Luther King gave his first national address in Washington, D.C. He told his audience, "Give us the ballot and we will quietly, lawfully, and nonviolently, without rancor or bitterness, implement the May 17, 1954, decision of the Supreme Court." For King, meaningful school desegregation depended on the power of the black voter.

As civil rights demonstrations increased in intensity, national leaders began to work for federal legislation. In 1957 and 1960, two ineffective forms of civil rights legislation were passed by Congress. The most important civil rights legislation was not enacted until 1964, when violence in Birmingham, Alabama, and a mass march on Washington forced a response from the federal government. The civil rights movement made Birmingham and its director of safety, Eugene "Bull" Connor, symbols of the oppression of black people in the United States. President John F. Kennedy was quoted as saying "Our judgment of Bull Connor should not be too harsh. After all, in his way, he has done a good deal for civil rights legislation this year."[7] The March on Washington symbolized to Congress and the American people the growing strength of the civil rights movement and provided the stage for television coverage of speeches by civil rights leaders.

The result of these activities was the Civil Rights Act of 1964. Under eleven different titles, the power of federal regulations was extended in the areas of voting rights, public accommodations, education, and employment. Titles IV and VI of the legislation were intended to end school segregation and provide authority for implementing the Brown decision.

Title VI, the most important section, establishes the precedent for using disbursement of government money as a means of controlling educational policies. Originally, President Kennedy merely proposed a requirement that institutions receiving federal funds must end discriminatory practices. In its final form, Title VI required mandatory withholding of federal funds to institutions that did not comply with its mandates. It states that no person, on the basis of race, color, or national origin, can be excluded from or denied the benefits of any program receiving federal financial assistance, and it requires all federal agencies to establish guidelines to implement this policy. Refusal by institutions or projects to follow these guidelines will result in the "termination of or refusal to grant or to continue assistance under such program or activity."

The power of Title VI rests in its ability to withhold federal money from financially pressed school systems. This became a more crucial issue after the passage in 1965 of the Elementary and Secondary Education Act. The rate of desegregation was more rapid after the 1964 Civil Rights Act than before, but abundant evidence by the end of the 1960s showed that segregated education continued in the South. One political scientist argued that school desegregation in the South by 1968 looked massive compared to the level in the early 1960s, but compared to an ideal of total integration, the actual results could be labeled as token. By defining a desegregated school as one that blacks attended and where more than 20 percent of the school population was white, a sample of 894 counties in the South found that 5 percent or less of the black pupils were attending integrated schools in 25 percent of the counties and 10 percent or less in 40 percent of the counties. At a level approaching genuine integration, in 20 percent of the counties 90 percent or more of the black pupils were reported to be attending integrated schools. For all southern counties, the median attending integrated schools was 15.6 percent.[8]

School desegregation moved at an even slower pace in the North. Originally it was believed that the Brown decision would affect only those states whose laws required segregated education. However, by the late 1960s, the courts began to rule that the Brown decision applied to all schools in the country, if it could be proved that segregation was the result of intentional actions by school boards or school administrators. In addition, forced integration by busing was ruled by the United States Supreme Court in *Swann v. Charlotte-Mecklenburg Board of Education* (1971) to be a legal means of desegregating a school district. In many communities, busing sparked violent demonstrations, and alternative, or magnet, schools became a popular, more conservative means of integrating school districts.

BUSING

In the Swann decision, the Supreme Court warned that "schools all or predominantly of one race in a district of mixed population will require close scrutiny to determine that school assignments are not part of state enforced segregation."[9] The implications of this decision were that de facto segregation in northern urban school districts would come under close scrutiny by the courts and that busing would be considered a legitimate tool for implementing desegregation plans. Traditional arguments about the value of neighborhood schools could no longer be used to avoid integration; now school districts would be viewed as unitary systems, and wherever possible, racial integration within those districts would be achieved.

Involuntary busing was never popular with large numbers of the white population or with those who were politically conservative. President Nixon promised in his national campaigns to curb the extent of involuntary busing. In March 1972 he sent a special message to Congress requesting a moratorium on student busing. Nixon's arguments were couched in the rhetoric of equality of opportunity: "Conscience and the Constitution both require that no child should be denied equal educational opportunity." He went on to argue that the purpose of the Brown decision was to eliminate the dual school system in the South. This purpose, he maintained, had been achieved. Nixon claimed that the major remaining problem was the maze of differing court orders that had developed to end segregation. Many of these plans, including busing, he argued, had resulted in violence and community disruption and had imposed hardships on children. Nixon felt that both wrong and right reasons could be given for opposing busing. The wrong reasons were those based on racial prejudice. The right reasons were a dislike of "wrenching of children away from their families, and from the schools their families may have moved to be near, and sending them arbitrarily to others far distant."[10]

Nixon went on to argue that the result of the substantial dismantling of the dual school system was a greater balance of "emphasis on improving schools, on convenience, on the chance for parental involvement." For Nixon, this meant that the argument for equality of educational opportunity should concentrate "much more specifically on education: on assuring that the opportunity is not only equal, but adequate."[11] He stated that the legitimate concerns in the busing issue were quality of education, transportation of children to distant schools, and equality of educational resources.

Nixon's attempt to stem the tide of busing was defeated, and busing continued to be a major national issue. In 1974, major community violence occurred as Boston began to use busing as a tool for racial integration of the schools. The violence in Boston screamed across newspaper headlines and seemed to provide a good case for conservatives that busing should be ended. The conservative argument received further reinforcement in 1975, when James Coleman issued a report detailing the negative consequences of involuntary school integration. Coleman's report argued that involuntary school integration was causing "white flight" from the affected school districts. In turn, white flight was heightening the degree of segregation by contributing to the concentration of dominated populations in particular communities.[12]

As mentioned earlier, it was ironic that conservative groups in local communities in the middle of the 1970s began to advocate alternative, or magnet, schools as a means of voluntary desegregation. Because of their effect on the curriculum, alternative schools caused a radical change in the traditional structure of American education. The irony in the conservative support of magnet schools was that the concept of magnet schools was a product of a radical reaction to the school system in the late 1960s and early 1970s.

MAGNET SCHOOLS

The magnet school movement was a product of conservative reaction to desegregation and the alternative school movement of the 1960s. The term *alternative* was most often used when referring to schools that were alternatives to the existing public school system. By the 1970s, the term also referred to public school programs that were alternatives to the standard public school curriculum. By the 1980s and 1990s, the magnet school movement became part of the debate over whether or not parents should be allowed to choose a particular public school or program for their child.

Alternatives to the public schools have a long tradition in American history. In one sense, the Catholic school system of the nineteenth century was an alternative to the Protestant-dominated public school system. In the early twentieth century, alternative schools were established in reaction to what was believed to be the authoritarian and oppressive atmosphere of the public schools. Some of these alternative schools were products of a reaction to the public school's political and economic doctrines. One school of this type was the Modern School, established by anarchists in Stelton, New Jersey. This school existed from the beginning of World War I until the 1950s. Its instructional methods were based on the idea that nothing should be imposed on the child and that learning should be a product of the child's interests. It was hoped that this form of education would create personalities that would not accept authoritarian institutions. The Manumit School for workers' children, another alternative school, was formed in the 1920s as an alternative to antiunion teachings in the public schools. The school operated on the principles of industrial democracy: The children were organized into trade unions, and some students actually organized labor strikes in protest over the conditions at the school.[13]

Summerhill, a more famous and influential alternative school, was started by A. S. Neill in England in the 1920s. In the 1950s a Summerhill society was organized in the United States, and during the student rebellions of the 1960s the Summerhill school was often cited as a model of alternative education.[14]

Neill organized Summerhill to create nonauthoritarian personalities, which he believed would result in a utopian society. Using a simplistic interpretation of the work of Sigmund Freud, Neill argued that children who commit crimes and violent acts are primarily the product of repressed conditions. Given a state of true freedom, children would grow to be loving and happy adults. At Summerhill, children were given complete freedom to attend classes or not and were allowed to participate in the operation of the school.

In the 1940s Neill developed a more sophisticated rationale based on the psychology of Wilhelm Reich. According to this theory, in a child, repression leads to a fear of pleasure. As a child develops, this fear or anxiety about pleasure causes him or her to seek the security of authoritarian institutions; for this reason, adults seek situations that are secure but provide little personal pleasure. Neill asked, for example, How would an individual accept a job in a factory or bureaucratic institution that is monotonous and does not provide for individual pleasure? Why would an individual support an authoritarian government like that of Nazi Germany? His answer in both cases was that children are repressed within the institution of the modern nuclear family and grow up willing to give up individual pleasure for the security of authority.

The problem with the nuclear family, Neill believed, is the repression of the wife by the husband. This repression in turn causes the wife to repress her children. Neill proposed two solutions to this situation: either the husband and wife must achieve true equality in their relationship or the child must leave the family structure. For Neill, Summerhill was a haven of liberation from the repression of the nuclear family.

When students protested in the 1960s against the repression in public schools and universities, the free school movement blossomed. Not all the alternative schools established in the 1960s and early 1970s followed the Summerhill model; some were more political, and some tried other educational methods. Most of the schools survived for only a short time and were often forced to close because of inadequate financial support.

For political conservatives, the free school movement was a threat to existing institutions and to the stability of society. In the early 1970s, some liberal communities—Minneapolis, for example—introduced alternative schools as part of their public school system. Initially, many of these alternative public schools were organized around the Summerhill philosophy, but as the movement spread, alternative schools began to offer a variety of curricula and teaching methods.

The exact time when "alternative" schools became "magnet" schools is not altogether clear, but beginning in the early 1970s, alternative schools began to be incorporated into desegregation plans. The term *magnet* came to describe the function of these schools in desegregation efforts. The idea was that a public school would offer a specialized curriculum or teaching method that would be attractive to a broad spectrum of a community. Parents and students would be allowed to choose that magnet school in place of their regular school. In other words, the school would act as a magnet to attract children from throughout the school district. A major consideration in admitting students to magnet schools was maintaining racial balance.

Magnet schools offered an attractive alternative to people opposed to involuntary busing because they were based on free choice and voluntary efforts at desegregation. They also appealed to many community members because they promised an elite, specialized education. For instance, the first magnet schools established in most communities were schools for creative and performing arts and schools for academic enrichment. Offering elite schools of this type, it was argued, would reduce the white flight from desegregated school districts.

The use of magnet schools to solve problems of segregation reinforced the twentieth-century trend toward a more differentiated curriculum. By the early 1980s, the variety of choices available to students in some school systems would have astounded educators in the early part of the century. For instance, the Houston school system offered alternative schools for engineering, criminal justice, the petrochemical industry, health sciences, advanced academic work, and creative and performing arts. Philadelphia offered the same range of alternatives along with special programs in foreign affairs. The Cincinnati school system offered alternative schools for computer sciences, athletics, advanced academic work, science and mathematics, creative and performing arts, and languages.[15]

The increased differentiation caused by magnet schools improved the ability of the schools to match their curricula to the needs of the labor market. In Houston, for example, most of the alternative schools were geared to preparation for specific segments of the labor market. Although the original vision of alternative schools was that they would aid in the creation of a free society, those that appeared as part of desegregation plans were more often concerned with creating a fully employed society.

During the Reagan administration years in the 1980s, magnet schools became the primary method used to continue desegregation of American education. In 1984 the administration, after many years of inaction on school integration, supported a court-ordered desegregation settlement in Bakersfield, California, that relied mainly on the use of magnet schools. That same year, the Cincinnati schools settled out of court with the NAACP on a desegregation plan that relied solely on magnet schools.

The development of a highly specialized and differentiated curriculum as a result of desegregation was a major break with Horace Mann's nineteenth-century vision of a common school providing a common education for all. It was also a major break with the idea of a comprehensive high school as presented in the *Cardinal Principles of Education* report in the early twentieth century. In this context, the goal that schooling should provide for social cohesion through a common curriculum and common schools was no longer a concern. The irony of the ending of desegregation is that it resulted in the final demise of the common school tradition.

NATIVE AMERICANS

As African Americans were leading the fight against segregated schooling, Native Americans were attempting to gain control of the education of their children and restore their cultural heritage and languages to the curriculum. Native Americans shared a common interest with Mexican Americans and Puerto Ricans in supporting bilingual and multicultural education.

During the 1940s and 1950s, federal Indian policy was directed at termination of tribes and reservations. The leader of the termination policy, Senator Arthur V. Watkins of Utah, declared in 1957, "I see the following words emblazoned in letters of fire above the heads of the Indians—THESE PEOPLE SHALL BE FREE!"[16] Freedom in this case meant freedom from federal supervision and control. It also meant the end of official tribal status.

Termination policies attempted to break up tribal relations by relocating Indians to urban areas. Relocation to urban areas was similar to the nineteenth-century federal policy which sent Native Americans to Indian territory and reservations. But, in this case, Indians were to be "civilized" by being dispersed throughout the general population.

Termination efforts met stiff resistance from Indian and white civil rights activists. In 1961, 450 Indian delegates from ninety tribes attended the American Indian Chicago Conference at the University of Chicago. The delegates issued a Declaration of Indian Purpose calling for the end of termination policies. In the end, termination policy resulted in about 3 percent of the Indian tribes being terminated, including the Menominee of Wisconsin and the Klamath Indians of Oregon.[17]

While resisting termination policies, Native Americans began to demand greater self-determination. This was reflected in policy changes in the Bureau of Indian Affairs after the election of John F. Kennedy in 1960. Condemning the termination policies of the 1950s, the Kennedy administration advocated Indian participation in decisions regarding federal policies. Kennedy's secretary of the interior, Stewart Udall, appointed a Task Force on Indian Affairs, which, in its 1961 report, states, "to insure the success of our endeavor we must solicit the collaboration of those whom we hope to benefit—the Indians themselves . . . equal citizenship, maximum self-sufficiency, and full participation in American life."[18]

One of the results of the drive for self-determination was the creation of the Rough Rock Demonstration School in 1966. Established on a Navajo reservation in Arizona, the school was a joint effort of the Office of Economic Opportunity and the Bureau of Indian Affairs. One of the major goals of the demonstration school was for Navajo parents to control the education of their children and to participate in all aspects of their schooling.[19]

Besides tribal control, one of the important features of the Rough Rock Demonstration School was the attempt to preserve the Navajo language and culture. In contrast to the deculturalization efforts of the nineteenth and early twentieth centuries (discussed in Chapter 6), the goal of learning both Navajo

and English was presented as a means of preparing children to "fend successfully in both cultures and see the Navajo way as part of a universal system
of values."[20]

The struggle for self-determination was aided by the development of a
pan-Indian movement in the United States. The pan-Indian movement was
based on the assumption that Native American tribes shared a common set of
values and interests. Similarly to the role played by CORE and SCLC among
African Americans, pan-Indian organizations, such as the American Indian
Movement (AIM) and the Indians of All Tribes, led demonstrations demanding self-determination. In 1969, members of the Indians of All Tribes seized
Alcatraz Island in San Francisco Bay as a means of calling attention to the
plight of Native Americans and demanded that the island, which Indians had
originally sold to the federal government for $24 worth of beads, be made an
Indian cultural and education center. In 1972, AIM organized a march on
Washington, D.C., called the Trail of Broken Treaties. Members of the march
seized the Bureau of Indian Affairs and hung a large sign at the entrance
declaring it the American Indian Embassy.[21]

INDIAN EDUCATION: A NATIONAL TRAGEDY

Throughout the 1960s and 1970s, federal administrations gave support to
Indian demands for self-determination. During his election campaign in 1968,
President Nixon declared, "The right of self-determination of the Indian
people will be respected and their participation in planning their own destiny
will actively be encouraged."[22]

It was in this climate of civil rights activism and political support for
Indian self-determination that the U.S. Senate Committee on Labor and
Public Welfare issued in 1969 the report *Indian Education: A National Tragedy—
A National Challenge*. The report opened with a statement condemning previous educational policies of the federal government: "A careful review of
the historical literature reveals that the dominant policy of the Federal Government toward the American Indian has been one of forced assimilation . . . [because of] a desire to divest the Indian of his land."[23]

After a lengthy review of the failure of past educational policies, the
report's first recommendation was "maximum participation and control by
Indians in establishing Indian education programs."[24] In its second recommendation, the report called for maximum Indian participation in the development of educational programs in federal schools and local public schools.
These educational programs were to include early childhood education, vocational education, work-study, and adult literacy education. Of special importance was the recommendation to create bilingual and bicultural education
programs.

Native American demands for bilingual and bicultural education were
aided by the passage of Title VII of the Elementary and Secondary Education
Act of 1968 or, as it was also called, the Bilingual Education Act. This was, as I

will explain later in this chapter, a product of political activism by Mexican-American groups. Native Americans used funds provided under this legislation to support bilingual programs in Indian languages and English. For instance, the Bilingual Education Act provided support for bilingual programs in Navajo and English at the previously mentioned Rough Rock Demonstration School.[25]

The congressional debates resulting from the criticism leveled at Indian education in the report *Indian Education: A National Tragedy—A National Challenge* eventually culminated in the passage of the Indian Education Act in 1972. The declared policy of the legislation was to provide financial assistance to local schools to develop programs to meet the "special" educational needs of Native American students. In addition, the legislation created a federal Office of Indian Education.[26]

In 1974, the Bureau of Indian Affairs issued a set of procedures for protecting student rights and due process. In contrast to the brutal and dictatorial treatment of Indian students in the boarding schools of the late nineteenth and early twentieth centuries, each Indian student was extended the right "to make his or her own decisions where applicable."[27] And, in striking contrast to earlier deculturalization policies, Indian students were granted "the right to freedom of religion and culture."[28]

The most important piece of legislation supporting self-determination was the 1975 Indian Self-Determination and Education Assistance Act, which gave tribes the power to contract with the federal government to run their own education and health programs. The legislation opened with the declaration that it was "An Act to provide maximum Indian participation in the Government and education of Indian people; to provide for the full participation of Indian tribes in programs and services conducted by the federal government."[29]

The Indian Self-Determination and Education Assistance Act strengthened Indian participation in the control of education programs. The legislation provided that in a local school district receiving funds for the education of Indian students which *did not* have a school board having a majority of Indians had to establish a separate local committee composed of parents of Indian students in the school. This committee was given the authority over any Indian education programs contracted with the federal government.

The principles embodied in the Indian Self-Determination and Education Assistance Act were expanded upon in 1988 with the passage of the Tribally Controlled Schools Act. In addition to the right to operate schools under federal contract as provided in the 1975 legislation, the Tribally Controlled Schools Act provided for outright grants to tribes to support the operation of their own schools.[30]

Efforts to protect Indian culture was strengthened with the passage in 1978 of a congressional resolution on American Indian religious freedom. The reader is reminded, as I discussed in Chapter 6, that missionaries and federal policies from the seventeenth to the early twentieth centuries attempted to eradicate Indian religions and replace them with Christianity. The resolution recognized these earlier attempts to abridge Indian rights to religious freedom, stating: "That henceforth it shall be the policy of the United States to protect and preserve for American Indians their inherent right of freedom to believe, express and exercise traditional religions . . . and the freedom to worship through ceremonial and traditional rites."[31]

In addition to the protection of religion, the federal government committed itself to promoting traditional languages with the passage of the Native American Languages Act of 1990. This act commits the federal government to "preserve, protect, and promote the rights and freedom of Native Americans to use, practice, and develop Native American languages."[32]

There is, of course, an ironic twist to federal legislation designed to promote self-determination and preservation of Native American languages, religions, and cultures when placed against the backdrop of history. As I discussed in Chapter 6, the Civilized Tribes in Indian territory were operating their own tribal governments and school systems in the nineteenth century. The Cherokees were conducting bilingual education programs and protecting their cultural and religious traditions. These forms of self-determination and protection of languages and cultures ended when Indian Territory was dissolved in 1907. Also, the tribes placed onto reservations in the nineteenth century were subjected to policies consciously designed to destroy their cultures, languages, and religions. Therefore, the federal legislation of the 1970s and 1980s which were designed to reverse these policies required many tribes to discover and resurrect languages and traditions that the federal government had already partially destroyed.

MEXICAN AMERICANS

As I discussed in Chapter 7, Mexican-American students were segregated throughout the Southwest. Similarly to African Americans, Mexican Americans turned to the courts to seek redress for their grievances. In Ontario, California, in 1945, Mexican-American parents demanded that the school board grant all requests for transfer out of the Mexican schools. When the board refused this request, Gonzalo Mendez and William Guzman brought suit for violation of the Fourteenth Amendment to the Constitution. The school board responded to this suit by claiming that segregation was not based on race or national origins but on the necessity of providing special instruction.[33]

In 1946 a U.S. District Court ruled in *Mendez et al.* v. *Westminster School District of Orange County* that Mexicans were *not* Indians as claimed under the 1935 California law discussed in Chapter 7. The judge argued that the only possible argument for segregation was the special educational needs of Mexican-American children. These needs centered around the issue of learning English. Completely reversing the educational justification for segregation, the judge argued that "evidence clearly shows that Spanish-speaking children are retarded in learning English by lack of exposure to its use by segregation."[34] Therefore, the court ruled that segregation was illegal because it was *not* required by state law and because there was no valid educational justification for segregation.[35]

Heartened by the Mendez decision, the League of United Latin American Citizens (LULAC), the Mexican-American equivalent of the NAACP, forged ahead in its legal attack on segregation in Texas. With support from LULAC, a group of parents in 1948 brought suit against the Bastrop Independent School District, charging that local school authorities had no legal right to segregate children of Mexican descent and that this segregation was solely because the children were of Mexican descent. In *Delgado v. Bastrop Independent School District*, the court ruled that segregating Mexican-American children was illegal and discriminatory. The ruling required that the local school district end all segregation. The court did give local school districts the right to separate some children in the first grade only if scientific tests showed that they needed special instruction in English and the separation took place on the same campus.[36]

In general, LULAC was pleased with the decision. The one point they were dissatisfied with was the provision for the separation of children in the first grade. This allowed local schools to practice what was referred to in the latter part of the twentieth century as second-generation segregation. Second-generation segregation refers to the practice of using educational justifications for segregating children within a single school building. In fact, many local Texas school districts did use the proviso for that purpose.[37]

While the Mendez and Delgado decisions did hold out the promise of ending segregation of Mexican Americans, local school districts used many tactics to avoid integration, including manipulation of school district lines, choice plans, and different forms of second-generation segregation. For instance, the California State Department of Education reported in 1966 that 57 percent of the children with Spanish surnames were still attending schools that were predominantly Mexican American. In 1973, a civil rights activist, John Caughey, estimated that two-thirds of the Mexican-American children in Los Angeles attended segregated schools. In *All Deliberate Speed: Segregation and Exclusion in California Schools, 1855–1975*, Charles Wollenberg estimates that in California by 1973 more Mexican and Mexican-American children attended segregated schools than in 1947.[38]

The continuation of de facto forms of segregation resulted in the formation in 1967 of the Mexican American Legal Defense and Education Fund (MALDEF). Initially, MALDEF focused on cases dealing with students who were punished for participating in civil rights activities. In 1968, MALDEF focused its attention on the inequitable funding of school districts in Texas that primarily served Mexican Americans. Not only were Mexican-American children facing de facto segregation, but the schools they were attending were receiving less funding than schools attended by Anglos.[39]

The case brought by MALDEF, *Rodriguez v. San Antonio Independent School District*, had major implications for financing of schools across the country. In the case, a group of Mexican-American parents brought a class action suit against the state of Texas for the inequitable funding of school districts. In 1971, a federal district court ruled that the Texas school finance system was unconstitutional. In its decision, the federal district court applied, as the U.S. Supreme Court had in the 1954 school desegregation case, the equal protection clause of the Fourteenth Amendment. The inequality in financing of school districts was considered a denial of equal opportunity for Mexican-American children to receive an education. The U.S. Supreme Court overturned the decision on March 12, 1973, with the argument that school finance was not a constitutional issue. This Supreme Court decision meant that all school finance cases would have to be dealt with in state courts. Since 1973, numerous cases involving inequality in the financing of public schools have been argued in state courts.[40]

In 1970, Mexican Americans were officially recognized by the federal courts as an identifiable dominated group in the public schools in a MALDEF case, *Cisneros* v. *Corpus Christi Independent School District*. A central issue in the case was whether or not the 1954 school desegregation decision could be applied to Mexican Americans. The original Brown decision had dealt specifically with African Americans who were segregated by state and local laws. In his final decision, Judge Owen Cox ruled that blacks and Mexican Americans were segregated in the Corpus Christi school system law and that Mexican Americans were an identifiable dominated group because of their language, culture, religion, and Spanish surnames.[41]

BILINGUAL EDUCATION: PUERTO RICANS AND MEXICAN AMERICANS

While MALDEF continued to wage its battles in the courts, other Mexican-American organizations turned to the issue of preserving Mexican-American culture. In addition, Mexican Americans were joined by Puerto Ricans in efforts to have the public schools preserve the use of the Spanish language. As I discussed in Chapter 6, Puerto Ricans were very concerned about preserving their use of Spanish against the forces of deculturalization.

During the 1960s, Mexican Americans began to demonstrate for the use of Spanish in schools and the teaching of Mexican-American history and culture. In 1968, Mexican-American students boycotted four East Lost Angeles high schools, demanding bilingual programs, courses in Mexican-American history and culture, and the serving of Mexican food in the school cafeterias. In addition, the students demanded the hiring of more Spanish-speaking teachers and the firing of teachers who appeared to be anti–Mexican American.[42]

The school boycotts in Los Angeles attracted the attention of the newly formed La Raza Unida. La Raza Unida was formed in 1967, when a group of Mexican Americans boycotted federal hearings on the conditions of Mexican Americans and started their own conference. At the conference, La Raza Unida took a militant stand on the protection of the rights of Mexican Americans and the preservation of their culture and language. A statement drafted at the first conference proclaimed: "the time of subjugation, exploitation, and abuse of human rights of La Raza in the United States is hereby ended forever."[43]

La Raza Unida's statement on the preservation of culture and language reflected the growing mood in the Mexican-American community that public schools needed to pay more attention to dominated cultures and languages. The statement drafted at the first conference affirmed "the greatness of our heritage, our history, our language, our traditions, our contributions to humanity and our culture."[44]

Politicians responded to Mexican-American and Puerto Rican demands for the presentation of Spanish in the schools. Liberal Democratic Senator Ralph Yarborough of Texas, believing that he would lose the 1970 election to a wealthy and conservative Democrat, decided that Hispanic support was crucial to his coalition of blacks, Mexican Americans, and poor whites. In an effort to win Hispanic support, Yarborough, after being appointed to a special subcommittee on bilingual education of the Senate Committee on Labor and Public Welfare, launched a series of hearings in major Hispanic communities.[45]

The testimony at these hearings came primarily from representatives of the Mexican-American and Puerto Rican communities, not educational experts or linguistic theorists. The hearings concluded in East Harlem, with Senator Edward Kennedy and Bronx Borough President Herman Badillo decrying the fact that there were no Puerto Rican principals and only a few Puerto Rican teachers in the New York City school system.[46]

Yarborough supported bilingual legislation that focused on students whose "mother tongue is Spanish." The legislation included programs to impart knowledge of and pride about Hispanic culture and language and to bring descendants of Mexicans and Puerto Ricans into the teaching profession. The legislation was clearly designed to win political support from the Hispanic community in Texas. Yarborough's efforts resulted in the passage of the previously mentioned Bilingual Education Act of 1968.

As I discussed earlier in this chapter, Native Americans, along with Mexican Americans and Puerto Ricans, welcomed the idea of bilingual education. The legislation promised that their cultures and languages would be preserved by the public schools. Bilingual education, as it was conceived of in Hispanic and Native American communities, involved teaching both English and Spanish or a Native American language. Some of the Civilized Tribes in Indian Territory, as I discussed in Chapter 6, had used bilingual methods in their schools. In addition, bilingual education existed at differing periods in Mexican-American and Puerto Rican schools. The goal is to teach students to be fluent in two languages. In addition, Mexican Americans, Puerto Ricans, and Native Americans consider bilingual education to be part of a general effort to transmit their cultural traditions to students.

By the 1980s, the two major U.S. political parties were divided over bilingual education. Traditionally, organized ethnic groups, including Mexican Americans and Puerto Ricans, were a strong force in the Democratic party. In contrast, bilingual education became a major target of attack during the Republican administrations of the 1980s and 1990s. In fact, some members of the Republican party joined a movement opposing bilingual education and supporting the adoption of English as the official language of the United States. The movement to make English the official language was led by an organization, U.S. English, founded in 1983 by S. I. Hayakawa, a former Republican senator.

In 1986, in reaction to the Reagan administration, the National Association of Bilingual Education increased its political activities and intensified its public relations efforts. In reference to S. I. Hayakawa and U.S. English, Gene T. Chavez, the president of the association, warned that "those who think this country can only tolerate one language" were motivated more by political than by educational concerns. At the same meeting, the incoming president of the organization, Chicago School Administrator Jose Gonzalez, attacked the Reagan administration and the Department of Education for entering an "unholy alliance" with right-wing groups opposing bilingual education, groups such as U.S. English, Save Our Schools, and the Heritage Foundation.[47]

Within the Reagan administration, Secretary of Education William Bennett attempted to reduce support for bilingual education by appointing opponents of it to the government's National Advisory and Coordinating Council on Bilingual Education. The new appointees expressed a preference for immersing non-English-speaking children in the English language, rather than teaching them in a bilingual context. In addition, the new appointees favored giving more power to local officials to determine programs. Of course, such a policy would undercut the power the Hispanic community had gained by working with the federal government. Originally, Hispanics had turned to the federal government for assistance because they lacked power in local politics.[48]

One of Bennett's appointees to the National Advisory and Coordinating Council on Bilingual Education, Rosalie Pedalino Porter, director of the Bilingual and English as a Second Language programs in Newton, Massachusetts, wrote a book on the controversy with the descriptive title *Forked Tongue: The Politics of Bilingual Education*. For Porter, the politics of bilingual education involves political struggle within the educational establishment and the broader issue of cultural politics. Like other Bennett appointees, Porter rejects bilingual education which is also bicultural. She believes that language training should be geared toward providing the student with the language tools necessary for equal opportunity within the mainstream economy. But, unlike the more conservative of Bennett's appointees, she does not support attempts to make English the official language of the United States.

Porter's conclusions regarding bilingualism are a reflection of her broader views on cultural politics. She argues against bilingualism that is also bicultural because it segregates dominated communities with the least power. In her words, "The critical question is whether education policies that further the cultural identity of dominated groups at the same time enable dominated children to acquire the knowledge and skills to attain social and economic equality."[49]

Porter opposes the efforts of U.S. English because their efforts are provocative and based on anti-immigrant attitudes and threaten special programs for language minority groups. She quotes a statement by Richard Rodriguez as representing her position on attempts to enact an amendment to the Constitution making English the official language:

> What bothers me most about defenders of English comes down to a matter of tone. Too shrill. Too hostile. Too frightened. They seem to want to settle the issue of America's language, once and for all. But America must risk uncertainty if it is to remain true to its immigrant character. . . . We must remind the immigrant that there is an America already here. But we must never forget that we are an immigrant country, open to change.[50]

Despite opposition from civil rights organizations and professional organizations, including the National Association of Bilingual Education, the National Council of Teachers of English, the Linguistics Society of America, and the Modern Language Association, efforts to make English the official language continue at the state and national level. In 1923, Nebraska made English the official state language, followed by Illinois in 1969. In 1978, Hawaii made English and Hawaiian the official state languages. Indicative of the concerns of the 1980s, between 1984 and 1988 fourteen other states made English the official state language.[51]

The major target of those supporting English as the official language is the ballot. Extensions to the 1965 Voting Rights Act granted citizens the right to voting information in their native languages. In communities where 5 percent or more of the population speak languages other than English, voting material must be provided in those languages. Supporters of English-language amendments argue that voters should be fluent in English and that naturalization procedures require a test given in English. Therefore, from their standpoint, ballots and election material should be kept in English. On the other hand, opponents argue that election materials should be presented in native languages so that all groups will be on an equal footing with those who are fluent in English.

Besides the issue of political power, language is considered a cultural issue by Mexican Americans, Puerto Ricans, and Native Americans. A person's cultural perspective is directly related to attitudes regarding making English the official language. This connection is exemplified by Humberto Garza's comment regarding a requirement that Los Altos, California, city employees speak only English on the job: "Those council people from Los Altos should be made to understand that they are advocating their law in occupied Mexico [referring to the U.S. conquest of Mexican territory, including California, as I discussed in Chapter 7]. . . . They should move back to England or learn how to speak the language of Native Americans."[52]

THE GREAT CIVIL RIGHTS MOVEMENT
EXPANDS ITS REACH

The great civil rights movement motivated other groups to demand equality of educational opportunity. Women, of course, had been battling for equal rights for several centuries. In response to the women's movement of the 1960s and 1970s, Congress passed the Higher Education Act of 1972, which provided for sexual equality in both employment and educational programs. The legislation applied to all educational institutions, including preschool, elementary, and secondary schools, vocational and professional schools, and public and private undergraduate and graduate institutions. A 1983 Supreme Court decision, *Grove City College* v. *Bell*, restricted the application of Title IX in its application to specific educational programs within institutions. In the 1987 Civil Rights Restoration Act, Congress overturned the Court's decision and amended Title IX to include all activities of any educational institution receiving federal aid.[53]

Parents of handicapped children and those needing special education had for years complained about lack of services for their children. The political movement for federal aid to help handicapped students followed a path similar to that of the struggles over segregation. First, finding themselves unable to change educational institutions by pressuring local and state governments, organized groups interested in improving educational opportunities for the handicapped turned to the courts. This was the path taken in the late 1960s by the Pennsylvania Association for Retarded Children (PARC).

PARC was one of many associations organized in the 1950s to aid handicapped and retarded citizens. These organizations were concerned with state laws that excluded retarded and handicapped citizens from educational institutions because they were considered ineducable and untrainable. State organizations like PARC and the National Association for Retarded Children campaigned to eliminate these laws and to demonstrate the educability of all children. But, as the civil rights movement discovered throughout the century, local and state officials were resistant to change and relief had to be sought from the judicial system.

In *Pennsylvania Association for Retarded Children (PARC)* v. *Commonwealth of Pennsylvania*, a case that was as important to the handicapped rights movement as the Brown decision was to the civil rights movement, PARC objected to conditions in the Pennhurst State School and Hospital. In framing the case, lawyers for PARC focused on the legal right to an education for handicapped and retarded children. PARC, working with the major federal lobbyist for handicapped children, the Council for Exceptional Children (CEC), overwhelmed the court with evidence on the educability of handicapped and retarded children. The state withdrew its case, and the court enjoined the state from excluding mentally retarded children from a public education and required that every mentally retarded child be allowed access to an education. The PARC case prompted lobbying groups representing the handicapped to file thirty-six cases against state governments. The CEC prepared model legislation and lobbied for its passage at the state and federal levels.[54]

One political problem facing advocates of federal aid for children with special needs was the possibility of excessive federal control resulting from attempts to define an appropriate education for each handicapped or retarded child. In fact, to do so would have raised the specter of federal control of local education and alienated many members of Congress.

The resolution of this political problem, as it appeared in 1975 in Public Law 94-142 (Education for All Handicapped Children Act), was the requirement that an individual educational plan (IEP) be developed for each child jointly by the local educational agency and the child's parents or guardians. This gives the child or the parents the right to negotiate with the local school system about the type of services to be delivered. The IEP was considered to be a brilliant political strategy. In their study of the legalization of special education, David Neal and David Kirp call the IEP "an ingenious device in terms of political acceptability." They write,

> It avoids attempting to mandate specific services; it recognizes the rights of recipients, empowers them, and involves them in the process; it avoids treading on the professional discretion of teachers and potentially enhances their influence over placement decisions; it provides a means of holding local administrators accountable while paying some deference to the belief that the federal government should not interfere too much with local autonomy in education; and it appeals to local school officials by fixing the upper limit of the liabilities with respect to the child.[55]

The gains made by women and children with special needs highlight the power and inclusiveness of the great civil rights movement. A broad range of groups who felt excluded from equal participation in education joined in a common struggle in the streets, in school systems, in the courts, in state legislatures, and in the halls of Congress. Also, the great civil rights movement illustrates the power people have to change social and political conditions if they are willing to organize and join in a common struggle.

NOTES

1. *Brown et al.* v. *Board of Education of Topeka et al.* (1954), reprinted in Albert P. Blaustein and Clarence C. Ferguson, Jr., *Desegregation and the Law* (New Brunswick, N.J.: Rutgers University Press, 1957), pp. 273–282.
2. "The Effects of Segregation and the Consequences of Desegregation: A Social Science Statement," appendix to Appellants' Brief filed in the School Segregation Cases in the Supreme Court of the United States, October term, 1952, in John Bracey, August Meier, and Elliott Rudwick, eds., *The Afro-Americans: Selected Documents* (Boston: Allyn & Bacon, 1972), pp. 661–671.

3. Ibid.
4. Gunnar Myrdal, *An American Dilemma: The Negro Problem and Modern Democracy* (New York: Harper & Row, 1944), pp. lxxii–lxxiii.
5. Martin Luther King, Jr., *Stride toward Freedom: The Montgomery Story* (New York: Harper & Row, 1958), p. 91.
6. Ibid., pp. 94–97.
7. Quoted in David Lewis, *King: A Critical Biography* (New York: Praeger, 1970), p. 171.
8. James W. Prothro, "Stateways versus Folkways Revisited: An Error in Prediction," *Journal of Politics,* Vol. 34 (May 1972), pp. 356–357.
9. For a discussion of this case, see Charles Tesconi and Emanual Hurwitz, eds., *Education for Whom?* (New York: Dodd, Mead, 1974), pp. 34–66, 174–188.
10. Richard Nixon, "Message to Congress," March 17, 1972, in Dwight W. Allen and Jeffrey C. Hecht, eds., *Controversies in Education* (Philadelphia: Saunders, 1974), pp. 530–534.
11. Ibid.
12. James S. Coleman et al., *Trends in School Segregation, 1968–1973* (Washington, D.C.: Urban Institute, 1975).
13. For a discussion of these schools, see Joel Spring, *Education and the Rise of the Corporate State* (Boston: Beacon Press, 1972).
14. For a discussion of Summerhill, see Joel Spring, *A Primer of Libertarian Education* (New York: Free Life Editions, 1975), pp. 81–111.
15. Kathryn Borman and Joel Spring, *Schools in Central Cities* (White Plains, N.Y.: Longman, 1984), pp. 160–172.
16. Francis Paul Prucha, *The Indians in American Society: From Revolutionary War to the Present* (Berkeley: The University of California Press, 1985), p. 70.
17. Ibid., pp. 72–75.
18. Ibid., p. 74.
19. Jon Reyhner and Jeanne Eder, *A History of Indian Education* (Billings, Montana: Eastern Montana College, 1989), pp. 125–126.
20. Ibid., p. 126.
21. Prucha, *Indians in American Society,* p. 82.
22. Ibid., p. 83.
23. U.S. Congress, Senate Committee on Labor and Public Welfare, *Indian Education: A National Tragedy—A National Challenge,* 91st Cong., 1st Sess. (Washington, D.C.: U.S. Government Printing Office, 1969), p. 9.
24. Ibid., p. 106.
25. Reyhner and Eder, *History of Indian Education,* pp. 132–135.
26. "Indian Education Act, June 23, 1972" in Francis Paul Prucha, ed., *Documents of United States Indian Policy,* (Lincoln: University of Nebraska Press, 1990), pp. 263–264.
27. "Student Rights and Due Process Procedures, October 11, 1974" in Prucha, *Documents,* p. 271.
28. Ibid.

29. "Indian Self-Determination and Education Assistance Act, January 4, 1975" in Prucha, *Documents*, p. 274.
30. "Tribally Controlled Schools Act of 1988" in Prucha, *Documents*, pp. 314–315.
31. "American Indian Religious Freedom, August 11, 1978," in Prucha, *Documents*, pp. 288–289.
32. Reyhner and Eder, *History of Indian Education*, p. 137.
33. Ibid., p. 126.
34. Quoted in ibid., p. 128.
35. Ibid., pp. 127–129. Also see Gilbert G. Gonzalez, *Chicano Education in the Era of Segregation* (Philadelphia: Balch Institute Press, 1990), pp. 147–156.
36. Guadalupe San Miguel, Jr., *"Let All of Them Take Heed": Mexican Americans and the Campaign for Educational Equality in Texas, 1910–1981* (Austin: University of Texas Press, 1987), pp. 123–124.
37. Ibid., p. 125.
38. Charles Wollenberg, *All Deliberate Speed: Segregation and Exclusion in California Schools, 1855–1975,* (Berkeley: University of California Press, 1976), p. 134.
39. San Miguel, *"Let All of Them Take Heed,"* pp. 169–173.
40. Ibid., pp. 173–174.
41. Ibid., pp. 177–179.
42. Wollenberg, *All Deliberate Speed,* pp. 134–135.
43. San Miguel, *"Let All of Them Take Heed,"* p. 168.
44. Ibid.
45. Hugh Davis Graham, *Uncertain Triumph: Federal Educational Policy in the Kennedy and Johnson Years* (Chapel Hill: University of North Carolina Press, 1984), p. 155.
46. Ibid., p. 156.
47. James Crawford, "Bilingual Educators Seeking Strategies to Counter Attacks," *Education Week*, Vol. 5, No. 28 (April 9, 1986), pp. 1, 9.
48. James Crawford, "Administration Panel Praises Bennett's Bilingual-Education Stance," *Education Week*, Vol. 5, No. 28 (April 9, 1986), p. 9.
49. Rosalie Pedalino Porter, *Forked Tongue: the Politics of Bilingual Education* (New York: Basic Books, 1990), p. 188.
50. Ibid., pp. 219–220.
51. Ibid., pp. 210–211.
52. Quoted in ibid., p. 216.
53. See Joel Spring, *American Education,* 5th ed. (White Plains, N.Y.: Longman, 1991), p. 114.
54. David Neal and David Kirp, "The Allure of Legalization Reconsidered: The Case of Special Education" in David Kirp and Donald Jensen, eds., *School Days, Rule Days: The Legalization and Regulation of Education* (Philadelphia: Falmer Press, 1986), pp. 346–348.
55. Ibid., pp. 349–350.

Education and National Policy

After World War II, American schools were increasingly linked to the policy needs of the federal government. The Cold War between the United States and the Soviet Union spawned demands for more academic courses in the schools and a greater emphasis on science and mathematics as a means of winning the weapons race with the Soviet Union. This emphasis on science and mathematics was considered essential to producing enough scientists and engineers to keep the United States technologically ahead of the Soviet Union. The federal government's concern with the school's role in the Cold War was behind its decisions to continue selective service into peacetime as a means of controlling human resources, to establish the National Science Foundation (NSF), and to pass the National Defense Educational Act (NDEA). These actions affected the curriculum of the schools and the educational choices made by students.

During the 1960s, when civil rights and poverty were national concerns, the federal government made education part of a national campaign against poverty. Like common school reforms of the nineteenth century, the federal government's War on Poverty of the 1960s attempted to eliminate poverty through special educational programs. In addition, civil rights legislation gave the federal government the responsibility to ensure that schools were not committing discriminatory actions against minority groups.

The expansion of the role of the federal government in education took place in a climate of strong public reaction against the schools. This negative reaction came from several sources. Immediately following World War II, members of the radical right charged that the schools had been infiltrated by communists. Right-wing groups demanded the removal of anti-American literature from the schools and the dismissal of left-leaning teachers. At the same time, those committed to victory for the United States in its technological race with the Soviet Union accused the public schools of being anti-intelligent and charged that professional educators had led the schools to ruin.

In addition, the civil rights movement of the 1950s was a grass-roots protest against school segregation and discriminatory educational policies. In 1954 the Supreme Court ruled that segregated education was unconstitutional, but the lack of quick enforcement of this ruling by federal officials and the courts convinced minority group leaders that direct action was required to achieve integrated quality education. Also, civil rights leaders wanted to end all forms of segregation and discrimination. These factors led to the emergence of a political and social protest movement that eventually forced the passage of federal civil rights legislation and special educational legislation. In a political context, by seeking redress against the discriminatory actions of local elites, the civil rights movement was forced to seek aid from the federal government. A major consequence was that the federal government increased its involvement with and power over local school systems.

Two major historical interpretations of these post–World War II events have been offered. One is presented in Joel Spring's *Sorting Machine: National Educational Policy since 1945;* the other is put forth by Diane Ravitch in *The Troubled Crusade: American Education, 1945–1980.* The interpretation given in *The Sorting Machine* stresses the expanded role of the corporate liberal state in the management of human resources. Within the framework of this interpretation, selective service, the NSF, the NDEA, and the War on Poverty are considered part of the general trend in the twentieth century to use the schools as a means of cultivating human resources for the benefit of industrial and corporate leaders. This interpretation recognizes the problems and failures of the schools in achieving these goals and the evolving complexity of political relationships in the educational community. Spring's major criticism of educational events is that schools were increasingly used to serve national economic and foreign policies and, as a result, failed to prepare students to protect their political, social, and economic rights.[1]

Ravitch, in contrast, provides a neoconservative interpretation of educational events after World War II. She argues that a major concern after the war was to provide equality of opportunity. "At every level of formal education, from nursery school to graduate school, equal opportunity became the overriding goal of postwar educational reformers." Ravitch does not link the evolution of educational policy with the needs of corporate and industrial leaders. Her major criticisms of events during this period are of the tendency, from her perspective, for the schools to dilute the curriculum and for the civil rights movement to expand its demands for equal treatment for minority groups to include a demand for special treatment to overcome previous discriminatory actions. She is highly critical of affirmative action programs for admission of minority groups to higher education and to employment opportunities. In general, Ravitch agrees with the critics of the 1950s who claimed that the schools had been made anti-intellectual by the control of professional educators.[2]

Spring's and Ravitch's major differences in interpretation are over the relationship between educational events and larger social and economic problems, and the criticism of programs designed to provide special advantages to social groups subjected to discriminatory actions. These differing frameworks lead to differing conclusions. Spring concludes that the major problem for the future is to separate educational policy from other national policy goals and to develop a philosophy of schooling based on concepts of liberty. *The Sorting Machine* ends with the hope that the book "will aid in an understanding of this issue [that education can be used for liberation or social enslavement] and that we might begin to formulate a national educational philosophy based on individual liberty, not on service to the state or corporate interests."[3] Ravitch concludes her book on an optimistic note, expressing confidence in the steady expansion of educational opportunities: "To believe in education is to believe in the future, to believe in what may be accomplished through the disciplined use of intelligence, allied with cooperation and good will. If it seems naively American to put so much stock in schools, colleges, universities, and the endless prospect of self-improvement and social improvement, it is an admirable, and perhaps even a noble, flaw."[4]

Discussions of the effects on education of the Cold War and the War on Poverty follows.

THE COLD WAR AND
NATIONAL EDUCATIONAL POLICY

Interrelated social and political problems and public criticism of the schools shaped national educational policy after World War II. First was the persistent youth problem. World War II had ended the Depression problem of youth unemployment, but government policymakers feared that the end of the war and the return of members of the armed forces to the labor market would create new mass unemployment. Second, the split between professional educators and the business community that occurred during the Depression widened. The conflict further intensified when the academic community and federal officials criticized the control of the schools by professional educators, claiming that control by this group had made the schools anti-intellectual and turned them into the weakest link in America's defense against the Soviet Union. Third, public criticism of the schools increased when the radical right charged that American education had been infiltrated by communists. Finally, the Cold War arms race generated demands by government and industry that the schools educate more scientists and engineers. All these factors became interwoven to form educational policy in the 1940s and 1950s.

During World War II, President Franklin D. Roosevelt wanted to solve the youth problem and maintain world peace by requiring universal military training for all males. This concept of a year of service had existed since World War I and had been one reason for the formation of the CCC during the Depression. In June 1945 the congressional Select Committee on Postwar Military Policy proposed a training plan that would "be universal and democratic, applicable to rich and poor alike, and with a minimum of exceptions." After Roosevelt's death in 1945, President Harry S. Truman quickly seized the banner of universal military training and proposed one year of training for all American youth. Truman believed that universal training would be a panacea for many of America's problems. He told a joint session of Congress that a plan of this type would provide for national security and "raise the physical standard of the Nation's manpower . . . lower its illiteracy rate, and . . . develop in our young men the ideals of responsible American citizenship."[5]

When Truman urged the establishment of a plan for universal training, Congress, which was hoping to solve any unemployment problems by providing funds for returning members of the military to attend school, expressed little enthusiasm. Like the NYA and CCC programs during the Depression, this approach to unemployment relied on reducing the available labor force by having large numbers of the population attend school rather than enter the labor market. Congress passed the Servicemen's Readjustment Act of 1944 (commonly known as the GI Bill of Rights) with provisions for educational benefits. Under the terms of the legislation, veterans would receive support for tuition, books, and living expenses. The legislation had a major impact on college enrollments. In 1945, 1,013,000 veterans attended college, doubling the existing college population. In the seven years in which benefits were provided, 7.8 million veterans received some form of postsecondary education.

Although the GI Bill solved part of the problem of youth unemployment, calls for universal service continued until the early 1950s, when the Korean War provided a final impetus for serious consideration of universal training. The drama that led to passage of the Universal Military Training and Service Act of 1951—legislation that directly affected the lives of young American men for the next two decades—began on the morning of January 10, 1951. On that day, Senator Lyndon B. Johnson, chairman of the Preparedness Subcommittee of the Committee on Armed Services, opened hearings on universal military service. The committee was in session for over three weeks. The major problem it considered was how to balance the security needs for more engineers and scientists with military needs. The agenda included debate of the concept that universal military service could be used to channel and control the distribution of human resources in American society.

The major witnesses testifying before the committee were officials of the Department of Defense and representatives of the academic and scientific establishments, all of whom agreed on compulsory military duty but differed on how deferments should be used for channeling human resources. The university community, of course, was concerned that a sudden introduction of universal training would greatly reduce college enrollments during the first years of operation, causing serious disruption and economic strain on universities. The Department of Defense feared it would be required to handle "all" American youth and wanted assurance that only individuals qualified to serve in the armed forces would be drafted.

Also, opposition to drafting all men came from the scientific establishment, which wanted potential scientists and engineers deferred from service. The scientific establishment included the growing number of scientists who, during and after World War II, began to move freely among centers of power in government, industry, and the military. These scientists began to exert a growing influence on national policies, and in discussion about human resource development and education, their point of view was received with a great deal of sympathy. Charles A. Thomas, chairman of the Scientific Manpower Advisory Committee of the National Security Resources Board and executive vice president of Monsanto Corporation, appeared before Lyndon Johnson's Preparedness Subcommittee in January 1951. The Scientific Manpower Advisory Committee, established to advise the President of the United States, included leaders from the military, industry, and the academic community. The group proposed the deferment each year of 75,000 men who would receive education as scientists and engineers, as well as additional deferments for those attending graduate school.

Vannevar Bush and James B. Conant, two other important representatives of the scientific establishment, also supported universal training. Bush and Conant had worked together on scientific research for the federal government during World War II and had been architects of the government's scientific policies during and after the war. Both had also worked for the establishment of the National Science Foundation (NSF). In 1944, President Roosevelt asked Bush to prepare a plan for continued government involvement in research after the war. Bush responded with an enthusiasm that reflected his own belief that science was the panacea for the world's problems.

Bush had unlimited faith in the power of science and technology to improve society. Even in his autobiography, written during the turmoil and student rebellions of the 1960s, he expressed faith that science and technology would end poverty, save the environment, and serve as the foundation stones of a better world. In 1945, Bush issued his reply to the President in a report with the glowing and hopeful title *Science—The Endless Frontier*.[6] Bush argued that continuation of basic scientific research was essential for maintaining full employment, world leadership, national security, and national health. The keys to increasing scientific capital were, first, ensuring that large numbers of men and women received scientific training and second, supporting basic scientific research in colleges, universities, and research institutes. This could be accomplished, Bush felt, through the establishment of a National Science Foundation that would become a focal point for planning and supporting a scientific work force.

In addition to supporting basic research, two important functions of the NSF, as envisioned by Bush, were improving science education in the public schools and establishing a system of undergraduate and graduate fellowships for training and scientific research. Bush believed that the improvement of science teaching in high schools was imperative if latent scientific talent were to be properly developed. He viewed the prospect of high school science teachers' failing to awaken interest or provide adequate instruction as a great danger. The NSF had an important effect on public education in later years, when the foundation began to support studies of science curricula and helped to introduce many new programs into the public schools.

Bush appeared before the Senate Preparedness Subcommittee in 1951, shortly after the passage of the National Science Foundation Act of 1950. The primary conflict in the battle to establish the foundation focused on the issue of executive versus independent control. The first act to establish a National Science Foundation was passed by Congress in 1947 but was vetoed by President Truman because he felt the board of the foundation was given too much independent power and he wanted the director to be appointed by the President. When the 1950 bill passed, Bush claimed that he was able to convince Truman not to veto it by arguing that an independent board with the power to select its own director would have an easier time working with the university community. The establishment of the NSF did not dissuade Bush from seeking additional measures to increase the number of scientists.

Bush's testimony before the Senate subcommittee was given in the name of a group called the Committee on the Present Danger. This group believed the first key step in the free world's defense was military manpower legislation that would act "both as a deterrent to a major aggression and as a defense if war should come."[7] The membership of this group included thirty-three important leaders from the military, industry, and universities.

James B. Conant, then president of Harvard University and the first chairman of the board of the NSF, also testified for the Committee on the Present Danger in support of universal military training and the channeling of human resources into science and engineering. Like Bush, Conant represented the new breed of scientists who were gaining influential positions and exerting power over national policy. Conant was an important figure in discussions on the channeling of human resources because of his leadership role in science and his later study of the American high school. His support of universal military training and the channeling of manpower provided the basic framework for his discussions about the American high school.

Conant's ideas on the channeling of human resources were given before a congressional hearing in 1947, when he was asked to testify in favor of legislation supporting the establishment of the NSF. He told the committee that his primary concern was to secure provisions for granting scholarships and fellowships: "It is men that count. And today we do not have the scientific manpower requisite for the job that lies ahead."[8]

For Conant, it was most important to tap the latent talent of many high school students who either did not enter a scientific career or were unable to pursue a college education because they lacked the financial resources to do so. A system of scholarships would ensure that superior high school students who needed financial aid could continue their education. During the discussion, one member of Congress asked Conant if he thought the public schools could accomplish more toward channeling scientific human resources if they set apart superior students and gave them special training. Conant replied that this was already being done to a certain extent in the public schools but required a greater emphasis. To emphasize the importance of this idea, Conant submitted an abstract of a speech he had given two days earlier to the American Association of School Administrators titled "The Dilemma of American Education."

The dilemma, as described by Conant, was similar to the dilemma facing those considering universal military training: How do you make treatment equal but at the same time make provision for channeling superior human resources into needed occupations? Conant never resolved the dilemma, but he did suggest that "we pay a price for the fundamental democracy of our undifferentiated system of public schools . . . if we are wise the price need not be as high as it is at the present moment."[9] For Conant, reducing the price of providing democratic schools meant increasing their role as social sorting institutions; this would be accomplished by placing greater emphasis on the guidance and counseling of superior students and by setting a greater intellectual pace for these students, who would be required to take four years of mathematics and three years of a foreign language and to gain a mastery of the English language. These superior students would be the pool from which scholars would be selected to receive federal subsidies for higher education. Conant made it clear to the congressional committee that he did not advocate a federal subsidy to enable *all* students to attend college—only to allow superior students to enter professions considered necessary to national interests.

Out of the hearings held by Lyndon Johnson came a plan for universal training that satisfied the concerns of both the scientific establishment and the academic world. The legislative compromise involved amending selective service legislation from World War II instead of passing entirely new legislation. The amendments of 1951 provided for the control and channeling of human resources by authorizing the President to defer individuals whose academic training was necessary to the national health, safety, or security interests. College students could be deferred by receiving a certain score on the national Selective Service College Qualification Test or by maintaining a certain class rank. Ultimate power over the system was placed into the hands of local draft boards, and restriction of presidential power was ensured by specifically exempting draft boards from the obligation to defer students solely on the basis of federally established criteria.

The 1951 amendments to the Selective Service Act established the major form of government youth policy in effect in the 1950s and 1960s. Young males could chose either to remain in school or to serve in the armed forces. Complaints about the inequalities inherent in the system began within a year after the passage of the amendments. Obviously, the system favored those who were able to attend universities and colleges, which often meant that the poor went into the military while the middle class and the rich attended college.

Administrators of college and universities were pleased with the selective service amendments because they guaranteed an increasing student population. In fact, by the late 1960s, when the selective service system was abandoned, the number of college graduates had increased to the point of flooding the labor market. The result was educational inflation—that is, a decline in the economic value of a college degree in the labor market. As a system of controlling human resources, selective service failed because it was based on the erroneous assumption that channeling talent into higher education would result in increased economic growth.

Both Conant and Bush were satisfied with the selective service legislation because it promised to channel more youth into science and engineering, but they also feared that public schools were not academically advanced enough to meet the challenge of the Cold War. In part, the NSF was designed to provide some impetus for public schools to emphasize science and mathematics, but it did not answer all concerns about the academic quality of American schools. Consequently, Conant and Bush joined the chorus of voices raising doubts about the academic quality of American schools. Two major groups led public criticism of the school system. One group, the radical right, linked the alleged decline of academic standards to communist infiltration of American education. The other group, primarily from the academic community, claimed that professional educators were anti-intellectual and that scholars should have the major influence over the public school curriculum.

The fears caused by the Cold War made the public receptive to the radical right's criticisms. In 1951 the executive secretary of the NEA's National Commission for the Defense of Democracy through Education reported in a slightly hysterical tone that the number of "attacks" on public schooling had increased rapidly since the closing days of World War II. According to the commission's survey, the pace of "attack" was so swift that more than twice as many attacks had occurred in the three-year period since 1948 as in the three-year period before 1948. The phraseology and reaction of educators often made them appear to be warriors doing battle with an enemy that was storming the walls of the public schools. Words like *attack, counterattack,* and *siege* were hurled around when describing the plight of the professional educator. The executive secretary of the National Commission for the Defense of Democracy through Education, in reporting the increasing criticism of the schools, exemplified the battle mentality. He stressed that the "attacking groups are not as dangerous as they seem. . . . But we all need to be alarmed as were the Minute Men by Paul Revere in 1775." He went on to call the educational troops together with this plea: "If, like the Minute Men, we are ready to carry out individual responsibilities of intelligent group planning, professional unity, organized action, and friendly contact with our allies, we will be as successful in defending our cause as were the gallant men at Concord."[10]

The incident that put right-wing attacks on the schools into the national press and probably left other school administrators in a state of apprehension was the forced resignation in 1950 of School Superintendent Willard Goslin of Pasadena, California. Goslin was a national figure in professional education circles, having served in 1948 as president of the American Association of School Administrators. In 1949, when Goslin proposed a tax increase, members of the local community mounted an attack charging that the schools had fallen under the control of communism. This charge, plus the publicity it aroused, forced Goslin's resignation.

The anticommunist campaign directed at Superintendent Goslin was based on pamphlets distributed by the National Council for American Education, headed by Allen Zoll—one of many national organizations focusing attention on subversion in the schools. Other organizations of this type included the American Coalition of Patriotic Societies, the American Council of Christian Laymen, the Anti-Communist League of America, the California Anti-Communist League, the Christian Nationalist Crusade, Defenders of American Education, the Daughters of the American Revolution, and the Sons of the American Revolution.

Zoll organized the National Council for American Education in 1948. He reportedly began his crusade with the "Michigan statement": "We form hell-raising groups to find out what is being taught in the schools, and then we raise hell about it." Pasadena, of course, was not the only community influenced by Zoll's pamphlets. In 1951 the *Saturday Review of Literature* devoted a large section of its education issue to school controversies around the country. In Denver, Zoll's pamphlets, including one titled *The Commies Are After Your Kids,* supposedly provided a good deal of ammunition for local citizen groups. In Englewood, New Jersey, and Port Washington, New York, Zoll's writings reportedly exerted a significant influence. In Pasadena, the Zoll pamphlet that attracted attention was *Progressive Education Increases Juvenile Delinquency,* which stated that "so-called progressive education, shot through as it is with the blight of Pragmatism, has had a very deleterious effect upon the original character of American education."[11]

The textbook industry was also being charged with communist infiltration. In 1949 Lucille Cardin Crain began issuing a quarterly newsletter, the *Educational Reviewer,* which had as its goal the weeding out of subversive material from public school textbooks. Her first target was a popular high school text, *American Government* by Frank Abbott Magruder. She claimed that Magruder's view of democracy led "straight from Rousseau, through Marx, to totalitarianism" and that the book gave a very favorable view of the workings of the government of the Soviet Union. Convinced that the text was designed to undermine the free enterprise system, she gave wide circulation to her critique of the book. Her arguments eventually reached the ears of national radio commentator Fulton Lewis, Jr., who used portions of Crain's analysis on a coast-to-coast broadcast and added a scare statement: "That's the book that has been in use in high schools all over the nation, possibly by your youngster."[12]

Other groups joined in the work of the *Educational Reviewer,* including Allen Zoll's National Council for American Education, the Daughters of the American Revolution, the Sons of the American Revolution, and the Guardians of American Education. These groups published their own lists of subversive books and texts. Throughout the country during the 1950s and 1960s, community members armed with one of these lists would demand that certain subversive books be removed from library shelves and from the curricula of the schools. Suggestions were even made that textbook writers be required to take a loyalty oath. These actions alarmed the textbook industry, and in 1953 an official statement of the American Textbook Publishers Institute warned against a loyalty oath for authors because it would lower the quality of textbook authorship and material. The institute claimed that the highly individualistic and competitive system in the textbook industry provided adequate safeguards against "the deliberate introduction of harmful or subversive material." To curb local attacks, it recommended that states establish public agencies to monitor complaints about textbooks.

The academics' attack against the public schools was led by historian Arthur Bestor. In 1952 he delivered a paper at the annual meeting of the American Historical Association titled "Anti-Intellectualism in the Schools: A Challenge to Scholars." As part of his presentation, Bestor submitted a series of proposals based on a detailed resolution he had drafted and started to circulate among scholarly friends for their approval and signatures. By the time of the meeting, he had collected 695 signatures. Of the signatories, 199 were historians, 93 were in English, 86 in the biological sciences, 77 in mathematics, and the others in a variety of academic fields. The preamble of the resolution expressed alarm at the "serious danger to American intellectual life arising from anti-intellectual tendencies" and the "anti-intellectualism conceptions of education among important groups of school administrators and educational theorists." The actual resolutions proposed a close working relationship between the scholarly community and professional educators.

What prompted Bestor to prepare his resolution was the life-adjustment education movement, which was launched in 1945 at a conference sponsored by the Vocational Education Division of the U.S. Office of Education. At this meeting, a well-known leader of vocational education, Dr. Charles Prosser, introduced the following resolution: "The vocational school of a community will be able better to prepare 20 percent of the youth of secondary school age for entrance upon desirable skilled occupations; and . . . the high school will continue to prepare another 20 percent for entrance to college." The question in Prosser's mind was what to do with the other 60 percent. He gave the following answer in his resolution: "We do not believe that the remaining 60 percent of our youth of secondary school age will receive the life-adjustment education they need . . . unless . . . the administrators of public education with the assistance of vocational education leaders formulate a similar program for this group."[13]

Bestor's anger was sparked by copies of the life-adjustment education materials distributed by the Illinois Secondary School Curriculum Program. He quickly recognized and criticized the methods used by educators to sell life-adjustment curricula to the public. In his criticisms of the public schools, Bestor quoted from the Illinois materials: "Given the American tradition of the local lay-control of public education, it is both necessary and desirable that a community (patrons, pupils, teachers) consensus be engineered in understanding support of the necessary changes before they are made."[14] Bestor responded, "We approach here the real meaning of what educationists euphemistically describe as 'democracy in education.' It is the democracy of the 'engineered consensus.'" He concluded that control of the educational system was not in public hands, but in the hands of professional educators or, as he referred to them, "educationists."[15]

Life-adjustment education also convinced Bestor that professional educators were responsible for the anti-intellectual quality of American schools. He notes, for example, that in one of the Illinois documents, "Problems of High School Youth," an overwhelming proportion of problems cited deal with what he calls trivia and that no mention is made of mathematics, science, history, or foreign languages. In the list of fifty-five "Problems of High School Youth," he cites as trivia such items as "the problem of improving one's personal appearance"; "the problem of selecting a family dentist"; "the problem of developing one or more 'making things,' 'making it go,' or 'tinkering' hobbies"; and "the problem of developing and maintaining wholesome boy-girl relationships."[16]

Bestor wanted the public schools to reject the traditional emphasis on socialization and the social-sorting function of schooling. From his perspective, curricula should be organized around traditional subject matter disciplines. In the schools, he argues, "the important books must be read. . . . Fundamental problems must be studied, not merely talked about."[17] This would occur in a climate where the basic scientific and scholarly disciplines were presented as systematic ways of thinking, with each discipline organized around a structure and methodology of its own. The disciplines to be studied would include mathematics, science, history, English, and foreign languages.

Bestor rejected the notion of a differentiated course of study based on the future social destination of the individual. He accepted the existence of differences in intellectual ability among students but argues, in reference to students of lower mental ability, "Most of them, I believe, can be brought at a slower pace along the same route."[18] Elimination of the emphasis on socialization and the sorting of human resources in the schools, Bestor felt, could curb the tide of anti-intellectualism in society by creating a new respect in the student and in the home for knowledge and cultural achievement.

In 1952 the American Historical Association was unable to reach a consensus on Bestor's proposal. In its place was substituted a weakly worded resolution supporting Bestor's basic concerns and calling for further study of the possibility of working with other learned societies. Undeterred by the setback, Bestor searched for another means of implementing his ideas. In 1956 he helped to organize the Council for Basic Education and became its first president. Shortly after the founding of this group, Mortimer Smith became its executive director and the major force behind the operations of the organization.

Within a short time after Bestor's initial criticism, a chorus of other voices joined in condemning the schools and their control by professional educators. Alan Lynd's *Quackery in the Public Schools,* published in 1953, criticized the anti-intellectual quality of college and university courses in teacher education. He blamed this situation on control of higher education by professional educators.

Smith made his views known nationally in two publications: *And Madly Teach: A Layman Looks at Public School Education* (1949) and *The Diminished Mind: A Study of Planned Mediocrity in Our Public Schools* (1954). Smith, like his colleagues, charged the schools with anti-intellectualism and domination by the professional educator, but he gave greater emphasis to the idea that the schools were undemocratic. Bestor had complained that a differentiated curriculum was undemocratic because it did not allow schools to prepare students equally for participation in the world. For Smith, a differentiated curriculum worked against the functioning of a democratic society because it resulted in inequality of individual educational development.

The most widely heard of the critics in the 1950s was Vice Admiral Hyman G. Rickover, often called "the father of America's nuclear navy." He carried his message of the dismal failure of American schools to such meetings as the one held by the Society of Business Magazine Editors in 1956, the Westinghouse Science Talent Search Award Ceremony in 1957, the Engineering Society of Detroit in 1957, and the Harvard Club of New York in 1958, and finally into a best-selling book, *Education and Freedom*. Admiral Rickover's basic message asserted that the United States was losing the technological and military race with the Soviet Union because America's public schools were failing to identify and adequately educate talented youth as future scientists and engineers. In an interview conducted by news commentator Edward R. Murrow, Rickover stated that education "is even more important than atomic power in the navy, for if our people are not properly educated in accordance with the terrific requirements of this rapidly spiraling scientific and industrial civilization, we are bound to go down. The Russians apparently have recognized this." Like other critics of the time, Rickover blamed professional educators for creating an anti-intellectual atmosphere in the schools and claimed that the schools were the weakest link in America's overall defense strategy.[19]

These attacks on the public schools provided the background for the most significant educational legislation of the 1950s. Throughout the late 1940s and 1950s, educators had been seeking some form of federal legislation to help build schools and pay teacher salaries. Local schools were seriously pressed for space and for money to educate the increasing number of children born in the baby boom period after World War II. National political leaders failed to respond to these requests; they neither passed nor approved legislation for federal aid to local school districts.

Resistance to federal aid to education rapidly disappeared on October 4, 1957, when the Soviet Union launched *Sputnik I*. That the Soviet Union was the first in space indicated to many Americans that America was losing the technological and military race. Of course, the public schools were blamed for the lag in technological development, and voices were lifted to demand a greater stress on mathematics and science.

In 1958, responding to *Sputnik I* and public outcries about conditions in the schools, Congress passed the National Defense Education Act (NDEA). The very name of the legislation defined its intended goals. Before the legislation was passed and immediately after the launching of *Sputnik I*, President Dwight D. Eisenhower had outlined the relationship between education and Cold War strategy and set the stage for passage of the legislation.

In Oklahoma City on November 13, 1957, Eisenhower gave a speech pointing out that the Soviet Union had converted itself in only forty years from a nation of peasants to an industrial nation that had accomplished major technological achievements and established a rigorous educational system. He went on to warn, "When such competence in things material is at the service of leaders who have so little regard for things human, and who command the power of an empire, there is danger ahead for free men everywhere." Eisenhower argued that the United States must meet the Soviet threat on its own terms by outmatching the Soviet Union in military power, technological advancement, and specialized research and education. Essential to a program of national defense was increased military research, which would be directed toward the production of intercontinental ballistic missiles. Eisenhower tried to assure the nation that it was well on the way to developing adequate missile power. "Young people now in college," he emphasized, "must be equipped to live in the age of intercontinental ballistic missiles." Specifically, Eisenhower called for a system of nationwide testing of high school students and a system of incentives to persuade students with high ability to pursue scientific or professional studies. He urged a program to stimulate quality teaching in mathematics and science and fellowships to increase the number of teachers.[20]

On January 27, 1958, Eisenhower delivered a special message to Congress outlining his program of education for national defense. The first item on his list of recommendations was a fivefold increase in appropriations for the educational activities of the NSF. Second, he called for reducing the waste of national talent by providing grants to states for improved testing programs and guidance and counseling services. This recommendation eventually became Title V of the 1958 NDEA. Title V appropriated $15 million for each of four succeeding fiscal years for guidance, counseling, testing, and identification of able students. All these programs were considered essential for controlling and developing human resources for the Cold War.

Third, Eisenhower recommended federal funds to improve the teaching of science and mathematics through the hiring of additional science teachers and the purchase of equipment and materials. This became Title III of the NDEA, which appropriated $70 million for each of the next four fiscal years to be used for equipment and materials and for the expansion and improvement of supervisory services in the public schools in science, mathematics, and modern foreign languages. Eisenhower's fourth recommendation was for a graduate fellowship program to prepare more students for college teaching careers. This became Title IV of the NDEA and resulted in the National Defense Fellowship program.

The issue of foreign languages and their relationship to national security was the subject of Eisenhower's fifth recommendation. Eisenhower argued: "Knowledge of foreign languages is particularly important today in the light of America's responsibilities of leadership in the free world. And yet the

American people generally are deficient in foreign languages, particularly those of the emerging nations in Asia, Africa, and the Near East."[21] The foreign-language sections of the NDEA were clearly seen as provisions to strengthen America's competition with the Soviet Union for influence over the developing nations of the world.

The categorical nature of aid given under the NDEA reflected the government's negative feelings toward professional educators and its decision to take responsibility for establishing educational policies that would serve other national policies, such as defense. At the hearings on the NDEA, the head of the NEA defended the schools and requested that money be appropriated for general use by local schools. On the other hand, there was strong testimony from scientists and other officials against giving general aid to the public schools, given the fact that professional educators had the power to determine the use of the funds. These critics of the schools and educators wanted the federal government to specify the categories under which the money could be used; this was written into the NDEA.

As a consequence, the NDEA became a means by which the federal government could control local educational policy simply by offering money for the establishment of specified educational programs. Local educators did not have to accept the federal money, but few refused because financial conditions in most school districts made them eager for the funds.

Cold War concerns also got the federal government involved in developing new curricula, particularly in the areas of mathematics and science. Money flowing from the NSF was used to develop curriculum materials and to train teachers. The most dramatic development in this area was the "new mathematics," as it was called in the early 1960s. The new mathematics was based on the idea of teaching students basic mathematical concepts such as set theory and functions. When it swept the nation, many parents found themselves unable to understand or to help their children with the material.

In summary, a major effect of the Cold War on educational policies was to link the youth issue to selective service and to push the federal government into a leadership role in educational policies. Mounting criticism of the schools, which had begun during the Depression years, created a major split between professional educators and the public. This split widened in the 1960s, when the schools were accused of being racist. Another major consequence of the Cold War was an emphasis on the idea that schooling is the key to the development of human resources and the distribution of human resources in the labor market. This continued to be an important theme through the 1980s.

THE WAR ON POVERTY

The federal government's War on Poverty during the 1960s was reminiscent of the beliefs of nineteenth-century common school reformers that education could reduce social-class divisions and eliminate poverty. In some ways, President Lyndon Johnson can be considered a twentieth-century version of

Horace Mann. But the difference between nineteenth-century reformers and twentieth-century leaders is the latter's belief that the schools should develop and sort human resources. By the 1960s, it was commonly believed that discrimination and poverty were the two basic problems preventing the use of the schools as a means of discovering and classifying talent for service to the national economy and national defense. Within this framework, school integration and the elimination of poverty were necessary to ensure unbiased development and selection of human talent.

Congress's response to the issue of poverty was passage of the Economic Opportunity Act of 1964 (EOA) and the Elementary and Secondary Education Act of 1965 (ESEA). Two of the most important programs of EOA were the Job Corps and Head Start. Head Start was established to provide an opportunity for children of the poor to enter the social-sorting process of education on equal terms with children from more affluent backgrounds. The ESEA contained major provisions for improving educational programs for children from low-income families.

The War on Poverty encompassed three major areas of concern: unemployed and delinquent youth; disadvantaged students for whom education did not provide equality of opportunity; and the cycle, or circle, of poverty.

The concept of a circle of poverty gained popularity with the publication of Myrdal's *American Dilemma*. This 1940 study describes poverty among poor blacks as a set of interdependent causal factors. For instance, a poor education restricts employment opportunities, which causes a low standard of living and consequently leads to poor medical care, diet, housing, and education for the next generation. This model of poverty suggests that one can begin at any point in the set of causal relationships and move around the circle of poverty.

This model captured the imagination of the Kennedy administration in the early 1960s. A story was told that the idea for launching a massive federal program against unemployment and poverty came directly from President Kennedy in 1962, when he told Walter Heller, chairman of the Council of Economic Advisers, to gather all the statistics on poverty. At the time, Kennedy requested copies of Michael Harrington's recently published *The Other America: Poverty in the United States*. By 1963, President Kennedy had decided to launch a War on Poverty that would attack the very social structure that caused poverty.

Michael Harrington's book influenced the final report on poverty written by the Council of Economic Advisers and presented to Congress as the basic program for the EOA. Harrington believed that insulation of the poor from the rest of America is dividing the nation into two cultures. Within the circle of poverty, the poor get sick more often because of unhealthy living conditions in slums and inadequate nutrition. Inadequate medical care causes their illnesses to last longer, resulting in lost wages and work. Because of lost wages, the poor cannot afford adequate housing, education, and medical care. Harrington argues that there is a much richer way of describing this circle—as a *culture*. The vicious circle of poverty has created its own cultural patterns. Its family structure is different from that of the rest of society—it has more homes without fathers, early pregnancy, different attitudes toward sex, and less marriage. Millions of children of the poor, Harrington claims, do not know affection or stability. The culture of poverty is also defined by the actions of other institutions in society. For instance, there is a marked difference between how the police treat the poor and how they treat the middle class.

Of significance for modern times, Harrington argues, is the fact that the culture of poverty is beginning to perpetuate itself under the pressures of modern technology. As technology increases, so do educational requirements for occupations. As technological progress sweeps through the rest of society, the poor are increasingly left behind, and it becomes more difficult for them to move up in the social structure. Poverty is passed on from generation to generation because of the increasing difficulty for children of the poor to receive adequate education and job training. The price of more complex technology is the growing existence of a culture that cannot participate in its benefits.

An attack on the culture of poverty became a central focus of the Kennedy administration. In October 1963, Walter Heller began to draw together various plans for an invasion of the culture of poverty. Heller sent government agencies a memorandum requesting plans that would help to avoid entrapment in the culture of poverty and would provide a means of escape. In November 1963, while responses to the memorandum were being reviewed, President Kennedy was assassinated. Almost immediately, President Johnson announced his intention of supporting the program and directed Heller to complete his task. In January 1964, Heller's report was included in *The Annual Report of the Council of Economic Advisers* as "The Problem of Poverty in America."

The report strongly emphasized the role of education in uprooting the culture of poverty. Certainly, social scientists such as Myrdal and Harrington considered education to be a link in the circle of poverty, but the Heller report placed education into the central role in the battle strategy: "Equality of opportunity is the American dream, and universal education our noblest pledge to realize it. But, for the children of the poor, education is a handicap race; many are too ill motivated at home to learn at school." The report goes on to claim that poverty is directly linked to education: "The chief reason for low rates of pay is low productivity, which in turn can reflect lack of education or training, physical and mental disability, or poor motivation." This argument places the responsibility for low incomes directly on the shoulders of wage earners, not on the economic system. "The importance of education," the report continues, "as a factor in poverty is suggested by the fact that families headed by persons with no more than 8 years of education have an incidence rate of 37 percent."[22]

The Heller report underlines the importance of education in the War on Poverty when it claims "The severely handicapping influence of lack of education is clear. The incidence of poverty drops as educational attainments rise for nonwhites as well as white families at all ages." One section of the report, labeled "The Vicious Circle," begins with the straightforward statement "Poverty breeds poverty." The report defines the role of education in this circle: "It is difficult for children to find and follow avenues leading out of poverty in environments where education is deprecated and hope is smothered."

The major strategy the report advocates is the use of education to end poverty. It flatly states, "Universal education has been perhaps the greatest single force contributing both to social mobility and to general economic growth." In addition, the report argues, if the children of poor families were given skills and motivation, they would not grow up to be poor adults. The current problem, the report maintains, is that many young people are condemned to inadequate schools and instruction, and many school systems concentrate their efforts on children from higher-income groups. Effective education for children at the bottom of the economic ladder requires special methods and greater expenses: "The school must play a larger role in the development of poor youngsters if they are to have, in fact, 'equal opportunity.'" In language pointing toward the eventual plans for Head Start, the report continues, "This often means that schooling must start on a pre-school basis and include a broad range of more intensive services." In addition, the report urges the development of a Youth Conservation Corps, adult education programs, day care centers for working mothers, improved health programs, and increased assistance to the aged. In sum, the Heller report outlines a total package designed to uproot and destroy the environment and culture of poverty.

President Johnson accepted the argument that the problem of poverty in the 1960s was different from that of the Depression. He wrote about his meeting with Heller, "The most significant aspects of this new poverty, once the spotlight of attention was thrown on it, were the dismaying nature of its stubborn entrenchment and total entrapment of its victims from one generation to the next." Johnson announced plans for the War on Poverty in his State of the Union Message to Congress on January 8, 1964. He told Congress it was its responsibility to replace despair with opportunity and declared, "this administration today, here and now, declares unconditional war on poverty in America." He also told Congress and the American people that the chief weapons of the battle would be better schools, better health, better homes, and better training and job opportunities. This would be a battle to help Americans escape squalor, misery, and unemployment.[23]

The War on Poverty began with the signing of the EOA on August 20, 1964. Part A of Title I of the EOA established the Job Corps—a unique combination of approaches to the youth problem. First, it attacked unemployment among youth by providing urban and rural residential training centers. This program was modeled on the CCC of the 1930s, in which residents devoted their time to conserving and managing natural resources. Parts B and C of Title I provided programs for work training and work-study. In both programs, youths were to learn skills while working on a government project.

Head Start was developed under Title II of the legislation, which provided for community action programs. It was the first and probably the most popular of the national community action programs. The Economic Opportunity Act of 1964 made no specific mention of the education of younger children as a component of the War on Poverty. One reason for this is that the highly explosive issues of race and church-state relationships had in the past hindered the passage of federal education bills. A congressional amendment to establish a preschool program had been attached to the original EOA but was withdrawn when assurances were given that the Office of Economic Opportunity would support the program. In January 1965, President Johnson announced the decision to fund a preschool program named Head Start under the antipoverty program. In February, Sargent Shriver, head of the Office of Economic Opportunity, announced that the program would be launched during the summer of 1965. The response to the announcement was immediate and enthusiastic, and during the first summer 560,000 children entered the Head Start program.

The ESEA was signed by President Johnson on April 11, 1965, in the one-room schoolhouse near Stonewall, Texas, where his own education had begun. For the occasion, his first schoolteacher was flown in from retirement in California to stand at his side. The most important section of the ESEA was Title I, which provided funds for improved educational programs for children designated as educationally deprived. Title I specifically states: "The Congress hereby declares it to be the policy of the United States to provide financial assistance . . . to expand and improve . . . educational programs by various means . . . which contribute particularly to meeting the special educational needs of educationally deprived children."[24]

In essence, Title I was the major educational component of the War on Poverty. At the opening congressional hearings on the bill, Health, Education and Welfare Secretary Anthony J. Celebrezze and Commissioner of Education Francis Keppel provided the President's justification and rationale for special educational assistance to the educationally deprived. In his opening statement to the committee, Celebrezze quoted President Johnson's statement "Just as ignorance breeds poverty, poverty all too often breeds ignorance in the next generation." Celebrezze went on to claim, "The President's program . . . is designed to break this cycle which has been running on from generation to generation in this most affluent period of our history." He stated that a clear link exists between high educational and high economic attainment.[25]

Commissioner Keppel's statement also drew on the rhetoric and arguments that had come to characterize the government's approach to the problem of poverty. But in this case, as in the report of the Council of Economic Advisers, education was viewed as the major element to be attacked in the cycle of poverty. Keppel told the committee: "Archimedes . . . told us many centuries ago: 'Give me a lever long enough and a fulcrum strong enough and I can move the world.' Today, at last, we have a prospect of a lever long enough and supported strongly enough to do something for our children of poverty." The lever, of course, was education, and the fulcrum was federal financial assistance.[26]

Other sections of the legislation covered a variety of special purposes, which in many cases were included to ensure passage of Title I. Title II provided financial assistance for school library resources, textbooks, and other instructional materials. A primary reason for including Title II was to win support from private school interest, because they would be eligible for the aid. Furthermore, Keppel supported Title II during the Congressional hearings with statistics showing that the quality of the school library was strongly associated with student performance.

Title III provided funds for the establishment of supplementary educational centers to promote local educational innovations. Educators who helped President Johnson draft the legislation hoped this could be one method for stimulating creativity in local school systems. Title IV provided money for educational research and for the establishment of research and development centers. Title IV was included because the drafters of the legislation believed it would receive minimal legislative support if it were submitted as a separate bill. In a sense, the concept of research and development in education rode in on the coattails of Title I.

Funds for strengthening state departments of education were designated under Title V. The purpose of providing these funds was to allay fears about federal control of education. One of the interesting results of federal support of education under the ESEA was the increased power it gave to state departments of education in relation to local school districts.

In general, the ESEA followed in the tradition of federal involvement in education that had been evolving since World War II. The basic thread was planning for the use of human resources in the national economy. In the 1950s, under pressure from the technological and scientific race with the Soviet Union, emphasis had been placed on channeling talented youth into higher education. In the early 1960s, the emphasis shifted to providing equality of opportunity as a means of utilizing the poor as human resources. President Johnson, who had chaired the Senate hearings on selective service in the early 1950s, clearly reiterated this in his message to Congress that accompanied the proposals for the ESEA: "Nothing matters more to the future of our country; not our military preparedness, for armed might is worthless if we lack the brainpower to build a world of peace; not our productive economy, for we cannot sustain growth without trained manpower."[27]

However, unlike the human resource policies of the 1950s, the approach of the 1960s was essentially to wage war on a culture. Within the theoretical framework of the War on Poverty, the social and economic system that had created poverty and allowed it to continue was not considered the problem; the problem was the culture of the poor. Indeed, the overall strategy was to integrate the poor into the existing social and economic system. Very simply, this can be called *blaming the victim*—placing the full responsibility for poverty on the shoulders of the poor. They—not the economic system that had produced poverty—were expected to change.

The ESEA can be considered a conservative approach to the problem of poverty because it did not propose any dramatic changes in the economic system. The same conservatism was evident in the issue of social-class differences. The approach of the War on Poverty was that no basic conflict exists among the interests of the different social classes. Within the context of the War on Poverty, the economic interest of the poor was to enter the middle class, not to change the economic and social system, and the interest of the middle class was not to repress the poor, but to solve such problems as crime, delinquency, and unemployment by bringing the poor into the mainstream of society. Education plays a major role in this particular analysis of social-class differences because it would supposedly provide the bridge for the poor to enter the opportunity structure of society. In the rhetoric of the War on Poverty, education was considered the hope of the poor and the method of the middle class.

CONCLUSION

The expanded role of the federal government in education during the 1950s and 1960s ensured that educational policy would be directly related to other national policies. Within the span of only two decades, educational policy had shifted from winning the scientific and technological war with the Soviet Union to winning the War on Poverty. One result of increased federal involvement was that education became an important factor in national politics. After the 1960s, presidential candidates began to address educational issues and define an educational constituency.

Federal protection of the rights of minority groups placed the federal government in the position of policing educational institutions. This was a necessary correction to the past discriminatory actions of local elites, school boards, and school administrators, but it increased the complexity of the distribution of power over the schools. The political structure of education that emerged in the 1980s pitted special-interest groups, politicians, business organizations, teachers' unions, and school administrators against one another. As in the nineteenth century, each pressure group viewed public schooling as the answer to social, political, and economic problems.

NOTES

1. Joel Spring, *The Sorting Machine: National Educational Policy since 1945* (New York: McKay, 1976).
2. Diane Ravitch, *The Troubled Crusade: American Education, 1945–1980* (New York: Basic Books, 1983).
3. Spring, *Sorting Machine*, p. 266.

4. Ravitch, *Troubled Crusade*, p. 330. A more extensive discussion of the differences in interpretation is provided in Joel Spring, *The Sorting Machine Revisited: National Educational Policy since 1945* (White Plains, N.Y.: Longman, 1988), pp. 177–185.
5. President's Advisory Commission on Universal Training, "Staff Study: Universal Military Training in the United States: A Brief Historical Summary" in *A Program for National Security: Report of the President's Advisory Commission on Universal Training* (Washington, D.C.: U.S. Government Printing Office, 1947), pp. 401–406.
6. Vannevar Bush, *Science—The Endless Frontier: A Report to the President* (Washington, D.C.: U.S. Government Printing Office, 1945).
7. U.S. Congress, Senate Committee on Armed Services, *Universal Military Training and Service Act of 1951—Hearings before the Preparedness Subcommittee of the Committee on Armed Services*, 82d Cong., 1st Sess., January 10–February 2, 1951 (Washington, D.C.: U.S. Government Printing Office, 1951), pp. 1082–1083.
8. U.S. Congress, Senate Committee on Interstate and Foreign Commerce, *Hearings before the Committee on Interstate and Foreign Commerce*, 80th Cong., 1st Sess., March 6–7, 1947 (Washington, D.C.: U.S. Government Printing Office, 1947), p. 147.
9. Ibid., pp. 155–157.
10. Richard Barnes Kennan, "No Ivory Tower for You," *NEA Journal*, Vol. 40 (May 1951), pp. 317–318.
11. Quoted in David Hulburd, *This Happened in Pasadena* (New York: Macmillan, 1951), pp. 90–91.
12. Quoted in Jack Nelson and Gene Roberts, Jr., *The Censors and the Schools* (Boston: Little, Brown, 1963), pp. 40–53.
13. Quoted in Franklin R. Zeran, "Life Adjustment in Action, 1944–1952" in Franklin R. Zeran, ed., *Life Adjustment Education in Action* (New York: Chartwell House, 1953), p. 86.
14. Arthur Bestor, *Educational Wastelands* (Urbana: University of Illinois Press, 1953), p. 86.
15. Ibid., pp. 36–38.
16. Ibid.
17. Ibid.
18. Ibid.
19. Quoted by Edward R. Murrow in the Foreword to Hyman G. Rickover, *Education and Freedom* (New York: Dutton, 1959), pp. 5–7.
20. Dwight D. Eisenhower, "Our Future Security" in U.S. Congress, Senate Committee on Labor and Public Welfare, *Science and Education for National Defense: Hearings before the Committee on Labor and Public Welfare*, 85th Cong., 2nd Sess., 1958 (Washington, D.C.: U.S. Government Printing Office, 1958), pp. 1357–1359.
21. Dwight D. Eisenhower, "Message from the President of the United States Transmitting Recommendations Relative to Our Educational System" in

Senate Committee on Labor and Public Welfare, *Science and Education for National Defense*, pp. 239–262.

22. "The Problem of Poverty in America" in *The Annual Report of the Council of Economic Advisors* (Washington, D.C.: U.S. Government Printing Office, 1964).

23. Lyndon B. Johnson, "The State of the Union Message to Congress, 8 January 1964" in *A Time for Action: A Selection from the Speeches and Writings of Lyndon B. Johnson* (New York: Atheneum, 1964), pp. 164–179.

24. "Elementary and Secondary Education Act of 1965, Public Law 89-10," reprinted in Stephen Bailey and Edith Mosher, *ESEA: The Office of Education Administers a Law* (Syracuse, N.Y.: Syracuse University Press, 1968), pp. 235–266.

25. U.S. Congress, House Committee on Education and Labor, *Aid to Elementary and Secondary Education: Hearings before the General Subcommittee on Education of the Committee on Education and Labor*, 89th Cong., 1st Sess., 1965 (Washington, D.C.: U.S. Government Printing Office, 1965), pp. 63–82.

26. Ibid., pp. 82–113.

27. Ibid., p. 63.

The Conservative Reaction and the Politics of Education

The conservative political and educational patterns of the 1970s emerged in reaction to the student protest and civil rights demonstrations of the 1960s and the policies of the War on Poverty. Ironically, the result of the continuing struggles of women, the handicapped, and minority groups for increased equality of educational opportunity was that these groups made most of their gains during the 1970s and 1980s, against a background of conservative political reaction.

Conservative educational policies were set into motion by student demonstrations that erupted on college and high school campuses in the late 1960s. The demonstrations were triggered mainly in reaction to the Vietnam War because the selective service system threatened most young men eligible for the draft. As the demonstrations escalated, they began to call into question many of the institutions and values of American life. Demands were made for greater freedom of expression and more equality in the distribution of wealth. Universities and public schools were attacked as institutions of oppression and racism. Alternative schools began to appear in both the private and the public educational systems.

The irony of the demonstrations is that the participants were mainly college students who were part of the large concentration of youths attending college on deferments from the selective service system. For national leaders, the demonstrations indicated failures in both the use of the selective service system to control human resources and the idea that simply sending youth to college would improve the national economy.

In 1968 Richard Nixon was elected President on a ticket promising to solve the problem of the Vietnam War and restore law and order to American campuses. Nixon's policies ran counter to the more liberal policies of the Kennedy and Johnson administrations. His administration questioned the value of the War on Poverty educational legislation in providing equality of opportunity for the poor, the use of selective service to control human resources, and the use of busing for desegregation. Nixon favored educational programs designed to prepare students for specific careers, a return to basic education, replacement of selective service with volunteer armed forces, and an expansion of vocational education.

Within the educational establishment, a period of conservative reaction began. The role and power of professional educators had been strongly criticized during the 1950s and in the demonstrations of the late 1950s and early 1960s, and now demands were made for greater public control of the educational system. One reaction by professional educators was to call for their own accountability to the public through the reporting of test scores. The accountability movement gave more power to professional educators.

Within the schools, educators began to rely heavily on teaching by specific behavior objectives and on using standardized methods of instruction. In other words, the tradition of behaviorism initiated in the early twentieth century by Edward Thorndike came to dominate the schools of the 1970s and 1980s. The tradition of behaviorism fit neatly into the accountability movement.

As a result of the accountability movement, by the 1990s the educational system was dominated by standardized testing. Students were given standardized tests annually. Often, principals were judged on the basis of how well their students performed on the tests. In turn, they placed pressure on teachers to teach to the tests. The mania for testing increased in the 1980s with state governments adopting policies requiring statewide testing of public school students. The frenzy over testing gripped teacher education as states imposed requirements that applicants for teaching licenses take a state or national teacher examination.

The fanatical pursuit of excellence through testing became a central plant in the conservative agenda. Without any proof that testing actually improved the quality of education, the Bush administration in the late 1980s and early 1990s made the creation of national achievement tests and national standards for curriculum a major feature of its educational agenda.

As the conservative reaction took place in the schools, a new style of educational politics emerged. As a result of the increased role of the federal government in education, education was given greater emphasis in national politics. One important cause of this change was the transformation in the 1960s of the NEA into a union primarily concerned with the wages and working conditions of teachers. In the late 1970s, the NEA began to play a major role in national politics and, along with its rival, the AFT, began to influence national elections.

In the 1980s and 1990s, a new wave of criticism accused the schools of causing an imbalance in international trade because of their low academic standards. The educational policies of the Reagan and Bush administrations in the 1980s and 1990s were focused on the role of schools in helping the United States compete in international trade. As in the movement for vocational education in the early twentieth century, a new cry was raised for high educational standards as a means of graduating students capable of improving American technology and thus winning the international trade war with West Germany and Japan. In addition, these critics felt that a closer relationship should exist between schooling and the needs of the labor market. This movement continued the dominant pattern in twentieth-century education—the use of schools to channel and improve human resources.

THE NIXON ADMINISTRATION
AND THE CONSERVATIVE REACTION

The years of the Nixon administration were a time of conservative reaction to student demonstrations and the demands of the civil rights movement. The conservative reaction included a retreat from the programs of the War on Poverty, the development of career education, a renewed emphasis on the power of the educational expert, the spread of the concept of accountability in education, increased emphasis on testing, and the use of behavioral psychology in the classroom. President Richard Nixon was elected in 1968 in the midst of national turmoil caused by the demonstrations against the war in Vietnam and widespread urban riots. Promises of maintaining law and order were an important part of Nixon's presidential campaigns in 1968 and 1972.

Student demonstrations, the civil rights movement, and urban riots convinced many Americans in the 1960s that the United States was on the verge of radical social change. Given this point of view, it was logical for national leaders to seek some means of restoring a sense of authority to society and the educational system.

The first major student demonstration took place at the University of California at Berkeley in 1964, when the chancellor announced that students would not be able to use an area in front of the entrance to the university for political activities. The students formed the Free Speech Movement and conducted a sit-in at one of the campus buildings.

The target of many students in the Free Speech Movement was university president Clark Kerr, who in articulating the modern role of higher education had likened universities to service stations providing help to business, government, and other private organizations. Many students objected to the role of universities in giving aid to the military and implementing American foreign policy. In addition, modern universities had grown to tremendous proportions compared with those in the earlier part of the century. As a result, Kerr and other administrators in higher education became targets of student demonstrators. The administrators were charged with using the university to aid in the war effort and with impersonal treatment of students.

The student demonstrations quickly spread from Berkeley to other campuses. In 1965, the first teach-in against the war was held at the University of Michigan. At other campuses, protesters blocked employment recruiting by Dow Chemical Corporation, a major producer of military chemicals for the

government. In 1968, the assassination of Dr. Martin Luther King, Jr., added more fuel to campus protests and sparked major urban riots. Campus protests continued after President Nixon's election and reached a high point in 1970 when Ohio National Guardsmen killed four students at Kent State University.

In the midst of these student demonstrations and urban riots, Nixon launched his campaign to restore law and order to American society. Part of Nixon's educational policy centered around the development of career education. In 1971 and 1972, Sidney Marland, Jr., Nixon's commissioner of education, began to earmark discretionary funds provided by Congress to the Office of Education for the development of career education projects. Marland's method of using discretionary funds turned career education into a reform movement originating at the top of the political structure of education. By 1972–1973, Marland was able to announce that in the first year of this program, 750,000 young people had participated.

Marland believed that career education was the answer to student rebellion, delinquency, and unemployment. In his first annual report to Congress, in 1971, he argued that disenchantment among youth existed because education did not lead to career opportunities. For Marland, the villain was general education programs that lacked specific goals and were not linked to the job market. Marland argued that education should be meaningful; by *meaningful,* he meant "related to a career objective." He stated, "When we use the word 'meaningful,' we imply a strong obligation that our young people complete the first 12 grades in such a fashion that they are ready either to enter into some form of higher education or to proceed immediately into satisfying and appropriate employment." This, of course, was a restatement of the traditional goal of the comprehensive high school, but he considered its primary weakness to be its general education programs, which were not directly related to entry into either the job market or higher education. "The emergence of the comprehensive high school, properly defined and implemented, carries the ultimate solution."[1]

Therefore, Marland believed, students and schools were in a state of turmoil because the school had never completely achieved the goal of sorting students for the labor market. In his first report to Congress, he stated, "We must eliminate anything in our curriculum that is unresponsive to either of these goals [higher education and employment], particularly the high school anachronism called 'the general curriculum,' a false compromise between college preparatory curriculum and realistic career development."[2] For Marland, all elements of school life needed to be justified by their contribution to career development. In the words of Marland's associate commissioner, "The fundamental conception of career education is that all educational experiences, curriculum, instruction, and counseling should be geared to preparing each individual for a life of economic independence, personal fulfillment, and an appreciation for the dignity of work."[3] This meant a complete alignment between the job market and the public schools. Marland believed career education offered one solution "to some of our more serious social and

economic problems, including high unemployment and the attendant problems of disaffection and drug excess among the young."[4]

Career education was unique in its attempt to make vocational guidance a part of the academic program of the school and to begin the program in the early grades. During the elementary and junior high school years, career education was to acquaint students with the world of work and the varieties of occupations by relating them to the subject matter of the curriculum. After study and preparation for an occupational choice in these early grades, the high school student was to begin preparing for entry into either an occupation or higher education. Advocates of career education also believed that higher education should be organized around this model. The real hope for higher education, Marland believed, was the community college. He argued that the community college should not be viewed as merely a "large anteroom for the four-year institutions"[5] but as a unique institution of higher learning whose developing philosophy was based on the concept of career education. Close ties with local businesses made it possible for the community college to gear its programs to the needs of the labor market.

At the same time that career education was becoming a major program of the Nixon administration, between 1970 and 1973, Nixon vetoed three of six appropriation bills for the Department of Health, Education and Welfare and pocket vetoed the 1973 appropriation bill. Nixon justified the vetoes as necessary to reduce the federal budget and on the grounds of lack of evidence that federal money for compensatory education programs resulted in any significant social change.

The individual in the Nixon administration responsible for formulating the argument that money spent on schooling had little effect on social change was White House counselor and Nixon confidant Daniel Patrick Moynihan. Moynihan believed that social change for the poor could be accomplished only through a national policy of economic support for the family. This idea was incorporated into a Nixon plan to provide a guaranteed family income that supposedly would break the cycle of poverty by stabilizing the family unit.

Moynihan was strongly influenced by the Coleman Report's findings on the social impact of education. This report was written to fulfill the requirements of Title IV of the 1964 Civil Rights Act, which gave the commissioner of education the responsibility for surveying the availability of equality of educational opportunity in the United States. The commissioner selected James Coleman of Johns Hopkins University to assume major responsibility for the design, administration, and analysis of a survey about the extent of equality of educational opportunity in the public schools.

Regarding the basic issue of school segregation, the Coleman Report found that almost "80 percent of all white pupils in the 1st grade and 12th grade" attended schools that were from "90 to 100 percent white." Sixty-five percent of black students in the first grade attended schools with student populations that were between 90 and 100 percent black. This meant that the majority of children in the United States attended segregated schools and that white children were the most segregated.[6]

In addition, the Coleman Report correlates differences in resources with student achievement. For purposes of the report, student achievement was determined by achievement tests. The report assumes that achievement tests measure "the skills which are among the most important in our society for getting a good job and moving up to a better one, and for full participation in an increasingly technical world." It found that, except for Asian Americans, all other minority groups scored significantly lower than whites and that the differences increased from the first through the twelfth grades: "For most minority groups . . . schools provide little opportunity for them to overcome . . . initial deficiency; in fact they fall farther behind the white majority in the development of several skills which are critical to making a living and participating fully in modern society."[7]

The report did demonstrate the possible benefits of integration. Differences were found in the effect of school resources on white and minority students. The achievement of white students seemed to be less affected by the strengths or weaknesses of curricula and school facilities, whereas these did seem to have some effect on the achievement of minority students. Student achievement was strongly related "to the educational backgrounds and aspirations of the other students in school." The Coleman Report concludes that if a white pupil from a family strongly supportive of education was put into a school with pupils who did not come from that type of background, the pupil's achievement would "be little different than if he were in a school composed of others like himself." On the other hand, if "a minority pupil from a home without much educational strength is put with schoolmates with strong educational backgrounds, his achievement is likely to increase." This conclusion provided support for integration.

In general, except for its finding on integration, the Coleman Report provides a pessimistic outlook on the ability of the schools to overcome poverty and solve social problems. In 1966 Moynihan and Frederick Mosteller conducted a faculty seminar at Harvard University on the findings of the Coleman Report. One aspect of the report that impressed Moynihan was its contradiction of what he called "conventional wisdom." The report seemed to show that things people assumed were important in improving achievement in the schools in fact had little relationship to achievement. This supposed contradiction of conventional wisdom provided Moynihan with the ammunition to attack social scientists as a group as well as federal education programs.[8]

In 1967, in a paper titled "On the Education of the Urban Poor," Moynihan accused social scientists of attempting to shape public opinion according to personal rather than objective findings. He argued that social scientists were committed to social change and tended to be at odds with people having wealth and political power. Social scientists, according to Moynihan, tended to be liberal or radical, which resulted in an assumption by poor and minority groups in America that social scientists would always be on their side.[9]

In 1970 Moynihan called for increased spending for educational research but not for educational programs. Part of his argument was that government

educational policies needed to be validated by research before being implemented. Writing in *The New York Times* in 1972, he gave support for recent
legislation for a National Institute of Education (NIE). The NIE was designed
to conduct basic research in education. Moynihan believed that the research
findings of the NIE would provide the basic facts for the future development
of educational legislation. According to Moynihan, past educational programs had failed because basic research had not been conducted before their
implementation. The NIE had been proposed to Congress in 1970 by President Nixon with the objective, as stated by Moynihan, "to bring 'big' science
to bear on education, especially the problem of low achievement among
students from low-income families."[10]

Moynihan provided the rationalization for the educational retreat of the
Nixon administration. "I for one would be willing to bet that the more we
learn about formal schooling the less we will come to value it." He even
suggested that research findings would show the need for a greater stress on
the placement of the school graduate in the job market: "Rather than spending more money on early education, for example, we are likely to conclude
that the transition we manage least well in our society is that of the young
person leaving the world of school for the world of work, and that accor-
dingly much more resources have to be applied to this period in individual
development rather than the much earlier one."[11]

One significant aspect of Moynihan's statement is that it represented an
abandonment of the attempt to make the system of social selection in the
schools operate fairly by providing equality of opportunity. Moynihan's attitude was essentially that educational research proved that nothing could be
done in the schools to increase achievement among the lower class and,
therefore, that such efforts were not worth the spending of federal dollars.

The reduction of spending for federal educational programs and the
establishment of the NIE represented an important shift in the relationship
between the educational establishment and the federal government. More
money for research and less money for the schools resulted in the funding of
college professors and research units in local school systems rather than
teachers and administrators of specific educational programs. The real shift
that occurred was away from providing financial support of education for the
poor to providing financial support for white-collar research workers. Thus,
the consequence of the great retreat of the Nixon administration was that, in
the tradition of administrative progressives, funding was given to educational
experts, and direct concern with the lives of the poor was diminished.

ACCOUNTABILITY AND THE INCREASING POWER
OF THE STANDARDIZED TEST

As government funding shifted from the clients to the experts, the rise of the
accountability movement attempted to restore power to the professional
educator. In part, the accountability movement was a reaction to attempts to

achieve community control of the schools. Community control received its first public attention when instituted in 1966 at Intermediate School 201 in Harlem and in 1968 in the Ocean Hill–Brownsville section of Brooklyn, both in New York City.

The concept of community control emerged from attempts to end racism and discrimination in the schools. In many ways, it was an attempt to capture the nineteenth-century ideal of democratic localism, according to which the schools were to reflect the values and desires of their users. Minority groups felt that racism existed in the schools because the community served by the schools had little power over the hiring of teachers, the spending of money, and the organization of the curriculum. Those in the community control movement believed that these decisions were made by a combination of elite school boards, educational administrators, and teachers' unions. Leaders of the movement felt that decisions made by these groups resulted in racists teaching in schools serving minority communities and in the use of a curriculum that reflected discriminatory attitudes.

The community control movement simply wanted to restore complete control of the schools to members of the local community. Of course, this proposal threatened the power of professional educators, school boards, and teachers' unions. In fact, the first major reaction to community control came from the teachers' union, when the local community in Ocean Hill–Brownsville dismissed a number of teachers for racist attitudes. The resulting reaction from the teachers' union, which viewed the actions of the community as a direct threat to the power of the union, ended the community control movement in New York City.

The accountability movement was an attempt to restore power to professional educators, who had been threatened by the community control movement and the public criticism of schools in the 1950s. Like the administrative progressives in the early twentieth century who argued for control by experts, the proponents of accountability considered education an arena for professional decision making.

Control by experts is an important theme of the book that sparked the accountability movement. Leon Lessinger's *Every Kid a Winner: Accountability in Education* considers the community control movement a threat to the quality of education.[12] Lessinger uses the model of the hospital to attack the concept of democratic control. He argues that in a hospital, patients and the community in general do not and should not participate directly in decisions regarding medical treatment or surgery because these are areas of decision making that require expert knowledge and training. For Lessinger, the idea of democratic control in surgery is ludicrous and dangerous to the patient. In his opinion, users of medical services have the right to complain, but decisions about how to deal with the complaint should remain in the hands of medical experts.

Lessinger feels that the same model is applicable to education. Modern schooling, he maintains, is based on professional knowledge gained through research and study. The average member of the community does not have the training necessary to make correct educational decisions. Like the hospital clientele, the community has the right to complain but does not have the right or the knowledge to make decisions regarding the resolution of complaints. Only the educational expert should be entrusted with decision-making power.

Even with his reliance on experts, Lessinger recognizes that in a democratic society the schools must be responsive to the public. He feels this responsiveness can be achieved by the schools reporting their accomplishments and failures to the public. This public accounting of the results of schooling was the heart of the accountability movement. Lessinger envisions the creation of a national educational accounting firm operated by educational engineers who will measure educational results by the use of achievement tests and report the results to the public. He assumes that these results will provide the public with expert data that can be used to express approval or criticism of the accomplishments of the school system.

As the accountability movement spread in the early 1970s, states and local communities began to require schools to publish achievement test scores annually. The use of test scores to measure the schools' success kept power in the hands of educational experts. In the schools, students found themselves taking an increasing number of achievement tests in order to satisfy the requirements of accountability. One result was that testing, or measurement, was restored to a central place in the educational process. Accompanying this rebirth of interest in standardized testing was an increasing emphasis on behaviorism and on teaching by specific behavioral objectives.

The accountability movement's emphasis on testing and instruction according to specific behavioral objectives fit the pattern of traditional approaches to classroom instruction. At the same time that these practices for reform of American schools were being advocated, a more progressive approach to classroom organization called the *open classroom* was being advocated. The differences between these two approaches to instruction highlight the continuing debate about instruction. In addition, as I will discuss later in this chapter, the creation of standardized achievement tests began a central feature on national educational policy in the early 1990s.

THE POLITICAL NATURE OF CLASSROOM INSTRUCTION

In Chapter 8, I discussed the differences in student-centered and teacher-centered classrooms as exemplified by the theories of John Dewey and Edward Thorndike. The tension between these two concepts of classroom instruction persisted through the twentieth century. Also, as I explained in Chapter 14, during the Cold War years of the late 1940s and early 1950s the progressive educational theories associated with John Dewey came under attack by conservatives and anticommunists. This attack helped to align political beliefs with theories of classroom management.

In general, conservatives tended to reject student-centered instruction in favor of traditional teacher-centered classrooms. Political conservatives in the 1950s believed that instruction based on the interests and choices of children undermined the intellectual content of schooling. In fact, conservatives charged progressive education with causing a decline in the quality of American schools. This argument continued into the 1960s and 1970s, when conservatives attacked student demands for choice in the classroom and curriculum. Excellence, standards, discipline, homework, and evaluation in the classroom became the typical concerns of political conservatives.

Liberals, on the other hand, tended to argue that classroom instruction should be geared to student needs and interests. They argued, as John Dewey had, that rigid classroom procedures primarily educated people to take orders and to be passive participants in a democratic society. They tended to reject excellence in favor of equality of educational opportunity. Those who advocated excellence most often wanted student performance to be measured by absolute standards. On the other hand, liberals tended to want students to be judged according to their own abilities and interests. Sometimes differences between the two groups were reflected in attitudes about report cards. Conservatives tended to want report cards to be based on absolute standards such as letter grades,[13] whereas liberals tended to want report cards to be a statement of progress of the individual student.

Of course, these political divisions cannot be rigidly applied because many people have a mixture of political beliefs. The differences in beliefs about the operation of classrooms were highlighted in the late 1960s and early 1970s by the development of open classrooms and the influence of the behaviorist theories of psychologist B. F. Skinner. Based on the idea that the classroom should be organized around the development and interests of the children, the open classroom operated in the tradition of John Dewey's progressivism. On the other hand, Skinner's theories were part of the tradition of Edward Thorndike, which emphasized managing the learning of children through the use of rewards. It was Skinner's theories that provided support for what Ira Shor has called the conservative restoration of the 1970s.[14]

In the early twentieth century, behaviorism received support from the theories of educational psychology advocated by William James and Edward Thorndike. The behaviorist model is extremely mechanistic—a concept of teaching based on the use of measurement (testing) to determine deficiencies and accomplishments and the use of reinforcement to teach specific objectives. This concept of teaching fit nicely into the technocratic worldview held by administrative progressives in the early part of the century.

Beginning in the 1940s, the behaviorist trend in education received an added boost from the work of B. F. Skinner. Skinner tried to apply behaviorism to the work of the school by developing programmed learning machines and writing about the relationship of behaviorism to the structure and functioning of society. The best introduction to Skinner's philosophy is his utopian novel, written in the 1940s, with the controversial title *Walden Two*.[15] The title was controversial because many readers could find little resemblance between the society described by Skinner and the Walden described in the original work by Henry David Thoreau. In Skinner's novel, Walden Two is a scientifically managed society organized around the principles of behavioral engineering. Skinner considered democratic control of his utopian society self-defeating, because behavioral engineering requires control by expert managers. The managers were to pay attention to community desires by measuring the degree of happiness and determining what things needed to be changed or improved to increase the happiness of the residents. In one sense, this novel depicts a society in which democracy is replaced by a public survey like the Gallup poll.

Control by experts and behavioral engineering of a society do not contradict Skinner's concept of freedom. He believed that if a science of behavior could exist and the laws of behavior could be discovered, traditional ideas regarding freedom would need to be changed. If laws of behavior that can predict human action exist, free will does not exist, and without free will, individual actions become the product of past actions and the influence of the environment. Within this framework, behavior is determined by reinforcements received from other individuals or social conditions, which means that individual behavior can be scientifically controlled and the individual does not have the ability to break out of that control.

Skinner changed the meaning of freedom to fit his concept of behavioral control. For Skinner, freedom exists when individuals are not restricted from doing those things they have been conditioned to do. Thus, freedom is a feeling achieved when one is able to act out behavior that has been determined by previous reinforcement. As a concept of society and the individual, behaviorism places the expert in charge of a society that is scientifically engineered. In this engineered society, behavioral control is exerted over citizens, who exist in a state of planned happiness.

In the 1950s Skinner joined the chorus of criticism of the public schools. From his perspective, a major problem with schools was that teachers did not use the scientific findings of behavioral psychology. His answer to this situation was the teaching machine or program. Based on the principles of behaviorism, teaching machines were to instruct by presenting students with small units of knowledge and providing constant reinforcement. By the late 1970s and 1980s, the original principles underlying the teaching machine were incorporated into many educational software programs for the microcomputer.

In the 1970s, the principles of behavioral psychology fit nicely into the use of increased measurement of students that was a result of the accountability movement. Philosophically, behaviorism was compatible with the conservative trends of the Nixon years. Like accountability, behaviorism rejects concepts of democratic control; like career education, with its emphasis on control, behaviorism was considered an antidote to the type of freedom expressed in student demonstrations. Behaviorism combined with accountability supported the competency-based education movement of the 1970s.

Competency-based education simply means teaching the student specific competencies and measuring the achievement of that learning before proceeding to new competencies. Like other forms of behaviorism, competency-based education uses a mechanistic model of learning and attempts to exert direct control over student behavior.

In contrast to the behaviorally managed classroom, the open classroom, or, as it was sometimes called, the *informal classroom,* emphasized active learning and student choice. A major source of the ideas associated with the open classroom was the primary school in England. In the United States the idea received popular attention with the publication in 1970 of Charles Silberman's *Crisis in the Classroom,* which, after criticizing the conditions in American classrooms, held up the open classroom as a panacea.[16]

The open classroom provided for individual instruction and choice through the establishment of learning stations in spaces larger than the traditional classroom. Ideally, students were to move from learning station to learning station according to their individual desires and learning rate. Each learning station had activities related to a particular area of learning. For instance, one learning station might be devoted to reading while another might focus on science. A characteristic of the open classroom was large informal open spaces without the traditional rows of desks.

A theoretical underpinning of the open classroom was provided by the psychological theories of Jean Piaget. Piaget worked within the tradition of Jean-Jacques Rousseau (discussed in Chapter 2). Like Rousseau, Piaget argued that instruction should match the child's stage of development. Piaget worked out an elaborate analysis of how each stage of cognitive development determined the ability of the child to understand different concepts. An important part of this theory was a stress on active learning and the child's developmental characteristics. Piaget's theories provided support for advocates of the open classroom. His emphases on relating instruction to development and on the importance of activity seemed to support the notions of individualized learning and movement between learning stations that were characteristic of the open classroom.[17]

During the early 1970s, the idea of the open classroom spread to many communities. Elementary and middle schools were built with large open spaces to accommodate this new form of classroom organization, but by the end of the 1970s, the concept was losing popularity and many of the open spaces built specifically for this type of instruction were being divided into traditional classrooms.

In *How Teachers Taught: Constancy and Change in American Classrooms 1890–1980,* Larry Cuban searched for the reasons for the demise of the open classroom idea. In 1981 he visited schools in North Dakota where the idea had had a major influence on school architecture. What he found were teachers who were pleased at the idea that central administrators had decided to construct walls to divide recently constructed open classrooms into smaller, traditional classrooms. From his study of North Dakota and other states and cities, he concluded that only a minority of teachers gave support to the open classroom concept. The majority of teachers continued to use traditional teacher-centered methods.[18]

Why wasn't the open classroom widely adopted? Cuban argues that in general, student-centered instruction has failed to have a major impact in American public schools because of the conservative nature of teacher culture, the structure of schools, and the fact that schools are primarily interested, in his words, in "social control and sorting." For example, instruction based on student interest is contrary to the idea that education should serve economic and political purposes. Cuban's argument highlights the political nature of classroom instruction.[19]

THE POLITICS OF EDUCATION

Conflict is the best word to describe the politics of education in the 1980s. The educational establishment was divided into differing groups. Teachers' unions were more militant and actively engaged in national politics. Many college professors of education and members of large central city educational bureaucracies lobbied for more federal funds for research. Other segments of the educational establishment wanted a greater emphasis on funding for compensatory education programs. School administrators started to unionize and could often be found bargaining with representatives from teachers' unions. A variety of public interest groups organized to put pressure on the school establishment and to seek aid from the courts and other parts of government. Court decisions were increasingly affecting the operation of schooling and were considered an important component of the political structure of education. Business elites continued to try to use the schools to further their own self-interest by working with state governments.

Certainly, the most important changes in the politics of education after World War II were the transformation of the NEA from an organization dominated by school administrators into a militant teachers' union and the use of strikes and collective bargaining by both the NEA and the AFT. The change in the NEA took place in 1962, when the organization launched a program for collective negotiations. This meant that local affiliates were to try to establish collective-bargaining agreements with local school systems. The result was a dramatic shift in the role of local NEA affiliates and a rewriting of local constitutions. Up to this time, many NEA locals, known in the organization as education associations, had been controlled by local administrators. Collective bargaining reversed this situation and turned the local affiliates into organizations that told boards and administrators what teachers themselves wanted.

A major factor in the growing militancy of the NEA was the success of the AFT in conducting strikes and gaining collective-bargaining agreements. Originally, neither organization supported the idea of teachers striking. In 1944, when the AFT local in Cicero, Illinois, signed the first collective-bargaining agreement between a school board and a teachers' organization, the national AFT maintained a no-strike policy. The national organization maintained the same policy in 1947 when the Buffalo teachers' union went on strike against the local school system. Other local unions joined in the support of this strike, which became a model for teachers around the country.

The major break in the no-strike policy came in 1960 when the New York affiliate of the AFT, the United Federation of Teachers (UFT), voted to strike over the issues of a dues check-off plan, the conducting of a collective-bargaining election, sick pay for substitutes, fifty-minute lunch periods for teachers, and changes in salary schedules. On November 7, 1960, the UFT officially struck against the New York City school system. The union declared the strike effective when 15,000 of the city's 39,000 teachers did not report to school, and 7,500 teachers joined picket lines around the schools. In the spring of 1961, the UFT won a collective-bargaining agreement with the school system and became one of the largest and most influential locals within the AFT.

The New York City strike acted as a catalyst for more teachers to join the union and to increase the level of militancy. In 1966 the membership of the AFT was 125,421; by 1981 it had more than quadrupled, to 580,000. This increased membership plus the increased militancy of the NEA heralded a new era in the relationship between teachers' organizations and the managers of American education.

As teachers' militancy increased during the 1970s, a major movement developed in the ranks of teachers for more power over educational policy. In part, this was a response to the troubled financial state of many school districts in the 1970s, which made it difficult for teachers to demand salary increases. The teacher power movement, as it came to be known, sought to have collective bargaining decide issues concerning classroom size, the counseling of new teachers, the establishment of teacher-controlled committees to approve policies of boards of education, and the formation of building committees to curb and challenge the power of principals.

The teacher power movement of the 1970s was reminiscent of the concerns of teachers in the early twentieth century, when reforms introduced by administrative progressives had left teachers feeling they were merely pawns in the educational plans of school administrators. The rebellions of teachers in the early part of the century were not successful against this threat to their power and status. Almost seventy years passed before teachers were able to challenge these earlier school reforms successfully.

The next major step for teachers' organizations was active involvement in politics—a step that represents another aspect of the teacher power movement. The most significant political step taken by the NEA was to give its support to the 1976 presidential campaign of Jimmy Carter. This step began a process of political involvement whereby teachers' organizations supported political candidates, who, in turn, promised political favors. In 1976, Carter promised the NEA, in exchange for its support, to establish a Department of Education having a secretary of education who would represent educational interests at presidential cabinet meetings. After his election, Carter fulfilled his promise to the NEA, thus launching a new era of federal involvement in education. The establishment of the Department of Education ensured the role of the federal government in establishing national educational policy.

The involvement of teachers' organizations in national politics caused a major change in the role played by education in national elections. Both the NEA and the AFT tended to favor the policies of the Democratic party. This left the Republican party without any clearly defined educational constituency. President Reagan tried to correct this situation for the Republican party in the 1980 and 1984 presidential elections by appealing to groups that were opposed to the teachers' unions and highly critical of the public school establishment. Part of his appeal went to private school groups that were hoping for some form of federal support through vouchers or tuition tax credits. Another part of his appeal went to groups that felt the schools had lost their role in shaping student character to conform to traditional Christian values. Individuals concerned with the teaching of moral values were organized into a number of groups, including the Moral Majority and groups supporting school prayer. Reagan hoped to win political support from these groups by promising tuition tax credits and a restoration of school prayer.

The fact that Reagan could appeal to groups outside the usual educational establishment that were interested in educational issues highlights one of the major changes in educational politics in the 1970s and 1980s. Beginning with the civil rights movement in the 1950s, an increasing number of organizations had appeared on the national scene to promote specific educational interests; civil rights organizations represented one type of special interest group. Also, after the 1954 Brown decision, courts continued to make controversial rulings that led to the creation of other special interest groups. The most visible of these court-created special interest groups were those opposed to the Supreme Court's decision in *Engel* v. *Vitale* (1962) that prohibited prayer in the public schools.

SCHOOL PRAYER

The Supreme Court's school prayer decision was greeted with as much controversy as the Brown desegregation decision. *Engel* denied the right of a public school system to conduct prayer services within school buildings during regular school hours. The case began in the state of New York when a local school system was granted the right by the New York Board of Regents to have a brief prayer said in each class at the beginning of the school day. The prayer, considered to be denominationally neutral, read, "Almighty God, we acknowledge our dependence upon Thee, and we beg Thy blessings upon us, our parents, our teachers and our country." The New York courts granted the right of local school systems to use this prayer.

When the U.S. Supreme Court ruled on the case, one of its major objections to school prayer was the fact that a government official had written the prayer. This seemed to violate the First Amendment, that is, it put the government directly in the business of establishing religion. The Court reviewed the early history of the United States, the struggle for religious freedom, and the ending of government support of churches. The writing of a school prayer, the Court argued, ran counter to the long tradition of separation of church and state.

The immediate reaction from one sector of the public to the school prayer decision was to claim that the Supreme Court had removed God from the schools. Historically, given the heavy religious content in nineteenth-century schools, this charge was to a certain extent correct. The only hopes for those groups in favor of school prayer were in the organization of a separate religious school system or the passage of a constitutional amendment allowing prayer in public schools. It was to this sector of the population that President Reagan appealed in the 1980 and 1984 elections by promising the passage of a school prayer amendment.

CHILDREN WITH SPECIAL NEEDS

At the same time that school prayer advocates were organizing to protest changes in the traditions of schooling, groups supporting better education for the handicapped were struggling against traditional discriminatory practices. Numerous organizations were formed to promote better education for the handicapped, the largest of these being the National Association for Retarded Citizens and the Council for Exceptional Children.

Throughout the 1960s, these organizations fought hard to gain special federal funding for educational programs for the handicapped and for protection of the civil rights of handicapped children. The first major breakthrough came in 1971, when a court in Pennsylvania ruled that state schools had to provide a suitable free public education for all retarded and handicapped children. This decision was followed in 1972 by a federal court ruling that the District of Columbia had to provide a suitable free education regardless of the emotional, mental, or physical condition of the child.

A major victory for these groups came in 1973 with the passage of the Rehabilitation Act of 1973. Section 504 of this legislation was equivalent to Title VI of the 1964 Civil Rights Act in that it required the withholding of federal funds from schools that discriminated against the handicapped. This legislation was followed in 1975 by Public Law 94-142, the Education for All Handicapped Children Act, which prescribed that each handicapped child receive an individualized educational program. The most controversial part of the legislation was the detailed requirements to be followed in the writing of each individualized program.

Public Law 94-142 was important because it demonstrated the power of special interest groups and the growing extent of federal involvement in education. For each handicapped child, the legislation required a written statement about the child's level of performance, a statement of annual goals, a statement of services to be provided, a date for initiation of services, and objective criteria for evaluation. In other words, the legislation actually outlined a specific method for treating each handicapped child that local school officials were required to follow.

This legislation provided new justification for the cries that were beginning to be heard from local school people about the burden of federal regulations. But given the long history of discrimination against minority groups and handicapped children, federal involvement was required to change local educational policies. This fact did not lessen the extreme level of protest heard from local school officials and from conservative groups opposed to any federal interference in local school practices.

THE REAGAN AGENDA

In the 1980 and 1984 elections, President Reagan directed his campaign toward those who were upset with federal interference in local schools. In these two national political campaigns, Reagan defined his educational constituency as those opposed to federal interference in the schools, those in favor of school prayer, private school interests, and those concerned with the values taught in the schools. To those opposed to federal interference in the schools, Reagan promised deregulation and the abolition of the Department of Education. The total educational package offered by the Republicans in 1980 and 1984 included a constitutional amendment for deregulation, abolition of the Department of Education, sanction of school prayer, and provision of tuition tax credits. Two aspects of the 1980 and 1984 presidential elections are important in this context. These were the first national elections in which each political party defined a clear educational constituency. The Democrats appealed to the two major teachers' unions and to members of the public who favored increased federal aid to local schools, whereas the Republicans appealed to the constituency described above. Second, these clear differences between the two parties meant that education was viewed as a national issue represented by various national constituencies.

An important consequence of making education part of national politics is that it ensured the linking of education to national issues. Of course, this process had begun during the 1950s, when the Cold War and educational policies were linked, and had continued in the 1960s, when education became an important part of the War on Poverty. Though President Reagan ran on a platform promising less federal interference in schooling, the actual consequence of making education a national political issue was to guarantee a continued dialogue about national educational policies.

Therefore, it is understandable that the administration that had promised less federal involvement in education issued a report in 1983, *A Nation at Risk*, that blamed the schools for America's difficulties in competing in world markets with Japan and West Germany. The allegedly poor academic quality of American public schools was seen as the cause of lower rates of productivity than those of Japan and West Germany, as well as of the declining lead of the United States in technological development. The report states, "If only to keep and improve on the slim competitive edge we still retain in world markets, we must rededicate ourselves to the reform of the educational system for the benefit of all."[20]

A similar argument was used in the early twentieth century to justify federal aid to vocational education. At that time, the major international competitor was Germany, and the American school system was compared unfavorably with the German school system. The difference between the earlier plea for vocational education and the reform proposals in *A Nation at Risk* is that the latter does not call for increased federal aid. *A Nation at Risk* exhorts states and local communities to increase academic standards, improve the quality of teachers, and reform the curriculum.

A Nation at Risk put the Reagan administration into an interesting political situation. On the one hand, blaming the public schools for international economic problems appealed to those members of the Republican constituency who were highly critical of the workings of the schools. On the other hand, the report could not call for federal intervention to aid the schools because of Republican promises to decrease federal involvement in education. Finally, the Reagan administration did place the issue of schooling on a national political agenda by linking it to national trade problems. In other words, the net effect of Republican actions was to ensure that education would remain a national issue.

A major strategy of the Republican administration was to increase the role of states in education as the federal role declined. The role of state governments in education had increased with federal legislation in the 1960s. Most federal monies were channeled through state departments of education, and funds were provided to increase the administrative staff at the state level. Thus, the actions of the Reagan administration reinforced existing trends in the distribution of political power. As power over education shifted back and forth between state and federal agencies, the power of local school boards over education declined.

Indicative of the increase of state power over education was state governors' increasing use of education as a political issue. In the 1980s, state governors jumped onto the bandwagon with others who blamed the schools for the problems in foreign trade. In addition, the governors promised voters that reforms in the educational system would lead to economic prosperity for their states. The increased involvement of governors in education resulted in dramatic changes.

One of the first important changes made was establishing career ladders for teachers. This educational reform was pioneered by Republican Governor Lamar Alexander of Tennessee and was quickly copied in differing forms by other states. The basic idea of career ladders is to provide some means by which the teacher can see his or her work leading to future advancement.

Traditionally, teaching was "careerless," because the only hope for advancement was to leave teaching for educational administration. Career ladders were designed to allow competent teachers to advance in rank and responsibilities while remaining in the classroom.

Governor Alexander proposed a career ladder to the Tennessee state legislature in 1983. The bill ran into heavy opposition from teachers' organizations, which were concerned with methods of evaluation and the consequences for teachers already covered by the state's existing certification program. In February 1984 the Tennessee legislature passed Alexander's legislation after a compromise had been reached with the state teachers' organization. At the time of its passage, the bill was hailed as the most ambitious program of its type ever put into law.

The career-ladder idea received national recognition among governors in *Action for Excellence,* the 1983 report of the Task Force on Education for Economic Growth. The task force was composed primarily of state governors and heads of American corporations. The report complains: "In every state . . . teachers are paid according to rigid salary schedules based primarily on training and years of experience. No state, to our knowledge, has a system for rewarding exceptional teachers for their superior performance." To solve this problem, the report recommends that "states should create 'career ladders' for teachers."[21]

An important aspect of the Task Force on Education for Economic Growth was the cooperation on educational policy it stimulated between big business and governors. What this meant was that business influence shifted from the local level to the state level. This shift reflected the increasing political role of state government in education. The task force consisted in part of twelve governors, three state legislators, one representative of organized labor, six educators, and four organizational leaders. The most impressive component of the membership was fourteen business leaders. The cochairs of the task force were Frank Cary, chairman of the executive committee of the IBM Corporation, and Pierre S. du Pont IV, governor of Delaware and an heir to the du Pont chemical fortune. Other members from the business community included the chief executive officers of Texas Instruments, RCA, Ford Motors, Xerox, Dow Chemicals, Control Data, Johnson Publishing, Time Inc., and SFN; the vice chairman of the board of directors of AT&T; and the chairman of the National Association of Manufacturers.

In addition to supporting the idea of career ladders, the report of the task force calls for closer relationships between American business and the schools. The introduction to the report states, "We believe especially that businesses, in their role as employers, should be much more deeply involved in the process of setting goals for education in America and in helping our schools to reach those goals." One of the "action recommendations" called for in the report states, "Business leaders should establish partnerships with schools." And in bold type in the section titled "Education and Growth," the report proclaims: "If the business community gets more involved in both the design and the delivery of education, we are going to become more competitive as an economy." The call for greater participation of the business community in establishing the goals of the public schools was couched in the traditional language of the promise of American schooling. Like the proclamations of school reformers and public leaders in the nineteenth century, the report proclaims education as a panacea for society's ills: "It is the thesis of this report that our future success as a nation—our national defense, our social stability and well-being and our national prosperity—will depend on our ability to improve education and training for millions of individual citizens."[22]

Within the framework of the traditional promise of American education to solve economic and social problems, business and state leaders banded together in the early 1980s to reform education. Although this strong coalition was formed at the state level, local schools also felt pressure from local business leaders. Many schools were adopted by business through an "adopt-a-school" program, and in communities with wide-ranging magnet, or alternative, schools, businesses often helped to plan educational goals according to the needs of the labor market.

In some communities, a formal relationship was established between business and the schools. In the early 1980s, business leaders and the Boston schools signed a formal compact stating that the schools would improve the quality of graduates to meet employers' needs, and, in exchange, local business would give preference to graduates of Boston schools. A similar alliance was established in Atlanta. Michael Timpane, in his 1981 study *Corporations and Public Education,* written for the Carnegie Corporation, details the extent of the new cooperative ties between business and the schools and argues that the basic reason for this alliance was the growing shortage of entry-level workers. "For the first time in a generation there will probably be, in several urban locations, an absolute shortage of labor supply for entry level positions. Urban employers already report great difficulty in locating qualified employees for entry level positions."[23]

It is important to place business involvement in the schools in the 1980s into the perspective of the wide range of political pressures on education. Business was only one of the groups attempting to shape education to serve their particular interests. The political pressures came from within and outside the educational establishment. Within the establishment, teachers' unions sought greater teacher power, while administrators fought to hold on to their control. Outside the educational establishment, special interest groups, such as those concerned with school prayer or the handicapped, tried to get the schools to serve their particular interests. Political leaders at the federal and state levels tried to use the schools as a scapegoat for current social and economic problems and, at the same time, tried to advance their own political fortunes by calling for educational reform to solve the problems the schools had supposedly created. The politics of education in the 1980s represents a new web of entangling political pressures that are pushing and pulling American schools in a multitude of directions.

THE BUSH YEARS: NATIONAL STANDARDS, CHOICE, AND SAVAGE INEQUALITIES

On April 18, 1991, President Bush unveiled plans for achieving national education goals by the year 2000. Similar to the rhetoric of the Reagan administration, these plans were presented as necessary for improving the ability of the U.S. companies to compete in international markets. Administration officials admitted that the plans were also designed to ward off criticism during the 1992 election campaign that Bush had no domestic agenda.[24]

The four main features of the plan were the creation of model schools, national standards, voluntary national achievement tests, and incentives for parental choice.[25] Bush's model schools plan was launched on July 8, 1990, with the establishment of a private, nonprofit corporation, the New American Schools Development Corporation (NASDC), which was funded by private corporations and was to work with the federal government. The Bush administration planned that the NASDC would develop 535 model schools with one experimental school in each congressional district and two more for each state.

The domination of the model schools program by large corporations was reflected in headlines in *The New York Times* ("Brought to You by Exxon— School Reform") and *Education Week* ("Educators Watch with a Wary Eye as Business Gains Policy Muscle").[26] These headlines were prompted by the announcement of the membership of the controlling board of the NASDC. Of the eighteen members of the board, twelve are heads of major corporations, including Nabisco, the Boeing Company, AT&T, B. F. Goodrich, and the Exxon Corporation. In addition, there are two politicians, two publishers, and the commissioner of the National Football League. The *only* educator on the board is Joan Cooney, chairman of the executive committee of the Children's Television Workshop.[27]

The lack of educators on the board caused Marc Tucker, president of the National Center on Education and the Economy, to declare, "It is clear that business has an open door to the top policymakers, including the President, in a way that professional educators would envy."[28]

Many believe, as expressed by David Hornbeck, former Maryland state superintendent, that "For the first time in American history, what is good for kids and what is good for business coincide almost on a one-for-one basis."[29] The assumption is that business will be able to help plan an educational system that will improve the American work force and economy.

This close relationship between business and educational policy could be criticized from the standpoint that while workers and business leaders share a common interest in an improved economy, there is an inherent conflict between the desire of workers for increased wages and the desire of business leaders to reduce wages. This is an important issue for the middle and lower classes because of the increasing inequality in the distribution of income.

During the 1980s, the rich got richer and the middle class and poor got poorer. A 1991 report by the U.S. Census Bureau states that between 1984 and 1988 the median income for the most affluent fifth of all households increased by 14 percent, from $98,411 to $111,770, while the median income of all households declined, from $37,012 to $35,752.[30] Also, between 1977 and 1990, the average pretax income of the richest fifth of the population increased by 9 percent, while that of the poorest fifth declined by 5 percent.[31]

I would argue that business has an interest in educating a skilled work force, but it does not have an interest in educating workers to become active in increasing their share of national wealth and increasing their wages. There is nothing in the current proposals of the secretary of labor's Commission on Achieving Necessary Skills (this commission is charged with determining the educational needs of the American work force) that suggests giving future workers the political and economic education needed to protect their share of the national income.[32] It could be that model schools will educate better workers who will willingly work for lower wages than previous generations would.

The Bush administration proposed creating voluntary "American Achievement Tests" for grades four, eight, and twelve. The tests would cover five core subjects, and students would be measured by "world class standards." To accomplish this goal, the Bush administration, in cooperation with Congress and the National Governors Association, created the National Council on Education Standards and Testing (NCEST).

Similarly to other reform proposals, the search for national standards was strongly influenced by economic concerns. The cochairman of the NCEST, Governor Roy Romer of Colorado, defined national standards as "guidelines for what youngsters should know and be able to do to be citizens who can compete in the world economy."[33]

There was a sharp reaction from the NEA to the proposal for national standards and tests. At its annual convention in July 1991, the NEA voted to "oppose development or implementation of new federally mandated national tests and a national testing program as being contrary to the diverse interests and needs of children."[34] Fearing that national standards and tests would result in a national curriculum, Robert Chase, vice president of the NEA, warned, "We can find ourselves in a situation where standardized testing becomes a driver as far as the curriculum is concerned."[35]

Ironically, the Bush plan for national standards seemed to contradict traditional Republican resistance to federal control of local schools. The establishment of federal standards and tests might result in direct federal control of the most important aspect of public schools—the curriculum. This seeming contradiction can be explained only by defining the new federalism of the Republican party as centralized control of policy objectives combined with management of those objectives at the state and local levels.

CHOICE

As I previously discussed, choice has been an important part of the Republican party's agenda since Reagan's election in 1980. Reagan wanted to give parents an opportunity to choose between public and private schools. Initially, President Bush supported choice only between public schools, but later he expanded the idea to include private schools.

Choice is important for the model schools program, which could create both privately operated model schools and model schools within public systems. In announcing support for school choice and vouchers, Secretary of Education Lamar Alexander suggested that schools might be run by corporations or even museums. In addition, choice is linked to the adoption of American Achievement Tests. Under the Bush plan, test results would supply parents with the information needed to choose among public schools or between public and private schools.[36]

The choice plan drew sharp criticism from the American Federation of Teachers, which warned that choice plans might destroy public schools and could result in dividing children by "class, race, political power, level of achievement, or behavior."[37]

Significantly, the state with the broadest choice plan, Minnesota, reported that 99 percent of the state's students remained in their local schools. Seven other states have adopted plans that allow a student to transfer to any other public school in the state. The only state with a voucher plan, Vermont, permits towns without public schools to pay residents' tuition at private schools.[38]

Reflecting the growing nationalization of the American educational system under the Bush administration, Secretary Alexander indicated the administration's willingness to seek federal funding for the National Board of Professional Teaching Standards for the creation of tests that would be used to issue national teaching certificates.[39] At the third annual meeting of the board in June 1991, Chairman James B. Hunt, Jr., stated that hostility to the creation of national certification was no longer apparent. At the meeting, the board announced that standards for thirty certificate areas would be ready by 1996.[40]

SAVAGE INEQUALITIES

While the Bush administration talked about reform, public schools around the country faced the worst financial crises in decades. Many state governments reported a sharp decline in tax revenues. For example, North Carolina is faced with a $1 billion deficit, requiring big cuts in the education budget. Rhode Island cut more than 10 percent from the state school budget. Pennsylvania has a $434 million budget deficit, and Governor John McKernan was forced to shut down the state government for two weeks because of a shortfall in revenue. These are just a few examples of the current fiscal crisis.[41]

Economist Robert Reich argues that states and local school systems are facing financial problems because of reductions during the 1980s in state and local taxes on corporations and the wealthy. Therefore, as corporate control of schools has increased, corporate support has declined.

As an example of the duplicity of corporations regarding education policy, Reich writes that the "executives of General Motors . . . who have been among the loudest to proclaim the need for better schools, have been the most relentless pursuers of local tax abatements." For instance, in Tarrytown, New York, General Motors was able to reduce its contribution to local tax revenues by $2.81 million. The result, according to Reich, was the laying off of scores of local teachers.[42]

Reich argues that after changes in federal, state, and local taxes in the 1980s, the income tax on the wealthiest citizens in the United States was the lowest of any industrialized nation in the world. In addition, the corporate share of local property tax revenues declined from 45 percent in 1957 to 16 percent in 1987. Reich states, "By the end of the 1980s, the top 1 percent of American earners were paying a combined federal-state-local tax rate of only 26.8 percent, compared with 29 percent in 1975 and 19.6 percent in 1966."[43] Based on Reich's argument, improving the current financial plight of public schools depends on a return to higher taxes on the wealthy and corporations.

By the 1990s, school systems were seriously hurt by a reduction in tax revenues caused by the combination of a depressed economy and tax cuts. In addition, the differences between rich and poor school districts were brought to the attention of the general public with the publication in 1991 of Jonathan Kozol's *Savage Inequalities: Children in America's Schools*. The book provided ample documentation of the differences between wealthy and poor school districts. In poor school districts, Kozol found overcrowded classrooms, a shortage of textbooks, science laboratories without equipment or running water, and vocational programs operating with antiquated equipment. In contrast, he found rich school districts operating with small class sizes, plenty of textbooks and equipment, and up-to-date computer and science facilities. From Kozol's perspective, these savage inequalities between schools reinforced the inequalities between social groups.[44]

HUMAN CAPITAL TRIUMPHS

The combination of business control with the emphasis on teaching work skills is ensuring the triumph of human capital goals for American education. As I discussed in Chapter 9, human capital goals attempt to align the curriculum of public schools with the needs of the labor market. This is exemplified by the major changes in high school graduation requirements in Oregon, the first state to enact the recommendations of the National Center on Education and the Economy. In July 1991, Oregon Governor Barbara Roberts signed a bill to end the traditional high school education at the tenth grade.

Educators in the early twentieth century debated whether there should be different high school educations for those going to college and those completing their formal education with high school graduation. The resolution of that debate was that a high school education should prepare all students for both college and life. This resulted in the creation of the comprehensive high school for all students. The Oregon legislation reverses that decision by giving students a Certificate of Initial Mastery after the tenth grade and then separating students into vocational and college preparatory programs.

Critics argue that the Oregon plan will create an elitist school system with children from lower-income families being channeled into the vocational programs—the very same concern that led to a rejection of this type of separate secondary education in the early twentieth century.[45]

The triumph of human capital reflects the increasing alignment of education policies with national economic and political interests. In addition, centralization of control at the national level is increasing with the creation of national standards and achievement tests, development of national certification for teachers, increasing cooperation between state governments, and increasing influence on educational policy by private foundations. Also, the control of the content of textbooks is increasing with the agreement of Texas and California to cooperate on textbook adoption in 1944.[46] These trends reflect increasing control over the dissemination of ideas through schools by major economic and political interests.

CONCLUSION: IDEOLOGICAL MANAGEMENT AND THE HISTORY OF EDUCATION

As I indicated in the Preface to this book, I consider the history of education to be one part of the study of ideological management in modern society. The term *ideological management* highlights an important phenomenon in the modern world. Particularly since the nineteenth century, the control of ideas has been viewed as a source of power. What people know, what they believe in, and how they interpret the world have an important effect on their choices and, consequently, their actions. In totalitarian societies, ideological management often takes place through a centralized bureau, with an attempt to coordinate the ideological messages conveyed to the public by the different media and the schools. In societies with less centralized control, such as the United States, there are often struggles between different political and economic groups over the ideas and values to be conveyed to the public, and there is no central agency coordinating the media and the schools.

The term *ideological management* is intended to convey a concept that is more complex and more inclusive than is ordinarily associated with the idea of propaganda. Usually propaganda is thought of as government officials manipulating information for the purpose of ideological control. Ideological management includes this concept of propaganda and, in addition, includes attempts by a variety of public and private groups to influence ideas and information conveyed to the public. Also, propaganda suggests that there is an agreed-upon ideological message to be distributed to the public. While ideological management does not exclude that possibility, the term is used here to suggest competition and conflict between groups over what ideas and information should be disseminated. In addition, I want to suggest the possibility of the distribution of conflicting information and ideas.

Against the background of this discussion, ideological management can be more specifically defined as the conscious exclusion or addition of information and ideas conveyed to the public. Therefore, the history of education is nested in this broader concept of how ideas are disseminated in modern society. In other words, the history of education can be considered as part of the study of the political and economic forces shaping both the process and the content of ideas disseminated to the public.

In the Western world of the nineteenth century, different political and economic groups believed that government-operated schools could be a mechanism for ensuring the distribution of their particular ideologies to the majority of the population. Also, the role of public schools expanded because students and parents wanted increased educational opportunities as a means of mobility in the job market, and because various social advocacy groups wanted the role of the school to expand to serve humanitarian functions. In addition, educational administrators and teachers worked to expand and define public schools according to their own self interest.

One could argue that the combination of these historical forces made modern public schools the first mass media designed to reach an entire generation. In the twentieth century, particularly in the United States, differing groups have battled to ensure that their concepts of politics, morality, and society are taught by the schools. In these situations, ideological management does not result from the action of a single individual or group but is the result of conflict, compromise, and negotiation. Of course, victory in these struggles often goes to the most powerful and most active groups.

I would also include in the framework of ideological management the creation of new ideas and the functions of the knowledge industry. In *Conflict of Interests: The Politics of American Education*, I discuss the political forces shaping the creation of new knowledge in modern society. Of major importance are decisions made by the federal government and private foundations regarding the types of research that will be funded, decisions that are based on political and economic goals. In other words, the types of new knowledge created through funded research are determined by political and economic objectives. I would argue that the process by which research is funded can have dramatic effects on the future development of society. In addition, the knowledge industry, which includes the publishing and testing industries, shapes its products for a market influenced by economic and political forces.[47]

As I discussed in Chapter 12, the process of ideological management affects other institutions for the dissemination of ideas. Movies, radio, and television are potent forces in the education of the public. Forces similar to those affecting the public schools shape the content of these media. Edward Herman and Noam Chomsky, in *Manufacturing Consent: The Political Economy of the Mass Media*, develop a useful model for describing the effect of these forces on the broadcast media.[48] Their model is based on five "filters" which shape the content of news broadcasts in the United States, and it is applicable also to other countries where the news media are privately owned in contrast to countries where a state bureaucracy exerts monopolistic control. In their model, the content of newscasts goes through a series of filters before reaching the public. While news broadcasters claim objectivity, these filters, the authors argue, have a determining effect on news content.

Herman and Chomsky's model is useful in analyzing the political and economic forces shaping the content of broadcasting, and it also has a certain applicability to movies and public schools. For instance, the first filter in their model is the economic structure of broadcasting, which in their analysis is concentrated in the United States in a few companies. These major corporations, they argue, are interlocked and share common interests, which affect the selection of news. The second filter is advertisers, who are reluctant to sponsor programs that might generate public controversy or convey a message to the public that is contrary to their interest. These first two filters reflect the structure of American broadcasting, which is privately owned and dependent on commercial advertising. The third filter in their propaganda model is news sources. Herman and Chomsky argue that broadcasters tend to rely on powerful corporate and government news sources because these are easily accessible and inexpensive. Broadcasters seldom contact marginal political and economic groups. In addition, broadcasters fear offending their major sources. The result, they argue, is a bias in content and selection of news.

The fourth filter affects public schools as well as the broadcasting industries. This filter, which refers to letters, speeches, phone calls, and other forms of group and individual complaints, Herman and Chomsky call "flak." Advertisers and broadcasters avoid programming content that might cause large volumes of flak. Advertisers are concerned that flak will hurt the sales of their products, while station owners fear that flak will threaten their government-granted licenses. The result is bland, noncontroversial programs. When the concept is applied to public schools, this filter represents the fear of school administrators that flak might threaten their jobs or cause a loss of public funding. Consequently, educators often avoid teaching anything that might cause controversy in the community.

Herman and Chomsky consider the ideology of anticommunism to be the final filter in news broadcasting. This ideology, they argue, tends to paint world events as a struggle between good and evil. In their words, this "ideology helps mobilize the populace against an enemy, and because the concept is fuzzy it can be used against anybody advocating policies that threaten property interests or support accommodation with Communist states and radicalism."[49] Therefore, they argue, under the fuzzy ideology of anticommunism, left and labor movements can be cast in the role of enemy, while fascist dictatorships can be considered on the side of good. Like the concept of flak, the ideology of anticommunism has played an important role in American schools.

Therefore, Herman and Chomsky's propaganda model can be applied to other conveyors of ideas and values to American society. For instance, as I discussed in Chapter 12, the ideas and values in movies and radio during their most influential period of the 1930s to 1950s were influenced by the economic organization of the industry, by the fear of "flak," and by the conservative political philosophy of their owners.

The role of flak in molding the content of media is an important part of Kathryn Montgomery's study *Target: Prime Time-Advocacy Groups and the Struggle over Entertainment Television.*[50] She traces the role of advocacy groups in influencing the content of television from the 1950s to the 1980s. She identifies four major advocacy groups, which have also in varying degrees affected the content of the public school curriculum, radio, and movies. The first advocacy group is organizations representing minorities, women, seniors, and the disabled. All of these groups campaigned for the presentation of more positive images on television programs. In a similar manner, organizations representing minorities, women, and the disabled work for the presentation of more positive images in the public school curriculum and in textbooks.[51]

The second group identified by Montgomery is conservative religious organizations. In my opinion, these groups play a major role in shaping the values disseminated not only by the broadcast media, but also by movies and the public schools. Conservative religious groups have acted as self-appointed moral guardians of American culture. As Montgomery indicates, these groups have a significant impact on television programming. As I discussed in Chapter 12, conservative religious leaders played a major role in the early censorship of movies and in the adoption of the movie code in the 1930s. The intent of this code, which was applauded by conservative religious leaders, was to turn entertainment into moral lessons for the public. Conservative religious groups have also acted as guardians over the moral content of schooling. Without a doubt, conservative religious organizations play a major role in ideological management in the United States.

Social-issue groups form the third set of advocacy organizations identified by Montgomery. These groups range from environmentalist organizations to those concerned with drug abuse. With regard to the media, these organizations pressure television broadcasters to use entertainment to teach social lessons: For instance, programs might include antidrug statements. These groups have applied similar pressures to public schools, which are now called on to solve a whole host of social problems ranging from drug abuse to saving the environment.

Of particular importance to broadcasting are what Montgomery calls antiviolence groups. She includes in these groups organizations such as the Parent-Teacher Association and the American Medical Association. These groups have been particularly vocal regarding children's programming. As described in Chapter 12, these groups had a major impact on children's radio programs in the 1930s and 1940s and on the development of the first censorship codes in the broadcast industry.

Of course, as Montgomery argues, there is no one-to-one correspondence between the demands of advocacy groups and the response of broadcasters. In reality, the final outcome is the result of negotiation between advocacy groups and broadcasters, on the one hand, and the organizational and economic needs of the broadcast industry, on the other. For instance, while some advocacy groups might condemn sex and violence in television programming and movies, the industries might find exploitation of these themes profitable. Also, as Todd Gitlin demonstrates in *Inside Prime Time: How the Networks Decide about the Shows That Rise and Fall in the Real World behind the TV Screen*, network executives must negotiate their way through cross-pressures from politicians, advocacy groups, the artistic concerns of producers, the desires of advertisers, and the quest for profits.[52]

Therefore, organizational factors, government intervention, economic factors, flak from advocacy groups, and the ideology of anticommunism are important factors determining ideological management in the United States. Information and ideas are consciously added or excluded in public schools, movies, and the broadcast industry as a result of these factors. Often this conscious inclusion or exclusion of information and ideas is a product of conflict and negotiation between these differing elements. It is in this arena of conflict and negotiation that decisions are made about the ideas and values to be disseminated to the American public.

As one part of the general study of the dissemination of ideas, the history of education can make an important contribution to the development of a general theory regarding the creation and distribution of ideas in modern society. In addition, we can reach a better understanding of how the control of knowledge can be used as an instrument of power. Also, as I stated in this book's Preface, the study of history is essential to understanding our society. A comprehension of history is also essential to making critical decisions about the future. To be a critical thinker about American schools requires being a critical thinker about the history of education.

NOTES

1. "Quoting Marland," *American Education*, Vol. 7 (January–February 1971), p. 4.
2. Sidney P. Marland, Jr., "The Condition of Education in the Nation," *American Education*, Vol. 7 (April 1971), p. 4.
3. Quoted in Robert M. Worthington, "A Home-Community Based Career Education Model," *Educational Leadership*, Vol. 30 (December 1972), p. 213.
4. Sidney P. Marland, Jr., "The School's Role in Career Development," *Educational Leadership*, Vol. 30 (December 1972), pp. 203–205.
5. Sidney P. Marland, Jr., "Career Education and the Two-Year Colleges," *American Education*, Vol. 8 (March 1972), p. 11.
6. James S. Coleman et al., *Equality of Educational Opportunity* (Washington, D.C.: U.S. Government Printing Office, 1966), pp. 3–20, 35–217.
7. Ibid., p. 21.

8. Frederick Mosteller and Daniel P. Moynihan, eds., *On Equality of Educational Opportunity* (New York: Random House, 1972).

9. Daniel P. Moynihan, "On the Education of the Urban Poor" in Daniel P. Moynihan, ed., *Coping: Essays of the Practice of Government* (New York: Random House, 1973), pp. 167–194.

10. Daniel P. Moynihan, "Can Courts and Money Do It?" *New York Times* (January 10, 1972), reprinted in Miriam Wasserman, *Demystifying School* (New York: Praeger, 1974), pp. 226–230.

11. Ibid., p. 229.

12. Leon Lessinger, *Every Kid a Winner: Accountability in Education* (New York: Simon & Schuster, 1970).

13. For a discussion of how the issue of types of report cards can divide communities, see Joel Spring, *Conflict of Interests: The Politics of American Education* (White Plains, N.Y.: Longman, 1988), pp. 102–105.

14. Ira Shor, *Culture Wars: Schools and Society in the Conservative Restoration 1969–1984* (Boston: Routledge & Kegan Paul, 1986), provides a strong argument linking conservative political thought to the accountability movement and instructional practices based on behavioral psychology.

15. B. F. Skinner, *Walden Two Revisited* (New York: Macmillan, 1976).

16. Charles Silberman, *Crisis in the Classroom* (New York: Random House, 1970).

17. For a discussion of instructional models based on the theories of Jean Piaget and B. F. Skinner, see Bruce Joyce and Marsha Weil, *Models of Teaching* (Englewood Cliffs, N.J.: Prentice-Hall, 1986).

18. Larry Cuban, *How Teachers Taught: Constancy and Change in American Classrooms 1890–1980* (White Plains, N.Y.: Longman, 1984), pp. 158–159.

19. Ibid., pp. 240–249.

20. National Commission on Excellence in Education, *A Nation at Risk* (Washington, D.C.: U.S. Government Printing Office, 1983).

21. Task Force on Education for Economic Growth, *Action for Excellence* (Denver: Education Commission of the States, 1983).

22. Ibid., pp. 3, 6–7, 18.

23. Michael Timpane, *Corporations and Public Education* (Report written for the Carnegie Corporation and distributed by Teachers College, Columbia University, New York, 1981).

24. John E. Yang, "Bush Unveils Education Plan: States, Communities Would Play Major Role in Proposed Innovations," *Compuserve Executive News Services Washington Post* (April 19, 1991).

25. Kenneth J. Cooper, "National Standards at Core of Proposal: Model Schools Envisioned," *Compuserve Executive News Service Washington Post* (April 19, 1991).

26. Karen DeWitt, "Brought to You by Exxon—School Reform," *The New York Times* (July 21, 1991), p. 4E; Jonathan Weisman, "Educators Watch with a Wary Eye as Business Gains Policy Muscle," *Education Week* (July 31, 1991), p. 1.

27. "Members of Board of New-Schools Corporation," *Education Week* (July 31, 1991), p. 24.

28. Jonathan Weisman, "Educators Watch with a Wary Eye as Business Gains Policy Muscle," *Education Week,* (July 31, 1991), p. 1.

29. Ibid., p. 25.

30. Pear, R., "Rich Got Richer in 80's; Others Held Even," *The New York Times* (January 11, 1991), pp. 1, 20.

31. Robert B. Reich, *The Work of Nations: Preparing Ourselves for 21st Century Capitalism* (New York: Knopf, 1991), p. 7.

32. Lonnie Harp, "Schools Urged to Revamp Instruction to Stress Workforce Skills," *Education Week* (July 31, 1991), p. 11.

33. "What Are 'National Standards'? Groups Define Them Differently," *Education Week* (July 31, 1991), p. 7.

34. Robert Rothman, "Efforts to Create National Testing System Move into High Gear," *Education Week* (July 31, 1991), p. 7.

35. Ibid.; Susan Chira, "A Sea of Doubt Swells around Bush's Education Plan," *The New York Times* (July 22, 1991), p. A12.

36. William Celis, "National Tests Aim at Gauging Critical Thought," *The New York Times* (April 22, 1991), p. A15.

37. Denis Searles, "Alexander-Choice," *Compuserve Executive News Service Associated Press* (April 12, 1991).

38. Kenneth Cooper, "Minnesota's School Option Inspires Few Students to Transfer; National Advocates Watch 7 States Pioneering Open Enrollment," *Compuserve Executive News Service Washington Post* (February 24, 1991).

39. Julie Miller and Karen Diegmuller, "Bush Shift Seen on Federal Aid to Teacher Board," *Education Week* (July 31, 1991), pp. 1, 22.

40. Karen Diegmuller, "Teachers, at Board's Forum, Uncertain about Certification," *Education Week* (July 31, 1991), p. 22.

41. Lonnie Harp, "Budget Troubles Hit Summer Crescendo in Many States," *Education Week* (July 31, 1991), pp. 28, 34–35.

42. Reich, *Work of Nations*, p. 281.

43. Ibid., pp. 200, 246, 281.

44. Jonathan Kozol, *Savage Inequalities: Children in America's Schools* (New York: Crown Publishers, 1991).

45. Brad Cain, "School Overhaul," *Compuserve Executive News Service Associated Press* (July 16, 1991); Ethan Rarick, "Oregon Moves to End High School at 10th Grade," *Compuserve Executive News Service Associated Press* (July 31, 1991).

46. Peter West, "Texas and California Plan Joint Adoption of Science Textbooks," *Education Week* (July 31, 1991), pp. 1, 21.

47. See Joel Spring, *Conflict of Interests: The Politics of American Education*, 2d Edition (White Plains, N.Y.: Longman, 1993).

48. Edward S. Herman and Noam Chomsky, *Manufacturing Consent: The Political Economy of the Mass Media* (New York: Pantheon, 1988).

49. Ibid., p. 29.
50. Kathryn C. Montgomery, *Target: Prime Time-Advocacy Groups and the Struggle over Entertainment Television* (New York: Oxford University Press, 1989).
51. Spring, *Conflict of Interests*, pp. 125–149.
52. Todd Gitlin, *Inside Prime Time: How the Networks Decide about the Shows that Rise and Fall in the Real World behind the TV Screen* (New York: Pantheon, 1985).

Index

Abbot, Lyman, 267
ABC (American Broadcasting Company), 320
Academic freedom, 51, 270–273
Academies 16–17, 20–23, 53, 224
Academy movement, 21, 23, 29
Accountability movement, 402
Adams, John, 38
Advertising, 329
African-American education, 164–168, 174–175
African Americans, 3, 15, 139, 141, 144, 162, 164–165, 167–175, 185, 338, 346–347, 357–358, 362
Alexander, Lamar, 409–410, 414
Allotment program, 148
Alternative schools, 354–356, 392, 411 (See also Magnet schools)
Alvord, John W., 168
American Association of University Professors (AAUP), 273
American Board of Commissioners for Foreign Missionaries, 133
American Council on Education, 298
American Federation of Labor (AFL), 289
American Federation of Teachers (AFT), 238, 281, 285, 393, 404–414
American Indian Movement (AIM), 358
American Indians (see Native Americans)
American Institute of Instruction, 65
American Lyceum, 65
American Medical Association (AMA), 419
Americanization, 130–131, 148, 151–152, 155–157, 182, 188–189, 196–198, 236–237 of Puerto Rico, 150–152
Anderson, James, 144, 170–172, 175

Apprenticeship, 7–8, 22
Aristotle, 10
Armstrong, Samuel, 170–171
Atkins, J. D. C., 145
Aylesworth, Merlin H., 323

Bacon, Francis, 19
Badillo, Herman, 363
Bagley, William C., 208, 217
Bailyn, Bernard, 17
Bainter, Edward, 154
Baldwin, William H., Jr., 172
Bangs, Reverend, 83
Barnard, Henry, 21, 64–65, 106, 110
Beecher, Lyman, 79
Behaviorism, 41, 401–403
Bell, Howard, 298
Benedict, John D., 141
Bennett, William, 364
Benson, Lee, 77–78
Bestor, Arthur, 379–381
Bible, 6, 9, 28, 34, 36, 39, 68–69, 81–82, 84, 125
Big Bird, 3, 302
Bigelow, John, 178
Bilingual education, 179, 357, 360, 362–364
Bilingual Education Act (see Elementary and Secondary Education Act)
Binet, Alfred, 262
Blank slate, 27–28
Bloomfield, Meyer, 232
Blumer, Herbert, 309
Boarding schools, 76, 145, 147, 157, 182, 359
Bobbit, Franklin, 259

425

Bond, Horace Mann, 172
Bonser, Frederick G., 231
Boston Prison Discipline Society, 47, 52
Boston School Committee, 47, 116, 165–167
Boulton, Matthew, 19
Bowers, C. A., 295
Boyer, Ernest, 338
Breen, Joseph, 317–318
Brigham, Carl, 264
Broadcast industry (*see* Radio; Television)
Brown, Oliver, 347–348
Brown v. Board of Education of Topeka, 347, 352, 366, 406
Brownson, Orestes, 79
Brumbaugh, Martin Grove, 151–152
Bullock, Henry, 164, 171
Bunker, Frank, 233
Bureau of Indian Affairs, 157
Burgess, Warren, 105
Bush, Vannevar, 374–375, 377
Bush (George) administration, 393, 412–414
Busing, 353, 393

California Bureau of Instruction, 179
Call, Arthur, 217
Callahan, Raymond E., 256, 258
Calvinism, 65–66, 124
Cardinal Principles of Secondary Education, 220–222, 224–225, 227, 234
Career education, 395–396
Carnegie, Andrew, 172, 305
Carr, Peter, 38
Carr, William G., 323
Carter, Jimmy, 405–406
Cary, Frank, 410
Catholic school system, 83, 85, 354
Catholicism, 6, 67, 80–85, 93
Cato's Letters, 18–19, 22
Caughey, John, 361
CBS (Columbia Broadcasting System), 320, 324, 328–330
Celebrezze, Anthony J., 387
Censorship, 302, 307, 313–315, 318, 323, 325, 327–328, 330, 332
Charity, 121, 123–124, 127
Charity school movement, 42, 44, 53, 65, 90
Charity school reformers, 47
Charity schools, 40, 42–43, 45, 48–49, 51, 53, 56, 62, 64, 74, 100, 134
Charles E. Stuart and Others v. School District No. 1 of the Village of Kalamazoo and Others, 215
Charters, W. W., 307–308
Chavez, Gene T., 364

Cherokee Nation, 140
Cherokees, 132, 134–135, 137, 140–142
Chicago Federation of Labor (CFL), 285
Chicago Federation of Teachers (CFT), 238, 283–289
Chickasaws, 132, 135, 141
Children's programming, 329–332, 335–336
Children's Television Workshop, 3, 303, 331, 333–336, 339–340, 412
Chippewas, 142
Choctaw Nation, 134–135, 137–140, 156
Choctaws, 132–135, 137–143
Chomsky, Noam, 417–418
Cicero, 10
Cisneros v. Corpus Christi Independent School District, 362
Civil Rights Act (1964), 352, 396, 407
Civil rights movement, 148, 158, 185, 276, 282, 346–367, 370–371, 392, 394, 406–407
Civilization Fund Act, 133–134
Clark, Jonas, 271
Clark, Kenneth, 348
Clinton, DeWitt, 43, 45–47
Codey, Thomas M., 215
Coffman, Lotus, 120
Cohen, Sol, 254
Cold War, 370, 372, 377, 382–383, 400, 408
Coleman, James, 353, 396
Colleges/universities, 49, 53, 74, 215–216, 267, 270, 273–275, 297, 299, 376, 392, 396
Collier, John, 305
Colonial education, 4–6, 9
Columbia University, 50
Commission on the Reorganization of Secondary Education (*see* Cardinal Principles of Secondary Education)
Committee of Ten on Secondary School Studies (NEA), 216–217, 221, 271
Common school ideology, 64–65
Common school movement, 48, 56, 62–73, 77, 80, 87–88, 90–93, 97, 101–103, 106–108, 242
Common school reform, 66, 88, 91
Common school reformers, 33, 48, 64–65, 75–76, 98, 102, 105–107, 109
Common school system, 34–35, 41, 69, 92, 97–98, 121, 125, 322
Common schools, 35, 62–63, 65, 68–73, 76–77, 80, 86–87, 89–90, 92–93, 106–108, 120, 125–126, 322, 383
Commons, John R., 89
Commonwealthmen, 19
Communism, 34

Community control movement, 399
Comstock, Anthony, 305
Conant, James B., 374–377
Condon, Ralph, 259–260
Congress on Racial Equality (CORE),
    350–351, 358
Connor, Eugene "Bull," 351
Cooley, Edwin, 286–287
Cooney, Joan, 332–333, 412
Cooperation, 219, 222, 238
Cornell, Ezra, 271
Corporation for Public Broadcasting, 332,
    339–340
Council for Exceptional Children (CEC),
    366–367
Counts, George, 255, 294–295
Cox, Owen, 362
Cox, Philip, 233
Crain, Cardin Lucille, 378
Crane, Theodore, 51
Creeks, 132, 135
Cremin, Lawrence, 10, 13, 65, 193, 236
Crime, 189–190
Cronin, Joseph M., 252
Crows, 143
Croy, Homer, 313
Cuban, Larry, 114, 198, 208, 403–404
Cubberley, Ellwood, 6, 45, 86–87, 89,
    116–117, 235–237, 274–275
Curry, Robert, 254
Curti, Merle, 7–8, 12, 57, 87, 237–238, 240
Curtis, Henry S., 193–194

Dale, Edgar, 310–311
Dame schools, 8, 25
Dartmouth College v. Woodward, 49, 53–55
Darwin, Erasmus, 19
Davis, Jerome, 321
Davis, Jesse B., 231–232
Davis, Maxine, 298
Dawes Act, 140
Dawes Commission, 141
Debs, Eugene V., 272
Deculturalization, 3, 130–131, 148, 156–158,
    182–183, 346, 357
De Garmo, Charles, 200
Delgado v. Bastrop Independent School District,
    361
Democracy, 36, 38, 204, 221–222, 249, 260,
    263–264, 349
Democrats, 77–80, 92–93, 218, 242, 408
De Montilla, Aida Negron, 151
Demos, John, 24

Depression, the, 276, 280, 282, 292–293,
    296–298, 300, 372, 383
Desegregation, 347, 349–350, 352, 355–356,
    393
Dewey, John, 190, 198, 200–204, 207, 209,
    400–401
Dexter, Edwin, 153
Donahue, John, 325
Duane, James, 133
Du Bois, W. E. B., 168–169, 173–174
du Pont, Pierre S., IV, 410
Dyer, Frank, 253–254

Economic Opportunity Act (EOA) (1964),
    384, 386–387
Eder, Jeanne, 140, 143–144
Education
    African American, 164–168, 174–175
    and americanization, 151
    and authoritarianism, 12, 57
    bilingual, 179, 357, 360, 362–364
    and building nationalism, 28
    career, 395–396
    and the civil rights movement, 367
    and the Cold War, 382, 408
    colonial, 4–6, 9
    to end crime and poverty, 58
    and the federal government, 281, 290,
        296
    as a government function, 29, 118
    and graduate schools, 267–268, 273–275
    of handicapped, 366–367, 407
    and improving material prosperity, 4, 188
    Indian, 147–148
    as a means of cultural imperialism, 16
    and nationalism, 32, 56
    as a panacea, 5–6
    public taxation for, 215
    and religion, 17–18
    science of, 243
    segregated industrial, 169, 171
    and social class, 5, 229
    and social control, 180
    social impact of, 396
    and social order, 34, 232
    and social science, 239
    vocational (*see* Vocational education)
    and the War on Poverty, 370, 384–387
    and women, 24–25, 100, 118
    and the working class, 241
    and workingmen's parties, 75–76
Education for All Handicapped Children
    (Public Law 94–142), 367, 407
Eisenhower, Dwight D., 382

Eisenhower, John, 177
Electric Company, The, 338
Elementary and Secondary Education Act
    (ESEA) (1965), 352, 358, 363, 384,
    387–389
Elementary schools, 97, 108–109, 118, 127,
    199, 208, 338
Eliot, Charles, 216, 223, 271
Elitism, 250–251
Elsbre, Willard, 101, 104, 117, 119, 200
Ely, Richard, 272
Emerson, Harrington, 256
Émile, 26–27
Engelhardt, Nicolaus, 275
Engels, Friedrich, 70
Equality of opportunity, 219, 249
Erasmus, Desiderius, 10
Ershkowitz, Herbert, 77
Extracurricular activities, 222–223, 225

Falkner, Roland, 153
FCC, 324–325, 327–328, 331
Federal Radio Commission (FRC), 320
Finberg, Barbara, 333
Finkelstein, Barbara, 109
First Amendment, 16
Fisher, Laura, 191
Fishlow, Albert, 97
Five Civilized Tribes, 135, 138, 140–142,
    144, 148, 156, 176, 360, 363
    (*See also* Cherokees; Chickasaws;
    Choctaws; Creeks; Seminoles)
Flak, 418, 420
Folsom, David, 134–135
Foraker Act, 151
Forman, Henry James, 308–310
Fourteenth Amendment, 347, 360, 362
Franklin, Benjamin, 14–15, 21–23, 29
Freedman's Bureau, 168
Freedom, 18–19, 33–34, 355, 357, 360, 402
    academic, 51, 270–273
    of ideas, 16–18, 20
    intellectual, 4–5, 16, 20–21
    of learning, 18
    of the press, 16
    of speech, 16, 18, 38, 322
    of thought, 4, 16, 18, 322
Fremont, John C., 177
Fretwell, Elbert K., 222
Freud, Sigmund, 355
Froebel, Friedrich, 190, 192
Frost, S. E., 320

Galton, Samuel, 19
Gamble, James N., 252
Gandhi, Mohandas K., 351
GI Bill of Rights (*see* Servicemen's
    Readjustment Act)
Gitlin, Todd, 420
Goddard, Henry Herbert, 261–263, 266, 276
Goggin, Catherine, 283, 286
Gonzalez, Gilbert, 181–182
Gonzalez, Jose, 364
Goodman, Ellen, 337
Gordon, Thomas, 18
Goslin, Willard, 377
Government-operated schools, 5, 16, 417
Graduate schools, 267–268, 273–275
Grammar schools, 4, 7–8, 10–12, 21, 23, 39,
    146, 154, 214
Grant, Ulysses S., 177
Griscom, John, 112–113
Grovas, Francisco, 154
Grubb, W. Norton, 229
Gutowski, Thomas, 222
Guzman, William, 360

Haley, Margaret, 238, 283, 286, 290
Hall, G. Stanley, 219–220, 272
Hall, Samuel, 99
Hampton Institute, 144, 170–171
Handicapped, education of, 366–367, 407
Hansot, Elisabeth, 274–275, 290, 293
Harrington, Michael, 384–385
Harris, William T., 115, 146, 191, 290
Harvard College, 11–12, 50
Hayakawa, S. I., 364
Hays, Will, 303, 306, 312, 327
Head Start, 332, 384–387
Heller, Walter, 384–386
Herbart, Johann, 198–200
Herbartian movement, 198–200
Herman, Edward, 417–418
Hickenlooper, Andrew, 252
High schools, 23, 127, 189, 212–226,
    233–235, 237, 242, 273, 293, 297, 299,
    319–320, 395
Hodgson, Adam, 135
Hofstadter, Richard, 50–51
Hornbeck, David, 412
Houses of refuge, 48–49
Howe, Daniel, 78–79
Howe, Harold, II, 333
Hughes, Bishop, 84
Hunt, James B., Jr., 414
Huyke, Juan B., 155

Ideological management, 1–3, 340, 416–419
Immigrants, 197–198
  Chinese, 162–164, 185
  Japanese, 162–164, 185
  Korean, 162–164
  Mexican, 180–185
Immigration, 188–189
Indian education, 147–148
Indian Education Act (1972), 359
Indian schools, 146–148
  Albuquerque Indian School, 147
  Armstrong Academy, 139
  Carlisle Indian School, 144–145
  New Hope Academy, 139–140
  Spencer Academy, 139–140
Indian Self-Determination and Education
  Assistance Act (1975), 359
Indian Territory, 131–144, 148, 154,
  156–157, 176, 179–182, 357, 360, 363
Indians of All Tribes, 358
Industrialization, 188–189
Integration, 347, 352–353, 384, 397
Intellectual freedom, 4–5, 16, 20–21
Intelligence testing, 260–263, 265

James, William, 198, 205–206, 401
Jefferson, Thomas, 11, 33, 37–40, 56–57, 65
Job Corps, 384
Johnson (Lyndon B.) administration, 332,
  373–374, 376, 383, 386–388, 392
Johnston, Charles, 232
Jones Act, 154
Junior high schools, 189, 226, 233–234, 242,
  293
Juvenile delinquency, 47
Juvenile reformatories, 42–43, 47–48, 112

Kaestle, Carl, 6, 44–45, 56–57, 79–80, 84,
  90–91, 97, 104
Kanter, Rosabeth, 118
Kantor, Harvey, 226
Karier, Clarence, 238, 240, 261
Katz, Michael, 88–89
Kearny, Stephen, 177
Kennedy (John F.) administration, 351–352,
  357, 363, 384–385, 392
Keppel, Francis, 387–388
Kerr, Clark, 394
Kilpatrick, William Heard, 204–205
Kindergarten, 190–194, 196, 198, 293, 332
King, Irving, 204
King, Martin Luther, Jr., 350–351

Kingsbury, Cyrus, 134–135
Kirp, David, 367
Klamath Indians, 357
Kozol, Jonathan, 415
Krug, Edward, 215, 217, 229, 232, 299

Labaree, David, 213
Laboratory school, 201–203
La Farge, Oliver, 147
La Raza Unida, 362–363
Lancaster, Joseph, 45–46, 110
Lancasterian system, 40, 42–43, 45–48,
  64–65, 134
Lannie, Vincent 82–83
Lazerson, Marvin, 191–192, 229
Lea, Luke, 142
League of United Latin American Citizens
  (LULAC), 183–185, 361
Lee, Joseph, 194
Leflore, Greenwood, 137–138
Lesser, Gerald, 333–337
Lessinger, Leon, 399–400
Lewin, William, 310–311
Lewis, Fulton, Jr., 378
Lewis, Samuel, 65
Lewis, William, 219
Life-adjustment curricula, 379–380
Lindsay, Samuel, 148, 153
Locke, John, 20, 27–28, 50
Loeb, Jacob, 288
Lord, Daniel S. J., 313–315
Lowe, Robert, 293
Lynd, Alan, 380

McAndrew, William, 223
MacCracken, John H., 320
McGuffey, William, 121–122
McGuffey *Readers*, 98, 121–126
McKenney, Thomas L., 134, 136, 139
McKernan, John, 414
McKinley, William, 149
Magnet school movement, 354
Magnet schools, 346, 354–356, 411
Magruder, Frank Abbott, 378
Manifest destiny, 130
Manual labor schools, 133, 143
Mann, Horace, 28, 35, 64–73, 75, 79–80, 87,
  93, 101–102, 116, 322, 356
Marland, Sidney, Jr., 338, 395–396
Marshall, John, 54–55
Martineau, Harriet, 103
Marx, Karl, 70, 378

Mass media, 3, 349
  (*See also* Movies; Radio; Television)
Massachusetts Bay Colony, 7, 13
Massachusetts Board of Education, 64, 72
Massachusetts Education Act (1789), 165
Massachusetts Law (1642), 7, 11
Massachusetts Temperance Society, 66
Mattingly, Paul, 100, 106–108
Mayo, Charles, 110
Mearns, William, 219
Mendez, Gonzalo, 360
*Mendez et al. v. Westminster School District of
  Orange County*, 360–361
Menominee, 357
Meriam, Louis, 147
Meriam Report, 147–148
Merit pay, 285
Meritocracy, 248, 250, 264, 267, 276
Mexican American Legal Defense and
  Education Fund (MALDEF), 361
Mexican Americans, 3, 15, 162–163, 176,
  178–185, 336, 346, 357, 360–365
Miller, Paul, 154
Milligan, Mrs. Harold V., 326–327
Minow, Newton, 331
Mirel, Jeffrey, 292–293
Missionary schools, 133, 135
Mix, Charles E., 142–143
Model schools program, 414
Modern School, 354
Molesworth, Robert, 17–19
Moley, Raymond, 307
Montejano, David, 176–178
Montgomery, Kathryn, 419
Moral education, 26, 68
Moral Majority, 406
Morgan, Joy Elmer, 321–322
Morgan, Thomas J., 145–147
Morrill, Justin, 269
Morrill Land Grant Act (1862), 268–269
Morrisett, Lloyd, 302, 332–333
Mort, Paul, 275
Mosier, Richard, 123–124
Mosteller, Frederick, 397
Motion Picture Producers and Distributors
  of America (MPPDA), 303, 305–307,
  310, 312–314, 327
Movies, 302–319, 321–324, 327–329, 331,
  417–420
Moynihan, Daniel Patrick, 396–398
Multicultural education, 357
Musterberg, Hugo, 231
Murrow, Edward, 381
Muste, A. J., 350
Myrdal, Gunnar, 348–349, 384–385

NAACP (National Association for the
  Advancement of Colored People), 169,
  173–174, 185, 346–348, 356, 361
Nation at Risk, A, 408–409
National Association of Broadcasters, 331
National Council for American Education,
  378
National Council on Education Standards
  and Testing (NCEST), 413
National Council of Teachers of English,
  310–312
National Defense Education Act (NDEA),
  370–371, 381–383
National Education Association (NEA), 190,
  203, 216, 220, 223–224, 237, 258, 271,
  273, 281–282, 286, 288, 290–292,
  294–296, 299–300, 303, 307, 313,
  320–321, 323, 377, 393, 404–406, 413
National Institute of Education (NIE), 398
National Science Foundation (NSF),
  370–371, 374, 377, 382
National Science Foundation Act (1950), 375
National Youth Administration (NYA), 296,
  298–300, 373
Nationalism, 32, 34, 36–37, 56, 63
Native American Languages Act (1990), 360
Native Americans, 3, 15, 130–148, 151–152,
  154, 156–158, 163, 170, 182, 185,
  357–360, 365
Navajo, 357
NBC (National Broadcasting Corporation),
  320, 323–324, 326, 328, 330
Neal, David, 367
Nearing, Scott, 255
Neill, A. S., 354–355
New American Schools Development
  Corporation (NASDC), 412
New England Primer, 8–10, 16, 25, 33, 35, 40,
  121
New England's First Fruits, 11–12
New York Free School Society, 42–45, 74,
  81
1930 Production Code, 313–318
Nixon (Richard) administration, 338, 353,
  358, 392–396, 398
Noble, David, 272
Normal schools, 106, 108, 273, 290
Norton, Mary, 99

Oberholtzer, Ellis, 304
Old Deluder Satan Law (1647), 7, 119
Olesen, Peter, 307
Olmsted, Frederick, 178
Open classroom, 400, 402–404

O'Shea, Michael V., 204
Oswego movement, 108, 110

Padin, Reform, 155
Paley, William, 324, 328
Palmer, Edward, 338
Pan-Indian movement, 358
Parker, Francis, 216
Parkhurst, Charles, 305
Parks, Rosa, 351
Parsons, Frank, 231–232
Patriotism, 2, 32–34, 36–37, 58, 147
Paulding, J. K., 195
Payne Studies, 307–310, 320, 323
Peabody, Elizabeth, 190
Peake, Mary, 168
Peirce, Cyrus, 110
Penn, John, 15
Penn, William, 14
*Pennsylvania Association for Retarded Children
    (PARC) v. Commonwealth of
    Pennsylvania*, 366
Pestalozzi, Johann, 98, 109–114, 190, 200
Pestalozzian methods, 98, 103, 109–111,
    113, 115, 200
Peterson, Paul, 254–255
Philbrick, John, 116
Piaget, Jean, 403
Pitchlynn, John, 135
Pitt, Leonard, 179
Plank, David, 254–255
Play movement, 192–194
Playground movement, 193
Playgrounds, 189, 193–194, 196, 198
Pledge of Allegiance, 34
Plessy, Homer, 347
Plessy v. Ferguson, 348
Plutarch, 10
Political freedom, 32
Polk, James, 177
Porter, Rosalie Pedalino, 364–365
Poverty, 189–190, 332, 370, 383–388
Powell, Arthur, 274
Pratt, Richard, 144
Price, Hiram, 144
Priestly, Joseph, 19–20
Private parochial system, 72
Private schools, 8, 14, 45, 54, 62, 87, 408
Production Code Administration, 313,
    317–319
Prosser, Charles, 379
Protestantism, 6, 67, 81–84, 90–93
PTA (Parent Teachers Association),
    325–328, 419

Public school reformers, 86
Public School Society, 83–84
Public school system, 62, 172, 354–355
Public schooling, 2, 34, 45, 62, 334–335,
Public schools, 1, 3, 6, 25, 28, 44–45, 54,
    134, 162, 165, 167, 173, 179, 194–195,
    197, 223, 234, 238, 248, 260, 275, 280,
    302, 310, 312, 322, 362–363, 374–375,
    377, 379–380, 383, 402, 404, 406,
    414–415, 418–420
Puerto Rican Commonwealth Bill, 156
Puerto Rican Teachers Association, 155–156
Puerto Ricans, 3, 15, 130–131, 148, 150–158,
    185, 326, 357, 362–365
Puffer, J. Adams, 230

Quigley, Martin, 313–315
Quincy School, 116–117

Radio, 302–303, 307, 319–331, 417–419
Radio Act of 1927, 320
Rauschenbusch, Walter, 350
Ravitch, Diane, 371–372
Reading and writing schools, 7–8, 10, 13,
    39, 53
Reagan (Ronald) administration, 356, 364,
    393, 406–409, 412
Reavis, William C., 275
Reese, William, 241
Rehabilitation Act (1973), 407
Reich, Robert, 415
Reich, Wilhelm, 355
Religion, 4–6, 8, 14, 17–18, 32, 38, 50, 68,
    83
Republicans, 77, 242, 406, 408, 413–414
Reyhner, Jon, 140, 143–144
Rickover, Hyman G., 381
Rishworth, Thomas, 325–326
Rivera, Munoz, 154
Robbins, Caroline, 20
Roberts, Barbara, 415
Roberts, Benjamin, 167
Rockefeller, John C., 272
Rodriguez, Richard, 365
*Rodriguez v. San Antonio Independent School
    Distrit*, 361
Rogers, Ferebe, 165
Rogers, John, 9
Romer, Roy, 413
Roosevelt, Franklin D., 155, 296, 372, 374
Roosevelt, Theodore, 164
Rose, Robert, 275
Rosenwald, Julius, 175

Ross, Edward, 239, 272
Rousseau, Jean-Jacques, 26–27, 112, 378, 403
Rudolph, Frederick, 51
Rush, Benjamin, 37, 41
Russell, William, 74
Russell Sage Foundation, 195–196, 306

Saenz, J. Luz, 184
Salinas, Ezequiel, 184
San Miguel, Guadalupe, Jr., 181
Saunders, Alfred, 307
School administrators, 250–251, 257–260, 280, 285, 292, 300, 389, 404
School boards, 250–255, 259, 280, 292, 389
School health programs, 188
School prayer, 406–408
Schultz, Stanley, 165
Schurz, Carl, 190
Scientific management, 248–250, 256–258, 276, 280–283, 285, 288
Scott, Anne, 100
Scott, Colin, 204
Scudder, H. E., 195
Segregated industrial education, 169, 171
Segregated schools, 163–169, 173, 199
Segregation, 3, 157, 162–164, 175, 179, 182, 346–347, 352–353, 356, 360, 396
Selective Service Act, 376
Selective service system, 392–393
Seminoles, 132, 135
Seneca, 10
Servicemen's Readjustment Act (1944), 373
Sesame Street, 3, 302–303, 331, 333, 335–339
Settlement house movement, 194
Seward, William, 78, 81, 83
Shade, William, 77
Shor, Ira, 401
Short, William, 308
Shriver, Sargent, 387
Sidney, Algeron, 22
Silberman, Charles, 403
Simon, Brian, 20
Sioux, 142–143
Sizer, Theodore, 274
Skinner, B. F., 401–402
Smith, Mortimer, 380–381
Smith, William, 15
Smith-Hughes Act (1917), 228–229, 282
Snyder, C. B. J., 198
Social center movement, 195–196
Social centers, 196, 198
Social Education Association, 204
Social efficiency, 217–221, 233, 256–257, 260
Social reconstruction, 294–296

Southern Christian Leadership Conference (SCLC), 350–351, 358
Spaulding, Frank, 257
Spring, Joel, 238, 240, 371–372
Spring, Pat, 139
Standardization, 62, 257, 393, 398, 400
Stanford, Leland, 272
Stowe, Calvin, 103–104, 113, 121
Stowe, Harriet Beecher, 103, 121
Strayer, George, 275
Student centered classrooms, 400–401
Student Nonviolent Coordinating Committee (SNCC), 350
Suffrage movement, 286
Summer school, 194
Summerhill, 354–355
Superintendents of education, 63, 119–120
Swann, v. Charlotte-Mecklenburg Board of Education, 352

Tappan, Henry, 268
Taylor, Frederick W., 256
Taylor, Zachary, 177
Teacher centered classrooms, 400–401
Teacher power movement, 405
Teachers' unions (*see specific union*)
Television, 302–303, 307, 331–334, 336, 339, 417–419
Terman, Lewis M., 265–266
Thomas, Charles A., 374
Thoreau, Henry David, 350, 402
Thorndike, Edward L., 198, 205–209, 262, 264, 266, 393, 400–401
3-2-1 Contact, 338
Timpane, Michael, 411
Tolstoy, Leo, 318
Treaty of Guadalupe Hidalgo, 177
Trenchard, John, 18
Tribal school systems, 137
Tribally Controlled Schools Act (1988), 359
Troen, Selwyn, 191
Tropea, Joseph, 266–267
Truman, Harry S., 156, 372, 375
Tucker, Marc, 412
Turner, Jonathan Baldwin, 269
Tuskegee Normal and Industrial Institute, 144, 170–172
Twelfth Annual Report, 68–71
Tyack, David, 114–116, 119–120, 240, 258–259, 274–275, 290, 293

Udall, Stewart, 357
Unification, 222
United Federation of Teachers (UFT), 405

Universal Military Training and Service Act
(1951), 373
Urban, Wayne, 283–284, 291
Urbanization, 188

Vinovskis, Maris, 79–80, 97, 213
Violas, Paul, 238, 240
Vocational education, 212, 226–230,
234–235, 238, 265, 282, 286, 288, 293,
379, 393–395, 409
Vocational guidance, 189, 212, 226, 230–232,
234–235, 238, 242, 396
Vocational schools, 221, 286
Voting Rights Act (1965), 365

Walker, David, 166–167
War on Poverty, 338, 370–371, 383–389,
392–393
Ward, Edward J., 196
Warfel, Harry, 35
Warner, Jack, 317–318
Warren, Earl, 348
Washington, Booker T., 144, 168–173, 175
Washington, George, 37, 133
Watkins, Arthur V., 357
Watt, James, 19
Weaver, Eli, 230
Webster, Daniel, 54–55
Webster, Noah, 10, 33–36, 56–57, 65, 91,
121
Wells, William, 120
Welter, Rush, 6, 9, 56–57, 89–90
Wertheim, Sally, 65
Western Literary Institute and College of
Professional Teachers, 65
Wheelock, Eleazor, 54
Wheelock, John, 54
Wheelock, Lucy, 192

Whigs, 77–82, 84, 86, 92, 218
Whipple, Guy M., 263
Willard, Emma, 100, 106–107
Wilson, Woodrow, 154
Winthrop, John, 5
Withrow, John, 252–254
Wollenberg, Charles, 163, 181
Women:
and charity, 121
and citizenship, 109
economic exploitation of, 97
education of, 24–25, 100, 118
moral character of, 101, 108–109, 118, 126
and republican motherhood, 108–110, 126
as teachers: charity schools, 100
and the common school movement,
101–103, 106–108
dame schools, 8
moral character education, 101–104,
106–108, 122
and Pestalozzian methods, 109–111,
115
and teacher training, 99, 106–110
Women's National Radio Committee,
326–327
Woodward, Calvin, 226–227
Work, Hubert, 147
Workingmen's parties, 73–76, 86, 89–90, 93
Wright, Fanny, 103
Wrigley, Julia, 240, 285–286

Yale College, 42, 50
Yale Report of 1828, 49, 51–53
Yarborough, Ralph, 363
Yerkes, Robert, 260
Young, Ella Flagg, 288

Zoll, Allen, 378